Charles Burke Elliott

The Principles of the Law of Public Corporations

Charles Burke Elliott

The Principles of the Law of Public Corporations

ISBN/EAN: 9783337233396

Printed in Europe, USA, Canada, Australia, Japan

Cover: Foto ©Suzi / pixelio.de

More available books at **www.hansebooks.com**

THE PRINCIPLES

OF THE LAW OF

PUBLIC CORPORATIONS

BY

CHARLES B. ELLIOTT, Ph. D., LL. D.

Judge of the District Court of Minnesota

CHICAGO
CALLAGHAN AND COMPANY
1898

TO THE

HON. ROBERT G. EVANS,

OF MINNESOTA,

THIS VOLUME IS CORDIALLY AND RESPECTFULLY

DEDICATED.

THIS book is the result of an attempt to state the law of Public Corporations in a manner suited to the needs of students. The plan made it necessary to pass rapidly over questions which are no longer controverted, and to treat very briefly matters which more properly belong to other titles of the law. A writer on this subject must necessarily be under unmeasured obligation to the Hon. John F. Dillon. I gladly acknowledge that obligation.

The authorities have been verified and the table of cases prepared by W. E. Hewett, Esq., of the Minneapolis bar.

MINNEAPOLIS, *April, 1893.*

TABLE OF CONTENTS.

CHAPTER I.
INTRODUCTORY.
DEFINITION, CLASSIFICATION AND HISTORY.

In general	§ 1
Different kinds of corporations	2
Classification of public corporations	3
School districts	4
Distribution of powers and duties	5
The county — Its organization and functions	6
The township	7
The town meeting	8
The township elsewhere than in New England	9
The English municipality	10
The American municipality	11

BOOK I.
THE CREATION AND CONTROL OF PUBLIC CORPORATIONS.

CHAPTER II.
THE CREATION OF PUBLIC CORPORATIONS.

CHAPTER III.
LEGISLATIVE CONTROL OVER PUBLIC CORPORATIONS.

CHAPTER IV.
CONSTITUTIONAL LIMITATIONS UPON LEGISLATIVE POWER OVER PUBLIC CORPORATIONS.

CHAPTER II.
THE CREATION OF PUBLIC CORPORATIONS.

Legislative authority	§ 12
The power to create	13
Compulsory incorporation	14
By the United States	15
By territorial legislatures	16
By implication	17

By prescription . . . . § 18
Manner of legislative action 19
Name, boundaries and powers 20

CHAPTER III.

LEGISLATIVE CONTROL OVER PUBLIC CORPORATIONS.

General statement 21
Dual character of municipal corporations 22
Local self-government 23
Power over charters 24
Public property 25
Roads and streets 26
Certain franchises 27
The private property of a corporation 28
Disposition of property upon dissolution 29

I. POWER OVER OFFICES AND OFFICERS.

Various kinds of officers 30
Police officials 31
Their appointment and payment 32
Park commissioners 33
Board of public works 34
Officers to lay out streets 35
Mayor 36

II. FUNDS AND REVENUES.

Power over revenue of public corporations 37

III. LEGISLATIVE CONTROL OVER CONTRACTS.

Relation of the corporation to the state 38
Rights of parties contracting with corporation 39
Illustrations 40
Rights in a sinking fund 41
Limitation on indebtedness 42

IV. THE POWER TO IMPOSE OBLIGATIONS.

Nature of the debt 43
Compulsory taxation 44
Construction of highways 45
Support of public schools 46
Local corporate purposes 47
Subscription for stock 48
Compulsory payment of claims 49

V. THE TERRITORY AND BOUNDARIES.

The general rule 50
What territory may be annexed 51
Illustrations 52
Property and debts upon division of territory 53

CHAPTER IV.

CONSTITUTIONAL LIMITATIONS UPON LEGISLATIVE POWER OVER PUBLIC CORPORATIONS.

In general	§ 54
General laws	55
The requirement of a "uniform system of government"	56
Illustrations	57
The requirement that "laws of a general nature shall have uniform operation throughout the state"	58
Illustrations	59
Local-option laws	60
Classification	61
Class containing but one member	62
Geographical conditions	63
Population	64
Illustrations	65
Possible accession to a class	66
Legislation regulating the "business," "affairs" and "internal affairs" of corporations	67
The prohibition of special legislation "where a general law can be made applicable"	68
Amendment or repeal of existing special charters	69

BOOK II.

THE POWERS OF PUBLIC CORPORATIONS.

CHAPTER V.
GENERAL POWERS — NATURE AND CONSTRUCTION.

CHAPTER VI.
PARTICULAR POWERS.

CHAPTER VII.
PARTICULAR POWERS — CONTINUED.

CHAPTER VIII.
PARTICULAR POWERS — CONTINUED.

CHAPTER IX.
MUNICIPAL SECURITIES.

CHAPTER X.
MUNICIPAL INDEBTEDNESS.

CHAPTER V.

GENERAL POWERS — NATURE AND CONSTRUCTION.

The general principle	§ 70
Comments upon the rule	71
Construction	72

Usage . . . . § 73
Delegation of powers 74
Illustrations 75

CHAPTER VI.
PARTICULAR POWERS.

Manner of granting powers 76
Statutory requirements 77
The exercise of power beyond corporate limits 78
Power to enact ordinances 79
General welfare clause 80

I. MISCELLANEOUS POWERS.

Power to contract 81
Letting contracts to lowest bidder 82
Remedy of bidder 83
Contracts for a term of years 84
Exclusive privileges 85
Power to borrow money 86
Compromise and arbitration 87
Powers of school boards — Text-books 88

II. POLICE POWERS.

Nature and scope of the police power 89
Regulation of occupations and amusements 90
The preservation of health 91
Nuisances 92
Regulation of wharves 93
Licenses 94
Markets 95
Prevention of fires 96
Care of indigent and infirm 97

CHAPTER VII.
PARTICULAR POWERS — CONTINUED.

I. POWERS RELATING TO STREETS AND HIGHWAYS.

Power over streets 98
Rights of abutting owners 99
The proper uses of a street 100
Obstructions 101
Temporary uses of a street 102
Power to improve streets 103
Gas and water pipes 104
Projecting doors, windows and porches 105
Railroads in streets 106
Conditions imposed 107
Telegraph and telephone poles 108

Additional servitudes — Compensation to abutting owners . . § 109
Railways as additional burdens 110
Telegraph and telephone poles as additional burdens 111

II. TAXATION AND SPECIAL ASSESSMENTS.

Power of taxation 112
Nature of special assessments 113
Their constitutionality 114
Purposes for which local assessments may be levied 115
Method of apportionment 116
By benefits 117
The frontage rule 118
Property exempt from taxation 119
Collection of assessments 120
Personal liability for assessments 121

CHAPTER VIII.

PARTICULAR POWERS — CONTINUED.

I. THE POWER OF EMINENT DOMAIN.

Definition 122
May be delegated 123
What may be taken 124
Must be for public use 125
Property already appropriated to public use 126
Meaning of "property" 127
What constitutes a taking 128
The proceedings 129
The tribunal 130
Notice 131
The compensation 132
Consequential injuries 133
Benefits 134
Manner of payment 135
Right of appeal 136

II. JUDICIAL POWER.

Power to establish courts 137
Jurisdiction 138
Qualifications of judges and jurors 139
Procedure — Jury trial 140

III. CORPORATE OR PRIVATE POWERS.

In general 141
Right to hold property 142
Parks and cemeteries 143
Wharves and ferries 144
Water and lights 145
Power to own and operate gas, light and water plants . . . 146

Nature of the power . . . . § 147
The acquisition of the plant 148
Contracts between municipalities and franchise companies . . 149

CHAPTER IX.
MUNICIPAL SECURITIES.
I. WARRANTS AND ORDERS.
Power to issue 150
Form 151
Negotiability 152
Effect of acceptance 153
Presentment and demand 154
Payable out of a particular fund 155
Rights of indorser 156
Defenses 157

II. MUNICIPAL BONDS.
Power of public *quasi*-corporations 158
Power of municipal corporations 159
Ratification of illegal bonds 160
Liability for money received 161
Right to restrain issue of illegal bonds 162

a. PURPOSES FOR WHICH BONDS MAY BE ISSUED.
Must be a public purpose 163
What are public purposes 164
Railways 165
Private purposes 166
How determined 167

b. CONDITIONS PRECEDENT TO LEGAL ISSUE.
In general 168
Consent of the people 169
Manner of obtaining consent 170
Majority of voters 171
Location and completion of roads 172

c. ESTOPPEL.
When estoppel arises 173
Authority of officers 174
Estoppel by conduct — Illustrations 175
By judgment 176

d. RIGHTS OF BONA FIDE HOLDERS.
Who are such 177
Defenses available against a *bona fide* holder 178
Recitals in bonds 179
Effect of recitals — Continued 180
Authority of officials to make recitals 181
Recital that bonds have been issued "in conformity to law" . . 182
Excessive issues 183

CHAPTER X.
MUNICIPAL INDEBTEDNESS.

Power to incur debts	§ 184
The meaning of indebtedness	185
Contingent obligations	186
Contracts requiring annual payments	187
Anticipation of revenues	188

BOOK III.

OF THE MODE AND AGENCIES OF CORPORATE ACTION.

CHAPTER XI.
OF THE MANNER OF EXERCISING CORPORATE POWER.
CHAPTER XII.
OF THE FORM AND ENACTMENT OF ORDINANCES.
CHAPTER XIII.
THE VALIDITY OF ORDINANCES.
CHAPTER XIV.
GOVERNING BODIES, OFFICERS AND AGENTS.

CHAPTER XI.
OF THE MANNER OF EXERCISING CORPORATE POWER.

Charter provisions	§ 189
Meaning of terms	190
Statutory directions	191
Procedure in the enactment of ordinances	192
Where no mode is prescribed	193
Illustrations	194

CHAPTER XII.
OF THE FORM AND ENACTMENT OF ORDINANCES.

The form	195
The title	196
The enacting clause	197
The penalty	198
Need not recite authority	199
Council meeting	200
Introduction — Notice	201
Readings	202
Suspension of the rules	203
Presumption as to regularity	204
Signing	205

xiv TABLE OF CONTENTS.

Approval	§ 206
Approval — Illustrations	207
The executive veto	208
Necessity for publication	209
Publication, when directory	210
Ultra vires acts of officials	211
Manner of publication	212
Designation of paper	213
Location of paper — "Printed and published in the city"	214
Manner and sufficiency	215
Distinction between publication and notice	216
Time and period	217
Proof of publication	218

CHAPTER XIII.

THE VALIDITY OF ORDINANCES.

General statement	219
Under express power	220
Motives of legislative body	221
Ordinances valid in part	222
Nature of an ordinance	223
Injunctions — Invalid ordinances	224

I. GENERAL PRINCIPLES GOVERNING VALIDITY.

Must conform to charter	225
Must be constitutional	226
Must conform to law	227
Must not contravene common right	228
Must be general and impartial	229
Must not be oppressive	230
Must be reasonable	231
Reasonableness a question for the court	232
Presumption of reasonableness	233

II. ILLUSTRATIONS OF VALID AND INVALID ORDINANCES.

Laying pipes in streets	234
Location and speed of vehicles	235
Handling of trains	236
Regulation of street railways	237
Parades, music and speaking in public places	238
Licenses	239
Discrimination against non-residents	240
Regulation of markets	241
Regulation of liquor traffic	242
Fire regulations	243
Quarantine regulations — Second-hand clothing	244
Hotel runners and hackmen	245
Miscellaneous decisions	246

III. ORDINANCES WHICH PROHIBIT ACTS WITHOUT THE CONSENT OF CERTAIN OFFICIALS.

General statement	§ 247
Cases sustaining such ordinances	248
Delegation of authority	249
Nature of prohibited acts	250
Uniform conditions — Unjust discrimination	251

CHAPTER XIV.

GOVERNING BODIES, OFFICERS AND AGENTS.

Distribution of powers	252
The corporate meeting	253
Notice of corporate meetings	254
The common council	255
Place of meeting	256
Majority and quorum	257
Who are officers	258
Election and appointment	259
Qualifications	260
Conditions precedent to entering upon an office	261
Relation of officer to corporations	262
Incompatible offices	263
Illustrations	264
Officers *de facto*	265
Officers *de facto* — Continued	266
Compensation	267
Compensation — *De facto* officers	268
Increase of salary — Misdemeanor	269
Compensation of employees — Attorneys	270
The mayor	271
Control by the courts	272
Holding over after expiration of term	273
Resignation	274
Amotion	275
Removal — Express authority — Proceedings	276
Personal liability on contracts	277
Liability in tort	278
Liability of officers acting judicially	279
Liability of recorder of deeds	280
Liability of sheriff	281
Liability of highway officers	282
Liability of various officers	283
Liability for loss of public funds	284
Manner of trying title to an office	285

… xvi TABLE OF CONTENTS.

BOOK IV.

THE LIABILITIES OF PUBLIC CORPORATIONS.

CHAPTER XV.
LIABILITY ON CONTRACTS.

CHAPTER XVI.
LIABILITY FOR TORT — GOVERNMENTAL AND CORPORATE DUTIES.

CHAPTER XVII.
MUNICIPAL DUTIES RELATING TO GOVERNMENTAL AFFAIRS.

CHAPTER XVIII.
THE CONSTRUCTION AND CARE OF PUBLIC WORKS.

CHAPTER XIX.
ACTIONS AND PROCEEDINGS.

CHAPTER XV.

LIABILITY ON CONTRACTS.

General liability	§ 286
Presentation and demand	287
Doctrine of *ultra vires*	288
Estoppel — Contract executed by one party	289
Contracts within scope of general powers	290
Contract in part *ultra vires*	291
Liability on implied contract	292
Illustrations	293
Right to recover back illegal taxes	294
Payment must be compulsory	295
Voluntary payment	296

CHAPTER XVI.

LIABILITY FOR TORT — GOVERNMENTAL AND CORPORATE DUTIES.

Nature of corporation	297
Nature of duty	298
Discretionary powers	299
Imposed and assumed duties	300
Liability for acts of agents — *Respondeat superior*	301
Ultra vires torts	302
Ratification of *ultra vires* acts	303
Increase of liability by contract	304
General rules	305

I. SOLELY GOVERNMENTAL DUTIES.

Definition	§ 306
Neglect to enact or enforce laws	307
Suspension of ordinances	308
Liability for acts of a mob	309
Acts of police officers	310
Prevention of fires	311
Destruction of property to prevent spread of fire	312
Acts of firemen	313
Acts of board of health — Care of hospital	314
Care of criminals	315
Care of the indigent	316
Care of school buildings	317

II. SOLELY CORPORATE DUTIES.

Rule of liability for negligence	318
As owner of property	319
Illustrations — Wharves	320
Private business enterprises — Gas and water	321

CHAPTER XVII.

MUNICIPAL DUTIES RELATING TO GOVERNMENTAL AFFAIRS.

General statement	322
Common-law duty to repair highways	323
Conflicting rules — Chartered municipalities	324
Liability of counties and towns	325
Extent of duty to care for highways	326
Lighting the streets	327
Necessary obstructions	328
Illustrations	329
Lack of funds as a defense	330
Liability for acts of licensees	331
Care of sidewalks	332
Obstructions on sidewalks	333
Ice and snow on highways	334
Care of bridges	335
Notice	336

CHAPTER XVIII.

THE CONSTRUCTION AND CARE OF PUBLIC WORKS.

Care of public property	337
Surface waters	338
Drainage and sewers	339
The plan of a public work	340
Direct injury to property	341
The construction and care of sewers	342
Consequential damages	343

CHAPTER XIX.

ACTIONS AND PROCEEDINGS.

The right to sue and be sued . . . . § 344
Notice of claim 345
Mandamus 346
Mandamus to enforce duties toward creditors 347
Further illustrations of the use of *mandamus* 348
Quo warranto 349
Remedy in equity 350
Certiorari 351
Levy of execution on corporate property 352
Liability to garnishment 353

TABLE OF CASES CITED.

References are to pages.

Aaron v. Broils (64 Tex. 316, 53 Am. St. Rep. 764), 253.
Abbett v. Johnson Co. (114 Ind. 61), 6.
Abbott v. Kimball (19 Vt. 551), 47 Am. Dec. 708), 251.
Abel v. Minneapolis (Minn., 70 N. W. Rep. 851), 313.
Adams v. Mayor, etc. (29 Ga. 56), 199.
Adams v. Selina (48 Pac. Rep. 918), 279.
Adams v. Smith (6 Dak. 94), 60.
Adams v. Tyler (121 Mass. 380), 326.
Addis v. Pittsburgh (85 Pa. St. 379), 77.
Agnew v. Corunna (55 Mich. 428, 54 Am. Rep. 388), 297.
Ah Yon, In re (83 Cal. 99, 11 L. R. A. 408), 182.
Aikman v. Edwards (55 Kan. 751, 30 L. R. A. 149), 41.
Alabama R. Co. v. Kidd (29 Ala. 221), 3.
Aldrich v. Gorham (77 Me. 287), 291.
Aldrich v. Tripp (11 R. I. 141, 23 Am. Rep. 434), 298.
Alexander v. Milwaukee (16 Wis. 264), 313.
Alexandria, etc. Ry. Co. v. Alexandria (75 Va. 780), 120.
Allamango v. Albany County (25 Hun, 551), 284.
Alleghany County v. Gibson (90 Pa. St. 387, 35 Am. Rep. 607), 278, 279.
Allegheney v. Millville, etc. R. Co. (159 Pa. St. 411, 28 Atl. Rep. 202), 102.
Allegheny v. Zimmerman (95 Pa. St. 287, 40 Am. Rep. 649), 101.
Allegheny County v. Paris (93 Va. 615, 25 S. E. Rep. 882), 258.

Allen v. Baltimore & Ohio Ry. Co. (114 U. S. 311), 323.
Allen v. Burlington (45 Vt. 22), 206.
Allen v. Chippewa Falls (52 Wis. 430, 38 Am. Rep. 748), 304, 310.
Allen v. Decatur (23 Ill. 332), 273.
Allen v. Drew (44 Vt. 174), 110.
Allen v. Jay (60 Me. 124, 11 Am. Rep. 185), 154.
Allen v. Jones (41 Ind. 438), 120.
Allen v. La Fayette (89 Ala. 641, 9 L. R. A. 497), 81, 133, 148, 151.
Allen v. Louisiana (103 U. S. 80), 156.
Allentown v. Henry (73 Pa. St. 404), 112.
Allison v. Juniata Co. (50 Pa. St. 351), 146.
Alney v. Pierce (1 R. I. 292), 226.
Altgeld v. San Antonio (81 Tex. 436), 81, 108.
Altnow v. Town of Liberty (80 Minn. 186, 44 Am. Rep. 191), 293.
Alton v. Mulledy (21 Ill. 76), 176.
Altoona v. Bowman (171 Pa. St. 307), 177.
Alvord v. Syracuse Savings Bank (98 N. Y. 599, 8 Am. & Eng. Corp. Cas. 598), 161.
Amberson Ave., In re (36 Atl. Rep. 854), 113.
American T. & T. Co. v. Pearce (71 Md. 535, 7 L. R. A. 200), 107.
Ames v. Lake Superior, etc. Co. (21 Minn. 241), 124.
Amey v. Watertown (130 U. S. 301), 318.
Ampt v. Cincinnati (35 L. R. A. 737), 134.
Anderson, In re (109 N. Y. 554), 79.

TABLE OF CASES CITED.

References are to pages.

Anderson v. Board (122 Mo. 61, 26 L. R. A. 707), 77.
Anderson v. City of Wellington (40 Kan. 173, 2 L. R. A. 110, 10 Am. St. Rep. 175), 69, 97, 201, 206, 214, 215, 216.
Anderson v. East (117 Ind. 126, 2 L. R. A. 712), 271, 277, 292.
Anderson v. Insurance Co. (88 Iowa, 579), 171.
Anderson v. Santa Anna Co. (116 U. S. 356), 151.
Anderson v. Trenton (42 N. J. L. 486), 53, 60.
Anderson v. Wilmington (Del., 19 Atl. Rep. 509), 292.
Andrews v. Nat. F. & P. Works (C. C. A., 61 Fed. Rep. 782), 136.
Andrews v. Portland (79 Me. 84, 10 Am. St. Rep. 280), 236, 237.
Anne Arundel County v. Diwell (54 Md. 350, 39 Am. Rep. 393), 270, 293.
Anthony v. Adams (1 Met. 284), 272.
Anthony v. Jasper Co. (4 Dill. C. C. 136), 163.
Argenti v. San Francisco (16 Cal. 255), 151, 260, 262.
Arkadelphia Lumber Co. v. City of Arkadelphia (56 Ark. 370, 19 S. W. Rep. 1003), 180.
Armour v. Concord (48 N. H. 211, 97 Am. Dec. 605), 278.
Armstrong v. Ackley (71 Iowa, 76), 301.
Armstrong v. St. Paul (30 Minn. 299), 314.
Arnold v. Hudson R. Co. (55 N. Y. 661), 123.
Arnott v. Spokane (6 Wash. 442), 145.
Aron v. City of Wausau (74 N. W. Rep. 354), 279.
Arras v. Stukely (2 Mod. 260), 237.
Ashley v. Calliope (71 Iowa, 466), 44.
Ashley v. Port Huron (35 Mich. 296), 311.
Askey v. Hals Co. (54 Ala. 639), 5.
Aspinwall v. Daviess Co. (22 How., U. S., 160, 364), 164.

Assessment for Grad. Prior Av., In re (71 N. W. Rep. 27), 116.
Aston v. Newton (134 Mass. 507), 294.
Astor v. Mayor (66 N. Y. 567), 31.
Astor v. New York (62 N. Y. 567), 26.
Atchison St. R. Co. v. Mo. Pac. R. R. Co. (31 Kan. 660), 101.
Atkins v. Phillips (26 Fla. 281, 10 L. R. A. 158), 182.
Atkins v. Town of Randolph (31 Vt. 226), 39.
Atkinson v. Bartholow (4 Kan. 124), 65.
Atlanta v. First Presb. Church (86 Ga. 730, 12 L. R. A. 852), 115, 116.
Atlanta v. Halleday (96 Ga. 546, 26 S. E. Rep. 509), 198.
Atlantic W. W. v. Atlantic City (48 N. J. L. 378), 79.
Atlantic City W. W. v. Atlantic City (39 N. J. Eq. 367), 138.
Atlantic City W. W. v. Read (49 N. J. L. 558, 50 N. J. L. 665), 169, 174.
Attaway v. Cartersville (68 Ga. 740), 280.
Attorney-General v. Boston (123 Mass. 460), 323.
Attorney-General v. Common Council (70 N. W. Rep. 450), 30, 32.
Attorney-General v. Common Council of Detroit (71 N. W. Rep. 632, 37 L. R. A. 211), 280.
Attorney-General v. Detroit (26 Mich. 262), 323.
Attorney-General v. Jochim (99 Mich. 358, 23 L. R. A. 699), 245.
Attorney-General v. Lathrop (24 Mich. 235), 31.
Attorney-General v. Marston (66 N. H. 485, 13 L. R. A. 670), 230.
Attorney-General v. Northampton (143 Mass. 589), 324.
Atwell v. Zeluff (26 Mich. 118), 266.
Aurora v. West (22 Ind. 88), 163.
Austin v. Austin Cemetery Ass'n (87 Tex. 330), 197, 202.
Austin v. Austin Gas Co. (69 Tex. 180), 108.
Austin v. Johns (62 Tex. 179), 238.
Austin v. Nalle (85 Tex. 520), 150.

TABLE OF CASES CITED. xxi

References are to pages.

Austin v. Seattle (2 Wash. 667), 172.
Austin v. Vrooman (128 N. Y. 229, 14 L. R. A. 138), 249.
Austin v. Wilson (4 Tex. 400), 256.
Ayers, Appeal of (122 Pa. St. 266), 55, 56, 63.

B.

Babcock v. Fond du Lac (58 Wis. 231), 265.
Back v. Carpenter (20 Kan. 349), 20.
Backus v. Detroit (49 Mich. 110, 43 Am. Rep. 447), 89.
Backus v. Lebanon (11 N. H. 19, 35 Am. Dec. 466), 125.
Bacon v. Savannah (86 Ga. 301), 114.
Badeau v. United States (130 U. S. 439), 230.
Badger v. United States (93 U. S. 599), 242, 318.
Bailey v. Mayor (3 Hill, N. Y., 531), 3.
Bailey v. New York (3 Hill, 531, 30 Am. Dec. 669), 3, 139, 267, 287.
Bailey v. Tabor (5 Mass. 286, 4 Am. Dec. 57), 163.
Bailey v. Woburn (126 Mass. 416), 121.
Baker v. Johnson (41 Me. 15), 319.
Baker v. Marshall (15 Minn. 177, Gil 136), 316.
Baker v. Portland (58 Me. 199, 10 Am. L. Reg., N. S., 559), 195.
Baker v. Seattle (2 Wash. 576), 169.
Baker v. Steamboat (14 Iowa, 214), 65.
Balch v. County Com'rs (103 Mass. 106), 121.
Baldwin v. Smith (82 Ill. 162), 198.
Ball v. Woodbine (61 Iowa, 83, 47 Am. Rep. 803), 273, 277.
Baltimore v. Cemetery Co. (7 Md. 517), 115.
Baltimore v. Gill (31 Md. 375), 170, 323.
Baltimore v. Hughes (1 Gill & J. 265), 114.
Baltimore v. Keeley Institute (81 Md. 106, 27 L. R. A. 647), 94, 317.
Baltimore v. Keyser (72 Md. 106), 79.

Baltimore v. Marriott (9 Md. 160), 292.
Baltimore v. O'Donnell (54 Md. 110), 207.
Baltimore v. Poultney (25 Md. 18), 221.
Baltimore v. Proprietors (7 Md. 517), 116.
Baltimore v. Radicke (49 Md. 217), 197, 201.
Baltimore v. Root (8 Md. 95), 326.
Baltimore v. State (15 Md. 376), 30.
Baltimore, etc. R. Co. v. M'Gruder (34 Md. 79, 6 Am. Rep. 310), 123.
Baltimore, etc. Ry. Co. v. Spring (80 Md. 510, 27 L. R. A. 72), 152, 154.
Bancroft v. Cambridge (126 Mass. 438), 121.
Bangor Sav. Bank v. Stillwater (49 Fed. Rep. 721), 151.
Bank v. Dibrell (3 Sneed, Tenn., 379), 326.
Bank v. Mayor (7 Ohio, pt. 2, 31), 149.
Bank v. School District No. 53 (3 N. Dak. 496, 28 L. R. A. 642), 163.
Bank of United States v. Planters' Bank (9 Wheat., U. S., 904), 3.
Bankhead v. Brown (25 Iowa, 545), 121.
Barber v. Abendroth (102 N. Y. 406), 287.
Barber Asphalt Pavement Co. v. Hunt (100 Mo. 22, 18 Am. St. Rep. 530), 77, 186.
Barbier v. Connelly (113 U. S. 27), 85, 199, 213, 214.
Barker v. People (3 Cowen, N. Y., 685, 15 Am. Dec. 322), 225.
Barling v. West (29 Wis. 307), 91.
Barnard v. Knox Co. (37 Fed. Rep. 563, 2 L. R. A. 426), 170.
Barnert v. Patterson (48 N. J. L. 395), 222.
Barnes v. Chicopee (138 Mass. 67, 52 Am. Rep. 259), 296.
Barnes v. District of Columbia (91 U. S. 540), 18, 270, 292.
Barnes v. Palestine (50 Tex. 588), 4.
Barnes v. Williams (53 Ark. 205, 13 S. W. Rep. 845), 233.

c

References are to pages.

Barnett v. Dennison (145 U. S. 136), 160, 163.
Barnett v. Newark (28 Iowa, 62), 188.
Barnum v. Gilman (27 Minn. 466, 38 Am. Dec. 304), 230, 322.
Barr v. Kansas City (105 Mo. 550), 296.
Barre Ry. Co. v. Montpelier, etc. Ry. Co. (61 Vt. 1, 4 L. R. A. 785), 121.
Barron v. Detroit (94 Mich. 601, 19 L. R. A. 452), 286.
Barry v. Good (89 Cal. 215), 82.
Bartle v. Des Moines (38 Iowa, 414), 169.
Bartlett v. Crosier (17 Johns. 449, 8 Am. Dec. 428), 252.
Barton v. Pittsburgh (4 Brew., Pa., 373), 184.
Barton v. Syracuse (36 N. Y. 54), 304.
Barton Co. v. Walser (47 Mo. 189), 5.
Bassett v. Atwater (65 Conn. 355, 32 L. R. A. 575), 316.
Bates v. Bassett (60 Vt. 530, 1 L. R. A. 66), 134.
Bates v. Houston (37 S. W. Rep. 383), 284.
Bates v. Westborough (151 Mass. 174, 23 N. E. Rep. 1070, 7 L. R. A. 156), 312, 313.
Bauer v. Franklin Co. (51 Mo. 205), 145.
Bauer v. Rochester (35 N. Y. State Rep. 959, 12 N. Y. Sup. 418), 295.
Bauman v. Campau (58 Mich. 444), 268.
Baumgartner v. Hastings (100 Ind. 575), 88, 93.
Baxter v. Turnpike Co. (10 Lea, Tenn., 488), 4.
Bayer v. Hoboken (44 N. J. L. 131), 180.
Beach v. Gaylord (43 Minn. 466), 308.
Beach v. Leahy (11 Kan. 30), 7, 63.
Beard v. Hopkinsville (Ky., 23 L. R. A. 402), 170, 173.
Beardon v. Madison (73 Ga. 184), 195.
Beardsley v. Hartford (50 Conn. 529, 47 Am. Rep. 677), 291, 302.
Beardsley v. Smith (16 Conn. 368, 41 Am. Dec. 147), 325.

Beardsley v. Steinberg (49 Pac. Rep. 499), 145.
Beatrice v. Leary (45 Neb. 149, 50 Am. St. Rep. 547), 310.
Beaumont v. Wilkesbarre (142 Pa. St. 198), 114.
Beaver Creek v. Hosbergs (52 Mich. 528), 220.
Becker v. Keokuk Water Works (79 Iowa, 419), 275.
Becker v. Philadelphia, etc. R. Co. (177 Pa. St. 252, 25 L. R. A. 583), 127.
Becker v. Washington (94 Mo. 375), 186.
Bedell, Ex parte (20 Mo. App. 125), 190.
Beecher v. People (38 Mich. 289, 31 Am. Rep. 316), 101.
Beiling v. Evansville (144 Ind. 644, 42 N. E. Rep. 621), 86.
Belcher's S. R. Co. v. Grain Elevator Co. (101 Mo. 192, 13 S. W. Rep. 822), 134.
Belfast v. Brooks (60 Me. 569), 157.
Belknap v. Louisville (Ky., 34 L. R. A. 256), 157.
Bell, Ex parte (32 Tex. Cr. Rep. 308, 42 Am. St. Rep. 778), 200.
Bell v. Foutch (21 Iowa, 119), 97.
Bell v. Mobile, etc. Ry. Co. (4 Wall. 598), 154.
Bell v. York (31 Neb. 842, 48 N. W. Rep. 878), 302.
Belleville v. Citizens' Horse Car Co. (152 Ill. 171, 26 L. R. A. 681), 104.
Belo v. Forsyth Co. (76 N. C. 489), 155.
Belton v. Boston (54 N. Y. 245), 303.
Bennett's Appeal (65 Pa. St. 242), 2.
Bennington v. Park (50 Vt. 178, 161.
Benson v. Green (80 Ga. 230), 250.
Benson v. Mayor (10 Barb., N. Y., 225), 136.
Bentley v. Board of Co. Com'rs (25 Minn. 259), 67.
Benton v. Trustees of Boston City Hospital (140 Mass. 113), 284.
Berford v. Grand Rapids (53 Mich. 98, 51 Am. Rep. 105), 277.
Bergman v. Cleveland (39 Ohio St. 651), 210.

TABLE OF CASES CITED. xxiii

References are to pages.

Bergman v. St. Louis, etc. R. Co. (88 Mo. 678), 181.
Berlin v. Gorham (34 N. H. 266), 18.
Bermonsey v. Ramsey (L. R. 6 C. P. 247), 117.
Bernards Tp. v. Morrison (133 U. S. 523), 165, 167.
Bessey v. Unity (65 Me. 342), 19.
Bethune v. Hughes (28 Ga. 560, 73 Am. Dec. 789), 92.
Betz v. Limingi (46 La. Ann. 1113, 46 Am. St. Rep. 344), 299.
Bickenstaff, In re (70 Cal. 35), 214.
Bieling v. Brooklyn (120 N. Y. 98), 302.
Bier v. Grell (30 W. Va. 96, 8 Am. St. Rep. 17), 237.
Bigelow v. Topliff (25 Vt. 282), 251.
Biggs v. McBride (17 Oreg. 640, 5 L. R. A. 115), 319.
Billings v. Lafferty (31 Ill. 318), 253.
Billingsley v. State (14 Md. 369), 248.
Bills v. Goshen (117 Ind. 221, 3 L. R. A. 261), 176, 182, 186, 193.
Birge v. Chicago, etc. Ry. Co. (65 Iowa, 440), 125.
Birmingham v. Alabama, etc. Ry. Co. (98 Ala. 134, 13 So. Rep. 141), 206.
Birmingham v. Lewis (92 Ala. 352, 9 So. Rep. 243), 298.
Bishop v. Macon (7 Ga. 200, 50 Am. Dec. 400), 281.
Bissell v. Davidson (65 Conn. 183, 29 L. R. A. 251), 83, 87.
Bissell v. Jeffersonville (24 How., U. S., 287), 161, 165.
Bissell v. Kankakee (64 Ill. 249, 21 Am. Rep. 554), 154, 160, 163.
Bittenhaus v. Johnson (92 Wis. 595, 32 L. R. A. 380), 84.
Bitting v. Commonwealth (12 Atl. Rep. 29), 64.
Bittinger v. Bell (65 Ind. 445), 157.
Bizzell, In re (112 Ala. 210, 21 So. Rep. 371), 194.
Black v. Columbia (19 S. C. 412, 45 Am. Rep. 785), 275, 281.
Black v. Cohen (52 Ga. 621), 151.
Blair v. Cummings (111 U. S. 363), 154.

Blair v. West Point Precinct (2 McCrary, 459), 19, 20.
Blanchard v. Bissell (11 Ohio St. 103), 18, 41, 74, 177, 180, 186, 187.
Blandin v. Burr (13 Cal. 343), 39, 40.
Bledsoe v. Gary (95 Ala. 70, 10 So. Rep. 502), 131.
Blen v. Bear River, etc. Co. (20 Cal. 60, 81 Am. Dec. 132), 150.
Bliss v. Hosmer (15 Ohio St. 44), 120.
Blizzard v. Danville (175 Pa. St. 479), 312.
Blodgett v. Boston (8 Allen, 237), 301.
Bloodgood v. Mohawk, etc. R. Co. (18 Wend. 9, 31 Am. Dec. 313), 129.
Bloom v. Xenia (32 Ohio St. 461), 177, 185.
Bloomfield v. Charter Oak Bank (121 U. S. 121), 11, 13, 220, 325.
Bloomington v. Latham (142 Ill. 462, 18 L. R. A. 487), 202.
Bloomington v. Richardson (38 Ill. 60), 206.
Bluffton v. Silver (63 Ind. 262), 322.
Bluffton v. Studabaker (106 Ind. 129), 65.
Board v. City of Springfield (63 Ill. 66), 33.
Board v. Harrell (Ind., 1897, 46 N. E. Rep. 124), 169.
Board v. Leahy (24 Kan. 54), 59.
Board v. Minor (23 Ohio St. 211, 13 Am. Rep. 233), 83.
Board v. Stevenson (46 N. J. L. 173), 47.
Board of Commissioners v. Board of Commissioners (26 Kan. 181, 201), 171.
Board of Commissioners v. Duprez (87 Ind. 509), 272.
Board of Commissioners v. Mitchell (Ind., 15 L. R. A. 520), 228.
Board of Commissioners v. Platt (C. C. A., 79 Fed. Rep. 572), 162, 172.
Board of Education v. Blodgett (155 Ill. 441, 31 L. R. A. 70), 148.
Board of Education v. Minor (23 Ohio St. 211, 13 Am. Rep. 233), 83.
Board of Education v. State (26 Kan. 44), 152.

Board of Park Commissioners v. Common Council of Detroit (28 Mich. 287), 5.
Board of Trade Tel. Co. v. Barnet (107 Ill. 507), 107.
Bodge v. Philadelphia (167 Pa. St. 492), 280.
Boehm v. Baltimore (61 Md. 259), 91.
Bogaert v. Indianapolis (13 Ind. 134), 86.
Bogie v. Waupun (75 Wis. 1), 303.
Bohan, In re (115 Cal. 372, 36 L. R. A. 618), 86.
Bohen v. Waseca (32 Minn. 176, 50 Am. Rep. 564), 101, 302.
Bolles v. Brimfield (120 U. S. 759), 151.
Bolton v. Velines (20 S. E. Rep. 847), 280.
Bonaparte v. Camden, etc. R. Co. (1 Bald. 205), 3.
Bonds of Madeira Irrigation District, In re (92 Cal. 296, 14 L. R. A. 755), 111.
Bonner v. State (7 Ga. 473), 256.
Boom Co. v. Patterson (98 U. S. 403), 126.
Boro v. Phillips Co. (4 Dill. C. C. 216), 147.
Borough v. Alabama, etc. Ry. Co. (Ala., 13 So. Rep. 141), 205.
Boss Machine Works v. Park Co. Com'rs (115 Ind. 244), 259.
Boston v. Baldwin (139 Mass. 315), 131.
Boston, etc. Co. v. Boston (4 Metc. 181), 264.
Boston & M. R. R. Co. v. Lowell, etc. R. Co. (124 Mass. 368), 122.
Boston Belting Co. v. Boston (149 Mass. 44), 311.
Boston Seaman's Friend Society v. Boston (116 Mass. 181, 19 Am. Rep. 153), 116.
Bott v. Pratt (33 Minn. 323), 195.
Boucher v. New Haven (40 Conn. 456), 295.
Boutte v. Emmer (43 La. Ann. 980, 15 L. R. A. 63), 247.
Bowditch v. Boston (101 U. S. 16), 281.
Bowdoinham v. Richmond (6 Me. 112, 19 Am. Dec. 197), 44.

Bowen v. Greensboro (79 Ga. 709), 157.
Bowen v. Mauzy (117 Ind. 258), 89.
Bowery Nat. Bank v. Wilson (122 N. Y. 478, 9 L. R. A. 706), 285.
Bowes v. Boston (155 Mass. 344, 15 L. R. A. 365), 297.
Bowling Green v. Carson (10 Bush, Ky., 164), 209.
Bowman v. St. John (43 Ill. 337), 182.
Boyd v. Chambers (75 Ky. 140), 130.
Boyd v. Insurance Patrol (113 Pa. St. 269), 283.
Boyden v. United States (80 U. S. 17), 254.
Bradley v. Fisher (13 Wall., U. S., 335), 249.
Bradley v. Rochester (54 Hun, N. Y., 140), 214.
Bradwell v. Illinois (16 Wall. 130), 224.
Brady v. New York (20 N. Y. 312), 78.
Bray v. Wallingford (20 Conn. 416), 326.
Breinger v. Beloibere (44 N. J. L. 350), 198.
Brenham v. Brenham Water Co. (67 Tex. 542), 69, 80, 138.
Brenham v. German Am. Bank (144 U. S. 191), 149, 150, 163.
Brennan v. City of St. Louis (92 Mo. 482), 297.
Brennan v. Guardians (L. R. 2 C. L. 42), 285.
Brewer v. Otoe Co. (1 Neb. 373), 148.
Brewster v. Syracuse (19 N. Y. 116), 39.
Brick Presbyterian Church v. New York (5 Cow., N. Y., 538), 70.
Bridgeport v. Housatonic Ry. Co. (15 Conn. 475), 68, 151.
Bridgeport v. Railway Co. (36 Conn. 255), 109, 115, 116.
Briegel v. Philadelphia (135 Pa. St. 451, 30 Am. & Eng. C. C. 501), 306.
Briggs v. Lewiston (29 Me. 472), 265.
Brighton v. Toronto (12 U. C. 433), 209.
Bristol v. New Chester (3 N. H. 524), 44.
Britton v. Steber (62 Mo. 370), 32.
Broadway Church v. McAtee (8 Bush, Ky., 508, 8 Am. Rep. 408), 118.

TABLE OF CASES CITED.

References are to pages.

Broburg v. Des Moines (63 Iowa, 523, 19 N. W. Rep. 340, 50 Am. Rep. 756), 302.
Brock v. Hishen (40 Wis. 674), 129.
Brodhead v. Milwaukee (19 Wis. 624, 88 Am. Dec. 711), 154.
Brohme v. Monroe (106 Mich. 401, 64 N. Y. 204), 177.
Brooklyn, In re (143 N. Y. 596, 26 L. R. A. 271), 123, 141.
Brooklyn v. Breslau (57 N. Y. 591), 193.
Brooklyn v. Meserole (26 Wend., N. Y., 132), 322.
Brooklyn Park Com'rs v. Armstrong (45 N. Y. 234, 243, 244, 6 Am. Rep. 70), 35, 120, 207.
Brooks v. Baltimore (48 Md. 265), 109.
Brooks v. Hyde (37 Cal. 366), 43.
Brooks v. Morgan (86 Mich. 576), 249.
Brookville v. Arthurs (130 Pa. St. 501), 202, 299.
Broughton v. Pensacola (93 U. S. 266), 26, 29.
Brown v. Atchison (39 Kan. 54), 261.
Brown v. Bon Homme Co. (1 S. Dak. 216, 46 N. W. Rep. 173), 15, 160, 163, 165, 166.
Brown v. Bradlee (156 Mass. 28, 15 L. R. A. 509), 246.
Brown v. City of Cory (175 Pa. St. 528, 34 Atl. Rep. 854), 174.
Brown v. Denver (7 Colo. 305), 63, 65.
Brown v. District of Columbia (127 U. S. 579), 222.
Brown v. Gates (15 W. Va. 131), 325.
Brown v. Guyandotte (12 S. E. Rep. 1207, 11 L. R. A. 121), 284.
Brown v. Ingalls Tp. (81 Fed. Rep. 485), 163.
Brown v. Jerome (102 Ill. 371), 130.
Brown v. Keener (74 N. C. 714), 87.
Brown v. Lester (21 Miss. 392), 253.
Brown v. Rundlett (15 N. H. 360), 247.
Brown v. Russell (166 Mass. 14, 43 N. E. Rep. 1005, 33 L. R. A. 253), 223, 225.
Brown v. Turner (70 N. C. 93), 256.
Brown v. Vinalhaven (65 Me. 402), 284.

Brownell v. Greenwich (114 N. Y. 518, 4 L. R. A. 685), 165.
Browning v. Board (44 Ind. 11), 272.
Brownville v. Cook (4 Neb. 105), 196.
Brownville v. Loague (129 U. S. 493), 318.
Brugerman v. True (25 Minn. 123), 125.
Brumm's Appeal (Pa. St., 12 Atl. Rep. 855), 24.
Brunswick v. Braxton (70 Ga. 193), 292.
Bryan v. St. Paul (33 Minn. 289), 270, 284.
Bryant v. Robbins (7 Iowa, 258), 51.
Bryden v. Campbell (40 Md. 338), 250.
Bubridge v. Astoria (25 Oreg. 417, 42 Am. St. Rep. 796), 187.
Buchanan v. Litchfield (102 U. S. 278), 161, 167.
Buck v. Eureka (109 Cal. 405, 30 L. R. A. 409), 238.
Buckner v. Gordon (81 Ky. 665), 225.
Buell v. Ball (20 Iowa, 282), 193.
Buell v. Buckingham (16 Iowa, 284), 223.
Buffalo, In re (68 N. Y. 167), 122.
Buffalo v. Bettinger (76 N. Y. 393), 257.
Buffalo v. Harling (50 Minn. 551, 52 N. W. Rep. 931), 315.
Buffalo v. New York, etc. Ry. Co. (152 N. Y. 276, 46 N. E. Rep. 496), 195, 205.
Buffalo City Cemetery v. Buffalo (46 N. Y. 506), 115.
Bulger v. Eden (82 Me. 352), 269, 272.
Bunch v. Edenton (90 N. C. 431), 292.
Bunting v. Willis (27 Grat. 144, 21 Am. Rep. 338), 242.
Burch v. Hardwicke (30 Grat. 24), 30, 31.
Bureau of Sayre v. Phillips (148 Pa. St. 482, 24 Atl. Rep. 76), 208.
Burford v. Grand Rapids (53 Mich. 98, 51 Am. Rep. 105), 268, 299, 311.
Burg v. Chicago, etc. Ry. Co. (90 Iowa, 106, 48 Am. St. Rep. 419), 205.

xxvi TABLE OF CASES CITED.

References are to pages.

Burkholtz v. Dinnie (N. D., 1897, 72 N. W. Rep. 931), 171.
Burleson v. Reading (117 Mich. 115, 68 N. W. Rep. 294), 305.
Burlington v. Dennison (42 N. J. L. 165), 178.
Burlington Water Co. v. Woodward (49 Iowa, 62), 173.
Burmeister, Petition of (76 N. Y. 174), 111.
Burmeister v. Howard (1 Wash. 207), 195.
Burnes v. City of Atchison (2 Kan. 454), 19.
Burnett v. Maloney (97 Tenn. 697, 34 L. R. A. 541), 148.
Burnham v. Fond du Lac (15 Wis. 193-211), 326.
Burns v. Bradford (137 Pa. St. 361, 11 L. R. A. 726), 293, 301.
Burns v. Cohoes (67 N. Y. 204), 309.
Burns v. Harper (59 Ill. 29), 326.
Burr v. Plymouth (48 Conn. 460), 303.
Burrill v. Augusta (78 Me. 118, 57 Am. Rep. 788), 282.
Burritt v. Commissioners of State Contracts (120 Ill. 322), 178, 182.
Burton v. Harvey Co. Bank (28 Kan. 390), 145.
Burwell v. Vance Co. (93 N. C. 73), 124.
Bush v. Portland (19 Oreg. 45, 20 Am. St. Rep. 789), 90.
Butchers v. Crescent City (111 U. S. 746), 86.
Butler v. Passaic (44 N. J. L. 171), 178.
Buttrick v. Lowell (1 Allen, 172), 270.
Butz v. Cavanaugh (Mo., 88 S. W. Rep. 1102), 277.
Byers v. Com. (42 Pa. St. 89), 196.

C.

Cairncross v. Pewaukee (78 Wis. 66, 10 L. R. A. 473), 291, 297.
Cairo, etc. R. Co. v. Sparta (77 Ill. 505), 39.
Calder v. Smalley (66 Iowa, 219), 300.

Caldwell v. Alton (33 Ill. 416, 85 Am. Dec. 282), 92, 93.
Caldwell v. Boone (51 Iowa, 647, 33 Am. Rep. 154), 280, 299.
California, etc. Ry. Co. v. Butte Co. (18 Cal. 671), 155.
Callan v. Wilson (127 U. S. 540), 132.
Callanan v. Gilman (107 N. Y. 360), 295, 301.
Callendar v. Marsh (1 Pick., Mass., 417), 313.
Camden v. Mulford (26 N. J. L. 49), 75, 82, 324.
Camden, etc. R. Co. v. May's Landing, etc. Co. (48 N. J. L. 530), 258.
Campana v. Calderhead (17 Mont. 548, 30 L. R. A. 277), 82.
Campbell v. Polk Co. (3 Iowa, 467), 147.
Campbell v. Polk Co. (76 Mo. 57), 147.
Campbell v. Race (7 Cush. 408), 294.
Campbell v. Stillwater (32 Minn. 308), 297.
Cannon v. New Orleans (20 Wall. 577), 136.
Canto, Ex parte (21 Tex. App. 61, 57 Am. Rep. 609), 92.
Canton v. Nist (9 Ohio St. 439, 34 Am. Dec. 625), 199.
Cantrill v. Sainer (59 Iowa, 26), 177, 194.
Cape Girardeau v. Forgen (30 Mo. App. 551), 179.
Cape Girardeau v. Riley (52 Mo. App. 424), 182.
Carpenter v. Cohoes (81 N. Y. 21, 37 Am. Rep. 408), 293.
Carpenter v. People (8 Colo. 116), 63.
Carr v. State (111 Ind. 1), 244.
Carr v. St. Louis (9 Mo. 191), 199.
Carrington v. St. Louis (89 Mo. 208), 283, 307.
Carroll v. Iowa Land Co. (39 Iowa, 151), 5.
Carroll Co. v. Smith (111 U. S. 556), 157, 162.
Carson v. McFettridge (15 Ind. 327), 227.
Carstesen v. Town of Stratford (67 Conn. 428), 303.

TABLE OF CASES CITED. xxvii

References are to pages.

Carter v. Bridge Co. (104 Mass. 236), 38, 40.
Carter v. Thorson (So. Dak., 24 L. R. A. 734), 170.
Carter Co. v. Linton (120 U. S. 517), 148.
Carthage v. Frederick (122 N. Y. 269, 19 Am. St. Rep. 490, 10 L. R. A. 178), 67, 68, 299, 303.
Cary v. North Plainfield (49 N. J. L. 110), 92.
Cary v. Somerset Co. (45 N. J. L. 445), 77.
Cass v. Dillon (2 Ohio St. 617), 53.
Cass v. Jordan (95 U. S. 373), 159.
Cass Co. v. Johnston (95 U. S. 360), 157.
Cater v. N. W. Tel. Exch. Co. (60 Minn. 539, 63 N. W. Rep. 111), 104, 106.
Central v. Sears (2 Colo. 588), 179.
Central v. Wilcoxen (3 Colo. 566), 146.
Central Bridge Corp. v. Lowell (15 Gray, 106), 220.
Central Trans. Co. v. Pullman P. C. Co. (139 U. S. 22), 259, 263.
Chaddock v. Day (75 Mich. 527, 13 Am. St. Rep. 468), 84.
Chadeayne v. Robinson (55 Conn. 345), 307.
Chadoburne v. Newcastle (48 N. H. 196), 279.
Chadwick v. Colfax (51 Iowa, 70), 325.
Chaffee Co. Com'rs v. Potter (142 U. S. 355), 167.
Chamberlain v. Doner (13 Me. 466, 29 Am. Dec. 517), 221.
Chamberlain v. Evansville (77 Ind. 542), 65.
Chambers v. Barnard (127 Ind. 365, 11 L. R. A. 613), 231.
Chambers v. Satterlee (10 Minn. 290), 116.
Champaign v. Jones (132 Ill. 304), 296.
Champer v. Greencastle (138 Ind. 339, 46 Am. St. Rep. 390), 92, 93, 201.
Chan Yen, Ex parte (60 Cal. 78), 193.
Chandler v. Boston (112 Mass. 200), 41.

Chandler v. Douglass (8 Blackf. 10, 44 Am. Dec. 732), 17.
Chandler v. Scott (127 Ind. 226, 10 L. R. A. 375), 250.
Chapman v. Douglas Co. (107 U. S. 348), 151, 262, 263.
Chapman v. Oshkosh, etc. Ry. Co. (33 Wis. 620), 126.
Chapman v. Rochester (110 N. Y. 273, 1 L. R. A. 296), 311.
Charleston v. Reed (27 W. Va. 681, 55 Am. Rep. 336), 93.
Charliton v. Fitzsimmons (87 Iowa, 226), 206.
Cheeney v. Brookfield (60 Mo. 53), 148.
Chemung Bank v. Chemung (5 Denio, 517), 148.
Chesapeake P. Tel. Co. v. Mackenzie (74 Md. 36, 21 Atl. Rep. 690, 28 Am. St. Rep. 219), 107.
Chicago v. Baptist Theo. Union (115 Ill. 245), 115.
Chicago v. Bartree (100 Ill. 57), 91.
Chicago v. Blair (149 Ill. 310, 24 L. R. A. 412), 111.
Chicago v. Keefe (114 Ill. 222), 292.
Chicago v. Larned (34 Ill. 253), 114.
Chicago v. McCoy (136 Ill. 344, 11 L. R. A. 413), 189.
Chicago v. McGiven (78 Ill. 347), 302.
Chicago v. O'Brien (111 Ill. 532, 53 Am. Rep. 640), 211, 303.
Chicago v. Seben (165 Ill. 371), 309.
Chicago v. Union Building Ass'n (102 Ill. 79), 328.
Chicago v. Stratton (162 Ill. 494, 35 L. R. A. 84), 214.
Chicago v. Trotter (136 Ill. 430), 216.
Chicago, etc. Co. v. Chicago (88 Ill. 221), 91.
Chicago, etc. Ry. Co. v. Dunbar (100 Ill. 110), 27.
Chicago, etc. Ry. Co. v. Iowa (94 U. S. 155), 4.
Chicago, etc. Ry. Co. v. Langlade (56 Wis. 614), 41.
Chicago, etc. Ry. Co. v. Minnesota (134 U. S. 418), 136.
Chicago, etc. Ry. Co. v. Oconto (50 Wis. 189, 36 Am. Rep. 840), 41.

TABLE OF CASES CITED.

References are to pages.

Chicago, etc. Ry. Co. v. Otoe Co. (16 Wall. 667), 154.
Chicago, etc. R. Co. v. Sawyer (69 Ill. 285, 18 Am. Rep. 618), 304.
Chicago, etc. R. Co. v. U. P. R. Co. (47 Fed. Rep. 15), 258.
Chicago, B. & Q. R. Co. v. Quincy (139 Ill. 355), 100.
Child v. Boston (4 Allen, 41, 81 Am. Dec. 680), 252, 313.
Childrey v. Huntington (34 W. Va. 459, 11 L. R. A. 313), 301.
Chin Tan, In re (60 Cal. 78), 201.
Chisholm v. Montgomery (2 Woods, C. C. 584), 160.
Chope v. Eureka (78 Cal. 588, 4 L. R. A. 327), 291.
Christianson, In re (43 Fed. Rep. 243), 214, 215.
City v. Erie Pass. Ry. Co. (7 Phila., Pa., 321), 206.
City v. Kingsboro (161 Ind. 290), 126.
City v. Nash (Neb., 69 N. W. Rep. 964), 299.
City Council v. Aherns (4 Strob., S. C., L. 241), 201.
City Council v. Lombard (25 S. E. Rep. 772), 287.
City Council v. Pepper (1 Rich., S. C., 364), 131.
City Council v. Van Dorn (41 Ala. 505), 326.
City of Augusta v. Sweeney (44 Ga. 463, 9 Am. Rep. 172), 236.
City of Burlington v. Putnam Ins. Co. (31 Iowa, 102), 180.
City of Caldwell v. Prunelle (57 Kan. 511), 280.
City of Chadron v. Glover (43 Neb. 732, 62 N. W. Rep. 62), 293.
City of Chicago v. Hesing (83 Ill. 204), 297.
City of Delphi v. Evans (36 Ind. 90), 178.
City of Detroit v. Fort Wayne, etc. R. Co. (95 Mich. 456, 35 Am. St. Rep. 580, 20 L. R. A. 79), 194.
City of Ellsworth v. Rossitter (46 Kan. 237, 26 Pac. Rep. 674), 238.
City of Eufaula v. McNab (67 Ala. 588), 258.

City of Flora v. Naney (136 Ill. 45, 26 N. E. Rep. 645), 299.
City of Goshen v. Craxton (34 Ind. 239), 196.
City of Indianapolis v. Bieler (138 Ind. 30, 36 N. E. Rep. 857), 208.
City of Indianapolis v. Emmelman (108 Ind. 530), 297.
City of Laredo v. Nalle (65 Tex. 359), 327.
City of Paterson v. Barnett (46 N. J. L. 62), 178, 179.
City of Pawtucket v. Bray (R. I.; 37 Atl. Rep. 1), 300.
City of Port Huron v. Jenkinson (77 Mich. 414, 18 Am. St. Rep. 409), 303.
City of Poughkeepsie v. Quintard (136 N. Y. 275, 32 N. E. Rep. 764), 171.
City of St. Paul v. Lawton (61 Minn. 537), 215.
City of Tarkio v. Cook (120 Mo. 1, 41 Am. St. Rep. 678), 194, 195.
City R. Co. v. Citizens' St. Ry. Co. (166 U. S. 557), 100.
City Ry. Co. v. Mayor (77 Ga. 731, 4 Am. St. Rep. 106), 195.
Citizens' Bank v. City of Terrell (78 Tex. 456, 14 S. W. Rep. 1003), 168.
Citizens' Gas & Mining Co. v. Ellwood (114 Ind. 336), 176, 195.
Cincinnati v. Buckingham (10 Ohio, 257), 92.
Cincinnati v. Cameron (33 Ohio St. 336), 80, 139.
Cincinnati, etc. R. Co. v. Belle Center (48 Ohio St. 273, 27 N. E. Rep. 464), 122.
Circleville v. Neuding (41 Ohio St. 465), 270.
Claghorn v. Cullen (13 Pa. St. 133, 53 Am. Dec. 450), 26.
Claiborne Co. v. Brooks (111 U. S. 400), 145, 149, 150.
Clapp v. Board of Police (72 N. Y. 415), 246.
Clapp v. Davis (25 Iowa, 315), 326.
Clark v. Chicago (166 Ill. 84, 46 N. E. Rep. 730), 115.

TABLE OF CASES CITED.   xxix

References are to pages.

Clark v. Des Moines (19 Iowa, 199), 67, 145, 147.
Clark v. Iowa City (20 Wall. 583), 148.
Clark v. Miller (54 N. Y. 528), 249, 253.
Clark v. Mobile (36 Ala. 621), 326.
Clark v. Rogers (81 Ky. 43), 18.
Clark v. Thompson (37 Iowa, 536), 5, 7.
Clark v. Worcester (125 Mass. 226), 120.
Clarke v. Irwin (5 Nev. 92), 63.
Clarke v. Rochester (24 Barb., N. Y., 446), 5.
Clason v. Milwaukee (30 Wis. 316), 202.
Clay v. Nicholas Co. (4 Bush, Ky., 154), 150.
Clement v. Town of Casper (Wyo., 35 Pac. Rep. 472), 203.
Cleveland, In re (52 N. J. L. 188), 54, 55.
Cleveland v. King (132 U. S. 295), 292, 295.
Cleveland v. Stewart (3 Ga. 283), 3.
Cleveland, etc. Ry. Co. v. Connersville (Ind., 1897, 38 L. R. A. 175), 206.
Cleveland, etc. Tel. Co. v. Met. Fire Com. (55 Barb. 288), 79.
Clifford v. Commissioners (59 Me. 262), 124.
Cline v. Crescent City R. Co. (41 La. Ann. 1031, 6 So. Rep. 851), 202.
Clinton v. Cedar Rapids, etc. Ry. Co. (24 Iowa, 455), 26.
Clinton v. Clinton Co. (61 Iowa, 205), 86.
Clinton v. Henry Co. (115 Mo. 557), 118.
Closson v. Trenton (48 N. J. L. 438), 57.
Coal Float v. Jeffersonville (112 Ind. 19), 193.
Coates v. New York (7 Cow. 585), 86, 183.
Cobb v. Portland (55 Me. 381, 92 Am. Dec. 598), 280.
Cochran v. Frostburg (81 Md. 54), 75, 277, 278.
Cochran v. McCleary (22 Iowa, 75), 221, 321.

Cochrane v. Malden (152 Mass. 365), 309.
Coe v. Railway Co. (27 Minn. 197), 155.
Coffin v. Kearney Co. Com'rs (57 Fed. Rep. 137), 165.
Coggshal v. Des Moines (78 Iowa, 235), 79.
Cohen v. Cleveland (43 Ohio St. 190), 313.
Cohen v. New York (113 N. Y. 532), 273, 296, 298, 299.
Col. Pav. Co. v. Murphy (78 Fed. Rep. 28, 49 C. C. A. 17), 79.
Coldwater v. Tucker (36 Mich. 474, 24 Am. Rep. 601), 74.
Cole v. Kegler (64 Iowa, 69), 88.
Cole v. Muscatine (14 Iowa, 296), 314.
Cole v. Nashville (4 Sneed, Tenn., 162), 298.
Cole v. State (102 N. Y. 48), 37.
Coleman v. Second Ave. Ry. Co. (38 N. Y. 201), 100.
Coler v. Cleburne (131 U. S. 162), 160.
Coler v. Dwight School Tp. (3 N. Dak. 249, 55 N. W. Rep. 587), 165.
Coletrain v. McKane (3 Dev., N. C., 238, 24 Am. Dec. 256), 252.
Collins v. Davis (57 Iowa, 256), 324.
Collins v. Hatch (18 Ohio, 523, 51 Am. Dec. 465), 75.
Collinswood v. New Whatcom (16 Wash. 224, 47 Pac. Rep. 439), 273.
Coloma v. Eaves (92 U. S. 484), 150.
Columbus W. W. v. Mayor of Columbus (48 Kan. 99, 25 L. R. A. 534), 79, 259.
Colville v. Judy (73 Mo. 65), 124.
Colwell v. Boone (51 Iowa, 687), 279.
Comanche Co. v. Lewis (133 U. S. 198), 149.
Comer v. Folsom (13 Minn. 219, Gil. 205), 151.
Commissioners v. Allen (70 Pa. St. 465), 240.
Commissioners v. Allman (142 Ind. 58), 277.
Commissioners v. Aspinwall (21 How., U. S., 539), 164.

TABLE OF CASES CITED.

References are to pages.

Commissioners v. Gas Co. (12 Pa. St. 318), 201, 204.
Commissioners v. Detroit (28 Mich. 228, 15 Am. Rep. 202), 24.
Commissioners v. Johnson (19 Am. St. Rep. 96), 226.
Commissioners v. Johnson (71 N. C. 309), 128.
Commissioners v. Jones (12 Pa. St. 365), 224.
Commissioners v. Loague (121 U. S. 493), 162.
Commissioners v. North Liberty Gas Co. (2 Jones, 318), 204.
Commissioners v. Railway Co. (63 Iowa, 297), 126.
Commissioners v. Reynolds (20 Atl. Rep. 1011), 64.
Commissioners v. Shoemaker (27 Kan. 77), 63.
Commissioners v. Shorter (50 Ga. 489), 156.
Commissioners v. Standley (49 Pac. Rep. 23), 147.
Commonwealth v. Abraham (156 Mass. 57), 214.
Com. v. Adams (114 Mass. 323, 19 Am. Rep. 362), 205.
Com. v. Baltimore (132 Pa. St. 389), 23, 149.
Com. v. Boston (97 Mass. 555), 104.
Com. v. Brooks (109 Mass. 55), 204, 209, 214.
Com. v. Cutler (156 Mass. 52, 29 N. E. Rep. 1146), 86, 212.
Com. v. Davis (140 Mass. 485), 75, 189.
Com. v. Denworth (145 Pa. St. 172), 54.
Com. v. Elliott (121 Mass. 367), 208.
Com. v. Fahey (5 Cush. 408), 183.
Com. v. Fenton (139 Mass. 195, 29 N. E. Rep. 653), 204.
Com. v. Gage (118 Mass. 328), 204.
Com. v. Halstead (7 Atl. Rep. 221), 55.
Com. v. Jacksonville (Fla., 29 L. R. A. 416, 18 So. Rep. 339), 27, 33.
Com. v. Look (108 Mass. 452), 127.
Com. v. Macferron (152 Pa. St. 244, 25 Atl. Rep. 557), 55.
Com. v. Matthews (122 Mass. 60), 191, 204.

Com. v. Meeser (44 Pa. St. 341), 256, 321.
Com. v. Mitchell (82 Pa. St. 343), 77, 79.
Com. v. McCafferty (145 Mass. 384, 14 N. E. Rep. 451), 189.
Com. v. Mulhall (162 Mass. 496, 44 Am. St. Rep. 387), 204.
Com. v. Passmore (1 Serg. & R. 217), 98.
Com. v. Patch (97 Mass. 221), 201.
Com. v. Philadelphia (132 Pa. St. 238), 212.
Com. v. Pittsburg (34 Pa. St. 496), 316, 318.
Com. v. Parks (155 Mass. 531, 30 N. E. Rep. 174), 75.
Com. v. Patch (97 Mass. 221), 203.
Com. v. Patton (88 Pa. St. 258), 57, 60.
Com. v. Plaisted (148 Mass. 375), 25, 50, 71, 206.
Com. v. Robertson (5 Cush. 439), 204.
Com. v. Roy (140 Mass. 432), 198.
Com. v. Roxbury (9 Gray, 451), 11.
Com. v. Stodder (2 Cush. 563), 204.
Com. v. Turner (1 Cush., Mass., 493), 176.
Com. v. Wilkins (121 Mass. 356), 209.
Com. v. Worcester (3 Pick. 462), 202, 205.
Compton v. Zabriskie (101 U. S. 601), 323.
Conastota Knife Co. v. Newington Tramway Co. (69 Conn. 146, 36 Atl. Rep. 1107), 105.
Concord v. Robinson (121 U. S. 165), 150, 153.
Condict v. Jersey City (46 N. J. L. 157), 307.
Conklin v. School District (22 Kan. 521), 7.
Conner v. Woodfill (126 Ind. 85), 308.
Converse v. Porter (45 N. H. 399), 251.
Converse v. United States (21 How., U. S., 470), 230.
Cook v. Anamosa (66 Iowa, 427), 304.
Cook v. Hall (6 Ill. 579), 250.
Cook v. March (54 Ga. 468), 280.
Cook v. Milwaukee (27 Wis. 191), 302.

TABLE OF CASES CITED. xxxi

References are to pages.

Cook Co. v. Industrial School (125 Ill. 540, 8 Am. St. Rep. 386), 83.
Coolidge v. Brookline (114 Mass. 592), 108.
Coonley v. Albany (57 Hun, 327), 277.
Cooper, In re Application of (38 Hun, N. Y., 515), 121.
Cooper v. Phipps (L. R. 2 H. L. 149), 265.
Corbalis v. Newberry Tp. (132 Pa. St. 9), 304.
Corliss, In re (11 R. I. 638), 227.
Corpus Christi v. Woessner (58 Tex. 462), 170.
Corry v. Holtz (29 Ohio St. 320), 114.
Costello v. Wyoming (49 Ohio, 202, 30 N. E. Rep. 613), 51, 63.
Cotton v. New Providence (47 N. J. L. 401), 167.
Cotton v. Phillips (56 N. H. 220), 230.
Council Bluffs v. K. C. etc. Ry. Co. (45 Iowa, 358), 27.
Council Bluffs v. Stewart (51 Iowa, 385), 170.
Council Grove, Corp. Powers of (20 Kan. 619), 47.
County v. Graves (84 Cal. 71), 57.
County v. People (11 Ill. 202), 33.
County v. St. Paul & Sioux City Ry. Co. (28 Minn. 503, 508, 11 N. W. Rep. 73), 6.
County Com'rs v. Gibson (36 Md. 229), 252.
County of Richland v. County of Lawrence (12 Ill. 1), 33.
County of San Luis Obispo v. Hendricks (71 Cal. 242), 184.
County of Tipton v. Kimberlin (108 Ind. 449, 9 N. E. Rep. 407), 315.
Covington v. St. Louis (78 Ill. 548), 200.
Cowan's Case (1 Overton, Tenn., 311), 97.
Cowdry v. Caneadea (16 Fed. Rep. 532), 156.
Cowert, Ex parte (92 Ala. 94, 9 So. Rep. 225), 194.
Cowley v. Sunderland (6 H. & N. 565), 287.
Craig v. Andes (93 N. Y. 405), 157.

Crane v. West Chicago Park Commissioners (153 Ill. 348, 26 L. R. A. 311), 111.
Craw v. Tolono (96 Ill. 255, 35 Am. Rep. 143), 14, 118.
Crawford Co. v. Wilson (7 Ark. 214), 145.
Crawfordsville v. Brader (130 Ind. 149, 14 L. R. A. 268), 72, 137, 138, 178.
Creely Co. v. Milne (36 Neb. 301, 19 L. R. A. 689), 236.
Creighton v. Com. (83 Ky. 147), 233.
Creighton v. Marson (27 Cal. 613), 176.
Creighton v. San Francisco (42 Cal. 446), 33, 37, 40.
Cricket v. State (18 Ohio St. 9), 51, 58.
Cromarty v. Boston (127 Mass. 329, 34 Am. Rep. 331), 296.
Cromwell v. Sac Co. (96 U. S. 51), 162.
Cronin v. People (82 N. Y. 318), 183.
Cross v. Mayor of Morristown (18 N. J. Eq. 305), 179.
Crow v. Oxford Tp. (119 U. S. 215), 163.
Crowder v. Town of Sullivan (128 Ind. 486, 28 N. E. Rep. 94), 174.
Crowley v. Christensen (137 U. S. 86), 85.
Cuddon v. Eastwick (1 Salk. 143), 5.
Culbertson v. Fulton (127 Ill. 30), 173.
Culler, In re (53 Hun, N. Y., 534), 40.
Culver v. Streator (130 Ill. 238), 30, 271, 279, 280.
Cumberland Co. v. Pennell (69 Me. 357, 31 Am. Rep. 284), 253.
Cummins v. City of Seymour (79 Ind. 491, 44 Am. Rep. 226), 272, 309.
Cupp v. Commissioners (19 Ohio St. 173), 123.
Curran v. Boston (151 Mass. 505, 8 L. R. A. 243), 268, 285.
Curry v. District (62 Iowa, 102), 7.
Curry v. Township of Sioux City (62 Iowa, 104), 5, 7.
Curryer v. Merrill (25 Minn. 1, 33 Am. Rep. 450), 82.
Cushing v. Boston (128 Mass. 330, 35 Am. St. Rep. 383), 101, 295.

TABLE OF CASES CITED.

References are to pages.

Cushing v. The John Frazer (21 How., U. S., 184), 89.
Cutcamp v. Utt (60 Iowa, 156), 185.
Cutler v. Houston (158 U. S. 423), 162.
Cutting v. Stone (7 Vt. 471), 21.
Czarnieck's Appeal (11 Atl. Rep. 660), 88.

D.

Dabney v. Hudson (68 Miss. 292, 24 Am. St. Rep. 276), 233.
Daggett v. Colgan (92 Cal. 53, 14 L. R. A. 474), 153.
Dailey v. State (8 Blackf., Ind., 329), 231.
Dakota County v. Parker (7 Minn. 267), 266.
Daley v. St. Paul (7 Minn. 390, Gil. 311), 32.
Dalrymple v. Whitingham (26 Vt. 345), 146.
Daly v. Georgia, etc. R. Co. (80 Ga. 793, 12 Am. St. Rep. 286), 102.
Daly v. Morgan (69 Md. 460), 41.
Damon v. Granby (2 Pick. 345), 221.
Damour v. Lyon City (44 Iowa, 276), 310.
Danaher v. Brooklyn (119 N. Y. 241), 307.
Danversberger v. Pendergast (128 Ill. 229), 194.
Danville v. Shelton (76 Va. 325), 177.
Darby v. Sharon Hill (112 Pa. St. 66), 43, 44.
Dargan v. Mobile (31 Ala. 469, 70 Am. Dec. 505), 279.
Darkin, In re (10 Hun, N. Y., 269), 189.
Darlington v. City of New York (31 N. Y. 164), 24, 26, 278, 279.
Darlington v. Ward (48 S. C. 570), 193.
Darrow v. People (8 Colo. 426), 57, 65, 225.
Dartmouth College v. Woodward (4 Wheat. 518), 23, 134.
Datz v. Cleveland (52 N. J. L. 188, 7 L. R. A. 431), 240.
Davenport v. Bird (34 Iowa, 524), 132.
Davenport v. Kleinschmidt (6 Mont. 502), 79, 81, 174.

Davenport v. Peoria Ins. Co. (17 Iowa, 276), 299, 325.
Davidson v. Ramsey Co. (18 Minn. 482, Gil. 432), 150, 153, 154, 161, 167.
Davis v. Burger (54 Mich. 692), 226.
Davis v. Com. (167 U. S. 43, 162 Mass. 510, 44 Am. St. Rep. 389), 26 L. R. A. 712), 207.
Davis v. Crawfordsville (119 Ind. 1, 12 Am. St. Rep. 361), 308, 309, 312.
Davis v. Gaines (48 Ark. 370), 63.
Davis v. Graves (38 N. J. L. 104), 326.
Davis v. Litchfield (145 Ill. 313), 115, 202.
Davis v. Lynchburg (84 Va. 861), 114.
Davis v. Mayor of New York (1 Duer, 451), 240.
Davis v. Montgomery (51 Ala. 139), 277.
Davis v. New York (14 N. Y. 506), 100.
Davis v. Sawyer (133 Mass. 289), 89.
Davis v. Winslow (51 Me. 264), 98.
Davis v. Woolonough (9 Iowa, 104), 65.
Davock v. Moore (105 Mich. 120, 28 L. R. A. 783), 30, 38.
Davos v. Portland Water Com. (14 Oreg. 98), 135.
Day v. Jersey City (19 N. J. Eq. 412), 176.
Day v. Milford (5 Allen, 98), 101.
Day v. Mt. Pleasant (70 Iowa, 103), 302.
Dean v. Davis (51 Cal. 406), 219.
Dean v. New Milford Tp. (5 W. & S., Pa., 545), 293.
Decie v. Brown (167 Mass. 290, 45 N. E. Rep. 765), 200.
Decker v. Sergeant (125 Ind. 404), 209.
Decorah v. Bullis (25 Iowa, 12), 232.
Deehan v. Johnson (141 Mass. 23), 317.
Deems v. Baltimore (80 Md. 164, 26 L. R. A. 541), 87.
Deering, In re (93 N. Y. 651), 121.
Defer v. Detroit (67 Mich. 346), 312.
Deitz v. City of Central (1 Colo. 332), 18, 19.

TABLE OF CASES CITED. xxxiii

References are to pages.

Delane v. McDonald (41 Conn. 517), 256.
Delaware Co. v. McClintock (51 Ind. 325), 150.
Delger v. St. Paul (14 Fed. Rep. 567), 298.
Demattos v. New Whatcom (4 Wash. 127, 29 Pac. Rep. 933), 45.
Demorest v. New York (147 N. Y. 203, 41 N. E. Rep. 405), 237.
Dempter v. People (158 Ill. 36), 117.
Dennis v. Maynard (15 Ill. 477), 33.
Denny v. Spokane (48 C. C. A. 282, 79 Fed. Rep. 719), 117.
Dent v. Cook (45 Ga. 323), 149.
Denton v. Jackson (2 Johns. Ch. 220), 19.
Denver v. Bayer (7 Colo. 113), 123.
Denver v. Coulehan (20 Colo. 471, 27 L. R. A. 751), 41, 42.
Denver v. Darrow (13 Colo. 460, 16 Am. St. Rep. 215), 244, 255.
Denver v. Dunsmore (7 Colo. 328), 292.
Denver v. Williams (12 Colo. 475), 292.
Depot v. Simmons (112 Pa. St. 384), 270.
De Puyster, Petition of (80 N. Y. 565), 125.
Des Moines v. Gilchrist (67 Iowa, 210), 93, 177.
Des Moines Co. v. Harker (34 Iowa, 84), 6.
Des Moines Gas Co. v. Des Moines (44 Iowa, 505, 24 Am. Rep. 756), 80, 195.
Des Plaines v. Poyer (123 Ill. 111), 88.
Detroit v. Blackeby (21 Mich. 84), 201.
Detroit v. Howell Plank R. Co. (43 Mich. 140), 29.
Detroit v. Martin (34 Mich. 170), 265.
Detroit v. Osborne (135 U. S. 492), 292.
Detroit v. Detroit City Ry. Co. (37 Mich. 558), 102.
Detroit v. Fort Wayne, etc. Ry. Co. (95 Mich. 456, 20 L. R. A. 79), 100, 201.

Detroit Citizens' St. Ry. Co. v. Detroit (68 N. W. Rep. 304, 35 L. R. A. 859), 67, 96, 101.
Detroit City Ry. Co. v. Mills (85 Mich. 634), 105.
De Turk v. Com. (129 Pa. St. 151, 15 Am. St. Rep. 705, 5 L. R. A. 853), 229.
Devine v. Cook Co. (84 Ill. 590), 55, 66.
De Vose v. Richmond (18 Gratt. 338, 98 Am. Dec. 646), 149.
Dew v. Judges (3 Hen. & Munf. 1, 3 Am. Dec. 639), 256.
Dewey v. Des Moines (70 N. W. Rep. 605), 111, 113, 117.
Dey v. Jersey City (19 N. J. Eq. 414), 186, 219, 221.
Diamond Match Co. v. New Haven (55 Conn. 510), 309, 310.
Dibble v. New Haven (56 Conn. 199), 78.
Dickinson v. Neeley (30 S. C. 587, 3 L. R. A. 672), 153, 158.
Diehn v. Cincinnati (25 Ohio St. 305), 285.
Dimock v. Suffield (30 Conn. 129), 297.
Dingley v. Boston (100 Mass. 544), 88, 121.
Directors v. Houston (71 Ill. 318), 3.
Disdall v. Olmstead Co. (30 Minn. 96), 292.
District v. Bradley (164 U. S. 112), 108.
District Attorney, In re (11 Phil. 645), 231.
District of Columbia v. Cornell (130 U. S. 655), 145.
District of Columbia v. Woodbury (136 U. S. 450), 270, 292, 301.
Dively v. Elmira (51 N. Y. 506), 131.
Dix v. Dummuston (19 Vt. 263), 82.
Dixon Co. v. Field (111 U. S. 83), 165, 167, 168.
Doane v. Chicago R. R. Co. (160 Ill. 22, 35 L. R. A. 588), 102.
Doane v. Lake Street Elevated R. Co. (165 Ill. 510, 46 N. E. Rep. 510, 36 L. R. A. 97), 106.
Dobbins v. Northampton (5 N. J. L. 496), 57.
Dobbs v. Stauffer (24 Kan. 127), 88.

xxxiv TABLE OF CASES CITED.

References are to pages.

Dodd v. Hartford (25 Conn. 232), 323.
Dodge v. Granger (17 R. L 664), 283.
Doggert v. Colgan (92 Cal. 53, 14 L. R. A. 474), 108.
Doherty v. Braintree (148 Mass. 495), 304.
Donaher v. Brooklyn (51 Hun, 563), 276.
Donahoe v. Kansas City (136 Mo. 657), 273.
Donahoe v. Richards (38 Me. 379, 61 Am. Dec. 256), 83.
Doniell v. Sinclair (L. R. 6 App. Cas. 181), 265.
Donohue v. County of Wills (100 Ill. 94), 245.
Donovan v. Board of Education (85 N. Y. 117), 285.
Doolittle v. Broome County (18 N. Y. 155), 323.
Doon Tp. v. Cummins (142 U. S. 366), 171.
Door v. Mickley (16 Minn. 20, Gil. 8), 251.
Dosdale v. Olmstead County (33 Minn. 96, 44 Am. Rep. 185), 6, 306.
Dougherty v. Austin (94 Cal. 601), 53.
Douglas Co. v. Wallbridge (38 Wis. 179), 156.
Douglass v. Com. (108 Pa. St. 559), 77, 108.
Douglass v. Virginia City (5 Nev. 122), 75, 149.
Douglass v. Yallup (Burr. 722), 253.
Douglassville v. Johns (62 Ga. 423), 264.
Dovack v. Moore (105 Mich. 120, 28 L. R. A. 783), 33.
Dow v. Chicago (11 Wall., U. S., 108), 323.
Dowlan v. Sibley (36 Minn. 431), 5.
Downing v. Mason County (87 Ky. 208), 306.
Doyle v. Austin (47 Cal. 353), 116.
Drake v. Hudson River R. Co. (7 Barb., N. Y., 539), 178.
Drew v. Rogers (Cal., 34 Pac. Rep. 1081), 227.

Driftwood Co. v. Board (72 Ind. 226), 272.
Droz v. Baton Rouge (36 La. Ann. 340), 327.
Drummer v. Cox (165 Ill. 648, 46 N. E. Rep. 716), 108.
Du Bois v. Augusta (Dudley, Ga., 30), 199.
Dubois v. Kingston (102 N. Y. 219), 301.
Duffield v. Williamsport (162 Pa. St. 476, 25 L. R. A. 152), 83.
Duffy v. Dubuque (63 Iowa, 171), 301.
Duffy v. New Orleans (49 La. Ann. 114), 120.
Dullan v. Wilson (53 Mich. 392), 245.
Duluth v. Dibblee (62 Minn. 18), 109, 110.
Duluth v. Mallett (43 Minn. 204), 203, 205.
Dunbar v. Augusta (90 Ga. 390), 94.
Dunham v. Hyde Park (75 Ill. 371), 120.
Dunlap v. Knapp (14 Ohio St. 64), 252.
Dunnell Mfg. Co. v. Newell (15 R. I. 233), 265.
Durango v. Pennington (8 Colo. 257), 74.
Durgan v. Mobile (31 Ala. 469), 280.
Dutton v. Aurora (114 Ill. 138), 81.
Duty v. State (Ind. App., 36 N. E. Rep. 655), 238.
Duval Co. Com. v. Jacksonville (Fla., 29 L. R. A. 416), 319.
Dwight v. Springfield (4 Gray, 107), 324.
Dyer v. Covington Tp. (19 Pa. St. 200), 146.

E.

Eagle v. Kohn (84 Ill. 292), 155.
Earley v. San Francisco (55 Cal. 489), 47.
Easterly v. Town of Erwin (68 N. W. Rep. 919), 280.
Eastern, etc. Ry. Co. v. Central Ry. Co. (52 N. J. Law, 267, 31 Am. & Eng. Corp. Cas. 262), 33.

TABLE OF CASES CITED.

References are to pages.

Easthampton v. County Com'rs (164 Mass. 424), 123.
East Hartford v. Hartford Bridge (10 How., U. S., 511), 26, 28.
Eastman v. Clackamas County (32 Fed. Rep. 24), 293.
Eastman v. Meredith (36 N. H. 284), 11, 201, 306.
Eastman v. New York (5 Robt., N. Y., 389), 279.
East Oakland Tp. v. Skinner (94 U. S. 256), 152.
Easton Com. v. Covey (74 Md. 262), 214.
East St. Louis v. Bux (43 Ill. App. 276), 92.
East St. Louis v. East St. Louis G. L. Co. (98 Ill. 415, 38 Am. Rep. 97), 75, 174, 261.
East St. Louis v. People (124 Ill. 655, 23 Am. & Eng. Corp. Cas. 408), 169.
East Union Tp. v. Ryan (80 Pa. St. 459), 146.
Eaton v. Berlin (49 N. H. 219), 145.
Eaton v. Boston, etc. R. Co. (51 N. H. 504), 123.
Eaton v. Manitowoc (44 Wis. 489), 5, 46.
Eddy v. Granger (19 R. I. 105), 277.
Edgerley v. Concord (59 N. H. 78), 280, 287.
Edgwood, In re (130 Pa. St. 348), 43.
Edmonds v. Herbrandson (2 N. D. 270, 14 L. R. A. 725), 55, 60, 63.
Edmondson v. School District (Iowa, 67 N. W. Rep. 671), 162.
Edwards v. Charlotte R. R. Co. (39 S. C. 472, 22 L. R. A. 246), 307.
Edwards v. Chicago (140 Ill. 440), 115.
Edwards v. Pocahontas (47 Fed. Rep. 268), 284.
Edwards v. United States (103 U. S. 471), 242.
Edwards v. Watertown (24 Hun, 428), 70.
Eels v. Am. T. & T. Co. (143 N. Y. 133, 38 N. E. Rep. 202), 107.
Effingham v. Hamilton (68 Mich. 523), 82.

Egan v. Chicago (5 Ill. App. 70), 180.
Egerton v. Third Municipality (1 La. Ann. 435), 326.
Ehrgott v. New York (96 N. Y. 264), 270, 292.
Eichels v. Evansville St. Ry. Co. (78 Ind. 261), 65, 105.
Eischenlaub v. St. Joseph (113 Mo. 395), 93, 240.
Eitel v. State (33 Ind. 201), 61.
Eldora v. Burlingame (62 Iowa, 32), 194.
Eldridge v. Smith (34 Vt. 482), 152.
Electric L. Co. v. Jacksonville (36 Fla. 229, 30 L. R. A. 540), 153.
Electric Ry. Co. v. Grand Rapids (84 Mich. 257), 102.
Elizabethtown v. Lefler (23 Ill. 90), 188.
Elliott v. Kalkaska Sup. (58 Mich. 452, 55 Am. Rep. 706), 86.
Elliott v. Lisbon (57 N. H. 27), 291.
Elliott v. Minneapolis (59 Minn. 126), 77.
Elliott v. Philadelphia (75 Pa. St. 342, 15 Am. Rep. 581), 280.
Ellis v. Pratt City (113 Ala. 541, 33 L. R. A. 264), 325.
Ellis v. Lewiston (89 Me. 60), 302.
Ellison v. Rawley (89 N. C. 125), 243, 319.
Elmendorf v. Mayor, etc. (25 Wend., N. Y., 693), 188.
Elmore v. Drainage Commissioners (135 Ill. 269, 25 N. E. Rep. 1010), 270.
Ely v. Grand Rapids (84 Mich. 337), 77.
Emery v. Bradford (29 Cal. 75), 117.
Emery v. Lowell (104 Mass. 13), 308.
Emery v. Mariaville (50 Me. 315), 145.
Emery Co. v. Burresen (14 Utah, 328, 37 L. R. A. 732), 325.
Empire State, The (1 Newb. Adm. 541), 135.
Emporia v. Volmer (12 Kan. 622), 132.
English v. Smock (54 Ind. 115, 7 Am. Rep. 215), 152.
Enterprise v. State (29 Fla. 128, 10 So. Rep. 740), 50.

Erie's Appeal, In re (91 Pa. St. 398), 171, 174.
Erie v. Knapp (29 Pa. St. 173), 326.
Erie v. Magill (101 Pa. St. 616, 47 Am. Rep. 739), 303.
Ernest v. Parke (27 Am. Dec. 288), 37.
Ernst v. Morgan (39 N. J. Eq. 391), 56.
Erskine v. Steele Co. (4 N. Dak. 339, 28 L. R. A. 645), 145.
Erwin v. G. S. Tel. Co. (37 La. Ann. 63), 106.
Esling's Appeal (89 Pa. St. 205), 181.
Essex County Ry. Co. v. Lunenburg (49 Vt. 143), 155.
Estelle v. Lake Crystal (27 Minn. 243), 294.
Eufalie v. McNab (67 Ala. 588, 42 Am. Rep. 118), 133, 152.
Evans v. Job (8 Nev. 322), 63.
Evans v. Philadelphia Club (50 Pa. St. 107), 243.
Evansville v. Bayard (39 Ind. 450), 65.
Evansville v. Decker (84 Ind. 325, 43 Am. Rep. 86), 309, 311.
Evansville v. Dennett (161 U. S. 434), 164.
Evansville v. Evansville, etc. Ry. Co. (15 Ind. 395), 149.
Evansville v. State (118 Ind. 426, 4 L. R. A. 93), 30, 63.
Evansville v. Summers (108 Ind. 189), 65.
Everett v. Marquette (53 Mich. 450), 88.
Everett v. Smith (22 Minn. 53), 157, 222.
Evergreen Cemetery Ass'n v. New Haven (43 Conn. 234), 122.
Everts v. District (77 Iowa, 37, 14 Am. St. Rep. 204), 83.
Evison v. C., M. & St. P. Ry. Co. (45 Minn. 370), 202, 205.
Ewing v. Hoblizelle (81 Mo. 64), 57.
Ewing v. State (81 Tex. 177), 42.
Ewing v. Webster City (Iowa, 72 N. W. Rep. 511), 196, 197.
Eyler v. Commissioners (49 Md. 257, 23 Am. Rep. 249), 293.

F.

F. & M. Bank v. Loftus (133 Pa. St. 97, 19 Atl. Rep. 347), 63.
Fairchild v. Ogdensburg, etc. Ry. Co. (15 N. Y. 337), 145.
Fallbrook Irrigation Dist. v. Bradley (164 U. S. 112), 112, 152.
Fanner v. Alliance (29 Fed. Rep. 169), 199.
Fargusson v. Winslow (34 Minn. 384), 266.
Farmington River W. P. Co. v. County Com'rs (112 Mass. 206), 129.
Farquar v. Roseburg (18 Oreg. 271, 17 Am. St. Rep. 272), 292, 295.
Farr v. Grand Rapids (70 N. W. Rep. 411), 149.
Farrar v. St. Louis (80 Mo. 379), 114.
Farris v. Dudley (78 Ala. 124), 307.
Farwell v. Des Moines (66 N. W. Rep. 176), 115.
Farwell v. Manufacturing Co. (66 N. W. Rep. 177), 117.
Fass v. Seehawer (60 Wis. 525), 129.
Fath v. Keppel (72 Wis. 289, 7 Am. St. Rep. 867), 248.
Fath v. Tower Grove, etc. R. Co. (105 Mo. 537, 13 L. R. A. 74), 102.
Faulkner v. Aurora (85 Ind. 130, 44 Am. Rep. 1), 278.
Fawcett v. Pritchard (14 Wash. 604), 130.
Felchlin, Ex parte (96 Cal. 360, 31 Am. St. Rep. 223), 193.
Ferguson v. Davis County (57 Iowa, 601), 304.
Ferguson v. Halsell (47 Tex. 42), 177.
Feske, Ex parte (72 Cal. 125), 214.
Field v. Com. (32 Pa. St. 478), 245.
Field v. Des Moines (39 Iowa, 557), 269, 281, 282.
Field v. West Orange (36 N. J. Eq. 118), 311.
Fife v. Oshkosh (89 Wis. 540), 299, 302.
Fifield v. Phœnix (Ariz., 24 L. R. A. 430), 273.

TABLE OF CASES CITED. xxxvii

References are to pages.

Finch v. Board of Education (30 Ohio St. 37), 285.
Findlay v. Pittsburgh (82 Pa. St. 351), 77.
Findlay, City of, v. Pertz (66 Fed. Rep. 427. 31 C. C. A. 340), 76.
Findley v. Salem (137 Mass. 171, 50 Am. Rep. 289), 273.
Fire Ins. Co. v. Keeseville (148 N. Y. 46), 24, 73, 138, 139.
First Municipality v. Cutting (4 La. Ann. 336), 178.
First Municipality v. McDonough (2 Rob., La., 244), 149.
First Nat. Bank v. Americus (68 Ga. 190), 264.
First Nat. Bank v. Saratoga Co. (106 N. Y. 488), 148.
First Nat. Bank v. Sarles (129 Ind. 201, 28 Am. St. Rep. 185), 210.
Fisher v. Boston (104 Mass. 87, 6 Am. Rep. 196), 282, 307.
Fisk, Ex parte (72 Cal. 125), 191.
Fisk v. Kenosha (26 Wis. 23), 150.
Fitzgerald v. Berlin (64 Wis. 203), 294.
Fitzsimmons v. Brooklyn (102 N. Y. 537, 7 N. E. Rep. 878), 236.
Flack v. Hughes (67 Ill. 384), 152.
Flagg v. Hudson (142 Mass. 280), 297.
Flagg v. School District (4 N. Dak. 30, 25 L. R. A. 363, 58 N. W. Rep. 499), 160, 164, 165.
Flaherty, In re (105 Cal. 558, 27 L. R. A. 529), 201, 207, 213, 215.
Fleming v. Guthrie (32 W. Va. 1, 3 L. R. A. 57), 319.
Flemming v. Appleton (55 Wis. 90), 258.
Flieth v. City of Wausau (93 Wis. 448), 257, 315.
Flint v. Webb (25 Minn. 93), 111.
Flood v. State (19 Tex. App. 584), 199.
Florence, Ex parte Mayor of (78 Ala. 419), 69.
Flori v. St. Louis (69 Mo. 341, 33 Am. Rep. 504), 286.
Florida, etc. R. Co. v. State (31 Fla. 482, 20 L. R. A. 419), 317.

Flynn v. Canton Co. (40 Md. 321, 17 Am. Rep. 603), 211, 300, 303.
Flynn v. Taylor (127 N. Y. 586), 301.
Fobes v. Rome, W. & O. R. Co. (121 N. Y. 505, 8 L. R. A. 453), 105.
Folds v. Curlin (105 Ind. 221), 229, 230, 231.
Fond du Lac v. Crane (16 Wis. 196), 5.
Fones Bros. H. Co. v. Erb (54 Ark. 645, 13 L. R. A. 353), 74, 79.
Foote v. Cincinnati (11 Ohio St. 408, 38 Am. Dec. 737), 26.
Fopper v. Wheatland (59 Wis. 623), 297.
Forbes v. Escambria Board of Health (48 Fla. 26, 13 L. R. A. 549), 284.
Force v. Town of Batavia (61 Ill. 100), 160.
Ford v. Delta, etc. Co. (164 U. S. 662), 115.
Forman v. Hennepin Co. (64 Minn. 371, 67 N. W. Rep. 207), 95.
Forsyth v. Atlanta (45 Ga. 152), 277.
Forsyth v. B. & O. Tel. Co. (12 Mo. App. 494), 106.
Foster v. Coleman (10 Cal. 278), 145.
Foster v. Fowler (60 Pa. St. 27), 4, 325.
Foster v. Kansas (112 U. S. 201), 244.
Foster v. Lane (30 N. H. 315), 7.
Foster v. Police Com'rs (102 Cal. 183, 41 Am. St. Rep. 194), 195.
Fouche v. Swain (80 Ala. 153), 250.
Fowle v. Alexandria (3 Pet., U. S., 398), 277.
Fox v. Ellison (43 Minn. 41), 130.
Fox v. McDonald (101 Ala. 51, 46 Am. St. Rep. 98, 21 L. R. A. 529), 224.
Foxworthy v. Hastings (25 Neb. 133), 294, 299.
Frame v. Felix (167 Pa. St. 47, 27 L. R. A. 802), 77.
Frances v. Howard Co. (54 Fed. Rep. 487), 168.
Franklin Co. v. German Sav. Bank (142 U. S. 93), 162.
Franklin Co. v. Mitchell (25 Ohio St. 143), 5.
Franklin Wharf Co. v. Portland (67 Me. 46), 98.

D

References are to pages.

Frazee, In re (63 Mich. 396), 69, 182, 202, 204, 206, 214, 215, 216.
Frazer v. Warfield (13 Md. 279), 70.
Freeholders v. Buck (51 N. J. L. 155), 61.
Freeholders v. Stevenson (46 N. J. L. 173), 51.
Freeport v. Isbell (83 Ill. 440), 295.
Freeport v. Marks (59 Pa. St. 253), 193.
French v. Boston (129 Mass. 592), 286.
French v. Kirkland (1 Paige, 117), 112.
French v. Brunswick (21 Me. 29), 101.
French v. Burlington (42 Iowa, 614), 169, 170, 175.
Frey v. Michie (68 Mich. 323), 256.
Friend v. Pittsburgh (131 Pa. St. 305, 6 L. R. A. 636), 146.
Fritz v.' Hobson (L. R. 14 Ch. Div. 542), 98.
Frost v. Beekman (1 Johns. Ch. 288), 250.
Frost v. Cherry (122 Pa. St. 417), 54, 61.
Ft. Smith v. York (52 Ark. 84), 291.
Ft. Wayne v. Lake Shore, etc. R. Co. (18 L. R. A. 367, 32 N. E. Rep. 215), 133, 134.
Ft. Wayne v. Rosenthal (75 Ind. 156, 39 Am. Rep. 127), 228.
Ft. Worth v. Crawford (74 Tex. 404), 307.
Fuller v. Grand Rapids (105 Mich. 529, 63 N. W. Rep. 530), 271.
Fulliam v. New Muscatine (70 Iowa, 436, 30 N. W. Rep. 861), 299.
Fulton v. Riverton (42 Minn. 395), 165.
Furnell v. St. Paul (20 Minn. 117, Gil. 101), 304.

G.

Gabel v. Houston (29 Tex. 336), 195.
Gahagan v. Railway Co. (1 Allen, 187), 205.
Gale v. Kalamazoo (23 Mich. 344, 9 Am. Rep. 80), 80.
Galena v. Corwith (48 Ill. 423, 95 Am. Dec. 557), 149.
Galesburg v. Hawkinson (75 Ill. 156), 5, 21, 41.

Galesburg v. Searles (114 Ill. 217), 114.
Gallerno v. Rochester (46 U. C. Q. B. 279), 190.
Galveston v. Posnainsky (62 Tex. 118), 6, 292.
Galveston & W. R. Co. v. Galveston (39 S. W. Rep. 96, 36 L. R. A. 33), 103.
Galveston, etc. Ry. Co. v. Harris (Tex. Civ. App., 36 S. W. Rep. 776), 182.
Galvin v. New York (112 N. Y. 223), 306.
Gambel v. Stolte (59 Ind. 446), 125.
Gannon v. Hargadon (10 Allen, 106), 307.
Garden City v. Abbott (34 Kan. 283), 193.
Gardner, In re (68 N. Y. 467), 256.
Gardner v. Newburg Tp. (2 Johns. Ch. 162), 122.
Gargan v. Louisville, etc. R. Co. (89 Ky. 212, 6 L. R. A. 340), 104.
Garham v. Conger (85 Ky. 583), 115.
Garrett v. Jones (65 Md. 260), 100.
Garrison v. Chicago (7 Biss. 480), 79.
Garvin v. Wiswell (83 Ill. 215), 145.
Garza, Ex parte (28 Tex. App. 381, 19 Am. St. Rep. 845), 69, 90.
Gas Co. v. Donnelly (93 N. Y. 557), 79.
Gas Co. v. San Francisco (9 Cal. 453), 178, 264.
Gaskill v. Dudley (6 Met. 546), 19.
Gay v. Mutual N. T. Co. (12 Mo. App. 485), 100.
Gelpcke v. Dubuque (1 Wall. 475), 153.
George v. Oxford Tp. (16 Kan. 72), 157.
George's Creek Coal Co. v. New Central Coal Co. (40 Md. 425), 125.
German Savings Bank v. Franklin Co. (128 U. S. 526), 159, 163.
Geuild v. Chicago (82 Ill. 472), 64.
Giaufortone v. New Orleans (61 Fed. Rep. 64, 24 L. R. A. 592), 278, 279.
Gibbs v. Morgan (39 N. J. Eq. 136), 57.
Gibson v. Huntington (38 W. Vá. 177), 297.
Gilbert-Arnold Land Co. v. Superior (91 Wis. 353, 64 N. W. Rep. 999), 195.

TABLE OF CASES CITED. xxxix

References are to pages.

Gilchrist v. Gough (63 Ind. 589), 250.
Giles v. School Dist. (31 N. H. 304), 7.
Gilham v. Well (64 Ga. 192), 210.
Gillespie v. Lincoln (35 Neb. 34, 16 L. R. A. 349), 283.
Gillespie v. Rogers (146 Mass. 612), 251.
Gillison v. Charleston (16 W. Va. 282, 37 Am. Rep. 763), 311.
Gilluly v. Madison (63 Wis. 518), 311, 312.
Gillvie v. Lockport (122 N. Y. 403), 303, 305.
Gilman v. Laconia (55 N. H. 130, 20 Am. Rep. 175), 303, 312.
Gilman v. Sheboygan (2 Black, 510), 35, 36.
Gilmore v. Holt (4 Pick. 257), 195.
Gilson v. Dayton (123 U. S. 59), 163.
Giozza v. Tiernan (148 U. S. 657), 209.
Girard v. Omaha, etc. Ry. Co. (14 Neb. 270), 125.
Girard v. Philadelphia (7 Wall., U. S., 1), 26.
Gladstone v. Throop (71 Fed. Rep. 341, 37 U. S. App. 481), 152.
Glantz v. Bend (106 Ind. 305), 296.
Glass Co. v. Ashbury (49 Cal. 571), 177.
Glasscock v. Lyons (20 Ind. 1, 83 Am. Dec. 299), 237.
Glessner v. Anheuser-Busch Ass'n (100 Mo. 508), 102.
Goddard's Case (16 Pick. 504, 28 Am. Dec. 259), 211.
Goddard v. Hartwell (33 Am. St. Rep. 373), 269.
Goddard v. Seymour (30 Conn. 349), 265.
Goesler v. Georgetown (6 Wheat., U. S., 593), 100.
Gooch v. McGee (83 N. C. 59), 4.
Goodale v. Fennell (27 Ohio St. 426), 35.
Goodfellow v. New York (100 N. Y. 15), 294, 300.
Goodnow v. Ramsey Co. (11 Minn. 31), 145, 147, 148, 149.
Goose River Bank v. Willow Lake School Tp. (1 N. Dak. 26), 259.
Goshen v. England (119 Ind. 368, 5 L. R. A. 253), 292.

Goshen v. Myers (119 Ind. 196), 303.
Gould v. Topeka (32 Kan. 485), 295.
Govern v. State (48 N. J. L. 612, 9 Atl. Rep. 577), 57.
Graham v. Albert Lea (48 Minn. 201, 50 N. W. Rep. 1108), 299.
Graham v. Carondelet (33 Mo. 262), 186.
Granby v. Thurston (23 Conn. 416), 44.
Grand Rapids v. Blakely (40 Mich. 367), 264.
Grand Rapids v. Braudy (105 Mich. 670, 32 L. R. A. 116), 204, 210, 211.
Grand Rapids v. Newton (Mich., 1896, 35 L. R. A. 226), 212.
Grand Rapids B. Co. v. Jarvis (30 Mich. 308), 123.
Grand Rapids Electric Co. v. Grand Rapids Gas Co. (33 Fed. Rep. 659), 69, 98.
Grank v. Stillwater (35 Minn. 242), 270.
Grant v. Davenport (36 Iowa, 396), 108, 170, 174.
Grant v. Erie (69 Pa. St. 420, 8 Am. Rep. 272), 275, 281.
Grant Co. v. Lake Co. (17 Oreg. 453), 170.
Gratiot v. Mo. Pac. Ry. Co. (116 Mo. 450, 16 L. R. A. 189), 205.
Graves v. Shattuc (35 N. H. 257), 98.
Gray v. Iowa Land Co. (26 Iowa, 387), 96.
Gray v. McWilliams (98 Cal. 157, 21 L. R. A. 593), 307.
Great Falls Bank v. Farmington (41 N. H. 32), 147.
Green v. Cape May (41 N. J. L. 46), 178, 179.
Green v. Harrison County (61 Iowa, 311), 293.
Green v. Reading (9 Watts, Pa., 382), 313.
Green v. Spenser (67 Iowa, 410), 257.
Green v. Savannah (6 Ga. 1), 86.
Green v. Ward (82 Va. 324), 70.
Green County v. Eubanks (80 Ala. 204), 5.
Greensborough v. Ehrenruch (80 Ala. 579, 60 Am. Rep. 130), 86, 88, 210.

References are to pages.

Greenville W. W. Co. v. Greenville (70 Miss. 669), 80.
Greenwood v. Louisville (13 Bush, 226, 26 Am. Rep. 263), 283, 292.
Gregory, Ex parte (20 Tex. App. 210, 54 Am. Rep. 516), 91.
Gregory v. Bridgport (41 Conn. 76), 75.
Gregory v. New York (113 N. Y. 416), 245.
Grenada Co. v. Brogden (112 U. S. 261, 7 Am. & Eng. Corp. Cas. 329), 151.
Gridley v. Bloomington (88 Ill. 554, 30 Am. Rep. 566), 211.
Griffin v. Inman (57 Ga. 370), 157.
Grim v. Weisenberg School District (57 Pa. St. 433), 265, 266.
Grimes v. Keene (52 N. H. 335), 289.
Grinnell v. Des Moines (57 Iowa, 144), 112, 178.
Grogan v. San Francisco (13 Cal. 500), 28, 39, 134.
Grossenbach v. Milwaukee (65 Wis. 31, 56 Am. Rep. 614), 302,
Grossman v. Oakland (37 L. R. A. 593), 88.
Grousch v. State (42 Ind. 547), 214.
Grove Street, In re (61 Cal. 438), 124.
Grube v. St. Paul (34 Minn. 402), 282.
Grummon v. Raymond (1 Conn. 40, 6 Am. Dec. 200), 249.
Gude v. Mankato (30 Minn. 256), 304.
Guerrero, In re (69 Cal. 88), 215.
Guilder v. Otsego (20 Minn. 74), 38.
Guilford v. Supervisors (18 Barb. 615, 13 N. Y. 144), 39, 40.
Gullikson v. McDonald (62 Minn. 278), 279, 280, 284.
Gunn, In re (9 L. R. A. 519), 233.
Gurnee v. Chicago (40 Ill. 165), 111.
Gustafson v. Hamm (56 Minn. 334), 102.
Guthrie v. Territory (1 Okla. 188, 21 L. R. A. 841), 320.
Gutzweller v. People (14 Ill. 142), 34.
Guy v. Washburn (23 Cal. 111), 266.

H.

H., etc. v. Norfolk (6 Allen, Mass., 353), 38.
Haag v. Board (60 Ind. 511, 28 Am. Rep. 654), 271, 272.
Hager v. Reclamation Dist. (111 U. S. 701), 112.
Hager v. Supervisors (47 Cal. 222), 112.
Hagerston v. Sehner (37 Md. 180), 279.
Halbren v. Campbell (82 Mich. 255, 9 L. R. A. 408), 256.
Haldeman v. Penn. Ry. Co. (50 Pa. St. 435), 120.
Hale v. Houghton (8 Mich. 458), 87.
Halgren v. Campbell (82 Mich. 255, 9 L. R. A. 408), 234, 244.
Hall v. Bray (51 Mo. 288), 63.
Hall v. Houghton (8 Mich. 451), 188.
Hall v. Lauderdale (46 N. Y. 70), 247.
Hall v. Ray (40 Vt. 576, 94 Am. Dec. 440), 221.
Hallenbeck v. Hahn (2 Neb. 377), 153.
Halsey v. Rapid Tr. St. Ry. Co. (47 N. J. Eq. 380, 20 Atl. Rep. 859), 105, 106, 178.
Hamilton Gas L. Co. v. Hamilton City (146 U. S. 258), 142.
Hamlin v. Meadville (6 Neb. 227), 23, 149.
Hamm v. New York (70 N. Y. 460), 285.
Hammer v. State (44 N. J. L. 667), 57, 62.
Hammett v. Philadelphia (65 Pa. St. 146), 110, 111.
Hampshire Co. v. Franklin Co. (16 Mass. 75), 44.
Hancock v. Chicot Co. (32 Ark. 575), 145.
Hancock v. Hazzard (12 Cush. 112, 59 Am. Dec. 171), 254.
Hand v. Brookline (126 Mass. 324), 288.
Hand v. Newton (92 N. Y. 88), 134.
Handley v. Howe (22 Me. 562), 250.
Haniford v. Kansas City (103 Mo. 172), 292.

TABLE OF CASES CITED. xli

References are to pages.

Hanlin v. Chicago, etc. Co. (61 Wis. 515), 307.
Hannibal v. Fauntleroy (105 U. S. 408), 157.
Hannibal v. Marion Co. (69 Mo. 571), 23.
Hanson v. Vernon (27 Iowa, 28, 53), 3.
Hardenbrock v. Town of Legonier (95 Ind. 70), 199.
Hardy v. McKinney (107 Ind. 367), 129.
Harker v. Des Moines Co. (34 Iowa, 84), 6.
Harmon v. Chicago (110 Ill. 400), 199.
Harmon v. St. Louis (38 S. W. Rep. 1102), 88, 89, 277.
Harper v. Milwaukee (30 Wis. 365), 310.
Harrington v. Buffalo (121 N. Y. 147), 302.
Harrington v. Lansingburg (110 N. Y. 145), 270.
Harrington v. Town of Plain View (27 Minn. 224, 229, 6 N. W. Rep. 777), 6, 152.
Harris v. Atlanta (62 Ga. 290), 280.
Harris v. School District (28 N. H. 58), 7.
Harris v. State (92 Miss. 960, 33 L. R. A. 85), 221.
Harrisburg v. Segelbaum (151 Pa St. 348), 110.
Harrison v. Baltimore (1 Gill, Md., 202), 86.
Harshman v. Bates (92 U. S. 569), 157.
Hart v. Bridgeport (13 Blatchf. 289), 278.
Hart v. Murray (48 Ohio St. 605), 53.
Hart v. New Orleans (12 Fed. Rep. 292), 325.
Hart v. Red Cedar (63 Wis. 634), 293.
Hartford v. Talcott (48 Conn. 525), 303.
Hartford County v. Wise (75 Md. 38), 304.
Harvard v. Drainage Co. (51 Ill. 130), 31.
Harvey v. Hillsdale (86 Mich. 330, 49 N. W. Rep. 141), 270.
Harwood v. Marshall (9 Md. 83), 256, 319.

Harwood v. Shaw (126 Ill. 53), 129.
Hasbroucke v. Milwaukee (21 Wis. 219), 39.
Haskell, In re (112 Cal. 412, 32 L. R. A. 527), 181, 194.
Haskell v. Bartlett (34 Cal. 281), 190.
Hathaway v. Hinton (1 Jones, N. C., 243), 252.
Haupt's Appeal (125 Pa. St. 211, 8 L. R. A. 536), 189.
Haus v. Bethlehem (134 Pa. St. 12, 19 Atl. Rep. 437), 313.
Hausmann v. Madison (85 Wis. 187, 21 L. R. A. 263), 302.
Havens v. Lathene (75 N. C. 505), 254.
Hawes v. Chicago (158 Ill. 653, 30 L. R. A. 225), 202.
Hawkins v. Carroll Co. (50 Miss. 735), 150.
Hawkins v. Huron (2 U. P. C. C. P. 72), 182.
Hawkins v. Sanders (45 Mich. 491), 101.
Hawley v. City of Atlantic (92 Iowa, 172, 60 N. W. Rep. 519), 297.
Hayden v. Noyes (5 Conn. 391), 201.
Hayes, Ex parte (98 Cal. 555, 20 L. R. A. 701), 86, 209.
Hayes v. Douglass Co. (92 Wis. 429, 31 L. R. A. 213), 153.
Hayes v. Holly Springs (114 U. S. 120), 156.
Hayes v. Hyde Park (153 Mass. 514, 12 L. R. A. 249), 296.
Hayes v. Oshkosh (33 Wis. 314, 14 Am. St. Rep. 760), 280, 282.
Hayes v. Porter (22 Me. 371), 253.
Hayne v. Cape May (50 N. J. L. 55), 193.
Haynes, In re (54 N. J. L. 6), 59.
Hays v. Oil City (11 Atl. Rep. 63), 238.
Hayward v. School District (2 Cush. 419), 220.
Haywood v. Buffalo (14 N. Y. 534), 322.
Hazzard v. Council Bluffs (79 Iowa, 106), 312.
Health Dept. v. Rector (145 N. Y. 32, 27 L. R. A. 710), 84.
Heath v. Des Moines, etc. R. Co. (61 Iowa, 11), 102.

References are to pages.

Heath v. Fond du Lac (63 Wis. 228), 811.
Heeney v. Sprague (11 R. I. 456, 23 Am. Rep. 502), 308.
Heine v. Levee Com'rs (19 Wall., U. S., 655), 318.
Heiser v. New York (104 N. Y. 68), 314.
Heiskell v. Baltimore (65 Md. 125, 57 Am. Rep. 308), 222, 223.
Heiskell v. Mayor (65 Md. 125, 4 Atl. Rep. 116), 68.
Helen v. Lowell (3 Allen, Mass., 407), 195.
Helena Consol. Wat. Co. v. Steele (49 Pac. Rep. 382, 37 L. R. A. 412), 14, 139.
Heller v. Sedalia (53 Mo. 159, 14 Am. Rep. 444), 281.
Heller v. Stremmel (52 Mo. 309), 7.
Henderson v. County Court (50 Mo. 317, 11 Am. Rep. 415), 63.
Henderson v. Davis (106 N. C. 88), 193.
Henderson v. Minneapolis (32 Minn. 319), 309, 314.
Henkes v. Minneapolis (42 Minn. 530), 302.
Henley v. Lyme (5 Bing. 91), 223.
Hennepin v. Bartleson (37 Minn. 343), 110.
Henry v. Sprague (11 R. I. 457, 23 Am. Rep. 502), 195.
Henry Co. v. Soper (26 Iowa, 264), 5.
Hensley v. People (82 Ill. 544), 152.
Herschoff v. Beverly (43 N. J. L. 139), 130.
Herzo v. San Francisco (33 Cal. 134), 177.
Hess v. Pegg (6 Nev. 23), 63.
Hewitt's Appeal (88 Pa. St. 55), 41.
Hewitt v. School Dist. (94 Ill. 528), 149.
Higby v. Bunce (10 Conn. 567), 188, 189.
Higginson v. Nahant (11 Allen, 532), 122.
Hill v. Boston (122 Mass. 344), 11, 291, 292, 306.
Hill v. Boyland (40 Miss. 618), 182.
Hill v. Charlotte (72 N. C. 55, 21 Am. Rep. 451), 278.
Hill v. Easthampton (140 Mass. 381), 153.
Hill v. Fond du Lac (56 Wis. 242), 294.
Hill v. McNichol (76 Me. 315), 250.
Hill v. Memphis (134 U. S. 198), 149, 150.
Hill v. Rensselaer County (119 N. Y. 344), 279.
Hill v. Territory (Wash., 7 Pac. Rep. 63), 227.
Hine v. Keokuk, etc. R. Co. (42 Iowa, 636), 101.
Hine v. Robbins (8 Conn. 347), 250.
Hines v. Charlotte (72 Mich. 278, 1 L. R. A. 844), 271.
Hines v. Lockport (50 N. Y. 236), 298.
Hinze v. People (92 Ill. 406), 65, 226.
Hitchcock v. Galveston (96 U. S. 351), 70, 259, 260.
Hitchins v. Frostburg (69 Md. 100), 311, 312.
Hoboken v. Gear (27 N. J. L. 267), 191.
Hockett v. State (105 Ind. 250), 4.
Hodges v. Buffalo (2 Denio, 110), 153, 274.
Hodgman v. Chicago, etc. Ry. Co. (20 Minn. 48), 152, 155, 156, 159.
Hoffmann v. Greenwood Co. (23 Kan. 307), 239.
Hoglan v. Carpenter (4 Bush, Ky., 86), 230.
Hogland v. Sacramento (15 Cal. 142), 38.
Holden v. Smith (8 Moore, P. C. C. 75), 249.
Holdenell, Ex parte (74 Mo. 401), 196.
Holland v. Baltimore (11 Md. 186), 323.
Hollandbeck v. Winnebago County (95 Ill. 148, 35 Am. Rep. 151), 286.
Hollenbeck v. Marshalltown (62 Iowa, 21), 132.
Holmes v. Shreveport (31 Fed. Rep. 113), 149.
Holt Co. v. Scott (Neb., 1898, 73 N. W. Rep. 681), 226, 231, 232.
Holton v. Milwaukee (31 Wis. 27), 100.

TABLE OF CASES CITED.

References are to pages.

Holwedell, Ex parte (74 Mo. 395), 132.
Homestead St. Ry. Co. v. Pittsburgh, etc. Ry. Co. (166 Pa. St. 162, 27 L. R. A. 383), 102.
Hood v. Lynn (1 Allen, 103), 70, 153.
Hoole v. Kincaid (16 Nev. 217), 77.
Hooper v. Creager (84 Md. 197), 222.
Hooper v. Emery (14 Me. 375), 13.
Hope v. Dederick (8 Humph., Tenn., 1, 47 Am. Dec. 597), 17.
Hope v. Henderson (15 N. C. 29, 25 Am. Dec. 677), 242.
Hope v. Henderson (4 Dev. N. C. L. 1), 242.
Hopkins v. Mayor (4 M. & W. 461, 640), 195.
Hopkins v. Ogden City (5 Utah, 390, 16 Pac. Rep. 596), 296.
Horton v. Mobile Com'rs (43 Ala. 598), 46.
Horton v. Shelby Co. (118 U. S. 425), 232.
Hotchkiss v. Marion (12 Mont. 218, 29 Pac. Rep. 821), 171.
Hough v. Cook (44 Iowa, 639), 224.
House, Re (23 Colo. 87, 33 L. R. A. 832), 95.
House v. State (41 Miss. 737), 214.
House Roll No. 284, In re (31 Neb. 505), 154.
Houston v. Houston C. Ry. Co. (84 Tex. 581), 80.
Hover v. Barkhoff (44 N. Y. 113, 125), 252.
How v. People (88 Ill. 389), 190.
Howard v. Huron (S. D., 59 N. W. Rep. 833, 60 N. W. Rep. 803), 162, 318.
Howard v. Manufacturing Co. (139 U. S. 199), 76.
Howard County Com'rs v. Legg (93 Ind. 523, 47 Am. Rep. 390), 293.
Howe v. Plainfield (8 Vroom, N. J., 151), 196.
Howe v. West End St. Ry. Co. (167 Mass. 46), 105.
Howe v. White (49 Cal. 659), 251.
Howe v. Wright Co. (82 Iowa, 164, 47 N. W. Rep. 1086), 234.

Howes v. Chicago (158 Ill. 653, 30 L. R. A. 225), 193.
Howsman v. Trenton Water Works (119 Mo. 304, 23 L. R. A. 146), 268, 281.
Hoyt v. Danbury (69 Conn. 341), 300.
Hoyt v. East Saginaw (19 Mich. 39), 109, 184.
Hoyt v. Hudson (27 Wis. 656, 9 Am. Rep. 473), 309.
Hubbard v. Concord (35 N. H. 52, 69 Am. Dec. 520), 294.
Hubbard v. Linden (48 Wis. 674), 145.
Hubbell v. Viroqua (67 Wis. 343, 58 Am. Rep. 866), 277.
Hudson v. Marlborough (154 Mass. 218, 28 N. E. Rep. 147), 296.
Hudson, Freeholders of, v. Buck (51 N. J. L. 155), 57.
Hudson R. T. Co. v. Waterveldt Tp. (135 N. Y. 393, 17 L. R. A. 674), 101.
Huesing v. Rock Island (128 Ill. 465, 15 Am. St. Rep. 129), 67, 86.
Hughes v. Lawrenceburg (37 S. W. Rep. 257), 284.
Hughes v. Milligan (42 Kan. 396, 22 Pac. Rep. 313), 63.
Hughes v. Monroe County (147 Ill. 49), 284, 285.
Hughes v. Recorder's Court (75 Mich. 574, 4 L. R. A. 863), 93.
Hughson v. Crane (115 Cal. 404), 152.
Huling v. Kaw Valley R. Co. (130 U. S. 559), 125.
Hume v. New Haven (40 Conn. 478), 213.
Hungerford v. Hartford (39 Conn. 279), 112.
Hunt v. Chicago, etc. Ry. Co. (121 Ill. 638), 102.
Hunt v. New York (109 N. Y. 134), 293.
Hunter v. Chandler (45 Mo. 452), 237.
Hunter v. Farren (127 Mass. 481), 89.
Hursh v. Warner (102 Mich. 238, 26 L. R. A. 484), 86.
Huston v. Council Bluffs (Iowa, 69 N. W. Rep. 1130, 36 L. R. A. 211), 302.

TABLE OF CASES CITED.

References are to pages.

Hutchings v. Sullivan (Me., 37 Atl. Rep. 883), 299.
Hutchins v. Mt. Vernon (40 Ill. App. 19), 191.
Hutchinson v. Ypsilanti (103 Mich. 12, 61 N. W. Rep. 279), 302.
Hutt v. Chicago (132 Ill. 352), 115.
Hyde v. Franklin Co. 27 Vt. 185), 145.
Hydes v. Joyes (4 Bush, 464, 96 Am. Dec. 311), 71.

I.

Inchbold v. Robinson (L. R. 4 Ch. App. 388), 89.
Indiana v. Consumers' Gas T. Co. (140 Ind. 107, 27 L. R. A. 514), 100.
Illinois v. Canal Co. (2 Dill. C. C. 70), 135.
Illinois Cent. R. Co. v. Bloomington (76 Ill. 447), 198.
Illinois Cent. R. Co. v. Decatur (126 Ill. 92, 1 L. R. A. 613), 115.
Illinois Cent. R. Co. v. People (143 Ill. 434, 19 L. R. A. 119), 316.
Illinois Cent. R. Co. v. People (161 Ill. 244), 117.
Illinois Trust & Savings Bank v. Arkansas City (76 Fed. Rep. 271, 40 U. S. App. 257, 34 L. R. A. 518), 23, 28, 76, 80, 81, 139, 177, 179, 259, 261.
Illinois & M. Canal v. Chicago (12 Ill. 403), 115.
Indianapolis v. Bieler (138 Ind. 30), 90.
Indianapolis v. Huffer (30 Ind. 235), 309.
Indianapolis v. Imbery (17 Ind. 175), 178, 179.
Indianapolis v. Indianapolis, etc. (66 Ind. 396), 79.
Indianapolis v. Indianapolis Home, etc. (12 Ind. 215), 33.
Indianapolis v. Ind. Gas L. Co. (66 Ind. 396), 100.
Indianapolis v. Miller (27 Ind. 394), 179.
Indianapolis v. Wann (144 Ind. 175, 4 N. E. Rep. 901, 31 L. R. A. 743), 79, 174.

Indianapolis, etc. Ry. Co. v. Hartley (67 Ill. 439, 16 Am. Rep. 624), 104, 107.
Indianapolis & C. R. Co. v. Lawrenceburg (34 Ind. 304), 103.
Indianola v. Jones (29 Iowa, 282), 188.
Indianola v. G. W. T. & P. R. Co. (56 Tex. 594), 103.
Ingaman v. Chicago (78 Ill. 405), 201.
Inhabitants of Quincy v. Kennard (151 Mass. 563), 215.
Inman v. Tripp (11 R. I. 520), 308.
International Bank v. Franklin Co. (65 Mo. 105, 27 Am. Rep. 241), 146.
Interstate V. B. & P. Co. v. Philadelphia (164 Pa. St. 477), 77.
Iowa Land Co. v. Carroll (39 Iowa, 151), 5.
Iowa Land Co. v. County of Sac (39 Iowa, 149), 177.
Irvine v. Wood (51 N. Y. 224, 10 Am. Rep. 603), 101.
Irwin v. Great So. Tel. Co. (37 La. Ann. 63), 104.
Israel v. Jewett (29 Iowa, 475), 128.
Ivanhoe v. Enterprise (35 L. R. A. 58, 29 Oreg. 245), 109, 117, 118.
Iverson v. Indianapolis, etc. (39 Fed. Rep. 735), 83.
Ives v. Hulet (12 Vt. 314), 247.
Ivory v. Deerpark (116 N. Y. 476), 294, 298.

J.

Jackson v. Michigan (9 Mich. 111), 324.
Jackson v. Newman (59 Miss. 385, 42 Am. Rep. 367), 91.
Jackson v. People (9 Mich. 11), 324.
Jackson Co. v. Brush (77 Ill. 59), 156.
Jackson Co. H. R. Co. v. Interstate, etc. (24 Fed. Rep. 306), 81.
Jacksonville v. Electric Light Co. (36 Fla. 229, 30 L. R. A. 540), 138.
Jacksonville v. Ledwith (26 Fla. 163, 23 Am. St. Rep. 558), 177, 184, 195.
Jacksonville, etc. Ry. Co. v. Adams (33 Fla. 608, 24 L. R. A. 272), 125.
Jacksonville, etc. Ry. Co. v. Walsh (106 Ill. 253), 126.

TABLE OF CASES CITED. xlv

References are to pages.

Jacksonville Elec. L. Co. v. Jacksonville (30 L. R. A. 540), 138.
Jacksonville R. R. Co. v. Virden (104 Ill. 339), 157.
Jacobs, In re (98 N. Y. 98, 50 Am. Rep. 636), 84.
Jameson v. Denny (118 Ind. 449, 4 L. R. A. 79), 23.
Jameson v. People (16 Ill. 257, 63 Am. Dec. 304), 17, 20.
Jefferson v. Chapman (127 Ill. 438), 270.
Jefferson Co. v. Arrighi (54 Miss. 668), 148.
Jefferson Co. Com'rs v. Lineburger (3 Mont. 231, 35 Am. Rep. 562), 254.
Jeffries v. Harrington (11 Colo. 191), 225.
Jeffries v. Rowe (63 Ind. 592), 227.
Jenks v. Township (45 Iowa, 554), 326.
Jenks Tp. v. Sheffield Tp. (135 Pa. St. 400, 19 Atl. Rep. 1004), 47.
Jenny v. Brooklyn (120 N. Y. 164), 307.
Jensen v. Board (47 Wis. 298), 38.
Jensen v. Waltham (166 Mass. 344), 271.
Jersey City, etc. Ry. Co. v. Railroad Co. (20 N. J. Eq. 61), 102.
Jewell v. Gilbert (64 N. H. 13, 10 Am. St. Rep. 357), 231.
Jewett v. New Haven (38 Conn. 368, 9 Am. Rep. 382), 282.
Jewhurst v. Syracuse (108 N. Y. 303), 294, 299.
John v. Mayor (7 Eng. Rul. Cas. 278), 91.
Johnson v. Board (107 Ind. 15), 63, 64.
Johnson v. Indianapolis (16 Ind. 227), 21.
Johnson v. Joliet, etc. R. Co. (23 Ill. 202), 125.
Johnson v. Mayor of Croyden (1886, 16 Q. B. D. 708, 7 Eng. Rul. Cas. 278), 202, 207.
Johnson v. San Diego (109 Cal. 468, 30 L. R. A. 178), 44.
Johnson v. Simonton (33 Cal. 242, 249), 195.
Johnson v. Wells Co. (107 Ind. 15), 63.
Johnson Co. v. Thayer (94 U. S. 631), 156, 159.
Jolly v. Hawesville (89 Ky. 278), 279.
Jones v. Boston (104 Mass. 75, 6 Am. Rep. 194), 101, 111.
Jones v. Clinton (Iowa, 69 N. W. Rep. 418), 305.
Jones v. Detroit Bd. etc. (88 Mich. 371), 83.
Jones v. Hannoran (55 Mo. 462), 307.
Jones v. Hilliard (68 Ala. 300), 214.
Jones v. Insurance Co. (2 Daly, N. Y., 307), 195.
Jones v. Jefferson (66 Tex. 573), 242.
Jones v. New Haven (34 Conn. 1), 307.
Jones v. Richmond (18 Grat. 517), 94.
Jones v. Robins (8 Gray, 329), 102.
Jones v. Scanlan (6 Humph., Tenn., 195), 231.
Jordan v. Benwood (W. Va., 26 S. E. Rep. 266), 309.
Jordan v. Hannibal (87 Mo. 673), 304.
Jordan v. Hansom (49 N. H. 199, 6 Am. Rep. 508), 248.
Jordon v. Cass Co. (3 Dillon, 185), 19.
Judge v. Meriden (38 Conn. 90), 312.
Julia Blug. Ass'n v. Bell Tel. Co. (88 Mo. 258), 104, 106.
Justices v. Armstrong (3 Dev. 284), 19.

K.

Kahn v. Sutro (114 Cal. 316, 46 Pac. Rep. 87, 33 L. R. A. 620), 5.
Kane v. Fond du Lac (40 Wis. 495), 82.
Kansas City v. Birmingham (45 Kan. 212, 25 Pac. Rep. 569), 202.
Kansas City v. Cook (30 Mo. App. 660), 203.
Kansas City v. Corrigan (86 Mo. 67), 198.
Kansas City v. Garnier (57 Kan. 412, 46 Pac. Rep. 707), 211.
Kansas City v. Kansas City Belt Ry. Co. (102 Mo. 633, 10 L. R. A. 851), 127.
Kansas City v. Marsh Oil Co. (41 S. W. Rep. 943), 120.

References are to pages.

Kansas City v. Whipple (136 Mo. 475, 35 L. R. A. 746), 225.
Kansas City Ry. Co. v. Alderman (47 Mo. 349), 159.
Karst v. St. Paul, etc. R. Co. (22 Minn. 118), 314.
Katzenberger v. Aberdeen (121 U. S. 172), 151.
Kauffman v. Griesemer (26 Pa. St. 407, 67 Am. Dec. 437), 308.
Kaukauna Water Co. v. Green Bay Canal Co. (142 U. S. 254), 120.
Kaufmann v. Stein (138 Ind. 49, 46 Am. St. Rep. 368), 210.
Keihl v. City of South Bend (76 Fed. Rep. 921), 173, 175.
Keller v. Corpus Christi (50 Tex. 614, 32 Am. Rep. 613), 282.
Kelley v. Madison (43 Wis. 638), 257.
Kelley v. Mayor (4 Hill, N. Y., 265), 145, 147.
Kelley v. Milan (127 U. S. 139), 149, 150, 151, 162.
Kelley v. Minneapolis (57 Minn. 294, 26 L. R. A. 92), 100.
Kellogg v. Malin (50 Mo. 496), 120.
Kellogg v. Janesville (34 Minn. 132), 300, 301.
Kelly v. Chicago (62 Ill. 279), 77, 79.
Kelly v. Minneapolis (63 Minn. 125, 65 N. W. Rep. 115, 30 L. R. A. 281), 36, 172.
Kelly v. Pittsburgh (104 U. S. 156), 5.
Kelly v. State (92 Ind. 236), 63.
Kelly v. Meeks (87 Mo. 396), 42.
Kelsey v. Marquette F. & W. Com'rs (71 N. W. Rep. 589), 137.
Kemper v. Louisville (14 Bush, 87), 131.
Kempster v. City of Milwaukee (Wis., 1897, 72 N. W. Rep. 734), 234, 237.
Kendall v. Frey (74 Wis. 26, 17 Am. St. Rep. 118), 228, 240.
Kennedy v. Cumberland (65 Md. 514), 292.
Kennedy v. New York (73 N. Y. 365), 287.
Kenner v. Louisiana (92 U. S. 480),
Kennelly v. Jersey City (57 N. J. L. 293, 26 L. R. A. 281), 101, 102, 105, 244.

Kenney v. Goergen (36 Minn. 90), 231.
Kennison v. Beverly (146 Mass. 467), 311.
Kentucky v. Dennison (24 How., U. S., 66, 97), 316.
Keokuk v. Independent District (53 Iowa, 352, 36 Am. Rep. 226), 299.
Keokuk v. Keokuk P. Co. (45 Iowa, 196), 136.
Kepner v. Commonwealth (40 Pa. St. 124), 176, 177, 187.
Kerr v. Jones (19 Ind. 351), 231.
Kessel v. Zeiser (102 N. Y. 114, 55 Am. Rep. 769), 237.
Ketchum v. Buffalo (14 N. Y. 356), 133.
Kichli v. Minn. Brush Electric Co. (58 Minn. 418), 174.
Kies v. Erie (135 Pa. St. 144), 279.
Kies v. Erie (169 Pa. St. 598), 297.
Kiley v. Forsee (57 Mo. 390), 184.
Kilgore v. Magee (85 Pa. St. 401), 55, 57.
Kimball v. Boston (1 Allen, 417), 30, 279.
Kimball v. Marshall (44 N. H. 465), 221.
Kimberlane v. Tow (130 Ind. 120, 14 L. R. A. 858), 241.
Kimble v. Peoria (140 Ill. 156, 29 N. E. Rep. 723), 189.
Kincaid v. Hardin County (53 Iowa, 430, 36 Am. Rep. 236), 306, 325.
Kincaid v. Indianapolis Nat. Gas. Co. (124 Ind. 577, 8 L. R. A. 602), 106.
Kindiger v. Saginaw (59 Mich. 355), 131.
King v. Butler (15 Johns., N. Y., 281), 247.
King v. Davenport (98 Ill. 305), 88, 93.
King v. Mahaska Co. (75 Iowa, 329), 259.
King v. Minneapolis (32 Minn. 224), 126, 127.
King v. Williams (2 Maule & Sel. 141), 221.
Kingsbury v. Sperry (119 Ill. 279), 47.
Kingsley v. Chicago (124 Ill. 359, 19 N. E. Rep. 260), 91.
Kingston v. Dubois (102 N. Y. 219), 295.

TABLE OF CASES CITED. xlvii

References are to pages.

Kinmundy v. Mahan (72 Ill. 463), 71, 214.
Kinney v. Troy (108 N. Y. 567), 302.
Kinney v. United States (60 Fed. Rep. 883), 234.
Kipp v. Paterson (26 N. J. L. 298), 202.
Kirth v. Howard (24 Pick. 292), 249.
Kistner v. Indianapolis (100 Ind. 210), 102.
Klatt v. Milwaukee (53 Wis. 196), 295.
Klein v. New Orleans (99 U. S. 149), 325.
Klinger v. Bickel (117 Pa. St. 326), 93.
Knapp v. Hoboken (39 N. J. L. 394), 149.
Kneedler v. Norristown (100 Pa. St. 368), 202.
Knickerbocker v. People (102 Ill. 218), 59.
Knight v. Nash (22 Minn. 456), 326.
Knightstown v. Musgrove (116 Ind. 121, 9 Am. St. Rep. 827), 292.
Knoedler v. Norristown (100 Pa. St. 368), 93.
Knoglauch v. Railway Co. (31 Minn. 402), 205.
Knox County v. Aspinwall (24 How., U. S., 376), 163, 318.
Knox County v. Goggin (105 Mo. 182, 16 S. W. Rep. 684), 133.
Knox County v. Johnson (124 Ind. 145, 7 L. R. A. 684), 226, 317.
Knox County v. Nichols (14 Ohio St. 260), 156.
Knoxville v. Bell (12 Lea, Tenn., 157), 292.
Knoxville v. Byrd (12 Lea, Tenn., 121), 93.
Kobs v. Minneapolis (23 Minn. 159), 270.
Koch v. North Ave. Ry. Co. (75 Md. 222, 15 L. R. A. 377), 101, 105, 194, 308.
Kochersperger v. Markley (166 Ill. 43, 46 N. E. Rep. 742), 110.
Kohl v. United States (93 U. S. 367), 119, 125.
Kosmak v. New York (117 N. Y. 361, 22 N. E. Rep. 945), 312.
Kratzenberger v. Law (90 Tenn. 235, 25 Am. St. Rep. 681), 199.
Kreitz v. Behrensmeyer (149 Ill. 496, 24 L. R. A. 59), 237.
Kuehn v. Milwaukee (92 Wis. 263), 284.
Kuhn v. Chicago (30 Ill. App. 203), 211.
Kuhn v. Milwaukee (92 Wis. 263), 269.
Kunkle v. Franklin (13 Minn. 127, Gil. 119), 151.
Kunz v. Troy (104 N. Y. 344, 10 N. E. Rep. 442), 269, 302.

L.

La Clef v. City of Concordia (41 Kan. 323, 13 Am. St. Rep. 385), 284.
Lafayette v. Allen (81 Ind. 166), 307.
La Fayette v. Fowler (34 Ind. 140), 111.
La Fayette v. Male Orphans' Asylum (4 La. Ann. 1), 115.
Lafayette v. Timberlake (88 Ind. 330), 299.
Lafferty v. Huffman (Ky., 35 S. W. Rep. 123, 32 L. R. A. 203), 241.
Lahr v. Metro. Elev. Co. (104 N. Y. 268), 97.
Lake v. Palmer (18 Fla. 501), 48.
Lake v. Williamsburgh (4 Denio, 520), 147.
Lake Co. v. Graham (130 U. S. 674), 167, 169.
Lake Co. v. Rollins (130 U. S. 662), 161, 170.
Lake Pleasanton Water Co. v. Contra Costa Water Co. (67 Cal. 659), 121.
Lake View v. Tate (130 Ill. 247, 6 L. R. A. 58), 202, 205.
Lake View School Trustees v. People (87 Ill. 303), 83.
Lakeville, In re (7 Kulp, 84), 43.
Lamar Water & E. L. Co. v. City of Lamar (128 Mo. 188, 32 L. R. A. 157), 174.
Lambert v. Alcorn (144 Ill. 313, 21 L. R. A. 611), 307.

References are to pages.

Lamborn v. Dickson Co. (97 U. S. 181), 205.
Lamoille, etc. Ry. Co. v. Fairfield (51 Vt. 257), 160.
Land Co. v. Oneida (83 Wis. 649), 44.
Land, etc. Co. v. Brown (73 Wis. 294, 3 L. R. A. 472), 48, 152.
Landis v. Borough of Vineland (37 Atl. Rep. 965), 110.
Landow West v. Burtram (26 Ont. Rep. 161), 179.
Lane v. Woodbury (58 Iowa, 462), 285.
Langan v. Atchison (35 Kan. 318, 57 Am. Rep. 165), 302.
Langdon v. Castleton (30 Vt. 285), 234, 238.
Langlois v. Cohoes (58 Hun, N. Y., 226), 301, 304.
Lansing v. County Treas. (1 Dill. C. C. 522), 85.
La Porte v. Gamewell Fire Alarm Tel. Co. (146 Ind. 466, 45 N. E. Rep. 588), 169, 173, 174, 175.
Laramie Co. v. Albany Co. (92 U. S. 307), 5, 23, 44.
Laredo v. Nalle (65 Tex. 359), 326.
Laredo, City of, v. Int. B. & T. Co. (66 Fed. Rep. 246, 30 U. S. App. 110), 81.
Larkin v. Burlington, etc. Ry. Co. (85 Iowa, 492, 52 N. W. Rep. 480), 205.
Larson v. Grand Forks (3 Dak. 307), 292.
Last Chance Min. Co. v. Tyler Min. Co. (157 U. S. 683), 162.
Latah Co. v. Peterson (2 Idaho, 1118, 16 L. R. A. 81), 121.
Lauenstein v. Fond du Lac (28 Wis. 336), 70, 71.
Launtz v. People (113 Ill. 137, 55 Am. Rep. 405), 222, 226.
La Valle v. Supervisors (62 Wis. 376), 51.
Law v. People (87 Ill. 385), 169, 172, 175, 190.
Lawrence v. Boston (119 Mass. 126), 126.

Lawrence v. Ingersoll (88 Tenn. 52, 6 L. R. A. 308, 17 Am. St. Rep. 870), 221, 222, 256, 320.
Lawrence v. Meecham (166 Mass. 206, 44 N. E. Rep. 247), 189.
Lawrence v. Monroe (44 Kan. 607, 10 L. R. A. 520), 74, 86.
Lawrence v. Webster (167 Mass. 513, 46 N. E. Rep. 123), 110.
Lawson v. Milwaukee, etc. Ry. Co. (30 Wis. 597), 157.
Laycock v. Baton Rouge (35 La. Ann. 475), 170.
Leach v. People (122 Ill. 420), 48.
Leavenworth v. Miller (7 Kan. 479), 153.
Leavenworth, etc. Ry. Co. v. Platte Co. (42 Mo. 171), 155.
Leavenworth, etc. R. Co. v. Douglas Co. (18 Kan. 160), 156.
Leavenworth Co. v. Brewer (9 Kan. 307), 238.
Leavenworth Co. Com'rs v. Sellew (99 U. S. 624), 318.
Lee v. Drake (2 Salk. 468), 287.
Lee v. Minneapolis (22 Minn. 13), 313.
Leech v. Wilson Co. (68 Tex. 353), 148.
Leeds v. Atlantic City (52 N. J. L. 333), 256.
Leeds v. Richmond (102 Ind. 372), 120, 273.
Leep v. St. Louis Iron Mountain R. Co. (58 Ark. 407, 23 L. R. A. 264), 52.
Leets v. Pilgrim Church (14 Mo. App. 590), 89.
Lehew v. Brummell (103 Mo. 546, 23 Am. St. Rep. 895), 83.
Lehigh Water Co.'s Appeal (102 Pa. St. 515), 69, 140.
Lehr v. Metr. Elev. Ry. Co. (104 N. Y. 268), 105.
Lent v. Tillson (140 U. S. 316), 110.
Leonard v. Brooklyn (71 N. Y. 498), 325.
Leonard v. Canton (35 Miss. 189), 69.
Levy v. New York (1 Sandf. 465), 277.
Levy v. Salt Lake City (3 Utah, 63), 292.
Lewis v. Colts (39 La. Ann. 259), 250.

References are to pages.

Lewis v. Llewellyn (58 Kan. 510, 28 L. R. A. 510), 244.
Lewis v. Newton (75 Fed. Rep. 884), 203.
Lewis v. Shreveport (108 U. S. 282), 150.
Lexington v. Mulliken (7 Gray, Mass., 280), 316.
L'Herault v. Minneapolis (Minn., 72 N. W. Rep. 78), 305.
Liberty Bell, The (23 Fed. Rep. 843), 153, 323.
Liddy v. Long Island City (104 N. Y. 218), 238.
Lima v. Cemetery Ass'n (42 Ohio St. 128), 115.
Lincoln v. Boston (148 Mass. 578, 3 L. R. A. 257), 271, 298.
Lincoln v. Smith (29 Neb. 228), 292.
Lincoln v. Smith (28 Neb. 762), 305.
Lincoln v. Washburn (148 Mass. 578, 3 L. R. A. 257), 278.
Lincoln v. Worcester (8 Cush. 55), 264.
Lindall v. Covington (90 Ky. 444, 29 Am. St. Rep. 398), 201.
Lindley v. Polk County (50 N. W. Rep. 975), 284.
Lindsay Irr. Co. v. Mehrtens (97 Cal. 676), 121.
Linegar v. Rittenhouse (94 Ill. 208), 240.
Linn v. Adams (2 Ind. 143), 252.
Linn v. Chambersburg (160 Mass. 511, 25 L. R. A. 217), 188.
Liquidators v. Municipality (6 La. Ann. 21), 36.
Lipes v. Hand (104 Ind. 503), 128.
Lippelman v. Cincinnati (4 Ohio C. C. 327), 71.
List v. Wheeling (7 W. Va. 501), 169.
Litchfield v. Ballou (114 U. S. 190), 169.
Little v. Madison (49 Wis. 605), 298, 299.
Littlefield v. State (42 Neb. 223, 47 Am. St. Rep. 697), 203, 208.
Littler v. Jayne (124 Ill. 123), 79.
Little Rock v. Parish (36 Ark. 166), 63.
Livingstone v. Wolf (136 Pa. St. 519, 20 Am. St. Rep. 937), 100.

Lloyd v. New York (5 N. Y. 369, 55 Am. Dec. 347), 267.
Loan Ass'n v. Topeka (20 Wall., U. S., 655), 52, 154, 160, 161.
Lock v. City of Central (4 Colo. 65, 34 Am. Rep. 66), 284.
Locke's Appeal (72 Pa. St. 491), 214.
Lockhart v. Railway Co. (139 Pa. St. 419), 105.
Logan v. Pyne (43 Iowa, 524, 22 Am. Rep. 261), 69, 80.
Lombard v. Culbertson (59 Wis. 433), 251.
London v. Wood (12 Mod. 674), 131.
Long v. Duluth (49 Minn. 287), 69, 80, 81, 139, 140.
Long v. Fuller (68 Pa. St. 170), 129.
Long Branch v. Sloane (49 N. J. L. 356), 56, 62.
Longe v. Benedict (73 N. Y. 12), 249.
Longworth v. Council (32 Ind. 322), 63, 65.
Look v. Industry (51 Me. 375), 264.
Lord v. Anoka (36 Minn. 176), 220.
Lord v. Mobile (Ala., 21 So. Rep. 366), 298, 300.
Lord v. Oconto (47 Wis. 386), 134.
Lorence v. Ellensburg (13 Wash. 341, 52 Am. St. Rep. 42), 305.
Los Angeles v. Teed (112 Cal. 319, 44 Pac. Rep. 580), 171.
Los Angeles v. Waldren (65 Cal. 283), 179.
Louis v. Bourbon Co. (12 Kan. 186), 156.
Louisiana v. Police Jury (111 U. S. 716), 318.
Louisiana v. Pilsbury (105 U. S. 278), 35.
Louisiana v. Wood (102 U. S. 294), 262, 263.
Louisville, etc. Co. v. N. R. Co. (14 L. R. A. 579), 226.
Louisville, etc. R. Co. v. Pritchard (131 Ind. 564, 11 Am. St. Rep. 395), 293.
Love v. Atlanta (95 Ga. 129, 51 Am. St. Rep. 64), 284.
Love v. Raleigh (116 N. C. 296, 28 L. R. A. 192), 271.

TABLE OF CASES CITED.

References are to pages.

Love v. Schenck (12 Ired., N. C., 304), 33.
Lover v. Glochin (28 Wis. 364), 232.
Lowber v. Mayor (5 Abb. Pr., N. Y., 325), 5.
Lowell v. Boston (111 Mass. 454, 15 Am. Rep. 39), 155.
Lowry v. Polk Co. (51 Iowa, 50, 33 Am. Rep. 113), 254.
Lowry v. Rainwater (70 Mo. 152, 35 Am. Rep. 420), 85.
Lozier v. Newark (48 N. J. L. 452), 199.
Luce v. Board of Exam. (153 Mass. 108), 256.
Ludlow v. Cincinnati S. R. Co. (78 Ky. 357), 114.
Lund v. Chippewa Co. (93 Wis. 640, 67 N. W. Rep. 927, 34 L. R. A. 131), 108, 148.
Lycoming v. Union (15 Pa. St. 166, 53 Am. Dec. 571), 18, 37, 39.
Lyell v. Lapeer Co. (6 McLean, C. C., 446), 146.
Lynch v. New York (76 N. Y. 60), 311.
Lynchburg v. Slaughter (75 Va. 57), 162.
Lyon v. Adamson (7 Iowa, 509), 247.
Lyon v. Cambridge (136 Mass. 419), 295.
Lyon v. Lynd (44 Pa. St. 336), 319.

M.

McAleer v. Angell (R. I., 1897, 36 Atl. Rep. 588). 170.
McAllister v. Clark (33 Conn. 91), 85.
McAunich v. M. etc. R. Co. (20 Iowa, 338), 47.
McBean v. Chandler (9 Heisk., Tenn., 349), 114.
McBean v. Fresno (Cal., 1897, 31 L. R. A. 794), 174.
McBride v. Grand Rapids (47 Mich. 236), 228.
McCann v. Waltham (163 Mass. 344), 271.
McCarthy v. Boston (135 Mass. 187), 271.
McCarthy v. Chicago (53 Ill. 38), 98.
McCarthy v. Chicago, etc. Ry. Co. (112 Ill. 611), 102.
McCaull v. Manchester (85 Va. 579, 2 L. R. A. 691), 278.
McChaon v. Leavenworth Co. (8 Kan. 438), 234.
McClure v. La Platte Com'rs (19 Colo. 122), 255.
McClure v. Oxford Tp. (94 U. S. 429), 162, 163.
McComb v. Akron Council (15 Ohio, 474), 313.
McConihe v. McMurray (17 Fla. 238), 49.
McConihe v. State (17 Fla. 238), 54.
McConnell v. Dewey (5 Neb. 385), 252.
McConnell v. Osage City (80 Iowa, 290), 300, 301.
McCool v. Grand Rapids (58 Mich. 41), 296.
McCormick v. District of Columbia (4 Mackey, 396, 54 Am. Rep. 284), 106.
McCormick v. Pratt (8 Utah, 294, 17 L. R. A. 243), 233.
McCoull v. Manchester (85 Va. 579), 292, 295.
McCoy v. Briant (53 Cal. 248), 152, 177.
McCracken v. San Francisco (16 Cal. 591), 170.
McCrowell v. Bristol (89 Va. 652, 20 L. R. A. 653), 70, 71, 118.
McCullough v. Mayor (23 Wend. 458), 147.
McCumber v. Waukesha Co. (91 Wis. 442, 65 N. W. Rep. 51), 234.
McDade v. Chester (117 Pa. St. 414, 2 Am. St. Rep. 681), 277.
McDermott v. Board (5 Abb. Pr., N. Y., 422), 195.
McDermott v. Miller (45 N. J. L. 251), 187.
McDonald v. Massachusetts General Hospital (120 Mass. 432), 284.
McDonald v. New York (68 N. Y. 23, 23 Am. Rep. 144), 260.
McDonald v. Red Wing (13 Minn. 38, Gil. 25), 94, 281, 282.
McDonald v. State (80 Wis. 411), 184.

TABLE OF CASES CITED.

References are to pages.

McDonald's Ex'r v. Murdock (15 How., U. S., 363), 133.
McDonough v. Virginia City (6 Nev. 431), 292.
McDougall v. Hennepin Co. (4 Minn. 184, Gil. 130), 326.
McDowell v. Mass. etc. Co. (96 N. C. 514), 158.
McElroy v. Albany (65 Ga. 387, 38 Am. Rep. 781), 280.
McGavock v. Omaha (40 Neb. 64, 58 N. W. Rep. 543), 178.
McGee v. Com. (46 Pa. St. 358), 114.
McGill v. State (34 Ohio St. 228), 53.
McGoffin v. Cohoes (104 N. Y. 387), 257.
McGraw v. Whitson (69 Iowa, 348), 184, 185.
McGuire, In re (57 Cal. 604), 210.
McHugh v. St. Paul (Minn., 70 N. W. Rep. 5), 294, 295.
McInerney v. Denver (29 Pac. Rep. 516), 57.
McInerny v. Reid (23 Iowa, 410), 117.
McKean v. Lee (51 N. Y. 300), 89.
McKeesport v. Soles (178 Pa. St. 363, 35 Atl. Rep. 927), 115.
McKenzie v. Wooley (39 La. Ann. 944), 186.
McLellan v. Young (54 Ga. 399, 21 Am. Rep. 276), 326.
McManus v. Duluth, C. & W. R. Co. (51 Minn. 30), 159.
McMillan v. Anderson (95 U. S. 37), 110.
McMillan v. Richards (45 Neb. 786, 64 N. W. Rep. 242), 241.
McNally v. Cohoes (127 N. Y. 350), 292.
McNeil v. Chamber of Com. (154 Mass. 277, 13 L. R. A. 559), 77.
McPherson v. Foster (43 Iowa, 48, 22 Am. Rep. 215), 161.
McPherson v. Leonard (29 Md. 377), 182.
McRae v. Hogan (39 Wis. 529), 50.
Macey v. City of Duluth (Minn., 1897, 71 N. W. Rep. 687), 238.
Macomber v. Nichols (34 Mich. 212, 22 Am. Rep. 522), 297.

Macomber v. Taunton (100 Mass. 255), 295.
Macon v. Patty (57 Miss. 378), 108, 109.
Madison v. Harbor Board (76 Md. 395, 25 Atl. Rep. 337), 79.
Magenan v. Fremont (30 Neb. 843, 9 L. R. A. 786), 194.
Magie v. Stoddard (25 Conn. 565, 68 Am. Dec. 375), 230.
Maguire v. Spence (91 N. Y. 302), 301, 302.
Mahan, In re (20 Hun, 301), 78.
Mallory v. Ferguson (50 Kan. 685, 22 L. R. A. 99), 250.
Mandlin v. Greenville (33 S. C. 1, 8 L. R. A. 291), 138.
Mangam v. Brooklyn (98 N. Y. 585, 5 Am. Rep. 705), 235.
Manhattan Co. v. Ironwood (43 U. S. App. 369, 74 Fed. Rep. 535), 163.
Manhattan L. Ins. Co. v. Broughton (109 U. S. 121), 150.
Manhattan Trust Co. v. Dayton Natural Gas Co. (55 Fed. Rep. 181), 137.
Mankato v. Arnold (36 Minn. 62, 30 N. W. Rep. 505), 196.
Mankato v. Fowler (32 Minn. 354), 75.
Mankato v. Fowler (32 Minn. 364), 86, 90, 208.
Manners v. Haverhill (135 Mass. 165), 273.
Mansfield v. Moore (124 Ill. 133), 299.
Marble Co. v. Harvey (91 Tenn. 125), 263.
March v. Com. (12 B. Mon., Ky., 25), 200.
Marcy v. Oswego Tp. (92 U. S. 637), 167.
Marion Co. Com. v. Barker (25 Kan. 258), 221.
Mark v. State (97 N. Y. 572), 200.
Markham v. Brown (37 Ga. 277, 92 Am. Dec. 76), 86.
Markle v. Akron (14 Ohio, 586), 199.
Marmet v. State (45 Ohio St. 63), 57, 210.
Marsh v. Fulton Co. (10 Wall., U. S., 676), 160, 262.
Marshall v. Silliman (61 Ill. 225), 30.

TABLE OF CASES CITED.

References are to pages.

Marshall v. Snediker (25 Tex. 460), 266.
Marshalltown v. Bloom (43 Am. Rep. 116, 58 Iowa, 184), 91.
Marshall Co. v. Johnson (127 Ind. 238, 26 N. E. Rep. 821), 235.
Martin v. Dicks (52 Miss. 53), 41.
Martin v. State (23 Neb. 371, 36 N. W. Rep. 554), 185.
Martin v. Tyler (4 N. Dak. 278, 25 L. R. A. 838), 125, 128, 129.
Martindale v. Palmer (52 Ind. 411), 185, 186, 221.
Mason v. Shawneetown (77 Ill. 533), 155.
Mather v. Ottawa (114 Ill. 659, 11 Am. & Eng. Corp. Cas. 248), 155.
Matthews v. Alexandria (68 Mo. 115, 30 Am. Rep. 776), 71.
Matthews v. Kelsey (58 Me. 56), 98.
Matthis v. Cameron (62 Mo. 504), 147.
Mauran v. Smith (8 R. I. 192, 5 Am. Rep. 554), 317.
Maus v. Springfield (101 Mo. 613, 20 Am. St. Rep. 634), 292.
Maximilian v. Mayor (62 N. Y. 160), 285.
Maxwell v. Board (119 Ind. 20), 132.
May v. Cincinnati (1 Ohio St. 268), 199.
May v. Rice (91 Ind. 546), 179, 182.
Maynard v. Board of District Canvassers (84 Mich. 298, 11 L. R. A. 332), 319.
Mayor v. Beasly (1 Humph., Tenn., 232), 201.
Mayor v. City Bank (58 Ga. 587), 163.
Mayor v. Dry Dock, etc. Ry. Co. (133 N. Y. 104, 28 Am. St. Rep. 609), 203.
Mayor v. Kelley (98 N. Y. 467), 235.
Mayor v. Keyser (72 Md. 106, 19 Atl. Rep. 706), 78.
Mayor v. Marriott (9 Md. 174, 66 Am. Dec. 326), 277.
Mayor v. Morgan (7 Mart., N. S., 1, 18 Am. Dec. 232), 240.
Mayor v. Porter (18 Md. 284, 79 Am. Dec. 686), 69, 177.
Mayor v. Ray (19 Wall., U. S., 468), 81, 144, 149.

Mayor v. Sikes (94 Ga. 30, 47 Am. St. Rep. 132), 307.
Mayor v. State (15 Md. 376, 74 Am. Dec. 572), 69.
Mayor v. Widfield (8 Humph., Tenn., 707), 201.
Mayor of Baltimore v. State (15 Md. 376, 74 Am. Dec. 572), 26, 27.
Mayor of Nashville v. Ray (19 Wall. 478), 145.
Mayor of New York, In re (11 John. 77), 115, 121.
Mayor, etc. of New York v. Bank (111 N. Y. 446), 37.
Mazet v. Pittsburgh (137 Pa. St. 548), 74, 77, 78, 79.
Meeker v. Van Rensaeller (15 Wend. 397), 94.
Melick v. Washington (47 N. J. L. 254), 192.
Memphis v. Memphis Water Co. (5 Heisk., Tenn., 529), 17.
Memphis v. United States (97 U. S. 293), 35.
Memphis v. Woodard (12 Heisk., Tenn., 499, 27 Am. Rep. 750), 237.
Mendel v. Healey (28 W. Va. 233, 57 Am. Rep. 664), 275.
Mendel v. Wheeling (28 W. Va. 233), 281, 289.
Mendenhall v. Burton (42 Kan. 570), 42.
Mercer v. Corbin (117 Ind. 450), 98.
Mercer County v. Fleming (111 Cal. 46), 202.
Merchants' Bank v. Bergen Co. (115 U. S. 348), 160.
Merrick v. Wallace (19 Ill. 486), 250.
Merrill v. Austin (53 Cal. 379), 165.
Merrill v. Campbell (49 Wis. 535), 326.
Merrill v. Chicago (45 Ill. 133), 326.
Merrill v. Monticello (138 U. S. 673), 140.
Merrill, etc. Ry. Co. v. Merrill (80 Wis. 358), 79.
Merriwether v. Garrett (102 U. S. 472), 26, 35, 134, 317, 325.
Metcalf v. State (76 Ga. 208), 209.
Methodist E. Church v. Baltimore (6 Gill, 391), 183.

TABLE OF CASES CITED.

References are to pages.

Metzger v. Beaver Falls (178 Pa. St. 1), 141.
Meyer v. Fromm (108 Ind. 208), 188.
Meyer v. Graham (33 Neb. 566, 18 L. R. A. 146), 99.
Meyer v. Muscatine (1 Wall., U. S., 384), 161.
Michel v. New Orleans (32 La. Ann. 1094), 237.
Michener v. Philadelphia (118 Pa. St. 535), 110, 113.
Michigan City v. Boeckling (122 Ind. 39), 294, 296.
Mifflin Bridge Co. v. Juniata Co. (144 Pa. St. 235, 13 L. R. A. 431), 127.
Milan v. Tennessee C. Ry. Co. (11 Lea, Tenn., 330), 150.
Miles v. Worcester (154 Mass. 511), 310.
Milhan v. Sharp (27 N. Y. 611, 15 Barb. 193, 84 Am. Dec. 314), 100.
Millen v. Lansing (11 Fed. Rep. 829), 150.
Miller v. Bradford (12 Iowa, 19), 250.
Miller v. Kister (68 Cal. 142), 53.
Miller v. School District (Wyo., 39 Pac. Rep. 879), 171.
Miller v. Ware (31 Iowa, 524), 250.
Mills v. Brooklyn (32 N. Y. 489), 309.
Mills v. Gleason (11 Wis. 470, 78 Am. Dec. 721), 150, 151.
Mills Co. Nat. Bank v. Mills Co. (67 Iowa, 697), 146.
Milne v. Davidson (5 Mart., N. S., La., 586), 195.
Milward v. Thatcher (2 T. R. 81, 7 Eng. Rul. Cas. 320), 228, 230.
Milwaukee v. Koeffler (116 U. S. 219), 323.
Milwaukee v. Milwaukee (12 Wis. 93), 134.
Mimms v. Mimms (35 Ala. 23), 250.
Miners' Bank v. United States (1 Greene, Iowa, 553), 3.
Miners' Ditch Co. v. Zellerbach (37 Cal. 543, 99 Am. Dec. 300), 3, 4, 260.
Minneapolis v. N. W. Ry. Co. (32 Minn. 452), 129.
Minneapolis Gas L. Co. v. Minneapolis (36 Minn. 159), 136.

Minneapolis W. R. Co. v. M. & St. L. R. Co. (61 Minn. 502), 122.
Minnesota Linseed Oil Co. v. Palmer (20 Minn. 424), 322.
Minturn v. Larue (23 How. 435), 69, 74.
Minot v. West Roxbury (112 Mass. 1), 107.
Mirande, Ex parte (73 Cal. 365), 85.
Mississippi, etc. R. Co. v. Camden (23 Ark. 300), 150.
Missouri Pac. Ry. Co. v. Humes (115 U. S. 512), 125.
Missouri Pac. Ry. Co. v. City of Wyandotte (38 Kan. 573, 23 Pac. Rep. 930), 181.
Missouri Pac. Ry. Co. v. Keys (55 Kan. 205, 49 Am. St. Rep. 249), 307.
Missouri Pac. Ry. Co. v. Tygard (84 Mo. 263, 54 Am. Rep. 97), 158.
Mitchell v. Franklin Co. (25 Ohio St. 143), 5.
Mitchell v. Illinois, etc. Ry. Co. (53 Ill. 286), 125.
Mitchell v. Negaunee (71 N. W. Rep. 646), 138.
Mitchell v. Rockland (52 Me. 118), 274.
Mittelstadt v. Morrison (76 Wis. 265), 205.
Moale v. Baltimore (61 Md. 224), 118.
Mobile v. Watson (116 U. S. 289), 35, 45.
Mobile v. Yuille (3 Ala. 137), 182.
Modock, The (26 Fed. Rep. 718), 304.
Moffett v. Asheville (103 N. C. 237, 14 Am. St. Rep. 810), 271, 276.
Monadnock Ry. Co. v. Petersboro (49 N. H. 281), 71.
Monk v. New Utrecht (104 N. Y. 552), 293, 298.
Monongahela Bridge Co. v. Pittsburg (114 Pa. St. 478), 304.
Monongahela City v. Fisher (111 Pa. St. 9), 294.
Monroe v. Lawrence (44 Kan. 607), 84.
Montague v. Horton (12 Wis. 668), 147.
Montclair v. Ramsdell (107 U. S. 147), 166.

E

References are to pages.

Montezuma v. Minor (73 Ga. 484), 131.
Montgomery v. Gilmer (33 Ala. 116, 70 Am. Dec. 562), 309, 312.
Montgomery v. Parks (Ala., 21 So. Rep. 452), 211.
Montgomery v. Wright (72 Ala. 411), 292.
Montgomery City Council v. Montgomery, etc. Ry. Co. (31 Ala. 76), 259.
Montgomery Co. v. Menifee (93 Ky. 33), 44.
Montgomery Co. v. Schuylkill Bridge Co. (110 Pa. St. 54), 127.
Monticello v. Fox (Ind. App., 28 N. E. Rep. 1025), 312.
Montpelier v. E. Montpelier (27 Vt. 704, 29 Vt. 12), 26, 28, 134.
Moody v. Moeller (72 Tex. 635), 221.
Moody v. Niagara County (46 Barb., N. Y., 659), 279.
Moon v. Ionia (81 Mich. 535, 46 N. W. Rep. 25), 301.
Moore v. Abbot (32 Me. 46), 291.
Moore v. Kenockee Tp. (75 Mich. 332), 304.
Moore v. Mayor (73 N. Y. 238, 29 Am. Rep. 134), 164.
Moore v. Minneapolis (19 Minn. 300, Gil. 259), 304, 305.
Moore v. Monroe (64 Iowa, 364, 52 Am. Rep. 444), 83.
Moore v. New York (73 N. Y. 38), 260, 274.
Moran v. Miami Co. (67 U. S. 722), 165.
Moran v. New Orleans (112 U. S. 69), 198.
Moran v. Palace Car Co. (138 Mo. 641, 56 Am. St. Rep. 543), 277.
Morford v. Unger (8 Iowa, 82), 41.
Morgan v. Chicago, etc. Ry. Co. (36 Mich. 428), 125.
Morgan v. Dubuque (28 Iowa, 575), 116.
Morgan v. Morley (1 Wash. 464), 292.
Morris v. Rome (10 Ga. 532), 209.
Morris v. State (62 Tex. 728), 35.
Morris v. Taylor (40 Pac. Rep. 23), 149.
Morrison v. Bachert (112 Pa. St. 322), 61.

Morrison v. Hershire (32 Iowa, 271) 117.
Morrison v. Hinckson (87 Ill. 588, 29 Am. Rep. 77), 325.
Morrison v. Lawrence (98 Mass. 219), 273.
Morrison v. St. Paul (5 Minn. 108), 115.
Morrison v. Semple (6 Binn., Pa., 94), 123.
Morse v. Richmond (41 Vt. 435, 98 Am. Dec. 600), 297.
Morton v. Nevada (41 Fed. Rep. 582), 151.
Mosher v. School District (44 Iowa, 122), 37.
Moss v. Augusta (93 Ga. 787), 280.
Moss v. Comings (44 Mich. 359), 248.
Moss v. Oakland (88 Ill. 109), 190.
Mostyn v. Fabrigas (Cowp. 161, Smith's L. C. 1027), 248.
Moulton v. Evansville (25 Fed. Rep. 383), 161.
Moulton v. Moulton (5 Barb. 286), 251.
Moulton v. Scarborough (71 Me. 267, 36 Am. Rep. 308), 286.
Moultrie Co. v. Rockingham Sav. Bank (92 U. S. 631), 165.
Mount Hope Cemetery v. Boston (158 Mass. 509), 134.
Mount Pleasant v. Beckwith (100 U. S. 514), 35, 41, 44.
Mount Pleasant v. Vancise (43 Mich. 361), 198.
Mouse's Case (12 Coke, 13, 63), 281.
Moutz v. Detroit (18 Mich. 495), 115.
Mower v. Leicester (9 Mass. 237), 291.
Mowry v. Providence (16 R. I. 422, 16 Atl. Rep. 511), 134.
Mugler v. Kansas (123 U. S. 623), 87.
Mullen v. Rutland (55 Vt. 77), 304.
Municipality v. Cutting (4 La. Ann. 335), 178.
Municipality v. Dunn (10 La. Ann. 57), 109.
Municipality v. Pease (2 La. Ann. 538), 135.
Munn v. Illinois (94 U. S. 113), 4, 84.
Murphy v. Kelley (68 Me. 521), 307.

TABLE OF CASES CITED. lv

References are to pages.

Murray v. Allen (R. I., 38 Atl. Rep. 497), 308.
Muscatine v. Hershey (18 Iowa, 39), 135.
Musser v. Hyde (2 W. & S. 314), 251.
Mutual Ben. Life Ins. Co. v. Elizabeth (42 N. J. L. 235), 161.
Myers v. Spooner (55 Cal. 262), 250.

N.

Nance v. Falls City (16 Neb. 85), 257.
Nansen v. Grizzard (96 N. C. 293), 224.
Napa v. Esterly (61 Cal. 509, 16 Pac. Rep. 256), 188.
Nappeau v. People (19 Mich. 352), 211.
Nash v. Lowry (37 Minn. 261), 81.
Nash v. Muldoon (16 Nev. 404), 251.
Nash v. St. Paul (11 Minn. 174, Gil. 110), 79, 148.
Nashville v. Sutherland (92 Tenn. 335, 19 L. R. A. 619), 258, 275.
Nashville v. Taney (10 Lea, Tenn., 643), 264.
National Bank of Commerce v. Grenada (44 Fed. Rep. 262), 176, 188.
National Life Ins. Co. v. Board of Education (62 Fed. Rep. 788), 164.
Neeld's Road (1 Pa. St. 353), 125.
Neeman v. Smith (50 Mo. 525), 117.
Neff v. Wellesley (148 Mass. 487, 2 L. R. A. 500), 285, 286.
Neier v. Missouri Pac. Ry. Co. (12 Mo. App. 25), 202.
Nelson v. Haywood Co. (87 Tenn. 781, 4 L. R. A. 648), 153, 156.
Nelson v. La Porte (33 Ind. 258), 100.
Nelson v. St. Martin's Parish (111 U. S. 716), 35.
Nesbit v. Atlanta (97 Ga. 650), 284.
Netzer v. Crookston (59 Minn. 244), 298, 310, 313.
Nevada v. Hampton (13 Nev. 441), 40.
Nevada Bank v. Steinmetz (61 Cal. 301), 159.
Newark v. Funk (15 Ohio St. 463), 326.
Newark, etc. v. Passaic (45 N. J. Eq. 393), 89.

Newark Pass. R. Co. v. Block (55 N. J. L. 605), 105.
Newberry v. Fox (37 Minn. 141, 15 Am. St. Rep. 830), 76, 258.
New Boston v. Dunbarton (12 N. H. 409), 17.
New Brunswick v. Fitzgerald (48 N. J. L. 457, 8 Atl. Rep. 729), 57.
Newcomb v. Boston Protection Dept. (151 Mass. 215, 24 N. E. Rep. 39), 283.
Newell v. Minneapolis, etc. R. Co. (35 Minn. 112, 59 Am. Rep. 303), 102, 106.
New Hampshire, etc. Ry. Co. v. Chatham (42 Conn. 465), 161.
New London v. Brainerd (22 Conn. 552), 323.
Newman v. Emporia (41 Kan. 583), 114.
Newman v. Metropolitan, etc. Ry. Co. (118 N. Y. 618), 128.
Newmeyer v. Missouri, etc. Ry. Co. (52 Mo. 81, 14 Am. Rep. 394), 323.
New Orleans v. Abagznatto (62 Fed. Rep. 240, 26 L. R. A. 329), 278.
New Orleans v. Clark (95 U. S. 644), 37, 39, 40, 100.
New Orleans v. Finerty (27 La. Ann. 681, 21 Am. Rep. 569), 236.
New Orleans v. Home Ins. Co. (23 La. Ann. 61), 325.
New Orleans v. Morris (105 U. S. 600), 325.
New Orleans v. New Orleans, etc. R. Co. (40 La. Ann. 587, 4 So. Rep. 512), 102.
New Orleans v. New Orleans, etc. Co. (35 La. Ann. 548), 108.
New Orleans v. Stafford (27 La. Ann. 393, 21 Am. Rep. 561), 92.
New Orleans v. Water-works (142 U. S. 79), 108.
New Orleans Gas Co. v. Hart (40 La. Ann. 474, 8 Am. St. Rep. 544), 85.
New Orleans Gas Co. v. Louisiana L. Co. (115 U. S. 650), 81, 100.
New Orleans G. etc. Co. v. New Orleans (42 La. 188), 79.

TABLE OF CASES CITED.

References are to pages.

New Orleans M. & T. Co. v. Ellerman (105 U. S. 166), 136.
New Orleans, etc. Ry. Co. v. Dunn (51 Ala. 128), 150.
New Orleans Water Works v. New Orleans (164 U. S. 481), 74, 195, 197.
New Orleans Water Works Co. v. Rivers (115 U. S. 674), 100.
Newport v. Newport Gas Co. (84 Ky. 466), 136.
New Providence v. Halsey (117 U. S. 336), 167.
Newsome v. Cook (44 Miss. 352, 7 Am. Rep. 686), 243.
Newson v. Galveston (76 Tex. 559, 7 L. R. A. 797), 92.
New York v. Bailey (2 Denio, 433), 270.
New York Bank v. Grace (102 N. Y. 313), 172.
New York & N. E. R. Co. v. Bristol (151 U. S. 556), 99.
New York R. Co. v. City of Waterbury (55 Conn. 19), 186.
New York, etc. R. Co. v. Long (69 Conn. 424), 121, 125.
New York, etc. R. Co., In re, v. Metropolitan Gas Co. (63 N. Y. 326), 3.
Nichols v. Bridgeport (23 Conn. 189), 119.
Nichols v. City of St. Paul (44 Minn. 494), 297, 303.
Nichols v. Duluth (40 Minn. 389), 314.
Nichols v. McLean (101 N. Y. 526, 64 Am. Rep. 730), 236, 237.
Nichols v. Walters (37 Minn. 264), 60.
Nickerson v. Tirrell (127 Mass. 236), 287.
Nickodemus v. East Saginaw (25 Mich. 456), 266.
Nicoulin v. Lowery (49 N. J. L. 391), 86.
Nightingale, Petitioner (11 Pick. 168), 208, 213.
Niles v. Muzzy (33 Mich. 61, 20 Am. Rep. 670), 228, 239.
Niles Water-works v. Niles (59 Mich. 311), 74, 174.
Ninkle v. Detroit (49 Mich. 249, 43 Am. Rep. 464), 93.

Nivens v. Rochester (75 N. Y. 619), 270.
Nixson v. Campbell (106 Ind. 47), 159.
Noble v. St. Albans (56 Vt. 522), 309.
Nolan v. King (97 N. Y. 565), 295, 301.
Noonan v. Albany (79 N. Y. 470), 310, 197.
Noonan v. Stillwater (33 Minn. 198), 118, 299, 300.
Norris v. Staps (1617, Hob. 210), 199.
Norris v. Waco (57 Tex. 635), 41.
Norristown v. Fitzpatrick (94 Pa. St. 121), 30.
Norristown v. Moyer (67 Pa. St. 355), 302.
North Birmingham v. Colderwood (89 Ala. 247, 18 Am. St. Rep. 105), 196.
North Carolina R. Co. v. Baltimore (21 Md. 93), 103.
Norfleet v. Cromwell (70 N. C. 634), 121.
Northampton Bridge Case (116 Mass. 442), 120.
Northern Liberties v. St. John's Church (13 Pa. St. 104), 115.
Northern Trans. Co. v. Chicago (99 U. S. 635), 96, 99, 313, 314.
Northern Trust Co. v. Porter Tp. (110 U. S. 608), 166.
North Hempstead v. Hempstead (2 Wend. 109, 110), 19, 44.
North Hudson Co. R. Co. v. Hoboken (41 N. J. L. 81), 208.
North Milwaukee, In re (93 Wis. 616, 67 N. W. Rep. 1033, 33 L. R. A. 638), 17.
North Vernon v. Voegler (103 Ind. 314), 309.
Northway v. Sheridan (Mich., 69 N. W. Rep. 82), 230.
Northwestern Union Packet Co. v. Shaw (37 Wis. 655, 19 Am. Rep. 781), 260.
North Mo. Ry. Co. v. McGuire (49 Mo. 490), 40.
North Yarmouth v. Shilling (45 Me. 133, 71 Am. Dec. 530), 20.
Norton v. Bedford (166 Mass. 48), 271.
Norton v. Dyersburg (127 U. S. 160), 150, 153.
Norton v. Nye (56 Me. 211), 251.

TABLE OF CASES CITED.

References are to pages.

Norton v. Peck (3 Wis. 714), 5.
Norwich v. Hampshire (13 Pick. 60), 38.
Norwich G. L. Co. v. Norwich, etc. (25 Conn. 20), 80, 81, 100, 136.
Nuhlenbrinck v. Com. (44 N. J. L. 365), 208.

O.

O'Brien v. New York (15 N. Y. Supp. 520), 270.
O'Brien v. St. Paul (25 Minn. 331), 309, 314.
O'Connor v. Pittsburg (18 Pa. St. 187), 96.
O'Gorman v. Morris (26 Minn. 267), 296.
O'Hara v. State (112 N. Y. 146), 37.
O'Hare v. Parker River (N. D., 47 N. W. Rep. 380), 188.
O'Leary v. Board of Commissioners (79 Mich. 281, 19 Am. St. Rep. 160, 7 L. R. A. 170), 270, 283.
O'Leary, Ex parte (30 Tex. App. 493, 17 S. W. Rep. 1057), 88.
O'Linda v. Lathrop (21 Pick. 292), 101.
O'Reilley v. Kingston (114 N. Y. 439), 114.
Oats v. Walls (28 Ark. 244), 250.
Oberg, In re (21 Oreg. 406, 14 L. R. A. 577), 52.
Odell v. Atlanta (97 Ga. 670, 25 S. E. Rep. 173), 85.
Odell v. Schroeder (58 Ill. 353), 279.
Ogden v. McLaughlin (5 Utah, 387), 74, 84.
Ogden v. Raymond (22 Conn. 379, 59 Am. Dec. 429), 223.
Ogg v. Lansing (35 Iowa, 495, 14 Am. Rep. 499), 284.
Oil City v. Oil City Boiler Works (152 Pa. St. 348), 110.
Old Colony Ry. Co. v. Farmington Water Co. (153 Mass. 561, 13 L. R. A. 333), 122.
Oliver v. Worcester (102 Mass. 489), 286.
Oliver Cemetery Co. v. Philadelphia (93 Pa. St. 129), 115.

Olney v. Harvey (50 Ill. 453), 44.
Olson v. Chippewa Falls (71 Wis. 558), 295.
Omaha v. Olmstead (5 Neb. 446), 131.
Omaha v. Richards (49 Neb. 244), 286, 297, 309.
Opelousas v. Andrus (37 La. Ann. 699), 186.
Opening First St., In re (66 Mich. 42), 99.
Opinion of the Justices (81 Me. 602, 18 Atl. Rep. 291), 171.
Opinion of the Justices (150 Mass. 392, 8 L. R. A. 487), 138.
Opinion of Justices (167 Mass. 599, 46 N. E. Rep. 118), 231.
Oregon v. Jennings (119 U. S. 74), 167.
Oregon St. Nav. Co. v. Winsor (20 Wall., U. S., 64), 261.
Orlando v. Pragg (31 Fla. 111, 34 Am. St. Rep. 17), 284.
Orth v. Milwaukee (59 Wis. 336), 303.
Osborne v. Adams Co. (106 U. S. 181, 109 U. S. 1), 154.
Oshkosh v. State (59 Wis. 425), 324.
Otoe Co. v. Baldwin (111 U. S. 1), 151.
Ottawa v. Carey (108 U. S. 110), 150, 160.
Ottawa v. Chinn (75 Iowa, 405), 89.
Ould v. Richmond (23 Gratt. 464, 14 Am. Rep. 139), 107.
Overing v. Foote (65 N. Y. 262), 110.
Overton Bridge Co. v. Means (33 Neb. 857, 51 N. W. Rep. 240, 29 Am. St. Rep. 514), 240, 325.
Owens v. City of Lancaster (182 Pa. St. 257, 38 Atl. Rep. 859), 312.
Owners v. Mayor (15 Wend. 374), 121.
Owners v. People (113 Ill. 296), 47, 63.

P.

Pacific Ry. Co. v. Leavenworth (1 Dill. C. C. 393), 103.
Packwood v. Kittitas Co. (15 Wash. 88, 33 L. R. A. 673), 157.
Paddock v. Symonds (11 Barb. 117), 146.
Palestine v. Barnes (50 Tex. 538), 4.
Palmer v. Concord (48 N. H. 211, 97 Am. Dec. 605), 279.

TABLE OF CASES CITED.

References are to pages.

Palmer v. Danville (158 Ill. 156), 202.
Palmer v. Danville (166 Ill. 42, 46 N. E. Rep. 629), 114.
Palmer v. Helena (Mont., 47 Pac. Rep. 209), 171.
Palmer v. Stumph (29 Ind. 329), 114.
Palmyra v. Morton (25 Mo. 594), 114.
Pana v. Bowler (107 U. S. 529), 156, 165.
Parch v. Bayonne (39 N. J. L. 559), 82.
Park Com'rs v. Mayor (29 Mich. 347), 31.
Park Com'rs v. Common Council of Detroit (28 Mich. 228, 15 Am. Rep. 202), 25.
Parker v. Challis (9 Kan. 155), 114.
Parker v. Dakota Co. (4 Minn. 59, Gil. 39), 236.
Parker v. Mill Dam Co. (20 Me. 353, 37 Am. Dec. 56), 127.
Parkersburg v. Brown (106 U. S. 487), 152, 154.
Parkersburg Gas Co. v. Parkersburg (30 W. Va. 435), 138.
Parks v. Rooss (11 How., U. S., 362), 247.
Parrott v. Bridgeport (44 Conn. 180, 3 L. R. A. 265), 317.
Parrott v. Shaubhut (5 Minn. 331), 251.
Parsons v. Jackson (99 U. S. 434), 163.
Passaic, In re (54 N. J. L. 156, 23 Atl. Rep. 517), 59.
Patch v. Covington (17 B. Mon. 722, 66 Am. Dec. 186), 281.
Paterson Horse Ry. Co. v. Grundy (51 N. J. Eq. 213, 228), 105.
Patten Paper Co. v. Kaukauna Water Co. (90 Wis. 370, 28 L. R. A. 443), 120.
Patterson v. Society (24 N. J. L. 385), 115.
Paul v. Brewster Co. (40 N. J. L. 585), 54.
Paul v. Detroit (32 Mich. 108), 125.
Paul v. Gloucester (50 N. J. L. 585), 50.
Paul v. Kenosha (22 Wis. 266), 263.
Paulson v. Pelican (79 Wis. 445, 48 N. W. Rep. 715), 302.

Paulson v. Portland (149 U. S. 30), 110.
Pawlet v. Clark (9 Cranch, 292), 134.
Paxson v. Sweet (13 N. J. L. 196), 303.
Paxton & Hershy Co. v. Farmers', etc. Co. (45 Neb. 884, 29 L. R. A. 853), 121.
Paxton v. Sweet (20 N. J. L. 196), 203.
Payne v. Pavey (29 La. Ann. 116), 250.
Peabody v. West. Water Works Co. (37 Atl. Rep. 807), 138.
Pearsall v. Eaton Co. Sup'rs (74 Mich. 558, 4 L. R. A. 193), 104.
Pearson v. Zable (78 Ky. 170), 313.
Pease v. Cornish (19 Me. 191), 147.
Peay v. Little Rock (32 Ark. 31), 114.
Peck v. Rochester (3 N. Y. Supp. 873), 187.
Pedrick v. Bailey (12 Gray, 161), 213.
Pekin v. McMaben (154 Ill. 141, 27 L. R. A. 206), 286.
Pekin v. Reynolds (31 Ill. 529, 28 Am. Dec. 244), 146.
Pell v. Newark (40 N. J. L. 71), 61.
Pendleton Co. v. Amy (13 Wall., U. S., 297), 161.
Pennie v. Reis (132 U. S. 464), 33.
Pennsylvania Co. v. Chicago (81 Fed. Rep. 317), 279.
Pennsylvania Co. v. Horton (132 Ind. 187), 205.
Pennsylvania Hall, In re (5 Pa. St. 204), 40.
Pennsylvania Ry. Co. v. Philadelphia (47 Pa. St. 189), 150.
People v. Albertson (55 N. Y. 50), 26, 30, 31.
People v. Armstrong (73 Mich. 288, 16 Am. St. Rep. 578), 97, 198.
People v. Barnett Tp. (100 Ill. 332), 242.
People v. Bartlett (6 Wend., N. Y., 422), 241.
People v. Batchellor (35 N. Y. 128, 13 Am. Rep. 480), 39, 319.
People v. Bennett (83 Mich. 457), 23, 74, 84.
People v. Bennett (29 Mich. 451), 5, 18.
People v. Bloomington Tp. Com'rs (130 Ill. 432, 6 L. R. A. 161), 320.

TABLE OF CASES CITED.   lix

References are to pages.

People v. Board of Co. Com'rs (129 N. Y. 395, 14 L. R. A. 624), 319.
People v. Board, etc. (49 Cal. 684), 83.
People v. Board of Supervisors (27 Cal. 655), 190.
People v. Board (50 Cal. 561), 38.
People v. Bogart (3 Park. Crim. Rep. 143), 238.
People v. Bond (10 Cal. 563), 35, 36.
People v. Brisbane (76 N. Y. 553, 32 Am. Rep. 337), 282.
People v. Brooklyn (106 N. Y. 64), 244.
People v. Brooklyn Council (22 Barb., N. Y., 404), 319.
People v. Broom (138 N. Y. 95, 20 L. R. A. 81), 320.
People v. C. P. R. Co. (43 Cal. 432), 51.
People v. Campbell (72 N. Y. 496), 78.
People v. Carpenter (24 N. Y. 86), 321.
People v. Carrique (2 Hill, N. Y., 93), 228.
People v. Chicago (51 Ill. 17, 2 Am. Rep. 278), 39, 153.
People v. Chenango County (11 N. Y. 563), 316.
People v. City of Butte (4 Mont. 174), 19.
People v. Cleveland (5 Hill, N. Y., 616), 316.
People v. Cline (63 Ill. 394), 157, 161.
People v. Commissioners of Highways (130 Ill. 482, 6 L. R. A. 161), 316.
People v. Common Council (77 N. Y. 503, 33 Am. Rep. 659), 230.
People v. Cooper (83 Ill. 585), 54, 64.
People v. Cratty (93 Ill. 181), 179, 180, 316.
People v. Creiger (138 Ill. 401, 28 N. E. Rep. 812), 203.
People v. Dayton (55 N. Y. 367), 40.
People v. Detroit (18 Mich. 338), 319.
People v. Detroit (28 Mich. 228), 24, 31, 39, 135, 153.
People v. Draper (15 N. Y. 532), 30, 31.
People v. Dwyer (90 N. Y. 402), 78.

People v. Eaton (100 Mich. 208), 106.
People v. Fairbury (51 Ill. 149), 319.
People v. Field (58 N. Y. 491), 323.
People v. Flagg (46 N. Y. 401), 38, 152, 319.
People v. Freeman (80 Cal. 233, 13 Am. St. Rep. 122), 224.
People v. French (52 Hun, N. Y., 464), 225.
People v. French (102 N. Y. 583), 245.
People v. Green (58 N. Y. 295), 229, 231.
People v. Gordon (Mich., 45 N. W. Rep. 658), 212.
People v. Governor (29 Mich. 320, 18 Am. Rep. 89), 317.
People v. Hager (52 Cal. 171), 110.
People v. Haines (49 N. Y. 587), 111.
People v. Hanrahan (75 Mich. 611, 4 L. R. A. 751), 181, 200.
People v. Harper (91 Ill. 357), 39.
People v. Hayden (113 N. Y. 198), 244.
People v. Hechst (105 Cal. 621, 27 L. R. A. 203), 232, 234.
People v. Henshaw (76 Cal. 436, 18 Pac. Rep. 413), 59.
People v. Higgins (15 Ill. 110), 246.
People v. Hoffman (116 Ill. 587, 56 Am. Rep. 793), 54, 214.
People v. Holden (82 Ill. 93), 159.
People v. Hurlbut (23 Mich. 44), 5, 24, 29, 32, 34.
People v. Ingersoll (58 N. Y. 491), 33, 134.
People v. Johnson (100 Ill. 537), 145.
People v. Kane (84 Mich. 223), 243.
People v. Kelly (5 Abb. New Cas. 383), 39.
People v. Kerr (27 N. Y. 188), 27, 105.
People v. Killduff (15 Ill. 492), 256.
People v. Lake Co. (33 Cal. 487), 48.
People v. Lawrence (82 Cal. 182), 130.
People v. Lee (112 Ill. 112), 182.
People v. Leonard (73 Cal. 230, 14 Pac. Rep. 853), 227.
People v. Little (86 Mich. 125), 205.
People v. Londoner (13 Colo. 303, 6 L. R. A. 444), 65, 321.

TABLE OF CASES CITED.

References are to pages.

People v. McFadden (81 Cal. 489), 5, 46, 68.
People v. McKinney (52 N. Y. 374), 226.
People v. Mahaney (13 Mich. 481), 30, 31.
People v. May (9 Colo. 80, 13 Am. & Eng. Corp. Cas. 307), 169, 170.
People v. Mayor (82 N. Y. 491), 244.
People v. Mayor (15 Md. 376), 30.
People v. Mayor (4 N. Y. 419), 40, 108.
People v. Mead (24 N. Y. 114), 316.
People v. Miller (24 Mich. 458, 9 Am. Rep. 131), 237.
People v. Mirton (19 Colo. 565, 24 L. R. A. 201), 245.
People v. Morris (13 Wend. 325, 327), 2, 5, 34.
People v. Morrow (21 Wend., N. Y., 563), 284.
People v. Mulholland (82 N. Y. 324), 207.
People v. Murray (57 Mich. 306), 182.
People v. Nally (49 Cal. 478), 26.
People v. New York (2 Hill, N. Y., 9), 324.
People v. New York Infants' Asylum (122 N. Y. 190, 10 L. R. A. 381), 319.
People v. Nortrand (46 N. Y. 378), 232.
People v. Oldtown (88 Ill. 202), 157.
People v. Preveens (84 Cal. 518), 239.
People v. Porter (6 Cal. 26), 242.
People v. Rice (129 N. Y. 449, 14 L. R. A. 643), 319.
People v. Richardson (4 Cow., N. Y., 91, 109), 321.
People v. Riverside (70 Cal. 461), 41.
People v. Robb (126 N. Y. 180), 243.
People v. Rochester (44 Hun, N. Y., 166), 206.
People v. Rogers (Cal., 46 Pac. Rep. 740, 50 Pac. Rep. 658), 227, 241.
People v. Rossau (15 La. Ann. 238), 237.
People v. Salem (20 Mich. 452, 4 Am. Rep. 400), 153.
People v. Schroeder (76 N. Y. 160), 186.
People v. Shepard (36 N. Y. 285), 31.

People v. Smythe (28 Cal. 21), 237.
People v. South Mich. Ry. Co. (3 Mich. 496), 129.
People v. Spencer (55 N. Y. 1), 157.
People v. Spring Valley (129 Ill. 169), 321.
People v. State Board of Canvassers (129 N. Y. 360, 14 L. R. A. 646), 231, 316.
People v. State Treasurer (23 Mich. 499), 153.
People v. Steward (74 Mich. 411, 16 Am. St. Rep. 644), 245.
People v. Sturtevant (9 N. Y. 263, 59 Am. Dec. 536), 240.
People v. Supervisors (70 N. Y. 228), 39.
People v. Thatcher (55 N. Y. 525), 321.
People v. Therrein (80 Mich. 187), 245.
People v. Thompson (98 N. Y. 6), 122.
People v. Vilas (36 N. Y. 459), 235.
People v. Wagner (86 Mich. 594, 24 Am. St. Rep. 141), 91, 181.
People v. Waite (70 Ill. 25), 322.
People v. Walsh (96 Ill. 232, 36 Am. Rep. 135), 28, 96.
People v. Warfield (20 Ill. 160), 157.
People v. Wiant (48 Ill. 263), 157.
People v. Williams (145 Ill. 573, 24 L. R. A. 492), 320.
People v. Whitlock (92 N. Y. 191), 244.
People v. Wood (71 N. Y. 371), 147.
People v. Wright (70 Ill. 358), 61.
People v. Wright (78 Ill. 338), 47.
People v. Yonkers Board of Health (140 N. Y. 1, 23 L. R. A. 481), 324.
Peoria v. Simpson (110 Ill. 294, 51 Am. Rep. 683), 300, 301.
Peoria Gas L. Co. v. Peoria R. Co. (146 Ill. 372, 21 L. R. A. 373), 127.
Perry v. John (79 Pa. St. 412), 292.
Perry v. Keene (56 N. H. 514), 153.
Perry v. Worcester (6 Gray, 544, 66 Am. Dec. 431), 304, 308, 309, 312.
Perry Co. v. Conway Co. (52 Ark. 430, 6 L. R. A. 665), 44.
Perkins v. Fayette (68 Me. 152), 294.
Perkins v. New Haven (53 Conn. 214), 30, 279.

TABLE OF CASES CITED. lxi

References are to pages.

Peters v. Fergus Falls (35 Minn. 549), 292.
Peters v. Lindsburg (40 Kan. 654), 280.
Petersburg v. Applegarth (28 Grat. 343. 26 Am. Rep. 357), 277.
Peterson v. Mayor (17 N. Y. 449), 264.
Pettengill v. Yonkers (116 N. Y. 558), 270. 295.
Pettigrew v. Evansville (25 Wis. 223), 123.
Phelan v. Granville (140 Mass. 386), 235.
Phelps v. Mayor of New York (112 N. Y. 216, 2 L. R. A. 625), 265.
Philadelphia v. Field (58 Pa. St. 320), 38.
Philadelphia v. Fox (64 Pa. St. 180), 24, 26, 134.
Philadelphia v. Ridge Ave. Ry. Co. (143 Pa. St. 444), 102.
Philadelphia v. Rule (93 Pa. St. 15), 115.
Phillips, Matter of (60 N. Y. 16), 111.
Phillips v. Denver (19 Colo. 189, 41 Am. St. Rep. 230), 193, 198, 201.
Phillips v. Ritchie County (31 W. Va. 477), 292.
Phœnix Iron Co. v. Com. (113 Pa. St. 563), 316.
Pierce v. Drew (136 Mass. 75), 106.
Pierce v. New Bedford (120 Mass. 534, 37 Am. Rep. 397), 278.
Pierce v. Smith (48 Kan. 331), 63.
Pierie v. Philadelphia (139 Pa. St. 573, 21 Atl. Rep. 90), 235.
Piesk v. Chicago, etc. R. Co. (94 U. S. 164, 178), 4.
Pince v. City of Fresno (88 Cal. 407, 26 Pac. Rep. 606), 234.
Pinck v. Milwaukee (46 Wis. 565, 32 Am. Rep. 735), 270.
Pine Grove Tp. v. Talcott (19 Wall. 666), 153.
Pinkham v. Topsfield (104 Mass. 78), 303.
Piollet v. Simmers (106 Pa. St. 95, 51 Am. Rep. 496), 297.
Pitts v. Opelika (79 Ala. 527), 189.
Pittsburg v. Reynolds (48 Kan. 360, 29 Pac. Rep. 757), 189.

Pittsburg, etc. Co. v. Benwood Iron Works (31 W. Va. 710, 2 L. R. A. 680), 121.
Pittsburg, etc. Ry. Co. v. Chicago (159 Ill. 369, 42 N. E. Rep. 781). 102.
Pittsburg, etc. R. Co. v. Crown Point (Ind., 35 L. R. A. 684), 205.
Pittsburg, etc. R. Co. v. Keokuk, etc. R. Co. (131 U. S. 371), 262.
Pitzman v. Freeburg (92 Ill. 111), 150.
Place v. Providence (12 R. I. 1), 323.
Placke v. Union Depot Co. (41 S. W. Rep. 915), 105.
Platter v. Elkhart Co. (103 Ind. 360), 184.
Platteville v. Galena (43 Wis. 493), 156.
Platteville v. McKennan (54 Wis. 487), 196.
Pleasant Hill v. Dasher (120 Mo. 675), 118.
Plimpton v. Somerset (33 Vt. 283), 40.
Pointdexter v. Greenhow (114 U. S. 305), 104.
Police Com'rs v. Louisville (3 Bush, Ky., 597), 31.
Police Jury v. Britton (15 Wall. 566), 145, 149.
Polk v. Tunica (52 Miss. 422), 147.
Pollock v. Louisville (13 Bush, 221), 279.
Poplin v. Mundell (27 Kan. 159), 250.
Ponca v. Crawford (18 Neb. 551, 28 Neb. 762, 8 Am. St. Rep. 144), 292.
Portage Co. v. Wis. etc. Ry. Co. (121 Mass. 460), 159.
Portland, etc. Ry. Co. v. Hartford (58 Me. 23), 158.
Portland, etc. Ry. Co. v. Portland (14 Oreg. 188, 12 Pac. Rep. 265), 27.
Portsmouth Savings Bank v. Springfield (4 Fed. Rep. 276), 161.
Potter v. Douglas Co. (87 Mo. 240), 170.
Potts v. Breen (167 Ill. 67, 60 Ill. App. 201, 47 N. E. Rep. 81), 83.
Powell v. Board of Education (97 Ill. 375), 37 Am. Rep. 123), 82.
Powell v. Boston (111 Mass. 454), 107, 108.
Powell v. City of Madison (107 Ind. 106, 8 N. E. Rep. 31), 171.

References are to pages.

Powell v. Pennsylvania (127 U. S. 678), 87.
Powell v. St. Croix County (46 Wis. 210), 265.
Powell v. Wytheville (Va., 27 S. E. Rep. 805), 313.
Powers' Appeal (29 Mich. 504), 120.
Powers v. Council Bluffs (50 Iowa, 197), 310.
Powers v. Grand Rapids (98 Mich. 293, 57 N. W. Rep. 250), 113.
Prather v. Lexington (13 B. Mon. 559, 56 Am. Dec. 585), 278.
Pratt v. Litchfield (62 Conn. 112), 93.
Pray v. Jersey City (32 N. J. Law, 406), 291.
Pray v. North Liberties (31 Pa. St. 69), 109.
Prescott v. Waterloo (26 Fed. Rep. 592), 274.
Preston v. Boston (12 Pick. 14), 265.
Preston v. Manvers (21 U. C. Q. B. 626), 185.
Preston v. United States (37 Fed. Rep. 417), 231.
Prewitt v. Missouri, etc. Ry. Co. (134 Mo. 615, 36 S. W. Rep. 667), 205.
Prince v. Crooker (166 Mass. 347, 32 L. R. A. 610), 96, 167.
Prince v. Quincy (105 Ill. 138), 170.
Princess Co. Com. v. Bladensburg (51 Md. 468), 41.
Prior, In re (55 Kan. 724, 29 L. R. A. 303), 137.
Pritchett v. Stanislaus Co. (73 Cal. 310), 55.
Pritz, Ex parte (9 Iowa, 30), 64, 65.
Privet v. Bickford (26 Kan. 53, 40 Am. Rep. 301), 227.
Propagation Society v. Dudley (4 Pet., U. S., 480), 19.
Proprietors of, etc. v. Inhabitants (153 Mass. 42, 26 N. E. Rep. 239), 133.
Protestant Episcopal Church v. Anamosa (76 Iowa, 538, 2 L. R. A. 606), 292.
Provost City v. Sheriff (4 Utah, 15, 5 Pac. Rep. 302), 209.
Puffer v. Orange (122 Mass. 389, 23 Am. Rep. 368), 296.

Pumpelly v. Green Bay, etc. Co. (13 Wall. 166), 123, 127.
Pumphrey v. Baltimore (47 Md. 145), 38.
Purdy v. Lansing (128 U. S. 557), 150.
Purple v. Greenfield (138 Mass. 1), 98.
Putnam v. Douglas Co. (6 Oreg. 328, 25 Am. Rep. 627), 128.
Putnam v. Grand Rapids (58 Mich. 417), 138.
Pye v. Peterson (45 Tex. 312), 93.
Pyre v. Mankato (36 Minn. 373, 1 Am. St. Rep. 671), 308.

Q.

Quaker City Nat. Bank v. Nolan Co. (59 Fed. Rep. 660), 168.
Queen v. Justices (4 Q. B. 522, 29 Moak's Eng. Rep. 61), 189.
Quill v. Indianapolis (124 Ind. 292, 7 L. R. A. 681), 169.
Quincy v. Barker (81 Ill. 300), 303.
Quincy v. Bull (106 Ill. 337), 100.
Quincy v. Chicago, etc. Ry. Co. (92 Ill. 23), 178.
Quincy, etc. Ry. Co. v. Morris (84 Ill. 410), 153.
Quinton v. Burton (61 Iowa, 471), 303.
Quong Woo (13 Fed. Rep. 229), 214.

R.

Rae v. Mayor (51 Mich. 526), 75.
Rahway Savings Inst. v. Rahway (49 N. J. L. 384), 318.
Railroad Commission Cases (116 U. S. 307), 4.
Railroad Co. v. Ellerman (105 U. S. 166), 28, 135.
Railway Co. v. East Orange (41 N. J. L. 127), 202, 205.
Railway Co. v. Huesen (95 U. S. 465), 86.
Railway Co. v. Renwick (102 U. S. 180), 124.
Railway Co. v. Richmond (96 U. S. 521), 201.
Raleigh v. Pease (110 N. C. 32, 17 L. R. A. 331), 108, 109, 114, 117.

TABLE OF CASES CITED. lxiii

References are to pages.

Ralls Co. Court v. United States (105 U. S. 733), 35.
Ramsey v. Riley (13 Ohio, 157), 250.
Randolph v. Wood (49 N. J. L. 85), 57, 59.
Ranney v. Baeder (50 Mo. 600), 156.
Rathburn v. Wirth (150 N. Y. 459, 34 L. R. A. 403), 225.
Rathke v. Gardner (134 Mass. 14), 308.
Rauch v. Chapman (Wash., 36 L. R. A. 407), 170.
Ray v. Wilson (29 Fla. 342, 14 L. R. A. 773), 316, 320.
Ray Co. v. Vansycle (96 U. S. 675), 161.
Raymond v. Fish (51 Conn. 80, 50 Am. Rep. 3), 84.
Raymond v. Lowell (6 Cush., Mass., 524, 53 Am. Dec. 57), 293.
Read v. Plattsmouth (107 U. S. 568), 152.
Reading v. Savage (124 Pa. St. 328), 54.
Reardon v. Madison (73 Ga. 184), 206.
Reardon v. St. Louis County (36 Mo. 555), 293.
Reclamation Dist. v. Goloman (65 Cal. 635), 110.
Redford v. Coggeshall (R. I., 36 Atl. Rep. 89), 273.
Redwood Co. Com'rs v. Towler (28 Minn. 45), 254.
Reed v. City of Madison (83 Wis. 171), 297, 301.
Reeder v. City of Wahoo (27 Neb. 770, 43 N. W. Rep. 1145), 5.
Reese v. Watertown (19 Wall., U. S., 107), 325.
Reeves v. Continental R. Co. (152 Pa. St. 153, 25 Atl. Rep. 517), 55.
Reeves v. Wood Co. (8 Ohio St. 333), 111.
Regan v. Farmers' L. & Tr. Co. (154 U. S. 362), 262.
Regina v. Church Wardens (1 App. Cas. 611, 35 L. T. 381), 256.
Reg. v. Justin (24 Ont. Rep. 327), 98.
Reg. v. Rogers (2 Lord Raym. 777), 131.
Reilly v. Albany (112 N. Y. 30, 19 N. E. Rep. 508), 117.
Reimer's Appeal (100 Pa. St. 182, 45 Am. Rep. 373), 101.
Reineman v. Covington, etc. Ry. Co. (7 Neb. 310), 150.
Reiter v. State (61 Ohio St. 74, 23 L. R. A. 681), 242.
Renick v. Davenport (47 Iowa, 511), 153.
Renken v. Fuehring (130 Ind. 382, 15 L. R. A. 624), 111.
Reno Co. School Dist. v. Shadduck (25 Kan. 467), 82, 83.
Reusch v. Chicago, etc. Ry. Co. (57 Iowa, 685), 120.
Rex v. Burder (4 T. R. 778), 242.
Rex v. Commissioners of Sewers (8 Barn. & Cress. 355), 307.
Rex v. Harrison (3 Burr. 1328), 183.
Rex v. Jones (2 Stra. 1146), 242.
Rex v. Lone (2 Stra. 920), 242.
Rex v. Maidston (3 Burr. 1837), 200.
Rex v. Mayor (5 Barn. & Ald. 692), 130.
Rex v. Mayor (2 T. R. 259, 7 Eng. Rul. Cas. 328), 256.
Rex v. Patteson (4 B. & Ad. 9), 228.
Rex v. Richardson (1 Burr. 517, 538), 243, 244.
Rex v. Saunders (3 East, 119), 321.
Rex v. Bower (1 Barn. & Cress. 585), 242.
Rex v. Pateman (2 T. R. 777), 228.
Reynolds v. Mandain (4 Harr., Del., 317), 205.
Rice v. Austin (19 Minn. 103, 18 Am. Rep. 330), 317.
Rich v. Mentz Tp. (134 U. S. 623), 156, 157.
Rich v. Naperville (42 Ill. App. 222), 206, 316.
Richard v. Clarkburg (30 W. Va. 591), 243.
Richards v. Cincinnati (52 Ohio St. 419, 27 L. R. A. 737), 18.
Richards v. Raymond (92 Ill. 612, 34 Am. Rep. 151), 82, 152.
Richardson v. Heydenfeldt (46 Cal. 68), 71.
Richey v. Griffith (1 Wash. 429, 12 L. R. A. 384), 250, 251.

TABLE OF CASES CITED.

References are to pages.

Richman v. Muscatine Co. (77 Iowa, 513, 4 L. R. A. 445), 64.
Richmond v. Long (17 Gratt. 375, 94 Am. Dec. 461), 277.
Richmond v. McGirr (78 Ind. 192), 149.
Richmond Co. v. Lawrence Co. (12 Ill. 1), 34.
Richmond, etc. Co. v. West Point (27 S. E. Rep. 460), 133.
Richter v. Harper (95 Mich. 221, 54 N. W. Rep. 768), 191.
Riddell v. Proprietors (7 Mass. 169, 5 Am. Dec. 43), 286, 291.
Riddick v. Amelia (1 Mo. 7), 19.
Rideout v. Knox (148 Mass. 368, 2 L. R. A. 81), 84.
Riggs v. Johnson County (6 Wall., U. S., 166), 318.
Ring v. Cohoes (77 N. Y. 83), 295.
Rippe v. Becker (56 Minn. 100, 22 L. R. A. 857), 85.
Ritchie v. People (155 Ill. 98, 29 L. R. A. 79), 84.
Rittenhouse v. Mayor (25 Md. 336, 76.
Rivers v. Augusta (67 Ga. 376, 38 Am. Rep. 787), 278.
Road in Sterritt Tp., In re (114 Pa. St. 637), 124.
Roane v. Anderson (89 Tenn. 259), 41.
Roanoke Gas Co. v. Roanoke (88 Va. 810), 100.
Robbins v. Milwaukee, etc. Co. (6 Wis. 637), 128.
Roberts v. Easton (19 Ohio St. 78), 102.
Robinson, Ex parte (30 Tex. App. 493, 17 S. W. Rep. 1057), 88.
Robinson's Case (131 Mass. 376), 224.
Robinson v. Franklin (1 Humph. 156, 34 Am. Dec. 625), 92, 93, 178, 199.
Robinson v. Greenville (42 Ohio St. 625, 51 Am. Rep. 857), 277, 278.
Robinson v. Jones (14 Fla. 256), 322.
Robinson v. Rohr (73 Wis. 436, 2 L. R. A. 366), 249, 271.
Robinson v. Ruggles (50 Iowa, 240), 266.
Roby v. Sedgwick (35 Barb. 319), 20.
Roby v. Sheppard (W. Va., 26 S. E. Rep. 278), 41.

Rochester v. Campbell (123 N. Y. 405, 20 Am. St. Rep. 760), 299, 300, 303.
Rochester v. Upham (19 Minn. 108, Gil. 78), 90.
Rochester White Lead Co. v. Rochester (3 N. Y. 463), 309, 310.
Rock Island County v. United States (4 Wall., U. S., 435), 318.
Roderick v. Whitson (51 Hun, N. Y., 620), 206.
Rodman v. Musselman (12 Bush, Ky., 354, 23 Am. Rep. 724), 326.
Roe v. Kansas City (100 Mo. 190), 299.
Roeck v. Newark (33 N. J. L. 129), 319.
Roeller v. Ames (33 Minn. 132), 326.
Rogers v. Bradshaw (20 Johns. 744), 129.
Rogers v. Burlington (3 Wall., U. S., 654), 152, 161.
Rogers v. Marlowe (55 Kan. 737, 42 Pac. Rep. 555), 246.
Rogers v. People (68 Ill. 154), 7.
Rolf v. Greenville (102 Mich. 544), 302.
Rollins v. Gunnison Co. (49 U. S. App. 399, 80 Fed. Rep. 682), 162.
Rollins v. Lake Co. (34 Fed. Rep. 845), 170.
Romero v. United States (24 Ct. of Cl. 331, 5 L. R. A. 69), 234, 236.
Rooney v. Randolph (128 Mass. 580), 294.
Roosevelt v. Draper (23 N. Y. 318), 323.
Roosevelt Hospital v. New York (84 N. Y. 108), 116.
Root's Case (77 Pa. St. 276), 128.
Rosenthal v. Board of Canvassers (50 Kan. 129, 19 L. R. A. 157), 318, 319.
Ross v. Winsor (48 N. J. L. 95), 56, 58, 62.
Rothschild v. Darien (69 Ga. 503), 198.
Rowe v. Portsmouth (56 N. H. 291), 313.
Royce v. St. Louis (49 Pac. Rep. 290), 274.
Royce v. Salt Lake City (49 Pac. Rep. 290), 284.

TABLE OF CASES CITED. lxv

References are to pages.

Ruan Street, In re (132 Pa. St. 257), 63.
Ruggles v. Collier (43 Mo. 353), 71.
Ruggles v. Fond du Lac (53 Wis. 436), 266, 315.
Ruilson v. Post (79 Ind. 567), 83.
Rumsey v. N. Y. & N. E. Ry. Co. (130 N. Y. 88, 15 L. R. A. 618), 120.
Rumsey Mfg. Co. v. Shell City (21 Mo. App. 175), 178, 181.
Rundle v. Delaware, etc. Canal (1 Wall. Jr. 275, 290), 3.
Rusher v. Dallas (83 Tex. 151), 39.
Rushville v. Adams (107 Ind. 475, 57 Am. Rep. 124), 297.
Rushville Gas Co. v. Rushville (121 Ind. 206, 23 N. E. Rep. 72, 6 L. R. A. 315), 149, 222.
Russell v. M'Lellan (14 Pick. 63), 18.
Russell v. Men of Devon (2 T. R. 672), 19, 291.
Russell v. Place (94 U. S. 606), 150.
Rutgers v. New Brunswick (42 N. J. L. 436), 55, 59, 60.
Rutherford v. Hamilton (97 Mo. 543), 59, 114.
Rutherford v. Heddens (82 Mo. 388), 57.
Ruttles v. Covington (10 Ky. L. Rep. 766, 10 S. W. Rep. 644), 101.
Rychlicki v. St. Louis (98 Mo. 497), 303, 311.
Ryerson v. Brown (35 Mich. 333, 24 Am. Rep. 564), 121.

S.

Sackett v. New Albany (88 Ind. 473, 45 Am. Rep. 467), 170.
Sacramento v. Colorado Stage Co. (12 Cal. 132), 92.
Sacramento v. Dillman (102 Cal. 107, 36 Pac. Rep. 385), 189.
Sadler v. Eureka Co. (15 Nev. 44), 177.
Safety Ins., W. & C. Co. v. Baltimore (66 Fed. Rep. 140, 25 U. S. App. 166), 23, 80.
Safety Ins., W. & C. Co. v. Mayor (66 Fed. Rep. 140), 76.
Sage v. Brooklyn (89 N. Y. 189), 128.

Sage v. Lorain (19 Mich. 137), 248.
Saginaw G. L. Co. v. Saginaw (28 Fed. Rep. 529), 80, 138, 262.
Salamauca Tp. v. Jasper Co. Bank (22 Kan. 696), 143.
Salem Water Co. v. Salem (5 Oreg. 30), 170, 174.
Saleno v. City of Neosho (127 Mo. 627, 27 L. R. A. 769), 170, 174, 185, 187.
Saline Co. Com'rs v. Anderson (20 Kan. 398, 27 Am. Rep. 171), 237.
Salisbury v. Andrew (128 Mass. 336), 100.
Salisbury v. Ithaca (94 N. Y. 27), 299.
Salisbury v. Herchenroder (106 Mass. 458, 8 Am. Rep. 354), 101.
Salt Lake City v. Hollister (118 U. S. 256), 151, 271.
Saltpetre Case (6 Coke, 206), 94.
Sanborn v. Neal (4 Minn. 126, 77 Am. Dec. 502), 247.
Sanborn v. Rice Co. (9 Minn. 273), 40.
San Francisco Gas Co. v. San Francisco (6 Cal. 190), 178.
Sangamon v. Springfield (63 Ill. 66), 34.
San Luis Water Co. v. Estrada (48 Pac. Rep. 1075), 140.
Santa Anna Co. v. San B. etc. (56 Fed. Rep. 339), 79.
Santo v. State (2 Iowa, 155, 63 Am. Dec. 487), 239.
Sargent v. Tuttle (67 Conn. 162, 34 Atl. Rep. 1028, 32 L. R. A. 822), 108.
Satterfield v. Malone (35 Fed. Rep. 445, 1 L. R. A. 35), 250.
Sauk v. Philadelphia (8 Phila., Pa., 118), 187.
Sault Ste. Marie v. Van Dusen (40 Mich. 429), 148.
Savannah v. Donnelly (71 Ga. 258), 296.
Savings Society v. Philadelphia (31 Pa. St. 175), 193.
Sawyer v. Adams (8 Vt. 172), 251.
Sawyer v. Concordia (12 Fed. Rep. 754), 35.
Sawyer, In re (124 U. S. 200), 221.
Saxton v. St. Joseph (60 Mo. 153), 176.

TABLE OF CASES CITED.

References are to pages.

Scales v. Chattahoochee Co. (41 Ga. 225), 7, 293.
Scanlon v. Wedger (16 L. R. A. 395), 278.
Schenly v. Com. (36 Pa. St. 39), 111.
Schipper v. Aurora (121 Ill. 154, 6 L. R. A. 318), 262.
School District v. Gage (39 Mich. 484), 326.
School District v. Smith (67 Vt. 566, 32 Atl. Rep. 484), 232.
School District v. Stough (4 Neb. 357), 145.
School District v. Thompson (5 Minn. 280), 147.
School District v. Weber (75 Mo. 558), 39.
School District v. Williams (38 Ark. 454), 5.
School District v. Wood (13 Mass. 192), 6, 19.
Schroeder v. Baraboo (93 Wis. 95, 67 N. W. Rep. 27), 310, 312.
Schultz v. Milwaukee (48 Wis. 254, 35 Am. Rep. 779), 278, 290.
Schumann v. Ft. Wayne (127 Ind. 109, 11 L. R. A. 378), 91.
Schumm v. Seymour (24 N. J. Eq. 143), 176.
Schwartz v. Oshkosh (55 Wis. 490), 188.
Schweizer v. Liberty (82 Mo. 309), 188.
Scotland Co. v. Hill (132 U. S. 107), 162.
Scott v. Davenport (34 Iowa, 208), 171.
Scott v. Fishbate (117 N. C. 265, 30 L. R. A. 696), 239, 249.
Scowden's Appeal (96 Pa. St. 422), 58, 61.
Scranton's Appeal (113 Pa. St. 190), 55.
Scranton v. Catterson (94 Pa. St. 202), 296.
Scranton v. Whyte (148 Pa. St. 419, 23 Atl. Rep. 1043), 55.
Screws v. Watson (48 Ala. 628), 251.
Scudder v. Hinshaw (134 Ind. 56), 205.
Seagraves v. Alton (13 Ill. 366), 263.

Seaman v. New York (80 N. Y. 239), 287.
Searcy v. Grow (15 Cal. 117), 227.
Seattle & Mont. R. Co. v. State (7 Wash. 150, 22 L. R. A. 217), 126.
Seben v. City of Chicago (165 Ill. 371), 286, 297.
Second Ward Sav. Bank v. City of Huron (80 Fed. Rep. 661), 164.
Sedgwick v. Bunker (16 Kan. 498), 44.
Seele v. Deering (79 Me. 343), 271.
Seeley v. Litchfield (49 Conn. 134, 44 Am. Rep. 213), 294.
Seeley v. Westport (47 Conn. 294), 266.
Seely v. Pittsburgh (82 Pa. St. 360, 22 Am. Rep. 760), 114, 115.
Seep v. St. Louis, etc. R. Co. (58 Ark. 407, 23 L. R. A. 264), 84.
Seibert v. Lewis (122 U. S. 284), 35, 36.
Seifert v. Brooklyn (101 N. Y. 136), 309, 310, 311, 312.
Selleck v. Tallman (93 Wis. 246), 300.
Selma & Gulf R. Co., Ex parte (45 Ala. 696, 732), 6, 153.
Selvin v. North, etc. (L. R. 9 Ch. App. 705), 89.
Senate Bill, In re (12 Colo. 188), 24, 32.
Senate of Happy Home Club v. Alpena Co. (99 Mich. 117, 23 L. R. A. 144), 95.
Sessions v. Boykin (78 Ala. 328), 316.
Severin v. Cole (38 Iowa, 463), 126.
Seybert v. Pittsburgh (1 Wall. 272), 149.
Seymore v. Turnpike Co. (10 Ohio, 477), 4.
Seymour v. Cummings (119 Ind. 148, 5 L. R. A. 126), 309.
Seymour v. School District (53 Conn. 502), 326.
Shad v. Crawford (3 Metc., Ky., 207), 30.
Shadler v. Blair County (136 Pa. St. 488), 293.
Shaefler v. Sandusky (33 Ohio St. 246), 303.
Shafer v. Mumma (79 Md. 331), 130, 196.

TABLE OF CASES CITED. lxvii

References are to pages.

Shaffel v. State (72 N. W. Rep. 888), 131.
Shane v. St. Paul (26 Minn. 543), 265.
Shannon v. Portsmouth (54 N. H. 183), 245.
Shapleigh v. San Angelo (167 U. S. 646), 35, 45.
Sharon R. Co.'s Appeal (122 Pa. St. 533), 122.
Shaw v. Independent School District (40 U. S. App. 475, 77 Fed. Rep. 277), 168.
Shaw v. Pickett (26 Vt. 482), 118.
Shawnee Co. Com'rs v. Carter (2 Kan. 115), 144.
Shawneetown v. Baker (85 Ill. 563), 82.
Shawneetown v. Mason (82 Ill. 337), 128.
Sharpless v. Philadelphia (21 Pa. St. 147, 27 L. R. A. 72), 152, 153, 154.
Shartle v. Minneapolis (17 Minn. 308, Gil. 284), 292.
Shaub v. Lancaster (156 Pa. St. 362, 21 L. R. A. 691), 196.
Sheehan v. Good Samaritan Hospital (50 Mo. 155, 11 Am. Rep. 112), 115.
Shelby v. Clagett (46 Ohio St. 549), 292.
Sheldon v. Fox (48 Kan. 356, 16 L. R. A. 257), 79.
Sheley v. Detroit (45 Mich. 431), 111, 114.
Shelle v. Bryden (114 Pa. St. 147), 251.
Shepard v. People (40 Mich. 487), 88.
Shepard v. Pulaski County (Ky., 18 S. W. Rep. 15), 306.
Shepardson v. Milwaukee, etc. R. Co. (6 Wis. 605), 129.
Sheperd v. Burkhalter (13 Ga. 447), 250.
Sheperd v. Sullivan (166 Ill. 78, 46 N. E. Rep. 720), 117.
Sherbourne v. Yuba Co. (21 Cal. 113), 6, 284.
Sheridan v. Salem (14 Oreg. 328), 292.
Sherlock v. Stuart (96 Mich. 193, 21 L. R. A. 580), 317.
Sherman v. Williams (84 Tex. 421, 19 S. W. Rep. 606), 325.

Sherman Co. v. Simmons (109 U. S. 735), 5, 167.
Sherwin v. Bugbee (17 Vt. 337), 220.
Sherwood v. C. W. Co. (90 Cal. 635), 137.
Sherwood v. City (109 Ind. 410), 126.
Sheuck v. Borough (181 Pa. St. 191), 178.
Shields v. Durham (118 N. C. 450), 284.
Shipley v. Baltimore, etc. R. Co. (34 Md. 336), 128.
Shirk v. Pulaski Co. (4 Dill. C. C. 209), 145.
Short v. Maryland (80 Md. 392), 225.
Short v. Symes (150 Mass. 298, 15 Am. St. Rep. 204), 228.
Short-Conrad v. School District (69 N. W. Rep. 337), 68.
Shrove v. Larson (22 Wis. 142), 251.
Shue v. Commissioners (41 Mich. 638), 124.
Shussler v. Hennepin County (Minn., 70 N. W. Rep. 6), 272, 273, 274.
Sibley v. Dowlan (36 Minn. 431), 5.
Sievers v. San Francisco (115 Cal. 648), 269.
Simms v. Hymmes (121 Ind. 534), 129.
Simon v. Atlanta (67 Ga. 618, 44 Am. Rep. 729), 283.
Simon v. Northrup (27 Oreg. 487, 30 L. R. A. 171), 28, 38.
Sinclair v. Baltimore (59 Md. 592), 205.
Sinclair v. Slasson (44 Mich. 127), 251.
Sinking Fund Cases (99 U. S. 700), 29.
Sinton v. Ashbury (41 Cal. 525), 39.
Sioux City v. Weare (59 Iowa, 195), 172, 300.
Sioux City, etc. St. Ry. Co. v. Osceola Co. (45 Iowa, 168, 52 Iowa, 26), 162.
Skaggs v. Martinsville (140 Ind. 476, 49 Am. St. Rep. 209, 33 L. R. A. 781), 193.
Skinner v. Henderson (26 Fla. 121, 8 L. R. A. 55), 34.
Skinner v. Santa Rosa (29 L. R. A. 512), 157.
Sloane v. Beebe (24 Kan. 343), 111.
Smith v. Appleton (19 Wis. 468), 35, 37.
Smith v. Com. (41 Pa. St. 335), 179.

TABLE OF CASES CITED.

References are to pages.

Smith v. Dedham (144 Mass. 177), 79, 174.
Smith v. Duncan (77 Ind. 92), 71.
Smith v. Gould (61 Wis. 31), 268.
Smith v. Emporia (27 Kan. 528), 177.
Smith, Ex parte (135 Mo. 223, 33 L. R. A. 606), 198, 212.
Smith, Ex parte (38 Cal. 702), 52.
Smith v. Farrelly (52 Cal. 77), 266.
Smith, In re (99 N. Y. 424), 111.
Smith v. Knoxville (3 Head, Tenn., 245), 209.
Smith v. Mayor (88 Tenn. 464), 138.
Smith v. Milwaukee Bldg. Ex. (91 Wis. 360, 30 L. R. A. 63), 26, 99.
Smith v. Nashville (88 Tenn. 464, 7 L. R. A. 469), 87, 138.
Smith v. Newbern (70 N. C. 14, 16 Am. Rep. 766), 67, 68.
Smith v. People (162 Ill. 534, 33 L. R. A. 470), 178.
Smith v. Philadelphia (81 Pa. St. 38, 22 Am. Rep. 731), 288.
Smith v. Rochester (76 N. Y. 506), 271.
Smith v. Sherry (50 Wis. 200), 41.
Smith v. Waterbury (54 Conn. 174, 7 Atl. Rep. 17), 238.
Smith v. Westcott (17 R. I. 366, 13 L. R. A. 217), 26.
Smith v. Whitney (116 U. S. 167), 322.
Smoot v. Wetumpka (24 Ala. 112), 292.
Snell, In re (58 Vt. 257), 200.
Snider v. St. Paul (51 Minn. 466), 271.
Snyder v. Albion (Mich., 71 N. W. Rep. 475), 305.
Snyder v. Rockport (6 Ind. 237), 135.
Society of Savings v. New London (29 Conn. 174), 153.
Somer v. Philadelphia (35 Pa. St. 231), 178, 179.
Somerville v. Dickerman (127 Mass. 272), 67.
Sommers v. Marshfield (90 Wis. 59), 299.
Sonoma County Tax Case (13 Fed. Rep. 791), 265.
Soon Hing v. Crowley (113 U. S. 703), 199, 214.

Soper v. Henry Co. (26 Iowa, 264), 5.
South Bend v. Martin (142 Ind. 31, 29 L. R. A. 531), 91.
South Cov. Ry. Co. v. Barry (93 Ky. 43, 18 S. W. Rep. 1020), 206.
South Omaha v. Powell (Neb., 70 N. W. Rep. 391), 209.
South Park Com'rs v. Williams (51 Ill. 57), 121.
Southern Bell Tel. Co. v. Richmond (78 Fed. Rep. 858), 107.
Southport v. Ogden (23 Conn. 128), 199, 200.
Sowles v. Soule (59 Vt. 131), 265.
Spangler v. San Francisco (84 Cal. 12), 310.
Spaulding v. Andover (54 N. H. 38), 33.
Spaulding v. Lowell (23 Pick. 71), 69.
Spaulding v. Peabody (153 Mass. 129, 26 N. E. Rep. 421), 137, 138.
Speakership, In re (15 Colo. 500, 11 L. R. A. 240), 220.
Speed v. Detroit (98 Mich. 360, 22 L. R. A. 842), 30, 245, 246.
Speir v. Brooklyn (138 N. Y. 6, 21 L. R. A. 641), 273, 273.
Spencer v. Merchant (125 U. S. 345), 110, 113.
Springfield v. Edwards (84 Ill. 626), 172, 173, 175.
Springfield v. Green (120 Ill. 269), 114.
Springfield v. Le Claire (49 Ill. 476), 304.
Springfield v. Spence (39 Ohio St. 665), 309.
Springfield Fire Insurance Co. v. Keeseville (148 N. Y. 46, 30 L. R. A. 660), 281, 287, 288.
Spring Valley Co. v. Spring Valley (65 Ill. App. 571), 279.
Spring Valley Water-works v. San Francisco (82 Cal. 286, 16 Am. St. Rep. 116), 240.
Spring Valley Water-works v. Schottler (110 U. S. 347), 4.
Staates v. Washington (44 N. J. L. 605), 184.
Stafford v. Oskaloosa (57 Iowa, 748), 294.

TABLE OF CASES CITED.

References are to pages.

Stanfield v. State (83 Tex. 370, 18 S. W. Rep. 577), 54.
Stanke v. St. Paul (Minn., 73 N. W. Rep. 629), 302.
Stanley v. Davenport (54 Iowa, 463, 37 Am. Rep. 216), 102, 272, 297, 299.
Starr v. Burlington (45 Iowa, 87), 195.
State v. Ackerman (51 Ohio St. 163, 24 L. R. A. 298), 322.
State v. Ames (31 Minn. 440), 316.
State v. Anderson (44 Ohio St. 247), 60.
State v. Anderson (58 N. J. L. 515, 38 Atl. Rep. 846), 224.
State v. Anderson (45 Ohio St. 196, 12 N. E. Rep. 656), 223.
State v. Anwerda (40 Iowa. 151), 89.
State v. Atlantic City (49 N. J. L. 558), 170.
State v. Atlantic City (52 N. J. L. 332, 8 L. R. A. 697), 319.
State v. Austin (114 N. C. 855, 41 Am. St. Rep. 817), 199.
State v. Ballin (144 U. S. 1), 222.
State v. Barrows (Minn., 1898, 73 N. W. Rep. 704), 226.
State v. Bayonne (35 N. J. L. 335), 177, 179.
State v. Bayonne (44 N. J. L. 114), 71, 214.
State v. Beverly (45 N. J. L. 289), 181.
State v. Bennett (29 Mich. 451, 18 Am. Rep. 107), 42.
State v. Bergen (33 N. J. L. 39, 72), 179, 184.
State v. Berka (30 N. W. Rep. 267), 55.
State v. Bill (13 Ired., N. C., 273), 324.
State v. Binder (38 Mo. 450), 221.
State v. Blair (76 N. C. 78), 254.
State v. Blossom (19 Nev. 312), 234.
State v. Blue (122 Ind. 600), 83.
State v. Board (24 Wis. 683), 79.
State v. Board of County Canvassers (120 N. Y. 395), 319.
State v. Board of Freeholders (52 N. J. L. 512, 19 Atl. Rep. 972), 55.
State v. Board of Pub. Works (27 Minn. 62), 113.
State v. Boneil (42 La. Ann. 1110, 21 Am. St. Rep. 413), 196.

State v. Boucher (8 N. Dak. 389, 21 L. R. A. 539), 224.
State v. Boyd (19 Nev. 43), 48, 60.
State v. Bridgeman (8 Kan. 458), 316.
State v. Brinkerhoff (66 Tex. 45), 230.
State v. Bronson (115 Mo. 271), 82.
State v. Brown (19 Fla. 563), 214.
State v. Bruggerman (31 Minn. 493), 129.
State v. Bulkley (61 Conn. 287, 14 L. R. A. 657), 241, 321.
State v. Buss (125 Mo. 335, 33 L. R. A. 616), 229, 231, 252.
State v. Camden (58 N. J. L. 515, 38 Atl. Rep. 846), 185.
State v. Caminade (54 N. J. L. 135, 23 Atl. Rep. 933), 59.
State v. Cantiney (34 Minn. 1), 181.
State v. Cantler (33 Minn. 69), 214.
State v. Carr (129 Ind. 44, 13 L. R. A. 127), 237.
State v. Carrigan, etc. R. Co. (85 Mo. 263), 101.
State v. Carrol (38 Conn. 449, 9 Am. Rep. 409), 232.
State v. Cassidy (22 Minn. 312), 91.
State v. Cassidy (22 Minn. 321, 21 Am. Rep. 765), 90.
State v. Chicago, etc. Ry. Co. (80 Iowa, 586), 125.
State, Childs v. Minnetonka (57 Minn. 526, 25 L. R. A. 755), 42.
State v. Choate (11 Ohio, 511), 256.
State v. Churchill (15 Minn. 455, Gil. 369), 320.
State v. Cincinnati (20 Ohio St. 18), 65.
State v. Cincinnati (52 Ohio St. 419, 27 L. R. A. 737), 18.
State v. Cincinnati, etc. Gas Co. (18 Ohio St. 262), 80, 100, 193, 322.
State v. City of Great Falls (Mont., 1897, 49 Pac. Rep. 15), 23.
State v. City of Hudson (29 N. J. L. 475), 184.
State v. City of Orange (N. J., 13 Atl. Rep. 240), 208.
State v. City of Trenton (53 N. J. L. 132, 20 Atl. Rep. 1076), 203.
State v. Clark (54 Mo. 17), 193, 200.

F

State v. Clark (3 Nev. 566), 227, 242.
State v. Clark (23 Minn. 422), 158.
State v. Clark (52 Mo. 508), 236.
State v. Clark (28 N. H. 176), 209.
State v. Clayton (27 Kan. 442, 41 Am. Rep. 482), 242.
State v. Clinton Co. (6 Ohio St. 280), 161.
State v. Comm. (51 N. J. L. 402, 14 Atl. Rep. 587), 57.
State v. County Com'rs (39 Ohio St. 189), 78.
State v. Considine (16 Wash. 358, 47 Pac. Rep. 75), 210.
State v. Cooley (83 Ill. 585), 47.
State v. Cooley (56 Minn. 540), 55, 56.
State v. Copeland (96 Tenn. 296, 31 L. R. A. 844), 253, 255.
State v. County Court (51 Mo. 83), 63.
State v. Covington (29 Ohio St. 102), 47, 51, 53.
State v. Covington (29 Ohio St. 109), 30.
State v. Covington (29 Ohio St. 111), 73.
State v. Craig (132 Ind. 54, 16 L. R. A. 688), 30.
State v. Croft (24 Ark. 560), 254.
State v. Daviess Co. (64 Mo. 30), 156.
State v. Deffes (44 La. Ann. 45, 12 So. Rep. 841), 216.
State v. De Gress (53 Tex. 387), 256.
State v. Delaney (N. J., 1893, 25 Atl. Rep. 946), 225.
State v. Denny (118 Ind. 382, 4 L. R. A. 79), 30, 31.
State v. Denny (118 Ind. 449, 4 L. R. A. 65), 25, 29, 30.
State v. Dering (84 Wis. 585, 19 L. R. A. 858, 36 Am. Rep. 948), 189, 206, 207, 215.
State v. Dickson County Com'rs (24 Neb. 106), 79.
State v. Dillon (32 Fla. 545, 22 L. R. A. 124), 223, 225.
State v. Dillon (125 Ind. 65, 5 N. E. Rep. 136), 222, 223.
State v. District Court (29 Minn. 62), 113.
State v. District Court (33 Minn. 235), 5.
State v. District Court (41 Minn. 518), 186.

State v. Dixon, etc. (31 Neb. 552), 82.
State v. Doherty (16 Wash. 382, 47 Pac. Rep. 958), 224.
State v. Donaldson (41 Minn. 74), 84.
State v. Donovan (20 Nev. 75, 15 Pac. Rep. 783), 57.
State v. Dousman (28 Wis. 541), 48, 50.
State v. Draper (45 Mo. 355), 229.
State v. Dunn (12 Am. Dec. 25), 256.
State v. Du Barry (44 La. Ann. —, 11 So. Rep. 718), 216.
State v. Dupaquier (46 La. Ann. 577, 26 L. R. A. 162), 87.
State v. Eau Claire (40 Wis. 533), 121.
State v. Eidson (76 Tex. 302, 7 L. R. A. 733), 42, 43.
State v. Elizabeth (37 N. J. L. 432), 179.
State v. Elizabeth (57 N. J. L. 71, 23 L. R. A. 525), 56.
State v. Ellet (47 Ohio St. 90, 23 N. E. Rep. 931), 52, 53, 60.
State v. Ermentrout (63 Minn. 106, 65 N. W. Rep. 251), 224.
State v. Essex County (23 N. J. L. 214), 317.
State v. Everly (12 Nev. 616), 327.
State v. Fagin (42 Conn. 32), 241.
State v. Ferguson (31 N. J. L. 170), 242.
State v. Ferris (53 Ohio St. 1, 30 L. R. A. 218), 47, 52.
State v. Finn (87 Mo. 310), 251.
State v. Fond du Lac, etc. (24 Wis. 683), 78.
State v. Forest (74 Wis. 610), 42.
State v. Forkner (94 Iowa, 733, 28 L. R. A. 206), 54.
State v. Fountain (14 Wash. 236), 182.
State v. Fourcade (45 La. Ann. 717, 40 Am. St. Rep. 249), 202, 203.
State v. Freeman (38 N. H. 426), 211.
State v. French (17 Mont. 54, 39 L. R. A. 415), 91, 208.
State v. Friedley (135 Ind. 119, 21 L. R. A. 634), 236, 246.
State v. Gardner (34 N. J. L. 327), 114.
State v. Gary (21 Wis. 406), 246.
State v. Gas Co. (29 Wis. 452), 137.
State v. Gas Light Co. (102 Mo. 472), 137.

TABLE OF CASES CITED.   lxxi

References are to pages.

State v. Gates (35 Minn. 385), 240.
State v. George (23 Fla. 585), 224.
State v. Glenn (54 Md. 571), 132.
State v. Goff (15 R. I. 207, 2 Am. St. Rep. 921), 229, 230.
State v. Goodville (30 W. Va. 179, 6 L. R. A. 621), 225.
State v. Govan (70 Miss. 535, 12 So. Rep. 959), 18.
State v. Graham (16 Neb. 74), 57.
State v. Green (37 Ohio St. 227), 222.
State v. Hamilton (47 Ohio St. 52, 23 N. E. Rep. 935), 138.
State v. Hammer (42 N. J. L. 435, 440), 56, 58, 60.
State v. Hannibal, etc. Ry. Co. (75 Mo. 209), 108.
State v. Hardy (7 Neb. 377), 191, 194.
State v. Harper (6 Ohio St. 607, 67 Am. Dec. 363), 254.
State v. Harrington (68 Vt. 622, 34 L. R. A. 100), 208.
State v. Harris (50 Minn. 128, 52 N. W. Rep. 387). 132, 183, 196.
State v. Harris (96 Mo. 29, 22 Am. & Eng. Corp. Cas. 43), 158.
State v. Harrison (113 Ind. 440), 241.
State v. Harshaw (73 Wis. 211), 44.
State v. Hart (33 L. R. A. 118), 134.
State v. Hawkins (44 Ohio St. 98), 245.
State v. Haworth (122 Ind. 462), 39, 82.
State v. Hellmon (56 Conn. 190), 209.
State v. Henderson (38 Ohio St. 644), 185.
State v. Hermann (75 Mo. 340), 60.
State v. Hill (32 Minn. 275), 318.
State v. Hitchcock (1 Kan. 178), 63.
State v. Horley (39 Kan. 657, 18 Pac. Rep. 942), 156.
State v. Houston (78 Ala. 576, 56 Am. Rep. 59), 255.
State v. Hoyt (2 Oreg. 246), 230.
State v. Hughes (72 N. C. 25), 206.
State v. Hughes County (1 S. D. 292, 10 L. R. A. 588), 324.
State v. Hunter (38 Kan. 578), 25, 30, 55.
State v. Hutt (2 Ark. 282), 230.
State v. Huyvenhan (42 La. Ann. 488, 7 So. Rep. 621), 211.

State v. Ironton Gas Co. (37 Ohio St. 45), 4.
State v. Itzkovitch (49 La. Ann. 366, 21 So. Rep. 544), 89.
State v. Jacksonville S. R. Co. (29 Fla. 590), 27.
State v. Janesville, etc. Ry. Co. (87 Wis. 72, 41 Am. St. Rep. 23), 204.
State v. Jersey City (25 N. J. L. 536), 245, 246, 319.
State v. Jersey City (27 N. J. L. 493), 178, 179.
State v. Jersey City (29 N. J. L. 441), 117.
State v. Jersey City (34 N. J. L. 429), 184.
State v. Jersey City (37 N. J. L. 128), 115.
State v. Johnson (30 Fla. 433, 18 L. R. A. 414), 244, 245.
State v. Johnson (35 Fla. 2, 35 L. R. A. 357), 320.
State v. Jones (100 U. S. 513), 124.
State v. Judge (38 La. Ann. 43, 59 Am. Rep. 159), 241.
State v. Judges (21 Ohio St. 1), 51.
State v. Judge, etc. (42 La. Ann. 1089, 10 L. R. A. 248), 324.
State v. Kemp (69 Wis. 470, 2 Am. St. Rep. 753), 240.
State v. Kiichli (53 Minn. 147, 54 N. W. Rep. 1069, 19 L. R. A. 779), 220, 223, 243.
State v. Kirk (44 Ind. 401), 231.
State v. Kirkwood (14 Iowa, 162), 317.
State v. Kolsen (130 Ind. 361), 26, 30, 34, 63.
State v. Labatate (39 La. Ann. 513, 2 So. Rep. 550), 200.
State v. Laclede Gas Co. (102 Mo. 472, 22 Am. St. Rep. 789), 134.
State v. Langlie (5 N. D. 594, 32 L. R. A. 723), 316, 320.
State v. Lanier (31 La. Ann. 423), 254.
State v. Leavey (22 Nev. 454), 30.
State v. Leavy (21 La. Ann. 538), 31.
State v. Lee (22 Minn. 407, 13 N. W. Rep. 913), 196.
State v. Lee (29 Minn. 445), 132.
State v. Leech (60 Me. 58, 11 Am. Rep. 172), 246.

TABLE OF CASES CITED.

References are to pages.

State v. Leffingwell (54 Mo. 458), 5, 6.
State v. Lincoln Co. (35 Neb. 346), 79.
State v. Long Branch (42 N. J. L. 364, 36 Am. Rep. 518), 210.
State v. Lusk (48 Mo. 242), 231.
State v. McCabe (74 Wis. 481, 43 N. W. Rep. 322), 316.
State v. McGarry (21 Wis. 496), 244.
State v. McGrath (91 Mo. 386), 77, 79.
State v. McMahon (Minn., 1897, 72 N. W. Rep. 79), 90, 215.
State v. McNally (48 La. Ann. 1450, 21 So. Rep. 27, 36 L. R. A. 533), 208.
State v. McQuay (12 Wash. 554, 14 Pac. Rep. 897), 244.
State v. McReynolds (61 Mo. 203), 321.
State v. Macklin (18 S. W. Rep. 680), 59.
State v. Madison St. Ry. Co. (72 Wis. 612, 1 L. R. A. 771), 103.
State v. Mahner (43 La. Ann. 496, 9 So. Rep. 840), 217.
State v. Maine (27 Atl. Rep. 80), 87.
State v. Manitowoc (52 Wis. 421), 316, 318.
State v. Marlow (15 Ohio St. 114), 240.
State v. Mayor, etc. (37 N. J. L. 348), 205.
State v. Mayor of Atlantic City (52 N. J. L. 332, 8 L. R. A. 967), 234.
State v. Mayor of Newark (53 N. J. L. 4, 20 Atl. Rep. 86), 62.
State v. Medbery (7 Ohio St. 523), 174.
State v. Merrill (37 Me. 329), 75.
State v. Messenger (27 Minn. 119), 120.
State v. Meyer (54 N. J. L. 111, 22 Atl. Rep. 1004, 14 L. R. A. 62), 100.
State v. Miller (100 Mo. 439), 59.
State v. Milner (Minn., 68 N. W. Rep. 732), 226.
State v. Milwaukee (20 Wis. 87), 5.
State v. Mitchell (31 Ohio St. 592), 60.
State v. Montgomery (74 Ala. 226), 156.
State v. Moore (90 Ind. 294), 226.
State v. Moore (74 Mo. 413, 41 Am. Rep. 322), 254.
State v. Moores (Neb., 1898, 73 N. W. Rep. 299), 227.

State v. Morristown (33 N. J. L. 57), 200.
State v. Morse (50 N. H. 9), 124.
State v. Moyer (5 Port., Ala., 279), 93.
State v. Municipal Court (32 Minn. 329), 198.
State v. Murray (29 Wis. 96, 9 Am. Rep. 489), 227.
State v. Nashville (15 Lea, Tenn., 697), 198, 239.
State v. Nelson (34 L. R. A. 318), 74.
State v. Nelson (41 Minn. 25, 4 L. R. A. 300), 266, 320.
State v. Nelson (Minn., 68 N. W. Rep. 1066), 207.
State v. Nelson Co. (45 N. W. Rep. 33, 8 L. R. A. 283), 154.
State v. Nevin (19 Nev. 162), 254.
State v. Newark (25 N. J. L. 309), 177, 187, 324.
State v. Newark (27 N. J. L. 185), 116.
State v. Newark (30 N. J. L. 303), 185.
State v. New Brunswick (58 N. J. L. 255), 177.
State v. New Orleans (37 La. Ann. 13), 35.
State v. New Orleans (109 U. S. 285), 278.
State v. Northumberland (46 N. H. 156), 304.
State v. Norton (63 Minn. 497), 114.
State v. Oats (86 Wis. 634, 39 Am. St. Rep. 912), 256.
State v. Ocean Grove, etc. Ass'n (55 N. J. L. 507, 26 Atl. Rep. 798), 208.
State v. Ocean Grove Camp Meeting Ass'n (57 N. J. L. 110, 35 Atl. Rep. 794), 183.
State v. O'Connor (54 N. J. L. 36, 22 Atl. Rep. 1091), 62.
State v. Ollinger (Iowa, 1897, 72 N. W. Rep. 441), 235.
State v. Orange (50 N. J. L. 389, 13 Atl. Rep. 240), 202.
State v. Orr (68 Conn. 101, 28 L. R. A. 270), 84.
State v. Osawkee Tp. (14 Kan. 418, 19 Am. Rep. 99), 154.
State v. Parker (25 Minn. 215), 321.
State v. Parkinson (5 Nev. 17), 175.

TABLE OF CASES CITED. lxxiii

References are to pages.

State v. Parsons (40 N. J. L. 1), 47.
State v. Paterson (34 N. J. L. 163), 71.
State v. Patterson (98 N. C. 660), 182.
State v. Patterson (40 N. J. L. 186), 238.
State v. Peterson (50 Minn. 241), 245.
State v. Pinkerman (63 Conn. 176, 22 L. R. A. 563), 234, 236, 239.
State v. Pond (93 Mo. 606, 6 S. W. Rep. 469), 54, 55.
State v. Porter (113 Ind. 79), 223.
State v. Powell (97 N. C. 417), 132.
State v. Powers (38 Ohio St. 54), 52.
State v. Powle (67 Mo. 395, 29 Am. Rep. 512), 254.
State v. Pratt (52 Minn. 131), 98.
State v. Priester (43 Minn. 373), 194.
State v. Pritchard (36 N. J. L. 101), 245.
State v. Pugh (43 Ohio St. 98), 60.
State v. Putnam Co. Com'rs (23 Fla. 632), 97.
State v. Rahway (33 N. J. L. 111), 319.
State v. Rahway (58 N. J. L. 578), 183.
State v. Redmon (43 Minn. 250), 214.
State v. Reis (38 Minn. 371), 109, 111, 114.
State v. Riordan (24 Wis. 484), 48, 49, 50.
State v. Roberts (74 Mo. 21), 83.
State v. Robinson (35 Neb. 401, 17 L. R. A. 383), 320.
State v. Robitshek (60 Minn. 123), 132, 196.
State v. Rogers (10 Nev. 250), 182.
State v. Rose (4 N. D. 319, 26 L. R. A. 593), 324.
State v. Ruff (4 Wash. 384, 16 L. R. A. 140), 226.
State v. Saline Co. (48 Mo. 390, 8 Am. Rep. 108), 156.
State v. Saline Co. (51 Mo. 350, 11 Am. Rep. 454), 323.
State v. Savage (89 Ala. 1, 7 L. R. A. 426), 246.
State v. Schar (50 Mo. 393), 251.
State v. Schweick (19 So. Rep. 97), 135.

State v. Seavey (22 Neb. 454), 30.
State v. Secrest (13 Minn. 381), 318.
State v. Segel (60 Minn. 507), 210.
State v. Sexton (42 Minn. 154), 132.
State v. Shannon (132 Mo. 139), 226.
State v. Shea (Iowa, 1897, 72 N. W. Rep. 300), 238.
State v. Shearer (46 Ohio St. 275), 52.
State v. Sheppard (64 Minn. 287, 36 L. R. A. 305), 202, 205.
State v. Sherwood (15 Minn. 221, 2 Am. Rep. 116), 320.
State v. Simon (53 N. J. L. 550, 22 Atl. Rep. 120), 57.
State v. Sloan (48 S. C. 21, 25 S. E. Rep. 598), 102.
State v. Smith (26 N. E. Rep. 1069), 60.
State v. Smith (87 Mo. 158), 241.
State v. Smith (44 Ohio St. 348), 31.
State v. Smith (22 Minn. 218), 320.
State v. Smith (14 Wis. 497), 226.
State v. Somerby (42 Minn. 55), 321.
State v. Somers' Point (52 N. J. L. 33, 6 L. R. A. 57), 56.
State v. Sonne (16 R. I. 620), 256.
State v. South Kingston (18 R. I. 258, 22 L. R. A. 65), 320.
State v. Southern Minn. Ry. Co. (18 Minn. 40, Gil. 21), 316.
State v. Spande (27 Minn. 322, 34 N. W. Rep. 164), 47, 55.
State v. Spaulding (Iowa, 72 N. W. Rep. 288), 222.
State v. Spondee (37 Minn. 322), 47.
State v. Squires (26 Iowa, 340), 64.
State v. Stark (18 Fla. 255), 49.
State v. Stone (120 Mo. 428, 23 L. R. A. 194), 317.
State v. Stout (58 N. J. L. 598, 33 Atl. Rep. 858), 17.
State v. Strauss (49 Md. 288), 210.
State v. St. Joseph (37 Mo. 270), 158.
State v. St. Paul (32 Minn. 329), 93.
State v. St. Paul (34 Minn. 250), 324.
State v. St. Paul, etc. R. Co. (35 Minn. 131, 59 Am. Rep. 313), 293.
State v. Sullivan (45 Minn. 309, 11 L. R. A. 272), 321.
State v. Superior (90 Wis. 612, 64 N. W. Rep. 304), 245.

References are to pages.

State v. Supervisors (25 Wis. 339), 48, 50.
State v. Sutton (63 Minn. 147, 65 N. W. Rep. 262, 30 L. R. A. 630), 227.
State v. Synott (89 Me. 41), 131.
State v. Taft (118 N. C. 1190, 23 S. E. Rep. 970, 32 L. R. A. 122), 85, 86, 87, 210.
State v. Tappan (29 Wis. 664, 9 Am. Rep. 622), 39, 40, 41.
State v. Tippecanoe County (45 Ind. 501), 317.
State v. Toledo (48 Ohio St. 112, 11 L. R. A. 729), 57.
State v. Tolle (71 Mo. 645), 57, 59.
State v. Tolon (33 N. J. L. 195), 322.
State v. Tracy (48 Minn. 497, 51 N. W. Rep. 613), 321, 322.
State v. Trenton (35 N. J. L. 485), 226.
State v. Trenton (42 N. J. L. 486), 55.
State v. Trenton (49 N. J. L. 339), 77, 79.
State v. Trenton (53 N. J. L. 132, 20 Atl. Rep. 1076), 102, 193, 206.
State v. Trenton (54 N. J. L. 444, 24 Atl. Rep. 478), 60, 62.
State v. Trenton R. Co. (58 N. J. L. 666, 33 L. R. A. 129), 105.
State v. Trumpf (50 Wis. 103), 227.
State v. Tryon (39 Conn. 183), 195.
State v. Tucker (46 Ind. 355), 63.
State v. Tyler (14 Wash. 495, 45 Pac. Rep. 31), 325.
State v. Wadham (64 Minn. 318, 67 N. W. Rep. 64), 234.
State v. Wagner (34 Neb. 116, 15 L. R. A. 740), 319.
State v. Walsen (17 Colo. 170), 255.
State v. Warner (4 Wash. 263, 17 L. R. A. 263), 26, 42.
State v. Weatherby (45 Mo. 17), 321.
State v. Webber (107 N. C. 962, 22 Am. St. Rep. 920), 85, 194, 196.
State v. Webber (108 Ind. 31, 58 Am. Rep. 30), 82.
State v. Weir (33 Iowa, 134, 11 Am. Rep. 115), 54.
State v. Welch (36 Conn. 215), 209.
State v. Wells (46 Iowa, 662), 131.
State v. West (42 Minn. 147), 196.

State v. Wheelock (95 Iowa, 577, 30 L. R. A. 429), 91, 208.
State v. White (64 N. Y. 48), 206.
State v. Whitesides (30 S. C. 579, 3 L. R. A. 777), 209, 316, 321.
State v. Williams (99 Mo. 291, 12 S. W. Rep. 905), 227.
State v. Williams (25 Minn. 340), 320.
State v. Wilson (12 Lea, Tenn., 246), 47.
State v. Withrow (108 Mo. 1), 322.
State v. Womack (4 Wash. 19), 82.
State v. Wood (49 N. J. L. 85, 7 Atl. Rep. 286), 57.
State v. Woodbury (17 Nev. 337), 57.
State v. Woodin (56 Conn. 216), 87.
State v. Worth (95 N. C. 615), 182.
State v. Wright (80 Wis. 648), 130.
State v. Wright (54 N. J. L. 130, 23 Atl. Rep. 117), 58.
State v. Wrightson (56 N. J. L. 126, 22 L. R. A. 538), 319.
State v. Van Aucken (Iowa, 68 N. W. Rep. 454), 238.
State v. Van Beek (87 Iowa, 569, 19 L. R. A. 622), 226.
State v. Village of Lambertson (37 Minn. 362), 324.
State v. Vuhler (90 Mo. 560), 316.
State v. Young (30 Kan. 445), 19, 130.
State v. York Co. Com'rs (13 Neb. 57), 79.
State v. Zigler (32 N. J. L. 264), 182.
State Bank v. Gibbs (3 McCord, S. C., 377), 3.
State Board v. Aberdeen (56 Miss. 518), 39.
State Board of Agri. v. Citizens' St. Ry. Co. (47 Ind. 407, 17 Am. Rep. 702), 259.
State Center v. Bartenstein (66 Iowa, 249), 91, 208.
State Railway Tax Cases (92 U. S. 575), 323.
State Reservation, Matter of (133 N. Y. 734), 129.
Stearns Co. v. St. Cloud, etc. (36 Minn. 425), 39.
Stebbins v. Jennings (10 Pick. 172), 19.

TABLE OF CASES CITED.   lxxv

References are to pages.

Stebbins v. Keene Township (55 Mich. 552), 300, 301.
Stebbins v. Mayor (88 Kan. 578, 16 Pac. Rep. 745), 181.
Steele v. Boston (126 Mass. 583), 299.
Steele v. Dunham (76 Wis. 393), 248.
Stein v. Bienville Water Supply Co. (141 U. S. 67), 143.
Steines v. Franklin Co. (48 Mo. 167, 8 Am. Rep. 87), 161.
Stephen, Ex parte (114 Cal. 278), 194.
Stephens v. Props. of Canal (12 Mass. 466), 123.
Stephlan v. Daniel (27 Ohio St. 527), 266.
Sterling's Appeal (111 Pa. St. 35), 106.
Sterling v. Merrill (124 Ill. 522), 304.
Steubenville v. Culp (38 Ohio St. 18, 43 Am. Rep. 417), 237.
Stevens v. Carter (27 Oreg. 553, 35 L. R. A. 343), 320.
Stevens v. Muskegon (69 N. W. Rep. 227), 277.
Stevenson v. Bay City (26 Mich. 44), 186.
Stewart v. Board of Police (25 Miss. 479), 125.
Stewart v. New Orleans (9 La. Ann. 461, 61 Am. Dec. 219), 280.
Stewart v. Palmer (74 N. Y. 183), 110, 125.
Stewart v. Polk Co. (30 Iowa, 9), 154.
Stickney v. Salem (3 Allen, 374), 304.
Stilling v. Thorp (54 Wis. 528), 293.
Stillwater v. Moor (Okla., 33 Pac. Rep. 1024), 188.
Stinson v. Smith (8 Minn. 366), 109.
Stock v. Boston (149 Mass. 410), 288.
Stockdale v. Wayland School District (47 Mich. 226), 167.
Stockton v. Powell (29 Fla. 1, 15 L. R. A. 42), 140, 225.
Stockton, etc. Ry. Co. v. Stockton (51 Cal. 328), 158.
Stoddard v. Saratoga Springs (127 N. Y. 261), 271, 312.
Stone v. Charlestown (114 Mass. 214), 45.
Stone v. Mobile (57 Ala. 61), 324.
Story v. N. Y. Elev. R. Co. (90 N. Y. 122), 97, 105.

Stout v. Glen Ridge (58 N. J. L. 578, 35 Atl. Rep. 913), 5.
Stoutenburgh v. Hennick (129 U. S. 141), 18.
Stow v. Wyse (7 Conn. 214, 18 Am. Dec. 69), 220.
Stowers v. Postal Tel. & C. Co. (68 Miss. 559, 12 L. R. A. 864), 107.
Striker v. Kelley (7 Hill, N. Y., 9, 2 Denio, 323), 188.
Strosser v. Ft. Wayne (100 Ind. 443), 42.
Strout v. Pennell (74 Me. 262), 255.
Stubbs v. Lee (64 Me. 195, 18 Am. Rep. 251), 230.
Stuher v. Kern (44 N. J. L. 181, 43 Am. Rep. 353), 237.
Stuhr v. Hoboken (47 N. J. L. 147), 188.
Sturtevant v. Liberty (46 Me. 457), 145.
Stuyvesant v. Mayor (7 Cow., N. Y., 588), 184.
St. Joe, etc. Ry. Co. v. Buchanan Co. (39 Mo. 485), 154.
St. Johnsbury v. Thompson (59 Vt. 300), 200.
St. Joseph Tp. v. Rogers (16 Wall. 644), 157, 163.
St. Louis v. Allen (13 Mo. 400), 23.
St. Louis v. Allen (53 Mo. 44), 118.
St. Louis v. Bell Tel. Co. (96 Mo. 623, 9 Am. St. Rep. 370, 2 L. R. A. 278), 67, 69, 137.
St. Louis v. Buckner (44 Mo. 19), 71.
St. Louis v. Buffinger (19 Mo. 13), 195.
St. Louis v. Fitz (53 Mo. 582), 85, 201.
St. Louis v. Foster (52 Mo. 313), 182, 188, 195.
St. Louis v. Green (70 Mo. 562), 204.
St. Louis v. Know (6 Mo. App. 247), 208.
St. Louis v. Russell (9 Mo. 508), 23.
St. Louis v. Russell (116 Mo. 248, 20 L. R. A. 721), 70, 214.
St. Louis v. Shields (52 Mo. 351), 34.
St. Louis v. Shields (62 Mo. 247), 63.
St. Louis v. St. Louis R. Co. (89 Mo. 44), 194, 206.
St. Louis v. Webber (44 Mo. 547), 84, 201, 202, 203, 209.

TABLE OF CASES CITED.

References are to pages.

St. Louis Co. v. Griswold (58 Mo. 175), 31.
St. Louis Co. Ct. v. Sparks (10 Mo. 117, 45 Am. Dec. 355), 256.
St. Louis, etc. Co. v. Gill (54 Ark. 105, 11 L. R. A. 452), 184.
St. Paul v. Byrnes (38 Minn. 176), 86.
St. Paul v. Colter (12 Minn. 41, 90 Am. Dec. 278), 74, 84, 190, 208.
St. Paul v. Gilfillan (36 Minn. 298), 88, 89.
St. Paul v. Laidler (2 Minn. 190, Gil. 159, 72 Am. Dec. 89), 68.
St. Paul v. Smith (27 Minn. 364), 204.
St. Paul v. Traeger (25 Minn. 248), 68, 91.
St. Paul G. L. Co. v. McCardy (62 Minn. 509), 138.
St. Paul, etc. Co. v. Minneapolis (35 Minn. 141), 122.
St. Paul Ry. Co., In re (34 Minn. 227), 121.
St. Vincent's Orphan Asylum v. Troy (76 N. Y. 108, 32 Am. Rep. 286), 98.
Suchaneck v. State (45 Minn. 26), 131.
Suffield v. Hathaway (44 Conn. 521), 87.
Suffolk v. Parker (79 Va. 660, 52 Am. Rep. 640), 286.
Suffolk Sav. Bank v. Boston (149 Mass. 364, 4 L. R. A. 516), 162.
Sullivan v. Gilroy (55 Hun, N. Y., 285), 225.
Sullivan v. Helena (10 Mont. 134, 25 Pac. Rep. 94), 292.
Summers v. Davis County (103 Ind. 263), 284.
Summerville v. Pressley (33 S. C. 56, 8 L. R. A. 854), 85, 86.
Supervisors v. Rogers (7 Wall., U. S., 175), 318.
Supervisors of Marshall County v. Schenck (5 Wall., U. S., 781), 161.
Sutcliffe v. Board (147 U. S. 230), 168.
Sutherland v. Town of Goldsboro (96 N. C. 49), 158.
Sutro v. Pettit (74 Cal. 332, 5 Am. St. Rep. 442), 258.
Sutton's Hospital Case (10 Reports, 31a), 200.

Swan v. Buck (40 Miss. 268), 234.
Swarth v. People (109 Ill. 621), 71, 214.
Swartout v. Michigan, etc. R. Co. (24 Mich. 394), 20.
Sweet v. Carver Co. (16 Minn. 106), 147.
Sweet v. Hulbert (51 Barb. 312), 154.
Swift v. Falmouth (167 Mass. 115, 45 N. E. Rep. 184), 258.
Swift v. Topeka (43 Kan. 671, 8 L. R. A. 772), 98, 204.
Swindell v. Moxey (143 Ind. 153, 42 N. E. Rep. 528), 185.
Swindell v. State (143 Ind. 153), 178, 320.
Sykes v. Columbus (55 Miss. 115), 151.
Sylvester Coal Co. v. St. Louis (130 Mo. 323, 51 Am. St. Rep. 556), 196, 197.
Symonds v. Clay County (71 Ill. 350), 285.
Syracuse W. Co. v. Syracuse (116 N. Y. 167, 5 L. R. A. 546), 80, 140.

T.

Tacoma v. Tacoma L. & W. Co. (15 Wash. 499, 46 Pac. Rep. 1119), 133, 138.
Tacoma G. & E. Co. v. Tacoma (14 Wash. 288, 44 Pac. Rep. 655), 137.
Taft v. Pittsford (28 Vt. 286), 148.
Taggart v. Newport St. Ry. Co. (16 R. I. 668, 7 L. R. A. 205), 105.
Tainter v. Worcester (123 Mass. 311, 25 Am. Rep. 90), 281, 287.
Talbot v. New York & Harlem R. R. Co. (151 N. Y. 155), 124, 128.
Talbot Co. v. Queen Anne Co. (50 Md. 245), 23.
Talbot Pav. Co. v. Detroit (67 N. W. Rep. 979), 79.
Tallahassee v. Fortune (3 Fla. 19, 52 Am. Dec. 358), 292.
Tarkio v. Cook Co. (120 Mo. 1, 41 Am. St. Rep. 678), 181, 182.
Tarney v. New York (12 Hun, 542), 270.
Tate v. Greenboro (114 N. C. 392, 24 L. R. A. 671), 70.

TABLE OF CASES CITED. lxxvii

References are to pages.

Tate v. St. Paul (56 Minn. 527), 310, 311.
Tatham v. Philadelphia (11 Phil. 276), 153.
Taunton v. Taylor (116 Mass. 254), 87.
Taylor v. Americus (39 Ga. 59), 324.
Taylor v. Austin (52 Minn. 247), 312.
Taylor v. Bay City R. Co. (80 Mich. 77), 67.
Taylor v. Cárondelet (22 Mo. 105), 195.
Taylor v. Com. of Newberne (2 Jones' Eq. 141, 64 Am. Dec. 566), 18.
Taylor v. Lambertville (43 N. J. Eq. 112), 176.
Taylor v. Owensboro (98 Ky. 271), 279.
Taylor v. Palmer (31 Cal. 241), 117.
Taylor v. Palmer (21 Cal. 240), 191.
Taylor v. Phila. Bd. of Health (81 Pa. St. 73, 72 Am. Dec. 724), 30.
Taylor v. Sullivan (45 Minn. 309, 11 L. R. A. 272), 227.
Taylor v. Taylor (10 Minn. 107, Gil. 81), 157.
Taylor v. Woburn (130 Mass. 494), 293.
Teass v. St. Albans (38 W. Va. 1, 19 L. R. A. 802), 99.
Templeton v. Linn County (22 Oreg. 313, 15 L. R. A. 730), 292.
Templeton v. Voshloe (72 Ind. 134, 37 Am. Rep. 150), 309.
Ten Eyck v. Canal Co. (18 N. J. L. 200), 2.
Terre Haute v. Lake (43 Ind. 480), 176.
Terrett v. Taylor (9 Cranch, 52), 29.
Terrill v. Taylor (9 Cranch, 43), 134.
Territory v. Oklahoma (2 Okla. 158), 174.
Territory v. Smith (3 Minn. 240, Gil. 164), 227.
Territory v. Stewart (1 Wash. 98, 8 L. R. A. 106), 17.
Terry v. Milwaukee (15 Wis. 543), 146.
Terry v. Richmond (Va., 27 S. E. Rep. 429, 38 L. R. A. 834), 275, 276, 313.
Texton v. B. & O. Ry. Co. (59 Md. 63, 43 Am. Rep. 340), 102.
Thayer v. Boston (19 Pick. 511), 272, 274.

Theisen v. McDaniel (34 Fla. 440, 26 L. R. A. 234), 199, 201.
Theobald v. Louisville, etc. Ry. Co. (66 Miss. 279, 4 L. R. A. 735), 104.
Thomas, Re (53 Kan. 659, 37 Pac. Rep. 171), 181.
Thomas v. Board (5 Ind. 4), 63.
Thomas v. Boonville (61 Mo. 282), 71.
Thomas v. Burlington (69 Iowa, 140), 170, 172, 266.
Thomas v. Findley (6 Ohio C. C. 241), 283.
Thomas v. Gaines (35 Mich. 155), 114.
Thomas v. Leland (24 Wend. 65), 38, 39, 40.
Thomas v. Markman (Minn., 62 N. W. Rep. 206), 251.
Thomas v. Mason (39 W. Va. 526, 26 L. R. A. 727), 86, 317.
Thomas v. Port Huron (27 Mich. 320), 153, 263.
Thomas v. Richmond (12 Wall., U. S., 349), 69, 148, 198.
Thompson v. Carroll (22 How., U. S., 422), 198.
Thompson v. Jackson (93 Iowa, 376, 27 L. R. A. 92), 249.
Thompson v. Lee Co. (3 Wall. 327), 69, 153.
Thompson v. Moran (44 Mich. 602), 120.
Thompson v. Pacific R. Co. (9 Wall., U. S., 579), 3.
Thompson v. Schermerhorn (6 N. Y. 92, 52 Am. Dec. 385), 70.
Thomson-Houston Elec. L. Co. v. Newton (42 Fed. Rep. 723), 138.
Thorp v. Witham (65 Iowa, 566), 125.
Throckmorton v. Price (28 Tex. 609), 251.
Tice v. Bay City (84 Mich. 461, 47 N. W. Rep. 1062), 301.
Tiedt v. Carstensen (61 Iowa, 334), 129.
Tie Lay, In re (26 Fed. Rep. 611), 199.
Tierney v. Dodge (9 Minn. 156), 132.
Tiger v. Morris (42 N. J. L. 631), 62, 65.
Tillinghast v. Merrill (151 N. Y. 135, 34 L. R. A. 678), 254.

TABLE OF CASES CITED.

References are to pages.

Tillmon v. Otter (93 Ky. 600, 29 L. R. A. 110), 221.
Times Pub. Co. v. Everett (9 Wash. 518), 78.
Tindley v. Salem (137 Mass. 171), 268.
Tipton v. Norman (72 Mo. 380), 178.
Tisdale v. Town of Minonk (46 Ill. 9), 190.
Tissot v. Great So. Tel. Co. (39 La. Ann. 996, 4 Am. St. Rep. 248), 88.
Title G. & T. Co. v. Chicago (162 Ill. 505), 110, 114.
Toledo v. Cone (41 Ohio St. 149), 287.
Toledo, etc. Ry. Co. v. Jacksonville (67 Ill. 37, 16 Am. Rep. 611), 206.
Tomlin v. Dubuque, etc. Ry. Co. (32 Iowa, 106, 7 Am. Rep. 126), 134.
Tomlinson v. Board of Equalization (88 Tenn. 1, 6 L. R. A. 207), 324.
Tomlinson v. Indianapolis (144 Ind. 142, 36 L. R. A. 413), 90, 92.
Topeka v. Boutwell (53 Kan. 20, 27 L. R. A. 593), 211.
Topeka v. Tuttle (5 Kan. 186), 292.
Topeka Board, etc. v. Welch (51 Kan. 797), 82.
Torbush v. Norwich (38 Conn. 225, 9 Am. Rep. 395), 283.
Torrey v. Millbury (21 Pick. 64), 264.
Toutloff v. Green Bay (91 Wis. 490), 300.
Town of Coloma v. Eaves (92 U. S. 484), 164.
Town of Douglass v. Niantic Savings Bank (97 Ill. 228), 160.
Town of Essex v. Day (52 Conn. 483, 11 Am. & Eng. Corp. Cas. 265), 161.
Town of Kosciusko v. Stomberg (68 Miss. 469, 9 So. Rep. 297), 210.
Town of Venice v. Murdock (92 U. S. 494), 165.
Townsend, In re (39 N. Y. 171), 155.
Train v. Boston, etc. (144 Mass. 523, 59 Am. Rep. 113), 86.
Trainor v. Board of Auditors (87 Mich. 162, 15 L. R. A. 95), 223, 243, 244, 245.
Transportation Co. v. Chicago (99 U. S. 635), 134, 268.

Travelers' Ins. Co. v. Oswego (59 Fed. Rep. 58, 7 C. C. A. 69), 223.
Treadway v. Schnauber (1 Dak. 233), 23.
Treadwell v. Hancock Co. (11 Ohio St. 183), 159.
Trento v. Clayton (50 Mo. 541), 214.
Trescott v. Moan (50 Me. 347), 248.
Trustees v. Milwaukee, etc. Co. (77 Wis. 158), 101.
Trustees v. People (87 Iowa, 305), 83.
Tryon v. Pingree (Mich., 1897, 70 N. W. Rep. 905, 37 L. R. A. 222), 240.
Tuller v. Redding (16 Misc. Rep. 634), 98.
Turner v. Fish (19 Nev. 295), 57.
Turner v. Forsyth (78 Ga. 683), 322.
Turner v. Newburgh (109 N. Y. 301), 270.
Turner v. Nye (154 Mass. 578, 14 L. R. A. 487), 121.
Turner v. People's Ferry (21 Fed. Rep. 90), 135.
Tuttel v. Everett (51 Miss. 27), 266.
Tuttle, Ex parte (91 Cal. 589), 84, 215.
Tweighton v. San Francisco (42 Cal. 446), 40.
Twilley v. Perkins (77 Md. 252), 98.
Tyler v. Beacher (44 Vt. 648, 8 Am. Rep. 398), 154.
Tyler v. Hudson (147 Mass. 609), 121.
Tyrrell v. Andrew Co. (44 Mo. 309), 251.

U.

Underhill v. Calhoun (63 Ala. 216), 326.
Underhill v. Manchester (45 N. H. 214), 279.
Union Bank v. Commissioners of Oxford (119 N. C. 214), 318.
Union Ferry Works, In re (98 N. Y. 139), 81, 120.
Union Pacific Ry. Co. v. Dodge County (98 U. S. 541), 265.
Union Pacific Ry. Co. v. Montgomery (49 Neb. 429, 68 N. W. Rep. 619), 191.
United States v. Addison (6 Wall. 291), 237.

TABLE OF CASES CITED. lxxix

References are to pages.

United States v. Alexander (46 Fed. Rep. 728), 255.
United States v. Baltimore & Ohio R. Co. (17 Wall., U. S., 322), 40, 325.
United States v. Behan (110 U. S. 338), 76.
United States v. Brindle (110 U. S. 688), 228.
United States v. Clough (55 Fed. Rep. 373, 5 C. C. A. 140), 235.
United States v. Dashiel (71 U. S. 182), 254.
United States v. Green (53 Fed. Rep. 769), 242.
United States v. Macon County Court (99 U. S. 582), 318.
United States v. Morgan (52 U. S. 151), 254.
United States v. New Orleans (98 U. S. 381), 107.
United States v. Prescott (44 U. S. 589), 254.
United States v. Thomas (82 U. S. 337), 254.
United States Bank v. Dandridge (12 Wheat. 64), 20.

V.

Valentine v. St. Paul (34 Minn. 446), 266.
Valley Co. v. McLean (49 U. S. App. 131, 79 Fed. Rep. 728), 158, 168.
Valparaiso v. Gardner (97 Ind. 1, 49 Am. Rep. 416), 79, 80, 174.
Van Arsdale v. Hazard (3 Hill, N. Y., 243), 242.
Van Baalen v. People (40 Mich. 258), 90.
Van Buren, Petition of (79 N. Y. 384), 112.
Vance v. Little Rock (30 Ark. 435), 198.
Vanderbilt v. Adams (7 Cow. 349), 213.
Vanderslice v. Philadelphia (103 Pa. St. 102), 313.
Vandines' Case (6 Pick. 187), 195.
Van Giesen v. Bloomfield (47 N. J. L. 422), 57.

Van Hoffman v. Quincy (4 Wall. 535), 34, 35.
Van Hook v. Selma (70 Ala. 361), 14, 203.
Van Horne v. Des Moines (63 Iowa, 447, 55 Am. Rep. 750), 275, 281.
Van Pelt v. Davenport (42 Iowa, 308), 309.
Van Riper v. Parsons (40 N. J. L. 123), 55, 57.
Van Schaick v. Sigel (60 How. Pr. 122), 250.
Varner v. Martin (21 W. Va. 528), 121.
Varner v. Nobleborough (2 Me. 121, 11 Am. Dec. 48), 146.
Vassar v. George (47 Miss. 713), 40.
Vaux v. Jeffrun (2 Dyer, 114), 237.
Veale v. Boston (135 Mass. 187), 293.
Vegelahn v. Guntner (167 Mass. 92), 197.
Veneman v. Jones (118 Ind. 41, 20 N. E. Rep. 644), 204.
Vestal v. Little Rock (54 Ark. 321, 11 L. R. A. 779), 42, 43.
Vickery v. Chase (50 Ind. 461), 63.
Village of Carterville v. Cook (129 Ill. 152), 297.
Village of Ponca v. Crawford (23 Neb. 662, 8 Am. St. Rep. 144), 296, 298.
Village of Rankin v. Smith (63 Ill. App. 522), 294.
Village of Ravenna v. Pennsylvania Co. (45 Ohio St. 118, 12 N. E. Rep. 445), 205.
Village of St. Johnsbury v. Thomson (59 Vt. 301), 195.
Vincennes v. City G. L. etc. Co. (132 Ind. 114), 79, 80.
Vincennes University v. Indiana (14 How., U. S., 268), 319.
Virginia v. Plummer (65 Ill. App. 419), 302.
Virginia, etc. Ry. Co. v. Lyon Co. (6 Nev. 68), 158, 159.
Vidal v. Girard (2 How., U. S., 127), 26.
Voegthy v. Pittsburgh, etc. Ry. Co. (2 Grant's Cas., Pa., 243), 126.
Vogel v. State (107 Ind. 374), 227.
Volk v. Newark (47 N. J. L. 117), 199.

W.

Wabash v. Pearson (120 Ind. 426), 304.
Wabash R. Co. v. Defiance (167 U. S. 88), 96, 99, 100.
Wade v. Oakmont (165 Pa. St. 479), 173, 174.
Waggener v. Point Pleasant (42 W. Va. 798), 299.
Wagner v. Rock Island (146 Ill. 139, 21 L. R. A. 519), 24, 28.
Wagner v. Town of Garrett (118 Ind. 114), 209.
Wahn v. Philadelphia (99 Pa. St. 330), 188.
Wahoo, City of, v. Reeder (27 Neb. 770, 43 N. W. Rep. 1145), 5.
Wakefield v. Newell (12 R. I. 75), 308.
Wales v. Muscatine (4 Iowa, 302), 326.
Walker v. Cincinnati (21 Ohio St. 14, 8 Am. Rep. 24), 51, 54.
Walker v. City of Aurora (140 Ill. 402, 39 N. E. Rep. 741), 199.
Walker v. Cook (129 Mass. 577), 327.
Wall v. Trumbull (16 Mich. 228), 249.
Walla Walla Water Co. v. City of Walla Walla (60 Fed. Rep. 957), 175.
Wallace v. Lawyer (54 Ind. 501, 23 Am. Rep. 661), 326.
Wallace v. Trustees (84 N. C. 104), 23.
Walnut Tp. v. Wade (103 U. S. 683), 157.
Walsh v. New York (41 Hun, 299), 270.
Walton v. Missouri (91 U. S. 275), 91.
Wampler v. State (Ind., 38 L. R. A. 829), 320.
Wang Hane, In re (108 Cal. 680, 49 Am. St. Rep. 138), 194.
Ward v. Colfax Co. (10 Neb. 293, 35 Am. Rep. 477), 234.
Ward v. Greenville (8 Bax., Tenn., 288), 210.
Ward v. Hartford County (12 Conn. 404), 315.
Ward v. Marshall (96 Cal. 153, 30 Pac. Rep. 113), 267.
Warden v. New Bedford (131 Mass. 23, 41 Am. Rep. 185), 286.

Ware v. Percival (61 Me. 391), 264.
Warner v. Hoagland (51 N. J. L. 62), 59.
Warnock v. Lafayette (4 La. Ann. 419), 223.
Warren v. Charlestown (2 Gray, 84); 11.
Warren v. Evansville (106 Ind. 104), 65.
Warren v. Henley (31 Iowa, 31), 115.
Warren v. Westbrook Mfg. Co. (86 Me. 32, 26 L. R. A. 284), 308.
Warren v. Whitney (24 Me. 561, 41 Am. Dec. 406), 37.
Warthman v. Philadelphia (33 Pa. St. 202), 92, 93.
Washburn v. Oshkosh (60 Wis. 453), 41.
Washington Ave., In re (69 Pa. St. 352), 110, 114, 152.
Washington Street, In re (132 Pa. St. 257, 7 L. R. A. 193), 55.
Waterbury v. Commissioners (10 Mont. 515, 24 Am. St. Rep. 67), 326.
Water Co. v. Hamilton (81 Ky. 517), 4.
Waterer v. Freeman (Hob. 366), 248.
Waterloo Mfg. Co. v. Shannahan (128 N. Y. 345), 121.
Waters v. Leach (3 Ark. 110), 212.
Watertown v. Cady (20 Wis. 501), 5.
Watertown v. Mayo (109 Mass. 315), 86.
Watson v. Carey (6 Utah, 150), 182.
Watson v. N. Y. etc. Ry. Co. (47 N. Y. 157), 125.
Wayne County Auditor v. Benoit (20 Mich. 176), 237.
Weaver v. Devendorf (3 Den., N. Y., 117), 248.
Weaver v. Mississippi & R. R. Boom Co. (28 Minn. 534), 311.
Webb's Case (8 Coke, 45), 237.
Webb v. Demopolis (95 Ala. 116, 21 L. R. A. 62), 135.
Webb v. Mayor (64 How. Pr. 10), 28.
Weed v. Ballston Spa (76 N. Y. 329), 208.
Weed v. Boston (126 Mass. 443), 74.
Weeks v. Milwaukee (10 Wis. 258), 115.

TABLE OF CASES CITED.

References are to pages.

Weese v. Barker (7 Colo. 181), 250.
Weil v. Kerfield (54 Cal. 111), 184.
Weil v. Record (24 N. J. Eq. 169), 210.
Weinman v. Pass. R. Co. (118 Pa. St. 192), 59.
Weis v. Madison (75 Ind. 241), 309, 311.
Weismer v. Douglas (64 N. Y. 91, 21 Am. Rep. 586), 40, 154.
Weiss v. Edgerton Board (76 Wis. 177, 7 L. R. A. 330), 83.
Weitz v. Independent Dist. (79 Iowa, 423), 74, 77.
Welch v. Rutland (56 Vt. 228, 48 Am. Rep. 762), 280, 282, 283, 286, 291, 307.
Welker v. Porter (18 Ohio St. 85), 47, 59, 177.
Weller v. St. Paul (Minn., 12 Am. St. Rep. 754), 312.
Wellington v. Gregson (31 Kan. 99, 47 Am. Rep. 482), 101.
Wellman v. Board (84 Mich. 558, 47 N. W. Rep. 559), 245.
Wells, Ex parte (21 Fla. 280), 57.
Wells v. Buffalo (80 N. Y. 253), 265.
Wells v. Burnham (20 Wis. 119), 74.
Wells v. Salina (119 N. Y. 280, 7 L. R. A. 799), 81.
Wells v. Somerset, etc. R. Co. (47 Me. 345), 120.
Wellsborough v. New York, etc. Ry. Co. (76 N. Y. 182), 157.
Welsh v. Boston (126 Mass. 442), 84.
Welsh v. St. Louis (73 Mo. 71), 313.
Welter v. St. Paul (40 Minn. 460, 12 Am. St. Rep. 752), 292.
Welton v. Dickson (38 Neb. 767, 32 L. R. A. 496), 121.
Wesch v. Common Council (Mich., 1895, 64 N. W. Rep. 1051), 238.
Wesson v. Collins (72 Miss. 844, 18 So. Rep. 360, 917), 203.
Wesson v. Saline Co. (34 U. S. App. 680, 73 Fed. Rep. 917), 167.
West v. Lynn (110 Mass. 514), 302.
Westberg v. Kansas City (64 Mo. 493), 245.
West Chicago Park Com'rs v. McMullen (134 Ill. 170, 25 N. E. Rep. 676), 38, 133.

Westerly Nat. Works Co. v. Westerly (80 Fed. Rep. 611), 136, 141.
Western R. Co. v. Alabama, etc. R. Co. (17 L. R. A. 474, 96 Ala. 272), 106.
Western Reserve College v. Cleveland (12 Ohio St. 375), 278.
Western Sav. F. Society v. Philadelphia (31 Pa. St. 183, 72 Am. Dec. 730), 139.
Western Savings Society v. Philadelphia (31 Pa. St. 175), 287.
Western Union Tel. Co. v. Burlington, etc. R. Co. (11 Fed. Rep. 1), 262.
Western Union Tel. Co. v. Williams (86 Va. 696, 8 L. R. A. 429), 107.
Westfield v. Mayo (122 Mass. 100, 23 Am. Rep. 292), 300.
West Jersey R. Co. v. Camden & W. R. Co. (52 N. J. 31, 29 Atl. Rep. 423), 105.
Westlake v. St. Louis (77 Mo. 47), 266.
Weston v. Syracuse (17 N. Y. 110), 174.
West Plains Tp. v. Sage (32 U. S. App. 725, 69 Fed. Rep. 943), 150.
Westport v. Kansas City (103 Mo. 141), 42.
West River Bridge Co. v. Dix (6 How., U. S., 507), 120.
Weymouth v. New Orleans (43 La. Ann. 244), 286.
Wharf Case (3 Bland, Ch. 361), 135.
Wheeler v. Cincinnati (19 Ohio St. 19, 2 Am. Rep. 358), 280.
Wheeler v. Philadelphia (77 Pa. St. 338), 55, 56, 57.
Wheeler v. Plymouth (116 Ind. 158, 9 Am. St. Rep. 837, 18 N. E. Rep. 532), 277, 298.
Wheeler v. Wayne (31 Ill. App. 598, 24 N. E. Rep. 625), 74.
Whidden v. Drake (5 N. H. 13), 326.
White v. Kent (11 Ohio St. 550), 203.
White v. Marshfield (48 Vt. 20), 284.
White v. Meadville (177 Pa. St. 643, 34 L. R. A. 567), 141.
White v. People (94 Ill. 604), 111, 114.
White v. Polk (17 Iowa, 413), 280.
White v. State (Ga., 1897, 37 L. R. A. 642), 206.

TABLE OF CASES CITED.

References are to pages.

Whitfield v. Meridian (66 Miss. 570, 14 Am. St. Rep. 206), 292, 298.
Whitfield v. Paris (84 Tex. 431, 15 L. R. A. 783), 280, 284.
Whiting v. Sheboygan, etc. Ry. Co. (25 Wis. 167, 3 Am. Rep. 30), 153, 154.
Whiting v. Townsend (57 Cal. 515), 114.
Whiting v. West Point (88 Va. 905, 15 L. R. A. 861), 74, 107, 108.
Whitney v. Port Huron (88 Mich. 268, 26 Am. St. Rep. 291), 187.
Whitney v. Town of Ticonderoga (127 N. Y. 40, 27 N. E. Rep. 403), 296.
Whittaker v. Tuolumne County (96 Cal. 100, 30 Pac. Rep. 1016), 315.
Whitten v. Covington (43 Ga. 421), 214.
Whitwell, Ex parte (98 Cal. 73, 19 L. R. A. 727), 84.
Wiggin v. St. Louis (135 Mo. 558), 294.
Wilcocks, Ex parte (7 Cow. 403), 223.
Wilcox v. Chicago (107 Ill. 337, 47 Am. Rep. 434), 282, 283.
Wilcox v. Hemings (58 Wis. 144), 75.
Wild v. Deig (43 Ind. 455), 121.
Wild v. Paterson (47 N. J. L. 406), 307.
Wilde v. New Orleans (12 La. Ann. 15), 274.
Wiley v. Blufton (111 Ind. 152), 63, 65.
Wiley v. Greenfield (30 Me. 452), 148.
Wilkins v. Rutland (61 Vt. 336), 289, 291.
Wilkins v. St. Paul (16 Minn. 271), 125.
Wilkinson v. Saginaw (Mich., 1897, 70 N. W. Rep. 142), 236.
Will v. Village of Mendon (Mich., 66 N. W. Rep. 588), 293.
Willard's Appeal (4 R. I. 595), 245.
Willard v. Presbury (14 Wall. 676), 111.
Willett v. Young (82 Iowa, 292, 11 L. R. A. 115), 247.
Willey v. Alleghany City (118 Pa. St. 490), 287.
Williams' Appeal (72 Pa. St. 215), 35.
Williams v. Boynton (147 N. Y. 426, 42 N. W. Rep. 184), 232.
Williams v. Brewster (148 Mass. 256), 243.
Williams v. Com. (4 B. Mon., Ky., 146), 132.
Williams v. Commack (27 Minn. 209), 112.
Williams v. Nashville (89 Tenn. 487, 15 S. W. Rep. 364), 47.
Williams v. New York Ferry Co. (105 N. Y. 419), 185.
Williams v. Pittsburg (83 Pa. St. 71), 125.
Williams v. School District (87 Vt. 271), 121.
Williams v. State (112 Ala. 688), 131.
Williamson v. Keokuk (44 Iowa, 88), 150, 160.
Williamson v. Lacey (86 Me. 80, 25 L. R. A. 506), 249.
Williamson v. New Orleans (130 U. S. 190), 108.
Williamsport v. Com. (84 Pa. St. 487), 5, 149.
Willis v. Erie L. & T. Co. (37 Minn. 347), 107.
Wilmington v. Von Degrift (29 Atl. Rep. 1047, 25 L. R. A. 538), 277, 299.
Wilson, In re (32 Minn. 145), 209, 214, 324.
Wilson v. Board (133 Ill. 148, 27 N. E. Rep. 209), 47, 63.
Wilson v. Dullan (53 Mich. 392), 244.
Wilson v. Granby (47 Conn. 59), 304.
Wilson v. Jefferson County (13 Iowa, 181), 293.
Wilson v. People, etc. (19 Colo. 199, 22 L. R. A. 449), 255.
Wilson v. Rochester (180 Pa. St. 509), 141.
Wilson v. School District (32 N. H. 118), 7.
Wilson v. White (71 Ga. 506, 51 Am. Rep. 269), 295.
Wilson Co. v. First Nat. Bank (103 U. S. 770), 159.
Winbigler v. Los Angeles (45 Cal. 36), 291.
Winchester & L. T. Co. v. Croxton (98 Ky. 739, 33 L. R. A. 177), 137.
Windsor v. McVeigh (93 U. S. 274), 125.

TABLE OF CASES CITED.

References are to pages.

Winn v. Rutland (52 Vt. 481), 313.
Winona v. Cowdry (93 U. S. 612), 159.
Winona v. Thompson (24 Minn. 199), 159.
Winona v. Winona School District (40 Minn. 13, 13 L. R. A. 45, 12 Am. St. Rep. 687), 41, 44, 45.
Winona & St. P. Ry. Co. v. Watertown (1 S. Dak. 46, 44 N. W. Rep. 1072), 115.
Winspear v. Holman (37 Iowa, 542), 5, 6, 7.
Winter v. Henry County (61 Iowa, 684), 270.
Wirth v. Wilmington (68 N. C. 24), 193.
Wisconsin Keeley Inst. v. Milwaukee Co. (36 L. R. A. 53), 84, 95, 108, 153.
Wisconsin Water Co. v. Winans (85 Wis. 26, 20 L. R. A. 662), 121.
Wistar v. Philadelphia (80 Pa. St. 505), 111.
Witham v. Portland (72 Me. 539), 301.
Wixon v. Newport (13 R. I. 454), 291, 306.
Wolcott v. Wells (21 Nev. 47, 37 Am. St. Rep. 478), 256.
Wolf, Ex parte (14 Neb. 24), 209.
Wolff v. New Orleans (103 U. S. 358), 35.
Wong Hane, In re (108 Cal. 680, 49 Am. St. Rep. 138), 194.
Wood v. Brooklyn (14 Barb., N. Y., 425), 199.
Wood v. Varnum (83 Cal. 46), 245.
Woodard v. Brien (14 Lea, Tenn., 520), 60.
Woodhull v. New York (150 N. Y. 450), 279.
Woodruff v. Stewart (63 Ala. 208), 186.
Woonsocket, etc. Ry. Co. v. Sherman (8 R. I. 564), 153.
Wooster v. Mullins (64 Conn. 340, 25 L. R. A. 694), 239.
Worcester Nat. Bank v. Cheney (87 Ill. 602), 250.
Worcester Nat. Bank v. Cheney (94 Ill. 430), 55, 59.
Worden v. New Bedford (131 Mass. 23), 306.
Worley v. Columbia (88 Mo. 106), 271.

Worth v. Springfield (78 Mo. 108), 186.
Wragg v. Penn Tp. (94 Ill. 23), 196.
Wray v. Pittsburgh (46 Pa. St. 365), 111.
Wright v. Boston (9 Cush. 233), 112.
Wright v. Defrees (8 Ind. 298), 193.
Wright v. Nagle (101 U. S. 791), 81.
Wrought Iron Bridge Co. v. Town of Attica (119 N. Y. 204), 39.
Wullenwaber v. Dunigan (30 Neb. 877, 13 L. R. A. 811), 153.
Wurts v. Hoagland (114 U. S. 606), 125.
Wyoming Coal Co. v. Price (81 Pa. St. 156), 120.

Y.

Yarnold v. City of Lawrence (15 Kan. 126), 77.
Yates v. Lansing (5 Johns. 282, 9 Johns. 395, 6 Am. Dec. 290), 248.
Yates v. Milwaukee (10 Wall. 497), 88.
Yesler v. Seattle (1 Wash. 308), 152.
Yick Wo v. Hopkins (118 U. S. 369), 85, 199, 214, 216.
York Co. v. Watson (15 S. C. 1, 40 Am. Rep. 675), 255.
Yorks v. City of St. Paul (62 Minn. 250, 64 N. W. Rep. 565), 236.
Young v. Charleston (20 S. C. 116, 47 Am. Rep. 827), 291, 292.
Young v. Clarendon Tp. (132 U. S. 340), 149, 150.
Young v. St. Louis (47 Mo. 492), 184.
Youngblood v. Sexton (32 Mich. 406, 2 Am. Rep. 65), 323.
Youngs v. Hall (9 Nev. 212), 33, 62.

Z.

Zable v. Louisville Orphan Asylum (92 Ky. 89, 13 L. R. A. 668), 71, 116.
Zanesville v. Fannan (53 Ohio St. 605, 53 Am. St. Rep. 664), 293, 300.
Zaume v. Mound City (103 Ill. 552), 201.
Zeigler v. Gaddis (44 N. J. L. 365), 60.
Zeiler v. Central Ry. Co. (84 Md. 304, 34 L. R. A. 469), 184, 223.
Zottman v. San Francisco (20 Cal. 96), 67, 69, 74, 177, 179.

PUBLIC CORPORATIONS.

CHAPTER I.

INTRODUCTORY.

DEFINITION, CLASSIFICATION AND HISTORY.

§ 1. In general.
2. Different kinds of corporations.
3. Classification of public corporations.
4. School districts.
5. Distribution of powers and duties.

§ 6. The county — Its organization and functions.
7. The township.
8. The town meeting.
9. The township elsewhere than in New England.
10. The English municipality.
11. The American municipality.

§ 1. *In general.*— The people residing within the territorial limits of a state constitute a public body, organized for the purpose of self-government. The powers of government are distributed by the organic law among the three departments, which take their names from the nature of the powers delegated to each. In order that these powers may be executed with the least confusion and expense, it has been found advisable to subdivide the territory of the state, and to create the people resident within these subdivisions into artificial persons or corporations, charging them with the execution and administration of certain of the functions of the state. When by reason of local conditions, such as a congestion of population, special laws and methods of administration are required, local corporations have been created, to which are delegated certain powers, and upon which is conferred the privilege of conducting the affairs peculiar to that locality. They differ from the ordinary territorial subdivisions in the possession of these special powers and franchises, which are granted for the benefit of the people of that particular locality, as distinguished from the people of the state at large of which they form a part. Many of these bodies are very old, and have grown out of conditions which have long since passed away. The state has confirmed their ancient privileges, and in addition has imposed upon them many duties in connection with the work of public administration. The common form of public corporation in this country is a distinct creation by the state, and is provided for in the constitution of the state. Ordinarily, they are inseparably connected with a portion of the territory of the state; but the state may, and often does, create corporations for public purposes, without reference to territory.

§ 2. *Different kinds of corporations.*— These corporations are literally *created* by the state for its own purposes, without reference to the wishes of the people who reside within the territory. It also grants to individuals the right or franchise of being a corporation for the purpose of advancing their individual interests. The difference between the two kinds of corporations is apparent. The one is public, the other private. The former is created by the state on its own initiative, as an aid in the work of public administration and the government of the people of the state. It consents to or authorizes the creation of the other for the purpose of enabling the individuals to more advantageously conduct their private business. They are both corporations as they are legal entities or artificial persons, endowed with certain powers in common, but having different objects, and possessed of different powers. Private corporations are the result of contract, while public corporations are involuntary; and there is no contractual relation between the members or between the members and the state.[1]

[1] Dean v. Davis, 51 Cal. 406; People v. Morris, 13 Wend. 325, 327; Bennett's Appeal, 65 Pa. St. 242. The supreme court of New Jersey in Ten Eyck v. Canal Co., 18 N. J. L. 200, said: "Public corporations are political corporations, or such as are formed wholly for public purposes, and the whole interest of which is in the public. The fact of the public having an interest in the works or the property or the object of a corporation does not make it a public corporation. All corporations, whether public or private, are, in contemplation of law, founded upon the principle that they will promote the interest or convenience of the public. A bank is a private corporation, yet it is, in the eye of the law, designed for public benefit. A turnpike or a canal company is a private company, yet the public have an interest in the use of their works, subject to such tolls and restrictions as the charter has imposed. The interest, therefore, which the public may have in the property or in the objects of a corporation, whether direct or incidental (unless it has the whole inter-

If the corporation was created for the benefit of the incorporators or members, it is a private corporation, although, as we shall hereafter see, the nature of the business in which it proposes to engage may be such as to justify the state in exercising over it some of the powers ordinarily exercised only over public corporations. If, however, it was created for public, political purposes, with the primary object of aiding in the work of government, it is a public corporation, notwithstanding the fact that it may involve some private interests. Such organizations as cities, towns, villages, counties and townships are clearly public corporations.

The fact that the state has an interest in a corporation does not make such corporation public,[1] nor does the fact that a corporation derives a part of its support from the state[2] or is employed in the service of the state.[3] The rule is that, "if the whole interest does not belong to the government, or if the corporation is not created for the administration of political or municipal power, it is a private corporation."[4]

An attempt has been made to create a third class of corporations under the name of *quasi*-public corporations, and to include therein such as are organized for the primary benefit of the members, but are engaged in enterprises in which the public interests are directly involved, such as railway and warehouse companies.[5] But this classification has not been generally accepted. It is the use and not the corporation which is of a public nature. And it is an old principle of the law that, when "private property is affected with a public interest, it ceases

est), does not determine its character as a public or private corporation." Approved, Hanson v. Vernon, 27 Iowa, 28, 53.

[1] Bank of United States v. Planters' Bank, 9 Wheat. (U. S.) 904.

[2] Cleveland v. Stewart, 3 Ga. 283.

[3] Thompson v. Pacific R. Co., 9 Wall. (U. S.) 579.

[4] Beach, Pub. Corp., § 3. Citing Rundle v. Delaware, etc. Canal, 1 Wall. Jr. 275–290; Vincennes University v. Indiana, 14 How. (U. S.) 268; Bank of United States v. Planters' Bank, 9 Wheat. (U. S.) 907; Bonaparte v. Camden, etc. R. Co., 1 Bald.

205; Alabama R. Co. v. Kidd, 29 Ala. 221; In re New York, etc. R. Co. v. Metropolitan Gaslight Co., 63 N. Y. 326; Bailey v. Mayor, 3 Hill (N. Y.), 581; Directors v. Houston, 71 Ill. 318; Miners' Bank v. United States, 1 Greene (Iowa), 553; State Bank v. Gibbs, 3 McCord (S. C.), 377. Becoming owner or stockholder, the state descends from its sovereign dignity to individuality so far as to place it on an even footing of legal liability with other corporations of like character and purposes.

[5] Miners' Ditch Co. v. Zellerbach, 37 Cal. 543.

to be *juris privati* only;"[1] or, as stated in a modern decision, when a person devotes his property "to a use in which the public has an interest, he, in effect, grants to the public an interest in that use, and must submit to be controlled by the public for the common good to the extent of the interest he has created. He may withdraw his grant by discontinuing the use, but, so long as he maintains the use, he must submit to the control."[2]

Corporations which have received aid from the government for public purposes are sometimes classed as public corporations, but they are private corporations charged with public duties; and, in order that they may properly perform such duties, the state grants to them certain privileges and exemptions. Thus, the property of such a corporation which is necessary to enable it to perform the public duties with which it is charged cannot be seized and sold to satisfy an ordinary judgment.[3] Such bodies are what the supreme court of California[4] has designated as "corporations technically private, but of a *quasi*-public character, having in view some public enterprise in which the public interests are involved."

§ 3. *Classification of public corporations.*— Public corporations fall into two classes: The first are known as municipal corporations, and what remains may for want of a better name be grouped under the head of public *quasi*-corporations. Distinguishing features of municipal corporations are the possession of certain powers of legislation, and of certain powers and privileges, which are to be exercised for the particular benefit of the inhabitants of the municipality.

The corporation includes both the territory and the inhabit-

[1] Lord Hale in *De Portibus Maris*, 1 Hargrave's Law Tracts, 78.
[2] Munn v. Illinois, 94 U. S. 113. This is the doctrine of the "Granger Cases" and "Railroad Commission Cases." Chicago, etc. R. Co. v. Iowa, 94 U. S. 155 (1876); Peisk v. Chicago, etc., R. Co., 94 U. S. 164-178; Railroad Commission Cases, 116 U. S. 307 (1886); Hockett v. State, 105 Ind. 250 (Tel. Co.); State v. Ironton Gas Co., 37 Ohio St. 45 (Gas and Water Cos.); Spring Valley Water Works v. Schottler, 110 U. S. 347.
[3] Overton Bridge Co. v. Means, 33 Neb. 857, 51 N. W. Rep. 240, 29 Am. St. Rep. 514; Gooch v. McGee, 83 N. C. 59; Baxter v. Turnpike Co., 10 Lea (Tenn.), 488; Water Co. v. Hamilton, 81 Ky. 517; Palestine v. Barnes, 50 Tex. 538; Gue v. Canal Co., 24 How. (U. S.) 257; Seymour v. Turnpike Co., 10 Ohio, 477; Foster v. Fowler, 60 Pa. St. 27. See § 352,*infra*.
[4] Miners' Ditch Co. v. Zellerbach, 37 Cal. 543.

ants residing therein;[1] and may be defined as "the incorporation by the authority of the government of the inhabitants of a particular place or district, and authorizing them in their corporate capacity to exercise subordinate specified powers of legislation and regulation with respect to their local and internal concerns."[2]

The word "municipal" is sometimes used in statutes as synonymous with public and political, thus including all the governmental subdivisions of the state. Thus, counties have been held to be municipal corporations for the purpose of bringing them within the provisions of certain statutes,[3] although they are not properly municipal corporations.[4]

---

[1] Kelly v. Pittsburgh, 104 U. S. 79; Galesburg v. Hawkinson, 75 Ill. 156; People v. Bennett, 29 Mich. 451; Lowber v. Mayor, 5 Abb. Pr. (N. Y.) 325; Clarke v. Rochester, 24 Barb. (N. Y.) 446.

[2] 1 Dill. Mun. Corp., sec. 20. The fundamental idea of a municipal corporation is "the investing of the people of a place with the local government thereof." Cuddon v. Eastwick, 1 Salk. 143, quoted with approval in People v. Morris, 13 Wend. (N. Y.) 325, 334. People v. Hurlbut, 23 Mich. 44; State v. Milwaukee, 20 Wis. 87; Watertown v. Cady, 20 Wis. 501; Crane v. Fond du Lac, 16 Wis. 196; Norton v. Peck, 3 Wis. 714. The words "city" and "village" refer only to municipal corporations. City of Wahoo v. Reeder, 27 Neb. 770, 43 N. W. Rep. 1145; Mitchell v. Franklin Co., 25 Ohio St. 143. A school district or township is included within the phrase "political or municipal corporation." Clark v. Thompson, 37

Iowa, 536; Winspear v. Township of Holman, 37 Iowa, 542; Curry v. Township of Sioux City, 62 Iowa, 104. See School District v. Williams, 38 Ark. 454. The "Board of Park Commissioners" of the city of Minneapolis is not a municipal corporation. State v. District Court, 33 Minn. 235. The city and county of San Francisco is a municipal corporation, to be regarded as a city in matters of government, but the territory over which government is exercised is at the same time a county. Kahn v. Sutro, 114 Cal. 316, 46 Pac. Rep. 87, 33 L. R. A. 620. As to construction of the word "town," see Stout v. Glen Ridge, 58 N. J. L. 578, 35 Atl. Rep. 913.

[3] Iowa Land Co. v. Carroll, 39 Iowa, 151. In Dowlan v. Sibley Co., 36 Minn. 431, the court, in considering the provision of the statute, "that the legislature may, by general law or special act, authorize a municipal corporation to levy assessments for local

[4] People v. McFadden, 81 Cal. 489; Soper v. Henry Co., 26 Iowa, 264; State v. Leffingwell, 54 Mo. 458; Barton Co. v. Walser, 47 Mo. 189; Board of Park Com'rs v. Common Council of Detroit, 28 Mich. 237; Green Co. v. Eubanks, 80 Ala. 204; Askew v. Hale Co., 54 Ala. 639; Sherman Co.

v. Simons, 109 U. S. 735; Laramie Co. v. Albany Co., 92 U. S. 307; Williamsport v. Commonwealth, 84 Pa. St. 487. The term "municipal corporation" does not include towns. Eaton v. Supervisors of Manitowoc Co., 44 Wis. 489.

Under the head of public *quasi*-corporations are included those bodies which are public in their nature, but in some cases have not all the characteristic powers and liabilities of corporations. It includes counties, townships, school districts, overseers of the poor, and many such bodies. There is here an increase of public functions at the expense of corporate character. The power of local action and initiative is diminished, and with the increase of governmental functions there is a decrease of liability to individuals.[1]

"They are created for a public purpose as an agency of state through which it can most conveniently and effectually discharge the duties of the state as an organized government to every person, and by which it can best promote the welfare of all."[2]

improvements, etc.," Dickinson, J., said: "The question now presented is whether the words 'municipal corporations,' as here employed, should be deemed to include counties. At the time of the adoption of this amendment, counties might with propriety be termed political corporations. The statute declared them to be such. Gen. Stat. 1866, ch. 8, sec. 75. They were not, however, in the proper and more general use of the term, municipal corporations. Yet, for the purposes of general designation, it is not uncommon to use that term in a sense including such *quasi*-corporations as counties and towns, and so sometimes to distinguish public or political corporations or functions from those which would be termed private. Thus, in our own decisions may be found such language as this: 'A municipal corporation,— a city, county or town' (Harrington v. Town of Plainview, 27 Minn. 224, 229, 6 N. W. Rep. 777), 'a county or any other municipal corporation.' County of Blue Earth v. St. Paul & Sioux City R. Co., 28 Minn. 503, 507, 11 N. W. Rep. 73. See, also, Winspear v. District Tp. of Holman, 37 Iowa, 542; Ex parte Selma & Gulf R. Co., 45 Ala. 696, 732. In considering a provision in the constitution of Missouri forbidding the creation of corporations by special acts, 'except for municipal purposes,' it was said that a corporation for municipal purposes is either a municipality, such as a city or town created expressly for local self-government, with delegated legislative powers, or it might be a subdivision of the state for governmental purposes, such as a county. State v. Leffingwell, 54 Mo. 458, 475. Our consideration of this question has led us to the conclusion that the words 'municipal corporations' in the proviso under consideration may be reasonably construed as having the broad rather than the restricted sense, and as including such *quasi*-corporations as counties and towns."

[1] Sherbourne v. Yuba Co., 21 Cal. 113; Abbett v. Johnson Co., 114 Ind. 61; Dosdall v. Olmsted Co., 30 Minn. 96.

[2] Galveston v. Posnainsky, 62 Tex. 118; School District v. Wood, 13 Mass. 192. As used in our jurisprudence, the term "corporation" applies to derivative creations only, and does not include the state. Des Moines Co. v. Harker, 34 Iowa, 84.

The difference between a municipal corporation and a county is thus explained by Mr. Justice Paxson: "A municipal corporation has for its object the interest, advantage and convenience of the locality and its people. A county organization is intended to subserve the policy of the state at large in such matters as finance, education, provision for the poor, military organization, means of travel and transport, and especially the administration of justice. A municipal corporation is a government possessing powers of legislation, and is charged with a general care for the welfare of the people; while a county organization is merely the involuntary agent of the state, charged with the interests of the state in a particular county, and clothed with certain administrative functions limited in extent and clearly defined by law."

§ 4. *School districts.*— The administrative area for educational purposes is a public corporation known as a school district. It is a territorial subdivision of the county or township, according to whether one or the other is the unit for local government. Like all such corporations, their powers are strictly limited to such as are necessary for the proper performance of the administrative duties with which they are charged. "These little corporations," says Mr. Justice Bell,[1] "have sprung into existence within a few years, and their corporate powers and those of their officers are to be settled by the construction of the courts upon a succession of crude, unconnected, and often experimental enactments. School districts are in New Hampshire *quasi*-corporations of the most limited powers known to the law. They have no powers derived from usage. They have the powers expressly granted to them, and such implied powers as are necessary to enable them to perform their duties and no more."[2] Like counties, school districts have been sometimes included within the general name of municipal corporations.[3]

[1] Harris v. School District, 28 N. H. 58.

[2] Wilson v. School District, 32 N. H. 118; Foster v. Lane, 30 N. H. 315; Giles v. School District, 31 N. H. 304; Scales v. Chattahoochee Co., 41 Ga. 225; Rogers v. People, 68 Ill. 154; Beach v. Leahy, 11 Kan. 80; Conklin v. School District, 22 Kan. 521.

[3] Winspear v. District, etc., 37 Iowa, 542; Curry v. District, 62 Iowa, 102; Clark v. Thompson, 37 Iowa, 536. *Contra,* Heller v. Stremmel, 52 Mo. 309 (Incorporated board of public schools). See "The Laws Relating to City School Boards," by James C. Boykin, in Report of Commissioner of Education for 1895-96, vol. 1, ch. 1.

§ 5. *Distribution of powers and duties.*— The state in modern times makes very large use of municipal corporations in the work of state government. But ordinarily local administration is conducted by the counties and townships. The distribution of powers and duties varies in the different states. We find at the present time three systems of local administration based upon the unit of administration: the New England system, the Southern system and the Compromise system. In the New England system the town, or, as it is known in the West, the township, is the unit of administration, while the county is almost ignored. In the Southern system the county is the administrative unit, and nearly all the administrative business, not municipal in character and not affecting education, is centered in the county officers. In some states the county officers attend to school business; while in others the school district has been created. In some of the Southern States there is an area lower than the county, called the township, but it is simply an administrative district, and not generally a corporation.[1]

The Compromise system is the most widely prevalent. It developed in New York and Pennsylvania, and provides for a distribution of administrative affairs somewhat equally between the county and the town. In the Pennsylvania, or Commissioner form of this system, the county authority consists of commissioners elected by the people of the county at large; while in the Supervisor, or New York, form, the governing board consists of supervisors elected from the towns of which the county is composed. The Supervisor form is found in New York, Michigan, Illinois, Wisconsin, Nebraska, and in a modified form in Virginia.[2] The Commissioner plan is found in Pennsylvania, Ohio, Indiana, Iowa, Kansas and Missouri, and in a modified form in Maine, Massachusetts, Minnesota and the Dakotas, and has "very generally been adopted as the form for the county authority in the commonwealths of the South, where there are in the county generally no lesser districts to be represented."[3]

§ 6. *The county — Its organization and functions.*— The American county was, in the first instance, "a frontier copy

[1] Goodnow, Administrative Law, I, p. 192; Howard, Local Const. Hist., I, ch. IX.
[2] Howard, Local Const. Hist., I, p. 439.
[3] Goodnow, Administrative Law, I, p. 180.

of the English shire," although its growth affords no analogy to that of its English prototype. The shire is an historical unit with boundaries as natural as that of the nation, while our counties have been deliberately "laid out" as a part of the machinery for the administration of the government of the state.[1]

In the West and Southwest the adaptability of the county to the needs of a widely-scattered population led to its adoption as the chief organ of local government, while the mental characteristics of the early inhabitants of the Eastern states, and the conditions imposed upon them by religious and climatic influences, there led to the adoption of the township as the administrative unit. Natural conditions have modified both the county and the township in the Western states. The Southern settlers adopted the county as the unit of administration,[2] while the immigrants from New England carried with them their ideas of the importance of the town and the town meeting. In New England the county was originally created solely for judicial purposes, although in the process of time certain other functions have been taken from the township and conferred upon it. In the West and Northwest the township and the county exist side by side with carefully differentiated functions. The power and importance of the county consequently depends much upon its location, and this must not be lost sight of in determining the bearing of the decisions of the various states. Thus, in New England, where its powers are most restricted, its functions scarcely extend beyond the maintenance of county buildings, the granting of certain licenses and a partial control over highways, while in the South it has a complete set of officers and is practically charged with the entire local government. Under the common form of organization we find the county commissioners, and under their general supervision a county

---

[1] Wilson, The State, § 1026.

[2] Doubtless because of the nature of the country and the character of the people, but contrary to the advice of its early statesmen. Jefferson wrote: "Those wards called townships in New England are the vital principle of their governments, and have proved themselves the wisest inventions ever devised by the wit of man for the perfect exercise of self-government and for its preservation. . . . As Cato, then, concluded every speech with the words, '*Carthago delenda est*,' so do I every opinion with the injunction, 'Divide the counties into wards.'" Works, VI, 544.

treasurer, auditor, superintendent of education, superintendent of roads and a superintendent of the poor. On the judicial side there is the sheriff, clerk of courts, surrogate or ordinary or probate judge, and the state's attorney, who frequently acts for a judicial district composed of several counties. Where the township exists the county organization varies greatly, almost the only common point of resemblance being its control over the administration of justice. The county commissioners are variously elected and constituted. Under the Commissioner system, as in Indiana, Pennsylvania, Ohio, Iowa, Kansas and Minnesota, they are elected by the electors of the county, while under the Supervisor system of New York, Michigan, Illinois, Nebraska and Wisconsin, the board is composed of all the township supervisors. Somewhat wider powers seem to be granted where the Commissioner system exists. In Rhode Island the only county officers are those connected with the administration of justice. Elsewhere than in New England the administration of schools, the relief of the poor, the construction and maintenance of highways and matters of sanitation, and the control of the police, commonly falls to townships, while the county is charged with the administration of justice, the maintenance of jails, court-houses and poor-houses, and the equalization of taxes. Wherever found, however, counties are public *quasi-*corporations and possess such powers only as are conferred upon them by statute.

§ 7. *The township.*—The township is older than the county or the English shire. It is the lineal descendant of the ancient Germanic mark, and was revived by the early settlers of New England as best adapted to their condition. It was "a case of revival of organs and functions on recurrence of the primative environment."[1] These towns were from the first the administrative units, but were ultimately grouped for judicial purposes into counties, to which certain of their functions were transferred. This system of government by the town meeting is practicable only where the numbers who are to participate are limited and the capacity for self-government is highly devel-

---

[1] Howard, Local Const. Hist., I, ch. 2; Adams, Germanic Origin of New England Towns, J. H. U. Studies, 1st Series, No. 11. Criticised, Doyle, The Puritans, I, p. 74.

oped. Hence, while the system is still efficient, it has been somewhat impaired by the influx of a foreign population, untrained in self-government, and the growth of great cities.

§ 8. *The town meeting.*— A New England town is the best modern representative of a pure democracy. All the qualified voters of the territory are members of the corporation, and meet at certain periods as a general assembly for the transaction of the business of the community. The representative system is unknown, and each voter is entitled to participate personally in the work of government. The regular annual sessions are generally held in the spring of the year. They are presided over by a moderator and are attended by the town officers, who render their accounts for the year and their estimates of the money required for the ensuing year. The meeting approves or disapproves of the action of its officers and elects their successors. The organization of the towns is not entirely uniform, although they are all apparently formed upon one model. The officers are commonly from three to nine selectmen, a town clerk, a treasurer, a collector of taxes, assessor, a school committee, and such other minor officers as constables, library trustees and surveyors of highways. All the functions of local government are in the hands of these officials. The taxes for the payment of county expenses are apportioned by the counties, but are raised by the towns.[1]

---

[1] Warren v. Charlestown, 2 Gray, 84; Hill v. Boston, 122 Mass. 344; Commonwealth v. Roxbury, 9 Gray, 451; Eastman v. Meredith, 36 N. H. 284. For the history, organization and value of the town meeting, see Bloomfield v. Charter Oak Bank, 121 U. S. 121; Quincy's Municipal Hist. of Boston, ch. 1; Bryce, American Commonwealth, chs. 48, 49; Howard's Local Const. Hist. of the U. S., vol. 1, ch. 2; Freeman's Growth of the English Constitution, 17; Lecky, History of the Eighteenth Century, I, 887; John Stuart Mill, Representative Government, p. 64; May, Constitutional Hist. of England, II, 460; De Tocqueville, Democracy in America, I, ch. V, p. 56; Adams, Germanic Origin of N. E. Towns; John Hopkins Univ. Studies, 1st Series, No. 11, p. 5; Channing, Town and County Govt. in the New England Colonies of N. Am.; J. Toulmin Smith, Local Self-Government and Centralization, 29. Special attention is directed to Hosmer's Life of Samuel Adams, ch. XXIII (American Statesmen Series), and the same learned author's work on "Anglo-Saxon Freedom," ch. XVII. For a Tory estimate of the town meeting see the letters of Gov. Hutchinson in Hosmer's Life of Hutchinson.

§ 9. *The township elsewhere than in New England.*— The New England township sprang out of the church, the western township out of the school. In the West the government surveyor preceded the settler, and laid out the land into regular squares to which he gave the name of townships; and of each of these congress reserved two square miles for the endowment of schools. The organization necessary for the administration of this grant became the basis of the township as a political organization. The township was organized on the county. "The Northwestern township," says Dr. Wilson,[1] "is more thoroughly integrated with the county than is the New England township. County and township fit together as pieces of the same organization. In New England the township is older than the county, and the county is grouping of townships for certain purposes; in the Northwest, on the contrary, the county has in all cases preceded the township, and townships are divisions of the county. The county may be considered as the central unit of local government; townships are differentiated within it."

The township organization is strongest in the East and weakest in the South. It has been most generally accepted in New York, Pennsylvania, Ohio, Indiana, Kansas, Michigan, Wisconsin, Illinois and Minnesota. "In the states of this group," says Prof. Howard, "localism finds its freest expression: the town meeting possesses powers commensurate with the requirements of modern life; the primitive and proper nexus between *scir* and *tunscipe* is restored; the township is under the county but represented there. The county board of supervisors is the old scire-moot over again. The township-county system of the Northwest is one of the most perfect products of the English mind, worthy to become, as it may not improbably become, the prevailing type in the United States."[2]

In the far West, in states such as California, Oregon and Nevada, the county is the unit of government, although the township is well developed in California. Virginia has had a complete township system since 1870, and the tendency throughout the South and West seems to be toward the strengthening

---

[1] Shaw, Local Government in Illinois, p. 10.

[2] Local Self-Government in the United State, I, p. 158, quoted in Hosmer's Anglo-Saxon Freedom, p. 290.

of the township. Its organization differs according to its development, ranging from the pure democracy of New England to the representative system of the West. Where the departure from the original type is greatest, the town meeting has given place to the ordinary process of election. The selectmen are nowhere found outside of New England, but their functions are discharged by supervisors, who have general charge of the affairs of the township. These officers vary in number from one to three, and are sometimes, as in Ohio, designated as trustees. The powers of all townships are such and such only as are conferred on them by statute.[1]

§ 10. *The English municipality.*— The origin of our municipalities is found very far back in English history.[2] The thickly-settled communities in England always had a peculiar organization. From the beginning of the Norman period the inhabitants of a town owed certain payments to the crown, which were collected by the sheriff, who was the fiscal representative of the crown. The towns finally contracted to pay a fixed sum, which they were allowed to raise in such manner as they saw fit. This privilege was called the *firmi burgi*. It was in fact a lease of the town by its inhabitants. For the collection of this quota, the people under the supervision of the crown selected an officer, who was called the fermor or mayor. In consideration of the payment of a sum of money, the crown also granted to the inhabitants of a special district the privilege of holding a court, and exempted them from the jurisdiction of the sheriff's tourn, which was the ordinary crown court. The union of these privileges, known as the court leet and the *firmi burgi*, constituted a municipal borough. The townsmen, meeting in court leet, found it a natural and easy matter to assume such other functions as were necessitated by the presence of a large number of persons in a small district. They established rules as to participation in the court leet and as to the election of a mayor or provost. The general rule was that no one could participate in

[1] Bloomfield v. Charter Oak Bank, 121 U. S. 121; Hooper v. Emery, 14 Me. 375.

[2] This and the following section is taken largely from Prof. Goodnow's valuable work on Administrative Law.

the leet who did not pay taxes, was not a householder, and was not, in the eye of the law, capable of participating in the administration of justice. In the quaint language of the period, only those could be members of the court leet who were freemen householders, paying scot and bearing lot; and the formal criterion of the existence of these qualities in a given person was the fact that he had been sworn and enrolled in the court leet. This body had thus the ultimate decision as to the qualifications of municipal citizenship.

After the formation of parliament, the quota of the town was fixed by that body, and nothing remained to be done by the town but to assess the quota. The judicial system also underwent a change. The royal courts gradually absorbed all judicial functions, and the court leet became a jury for the determination of questions of fact. Such questions and the assessment of the quota could be more easily settled by a committee than by the large assembly, and the result was a formation of a committee of the original court leet for the transaction of both financial and judicial business. This committee gradually assumed the performance of all municipal business. It was composed of the largest taxpayers, who generally also held the commission of the peace. The smaller taxpayers gradually lost their equal privileges by neglecting to exercise them. As social and economic conditions changed, the qualifications for membership changed. In the larger cities membership in one of the great trade guilds became essential to the exercise of municipal functions. The limited body thus organized became finally the town council or leet jury.[1]

About this time the crown began to grant charters of incorporation to the body of rich and influential citizens who constituted the town council. The original object was to enable the district to hold property and to sue and be sued. Finally these bodies were granted representation in parliament, and thereafter their charters were granted and revoked by the crown when necessary to increase or maintain the political influence

[1] See Gneist, Self-Government, 318–325; Const. Hist. of England, II, pp. 140, 141; Pollock & Maitland, Hist. of Eng. Law, I, p. 625. For a description of modern English municipal corporations, see Pol. Sci. Quar., IV, pp. 197, 216.

of the crown in parliament.[1] The result was the system of rotten boroughs so well known in history.

§ 11. *The American municipality.*— The early American municipalities were modeled upon the English municipality as it existed in the seventeenth century. The city authority was in the town council, which was composed of the mayor, recorder, aldermen and councilmen. They were organized for the satisfaction of purely local needs, such as the management of the corporate property and finances, and the enactment of local police ordinances. The affairs of the colony within the municipality were attended to by a body of officers similar to those in the county and rural districts. But gradually the municipalities lost their local character and began to be used by the state as agencies of the state government. The corporation, which originally consisted of the members of the council, came to be regarded as consisting of the people residing within the district. The state made use of the city officials for the purposes of state administration, and used the municipality as an agent for the collection of taxes. The cities thus largely lost the power of regulating their purely local affairs; and instead of being organs for the satisfaction of local needs in accordance with the wishes of the inhabitants became the agencies of the state government, very much in the same manner as counties and other such subdivisions of the state.[2]

The plan of organization also changed. Instead of the consolidation of powers and functions in the council, they were separated and distributed among the council and the executive officers. The duty of deliberation is now generally left to the council, although it often exercises administrative power; while that of execution and administration is left to officers selected for that purpose.

[1] Dillon, Mun. Corp., I, § 18; Allison & Penrose, Hist. of Phila., p. 10; Rex v. London, 8 Howell, St. Trial, 1039. The judgment passed on London was followed by similar informations against the other towns. Most of the towns anticipated the attack by voluntarily surrendering their charters, in the place of which they received new ones "after a conservative pattern." The justices of assize especially abused their official powers to this end. Jeffreys, on the northern circuit, "made all charters fall before him like the walls of Jericho, and returned to London laden with surrenderings, the spoils of the towns." Gneist, Const. Hist. of England, II, p. 308.

[2] United States v. B. & O. Ry. Co., 17 Wall. (U. S.) 322.

BOOK I.

THE CREATION AND CONTROL OF PUBLIC CORPORATIONS.

CHAPTER II.

THE CREATION OF PUBLIC CORPORATIONS.

§ 12. Legislative authority.
13. Power to create.
14. Compulsory incorporation.
15. By the United States.
16. By territorial legislatures.

§ 17. By implication.
18. By prescription.
19. Manner of legislative action.
20. Name, boundaries and powers.

§ 12. *Legislative authority.*— All public corporations in this country are the creatures of legislation; and no place or locality can, by its act alone, obtain the rights and privileges, or subject itself to the liabilities, of a corporation.[1] In order that there may be such a corporation, there must have been legislative action under the form and subject to the limitations prescribed by the organic law. But this, as will hereafter be seen, may, under certain circumstances, be presumed.

§ 13. *The power to create.*— The creation of corporations for the purpose of aiding the central government and carrying on the work of local government is a legitimate exercise of the power of the state.[2] As there cannot be a municipal corpora-

[1] New Boston v. Dunbarton, 12 N. H. 409. The power to create municipal corporations is legislative, and cannot be delegated to the courts. Territory v. Stewart, 1 Wash. 98, 8 L. R. A. 106; Re North Milwaukee, 93 Wis. 616, 67 N. W. Rep. 1033, 33 L. R. A. 638. But the power to determine the boundaries may be delegated to the courts. State v. Stout, 58 N. J. L. 598, 33 Atl. Rep. 859.

[2] Hope v. Dederick, 8 Humph. (Tenn.) 1, 47 Am. Dec. 597; Memphis v. Memphis Water Co., 5 Heisk. (Tenn.) 529. The legislative power in this respect is supreme, except when restrained by constitutional limitation. See Chandler v. Douglass, 8 Blackf. 10, 44 Am. Dec. 732, and note; Jameson v. People, 16 Ill. 257, 63 Am. Dec. 304.

tion without territory, the legislature in creating the corporation must necessarily determine its territorial limits.[1]

§ 14. *Compulsory incorporation.*—While the legislature may, and now commonly does, require the consent of the people of the territory to their incorporation, it is not necessary that it should do so.[2] But compulsory incorporation can result only from direct legislative action, or the action of such persons or bodies as may by the law of the land be vested with sufficient delegated authority to bind the community.[3] A charter accepted by a majority of the people is binding upon all within the corporation.[4] When it is necessary that a charter or amendment thereto shall be accepted by the people, such acceptance must clearly appear; but it is not necessary that the acceptance should appear upon the records of the corporation, as it may be implied from the exercise of corporate power.[5]

§ 15. *By the United States.*—The power to create public corporations may be exercised by the federal legislature in a proper case. No express power for this purpose is granted to congress by the constitution, and it may therefore be exercised only when proper as a means of executing a granted power. Congress has express power "to exercise legislation in all cases whatsoever" over the District of Columbia; and may thus exercise the same power in creating public corporations within the District that an ordinary state legislature may exercise within the state.[6] It may also create such corporations in the territories by virtue of the general grant of power over the public domain.[7]

---

[1] Richards v. Cincinnati, 52 Ohio St. 419, 27 L. R. A. 737, and cases cited in the notes.

[2] Lycoming v. Union, 15 Pa. St. 166, 53 Am. Dec. 571; Berlin v. Gorham, 34 N. H. 266; Clarke v. Rogers, 81 Ky. 43; Blanchard v. Bissell, 11 Ohio St. 96; State v. Cincinnati, 52 Ohio St. 419, 27 L. R. A. 737. "The right to refer any legislation of this character to the people peculiarly interested does not seem to be questioned, and the reference is by no means unusual." Cooley, Const. Lim. (4th ed.), 143, citing many cases. It may be left with the people of a city to say whether they will come under a general law or retain their old organization. State v. Govan, 70 Miss. 535, 12 So. Rep. 959; § 60, *infra.*

[3] People v. Bennett, 29 Mich. 451, 18 Am. Rep. 107.

[4] Taylor v. Com. of Newberne, 2 Jones' Eq. 141, 64 Am. Dec. 566.

[5] Russell v. M'Lellan, 14 Pick. 63; Taylor v. Com. of Newberne, *supra.*

[6] Stoutenburgh v. Hennick, 129 U. S. 141; Barnes v. District of Columbia, 91 U. S. 540.

[7] Deitz v. City of Central, 1 Col. 332.

§ 16. *By territorial legislatures.*— As congress may create public corporations within a territory, it may delegate its powers in this respect to the legislature of the territory.[1] Under such a grant, the territorial legislature may confer upon municipal corporations the usual power to make and enforce proper ordinances for the government of the people.[2] The authorization of the territorial legislature is generally contained in a clause in the organic act, to the effect that its power shall extend to all rightful subjects of legislation.[3]

§ 17. *By implication.*— When not governed by an express constitutional provision, the legislature need not use any particular form of words or proceed in any particular manner in creating a public corporation. It is not even necessary that express words should be used. Thus, where the legislature confers or imposes upon a certain community or body of persons, by a collective name, powers or liabilities of such a character that they can only be exercised by or attached to the place in a corporate capacity, it will be deemed to have created a corporation, in so far at least as is necessary to give effect to the legislative intention.[4] But it is only in cases of necessity, in order that the grant may be enjoyed, that such corporate powers will be admitted;[5] and it has been said that the authorities will show that it is only when a *bona fide* con-

---

[1] Deitz v. City of Central, 1 Col. 323; Riddick v. Amelin, 1 Mo. 7; People v. City of Butte, 4 Mont. 174.

[2] State v. Young, 3 Kan. 445.

[3] Vincennes University v. Indiana, 14 How. (U. S.) 268; Burnes v. City of Atchison, 2 Kan. 454; People v. City of Butte, 4 Mont. 174.

[4] Russell v. Men of Devon, 2 T. R. 672. In Jordan v. Cass County, 3 Dillon, 185, the court said: "Undoubtedly the legislature designed that there should be a remedy upon these bonds, and if it were consistent with the legislative intent the court would be justified in holding, if necessary to afford an effectual remedy, that the township was created by implication, as to this particular matter, a body corporate, and as such liable to be sued." Denton v. Jackson, 2 Johns. Ch. 320; North Hempstead v. Hempstead, 2 Wend. 109; Dean v. Davis, 51 Cal. 406; Justices v. Armstrong, 3 Dev. 284; Bessey v. Unity, 65 Me. 342; School District v. Wood, 13 Mass. 193; Gaskill v. Dudley, 6 Met. 546. See Propagation Society v. Pawlet, 4 Pet. (U. S.) 480; Blair v. West Point Precinct, 2 McCrary, 459. Where the law imposes a duty or obligation upon and gives a remedy against an aggregate body, it gives a right of action, and to that extent, by implication, creates it a corporation.

[5] Stebbins v. Jennings, 10 Pick. 172.

tract cannot be otherwise enforced that a corporation will be admitted to have been created by implication.[1]

§ 18. *By prescription.*— In a few instances corporations have been recognized in this country as having been created by prescription. That is, when corporate powers have been exercised through a long term of years, it will be presumed that the power was originally granted, and the state will be estopped from asserting the contrary.[2] Thus, the existence of a school district may be proved by prescription; and it will then be presumed to possess the powers ordinarily conferred by the legislature upon such bodies.[3]

§ 19. *Manner of legislative action.*— In the absence of constitutional limitations, the legislature may create public corporations by special act or general law, as it deems most proper. Until within a comparatively recent time it was customary to create such bodies by special acts, which then became the charters of the corporations; and this method is still permissible in Alabama, Michigan, Oregon, Louisiana, Nevada, Maine, Maryland, New York, North Carolina, Wisconsin and Texas. In Missouri it may be by special act when the city contains at least five thousand inhabitants, and the charter is approved by a vote of the people within the territory to be incorporated. In these states it will be understood that the legislature may exercise its discretion, and in some cases it has provided for the creation of public corporations under a general law. But the inconvenience of having numerous public corporations within the state with different powers and liabilities, together with the evils incident to all special legislation, has led to the very general adoption of constitutional provisions forbidding the creation of either public or private corporations by special act, and requiring that the legislature shall provide for a uniform system of county, town and municipal government. Provisions of this general

[1] Blair v. West Point Precinct, 2 McCrary, 459.

[2] Jameson v. People, 16 Ill. 257, 63 Am. Dec. 304; Back v. Carpenter, 29 Kan. 349. "Municipal corporations are created for the public good — are demanded by the wants of the community; and the law, after long-continued use of corporate powers and the public acquiescence, will indulge in presumptions in favor of their legal existence." United States Bank v. Dandridge, 12 Wheat. 64; Swartout v. Michigan, etc. R. Co., 24 Mich. 394.

[3] Roby v. Sedgwick, 35 Barb. 319.

character are now in force in Illinois, Ohio, Kansas, Wisconsin, Michigan, Nebraska, Virginia, North Carolina, Missouri, Nevada, California, Iowa, Arkansas, New Jersey, West Virginia, Tennessee, Florida, Indiana and Minnesota. In some states the legislature is required to provide for a uniform system of county, town and municipal government; while in others, cities of a certain size are allowed to frame their own charters. Thus, in Missouri and California, cities having a population of over one hundred thousand may, under certain prescribed restrictions, frame a charter for themselves; and a similar law is in effect in Minnesota.[1] In Pennsylvania and Texas the legislature may by special act incorporate communities having over a specified number of inhabitants. Territorial legislatures are forbidden by act of congress from granting private charters or special privileges.[2]

§ 20. *Name, boundaries and powers.*— The creation of a corporation involves the fixing of its boundaries and the determining of its powers. Ordinarily the law provides a name for the corporation; but this need not be stated in the charter. Under general incorporation laws the name is commonly selected by the corporation.[3]

[1] Gen. Laws 1897, ch. 280, Const. Amend. adopted at Gen. Election, 1896. See "The People and their City Charters," in Oberholzer's The Referendum in America, ch. IV, and "Home Rule for our American Cities," in Annals of Am. Acad. of Pol. and Soc. Science for May, 1893, vol. III, p. 736.

[2] The various constitutional provisions are collected in Stimson, Am. St. Law, sec. 395 (44), and in Goodnow's Municipal Home Rule, ch. V (1895).

[3] Johnson v. Indianapolis, 16 Ind. 227; Cutting v. Stone, 7 Vt. 471; Galesburg v. Hawkinson, 75 Ill. 156.

CHAPTER III.

LEGISLATIVE CONTROL OVER PUBLIC CORPORATIONS.

§ 21. General statement.
22. Dual character of municipal corporations.
23. Local self-government.
24. Power over charters.
25. Public property.
26. Roads and streets.
27. Certain franchises.
28. The private property of a corporation.
29. Disposition of property upon dissolution.

I. POWER OVER OFFICES AND OFFICERS.

30. Various kinds of officers.
31. Police officials.
32. Their appointment and payment.
33. Park commissioners.
34. Board of public works.
35. Officers to lay out streets.
36. The mayor.

II. FUNDS AND REVENUES.

37. Power over revenue of public corporations.

III. LEGISLATIVE CONTROL OVER CONTRACTS.

§ 38. Relation of the corporation to the state.
39. Rights of parties contracting with corporation.
40. Illustrations.
41. Rights in a sinking fund.
42. Limitation of indebtedness.

IV. THE POWER TO IMPOSE OBLIGATIONS.

43. Nature of the debt.
44. Compulsory taxation.
45. Construction of highways.
46. Support of public schools.
47. Local corporate purposes.
48. Subscription for stock.
49. Compulsory payment of claims.

V. THE TERRITORY AND THE BOUNDARIES.

50. The general rule.
51. What territory may be annexed.
52. Illustrations.
53. Property and debts upon division of territory.

§ 21. *General statement.*— In considering the extent of legislative power over public corporations it must be remembered that such power is subject to the constitutional limitations upon legislative action in general, both as to substance and manner of execution. Constitutional provisions regarding general and special laws, titles of acts, and the like, must, as a matter of course, be observed in legislation with reference to public corporations as well as in all other cases. But, from the fact that such corporations are created by the legislature for governmental purposes, and that their rights rest on legislation and not on contract, it follows that the legislative control over such bodies is practically absolute unless restricted by express or implied constitutional limitations. That is, unless there is an express limitation upon the general power of the legislature, it may create, change or abolish public corporations with or without the consent of the inhabitants.[1] This is literally true with reference to public corporations which are purely governmental agencies, such as counties;[2] but municipal corporations have certain powers of a private nature in relation to which they act more as private corporations and are governed by the principles of private law.[3]

§ 22. *Dual character of municipal corporations.*— The extent of legislative power over municipal corporations is largely determined by the nature of the action sought to be controlled, or the interest affected. Such corporations have a twofold character. They are endowed with certain functions and possess powers and capacities which are granted to them for the benefit of their own citizens, and which are distinct from those which they possess as agencies of the state government. These powers and capacities are commonly called private, in order to distinguish them from the public powers in which the state is more directly concerned. As regards such private powers and capacities, municipal corporations are substantially on the same footing as private corporations.[4] Thus, when a municipal cor-

[1] St. Louis v. Russell, 9 Mo. 508; St. Louis v. Allen, 13 Mo. 400; Dartmouth College v. Woodward, 4 Wheaton, 518; Laramie Co. v. Albany Co., 92 U. S. 307; People v. Bennett, 29 Mich. 451; Wallace v. Trustees, 84 N. C. 164.

[2] "A county organization is created almost exclusively with a view to the policy of the state at large for purposes of political organization and civil administration in matters of finance, of education, of provision for the poor, of military organization, of the means of travel and transport, and especially for the general administration of justice. With scarcely an exception, all the powers and functions of the county organization have a direct and exclusive reference to the general policy of the state, and are in fact but a branch of the general administration of that policy." Treadway v. Schnauber, 1 Dak. 233; Hamlin v. Meadville, 6 Neb. 227; Talbot Co. v. Queen Anne Co., 50 Md. 245; Hannibal v. Marion Co., 69 Mo. 571.

[3] Illinois Trust & Sav. Bank v. Arkansas City, 76 Fed. Rep. 271, 34 L. R. A. 518; State v. City of Great Falls (Mont.), 49 Pac. Rep. 15 (1897).

[4] Illinois Trust & Sav. Bank v. Arkansas City, 76 Fed. Rep. 271, 34 L. R. A. 518; Safety I. Wire Co. v. Baltimore, 66 Fed. Rep. 140; Commonwealth v. Philadelphia, 132 Pa. St. 288; State, Jameson v. Denny, 118

poration supplies its inhabitants with gas or water, it is generally held to do so in its private corporate capacity, and not in the exercise of a power of local sovereignty.[1] As said by the supreme court of Pennsylvania in a recent case:[2] "If this power is granted to a borough or city, it is a special private franchise, made as well for the private emolument and advantage of the city as for the public good. In separating the two powers . . . public and private, regard must be had to the object of the legislature in granting them. If granted for public purposes exclusively, they belong to the corporate body in its public, political or municipal character; but if the grant was for the purpose of private advantage and emolument, though the public may derive a common benefit therefrom, the corporation *quo ad hoc* is to be regarded as a private company. It stands upon the same footing as would any individual or body of persons upon whom the like special franchises had been conferred."

The legislature has absolute authority over municipal corporations in matters of a governmental nature, and may enforce the performance of governmental duties, either through local officers or through agents or officers of its own appointment.[3]

§ 23. *Local self-government.*— In the absence of constitutional restrictions there is no question of the power of the legislature to control the local matters of municipalities, although in certain cases there is shown a strong disposition to protect the people from legislative interference in the management of their local affairs. Thus, in well-considered decisions in Indiana and Michigan it is held that the right of the people to the local

Ind. 449, 4 L. R. A. 79; Wagner v. Rock Island, 146 Ill. 139, 21 L. R. A. 519; Board of Commissioners v. Detroit, 28 Mich. 228, 15 Am. Rep. 202; Philadelphia v. Fox, 64 Pa. St. 180; People v. Hurlbut, 24 Mich. 44, 9 Am. Rep. 103.

[1] But see Fire Ins. Co. v. Keeseville, 148 N. Y. 46.

[2] Brumm's Appeal (Pa. St.), 12 Atl. Rep. 855. See, also, Wagner v. Rock Island, 146 Ill. 139, 21 L. R. A. 519. As said by Judge Cooley in People v. Detroit, 28 Mich. 228, 15 Am.

Rep. 202, 211: "Whoever insists upon the right of the state to interfere and control by compulsory legislation the action of a local constituency in matters exclusively of local concern should be prepared to defend a like interference in the action of private corporations and natural persons."

[3] This dual character was denied in some of the earlier cases. See Darlington v. City of New York, 31 N. Y. 164; In re Senate Bill, 12 Colo. 188.

self-government which existed at the time of the adoption of the state constitution is inherent and not subject to legislative interference.[1] But these decisions are based upon the peculiar conditions existing in these states, and do not affect the general statement as to legislative power. It is true the courts will not presume that the legislature intends to interfere with local self-government; but if in the legislative judgment the public interest will be best served by such interference, the power of the legislature cannot be successfully questioned. The rule is as stated in Massachusetts:[2] "We cannot declare an act of the legislature invalid because it abridges the privileges of self-government in a particular in regard to which such privilege is not guaranteed by the provisions of the constitution."

In some states the right of local self-government is secured by constitutional provision. Thus, the constitution of New York provided[3] that "all city, town and village officers, whose election or appointment is not provided for by the constitution, shall be elected by the electors of such cities, towns or villages, or appointed by such authorities thereof as the legislature thereof shall designate." This provision was held to secure to

[1] State v. Denny, 118 Ind. 382, 4 L. R. A. 65; State v. Denny, 118 Ind. 449, 4 L. R. A. 79; People v. Hurlbut, 24 Mich. 44, 9 Am. Rep. 103; Cooley, Const. Lim. 222. In Board of Park Com'rs v. Common Council of Detroit, 28 Mich. 228, 15 Am. Rep. 203, Cooley, J., said: "While it is a fundamental principle in the state, recognized and perpetuated by express provisions of the constitution, that the people of every hamlet, town and city of the state are entitled to the benefits of local self-government, the constitution has not pointed out the precise extent of local powers and capacities, but has left them to be determined in each case by the legislative authority of the state, from considerations of good policy as well as those which pertain to the local benefit and local desires." In State v. Hunter, 38 Kan. 578, the supreme court of Kansas said: "In effect it is said to be opposed to the fundamental theory of self-government, and denies to the people of the district the right to select their own officers from among their own number. Whatever may be said regarding the policy of placing the police administration of cities in a board of police commissioners who are chosen by state officers rather than through the electors of the cities, there can be no doubt that the legislature has the power to do so." State v. Seavey, 22 Neb. 455, 467. For a discussion of the tendency toward depriving municipalities of the right of self-government, see Goodnow's Municipal Problems, p. 9; Bryce, Am. Comw., I, p. 630, chapter on Municipal Government, contributed by Pres. Low of Columbia University.

[2] Commonwealth v. Plaisted, 148 Mass. 375.

[3] Const. of N. Y., art. 10, sec. 2.

the citizens of the municipalities immunity from legislate interference with the election or appointment of purely municipal officers;[1] but not to prevent the appointment by the legislature of commissioners for the improvement of the streets of a city.[2]

§ 24. *Power over charters.*— The transactions between a legislature and a municipal corporation are in the nature of legislation and not of contract.[3] Hence, municipal charters, not being contracts, may be changed by the legislature at pleasure when the rights of creditors of such corporations are not thereby affected.[4] This legislative power is not affected by the fact that the corporation is by its charter made the trustee of a charity or of other private rights and interests. If the legal existence of the trustee is destroyed, a court of chancery will assume the execution of the trust, and, if necessary, appoint a new trustee.[5] The legislature may, however, submit the question of the acceptance of an amendment to its charter to the people, although it is under no obligation to do so.[6] The fact that a city charter is recognized in the constitution of the state does not place it beyond the control of the legislature.[7] The annexation of territory to a city is not an amendment of its charter.[8]

§ 25. *Public property.*— The public property of a public corporation is under the exclusive control of the legislature. This includes all property acquired by the exercise of the power of eminent domain, or which is dedicated to a public use.[9] In

[1] People v. Albertson, 55 N. Y. 50.
[2] Astor v. New York, 62 N. Y. 567.
[3] East Hartford v. Hartford Bridge, 10 How. (U. S.) 511.
[4] State v. Kolsem, 130 Ind. 434, 14 L. R. A. 566; North Yarmouth v. Skilling, 45 Me. 133, 71 Am. Dec. 530; Claghorn v. Cullen, 13 Pa. St. 133, 53 Am. Dec. 450, cases cited on page 470 of note; Smith v. Wrescott, 17 R. I. 366, 13 L. R. A. 217; Meriwether v. Garrett, 102 U. S. 472; Broughton v. Pensacola, 93 U. S. 266.
[5] Girard v. Philadelphia, 7 Wall. (U. S.) 1; Vidal v. Girard, 2 How. (U. S.) 127. As to the power to take and hold property in trust, see Smith v. Wescott, 17 R. I. 366, 13 L. R. A. 217, and cases cited in note. The legislature may place the administration of trusts vested in the city in the hands of a board of trustees. Philadelphia v. Fox, 64 Pa. St. 160; Montpelier v. E. Montpelier, 27 Vt. 704, 29 Vt. 12.
[6] People v. Nally, 49 Cal. 478; Foote v. Cincinnati, 11 Ohio, 408, 38 Am. Dec. 737.
[7] Mayor of Baltimore v. State, 15 Md. 376, 74 Am. Dec. 572, and note.
[8] State v. Warner, 4 Wash. 263, 17 L. R. A. 263.
[9] Clinton v. Cedar Rapids, etc. Ry. Co., 24 Iowa, 455; Darlington v. Mayor, 31 N. Y. 164.

considering the nature of station-houses, fire-alarm telegraph and watch-boxes, the supreme court of Maryland says:[1] "There is no doubt that taking private property is beyond the scope of legislative authority, except when required for public use, and upon just compensation being made. But does this property come within such description? Let us test this by the very exception stated in the argument. If private, the state may take it for public use on making compensation; but to whom is the compensation to be made? Not to the mayor and city council as individuals, but to them as representing the people; and how made? By a tax levied upon the people themselves; that is, the people are to be taxed to buy property from themselves, for which they have already been taxed, and have paid. City property may be taken for public purposes other than the use of the city; that is, we suppose that property owned by the city might be condemned in some instances as any other property. But when the use would pass from the city into other hands, from whom would the payment or compensation be made to the city as recent owner? But this doctrine cannot apply where the design is merely to take city property dedicated to particular uses and apply the same property to the same purposes, by merely changing the agency by which the use is to be directed."

§ 26. *Roads and streets.*— The legislature as the representative of the whole people may regulate the use of streets, highways and other such public places. The municipality has no property interest in the streets even where it holds the title in fee. The title is held by the corporation in trust for the public, and "is as directly under the power and control of the legislature for any public purpose as any property held by the state or any public body or officers, and its application cannot be challenged by a corporation which in respect to such property, at least, is a mere agent of the sovereign power of the people."[2] Hence, the legislature may transfer the control of

[1] Mayor of Baltimore v. State, 15 Md. 376, 74 Am. Dec. 572.
[2] People v. Kerr, 27 N. Y. 188; Duval County Com. v. Jacksonville, 29 L. R. A. 416; State v. Jacksonville S. R. Co., 29 Fla. 590; Portland, etc. Ry. Co. v. Portland, 14 Oreg. 188, 12 Pac. Rep. 265; Council Bluffs v. K. C., etc. Ry. Co. '45 Iowa, 358; Chicago, etc. Ry. Co. v. Dunbar, 100 Ill. 110; Elliott, Roads and Streets, § 656.

the streets of a city to park commissioners, to be by them controlled as boulevards.[1]

§ 27. *Certain franchises.*— A public corporation has no property right in a ferry franchise acquired under a legislative grant.[2] So the power to maintain wharves and charge wharfage may be revoked at any time. Such powers "are merely administrative and may be revoked at any time, not touching, of course, any property of the city actually acquired in the course of administration."[3]

§ 28. *The private property of a corporation.*— The dual character of a municipal corporation has been already explained. Its property, like its powers, may be either public or private. It may own property as an individual or private corporation owns property; and in legislating with reference to such property the state must observe the principles of private law.[4] In exercising powers granted for the private benefit of the municipality and its inhabitants, it is governed by the same rules that govern the private individual or corporation. It has uniformly been held that municipal corporations may have private rights and interests vested in them under their charters; and that the grants of property to them for other than public purposes are no more the subjects of legislative control than are the private and vested rights of individuals.[5] Thus, where a city held certain real estate in fee-simple absolute, under ancient grants, and had at the expense of the citizens constructed reservoirs upon a portion of such real estate, it was held that the legislature had no power to require that the reservoir be destroyed and the land converted into a public park without compensation to the city.[6]

[1] People v. Walsh, 96 Ill. 232, 36 Am. Rep. 135; Simon v. Northrup, 27 Oreg. 487, 30 L. R. A. 171.
[2] E. Hartford v. Hartford Bridge, 10 How. (U. S.) 511, 16 Conn. 149.
[3] Railway Co. v. Ellerman, 105 U. S. 166.
[4] Illinois Trust & Sav. Bank v. Ark. City, 76 Fed. Rep. 271, 34 L. R. A. 518; Wagner v. Rock Island, 146 Ill. 139, 21 L. R. A. 519.
[5] Montpelier v. E. Montpelier, 29 Vt. 12, 27 Vt. 704. The private property of a municipal corporation is protected by the constitution of the United States in the same manner and to the same extent as the property of an individual. Grogan v. San Francisco, 18 Cal. 590, per Field, Ch. J.; Cooley, Const. Lim. *238.
[6] Webb v. Mayor, 64 How. Pr. 10. "It seems to me," said McComber, J., "that the weight of authority is to the effect that the property which

§§ 29, 30.] LEGISLATIVE CONTROL. 29

§ 29. *Disposition of property upon dissolution.*— The power to amend and repeal the charter of a private corporation cannot be used to take away property under the operation of a charter.[1] Upon dissolution, so much of the assets as are not public become subject to a charge for the benefit of the creditors. The private property of a public corporation is in like manner stamped with a trust for the payment of its debts,[2] and cannot be diverted to other uses by the legislature.[3]

I. POWER OVER OFFICES AND OFFICERS.

§ 30. *Various kinds of officers.*— The question of the legislative control over the officers who manage the affairs of public corporations is determined by the distinction between state and municipal officers. This distinction rests not upon the name or locality of the office, but upon the nature of the functions to be performed. If the duties of the office concern the state at large or the general public, although exercised within defined territorial limits, it is a state office, and under the absolute control of the legislature. But if such duties relate exclusively to the local concerns of a particular municipality, the office is strictly municipal, and any attempt on the part of the legislature to control the appointment of such officer is an interference with the right of local self-government.[4]

New York holds in its proprietary or private character, though originally derived from a power claiming the ultimate title, and which concerns the private advantage of the corporation as a distinct legal personality, is stamped with so many of the rights and powers of natural persons or private corporations as that the city cannot be deprived of this reservoir without due process of law and without just compensation. It admits of no doubt that the legislature may change, modify, enlarge or restrain the powers of a corporation which it has created. But whenever this is done, and a municipal corporation is relieved of the privilege and duty of maintaining a jurisdiction over the property and property rights, care has invariably been taken to restore to the original owner or proprietor the rights which the municipal corporation were for a time permitted to exercise. Terrett v. Taylor, 9 Cranch, 52; 2 Kent, Com. 257."

[1] The Sinking Fund Cases, 99 U. S. 700; Detroit v. Howell Plank Road Co., 43 Mich. 140.

[2] "If a municipal corporation, upon the surrender or extinction in other ways of its charter, is possessed of any property, a court of equity will take possession of it for the benefit of the creditors of the corporation." Broughton v. Pensacola, 93 U. S. 266.

[3] Hare, Am. Const. Law, p. 636, and cases cited.

[4] People v. Hurlbut, 24 Mich. 44, 9 Am. Rep. 103; State ex rel. Holt v. Denny, 118 Ind. 449, 4 L. R. A. 65;

§ 31. *Police officials.*— The various kinds and grades of police officials, although ordinarily performing their duties and exercising their powers within the limits of a single municipality, are state and not municipal officers.[1]

§ 32. *Their appointment and payment.*— The legislature may provide a permanent police for a municipal corporation, and place it under control of a board composed of members appointed by the legislature, and require the transfer to such board of all station-houses belonging to the corporation.[2] As said by Chief Justice Elliott,[3] "The power of the legislature to provide for the appointment of the members of a municipal board of police has been affirmed in every instance in which it has been so challenged and presented as to require the judgment of courts. Those courts which hold to the doctrine that the control of matters of purely local concern cannot be taken from the people of the locality place their decisions upon the ground that the selection of purely peace officers is not a local matter, but is one of state concern, inasmuch as such officers belong to the constabulary of the state. But while the reasoning of the courts is diverse, the ultimate conclusion reached by all the cases is the same." The maintenance of a police

State v. Hunter, 38 Kan. 578; People v. Draper, 15 N. Y. 532; Attorney-General v. Common Council of Detroit (Mich.), 70 N. W. Rep. 450. A member of a city council is not an officer of the ward from which he is chosen. He is a city officer. State v. Craig, 132 Ind. 54, 16 L. R. A. 688.

[1] Commonwealth v. Plaisted, 148 Mass. 375; Kimball v. Boston, 1 Allen (Mass.), 417; Rusher v. Dallas, 83 Tex. 151; Culver v. Streator, 130 Ill. 238; Perkins v. New Haven, 53 Conn. 214; Norristown v. Fitzpatrick, 94 Pa. St. 121; Burch v. Hardwicke, 30 Grat. (Va.) 24; State v. Seavey, 22 Nev. 454; State v. Hunter, 38 Kan. 578. "As a political society the state has an interest in the suppression of disorder and the maintenance of peace and security in every locality within its limits." Denio, J., in People v. Draper, 15 N. Y. 544; People v. Mayor, 15 Md. 376. In Shad v. Crawford, 3 Metc. (Ky.) 207, and People v. Albertson, 55 N. Y. 50, they were held to be local officers. The members of a board of health are state officers. Davock v. Moore, 105 Mich. 120, 28 L. R. A. 783; Taylor v. Philadelphia Board of Health, 31 Pa. St. 73, 72 Am. Dec. 724. Jury commissioners are state officers. Speed v. Detroit, 100 Mich. 92.

[2] Baltimore v. State, 15 Md. 376; People v. Mahaney, 13 Mich. 481; State v. Covington, 29 Ohio St. 102; State v. Seavey, 22 Neb. 454; State v. Hunter, 38 Kan. 578; State ex rel. Holt v. Denny, 118 Ind. 449, 4 L. R. A. 65; State ex rel. Jameson v. Denny, 118 Ind. 382, 4 L. R. A. 79. But see Evansville v. State, 118 Ind. 426, 4 L. R. A. 93.

[3] State v. Kolsen, 130 Ind. 434, 14 L. R. A. 566.

department is commonly left to municipal authority, but the legislature may establish a municipal board of police, with power to estimate the expense of such department and compel the municipality to provide by taxation for the payment of the amount so required.[1]

§ 33. *Park commissioners.*— The legislature may create a board of park commissioners, with members to be elected by the people of the municipality, and confer on it authority to purchase a public park. But such commissioners are primarily municipal officers, exercising powers of a nature purely municipal. In a leading case in Michigan a statute created a board and named the members and authorized it to select the land for a park and to make contracts therefor, subject to ratification by the city council and a vote of the people. Before the acts of the board were ratified the statute was amended, and the board authorized to "acquire by purchase" the necessary lands, and to require the council to provide the necessary money. It was held that the council could not be compelled to raise the money for such a local purpose, and that the fact that the council recognized the board as a municipal agent before the amendment did not make it the representative of the city with reference to powers conferred by the amendment.[2]

§ 34. *Board of public works.*— The legislature cannot create a body known as the board of public works, appoint the members and vest in such body complete and exclusive control over the streets and bridges of a city.[3] So, under a constitutional provision which authorizes the legislature to confer upon cities and villages such powers of local legislative and administrative character as it shall deem proper, and provides that "judicial officers of cities and villages shall be elected,

---

[1] People v. Mahaney, 13 Mich. 481; Burch v. Hardwicke, 30 Grat. (Va.) 24; Police Com'rs v. Louisville, 3 Bush (Ky.), 597; State v. Leovy, 21 La. Ann. 538. In People v. Albertson, 55 N. Y. 50, the case of People v. Draper, 15 N. Y. 532, is distinguished, and People v. Shepard, 36 N. Y. 285, doubted.

[2] People v. Detroit, 28 Mich. 328, 15 Am. Rep. 202; Attorney-General v. Lathrop, 24 Mich. 235; Park Com. v. Mayor, 29 Mich. 347. See St. Louis Co. v. Grisold, 58 Mo. 175; Harvard v. Drainage Co., 51 Ill. 130; People v. Mayor, 51 Ill. 17; Astor v. Mayor, 66 N. Y. 567. .

[3] State ex rel. Jameson v. Denny, 118 Ind. 382, 4 L. R. A. 79; State v. Smith, 44 Ohio St. 348.

and all other officers shall be elected or appointed at such times and in such manner as the legislature may direct," the legislature may appoint officers not municipal, such as police commissioners; but it cannot appoint officers whose duties are exclusively local, such as the members of a board of water commissioners for a particular city.[1]

§ 35. *Officers to lay out streets.*— The legislature may appoint officers within the city for specific purposes, such as laying out streets, and assessing damages arising therefrom, and authorize them to bind the corporation by their acts. Such an act is not an improper or extraordinary exercise of legislative power, and does not conflict with constitutional principles.[2]

§ 36. *The mayor.*— The chief executive officer of a city has been held to be a municipal and not a state officer.[3] But in a recent well-considered case,[4] it was held that the mayor was a state officer, within the meaning of a constitutional provision to the effect that no person holding an office under the state shall at the same time hold the office of governor. The court said: "Many cases have arisen upon similar provisions of the various constitutions, and while the decisions are not altogether uniform, we shall find them in substantial harmony upon two propositions, viz.: First, that an officer of a city, whose duties are purely and simply municipal, and who has no functions pertaining to state affairs, does not come within the constitutional description of officers holding office under the state. And sec-

[1] People v. Hurlbut, 24 Mich. 44, 9 Am. Rep. 103. The constitution of Colorado, article 5, section 25, which provides that the legislature "shall not delegate to any special commission, private corporation or association, any power to make, supervise or interfere with any municipal improvement, money, property or effects, or perform any municipal functions whatever," does not prevent the legislature creating a board of public works for the city of Denver charged with the making of public improvements, composed of members appointed by the governor by and with the advice and consent of the senate. In re Senate Bill, 12 Colo. 188.

[2] "When officers are thus appointed for purposes within the limits and sphere of the municipal government of a city, their acts are the acts of the city, precisely as if they had been done by the municipal authorities selected under the provisions of the charter." Daley v. St. Paul, 7 Minn. 390 (Gil. 311).

[3] Britton v. Steber, 62 Mo. 370.

[4] Attorney-General v. Common Council of Detroit (Mich.), 70 N. W. Rep. 450.

ond, where officers in cities are appointed or elected by the community in obedience to laws which impose duties upon them in relation to state affairs, as contradistinguished from affairs of interest to the city merely, such as relate to gas-works, sewers, water-works, lighting, etc., they are upon a different footing, and may properly be said to hold office under the state."

II. FUNDS AND REVENUES.

§ 37. *Power over revenue of public corporations.*—The legislature has the same power over the revenues of a city, county or township that it has over the immediate funds of the state;[1] and in the exercise of its authority it may appropriate such revenues to such public purposes as it deems most conducive to the public good.[2] The revenues of a county are not its property in the sense in which private property belongs to an individual. They are the result of taxation exercised for the public good, and the public interest requires that the legislature shall have power to direct and control their application.[3] Hence, until actually appropriated, the public funds are subject to the control of the legislature. Thus, no vested rights are acquired in a fund set apart for the relief of disabled officers. "The direction of the state," said Mr. Justice Field,[4] "that the fund should be for the benefit of the police officer or his representatives, under certain conditions, was subject to change or revocation at any time at the will of the legislature. There was no contract on the part of the state that its disposition should always continue as originally provided. Until the particular

[1] Dovack v. Moore, 105 Mich. 120, 28 L. R. A. 783; County v. People, 11 Ill. 202; County of Richland v. County of Lawrence, 12 Ill. 1; Trustees v. Tatam, 13 Ill. 28; Dennis v. Maynard, 15 Ill. 477; People v. Power, 25 Ill. 169; Love v. Schenck, 12 Ired. (N. C.) 304; Youngs v. Hall, 9 Nev. 212; Indianapolis v. Indianapolis Home, etc., 50 Ind. 215; Duval Co. Com. v. Jacksonville (Fla.), 29 L. R. A. 416, 18 So. Rep. 339.

Misappropriation of funds—Action—When the funds of the county or city are misappropriated, an action to recover the same must be brought in the name of the municipality. People v. Ingersoll, 58 N. Y. 1; People v. Fields, 58 N. Y. 491; Love v. Schenck, 12 Ired. (N. C.) 304; Dennis v. Maynard, 15 Ill. 477; Spaulding v. Andover, 54 N. H. 38. See Trustees of Aberdeen Academy v. Aberdeen, 13 S. & M. (Miss.) 645.

[2] Creighton v. San Francisco, 42 Cal. 446.

[3] Board v. City of Springfield, 63 Ill. 66.

[4] Pennie v. Reis, 132 U. S. 464.

event should happen upon which the money or a part of it was to be paid, there was no vested right in the officer to such payment."

Where the constitution of the state prohibited the legislature from authorizing counties to levy taxes for any other than county purposes, it was held that the legislature might nevertheless require the county to turn over a certain portion of a tax levied for county purposes to a municipality to be used in repairing the streets of a city.[1]

III. Legislative Control Over Contracts.

§ 38. *Relation of the corporation to the state.*— Neither public corporations nor their officers or agents[2] can acquire vested rights in the powers which are conferred upon them. "It is an unsound and even absurd proposition that political power conferred by the legislature can become a vested right as against the government in any individual or body of men.[3] Such power exists subject to the will of the legislature, and in the absence of a constitutional limitation may be repealed or withdrawn either by general law or special statute.[4] Thus, the legislature may repeal a grant of power to levy and collect wharfage, although the income of the wharf has been pledged by the corporation along with other revenues for the payment of bonds issued in order to obtain money to maintain and improve the wharf.[5] So, it may repeal a statute which gives to a city the right to license the sale of intoxicating liquors, and provides that the money received from such licenses shall be appropriated to the support of paupers within the city.[6] "Such authority," said Caton, J.,[7] "gives the city no more a vested right to issue licenses because the legislature specified the object to which the money should be applied, than if it had been put into the general fund of the city."

---

[1] Duval Co. Com. v. Jacksonville, (Fla.), 29 L. R. A. 416; Skinner v. Henderson, 26 Fla. 121, 8 L. R. A. 55.

[2] People v. Hurlbut, 24 Mich. 44.

[3] People v. Morris, 13 Wend. 335, Nelson, J.

[4] Sloan v. State, 8 Blackf. (Ind.) 361; State v. Kolsen, 130 Ind. 434, 14 L. R. A. 566.

[5] St. Louis v. Shields, 52 Mo. 351. Distinguishing Van Hoffman v. Quincy, 4 Wall. 535.

[6] Gutzweller v. People, 14 Ill. 142.

[7] See Richmond Co. v. Lawrence Co., 12 Ill. 1; Sangamon v. Springfield, 63 Ill. 66.

§ 39. *Rights of parties contracting with corporation.*— But in the exercise of this general power of control over the corporation, the legislature must not impair any of the constitutional rights of third persons who have become creditors of the corporation. The corporation itself may not acquire rights as against its creator in such cases; but its transactions with its creditors may give rise to contracts which are protected by the constitutional provision.[1]

§ 40. *Illustrations.*— Where a public corporation has been given authority to incur indebtedness, and to levy a tax for the purpose of providing the means to pay such debt, parties who become creditors of the corporation upon the faith of this taxing power are presumed to have contracted with reference to the means of payment thus provided, and the legislature cannot destroy their remedy by depriving the municipality of the right to levy the tax. The power of taxation as it existed at the date of the contract is read into the contract and becomes a part of the obligation.[2] The rights of creditors can no more be affected by constitutional amendment than by the repeal of the law authorizing the levying of the tax.[3] Subsequent changes which substantially modify the manner of levying the tax, so as to affect rights under the contract, violate the rule against the impairment of contracts.[4] But an alteration in the manner of levying such tax, which does not substantially affect the security of the creditor, is valid.[5] So, exempting certain property from the operation of the tax is not objectionable,

[1] Shapleigh v. San Angelo, 167 U. S. 654; Wolff v. New Orleans, 103 U. S. 358; Williams' Appeal, 72 Pa. St. 215; Memphis v. United States, 97 U. S. 293; Van Hoffman v. Quincy, 4 Wall. 536; Morris v. State, 62 Tex. 728; Brooklyn Park Commissioners v. Armstrong, 45 N. Y. 234; Mt. Pleasant v. Beckwith, 100 U. S. 514; Merriweather v. Garrett, 102 U. S. 472; Lansing v. County Treasurer, 1 Dill. C. C. 522; People v. Bond, 10 Cal. 563; Smith v. Appleton, 19 Wis. 468.

[2] Nelson v. St. Martin's Parish, 111 U. S. 716; Wolff v. New Orleans, 103 U. S. 358; Louisiana v. Pilsbury, 105 U. S. 278; Ralls Co. Court v. United States, 105 U. S. 733; Mobile v. Watson, 116 U. S. 289; Von Hoffman v. City of Quincy, 4 Wall. 535; Gilman v. Sheboygan, 2 Black, 510; Goodale v. Fennell, 27 Ohio St. 426, 22 Am. Rep. 321; State v. New Orleans, 37 La. Ann. 13.

[3] Sawyer v. Concordia, 12 Fed. Rep. 754.

[4] Seibert v. Lewis, 122 U. S. 284.

[5] People v. Bond, 10 Cal. 563.

when not carried to such an extent as to affect the substantial rights of the creditors.[1]

§ 41. *Rights in a sinking fund.*— The creditors of a public corporation may acquire contract rights in a fund which is raised for the payment of their debt, and upon the faith of which they have acted. Thus, where certain creditors surrendered their claims against the city, and accepted new obligations upon a pledge that certain revenues and property should be applied to the payment of such new obligations in a specific manner, the security thus provided for cannot be diverted to other purposes by either the municipality or the legislature. The provision for payment thus made becomes a part of the contract, and cannot be materially altered without the consent of such creditors.[2] So, where an act of a legislature provides for the creation of a sinking fund, which is to be deposited and applied in a certain manner, and creditors acting on the faith of such provision for the payment of their debts surrender their obligations and receive new bonds for the payment of which the fund is pledged, the legislature cannot, by subsequent act, provide for a different depositary of the fund.[3] It may be stated as a general rule that such provisions as were intended to, and probably did, operate as an inducement to the creditors to accept the new security, cannot subsequently be modified to the prejudice of the creditors.

§ 42. *Limitation on indebtedness.*— Where a city was authorized to issue a certain amount of bonds in payment for an equal amount then outstanding, and a provision of the act prohibited the city from thereafter issuing its bonds " except in payment of its bonded debts," it was held that, after the creditors had accepted this proposition, the prohibition against the

---

[1] Gilman v. Sheboygan, 2 Black, 510; Seibert v. Lewis, 122 U. S. 284. The rights of a contractor, who has agreed to take his compensation in assessments, cannot be destroyed by a subsequent statute restricting the power of assessment. Goodale v. Fennell, 27 Ohio St. 426, 22 Am. Rep. 321.

[2] People v. Bond, 10 Cal. 563. As to the nature of a sinking fund, see Kelly v. City of Minneapolis, 63 Minn. 125, 30 L. R. A. 281, 65 N. W. Rep. 115.

[3] The Liquidators v. Municipality, 6 La. Ann. 21.

issue of additional bonds became a contract between the municipality and the bondholders, which was impaired by subsequent legislation authorizing the issue of bonds for other purposes.[1]

IV. THE POWER TO IMPOSE OBLIGATIONS.

§ 43. *Nature of the debt.*— Where a debt or liability would arise out of the performance of a public duty, and is to be incurred for public or state purposes, the legislature may impose the same upon the corporation without its consent. The question can seldom arise in reference to public corporations other than municipal, and the power is frequently restricted by constitutional provisions. In the absence of such provisions, the question whether a city can be compelled by an act of the legislature to incur a debt or assume a liability against its will must be determined by the nature of or purpose for which such liability is to be incurred.[2] A city may be compelled to pay a debt even in excess of a legislative limit upon indebtedness;[3] but otherwise when the limitation is impose by the constitution.[4] It is often said that there must be some basis in morals and justice in order to justify the legislature in such compulsory action. Thus, a county which is under a moral obligation to reimburse another county for certain expenses may by subsequent act of the legislature be compelled to satisfy the claim.[5] But the moral obligation does not constitute a consideration;[6] and the legislature might compel the payment of the debt without reference to the existence of the moral element. The legislature cannot, however, require a court to render judgment upon a claim against a corporation upon mere proof of the

---

[1] Smith v. Appleton, 19 Wis. 468.
[2] Simon v. Northrup, 27 Oreg. 487, 30 L. R. A. 171; Lycoming v. Union, 15 Pa. St. 166, 53 Am. Dec. 575.
[3] Mosher v. School District, 44 Iowa, 122.
[4] Creighton v. San Francisco, 42 Cal. 446; New Orleans v. Clark, 95 U. S. 644.
[5] Lycoming v. Union, 15 Pa. St. 166, 55 Am. Dec. 575; Cole v. State, 102 N. Y. 48; O'Hara v. State, 112 N. Y. 146. "The legislature may determine what moneys they may raise and spend, and what taxation for municipal purposes may be imposed; and it certainly does not exceed its constitutional authority when it compels a municipal corporation to pay a debt which has some meritorious basis to rest upon." Mayor, etc. of New York v. Tenth Nat. Bank, 111 N. Y. 446.
[6] Warren v. Whitney, 24 Me. 561, 41 Am. Dec. 406, and note to Ernest v. Parke, 27 Am. Dec. 288.

amount of the claim, as this would be an attempt to exercise judicial power.[1]

§ 44. *Compulsory taxation.*—The state may direct and levy compulsory taxation whenever necessary to compel a public corporation to perform its duties as an agency of the state government, or to fulfill any legal or equitable obligation resting upon it in consequence of any corporate action. The people have no absolute right to be heard except through their representatives in the legislature of the state.[2]

§ 45. *Construction of highways.*—The control of public highways, bridges and canals is a matter of general, or state, as distinguished from municipal concern, and the legislature may require a municipal corporation to build and maintain a bridge over a stream within its limits,[3] or to expend money for the improvement of docks, wharves or levees.[4] So a county or town may be compelled to issue bonds for the purpose of raising money to be expended in the construction and maintenance of highways within their limits.[5] This duty to maintain streets and highways may be enforced by *mandamus* at the instance of a private person, without showing injury or interest.[6]

§ 46. *Support of public schools.*—Where the state has established a system of public schools, it may by compulsory taxation

[1] Hogland v. Sacramento, 15 Cal. 142.

[2] Cooley, Taxation, 684; Davock v. Moore, 105 Mich. 120, 28 L. R. A. 783.

[3] Simon v. Northrup, 27 Oreg. 487, 30 L. R. A. 171; Philadelphia v. Field, 58 Pa. St. 320; Thomas v. Leland, 24 Wend. 65; Guilder v. Otsego, 20 Minn. 74; Pumphrey v. Baltimore, 47 Md. 145. A county may be compelled to contribute toward the erection and maintenance of a bridge situated in another county. Carter v. Bridge Proprietors, 104 Mass. 236; Commonwealth v. Newburyport, 103 Mass. 129. "The general rule that bridges and highways shall be maintained by the counties and towns within which they are situated originated in the legislature, and the power that established it can repeal or modify it." Chapman, C. J., in Carter v. Bridge Proprietors, *supra*. The legislature may charge the cost of an authorized public improvement upon the particular public corporation chiefly benefited. Norwich v. Hampshire, 13 Pick. (Mass.) 60; H. etc. v. Norfolk Co., 6 Allen (Mass.), 353.

[4] Eastern, etc. Ry. Co. v. Central Ry. Co., 52 N. J. L. 267, 31 Am. & Eng. Corp. Cas. 262.

[5] People v. Flagg, 46 N. Y. 401; Jenson v. Board of Supervisors, 47 Wis. 298; People v. Board of Supervisors, 50 Cal. 561. May impose a tax to pay for the construction of a canal. Thomas v. Leland, 24 Wend. 65.

[6] Pumphrey v. Baltimore, 47 Md. 145.

compel the proper political division of the county to maintain the same. Such schools concern the state at large, and the unrestricted control by the legislature in no way conflicts with the privilege of local self-government.[1] So, it is competent for the legislature to provide for the distribution of money raised by taxation for school purposes after it has been collected.[2]

§ 47. *Local corporate purposes.*—The law is equally well settled that it rests with the citizens of the corporations and not with the legislature to determine whether a debt shall be incurred for a purpose purely municipal.[3]

§ 48. *Subscription for stock.*—A corporation is deemed to act as a private corporation when it becomes a stockholder in a railway company; and a mandatory statute enacted without the consent of the inhabitants of the town, requiring the corporation to become a shareholder in a private corporation by exchanging its bonds for stock upon the terms prescribed by the statute, is invalid.[4]

§ 49. *Compulsory payment of claims.*—The legislature may use the power of compulsory taxation in order to compel a public corporation which exists and exercises authority by its permission to pay a debt which is just and equitable in its character and involves a moral obligation, although not binding in strict law, and not enforceable in law or equity.[5] "The

[1] State v. Haworth, 122 Ind. 462; State v. Blue, 122 Ind. 600.
[2] School District v. Weber, 75 Mo. 558; State Board of Education v. Aberdeen, 56 Miss. 518.
[3] People v. Detroit, 28 Mich. 228, 15 Am. Rep. 202; People v. Chicago, 51 Ill. 17, 2 Am. Rep. 278; Cairo, etc. R. Co. v. Sparta, 77 Ill. 505; Marshall v. Silliman, 61 Ill. 225; People v. Batchelor, 53 N. Y. 128, 13 Am. Rep. 480; People v. Harper, 91 Ill. 357; Atkins v. Town of Randolph, 31 Vt. 226. Compare State v. Tappan, 29 Wis. 669.
[4] People v. Batchelor, 53 N. Y. 128. See opinion of Grover, J., reviewing the authorities. In People v. Kelly

(Brooklyn and New York Bridge Case), 5 Abb. New Cas. 383, it was held that the erection of a bridge to connect the two cities was a city purpose, for which indebtedness might be incurred.
[5] New Orleans v. Clark, 95 U. S. 644; Blandin v. Burr, 13 Cal. 343; Guilford v. Supervisors, 18 Barb. 615, 13 N. Y. 144; Brewster v. Syracuse, 19 N. Y. 116; Thomas v. Leland, 24 Wend. 65; People v. Supervisors, 70 N. Y. 228; Wrought Iron Bridge Co. v. Town of Attica, 119 N. Y. 204; Lycoming v. Union, 15 Pa. St. 166; Hasbrouck v. Milwaukee, 21 Wis. 219; Grogan v. San Francisco, 18 Cal. 390; Sinton v. Ashbury,

sovereign power of appropriation of the public funds already in the treasury, or to be raised by taxation, in favor of individuals, is one the exercise of which must depend largely upon the legislative conscience; and, like most of the great powers of government, cannot be interfered with by us, except in exceptional cases. The most usual cases in which this power has been exercised are those like the one under consideration, where an individual having no legal claim, in the sense of being capable of enforcement by judicial proceeding against a municipal government, has nevertheless in equity and justice, in the larger sense of those terms, a right to indemnity and compensation out of the public treasury."[1]

In a leading case in New York[2] it was held that the legislature might legally levy a tax upon the taxable property of a town, and appropriate the same to the payment of a claim made by an individual against the town, although the claim had been expressly rejected by the voters of the town at an election authorized by an act of the legislature, and which declared that their action should be final and conclusive. This case, although carrying the doctrine of legislative power to the farthest limit, has been generally approved, although it has met with criticism by courts of high standing. It may be defended, says Judge Cooley,[3] upon the ground that it is the right and duty of the state to see that the powers it confers are not abused to the injury of those who have relied upon

41 Cal. 525: Tweighton v. San Francisco, 42 Cal. 446; Nevada v. Hampton, 13 Nev. 441.

[1] Creighton v. San Francisco, 42 Cal. 446. Citing Guilford v. Supervisors, 18 Barb. 615; Vassar v. George, 47 Miss. 713. The liability of this power to abuse is pointed out by Mr. Justice O'Brien, in Matter of Culler, 53 Hun (N. Y.), 534. As to the right of the corporation to an ordinary trial, see Cooley, Taxation, p. 687; Sanborn v. Rice Co., 9 Minn. 273; State v. Tappan, 29 Wis. 664; Plimpton v. Somerset, 33 Vt. 283; In re Pennsylvania Hall, 5 Pa. St. 204.

[2] Guilford v. Supervisors, 18 Barb. 615; also 13 N. Y. 143; Brewster v. Syracuse, 19 N. Y. 113: People v. Mayor of Brooklyn, 4 N. Y. 419; Thomas v. Leland, 24 Wend. 65 (1840); People v. Dayton, 55 N. Y. 367 (1874); Guilford v. Supervisors, followed in Blandin v. Burr, 13 Cal. 343 (1859); N. Mo. R. R. Co. v. McGuire, 49 Mo. 490 (1872). Criticised in Weismer v. Village of Douglas, 64 N. Y. 91, 21 Am. Rep. 586. Approved, *arguendo*, in United States v. Baltimore & Ohio R. R. Co., 17 Wall. 322 (1872); New Orleans v. Clark, 95 U. S. 654 (1877). Same principle affirmed in Massachusetts in Carter v. Bridge Proprietors, 104 Mass. 236 (1870). See, also, Cooley, Const. Lim. 380, 491, notes.

[3] Cooley, Taxation (2d ed.), 685.

them, and that when a political corporation has contracted a debt or incurred an obligation, it has already taken the initiatory step in taxation; and has in effect given its consent that the subsequent steps, so far as they may be essential to the discharge of such debt or debts, may be taken.

But in Wisconsin an act of the legislature compelling the taxation of a town to pay for a bounty to a volunteer and the expenses of an unsuccessful suit to recover the same was held invalid, on the ground that it was not for a legitimate public purpose.[1]

V. THE TERRITORY AND BOUNDARIES.

§ 50. *The general rule.*— Unless restricted by the constitution, the legislature has general power to determine[2] and alter the territorial and boundaries of all public corporations.[3] After the territorial limits are once determined, it may "annex or authorize the annexation of the contiguous or other territory; and this without the consent, or even against the remonstrance, of the majority of the persons residing in the corporations or on the annexed territory."[4] But some limitations have been placed by the courts upon this general power. Thus, it has been held that non-contiguous territory cannot be annexed;[5] and that an unoccupied tract of country cannot be made a part of a village for the mere purpose of increasing the village revenue.[6] As said in a recent well-considered case,[7] the legislature has power to extend the boundaries and thus enlarge the territorial

---

[1] State v. Tappan, 29 Wis. 664, 9 Am. Rep. 622.
[2] Roane v. Anderson, 89 Tenn. 259; Washburn v. Oshkosh, 60 Wis. 453.
[3] Blanchard v. Bissell, 11 Ohio St. 96; Winona v. School District, 40 Minn. 13, 3 L. R. A. 45; State v. Lake City, 25 Minn. 404; Galesburg v. Hawkinson, 75 Ill. 152; Martin v. Dicks, 52 Miss. 53, 24 Am. Rep. 661; Daly v. Morgan, 69 Md. 460; Norris v. Waco, 57 Tex. 635; Chandler v. Boston, 112 Mass. 200; Mt. Pleasant v. Beckwith, 100 U. S. 514; Morford v. Unger, 8 Iowa, 82; Hewitt's Appeal, 88 Pa. St. 55; Chicago, etc. Ry. Co. v. Langlade, 56 Wis. 614; People v. Riverside, 70 Cal. 461; Roby v. Sheppard (W. Va.), 26 S. E. Rep. 278. A judicial district may be abolished by transferring all the counties comprising it to another district. Aikman v. Edwards, 55 Kan. 751, 30 L. R. A. 149.
[4] Dillon, Mun. Corp., § 185.
[5] Denver v. Coulehan, 20 Colo. 471, 27 L. R. A. 751; Chicago, etc. Ry. Co. v. Oconto, 50 Wis. 189, 36 Am. Rep. 840.
[6] Smith v. Sherry, 50 Wis. 200; Princess Co. Com. v. Bladensburg, 51 Md. 468.
[7] Denver v. Coulehan, 20 Colo. 471, 27 L. R. A. 751.

limits of a city or town; but such acts are to be interpreted and applied according to the essential nature as well as the subject-matter of the legislation. "Territory not in fact connected with or adjacent to a city cannot be regarded as a part of a municipal corporation, or as an addition thereto, in any true sense of the term." It was consequently held that the legislature had not the power to extend or enlarge the limits of a specially chartered town or city by adding thereto non-contiguous lands,— that is, lands entirely separated from the municipality by intervening territory. The power to annex territory may be delegated to the municipality,[1] and it is then for the court to determine whether the power has been properly exercised.[2]

§ 51. *What territory may be annexed.*— The authority delegated is generally to annex adjacent or contiguous territory. Adjacent lands means those lands lying so near and in such close proximity to the territory of a municipality as to be suburban in their character and to have some unity of interest with the city.[3] Contiguous lands are such as are not separated from the corporation by outside lands.[4] Corporate limits may reasonably and properly be extended so as to take in contiguous lands —

1. When they are platted and held for sale or use as town lots.

2. Whether platted or not, if they are held to be bought on the market, and sold as town property when they reach a value corresponding with the views of the owner.

[1] State v. Forest, 74 Wis. 610; Kelly v. Meeks, 87 Mo. 396; Strosser v. Ft. Wayne, 100 Ind. 443; Mendenhall v. Burton, 42 Kan. 570, 22 Pac. Rep. 558. In State v. Warner, 4 Wash. 773, 17 L. R. A. 263, it was held that the annexation of territory to a city is not an amendment of its charter within the meaning of the provision of the constitution which requires amendments to be submitted to the vote of the people. To the contrary see Westport v. Kansas City, 103 Mo. 141.

[2] Ewing v. State, 81 Tex. 177; State v. Eidson, 76 Tex. 302, 7 L. R. A. 733; State v. Bennett, 29 Mich. 451, 18 Am. Rep. 107; Vestal v. Little Rock, 54 Ark. 321, 11 L. R. A. 778.

[3] State, Childs v. Village of Minnetonka, 57 Minn. 526, 25 L. R. A. 755. The cases are digested in a note to this case.

[4] Vestal v. City of Little Rock, 54 Ark. 321, 11 L. R. A. 778. Lands on the opposite side of a river from a city may be contiguous to the city. Ibid.; Denver v. Coulehan, 20 Colo. 471.

3. When they furnish the abode for a densely-settled community or represent the actual growth of a town beyond its legal limits.

4. When they are needed for any proper town purpose, as for the extension of the streets or sewer, gas or water system, or to supply places for the abode or business of its citizens, or for the extension of needed police regulations.

5. When they are valuable by reason of their adaptability for prospective town uses. But the mere fact that their value is enhanced by reason of their nearness to the corporation is no ground for their annexation, unless it appears that the enhanced value is due to adaptability to town uses.

But city limits should not be extended so as to take in contiguous lands —

1. When they are used only for agriculture or horticulture, and are valuable on account of such use.

2. When they are vacant and do not derive special value from their adaptability for city uses.[1]

§ 52. *Illustrations.*— There are many cases illustrating the principle stated in the preceding section. Thus, a city comprising two miles of territory cannot incorporate an area of ten square miles, including farms and unoccupied country.[2] Three square miles of territory containing two settlements separated by unoccupied farm lands, unconnected by lines of buildings or improvements, cannot be incorporated.[3] A ravine dividing two areas of population is not such a natural barrier as will prevent the including of both in one village.[4] Lands occupied by the owner exclusively as a florist and farmer, to which no streets or town improvements extend, and which the line of settlement has not reached, cannot be annexed and subjected to municipal taxation.[5] A boundary cannot be extended so as to include territory already included in another city without direct legislative authority, which must authorize the restriction of the territory of the other corporation.[6]

---

[1] Vestal v. City of Little Rock, *supra*, and cases cited in annotation, 11 L. R. A. 778.

[2] State v. Eidson, 76 Tex. 302, 7 L. R. A. 733.

[3] In re Lakeville, 7 Kulp. 84.

[4] In re Edgewood, 130 Pa. St. 348.

[5] Vestal v. City of Little Rock, *supra*.

[6] Darby v. Sharon Hill, 112 Pa. St.

§ 53. *Property and debts upon division of territory.*— The right of the legislature to alter, divide or abolish public corporations, and to make such a division of property and apportionment of debts as is deemed equitable, is well settled.[1] The power is strictly legislative,[2] and not subject to the control of the courts. The apportionment may be made at the time of the division of the territory or at a subsequent time. Where the original act does not make a disposition of the common property and debts, "the legislature may at any subsequent time, by a later act, apportion them in such manner as seems to be just and equitable."[3]

When a portion of the territory of a public corporation is detached and created into a new corporation, or attached to another existing corporation, and the legislature makes no apportionment of property or debts, the old corporation retains all the public property, including what falls within the limits of the new corporation, and is responsible for all the debts contracted by it before the separation, without claim to contribution.[4] Thus, where the limits of a school district were so changed as to leave the school-house within the territory of another district, the original district was held to retain its ownership of the building.[5] But, when the old corporation is

66. As to severance of territory in which rival villages have grown up, see Ashley v. Calliope, 71 Iowa, 466.

[1] Winona v. School District, 40 Minn. 13, 3 L. R. A. 45; Johnson v. San Diego, 109 Cal. 468, 30 L. R. A. 178; State v. Harshaw, 73 Wis. 211; Granby v. Thurston, 23 Conn. 416; Olney v. Harvey, 50 Ill. 453; Larimie Co. v. Albany Co., 92 U. S. 307; Darby v. Sharon Hill, 140 Pa. St. 250.

[2] Bristol v. New Chester, 3 N. H. 524; Land Co. v. Oneida, 83 Wis. 649.

[3] Montgomery Co. v. Menifee, 93 Ky. 33; Sedgwick v. Bunker, 16 Kan. 498.

[4] Johnson v. San Diego, 109 Cal. 468, 30 L. R. A. 178, and cases cited; Perry Co. v. Conway Co. 52 Ark. 430, 6 L. R. A. 665. *Contra*, Bowdoinham

v. Richmond, 6 Me. 112, 19 Am. Dec. 197; Hampshire Co. v. Franklin Co., 16 Mass. 76. It has been said that when territory is detached from a public corporation, the old corporation has no claim upon the corporate property which falls without its new boundaries. Language to this effect was used in Larimie Co. v. Albany Co., 92 U. S. 307, and in Mt. Pleasant v. Beckwith, 100 U. S. 514. But as said by Mr. Justice Mitchell in Winona v. School Dist. Sup't: "It is a remarkable fact that these suggestions of a limitation or qualification of the rule are not only purely *obiter*, but the question is not discussed; no reason is assigned and no authority cited in its support, unless it be the old case of North Hempstead v. Hempstead, 2 Wend. 110."

[5] Winona v. School District, 40

abolished and new ones created out of its territory, the new corporations are treated as successors of the old, and as such liable for its debts and entitled to its property. Each of the corporations will then take the public property which falls within its limits.[1]

[1] Shapleigh v. San Angelo, 167 U. S. 646; Mobile v. Watson, 116 U. S. 289; Minn. 13, 8 L. R. A. 45, 12 Am. St. Rep. 687. Winona v. School District, *supra;* Demattos v. New Whatcom, 4 Wash. 127, 29 Pac. Rep. 933; Stone v. Charlestown, 114 Mass. 214.

CHAPTER IV.

CONSTITUTIONAL LIMITATIONS UPON LEGISLATIVE POWER
OVER PUBLIC CORPORATIONS.

§ 54. In general.
55. General laws.
56. The requirement of a "uniform system of government."
57. Illustrations.
58. The requirement that "laws of a general nature shall have uniform operation throughout the state."
59. Illustrations.
60. Local-option laws.
61. Classification.
62. Class containing but one member.

§ 63. Geographical conditions.
64. Population.
65. Illustrations.
66. Possible accession to a class.
67. Legislation regulating the "business," "affairs" and "internal affairs" of corporations.
68. The prohibition of special legislation "where a general law can be made applicable."
69. Amendment or repeal of existing special charters.

§ 54. *In general.*— The evils incidental to special legislation and the consequent lack of uniformity have led to the general adoption of constitutional provisions prescribing the manner in which the legislature shall exercise power over public corporations. Such provisions, in so far as they affect the manner of creating, have been referred to in a former chapter.[1] Where no such limitations are found, the legislature may exercise its powers by either special or general laws. These constitutional provisions vary in form and language. In some states they refer only to private corporations, while in others they refer to all corporations except those created for municipal purposes. This phrase has no definite technical import. It has been construed as applying to a corporation established for the purpose of raising funds and conducting a public school.[2] It does not include a county[3] nor a town.[4] Neither a drainage

---

[1] For a detailed examination of the law of the subject considered in this chapter, see Binney's Restrictions upon Local and Special Legislation in the United States.

[2] Horton v. Mobile School Commissioners, 43 Ala. 598.

[3] People v. McFadden, 81 Cal. 489.

[4] Eaton v. Manitowoc, 44 Wis. 489.

district[1] nor a sanitary district[2] are included in the provision prohibiting the formation of "cities, towns and villages" by special legislation. So, poor districts are not included within a provision prohibiting special legislation "regulating the affairs of counties, townships, wards, boroughs and school districts."[3]

§ 55. *General laws.*— A general law is one which operates equally and uniformly upon all persons, places and things brought within the relations and circumstances for which it provides;[4] or, in the words of a leading Pennsylvania case,[5] "a statute which relates to persons or things as a class is a general law; while a statute which relates to particular persons or things of a class is special." The mere grouping together in a single act of a number of special or local laws does not make a general law. Thus, an act providing that in eight designated counties of the state a certain official should receive a fixed annual salary named therein is a special law.[6] The words

---

[1] Owners of Lands v. People, 113 Ill. 296.

[2] Wilson v. Board, 133 Ill. 143, 27 N. E. Rep. 203.

[3] Jenks Township v. Sheffield Township, 135 Pa. St. 400, 19 Atl. Rep. 1004. See (Board of Police Commissioners) State v. Covington, 29 Ohio St. 102. A provision that "no corporation shall be created or its powers increased or diminished by special law" applies to private corporations only. Williams v. Nashville, 89 Tenn. 487, 15 S. W. Rep. 364; State v. Wilson, 12 Lea (Tenn.), 246. But see Corporate Powers of Council Grove, 20 Kan. 619.

[4] State v. Ferris, 53 Ohio St. 1, 30 L. R. A. 218; People v. Wright, 78 Ill. 338; State v. Cooley, 56 Minn. 543. In People v. Cooper, 83 Ill. 585, the court said: "The number of persons upon whom the law shall have any direct effect may be very few by reason of the subject to which it relates, but it must operate equally and uniformly upon all brought within the relations and circumstances for which it provides." In McAunich v. M. etc. R. Co., 20 Iowa, 338, the court said: "These laws are general and uniform, not because they operate upon every person in the state, for they do not, but because every person who is brought within the relations and circumstances provided for is affected by the laws that are general and uniform in their operation upon all persons in like situation, and the fact of their being general and uniform is not affected by the number of those who are in the scope of their operation." See, also, Welker v. Potter, 18 Ohio St. 85; Kingsbury v. Sperry, 119 Ill. 279; State v. Parsons, 40 N. J. L. 1.

[5] Wheeler v. Philadelphia, 57 Pa. St. 338; State v. Spondee, 37 Minn. 322; Earley v. San Francisco, 55 Cal. 489.

[6] Board of Freeholders v. Stevenson, 46 N. J. L. 173.

"laws of a general nature" have practically the same meaning. A law is of a general nature if it affects the whole of a class of persons or things.[1]

§ 56. *The requirement of a "uniform system of government."* A constitutional provision to the effect that "the legislature shall establish but one system of town and county government, which shall be as nearly uniform as practicable," is mandatory.[2] Its purpose is to prevent the legislature from establishing different systems of town and county government as well as to prevent special legislation. But "where the legislature has established a system of town and county government substantially uniform throughout the state, it may be conceded that its action is final upon the matter. The court in such case would not attempt to review the action of the legislative body and decide whether it might not have perfected a system more nearly uniform. But when a law like the one before us breaks the uniformity of a system already in operation, it seems to us that it is a proper exercise of judicial power to declare that the act is void because it departs from the rule of uniformity which the constitution enjoins.[3] The requirement of a uniform system of government does not prohibit the classification of public corporations for legislative purposes;[4] but all in the same class must possess the same power and be subject to the same restrictions, as "a system of municipal government in which cities of the same class may have dissimilarity in char-

[1] Brooks v. Hyde, 37 Cal. 366.
[2] State v. Dousman, 28 Wis. 541, per Lyon, J.; State v. Riordan, 24 Wis. 484; State v. Supervisors, 25 Wis. 339; Land, etc. Co. v. Brown, 73 Wis. 294, 8 L. R. A. 472. See, also, State v. Boyd, 19 Nev. 43. The provision in the constitution of Illinois that "the general assembly shall provide by a general law for a township organization," etc., has no reference to counties. Leach v. People, 122 Ill. 420. In New Jersey "town" includes cities. State v. Parsons, 40 N. J. L. 1. In People v. Lake County, 33 Cal. 487, a provision "That the legislature shall provide a system of county . . . government which shall be as nearly as practicable uniform throughout the state," was held to be directory only. Rhodes, J., said: "We have no hesitation in saying that policy forbids the attempt on the part of the judiciary, at this late day, to determine how far it is practicable to maintain uniformity in the system of county governments. They are now so diverse in most respects, except the names of the bodies invested with governmental functions, that scarcely any two counties have governments similar in all respects."

[3] State v. Riordan, 24 Wis. 484.
[4] Lake v. Palmer, 18 Fla. 501.

acter of organization as well as different powers is not a uniform system within the meaning of the constitution."[1] The mere fact that diverse results may flow from the execution of granted powers of local government does not render the enabling statute special or local.[2] If the same powers are possessed by all municipalities of the same class, the law is gen-

[1] McConihe v. McMurray, 17 Fla. 238; State v. Stark, 18 Fla. 255.

[2] In re Petition of Cleveland, 52 N. J. L. 188. Said Van Syckel, J.: "Uniformity in results cannot coexist with the right of local self-government until all men shall be of one mind. No one will assert that an act is local or special which gives to all the cities of this state the right to establish, by ordinance, the mode in which their subordinate officers shall be elected. Under such a statute one city might make the tenure of office a term of years, another during good behavior, and a third at the will of the common council. Such diverse results in the execution of the granted power, obviously, could not outlaw the act of the legislature. The authority granted to all is the same; the dissimilarity is in its use — a dissimilarity inherent in the idea of local government. The uniformity exacted by the constitutional mandate must be sought for, not in the results which flow from the free, unhampered exercise of the granted power of local government, but in the fact that every locality is afforded a like right to adopt and exercise, in its own way, the same powers which are bestowed upon every other like political body. To the one no privilege must be offered for acceptance which is not extended to the other. The authority given must be the same; it may be executed in a different way, or in the same way, at the option of the recipient. That is the uniformity to which the judicial declarations in the adjudged cases in this state must be referred. One of the conspicuous evils at which this constitutional amendment was aimed was, in my judgment, this: that prior to the amendment a few persons could go before the legislature and secure the passage of a special law to promote their own purposes, which might be obnoxious to the body of citizens. In such event, the only remedy was by an appeal to a subsequent legislature, and that might be too late to wholly repair the mischief. Such enactments are now forestalled by the fact that they cannot be made applicable without being submitted to the approval of the entire body of voters. In this way the people of every city are left free to select the mode in which they will regulate and conduct their local affairs, and it is this which impresses such legislation with the character of general, and not special, legislation. Gauged by this standard, there is no infirmity in the legislation which is the subject of this controversy. It applies to the entire class; there is no exception. It is held out to the free acceptance of all, and is capable of being accepted or rejected by every city in the state. In determining whether an act is general or special, we must regard the time of its enactment. If it applies to all cities then in existence, it seems to be a contradiction, in terms, to say that it is special. To be special, it must exclude some; if it excludes none, and expressly embraces all, it must be general."

eral. It has been held that such a provision is not intended to secure uniformity in the exercise of delegated police powers.[1] As a matter of course, the legislature cannot do indirectly what it cannot do directly. Hence, it cannot enact a special law to legalize a defective incorporation under the general law, without violating the provision that the legislature shall establish a uniform system of county, town and municipal government.[2]

§ 57. *Illustrations.—Under the provision requiring uniformity.*—An act which provides for a county board of supervisors of eight members in a certain county, while under the general law in force in all parts of the state such boards have three members, violates the provision requiring uniformity.[3] Where by an existing general law the power was conferred upon all county boards "to build and keep in repair county buildings," it was held that an act appointing three commissioners "to superintend the erection of a court-house in the county of M." was invalid.[4] So, an act restricting the power of the supervisors of Milwaukee county to act upon claims against the county and enter into contracts in its behalf without previous action thereon by the county auditor was held void as an attempt to take from that board important powers, which it possessed under the general statute of the state.[5] An act relating to county aid in the construction of bridges, which provided

[1] Paul v. Gloucester, 50 N. J. L. 585.
[2] Enterprise v. State, 29 Fla. 128, 10 So. Rep. 740.
[3] State v. Riordan, 24 Wis. 484.
[4] Said Paine, J.: "It takes an important power of the county board in that county (Milwaukee), and confers it upon special commissioners designated by the legislature. That it is not a uniform system to provide that in one county the power to build the county buildings shall be vested in special commissioners selected by the legislature, while in other counties the same power is vested in the boards of supervisors elected by the people, is obvious. It is equally obvious that it is not as uniform as practicable, because it is self-evident that this power might be vested in the county boards in all the counties. Independent of this act, it was so vested in fact. There was, under the existing law, complete uniformity." State v. Supervisors, 25 Wis. 339.
[5] State v. Dousman, 28 Wis. 541. In McRae v. Hogan, 39 Wis. 529, an act which attempted to take from the possession and control of the town officers in Chippewa county a portion of the moneys raised in their towns for highway purposes, and intrust its expenditure to the county board, contrary to the general law, was held void.

that "this act shall not apply to the county of Grant," violates the requirement of uniformity.[1] But "the power to construct drains is in no proper sense a part of the usual powers belonging to town and county government, but is a special authority given for a particular purpose, which may be conferred upon any persons or body upon which the legislature may see fit to confer it." Hence, an act providing for lowering the ordinary level of water in certain lakes in a designated county and for the drainage of wet and overflowed lands in any part of said county, different from the system of drainage in the remainder of the state, is valid.[2]

Under the provisions requiring uniformity in legislation affecting public corporations, an act which tends to remove existing diversity is valid. Thus, where the peculiarities which the act sought to abolish existed in but one county, it was said that "whenever an act of the legislature is general in its terms, and the only effect is to remove in some degree the differences in the various regulations of the internal affairs of towns or counties, and to subject those internal affairs to the operation of a general law, the act is not prohibited by the constitution, but is in strict accordance with the command of that instrument, which expressly enjoins upon the legislature the passage of laws for such cases."[3]

§ 58. *The requirement that "laws of a general nature shall have uniform operation throughout the state."*— This provision is found in the constitutions of many of the states.[4] Its effect is to prevent the legislature from restricting the operation of laws of a general nature to any part of the state less than the whole.[5] As it applies to general laws only, it does not prohibit proper local legislation.[6] It is construed as meaning "not that general laws must act alike upon all subjects of legislation, or upon all citizens and persons, but that they shall operate uni-

---

[1] La Valle v. Supervisors, 62 Wis. 376.
[2] Bryant v. Robbins, 7 Iowa, 258.
[3] Freeholders v. Stevenson, 46 N. J. L. 173.
[4] For its history see McGill v. State, 34 Ohio St. 228.
[5] Costello v. Wyoming, 49 Ohio, 202, 30 N. E. Rep. 613.
[6] State v. Judges, 21 Ohio St. 1; State v. Covington, 29 Ohio St. 102; Ruffner v. Commissioners, Disn. (Ohio), 196; Cricket v. State, 18 Ohio St. 9; People v. C. P. R. Co., 43 Cal. 432.

formly or in the same manner upon all persons who stand in the same category; that is to say, upon all persons who stand in the same relation to the law in respect to the privileges and immunities conferred by it, or the acts which it prohibits."[1] It does not prevent a proper classification of persons and subjects for purposes of legislation, as laws which operate uniformly upon members of a class have uniform operation. Of course, a law which is in full force in every part of the state has a uniform operation throughout the state.[2]

The taking of a class out of the general terms of a statute by an exception is as obnoxious to the restraint imposed by this provision as the passage of a special act affecting and relating to the excluded corporation only. Thus, a provision in an act relating to police, that it "shall not apply in and to cities commonly known as seaside and summer resorts," renders the act invalid.

§ 59. *Illustrations.*—Whether a statute is of a general nature depends not upon its form, but upon its application to the subject-matter.[3] A law may thus be special in form, and yet come within this provision. The courts will go behind the form of the enactment in order to determine its character. If it could be assumed merely from the fact of the enactment of a statute that the legislature had information showing that there was a necessity for such legislation in respect to the particular locality, all such legislation would have to be upheld regardless of the subject-matter.[4] On the other hand, a law may relate to a subject-matter which is general, and still not be of a general nature. The subject may be general, while the purpose of the act may be special and local.[5] Thus, the subject of common schools is of a general nature, but it is held in Ohio that a special school district may be formed from territory within the limits of the township, without conflicting with a constitutional provision.[6] The following acts have been

[1] Ex parte Smith, 38 Cal. 702; Leep v. St. Louis, Iron Mt. Ry. Co., 58 Ark. 407, 23 L. R. A. 264; In re Oberg, 21 Oreg. 406, 14 L. R. A. 577.

[2] State v. Ferris, 53 Ohio St. 1, 30 L. R. A. 218.

[3] State v. Ellet, 47 Ohio St. 90, 23 N. E. Rep. 931.

[4] State v. Ellet, 47 Ohio St. 90, 23 N. E. Rep. 931.

[5] State v. Shearer, 46 Ohio St. 275, 20 N. E. Rep. 335.

[6] State v. Powers, 38 Ohio St. 54. Such laws, although dealing with a general subject-matter, are intended to meet purely local conditions and

held invalid because contravening the constitutional requirement that all laws of a general nature must have uniform operation throughout the state: An act relating to salaries of county officers in counties of certain classes, as it prevented the county government act, which was essentially a law of a general nature, from having uniform operation.[1] An act providing that the salaries fixed by the act should take effect at different times in different counties.[2] An act providing for the construction, improvement and repair of sidewalks in or leading out of villages, because the subject-matter was of a character that concerned the inhabitants of every village in the state.[3] But acts designed to regulate the amount of compensation of local officers, regulating the police force in the city of Cincinnati through a board of commissioners to be appointed by the governor;[4] conferring power upon county commissioners to erect public buildings;[5] requiring county commissioners to subscribe on behalf of the county to the stock of a railroad company;[6] providing a special mode of selecting jurors in a designated county,[7] have been held to be of a local nature and not affected by this provision.

requirements. In McGill v. State, 34 Ohio St. 228, the court said: "It is easy to comprehend that a law defining burglary or bigamy and its penalty, or regulating descent and distribution, or prescribing the capacity requisite for the testamentary disposition of property, regulating conveyances, or prescribing a rate of interest for the use of money, and others of similar effect and operation, are laws of a general nature requiring a uniform operation throughout the state. To discriminate between localities or citizens in the enactment of laws of such a nature would be to grant privileges or impose burdens of a character which it was the clear purpose of the constitution to provide against. But that a law may be general and concern matters purely local or special in their nature, or may be local or special and relate to a matter that may be made the subject of a general law, not only rests upon sound reason but is well supported by authority." But in State v. Ellet, 47 Ohio St. 90, 23 N. E. Rep. 931, the court said: "The local statute must be upon a subject in its nature local as well as local in its operation."

[1] Dougherty v. Austin, 94 Cal. 601.
[2] Miller v. Kister, 68 Cal. 142.
[3] Crickett v. State, 18 Ohio St. 9; Hart v. Murray, 48 Ohio St. 605.
[4] State v. Covington, 29 Ohio St. 102.
[5] Ruffner v. Com., Disn. (Ohio), 196.
[6] Cass v. Dillon, 2 Ohio St. 617.
[7] McGill v. State, 34 Ohio St. 228. In this case it was not doubted that the matter of selecting jurors was a general subject in which the people of the state at large was interested, and that since the organization of the state it had been provided for by the general law, so that the law providing a special mode of selecting jurors in that county was one

§ 60. *Local-option laws.*— Statutes allowing the people of a particular locality to elect between different systems of police regulation or local government necessarily tend to prevent general laws from having a uniform operation throughout the state. In some states it is held that the restrictions upon local and special laws have no effect upon these subjects; at least so long as the communities of the same class have the same option.[1] In Florida it was held that an option, although granted to every member of a class, violated the constitutional provision. The court said:[2] "The government of each class must be the same, and such must be the result of the action of the legislature, independent of the contingency of local discretion or option in the premises." In Pennsylvania it is held that changes in the general municipal corporation law cannot be limited to such cities as adopt the new law.[3] So, a law repealing a general fence law, but to take effect only in such counties as should vote for the repeal of the general law, is invalid.[4] The great weight of authority supports the principle that the legislature may permit a locality to determine whether intoxicating liquors shall be sold within its limits. If the law is complete when it comes from the hands of the legislature, it is a general law operative throughout the state; thus, a statute permitting a certain penalty in a prohibitory liquor law to be suspended in any city upon the filing of the written consent of a certain proportion of the voters is not local or special; and it does not tend to produce diversity of laws in the different parts of the state. The court said: "The act is complete in itself, requires nothing further to give it validity, and does not depend upon the popular vote of the people."[5] An act which

treating of a general subject already embraced in general laws, making provisions applicable to all counties in the state; but the court held that this act was not a law of a general nature requiring uniformity of operation throughout the state, but was designed to meet a special want in a particular county and was not in conflict with the constitution.

[1] Paul v. Brewster County, 40 N. J. L. 585; In re Cleveland, 52 N. J. L. 188; State v. Pond, 93 Mo. 606; People v. Hoffman, 116 Ill. 487; People v. Cooper, 83 Ill. 585.

[2] McConihe v. State, 17 Fla. 238.

[3] Commonwealth v. Denworth, 145 Pa. St. 172; People v. Cooper, 83 Ill. 585.

[4] Frost v. Cherry, 122 Pa. St. 417.

[5] State v. Forkner, 94 Iowa, 733, 28 L. R. A. 206, reviewing many authorities; State v. Weir, 33 Iowa, 134, 11 Am. Rep. 115. For a discussion of the submission of state and local laws to the vote of the people, see Ober-

tends to diminish diversity and establish greater uniformity in the system is not invalidated by a provision that it shall be operative only on such members of the class to which it relates as shall accept its provisions.[1] But where the exercise of this discretionary power would tend toward diversity instead of uniformity, as where corporations existing under the control of the general law would by accepting the act become members of a class by themselves, the act is invalid.[2]

§ 61. *Classification.*— The legislature may, for purposes of legislation, divide the subject-matter of legislation into classes and then legislate for each class as a whole.[3] But a valid classification must have a basis in reason, and not be adopted arbitrarily as a mere cover for special legislation under the form of general legislation.[4] "The underlying principle of all cases,"

holtzer, The Referendum in America, Phila., 1893.

[1] Reading v. Savage, 124 Pa. St. 328. In Re Cleveland, 52 N. J. L. 188, a law authorizing the mayors of all cities of the state to appoint the principal municipal officers, to become operative in such cities as elect to accept it, was held general. In Stanfield v. State, 83 Tex. 370, 18 S. W. Rep. 577, an act authorizing the commissioners' court to abolish the office of county superintendent "when, in their judgment, such court may deem it advisable," was held general, as it related to the entire state. In State v. Hunter, 38 Kan. 578, 17 Pac. Rep. 177, an act providing for the appointment of a board of police commissioners by the executive council, upon the petition of two hundred *bona fide* householders, or when the council shall deem it advisable for the better government of such cities, was held to be a general law. In State v. Pond, 93 Mo. 606, 6 S. W. Rep. 469, Norton, J., said: "The fact that one or more counties, or one or more cities or towns, may by a majority vote put the law in operation in said county or counties, cities and towns, and other counties, cities and towns may not do so, does not affect the rule, nor furnish a test by which to decide whether the law is local or general."

[2] Scranton's Appeal, 113 Pa. St. 190. Affirmed in Com. v. Halstead (Pa.), 7 Atl. Rep. 221.

[3] State v. Cooley, 56 Minn. 540; In re Washington Street, 132 Pa. St. 257, 7 L. R. A. 193; Van Riper v. Parsons, 40 N. J. L. 123; Rutgers v. New Brunswick, 42 N. J. L. 51; State v. Trenton, 42 N. J. L. 486; State v. Board of Freeholders, 52 N. J. L. 512, 19 Atl. Rep. 972; Worcester National Bank v. Cheney, 94 Ill. 430; Devine v. Commissioners, 84 Ill. 590; Pritchett v. Stanislaus Co., 73 Cal. 310; State v. Berka (Neb.), 30 N. W. Rep. 267; State v. Spaude, 27 Minn. 322, 34 N. W. Rep. 164; Edmonds v. Herbrandson, 2 N. D. 270, 50 N. W. Rep. 970; Wheeler v. Philadelphia, 77 Pa. St. 338; Kilgore v. Magee, 85 Pa. St. 401; City of Scranton v. Whyte, 148 Pa. St. 419, 23 Atl. Rep. 1043; Commonwealth v. Macferron, 152 Pa. St. 244, 25 Atl. Rep. 557; Appeal of Ayers, 122 Pa. St. 266. "Legislation which applies to all members of a class is not local or special, but general." Reeves v. Continental R. Co., 152 Pa. St. 153, 25 Atl. Rep. 517.

[4] Edmonds v. Herbrandson, 2 N. D.

says Mr. Justice Sterrett,[1] "is that all classification with a view of legislating for either class separately is essentially unconstitutional, unless a necessity therefor exists, a necessity springing from manifest peculiarities, clearly distinguishing those of one class from each of the other classes, and imperatively demanding legislation from each class separately that would be useless and detrimental to the others. Laws enacted in pursuance of such classification and for such purposes are, properly speaking, neither general nor special." There must be something more than a mere designation of the subjects of a class. The characteristics which serve as the basis of classification must be of such a nature as to make the objects so designated peculiarly require special legislation. There must be a substantial distinction, having reference to the subject-matter of the proposed legislation, between the objects and places embraced in such legislation and the objects or places excluded."[2] The following are illustrations of cases in which the basis of classification was improper: Counties having a population of sixty thousand in which the fees allowed county clerks are turned over to the county.[3] Seaside resorts where there is taxable property to the amount of $10,000 embraced within an area not exceeding two square miles.[4] Seaside resorts governed by municipalities, the purpose being to take from a township committee, and to confer upon the borough commissioners, the right of expending the road taxes.[5] Cities and towns having race courses.[6] Municipalities governed by commissioners.[7] Cit-

270, 14 L. R. A. 725; State v. Cooley, 56 Minn. 540.

[1] Ayer's Appeal, 122 Pa. St. 266, 2 L. R. A. 577.

[2] State v. Hammer, 42 N. J. L. 435; Wheeler v. Philadelphia, 77 Pa. St. 338; Ayar's Appeal, 122 Pa. St. 266.

[3] Ernst v. Morgan, 39 N. J. Eq. 391.

[4] State v. Somers' Point, 52 N. J. L. 33, 6 L. R. A. 57. Said Depue, J.: "Municipal powers and franchises, such as this act confers, are as appropriate to places in an inland situation as to those located on the seashore, and are as suitable to localities inhabited or frequented by other individuals as to resorts for summer visitors. . . . If taxable property, irrespective of population, be a proper classification on which to base a grant of municipal powers to the scope of those granted by this act, such property presents the same characteristics wherever situated." State v. Philbrick (N. J.), 15 Att. Rep. 579.

[5] Ross v. Winsor, 48 N. J. L. 95; State v. Elizabeth, 57 N. J. L. 71, 23 L. R. A. 525.

[6] State v. Elizabeth, 56 N. J. L. 71, 23 L. R. A. 525.

[7] Long Branch v. Sloane, 49 N. J. L. 356.

ies and towns in which the streets have been lighted by legislative authority.¹ Townships not containing an incorporated city or borough.² Cities of not less than ten thousand inhabitants divided into not less than two nor more than three wards.³ Counties where the clerks are at the time of the passage of the law paid an annual salary.⁴ Cities of more than fifteen thousand inhabitants not having a board of excise, nor where licenses are granted by court of common pleas.⁵ Cities where a board of assessment and revision of taxes is in existence.⁶

§ 62. *Class containing but one member.*— The basis of classification must be characteristics and not numbers. There may be a public corporation in the state with such characteristics as to effectually distinguish it from all others. The fact that an act at the time of its passage affects but one corporation does not make it a special law, if there is nothing to prevent other corporations from becoming members of the class when they acquire the necessary population or comply with the other conditions.⁷

---

¹ Van Giesen v. Bloomfield, 47 N. J. L. 422.

² State v. Township Com. of Northampton, 51 N. J. L. 402, 14 Atl. Rep. 587. In Dobbins v. Northampton, 5 N. J. L. 496, the court said: "The classification on which this act rests is a classification setting apart townships not having an incorporated city or borough within the township bounds from the other townships in this state. The subject of the legislation — grading, making and working roads — is one that is common to all townships in this state as well as to the township set apart for this scheme of legislation."

³ Randolph v. Wood, 49 N. J. L. 85.

⁴ Gibbs v. Morgan, 39 N. J. Eq. 136.

⁵ Closson v. Trenton, 48 N. J. L. 438.

⁶ Hammer v. State, 44 N. J. L. 667; Van Giesen v. Bloomfield, 47 N. J. L. 422; Freeholders of Hudson v. Buck, 51 N. J. L. 155; State v. Wood, 49 N. J. L. 85, 7 Atl. Rep. 286; City of New Brunswick v. Fitzgerald, 48 N. J. L. 457, 8 Atl. Rep. 729; State v. Simon, 53 N. J. L. 550, 22 Atl. Rep. 120; Turner v. Fish, 19 Nev. 295; County of San Luis Obispo v. Graves, 84 Cal. 71.

⁷ State v. Toledo, 48 Ohio St. 112, 11 L. R. A. 729; Govern v. State, 48 N. J. L. 612, 9 Atl. Rep. 577; Ex parte Wells, 21 Fla. 280; State v. Donovan. 20 Nev. 75, 15 Pac. Rep. 783; State v. Woodbury, 17 Nev. 337; State v. Graham, 16 Neb. 74; Walker v. Cincinnati, 21 Ohio St. 14; Marmet v. State, 45 Ohio St. 63; Wheeler v. Philadelphia, 77 Pa. St. 338; Commonwealth v. Patton, 88 Pa. St. 258; Kilgore v. Magee, 85 Pa. St. 401; State v. Tolle, 71 Mo. 645; Ewing v. Hoblitzell, 81 Mo. 64; Rutheford v. Heddens, 82 Mo. 388; Darrow v. People, 8 Colo. 417; McInerney v. Denver (Colo.), 29 Pac. Rep. 516. In Van Riper v. Parsons, 40 N. J. L. 123, the court said: "The law in all its provisions is general, broad enough to reach every portion of the state, abating legislative commissioners for the regulation of mu-

§ 63. *Geographical conditions.*— Whether geographical conditions are a proper basis for classification depends upon the nature of the legislation. Such distinctions necessarily exclude the possibility of accession to the class. A classification of counties and towns with reference to the number and geographical location of the cities they contain cannot be sustained.[1] But for the purpose of legislation authorizing the construction of drives upon the beach, a classification based upon location upon the seashore would be proper.[2]

§ 64. *Population.*— For the purpose of appropriate legislation, population furnishes such a distinguishing characteristic as to render it a proper basis for classification. The needs of a great city are different from those of a small city or village. The organization of local government and the management of municipal affairs are unlike. Mere size, as measured by the number of inhabitants, necessarily creates conditions which call for different kinds of legislation. Hence, population has been universally recognized as a proper basis for the classification

nicipal affairs wherever they exist. Such commissions are distinguished from other sorts of municipal governments by characteristics sufficiently marked and important to make them clearly a class by themselves, and upon the whole of this class this law operates equally by force of terms which are restricted to no locality. A law so framed is not a special or local law, but a general law, without regard to the consideration that within the state there happens to be but one individual of the class or one place where it produces effect." In West Chicago Park Commissioners v. McMullen, 134 Ill. 171, 25 N. E. Rep. 676, the court said: "If it is true, as suggested, that the act is applicable as to conditions existing in a single city in the state, that fact does not necessarily render it local or special legislation. It is general in its terms and applies to all cities of the state which, at the time of its passage, had parks under the control of park commissioners, or that might, at any time thereafter, so have parks." The decision in Devine v. Cook County, 84 Ill. 590, was controlled not by the fact that it could apply to but one city in the state, but that it was so limited in duration as to convince the court that it was physically impossible for any other city to come within the class during the existence of the law."

[1] Scowden's Appeal, 96 Pa. St. 422.
[2] State v. Wright, 54 N. J. L. 130, 23 Atl. Rep. 117; Anderson v. Trenton, 42 N. J. L. 486. In State v. Hammer, 42 N. J. L. 440, it was said, by way of illustration, that "a sample of the other or legitimate kind would be signified in a law that should give to all cities in the state situated on tide-water the privileges of using such water in connection with their sewers." But see Ross v. Winsor, 48 N. J. L. 95.

of public corporations. The cases supporting this are very numerous.[1]

§ 65. *Illustrations*.— The following acts have been held constitutional: An act providing that in cities having a population of less than twelve thousand the term of office of councilman should be for as many years as there are councilmen in each ward.[2] An act providing for a police court in all cities of the second class; that is, containing a population of not less than fifty thousand or more than one hundred thousand.[3] An act fixing fees and salaries of county officers in counties having a designated population.[4] An act regulating the construction of water-works and streets in cities having a certain designated population.[5] An act prescribing a sewerage system in cities containing over thirty thousand and under fifty thousand inhabitants.[6] An act prescribing the number of school directors "in all cities of this state now having or hereafter attaining a population of over three hundred thousand inhabitants."[7] An act requiring the judges to let contracts for publishing judicial notices in cities having over one hundred thousand inhabitants.[8] But population is not a proper basis of classification for legislation authorizing the issue of bonds to pay a floating debt, as

---

[1] In re Passaic. 54 N. J. L. 156, 23 Atl. Rep. 517; Welkes v. Potter, 18 Ohio St. 85; Weinman v. Pass. R. Co., 118 Pa. St. 192. The court will take judicial notice of what the population of a county was according to the last census. Worcester National Bank v. Cheney, 94 Ill. 430.

[2] Randolph v. Wood, 49 N. J. L. 85.

[3] A difference in population requires different police regulations. State v. Caminade, 54 N. J. L. 135, 25 Atl. Rep. 933; People v. Henshaw, 76 Cal. 436, 18 Pac. Rep. 413 (Probate Courts); Knickerbocker v. People, 102 Ill. 218; Rutgers v. New Brunswick, 42 N. J. L. 51.

[4] Board v. Leahy, 24 Kan. 54.

[5] Warner v. Hoagland, 51 N. J. L. 62. There is a real and essential difference between the methods required in the management of public works in large and small cities, and population, hence, becomes a proper basis for classification. As said by Chief Justice Beasley, In re Haynes, 54 N. J. L. 6: "In a small city the supervision and control of the streets and of the water supply may well be, as it has been, left in the hands of those intrusted to administer generally its affairs; but all experience has shown that such matters in large cities can be properly managed only by independent boards, duly organized for the purpose."

[6] Rutherford v. Hamilton, 97 Mo. 543.

[7] State v. Miller, 100 Mo. 439; State v. Macklin (Mo.), 13 S. W. Rep. 680.

[8] State v. Tolle, 71 Mo. 645.

the object of the law has no natural relation to the basis of classification adopted.[1]

§ 66. *Possible accession to a class.*— Where the classification is based upon conditions and facts whereby other corporations of like nature are excluded from ever coming within the class, it is necessarily arbitrary, and legislation based upon it is not general.[2] Thus, an act applying only to counties where there were cast more than one thousand one hundred and fifty votes and less than one thousand three hundred and fifty votes at a specified election is invalid.[3] So an act granting courts power to grant licenses to inns and taverns in cities having a designated population by the census of 1875.[4] So an act regulating the relocation of county seats in all counties wherein at the date of the act the court-house and jail was not worth a designated amount of money.[5] So an act applying to cities in which a German newspaper had been published for three years before its passage, but not applying to cities which should thereafter come within the qualification.[6] In each of these cases the classification was arbitrary, and it was impossible in the nature of things that there should be any accessions to the class. The same difficulty may arise when the life of a statute is made so short as to render it impossible for any other city to acquire the necessary population; and in such a case the court will take judicial notice of the fact that no city can possibly grow so rapidly.[7]

[1] Anderson v. Trenton, 42 N. J. L. 486.

[2] Commonwealth v. Patton, 88 Pa. St. 258; Rutgers v. New Brunswick, 44 N. J. L. 551; Nichols v. Walter, 37 Minn. 264; State v. Mitchell, 31 Ohio St. 592; State v. Pugh, 43 Ohio St. 98; State v. Anderson, 44 Ohio St. 247; State v. Ellet, 47 Ohio St. 90, 23 N. E. Rep. 931; State v. Smith (Ohio), 26 N. E. Rep. 1069; Woodard v. Brien, 14 Lea (Tenn.), 520. See State v. Herrmann, 75 Mo. 340.

[3] State v. Boyd, 19 Nev. 43.

[4] Zeigler v. Gaddis, 44 N. J. L. 365; Adams v. Smith, 6 Dak. 94.

[5] Edmonds v. Herbrandson, 2 N. D. 270, 50 N. W. Rep. 970. The act under consideration in State v. Hammer, 42 N. J. L. 435, applied to any city "where a board of assessment and revision of taxes now exists," and the court said: "The result, therefore, is that the act was intended to apply to those two cities alone, and the legal effect of the law as now constituted is the same as though it had in express terms declared that it was not to be operative through the state at large, but only in the cities of Elizabeth and Newark."

[6] State v. Trenton, 54 N. J. L. 444, 24 Atl. Rep. 478.

[7] In Devine v. Cook Co., 84 Ill. 590, in construing an act which, by its terms, applied only to counties hav-

§ 67.]   CONSTITUTIONAL LIMITATIONS.   61

§ 67. *Legislation regulating the "business," "affairs" and "internal affairs" of corporations.*— In some states we find a provision that the legislature shall pass no local or special law regulating the business, affairs or internal affairs of public corporations.[1] Various constructions have been given these terms. In Indiana an act which created a court for a particular county was held not to regulate county business.[2] In Pennsylvania an act which authorized the holding of special sessions of the courts in a certain county in a place other than the county seat was held invalid as an attempt to regulate county business.[3] And subsequently, after the word "affairs" had been substituted for the word "business" in the constitution, it was held that an act to ascertain and appoint the fees to be received by certain county officers regulated the affairs of such counties.[4] So an act for regulating and maintaining fences and providing for a county election to determine the adoption or rejection of a repealing act was held invalid for the same reason.[5]

These provisions do not limit the power of the legislature to

ing a population of over one hundred thousand inhabitants, and which expired within six years from the date of its passage, the court said that it would take judicial notice of the fact that Cook county was the only county in the state containing over one hundred thousand inhabitants, and that it could not be expected, "by any ordinary influx of population, that any other county will have that population within the brief period fixed for the duration of this law, viz., within a period of six years from the time the act should take effect. . . . The court will take judicial notice not only that no other county in the state than Cook county had one hundred thousand inhabitants, but also that, without some supernatural interposition, no other county in the state can have one hundred thousand inhabitants until after July 1, 1879. But it seems to me it is going too far to hold that the mere fact that a statute is applicable only to counties having one hundred thousand inhabitants renders it a local law. In the course of time several counties may have that number. A law intended to be perpetual may not, in my judgment, be subject to objection, although thus limited." In Topeka v. Gillett, 32 Kan. 431, an act which excluded all cities from its operation which failed to take advantage of its provisions within ten days after its taking effect, and there being but three cities which could possibly possess the necessary qualifications within the time, all others being forever excluded, was held special. But the mere fact that an act is limited in the time of its duration does not necessarily make it special. People v. Wright, 70 Ill. 358.

[1] See Pell v. Newark, 40 N. J. L. 71; Freeholders v. Buck, 51 N. J. L. 155.
[2] Eitel v. State, 33 Ind. 201.
[3] Scowden's Appeal, 96 Pa. St. 422.
[4] Morrison v. Bachert, 112 Pa. St. 322.
[5] Frost v. Cherry, 122 Pa. St. 417.

create a new corporation or to repeal the charter of an existing one, thus leaving no internal affairs to be regulated, but to be valid the act must be limited to the mere creation of a new division or the alteration of an existing one. If the act is single and a new body finds the rules for its internal government in some general law, it is unobjectionable; but if the act of creation or alteration includes provisions looking to the regulation or government of the newly-created or altered district, it is an attempt to regulate the internal affairs of such district, and is invalid unless general.[1] While a corporation may thus be extinguished by a special law, it cannot be taken apart piecemeal, as by the repeal of a section here and there at different times. Its affairs would be as effectually regulated by thus depriving it of certain functions as by conferring new powers and attributes upon it.[2] The wards of a city are not public corporations, but are simply divisions created for the purpose of better enabling the municipality to exercise the authority with which it is vested. Hence, a limitation of the boundaries of a ward is not a regulation of the "internal affairs" of a public corporation.[3]

An act prohibiting the removal of a soldier or sailor from a public office " under the government of any city or county of this state " is a regulation of the internal affairs of counties.[4] So an act designating the newspapers which shall be selected as the official papers of cities regulates their internal affairs.[5] An act prescribing the manner in which the indebtedness of a county shall be conducted is a law "regulating county business."[6] An act regulating the assessment and revision of taxes in cities regulates their internal affairs.[7] The same is true of an act taking from the township committee and conferring upon the borough commissioners the right to expend the road tax appraised in the township.[8] But a law providing that no married woman holding any indebtedness of the state or the city may sell and transfer the same as though unmarried does not violate a constitutional provision forbidding legislation reg-

[1] Long Branch v. Sloane, 49 N. J. L. 356.
[2] Tiger v. Morris, 42 N. J. L. 631.
[3] State v. Mayor of Newark, 53 N. J. L. 4, 20 Atl. Rep. 86.
[4] State v. O'Connor, 54 N. J. L. 36, 22 Atl. Rep. 1091.
[5] State v. Trenton, 54 N. J. L. 444, 24 Atl. Rep. 478.
[6] Youngs v. Hall, 9 Nev. 212.
[7] Hammer v. State, 44 N. J. L. 667.
[8] Ross v. Winsor, 48 N. J. L. 95.

ulating the affairs of municipal corporations, as it "is simply the regulation of the mode and transfer, in certain counties, of property for the public convenience."[1]

§ 68. *The prohibition of special legislation "where a general law can be made applicable."*—In a number of states we find provisions forbidding special legislation in all cases where a general law can be made applicable. Courts have with practical unanimity held that it was for the legislature to determine whether or not a general law could be made applicable in a particular case.[2] But the evident disposition of the legislatures to extend the exception beyond its proper limits has led to the enactment of amendments in some states declaring it to be a judicial question. Thus, the constitution of Minnesota now provides[3] that "whether a general law could have been made applicable in any case is hereby declared to be a judicial question, and as such shall be judicially determined without regard to any legislative assertion on that subject." The language has generally been given a liberal construction for the purpose of advancing the legitimate purposes of ordinary legislation. A contrary construction, instead of placing on the legislature a wholesome limitation, as is the manifest in-

---

[1] F. & M. Bank v. Loftus, 133 Pa. St. 97, 19 Atl. Rep. 347.

[2] State v. Hitchcock, 1 Kan. 178; Beach v. Leahy, 11 Kan. 23; Commissioners v. Shoemaker, 27 Kan. 77; Hughes v. Milligan, 42 Kan. 396, 22 Pac. Rep. 313; Pierce v. Smith, 48 Kan. 331, 29 Pac. Rep. 565; Edmonds v. Herbrandson, 2 N. D. 270, 50 N. W. Rep. 970; Henderson v. County Court, 50 Mo. 317, 11 Am. Rep. 415; State v. County Court, 51 Mo. 83; Hall v. Bray, 51 Mo. 288; City of St. Louis v. Shields, 62 Mo. 247; Little Rock v. Parish, 36 Ark. 166; Davis v. Gaines, 48 Ark. 370; Owners of Land v. People, 113 Ill. 296; Wilson v. Board, etc., 133 Ill. 443, 27 N. E. Rep. 203; People v. McFadden, 18 Cal. 469, 15 Am. St. Rep. 66; Ayers' Appeal, 122 Pa. St. 266; In re Ruan Street, 132 Pa. St. 257; Brown v. City of Denver, 7 Colo. 305; Carpenter v. People, 8 Colo. 116; Longworth v. Common Council, 32 Ind. 322; State v. Tucker, 46 Ind. 355; Vickery v. Chase, 50 Ind. 461; Kelly v. State, 92 Ind. 236; Johnson v. Wells Co., 107 Ind. 15; Wiley v. Blufton, 111 Ind. 152; Evansville v. State, 118 Ind. 426; State v. Kolsem, 130 Ind. 434, 29 N. E. Rep. 595; Costello v. Wyoming, 49 Ohio, 202, 30 N. E. Rep. 613. But in a few cases it has been held to be a judicial question. Clarke v. Irwin, 5 Nev. 92; Hess v. Pegg, 6 Nev. 23; Evans v. Job, 8 Nev. 322. This last case was decided upon the authority of Thomas v. Board of Commissioners, 5 Ind. 4, which was subsequently overruled by Johnson v. Board, 107 Ind. 15.

[3] Constitution of Minnesota, art. LV, sec. 33, as amended in 1892. To the same effect, Constitution of Missouri of 1875, art. IV, sec. 53, cl. 32.

tention, would result in an absolute prohibition of special legislation. To give this provision the strictest possible construction of which its language will admit will result in rendering certain necessary legislation impossible, or in causing it to seek refuge under the mere form of general legislation. The provision is not intended to prohibit special legislation, but simply to restrict it to the narrowest field consistent with the practical work of legislation.[1] No general rule can be laid down, but each case must be determined by its peculiar facts and circumstances, interpreted in the light of the intent which the people must be presumed to have entertained when they inserted this saving provision in the constitution.[2]

When a general law could have no other or greater operation than a special law, so that no advantage could be derived nor evil avoided by enacting a law having a general instead of a special operation, a special law is permissible. Hence, where it appeared that there were certain irregularities in the manner of organizing a particular school district under the general law, and no other such case existed in the state, it was held that, although the legislature had no power under the constitution to directly create such a district by a special act, it might provide for a case of this kind by a special law legalizing the defective organization. Such a curative act is a local or special law, but a general law could not be made applicable to the case within the meaning of the constitution.[3]

§ 69. *Amendment or repeal of existing special charters.*— Constitutional provisions prohibiting special legislation relating to public corporations do not repeal special charters in force at the time of their adoption. Thus, such a charter is not repealed by the adoption of a provision requiring the legislature to provide by general laws for the organization of cities and

[1] In Richman v. Muscatine Co., 77 Iowa, 513, 4 L. R. A. 445, it was said that, "except where it clearly appears that the legislature was mistaken in its belief that a general law could not be made applicable," the courts will not interfere. See the earlier Iowa case, Ex parte Pritz, 9 Iowa, 30.

[2] State v. Squires, 26 Iowa, 340 Richman v. Supervisors, 77 Iowa, 513.

[3] People v. Cooper, 83 Ill. 585; Geuild v. Chicago, 82 Ill. 472; Commissioners v. Reynolds (Pa.), 20 Atl. Rep. 1011; Bitting v. Commonwealth (Pa.), 12 Atl. Rep. 29.

towns, and to make provision by general law whereby any city, town or village already incorporated may become subject to the general law.[1] But where a special law has been enacted for the benefit of a public corporation, subject to adoption or rejection by the inhabitants, it cannot be accepted by the corporation after the adoption of the constitutional provision. Such special law is repealed by the constitutional amendment.[2] Where cities elect to retain their special charters after the adoption of a constitutional amendment, it has been held that amendments thereto may be made without violating the constitution.[3] The weight of authority, however, is to the effect that this power of amendment is simply an evasion of the constitutional provision,[4] and that under a proper construction the legislature has neither the power to amend[5] or repeal[6] pre-existing special charters. Any change in a special municipal charter is a regulation of the internal affairs of a municipality.[7]

[1] Darrow v. People, 8 Colo. 426.
[2] Hinze v. People, 92 Ill. 406.
[3] Brown v. City of Denver, 7 Colo. 305; People v. Londoner, 13 Colo. 303.
[4] Atkinson v. Bartholow, 4 Kan. 124. In Ex parte Pritz, 9 Iowa, 30, it was held that a constitutional provision forbidding local or special laws "for the incorporation of cities and towns" forbade the enactment of special laws for the amendment of acts of incorporation in existence before the adoption of the constitution. Said Wright, C. J.: "In the interpretation of the constitution as in the interpretation of laws, however, we are to ascertain the meaning by getting at the intention of those making the instrument. . . . There can be no question but that it was designed to confine the legislature to general legislation, and leave the people in their municipal capacity to organize and carry on their government under such general laws. If this be so, then to say that the legislature may not pass a law to incorporate a city, but may to amend an act of incorporation in existence before the adoption of the constitution or charters under the general law, would make this provision of the constitution practically amount to nothing; for, if they may amend, they may to the extent of passing another new law, except as to one section, or they may at one session amend one-half the law, and at the next the other half; and thus the plain and positive prohibition of the fundamental law would be evaded. By such a construction the evil sought to be prohibited would continue, if possible, in a more objectionable form."
[5] Davis v. Woolonough, 9 Iowa, 104; Baker v. Steamboat, 14 Iowa, 214.
[6] State v. Cincinnati, 20 Ohio St. 18; Wiley v. Bluffton, 111 Ind. 152. Citing Longworth v. Evansville, 32 Ind. 322; Evansville v. Bayard, 39 Ind. 450; Chamberlain v. Evansville, 77 Ind. 542; Eichels v. Evansville Street Railway, 78 Ind. 261, 41 Am. Rep. 561; Warren v. Evansville, 106 Ind. 104; Bluffton v. Studabaker, 106 Ind. 129; Evansville v. Summers, 108 Ind. 189.
[7] Tiger v. Morris Common Pleas, 42 N. J. L. 631. See § 227.

BOOK II.

THE POWERS OF PUBLIC CORPORATIONS.

CHAPTER V.

GENERAL POWERS—NATURE AND CONSTRUCTION.

§ 70. The general principle.
71. Comments upon the rule.
72. Construction.

§ 73. Usage.
74. Delegation of powers.
75. Illustrations.

§ 70. *The general principle.*—The legislature in creating public corporations confers upon them such powers as it deems most conducive to the public good. The powers of counties and townships are generally uniform, and are determined by general laws. Those of municipal corporations are often conferred by special charters, which results in great lack of uniformity. The powers of corporations, stated in general language, are such and such only as the legislature has conferred upon them. Those of municipal corporations, as classified by Judge Dillon, and approved by many courts, are:

1. Those granted in express words.
2. Those necessarily or fairly implied in or incident to the powers expressly granted.
3. Those essential to the declared objects and purposes of the corporation, not simply convenient, but indispensable.[1]

The express powers are found in the words of the charter or general statute of incorporation. The implied powers arise out of the language of the grant of express power. The necessary

[1] Detroit Citizens' St. Ry. Co. v. Detroit (Mich.), 68 N. W. Rep. 304, 35 L. R. A. 859; St. Louis v. Bell Tel. Co., 69 Mo. 623, 9 Am. St. Rep. 370; Huesing v. Rock Island, 128 Ill. 465, 15 Am. St. Rep. 129; Village of Carthage v. Frederick, 122 N. Y. 268, 19 Am. St. Rep. 490; Smith v. Newbern, 70 N. C. 14, 16 Am. Rep. 766; Somerville v. Dickerman, 127 Mass. 272; Bentley v. Bd. Co. Com., 25 Minn. 259; Clark v. Des Moines, 19 Iowa, 199, 87 Am. Dec. 423; Zottman v. San Francisco, 20 Cal. 96, 81 Am. Dec. 96; Taylor v. Bay City St. R. Co., 80 Mich. 77.

powers are such as are essential in order to effect the objects for which the corporation was created.[1] But it must be remembered that a municipal corporation is a body with special and limited jurisdiction, and that its powers can neither be extended or diminished by its own acts.[2] Thus, where a charter authorized a municipal board to act by a majority vote, a by-law providing that a two-thirds vote should be required was held invalid.[3] In a somewhat similar case, the court said[4] that "in authorizing the city council to settle their rules of procedure, the legislature did not confer on the council the power to declare by rule what number of their body should constitute a quorum for the transaction of business. A mere majority of the members elected being present, the acts of the city council are valid, notwithstanding the existence of a rule adopted by the council requiring that two-thirds of the members elected shall be necessary to constitute a quorum. A municipal corporation cannot, by rule made by itself, either enlarge or diminish its own powers."

§ 71. *Comments upon the rule.*— The general principles as stated in the preceding section have been often approved by the courts. Thus Chief Justice Church said: " In this country all corporations, whether public or private, derive their powers from legislative grant, and can do no act for which authority is not expressly given or may not be reasonably inferred. But if we were to say that they can do nothing for which a warrant could not be found in the language of their charter, we would deny them in some cases the power of self-preservation as well as many of the means necessary to the essential object of their incorporation. And, therefore, it has long been an established principle of the law of corporations, that they may exercise all the powers within the fair intent and purpose of their creation which are reasonably proper to give effect to powers expressly granted. In doing this they must have a

[1] Smith v. City of Newbern, 70 N. C. 14, 16 Am. Rep. 766; Bridgeport v. Railroad Co., 15 Conn. 475; Village of Carthage v. Frederick, 122 N. Y. 268, 19 Am. St. Rep. 490.
[2] City of St. Paul v. Laidler, 2 Minn.
190 (Gil. 150), 72 Am. Dec. 89; City of St. Paul v. Traeger, 25 Minn. 252.
[3] Short-Conrad Co. v. School District of Eau Claire (Wis.), 60 N. W. Rep. 337.
[4] Heiskell v. Mayor, 65 Md. 125, 4 Atl. Rep. 116.

choice of means adapted to ends and are not to be confined to any one mode of operation."[1] They can exercise no powers, said Chief Justice Shaw,[2] " but those which are conferred upon them by the act by which they are constituted, or such as are necessary to the exercise of their corporate powers, the performance of their corporate duties and the accomplishment of the purposes of their association. The principle is derived from the nature of corporations, and the mode in which they are organized and in which their affairs must be conducted."

§ 72. *Construction.*— It is a well-settled rule of construction that in grants to corporations, whether public or private, only such powers and rights can be exercised under them as are clearly comprehended within the words of the act or derived therefrom by fair and reasonable implication, regard being had to the object of the grant. Any ambiguity or doubt arising out of the terms used by the legislature must be resolved in favor of the public.[3] All charters and city laws must be construed in conformity to constitutional principles and in harmony with general laws.[4]

---

[1] Bridgeport v. Railroad Co., 15 Conn. 475. But where the manner in which power is to be executed is expressly prescribed, that method must be followed. Mayor of Baltimore v. Porter, 18 Md. 284, 79 Am. Dec. 686; Zottman v. San Francisco, 20 Cal. 96, 81 Am. Dec. 96.

[2] Spaulding v. Lowell, 23 Pick. 71.

[3] St. Louis v. Bell Tel. Co., 96 Mo. 623, 9 Am. St. R. 370; Minturn v. Larue, 23 How. 435; Thompson v. Lee Co., 3 Wall. 327; Thomas v. Richmond, 12 Wall. 348; Lehigh Water Company's Appeal, 102 Pa. St. 515; Leonard v. Canton, 35 Miss. 189; Long v. Duluth, 49 Minn. 287; Brenham v. Brenham Water Co., 67 Tex. 542. With reference to this rule Judge Dillon says: "If upon the whole there be a fair, reasonable, substantial doubt whether the legislature intended to confer the authority in question, particularly if it refers to a matter extra-municipal or unusual in character, and the exercise of which will be attended by taxes, tolls, assessments or burden upon the inhabitants, or oppress them, or abridge natural or common rights, or divest them of their property, the doubt should be resolved in favor of the citizen and against the municipality." Municipal Corporations, § 891, note. See Ex parte Mayor of Florence, 78 Ala. 419; Grand Rapids Electric Co. v. Grand Rapids Edison Co., 33 Fed. Rep. 659; Logan v. Pyne, 43 Iowa, 524, 22 Am. Rep. 261; Anderson v. Wellington, 40 Kan. 173, 10 Am. St. Rep. 175, note. In Ex parte Garza, 28 Tex. Ap. 381, 19 Am. St. Rep. 845, it was said that all reasonable intendment in support of the validity of an ordinance should be indulged.

[4] In re Frazee, 63 Mich. 396, 6 Am. St. Rep. 311; Mayor v. State, 15 Md. 376, 74 Am. Dec. 572.

§ 73. *Usage.*— In this country power cannot be conferred upon public corporations by usage, but the usage may properly be considered in aid of construction.[1] Thus, an unlawful expenditure of money by a town cannot be made valid by usage however long continued. Abuses of power and violations of right derive no sanction from time or custom.[2]

§ 74. *Delegation of powers.*— As a public corporation exercises powers delegated to it by the legislature, the general rule is that it must itself exercise its powers, and cannot delegate them to any other body or person.[3] But a distinction is made between acts which involve discretion and those which are merely ministerial in their nature. Thus, in a case[4] which involved the rights of a council to direct the mayor and chairman of the committee on streets and alleys to make a contract on behalf of the city for the construction of sidewalks, it was said: "It is true that the council could not delegate all the power conferred upon it by the legislature, but like every other corporation it could do its ministerial work by agents. Nothing more was done in this case. The council directed the pavements, ordering them to be constructed of one or the other of several materials, but giving to the owners of abutting lots the privilege of selecting which, and reserving to the chairman of the committee authority to select in case the lot owner failed. The council also directed how the preparatory work should be done. There was, therefore, no unlawful delegation of power."

§ 75. *Illustrations.*— There are many cases illustrating the principles of the preceding section. Thus, a council having authority to lease certain rooms may appoint a committee to procure furniture and arrange the rooms.[5] So the power of a city over its streets may be delegated to a street committee composed of members of the board of aldermen.[6] Power to license the sale of liquor, expressly conferred on the city coun-

[1] Frazer v. Warfield, 13 Md. 279.
[2] Hood v. Lynn, 1 Allen, 103.
[3] St. Louis v. Russell, 116 Mo. 248, 20 L. R. A. 721 and note; Thompson v. Schermerhorn, 6 N. Y. 92, 55 Am. Dec. 385; McCrowell v. Bristol, 89 Va. 65, 20 L. R. A. 653; Lauenstein v. Fond du Lac, 28 Wis. 336.
[4] Hitchcock v. Galveston, 96 U. S. 341; Green v. Ward, 82 Va. 324.
[5] Edwards v. Watertown, 24 Hun (N. Y.), 428.
[6] Tate v. Greensboro, 114 N. C. 392, 24 L. R. A. 671.

cil, cannot, however, be delegated to the mayor.[1] When the mayor and aldermen are authorized to purchase a site and erect thereon a market building, they cannot delegate such power to commissioners.[2] The council cannot delegate to a board of public works the power given it, in conjunction with the board of education, to purchase a school-house site.[3] The power to determine which of several railroad companies shall receive municipal aid cannot be delegated.[4] Nor can a city with authority to build and maintain a wharf lease the same to some person, and authorize the lessee to fix the rates of wharfage.[5] A city cannot delegate its power to establish the grade of streets,[6] nor to prescribe the width of sidewalks,[7] nor to decide the manner in which streets shall be improved,[8] nor to decide the kind of paving blocks which shall be used,[9] nor to determine the dimensions and material of a sewer.[10] But the city may authorize a board to make rules and regulations governing the use of the streets.[11] But mere ministerial powers may be delegated.[12] Thus, a village may by ordinance empower the village recorder to license peddlers, where he is given only the ministerial power of issuing the license upon certain prescribed conditions being complied with.[13]

[1] State v. Bayonne, 44 N. J. L. 114; Kinmundy v. Mahan, 72 Ill. 462.
[2] State v. Paterson, 34 N. J. L. 163.
[3] Lauenstein v. Fond du Lac, 28 Wis. 336.
[4] Monadnock Ry. Co. v. Petersboro, 49 N. H. 281.
[5] Matthews v. Alexandria, 68 Mo. 115, 30 Am. Rep. 776.
[6] Lippelman v. Cincinnati, 4 Ohio C. C. 327.
[7] McCrowell v. Bristol, 89 Va. 652, 20 L. R. A. 653.
[8] Richardson v. Heydenfeldt, 46 Cal. 68.
[9] Smith v. Duncan, 77 Ind. 92; Hydes v. Joyes, 4 Bush, 464, 96 Am. Dec. 311; Thomson v. Boonville, 61 Mo. 282; Zabel v. Louisville (Ky.), 13 L. R. A. 668.
[10] St. Louis v. Buckner, 44 Mo. 19.
[11] Commonwealth v. Plaisted, 148 Mass. 375.
[12] Ruggles v. Collier, 43 Mo. 353.
[13] Swarth v. People, 109 Ill. 621.

CHAPTER VI.

PARTICULAR POWERS.

§ 76. Manner of granting powers.
77. Statutory requirements.
78. The exercise of powers beyond corporate limits.
79. Power to enact ordinances.
80. General-welfare clause.

I. MISCELLANEOUS POWERS.

81. Power to contract.
82. Letting contracts to lowest bidder.
83. Remedy of lowest bidder.
84. Contracts for a term of years.
85. Exclusive privileges.
86. Power to borrow money.
87. Compromise and arbitration.

§ 88. Powers of school boards — Text-books.

II. POLICE POWERS.

89. Nature and scope of the police power.
90. Regulation of occupations and amusements.
91. The preservation of health.
92. Nuisances.
93. Regulation of wharves.
94. Licenses.
95. Markets.
96. Prevention of fires.
97. Care of indigent and infirm.

§ 76. *Manner of granting powers.*— It must be remembered that public corporations are created by the state for the primary purpose of aiding in the work of government; and that it delegates to them such powers as are deemed advisable for that purpose. Municipal corporations have largely lost their original character, and become, like counties and towns, essentially public agencies, with certain private powers and franchises, however, to be used for the benefit of its citizens. In this country the legislatures generally attempt to enumerate all the powers which public corporations may exercise, but such an enumeration does not deprive the corporation of its common-law powers.[1] It is impracticable for any charter to contain an enumeration of all the powers which it may be advisable that such a corporation should exercise under all possible future conditions. Hence, it has become customary to apply to the legislature for additional powers upon the occurrence of every new demand. As a result there is no such systematic classification of corporate powers as probably would have been made under a system where power is granted in general terms, as is

[1] Crawfordsville v. Brader, 130 Ind. 149, 28 N. E. Rep. 851, 30 Am. St. Rep. 214.

common in many European countries. Thus, in France, all municipal power is derived from the simple provision that "the municipality regulates by its deliberations the affairs of the commonwealth."[1]

An examination of the laws of the several states and of the special charters of municipal corporations will show that many powers are common to all. Municipal corporations are ordinarily classified, and a grant of enumerated powers is then made by general laws to each class. Cities of the highest class naturally require and ordinarily possess many powers and privileges not granted to smaller corporations.

Municipal corporations are generally granted power to manage and control the finances and property of the city, and to make proper ordinances for the government and good order of the city, the suppression of vice and intemperance, and the prevention of crime. For these purposes they are authorized to enact ordinances licensing amusements, prohibiting gaming, establishing boards of health and public markets, providing for a standard of weights and measures, a system of quarantine, taxing animals running at large, abating nuisances, regulating driving, slaughter-houses, butcher shops and various other occupations. The powers of counties and townships vary according to locality. In the western states, where the powers are divided between the two bodies, the county ordinarily has power to sue and be sued, to purchase and hold real and personal estate for the use of the county, lands sold for taxes, and under judicial proceedings in which the county is plaintiff, to sell and convey real and personal estate owned by the county, and to make all contracts and do all other acts in relation to the property and concerns of the county necessary to the exercise of its corporate powers. It is impossible to enumerate or even to classify all the powers possessed by public corporations. Local statutes and special charters must be examined. A broad division may however be made into powers of a governmental nature and powers of a private or corporate character.[2]

§ 77. *Statutory requirements.*— When the manner in which the powers of a public corporation may be exercised is pre-

[1] Goodnow, Municipal Problems, p. 252. N. Y. 46; State v. Covington, 29 Ohio St. 111.
[2] Fire Ins. Co. v. Keeseville, 148

scribed by the charter, that mode is the measure of power and must be strictly followed. "When any power is granted and the mode of its exercise prescribed, that mode must be strictly pursued."[1] Thus, a contract executed in a manner other than that prescribed by the statute is void.[2]

§ 78. *The exercise of power beyond corporate limits.*—As a general rule a corporation cannot exercise its powers beyond its corporate limits.[3] But authority to do so may be conferred by statute based upon a public necessity,[4] as where a city is authorized to construct water-works at a distance beyond its limits. Under a charter containing general authority over drainage, the city may enter into contracts or prosecute work beyond its limits for the purpose of discharging sewage where it will not endanger the health of the community.[5] So a city may by ordinance require that an applicant for milk license shall consent that the dairy herd from which he obtains his milk may be inspected by the commissioner of health, although the herd is kept outside of the city limits.[6]

§ 79. *Power to enact ordinances.*—The legislature may properly delegate to a municipal corporation the right to exercise certain legislative powers.[7] The laws which a municipal corporation may thus pass are commonly called ordinances. "It cannot be doubted," says Mr. Justice Harlan,[8] "that the legislature may delegate to municipal corporations the power of enacting ordinances that relate to local matters, and that such ordinances, if legally enacted, have the force of laws passed by

---

[1] Whiting v. West Point, 88 Va. 905, 15 L. R. A. 861; Minturn v. Larue, 23 How. (U. S.) 435.
[2] Fones Bros. H. Co. v. Erb, 54 Ark. 645, 13 L. R. A. 353; Durango v. Pennington, 8 Colo. 257; Mazet v. Pittsburgh, 137 Pa. St. 548; Wells v. Burnham, 20 Wis. 119; Wheeler v. Wayne Co., 31 Ill. App. 598, 24 N. E. Rep. 625; Weitz v. Independent District, 79 Iowa, 423; Zottman v. San Francisco, 20 Cal. 96, 81 Am. Dec. 96; Niles W. W. v. Niles, 59 Mich. 311.
[3] People v. Bennett, 83 Mich. 457; Weed v. Boston, 126 Mass. 443; Ogden v. McLaughlin, 5 Utah, 387; Lawrence v. Monroe, 44 Kan. 607.
[4] Van Hook v. Selma, 70 Ala. 361, 45 Am. Rep. 85; Coldwater v. Tucker, 36 Mich. 474, 24 Am. Rep. 601.
[5] McBean v. Fresno, 112 Cal. 159, 44 Pac. Rep. 358, 31 L. R. A. 794; Coldwater v. Tucker, 36 Mich. 474, 24 Am. Rep. 601.
[6] State v. Nelson (Minn.), 34 L. R. A. 318 (1896).
[7] St. Paul v. Colter, 12 Minn. 41; Blanchard v. Bissell, 11 Ohio St. 96.
[8] New Orleans Water-works v. New Orleans, 164 U. S. 481.

the legislature of the state and are to be respected by all." When such an ordinance is enacted without authority it is void, and all proceedings under it are void; but if the power to enact the ordinance exists and is exercised in an irregular or unauthorized manner, the ordinance is treated as valid until set aside in proper legal proceedings.[1]

§ 80. *General-welfare clause.*— In addition to the grant of specific powers, most charters contain a clause granting power to provide for the preservation and promotion of the public welfare, and the peace and safety of the community. This provision is generally given a liberal construction, and under it ordinances have been enacted providing for and regulating the blasting of rocks, street preaching, destruction of trees in public places, and other such purposes.[2] It is generally held that, in the absence of statute or charter provision requiring a different interpretation, the general-welfare clause will authorize a corporation to restrain animals from running at large.[3] The mere fact that the charters of some cities in a state contain express provision authorizing the enactment of ordinances for this purpose, and that no such provision is contained in other charters, does not in itself prevent such cities from enacting such ordinances under the general-welfare clause.[4]

I. MISCELLANEOUS POWERS.

§ 81. *Power to contract.*— Unless restricted by its charter, a municipal corporation has implied power to make such contracts as are reasonably necessary for the purpose of carrying into effect the objects of its creation.[5] Power to contract conferred in general terms only authorizes the making of such contracts as are necessary and usual.[6] A municipal corporation can bind itself by such contracts only as it is authorized to

[1] Camden v. Mulford, 26 N. J. L. 49.
[2] Commonwealth v. Parks, 155 Mass. 531, 30 N. E. Rep. 174; Commonwealth v. Davis, 140 Mass. 485; Mankato v. Fowler, 32 Minn. 354; State v. Merrill, 37 Me. 329.
[3] Collins v. Hatch, 18 Ohio, 523, 51 Am. Dec. 465; Wilcox v. Hemming, 58 Wis. 144.
[4] Cochran v. Frostberg, 81 Md. 54, 27 L. R. A. 728.
[5] Douglass v. Virginia City, 5 Nev. 122; East St. Louis v. East St. Louis Gas L. Co., 98 Ill. 415.
[6] Rae v. Mayor, 51 Mich. 526; Gregory v. Bridgeport, 41 Conn. 76.

make, and it is not estopped by a contract made in violation of its charter provisions.[1] A city cannot by contract deprive itself of the power of performing its governmental duties;[2] and the distinction between corporate and governmental powers must not be lost sight of in considering the validity of contracts. As to powers of a private character, and property acquired thereunder and contracts made with reference thereto, the corporation is to be regarded *quoad hoc* as a private corporation.

When a contract will interfere with the duties of the corporation in preserving the public health and morals of the city, or will create a nuisance, the corporation cannot be required to perform it, but it must reimburse the other party for disbursements made under the contract, and pay resulting damages.[3]

A contract with a municipal corporation which is the owner of certain telegraph and telephone lines to put the wire in conduits underground is for the private advantage of the corporation. When a city, in the exercise of its governmental powers, and of its discretion as to time and manner, decides to make a certain improvement, the contracts made for the purpose of carrying on the work cannot be revoked by the corporation. An attempted revocation on the ground that the city attorney had advised that the ordinance authorizing the work was invalid is no defense to an action on the contract.[4] A municipal corporation may ratify a contract made by a party who was wrongfully acting for both parties, if it is not unlawful or immoral and might originally have been made by the corporation.[5]

§ 82. *Letting contracts to lowest bidder.*—Where a city council does not abuse its discretionary powers, and does not act

[1] Newberry v. Fox, 37 Minn. 141, 5 Am. St. Rep. 830. The doctrine of *ultra vires* is applied with greater strictness to municipal bodies than to private corporations.

[2] Illinois S. & T. Co. v. Arkansas City, 76 Fed. Rep. 271, 40 C. C. A. 257, and cases cited.

[3] Brick Presbyterian Church v. City of New York, 5 Cow. (N. Y.) 538; Rittenhouse v. Mayor, 25 Md. 336; United States v. Behan, 110 U. S. 338; Howard v. Manufacturing Co., 139 U. S. 199.

[4] Safety Ins. W. & C. Co. v. Mayor of Baltimore (C. C. A.), 66 Fed. Rep. 140.

[5] City of Findlay v. Pertz, 66 Fed. Rep. 427, 31 C. C. A. 340.

fraudulently, and the charter does not prescribe the mode of entering into contracts in purchasing material for the use of the city, it may award contracts without letting them to the lowest bidder, if the contract is otherwise within the scope of its corporate power.[1] But when the charter requires that such contracts shall be let to the lowest bidder, a contract let in any other manner is invalid and incapable of ratification.[2] When the right is reserved to reject any and all bids, it is equivalent to an offer to contract, and a bidder acquires no rights until his bid is actually accepted.[3] The advertisement for bids must be in such form as to permit of *bona fide* competitive bidding.[4] Charter provisions ordinarily require that the contract shall be let to the lowest responsible bidder. A certain discretion is then left to the awarding officers, which will not be controlled by the courts. A responsible bidder is one who has judgment and skill in addition to pecuniary responsibility.[5]

[1] Yarnold v. City of Lawrence, 15 Kan. 126; Elliott v. Minneapolis, 59 Minn. 111. In the case last above cited the court said: "But the powers of a city council are not unlimited. However difficult it might be to investigate the motives of the members of a city council, yet whenever they undertake to use their corporate power fraudulently for their own advantage or for the benefit or injury of others, such acts are void. Any other rule would be disastrous, and the most salutary doctrine that can be upheld, and which we uphold as the law, is to allow fraudulent contracts on the part of municipal corporations to be impeached.

[2] Cary v. Somerset Co., 45 N. J. L. 445; Addis v. Pittsburgh, 85 Pa. St. 379; McNeil v. Boston Chamber of Commerce, 154 Mass. 277, 13 L. R. A. 559; Frame v. Felix, 167 Pa. St. 47, 27 L. R. A. 802; Weitz v. Independent District, 79 Iowa, 423.

[3] Anderson v. Board, 122 Mo. 61, 26 L. R. A. 707, and note.

[4] Mazet v. Pittsburgh, 137 Pa. St. 548; Ely v. Grand Rapids, 84 Mich. 337; Barber Asphalt Pav. Co. v. Hunt, 100 Mo. 22.

[5] Kelly v. Chicago, 62 Ill. 279; Douglass v. Commonwealth, 108 Pa. St. 559; State v. M'Grath, 91 Mo. 386; State v. Trenton, 49 N. J. L. 339; Hoole v. Kincaid, 16 Nev. 217. In Frame v. Felix, 167 Pa. St. 47, the court said: "The provision that contracts for municipal work shall be given to the lowest responsible bidder does not have sole reference to the mere pecuniary liability of the contractor, but involves a discretion on the part of the municipal authorities in the selection of the agency best fitted for the performance of the work required. Commonwealth v. Mitchell, 82 Pa. St. 343; Findlay v. Pittsburg, id. 351; Douglass v. Commonwealth, 108 Pa. St. 559; Interstate Vitrified Brick & Paving Co. v. Philadelphia et al., 164 Pa. St. 477. But that discretion being granted, the purpose of the provision which was based upon motives of public economy, and originated perhaps from some degree of mistrust of the officers to whom the duty of making contracts for the public service

§ 83. *Remedy of bidder.*— Mandamus or mandatory injunction to require the execution of the contract to the lowest bidder is generally refused on the ground that there is a discretion vested in the awarding officers, that there is an adequate remedy at law, or that the provision is for the benefit of the public, and not the bidder.[1]

In a recent case[2] the circuit court of appeals said: "That taxpayers whose taxes are to be increased, or whose property is to be depreciated in value, by the fraudulent or arbitrary violation of this provision by the officers of a municipality, may maintain a bill to enjoin their proposed action, is a proposition now too well settled to admit of question.[3] These suits, however, stand upon the ground that the statutes upon which they are based were enacted, and the duties there specified were imposed upon the public officers, for the express benefit of the taxpayers and property holders who bring the suit. The appellee pays no taxes for this paving. He has no property which will be injured by the violation of the provisions relied upon, and no one who has is here to complain of their violation. So far as the purpose of the enactment is concerned, the complainant is a stranger to the statute, one whose interests were not considered, or intended to be considered, by the enactment. He is a mere bidder for some of the public work of this city, a contractor, or one who desires to become a contractor. . . . It is upon this principle that it is now settled by the great

was committed (Brady v. New York, 20 N. Y. 312), clearly was to secure to the city the benefit and advantage of fair and just competition between bidders and at the same time close as far as possible every avenue to favoritism and fraud in its various forms (Mazet v. Pittsburgh, 137 Pa. St. 548), and to insure the accomplishment of the work at the lowest price by subjecting the contract for it to public competition. In re Mahan, 20 Hun (N. Y.), 301. In order to effectuate this purpose it is manifest that where something is to be done that is required to be submitted to competition, every essential part of it that goes to make up the whole of it must be submitted to such competition."

[1] Dibble v. New Haven, 56 Conn. 199; State v. Fond du Lac Board of Education, 24 Wis. 683; People v. Campbell, 72 N. Y. 496. *Contra,* State v. Marion Co. Com'rs, 39 Ohio St. 188; Times Pub. Co. v. Everett, 9 Wash. 518 (1894). See annotation to Anderson v. Board, in 26 L. R. A. 707, 122 Mo. 61.

[2] Colorado Pav. Co. v. Murphy, 78 Fed. Rep. 28.

[3] Times Pub. Co. v. Everett, 9 Wash. 518, 37 Pac. Rep. 695; Beach, Pub. Corp., § 634; High, Inj., § 1251; Mayor v. Keyser, 72 Md. 106, 19 Atl. Rep. 706; People v. Dwyer, 90 N. Y. 402.

weight of authority that the lowest bidder cannot compel the issue of a writ of *mandamus* to force the officers of a municipality to enter into a contract with him."[1] Nor can he maintain an action at law for damages for the refusal to enter into the contract.[2] "This principle is as fatal to a suit in equity as to an action at law. It goes not to defeat one particular cause of action, but to defeat the right to any relief."[3] The bidder has no remedy in the absence of a mandatory statute or when the right to reject is reserved.[4] But when the bid is rejected upon grounds not within the province of the board to pass upon,[5] or when the officers act fraudulently,[6] the rights of the lowest bidder will be protected. A bidder whose bid is fraudulent,[7] obscure, or so framed as to prevent competition, is not entitled to the contract.[8]

§ 84. *Contracts for a term of years.*— A city council, in the absence of a charter restriction,[9] may enter into a valid contract for a term of years extending beyond the life of the council or the official term of the officers, if the time be not unreasonable under all the circumstances.[10] But the council must not by such contract preclude itself from exercising its

[1] High, Extr. Rem., § 92; State v. Board, 24 Wis. 683; Commonwealth v. Mitchell, 82 Pa. St. 343; Kelly v. Chicago, 62 Ill. 279; State v. McGrath, 91 Mo. 386; Douglass v. Commonwealth, 108 Pa. St. 559; Madison v. Harbor Board, 76 Md. 395, 25 Atl. Rep. 337.

[2] Talbot Pav. Co. v. City of Detroit (Mich.), 67 N. W. Rep. 979; Gas Light Co. v. Donnelly, 93 N. Y. 557.

[3] Colorado Pav. Co. v. Murphy, 78 Fed. Rep. 28, 49 C. C. A. 17.

[4] State v. Lincoln Co., 35 Neb. 346; State v. Dickson Co. Com., 24 Neb. 106.

[5] Cleveland, etc. Tel. Co. v. Metropolitan Fire Com., 55 Barb. (N. Y.) 288.

[6] State v. Trenton, 49 N. J. L. 339.

[7] Baltimore v. Keyser, 72 Md. 106; State v. York Co. Com., 13 Neb. 57.

[8] Fones Bros. H. Co. v. Erb, 54 Ark. 645, 13 L. R. A. 353; Mazet v. Pittsburgh, 137 Pa. St. 548; Coggshal v. Des Moines, 78 Iowa, 235; In re Anderson, 109 N. Y. 554; Littler v. Jayne, 124 Ill. 123. See Nash v. St. Paul, 11 Minn. 174.

[9] Indianapolis v. Wann, 144 Ind. 175, 42 N. E. Rep. 901, 31 L. R. A. 743.

[10] Garrison v. Chicago, 7 Biss. 480; New Orleans G. L. Co. v. New Orleans, 42 La. 188; Valparaiso v. Gardner, 97 Ind. 1; Indianapolis v. Ind. G. L. Co., 66 Ind. 396; Vincennes v. Citizens', etc. Co., 132 Ind. 114; Smith v. Dedham, 144 Mass. 177; Merrill, etc. Ry. Co. v. Merrill, 80 Wis. 358; Columbus W. W. Co. v. Columbus, 48 Kan. 99; Davenport v. Kleinschmidt, 6 Mont. 502; Atlantic City W. W. v. Atlantic City, 48 N. J. L. 378; Santa Anna W. Co. v. San Buenaventura, 56 Fed. Rep. 339. See note to Sheldon v. Fox, 48 Kan. 356, 16 L. R. A. 257.

legislative powers,[1] create a perpetuity or monopoly,[2] or absolutely surrender its control over the subject-matter of the contract.[3] But every contract, or ordinance in the nature of a contract, to some extent necessarily limits and controls the power and authority of future councils. This is the unavoidable result of any binding contract.[4] The power to execute a contract for goods, houses, gas, water, and the like, is neither a judicial nor a legislative power, but is a purely business power.[5] The purpose is not to govern the inhabitant, but to obtain a private benefit for the city and its people.[6]

§ 85. *Exclusive privileges.*— It is well settled that a municipal corporation cannot without express authority grant exclusive franchises or privileges, such as the right to put mains, pipes or hydrants in streets.[7] The general rule is that the leg-

[1] Brenham v. Brenham W. Co., 67 Tex. 543.
[2] Greenville W. W. Co. v. Greenville, 70 Miss. 669 (1890). See note to Altgeld v. San Antonio, 81 Tex. 436, 13 L. R. A. 383.
[3] Houston v. Houston City R. R. Co., 84 Tex. 581 (1892).
[4] Vincennes v. Citizens' G. L. etc. Co., 132 Ind. 114.
[5] Valparaiso v. Gardner, 97 Ind. 1, 49 Am. Rep. 416.
[6] Cincinnati v. Cameron, 33 Ohio St. 336; Safety Ins. Wire & C. Co. v. Baltimore, 66 Fed. Rep. 140, 25 U. S. (App.) 166. In Illinois T. & S. Bank v. Arkansas City, 40 C. C. A. 257, 76 Fed. Rep. 271, 34 L. R. A. 518, the court said: "But it is insisted that this contract is beyond the powers of the city and void, because it grants the right to use the streets of the city to the water company, and promises to pay rental for the hydrants for twenty-one years. The proposition on which this contention rests is that the members of the city council are trustees for the public; that they exercise legislative powers, and that they can make no grant and conclude no contract which will bind the city beyond the terms of their offices, because such action would circumscribe the legislative powers of their successors, and deprive them of their right to their unrestricted exercise as the exigencies of the times might demand. . . . This proposition ignores the settled distinction between the governmental or public, and the proprietary or business, powers of a municipality, and erroneously seeks to apply to the exercise of the latter a rule which is only applicable to the exercise of the former."
[7] Syracuse W. Co. v. Syracuse, 116 N. Y. 167, 5 L. R. A. 546; Altgeld v. San Antonio, 81 Tex. 436, 13 L. R. A. 383, note; State v. Cincinnati Gas Co., 18 Ohio St. 262; Gale v. Kalamazoo, 23 Mich. 344, 9 Am. Rep. 80; Logan v. Pyre, 43 Iowa, 524, 22 Am. Rep. 261; Des Moines Gas Co. v. Des Moines, 44 Iowa, 505, 24 Am. Rep. 756; Saginaw G. L. Co. v. Saginaw, 28 Fed. Rep. 529; Norwich G. L. Co. v. Norwich City Gas Co., 25 Conn. 20; Long v. City of Duluth, 49 Minn. 280, and cases there cited and reviewed. As to power of creating monopolies, see Saginaw Gas L. Co.

islature alone has the power to make exclusive grants of this character, and that this authority does not vest in the municipality, unless it is expressly granted to it by its charter.[1] Exclusive rights of this nature are not favored. If there is any ambiguity or reasonable doubt arising from the terms used by the legislature or granting body as to whether an exclusive franchise has been conferred or authorized to be conferred, the doubt is to be resolved against the party claiming such grant.[2] Power to light its streets is authority to give the use, although not the exclusive use, of the streets to the party with whom the contract for lighting is made.[3] Power to provide a water supply,[4] or "to cause said city or any part thereof to be lighted with oil or gas, and to levy a tax for that purpose," will not authorize contracts giving the exclusive right to furnish water or light for a fixed period.[5] So a city cannot, without express authority, grant to a street railway company the sole and exclusive right to construct and operate street railways in its streets.[6]

§ 86. *Power to borrow money.*— The power to borrow money must be conferred by express authority, or result as an incident to an express power coupled with the imposition of duties which are incapable of exercise and performance without the power to borrow.[7] It is not sufficient that it would be convenient to borrow: it must be necessary to the discharge of the duties imposed.[8] A limitation on the power to borrow money is destroyed by a general act empowering the city to construct water-works and to borrow money therefor.[9]

v. Saginaw, 28 Fed. Rep. 529; City of Laredo v. Int. Bridge & T. Co., 66 Fed. Rep. 246, 30 U. S. (App.) 110. The state may grant an exclusive franchise. N. O. Gas Co. v. La. Light Co., 115 U. S. 650.

[1] Illinois Trust & Sav. Bank v. Arkansas City, 40 C. C. A. 257, 34 L. R. A. 518, 76 Fed. Rep. 271, and cases cited.

[2] Long v. City of Duluth, 49 Minn. 280; Nash v. Lowry, 37 Minn. 261; Wright v. Nagle, 101 U. S. 791.

[3] Norwich G. L. Co. v. Norwich City G. Co., 25 Conn. 20.

[4] Altgeld v. San Antonio, 81 Tex. 436.

[5] Davenport v. Kleinschmidt, 6 Mont. 502; In re Union Ferry Co., 98 N. Y. 139.

[6] Jackson Co. H. R. Co. v. Interstate R. Co., 24 Fed. Rep. 306; Nash v. Lowry, 37 Minn. 261.

[7] Mayor v. Ray, 19 Wall. (U. S.) 468; Allen v. La Fayette, 89 Ala. 641, 9 L. R. A. 497.

[8] Wells v. Salina, 119 N. Y. 280, 7 L. R. A. 799.

[9] Dutton v. Aurora, 114 Ill. 138.

§ 87. *Compromise and arbitration.*— A public corporation may compromise claims held against it or held by it against other persons; or it may submit claims to arbitration the same as natural persons.[1]

§ 88. *Powers of school boards — Text-books.*— The powers of school boards and trustees are purely statutory,[2] and vary greatly in the different states. The board generally has authority to prescribe the text-books which shall be used in the district. The duty of establishing and maintaining a "general, uniform and thorough system of public free common schools," imposed by the constitution upon the legislature, does not necessarily imply that that body shall establish and maintain a uniform system of text-books throughout the state. A uniform system of free common schools does not require that the text-books used in the schools shall be uniform throughout the state.[3] When the legislature has not prescribed what books shall be used, and has not delegated the power to any other person or body, the trustees of a school district may do so by virtue of the general control over the school given them by statute.[4] The power may be delegated by the legislature to a school-book commission.[5] An act of the legislature prescribing the text-books which shall be used in the public schools does not violate the right of local self-government. It is a power which may be conferred upon a school board, and in such case the courts will not interfere.[6] The state may prescribe the text-books and make an exclusive contract to furnish the books for a certain term.[7] The school directors may be compelled by

[1] Shawneetown v. Baker, 85 Ill. 563; Kane v. Fond du Lac, 40 Wis. 495; Dix v. Dummuston, 19 Vt. 263; Paret v. Bayonne, 39 N. J. L. 559. See Somerville v. Dickerman, 127 Mass. 272.
[2] Barry v. Good, 89 Cal. 215.
[3] Campana v. Calderhead, 17 Mont. 548, 36 L. R. A. 277, 44 Pac. Rep. 84; Curryer v. Merrill, 25 Minn. 1, 33 Am. Rep. 450; State v. Haworth, 122 Ind. 462, 7 L. R. A. 240; State v. Womack, 4 Wash. 19; Effingham v. Hamilton, 68 Mich. 523; Reno County School District v. Shadduck, 25 Kan. 467; Topeka Board of Education v. Welch, 51 Kan. 797; Powell v. Board of Education, 97 Ill. 375, 37 Am. Rep. 123; Richards v. Raymond, 92 Ill. 612, 34 Am. Rep. 151.
[4] Campana v. Calderhead, 17 Mont. 548, 36 L. R. A. 277, annotated, 44 Pac. Rep. 84; State v. Webber, 108 Ind. 31, 58 Am. Rep. 30; State v. Dixon County School District, 31 Neb. 552.
[5] State v. Bronson, 115 Mo. 271.
[6] Cincinnati Board of Education v. Minor, 23 Ohio St. 211, 13 Am. Rep. 233.
[7] Curryer v. Merrill, 25 Minn. 1, 33 Am. Rep. 450; State v. Haworth, 122

mandamus to introduce the books which have been adopted according to statute,[1] and a pupil may be suspended for refusing to procure a prescribed book.[2] A parent cannot insist that his child shall be permitted to use a text-book other than that prescribed by the board.[3] The reading of the Bible as a textbook in the public schools violates the constitutional provision prohibiting sectarian instruction,[4] but a requirement that the Bible shall be used as a mere reading book is valid.[5] A school board may prescribe reasonable regulations for the health of the children and the community.[6] For this purpose it may require all pupils to be vaccinated as a condition precedent to the right to attend school, although there are no present indications of an epidemic.[7] But it has been held that such a requirement is unreasonable, unless it appears that small-pox actually exists or there is reasonable cause to anticipate its appearance.[8]

II. POLICE POWERS.

§ 89. *Nature and scope of the police power.*—The police power of the state is incapable of exact limitation and definition. Within its scope are included those paramount powers which may be exercised for the purpose of promoting the general

Ind. 462, 7 L. R. A. 240; State v. Blue, 122 Ind. 600.

[1] State v. Roberts, 74 Mo. 21. For the construction of particular statutes regulating the adoption of textbooks, see Iverson v. Indianapolis School Commissioners, 39 Fed. Rep. 735; People v. State Board of Education, 49 Cal. 684; Jones v. Detroit Board of Education, 88 Mich. 371.

[2] But see Ruilson v. Post, 79 Ind. 567; Trustees v. People, 87 Iowa, 305.

[3] Lake View School Trustees v. r.. ple, 87 Ill. 308. See Reno County School District v. Shadduck, 25 Kan. 467; Dobbs v. Stauffer, 24 Kan. 127.

[4] Weiss v. Edgerton School District Board, 76 Wis. 177, 7 L. R. A. 330, 20 Am. St. Rep. 41, note, p. 69. As to what constitutes a sectarian school, see Cook Co. v. Industrial School, 125 Ill. 540, 8 Am. St. Rep. 386, annotated.

[5] Donahoe v. Richards, 38 Me. 379,

61 Am. Dec. 256. See Board v. Minor, 23 Ohio St. 211, 13 Am. Rep. 233. A statute to the effect that the Bible shall not be excluded, but that no pupil shall be required to read it contrary to the wishes of his parents, is constitutional. Moore v. Monroe, 64 Iowa, 364, 52 Am. Rep. 444.

[6] Duffield v. Williamsport School District, 162 Pa. St. 476, 25 L. R. A. 152.

[7] Bissell v. Davidson, 65 Conn. 183, 29 L. R. A. 251.

[8] Potts v. Breen, 167 Ill. 67, 60 Ill. App. 201, 47 N. E. Rep. 81. Power of school directors to contract, see Everts v. District Township, 77 Iowa, 37, 14 Am. St. Rep. 264. As to separate schools for black and white children, see Lehew v. Brummell, 103 Mo. 546, 23 Am. St. Rep. 895, annotated.

comfort and welfare of society. Being a governmental power, it may be delegated by the legislature to a public corporation. It extends to the protection of the lives, persons and health of the people, and to all the property within the state. Any occupation which is of such a nature as to be liable to create a nuisance, unless subjected to special regulation, comes within the scope of its operation.[1] All property is held subject to its proper exercise.[2] While a wide range of discretion must be left to the body exercising this power, it is necessarily limited by the purpose for which the power exists. Acts done under it must have some relation to the appropriate end. The rights of property cannot be invaded under a pretense of the police power, when it is apparent that the power is in fact sought to be used for a different purpose.[3] The power must be exercised so as not to conflict with the constitutional rights of the people.[4] The various powers which fall under the general name of police powers are ordinarily specifically enumerated. In addition thereto, municipal charters commonly contain a general provision authorizing the exercise of powers necessary to preserve the peace and good order of the community and promote the public welfare. Much discretion must necessarily be left to the corporation; and it has been held that where a council is given power to make such regulations as it shall deem necessary and requisite for the security, welfare and convenience of the corporation, it has the right to judge as to what ordinances are necessary to preserve the health of the people of the municipality.[5]

[1] Munn v. Illinois, 94 U. S. 113; Raymond v. Fish, 51 Conn. 80, 50 Am. Rep. 3; State v. Orr, 68 Conn. 101, 28 L. R. A. 270; People v. Bennett, 83 Mich. 457; Welsh v. Boston, 126 Mass. 442, note; Ogden City v. McLaughlin, 5 Utah, 387; Monroe v. City of Lawrence, 44 Kan. 607; Bittenhaus v. Johnson, 92 Wis. 595, 32 L. R. A. 380. A statute which is for the benefit of private parties, which requires a county to pay for the treatment of habitual drunkards who are not financially able to pay for their own treatment, cannot be sustained under the police power. Wisconsin Keeley Institute v. Milwaukee Co. (Wis.), 36 L. R. A. 58. See § 97.

[2] Rideout v. Knox, 148 Mass. 368, 2 L. R. A. 81; Health Dept. v. Rector, 145 N. Y. 32, 27 L. R. A. 710.

[3] Chaddock v. Day, 75 Mich. 597, 13 Am. St. Rep. 468; Ex parte Tuttle, 91 Cal. 589; Ritchie v. People, 155 Ill. 98, 29 L. R. A. 79; State v. Donaldson, 41 Minn. 74.

[4] In re Jacobs, 98 N. Y. 98, 50 Am. Rep. 636; St. Louis v. Webber, 44 Mo. 547; Ex parte Whitwell, 98 Cal. 73, 19 L. R. A. 727; Seep v. St. Louis, etc. R. Co., 58 Ark. 407, 23 L. R. A. 264.

[5] City of St. Paul v. Colter, 12 Minn.

§ 90. *Regulation of occupations and amusements.*— Neither the state nor municipalities can prohibit the prosecution of a harmless business; but it may subject all manner of occupations and amusements to such reasonable regulations as are necessary in order to protect the interests of the public. When the business or occupation is of such a character as to threaten possible injury to the public, it becomes subject to reasonable restrictions by virtue of the police power. But it is only for the purpose of promoting the public health, welfare and morals that such interferences with private rights will be upheld.[1] Certain kinds of occupations which are illegal or immoral *per se*, such as gambling,[2] may be prohibited; but an ordinance which authorizes the police to seize and destroy gambling implements without notice to the owner is void, because depriving the owner of his property without due process of law.[3] But occupations not unlawful can only be regulated. Thus, a city council may prohibit the carrying on of a laundry except in certain localities and during certain hours; but it cannot arbitrarily refuse to issue a license to run a laundry to a person without reference to the character or qualifications of the applicant.[4] So a city may prohibit the keeping of a house of ill-fame, and impose penalties upon the owners of a building leased for that purpose;[5] but it cannot prohibit the leasing of a house to a prostitute simply as a place of residence.

Power to regulate a business must be exercised through the adoption of rules and regulations as to the manner in which it shall be conducted, and not by the municipality itself engaging in the business.[6] The business of selling intoxicating liquors is a proper subject of police regulation.[7] Thus, a city may by ordinance prohibit the sale of liquors and wines in places where musical or theatrical entertainments are given and where fe-

---

[1] 90 Am. Dec. 278; Summerville v. Pressley, 33 S. C. 56, 8 L. R. A. 854; New Orleans Gas Light Co. v. Hart, 40 La. Ann. 474, 8 Am. St. Rep. 544, note.

[1] Ex parte Mirande, 73 Cal. 365; St. Louis v. Fitz, 53 Mo. 582.

[2] Odell v. Atlanta, 97 Ga. 670, 25 S. E. Rep. 173.

[3] Lowry v. Rainwater, 70 Mo. 152, 35 Am. Rep. 420.

[4] Barbier v. Connelly, 113 U. S. 27; Yick Wo v. Hopkins, 118 U. S. 356; State v. Taft, 118 N. C. 1190, 23 S. E Rep. 970, 32 L. R. A. 122.

[5] McAllister v. Clark, 33 Conn. 91. *Contra*, as to the owners of the premises, State v. Webber, 107 N. C. 962.

[6] Rippe v. Becker, 56 Minn. 100, 22 L. R. A. 857.

[7] Crowley v. Christensen, 137 U. S. 86.

males attend as waitresses.[1] So it may provide that cider shall not be sold in quantities of less than a gallon, or drank on the premises.[2] A wider discretion on the part of the corporation is recognized in respect to exhibitions and amusements than in the case of trades and useful occupations; and a still wider discretion is allowed where the business is of such a nature as to be liable to degenerate into a nuisance, or tend to promote disorder and crime.[3]

§ 91. *The preservation of health.*—The protection of the health of the people is one of the principal purposes for which muicipal corporations are created, and every presumption will be indulged in favor of an ordinance having this for its object.[4] The instances in which this power has been exercised are innumerable. For illustration, a municipality may regulate slaughter-houses,[5] the burial of the dead,[6] the cleaning and care of sinks and cesspools,[7] and the kind and quantity of certain products, such as rice, which may be cultivated within the corporation limits.[8] So it may establish quarantine regulations,[9] and remove persons who are affected by a contagious disease, or who have been exposed to the same, to places of detention, and prevent communication with them.[10] It has been held that

[1] Ex parte Hayes, 98 Cal. 555, 20 L. R. A. 701.
[2] Lawrence v. Monroe, 44 Kan. 607, 10 L. R. A. 520.
[3] Mankato v. Fowler, 32 Minn. 364.
[4] Greenboro v. Ehrenreich, 80 Ala. 579, 60 Am. Rep. 130.
[5] Watertown v. Mayo, 109 Mass. 315; St. Paul v. Byrnes, 38 Minn. 176; Huesing v. Rock Island, 128 Ill. 465, 15 Am. St. Rep. 129; The Slaughter House Cases, 16 Wall. (U. S.) 36; Butchers v. Crescent City, 111 U. S. 746; Beiling v. Evansville, 144 Ind. 644, 42 N. E. Rep. 621.
[6] Bogaert v. Indianapolis, 13 Ind. 134; Coates v. Mayor, 7 Cow. (N. Y.) 585; Re Bohan, 115 Cal. 372, 36 L. R. A. 618.
[7] Nicoulin v. Lowery, 49 N. J. L. 391; Commonwealth v. Cutter, 156 Mass. 52, 29 N. E. Rep. 1146.
[8] Green v. Savannah, 6 Ga. 1; Summerville v. Pressley, 33 S. C. 56.
[9] Railway Co. v. Huesen, 95 U. S. 465; Train v. Boston Disinfecting Co., 144 Mass. 523, 59 Am. Rep. 113; Markham v. Brown, 37 Ga. 277, and note to this case, 92 Am. Dec. 76, where the cases are collected; Thomas v. Mason, 39 W. Va. 526, 26 L. R. A. 727, and extensive note on powers and liabilities of municipalities in times of epidemics; Hurst v. Warner, 102 Mich. 238, 26 L. R. A. 484, and note on quarantine regulations by health authorities. Parties dealing in second-hand clothing may be required to disinfect it. State v. Taft, 118 N. C. 1190, 32 L. R. A. 122.
[10] Harrison v. Baltimore, 1 Gill (Md.), 202; Clinton v. Clinton Co., 61 Iowa, 205; Elliott v. Kalkaska Sup., 58 Mich. 452, 55 Am. Rep. 706.

§ 91.]

by virtue of the police power the city may contract for the boring of an artesian well,[1] on the theory that nothing can be of greater concern to the community than a sufficient supply of wholesome water.[2] So a city may provide that an article of food, such as milk, which does not reach a prescribed standard, or trees which have the contagious disease known as the "yellows,"[3] shall be destroyed without compensation to the owner. Every man holds his property under the implied obligation that it shall not be injurious to the community. "The exercise of the police power," said Mr. Justice Harlan, "by the destruction of property which is itself a public nuisance, or the prohibition of its use in a particular way, whereby its value becomes depreciated, is very different from taking property for public use, or from depriving a possessor of his property without due process of law."[4] An ordinance requiring venders of milk to furnish gratuitously, on application of sanitary inspectors, samples of milk not exceeding a half pint for inspection and analysis, is within the exercise of police power.[5] Although a corporation has power to prevent articles of merchandise or other things which have been used by persons or in places infected with contagious disease from being brought within its limits, establish quarantine and reasonable inspection regulations, and provide for disinfecting and destroying the germ of the disease as far as practicable, it can go no further than is necessary in order to secure protection. Thus, it has no power to declare it unlawful to sell meat or other food, or to deal in

---

[1] Hale v. Houghton, 8 Mich. 458; Suffield v. Hathaway, 44 Conn. 521.

[2] Smith v. Nashville, 88 Tenn. 464, 12 S. W. Rep. 924.

[3] State v. Maine (Conn.), 37 Atl. Rep. 80 (1897). Mr. Justice Baldwin said: "A widespread apprehension throughout the community justifies itself, and is a sufficient basis for legislative action toward the removal of the cause, real or supposed, of the danger apprehended, where this cause is a deadly disease of a food-producing tree. Bissell v. Davison, 65 Conn. 183, 191, 32 Atl. Rep. 348. The destruction of the infected trees by order of a public official, after due inspection, is a remedy which, however severe, is one appropriate to the end in view, and may properly be enforced without any preliminary judicial inquiry, as well as without any compensation to the owner for resulting loss." State v. Woodin, 56 Conn. 216; Powell v. Pennsylvania, 127 U. S. 678.

[4] Mugler v. Kansas, 123 U. S. 623; Deems v. Baltimore, 80 Md. 164, 26 L. R. A. 541; Taunton v. Taylor, 116 Mass. 254; Brown v. Keener, 74 N. C. 714.

[5] State v. Dupaquier, 46 La. Ann. 577, 26 L. R. A. 162.

second-hand or cast-off clothing.¹ A lawful business, not in itself necessarily a nuisance, which may be conducted without danger to the community when properly regulated, cannot be prohibited.²

§ 92. *Nuisances.*—Municipal corporations are ordinarily given power to abate nuisances. It can be exercised only when the act or thing is an actual nuisance, and its abatement required in order to preserve the health and safety of the community.³ A corporation cannot make a thing a nuisance by merely saying that it is one.⁴ "It is a doctrine not to be tolerated in this country," said Mr. Justice Miller, "that a municipal corporation without any general laws, either of the city or of the state, within which a given structure can be shown to be a nuisance, can, by its mere declaration that it is one, subject it to removal by any person supposed to be aggrieved, or even by the city itself. This would place every house, every business, and all the property in the city at the uncontrolled will of the temporary local authorities."⁵ Ordinarily, there must be a judicial determination of the fact that the thing complained of is a nuisance, although the state may confer upon the municipality the power to abate nuisances summarily without formal legal proceedings.⁶ The remedy must not be more stringent than the necessities of the case require. Thus, where the nuisance consists in the improper use of a building, a city cannot legally

---

¹ Greenboro v. Ehrenreich, 80 Ala. 579, 60 Am. Rep. 130.
² State v. Taft, 118 N. C. 1190, 23 S. E. Rep. 970, 32 L. R. A. 122.
³ Ex parte Robinson, 30 Tex. App. 493, 17 S. W. Rep. 1057.
⁴ Des Plaines v. Poyer, 123 Ill. 111; Ex parte O'Leary, 65 Miss. 80, 7 Am. St. Rep. 640; Tissot v. Greath South. Tel. Co., 39 La. Ann. 996, 4 Am. St. Rep. 248; State v. Mott, 61 Md. 297, 48 Am. Rep. 105; Cole v. Kegler, 64 Iowa, 60; Grossman v. Oakland (Oreg.), 37 L. R. A. 593, and note on power of municipal corporation to define, prevent and abate nuisances.
⁵ Yates v. Milwaukee, 10 Wall. (U. S.) 497. See, also, St. Paul v. Gil-

fillan, 36 Minn. 298; Dingley v. Boston, 100 Mass. 544; Cole v. Kigler, 64 Iowa, 59; Everett v. Marquette, 53 Mich. 450. "An ordinance cannot transform into a nuisance an act or thing not treated as such by the statutory or common law." Grossman v. Oakland (Oreg.), 37 L. R. A. 593. In this case an ordinance absolutely prohibiting a railroad company from inclosing its track in the platted portions of the city, and providing that such inclosure should be a nuisance, was held invalid, although the charter conferred power to declare what shall constitute a nuisance.
⁶ Baumgartner v. Hasty, 100 Ind. 575; King v. Davenport, 98 Ill. 305.

cause the building to be destroyed.[1] What constitutes a nuisance must depend upon the particular circumstances of the case. Thus, a structure or act may be a nuisance in a certain locality and not so in another. This is true of smoke, ringing of bells, a tallow factory, blacksmith shop, blasting of rocks, sawing of marble, and the noise of a circus.[2] The ordinary remedy for the abatement of a nuisance is by indictment, although the municipality is also entitled to proceed by way of injunction.[3]

§ 93. *Regulation of wharves.*— A city may, under the police power, require that certain wharves and waters shall be used by certain classes of boats only. Such regulations do not deprive the owners of the wharves of their property without due process of law. They are valid because rendering more convenient and safe the transaction of business in the harbor.[4]

§ 94. *Licenses.*— Power to license occupations and amusements must be plainly conferred, or it cannot be exercised by a municipal corporation.[5] A license may be imposed either as a tax or as a police regulation. When imposed as a tax, its validity is determined by the principles governing taxation. When imposed as a police regulation, it must be for the pur-

---

[1] Shepard v. People, 40 Mich. 487; Czarniecke's Appeal (Pa. St.), 11 Atl. Rep. 660.

[2] Harmon v. Chicago, 110 Ill. 400; St. Paul v. Gilfillan, 36 Minn. 298; Davis v. Sawyer, 133 Mass. 289; Leets v. Pilgrim Church, 14 Mo. App. 590; Bowen v. Mauzy, 117 Ind. 258; McKean v. See, 51 N. Y. 300; Hunter v. Farren, 127 Mass. 481; Inchbold v. Robinson, L. R. 4 Ch. App. 388. The fact that the conditions constituting a nuisance are not the same at all times and places, and that esthetic ideas must sometimes be sacrificed to the demands of commerce, is thus expressed by Lord Justice James in Selvin v. North Brancepeth Coal Co., L. R. 9 Ch. App. 705: "If some picturesque haven opens its arms to invite the commerce of the world, it is not for this court to forbid the embrace, although the fruit of it should be the sights and sounds and smells of a common seaport and ship-building town, which would drive the dryads and their masters from their ancient solitudes."

[3] State v. Anwerda, 40 Iowa, 151; Ottawa v. Chinn, 75 Iowa, 405; Newark Aqueduct Board v. Passaic, 45 N. J. Eq. 393; Stearns Co. v. St. Cloud, etc. Co., 36 Minn. 425.

[4] Cushing v. The John Frazer, 21 How. (U. S.) 184; Backus v. Detroit, 49 Mich. 110, 43 Am. Rep. 447, where the right of a city to establish a public wharf without regard to the question whether a riparian owner has title to the land under water is fully discussed.

[5] State v. Itzkovitch, 49 La. Ann. 366, 21 So. Rep. 544.

pose of preventing some threatened evil, and must not exceed in amount a sum sufficient to cover the expenses of issuing the license and the expense of police supervision.[1] It may be required "for the purpose of insuring the proper police supervision, whenever the character of the trade or business is such that the absence of police supervision would occasion injury to the public dealing with those engaged therein, either because the trade requires a certain degree of skill and professional qualification, or because it furnishes abundant opportunities for the perpetration of fraud, which, without police supervision, would very likely prove successful."[2] As stated by Mr. Justice Mitchell,[3] "It is undoubtedly the law that the right to license must be plainly conferred or it will be held not to exist. The power to make by-laws relative to specified lawful occupations, or the general power to pass prudential by-laws in reference to them, would not as a general rule authorize the municipal corporation to exact a license from those carrying on such business. But in view of the very important bearing which the scavenger business has upon the public health, and the imperative necessity, from sanitary considerations, that such work should be intrusted only to those who are competent and prop-

[1] Mankato v. Fowler, 32 Minn. 364; Von Baalen v. People, 40 Mich. 258, 36 Am. Rep. 522, and authorities cited in note. In Tomlinson v. Indianapolis, 144 Ind. 142, 36 L. R. A. 413, the court said: "The only contention, in truth, which can be plausibly urged against the ordinance is that it charges those who drive upon the streets but live outside the city limits the same license fees charged against those who reside within the city; but we do not think that the ordinance can for this reason be held invalid. The common council, as we have seen, is given by the statute power to pass ordinances 'to regulate the use of streets and alleys by vehicles.' This provision would of itself be sufficient authority to sustain the ordinance. The power to regulate implies the power to license and to exact a reasonable fee for such license. But the statute further expressly provides that the council may pass ordinances 'to license, tax and regulate wheeled vehicles.' This is a police power and not a taxing power. Indianapolis v. Bieler, 138 Ind. 30. The fee charged is but $3 per year. Nor is it any objection to this conclusion that some revenue arises to the city from the fees collected, or that such revenue is applied to the repair of the streets. The streets are used, and in part worn out, and put in a condition needing repair, by the vehicles that are charged the license fee. See Rochester v. Upham, 19 Minn. 108 (Gil. 78); State v. Cassidy, 22 Minn. 321, 21 Am. Rep. 765."

[2] Tiedeman, Limitations on Police Power, § 101.

[3] State v. McMahon (Minn.), 72 N. W. Rep. 79 (1897); Ex parte Garza, 28 Tex. App. 381, 19 Am. St. Rep. 845.

erly equipped to perform it, we are of the opinion that the grant of power to make such regulations and to ordain such ordinances as may be necessary and expedient for the preservation of health and to prevent the introduction of contagious diseases, conferred authority on the common council, as one means of regulating the scavenger business, to require a license from those carrying it on and to prohibit any one from doing so without a license."[1]

The power to tax is distinct from the police power. Its purpose is revenue, while police power is for the purpose of regulation. Thus, a license charge imposed on hackmen of forty dollars per year is clearly intended for the purpose of raising revenue, and not for the purpose of regulation, and hence cannot be sustained under the police power.[2] But an annual license fee of eight dollars, and the cost of numbering the hack, not exceeding twenty-five cents, is valid as a police regulation.[3] Under the police power a municipal corporation may, under proper authority, require a license from peddlers, hackmen, draymen, omnibus drivers, retail liquor dealers, showmen, green grocers, billiard saloons, pawnbrokers, milk dealers, livery-stable keepers, plumbers, bakers and auctioneers.[4] An ordinance providing for a peddler's license which discriminates against nonresidents and goods not manufactured within the municipality is void as an attempt to regulate commerce.[5] Power to license and regulate saloons will not authorize an ordinance forbidding the use of door screens and window blinds in the windows and

[1] Boehm v. Baltimore, 61 Md. 259; Chicago, etc. Co. v. Chicago, 88 Ill. 221; Kinsley v. Chicago, 124 Ill. 359, 19 N. E. Rep. 260. Under a statute authorizing a city "to restrain hawking and peddling," a city may require a license from peddlers. South Bend v. Martin, 142 Ind. 31, 29 L. A. 531.
[2] Jackson v. Newman, 59 Miss. 385, 42 Am. Rep. 367.
[3] Ex parte Gregory, 20 Tex. App. 210, 54 Am. Rep. 516.
[4] Schumann v. Ft. Wayne, 127 Ind. 109, 11 L. R. A. 378; Chicago v. Bartree, 100 Ill. 57; State Centre v. Barenstein, 66 Iowa, 249; St. Paul v. Traeger, 25 Minn. 248; Barling v. West, 29 Wis. 307; People v. Wagner, 86 Mich. 594; State v. Cassidy, 22 Minn. 312. For a collection of cases and illustrations of ordinances imposing license fees, see State v. French, 17 Mont. 54, 39 L. R. A. 415, and note. As to the reasonableness of ordinances of that character, see § 239, and also English and American notes to the case of John v. Mayor of Congdon, 7 Eng. Rul. Cas. 278.
[5] Walton v. Missouri, 91 U. S. 275; Marshalltown v. Bloom, 43 Am. Rep. 116, 58 Iowa, 184. See State v. Wheelock, 95 Iowa, 577, 30 L. R. A. 429.

openings of a saloon. Such an ordinance to be reasonable must be confined in its operations to such times as the saloon is not allowed to do business, as on Sundays and holidays.[1] A city may be authorized to require a license for the use of the streets by vehicles without reference to their business.[2] So it may require a license from those engaged in a business which requires them to go from a place outside of the city to a place within the city, such as a stage[3] or dray line.[4]

§ 95. *Markets.*— The state commonly delegates to municipal corporations power to establish and regulate markets. This power is of a police nature and is designed to protect the health and well-being of the community. A market "is a designated place in a town or city to which all persons can repair who wish to buy or sell articles there exposed for sale. They have been found to be a public convenience when properly regulated. Such regulations as the city authorities may adopt in regard to them should have and generally have reference to the preservation of peace and good order and the health of the city. They should be of a police and sanitary character, and an attempt by color of regulations to restrain trade is an abuse of the power."[5] The market may be placed under the general supervision of the police or of an officer specially appointed for that purpose. Those enjoying market privileges may be required to pay a license therefor.[6] Under power to establish and regulate markets, a city may prohibit the sale of certain articles, such as oysters or beef, at any place other than the market during market hours.[7] But the authority to prohibit the "sale of vegetables during market hours" will not author-

[1] Champer v. Greencastle, 138 Ind. 339.

[2] Tomlinson v. Indianapolis, 144 Ind. 142. See cases collected in a note to this case in 36 L. R. A. 413.

[3] Sacramento v. Colorado Stage Co., 12 Cal. 132.

[4] East St. Louis v. Bux, 43 Ill. App. 276. See Cary v. North Plainfield, 49 N. J. L. 110.

[5] Caldwell v. City of Alton, 33 Ill. 416, 85 Am. Dec. 282, and note citing many cases. See, also, Warthman v. City of Philadelphia, 33 Pa. St. 202; New Orleans v. Stafford, 27 La. Ann. 898, 21 Am. Rep. 561; Robinson v. Mayor of Franklin, 1 Humph. 156, 34 Am. Dec. 625, note; Bethune v. Hughes, 28 Ga. 560, 73 Am. Dec. 789, and note on page 793.

[6] Cincinnati v. Buckingham, 10 Ohio, 257.

[7] Ex parte Canto, 21 Tex. App. 61, 57 Am. Rep. 609; Newson v. Galveston, 76 Tex. 559, 7 L. R. A. 797.

ize the prohibition of such sales at other times.[1] Power to establish and regulate markets carries with it power to purchase a site and erect the necessary buildings thereon.[2] Such power will not authorize the construction of a market building in a public street.[3] But when a city establishes a market in a portion of a public street duly condemned for that purpose, the owners of abutting property have no right of action against the city for damages caused thereby.[4] An ordinance which deprive the producers of market articles of their own raising from selling their produce at first hand to consumers in the principal city market, and compels them to be sold by holders of stalls at second hand, is void.[5]

§ 96. *Prevention of fires.*— A municipal corporation may, in the exercise of its power to protect the lives and property of its citizens, take all reasonable measures to prevent the rise and spread of conflagrations. It may prescribe fire limits and prohibit the construction of wooden buildings within such limits. When it has enacted such a prohibition, it may destroy a building erected in violation thereof without judicial proceedings. This power is generally held to be inherent in the corporation,[6] although some courts hold that it must be expressly conferred.[7] The municipality may legally forbid the erection of a wooden building within the fire limits, although the contract for its construction was made before the ordinance determining the limits was enacted.[8] Under the pressure of a

---

[1] State v. St. Paul, 32 Minn. 329. The authorities upon this point are conflicting. See note to Robinson v. Franklin, 34 Am. Dec. 638, 1 Humph. 156.
[2] Caldwell v. City of Alton, 33 Ill. 416.
[3] Warthman v. Philadelphia, 33 Pa. St. 203; State v. Moyor, 5 Port. (Ala.) 279; St. John v. Mayor, 3 Bosw. (N. Y.) 483.
[4] Ninkle v. City of Detroit, 49 Mich. 249, 43 Am. Rep. 464.
[5] "A city has no right, and the city has never been empowered, to shut out the producers of fresh provisions and similar farm and garden articles from having convenient access to customers. Hughes v. Recorder's Court of Detroit, 75 Mich. 574, 4 L. R. A. 863.
[6] See Baumgartner v. Hastings, 100 Ind. 575; Eischenlaub v. St. Joseph, 113 Mo. 395, 18 L. R. A. 590; King v. Davenport, 98 Ill. 305, 38 Am. Rep. 89; Charleston v. Reed, 27 W. Va. 681, 55 Am. Rep. 336; Klinger v. Bickel, 117 Pa. St. 326; Pratt v. Litchfield, 62 Conn. 112.
[7] Des Moines v. Gilchrist, 67 Iowa, 210; Knoedler v. Norristown, 100 Pa. St. 368; Pye v. Peterson, 45 Tex. 312.
[8] Knoxville v. Byrd, 12 Lea (Tenn.), 121.

controlling public necessity, even "where the owners themselves have fully observed all their duties to their fellows and to the state," private property may be taken and destroyed when necessary to prevent the spread of fire, "the ravages of pestilence, the advance of a hostile army, or any other great public calamity."[1]

§ 97. *Care of the indigent and infirm.*— The care of the indigent and the infirm in body, mind and morals is a duty which may properly be imposed upon a public corporation. The insane, the criminal and the pauper constitute a charge upon the community, and the expenses of their care may be met by taxation. Schools, almshouses and hospitals, when under the control of the public and open to all who need aid, are public institutions. But the power of taxation cannot be employed to support such institutions when they are under the control of private persons who are not accountable to the government.[2] These general principles have been recently discussed in connection with cases growing out of the movement for the care and treatment of habitual drunkards. The decisions have not been uniform, but the rule will probably be established that the public money may legally be used for this purpose. It was held in Maryland that an act authorizing the sending of any habitual drunkard for treatment to any institution within the state at the expense of the county or city, if neither the patient nor the petitioning kinsmen are financially able to pay the expenses, is valid.[3] The court said: "There can be no doubt as to the power of the legislature to require the payment by the city of a sum requisite to defray the expense of maintenance and medical treatment of an habitual drunkard residing within the corporate limits." The decision seems to regard the act as a proper exercise of the police power. The same principle appears to be recognized in Colorado, although the decision turned upon questions of construction. It was there held that

[1] Cooley, Const. Lim. (4th ed.) 746; Saltpetre Case, 6 Coke, 206; Meeker v. Van Rensaeller, 15 Wend. 397; McDonald v. Red Wing, 13 Minn. 38, Gil. 25; Jones v. Richmond, 18 Grat. 517. If damaged grain stored within the limits of a city be found detrimental to the public health it may be destroyed. Dunbar v. Augusta, 90 Ga. 390.
[2] Hare, Am. Const. Law, I. p. 280.
[3] Baltimore v. Keeley Inst. of Maryland (Md.), 27 L. R. A. 647 (1895).

the treatment of inebriates by a private corporation at the expense of a county is not the performance of a municipal function, and that such an appropriation of the county funds is not an appropriation of state moneys within the meaning of the constitution.[1] In Wisconsin a statute providing for the commitment of habitual drunkards who have not the means to pay for treatment to some institution within the state to be designated in the order, " provided that the expense of treatment in each case shall not exceed the sum of one hundred and thirty dollars, which sum shall cover and include all expenses for treatment, medicines and board for four weeks, and such expense shall be paid by the county," was held not within the police power of the state and hence unconstitutional, because requiring the county to expend the proceeds of taxation for a private purpose. The beneficiaries were not "poor" in the technical sense of the word,— destitute, in extreme want or helplessness. They were not the subjects of public charity, nor afflicted with a contagious or infectious disease. "The question then arises," says Chief Justice Cassoday, " whether any county can be compelled to pay any private party for treatment, medicines and board of any resident therein having a disease not contagious or infectious, merely because such diseased person has not the means to pay for such treatment. If a county may be compelled to make such payment for such treatment, medicine and board of a person having such a disease, then it logically follows that every county may be compelled to pay private parties for treatment, medicines and board of any person having any disease, though not contagious or infectious, provided the victim has not the present means of making such payment himself. We are clearly of the opinion that no such power exists."[2]

[1] Re House, 23 Colo. 87, 33 L. R. A. 832 (1896). The case of Senate of Happy Home Club v. Alpena County, 99 Mich. 117, 23 L. R. A. 144, sustains the constitutionality of the Michigan "Jag Law." In Forman v. Hennepin Co., 64 Minn. 371, 67 N. W. Rep. 207 (1896), the act was held invalid because attempting to make an improper delegation of authority. But it may reasonably be inferred that the act would have been sustained on general principles.

[2] Wisconsin Keeley Inst. Co. v. Milwaukee County (Wis.), 36 L. R. A. 55 (1897). See a criticism of this case in 31 Am. Law Rev. 616.

CHAPTER VII.

PARTICULAR POWERS — CONTINUED.

I. POWERS RELATING TO STREETS AND HIGHWAYS.

§ 98. Power over streets.
99. Rights of abutting owners.
100. The proper uses of a street.
101. Obstructions.
102. Temporary uses of street.
103. Power to improve streets.
104. Gas and water pipes.
105. Projecting doors, windows, porches.
106. Railroads in streets.
107. Conditions imposed.
108. Telegraph and telephone poles.
109. Additional servitudes — Compensation to abutting owners.
110. Railways as additional burdens.

§ 111. Telegraph and telephone poles as additional burden.

II. TAXATION AND SPECIAL ASSESSMENTS.

112. Power of taxation.
113. Nature of special assessments.
114. Their constitutionality.
115. Purposes for which local assessments may be levied.
116. Method of apportionment
117. By benefits.
118. The frontage rule.
119. Property exempt from taxation.
120. Collection of assessments.
121. Personal liability for assessments.

I. POWERS RELATING TO STREETS AND HIGHWAYS.

§ 98. *Power over streets.*— The legislature has paramount authority over the streets and highways of a city, and may delegate this power to municipal corporations. It may open and vacate such streets and highways at its will.[1] This general power is not taken away and conferred upon municipalities by a constitutional provision to the effect that the state shall not be interested in any work of internal improvement or vacate or alter any road laid out by the commissioners of highways or any street in any city or village. The municipality continues to act as the agent of the legislature in granting privileges in its streets.[2] But the people have a right to use

[1] Wabash R. Co. v. Defiance, 167 U. S. 88; Gray v. Iowa Land Co., 26 Iowa, 387; O'Connor v. Pittsburgh, 18 Pa. St. 187; People v. Walsh, 96 Ill. 232; Northern Transportation Co. v. Chicago, 99 U. S. 635; Elliott, Roads and Streets, § 562; Prince v. Crocker, 166 Mass. 347, 32 L. R. A. 610.

[2] Detroit Citizens' St. Ry. Co. v. Detroit (Mich.), 68 N. W. Rep. 304, 35 L. R. A. 859 (1896).

the streets for proper purposes, and the legislature cannot under this general power prevent such use.[1] The control over streets and highways is ordinarily given to cities when they fall within municipal limits, and to counties and towns when within their limits. Conflicting claims must be determined by an examination of the charter of the municipality or of the general laws of the state.[2]

§ 99. *Rights of abutting owners.*— The rights of the public and of an owner of property abutting on a street are sometimes conflicting. Such an owner has the rights common to the general public, and in addition thereto certain rights not shared by the public at large which arise out of the relation in which his lot stands to the street in front of it. "These rights," says Judge Dillon, "whether the fee of the street is in the lot-owner or in the city, are rights of property, and are as sacred from legislative invasion as the right to the lot itself. In cities the abutting property is especially dependent upon sewer, gas and water connections; for these the owner has to pay or contribute out of his own purse. He has also to pay or contribute toward the cost of sidewalks and pavements. These expenditures, as well as the relations of his lot to the street, give him a special interest in the street in front of him distinct from that of the public at large. He may make, as of right, all proper uses of the street, subject to the paramount right of the public for all street uses proper, subject to reasonable and proper municipal regulations. Such rights being property rights are, like other property rights, under the protection of the constitution."[3]

§ 100. *The proper uses of a street.*— The primary purpose for which streets and highways are dedicated is free and unobstructed passage. But this means more than the mere right to drive or walk along the street. In an ordinary highway

---

[1] Anderson v. Wellington, 40 Kan. 173, 2 L. R. A. 110; People v. Armstrong, 73 Mich. 288.

[2] Cowan's Case, 1 Overton (Tenn.), 311; Bell v. Foutch, 21 Iowa, 119; State v. Putnam Co. Com'rs, 23 Fla. 632.

[3] The conflicting rights of the public and abutting owners are elaborately discussed in the New York Elevated Railway cases. See Story v. N. Y. Elev. R. Co., 90 N. Y. 122, and Lahr v. Metro. Elev. R. Co., 104 N. Y. 268.

the public requires only the easement of passage and its incidents, but a wider use is required of the streets of a city. Hence the municipality, when acting under proper authority, may permit the streets to be used for any purposes which are not inconsistent with the primary purpose for which they were dedicated.[1]

§ 101. *Obstructions.*— The right of free transit is thus subject to certain necessary and reasonable restrictions. Certain things may constitute a partial obstruction which are nevertheless in aid of the primary purpose of the street. Others may be legally authorized for a short time because of the necessities of the case. But such obstructions must be reasonable; and if an abutting owner is thereby deprived of his easement of access, he can recover damages from the person placing the obstruction in the street, although it was placed there with the consent of the authorities.[2]

§ 102. *Temporary uses of street.*— A city may properly permit the use of a street for the temporary deposit of building material, and may require persons desiring to thus temporarily use the street to give a bond for the protection of the city against damages caused by the improper use of the privilege.[3] But such obstructions must not be permitted to remain so long as to create a nuisance.[4] So, a street may be used temporarily for moving buildings[5] or unloading cars;[6] but in all such instances, those using the right "must so conduct themselves as to discommode others as little as is reasonably practicable, and remove the impediment within a reasonable time, having regard to the circumstances of the case; and when they have done this the law holds them harmless."[7] Under a charter

---

[1] Grand Rapids Elec. L. Co. v. Grand Rapids Gas Co., 33 Fed. Rep. 659.

[2] Fritz v. Hobson, L. R. 14 Ch. Div. 542, annotated in 19 Am. L. Reg. (N. S.) 615; St. Vincent's Orphan Asylum v. Troy, 76 N. Y. 108, 32 Am. Rep. 286. A city may permit the use of bicycles on the sidewalks, provided they do not become a nuisance. See generally, Twilley v. Perkins, 77 Md. 252; Tuller v. Redding, 16 Misc. Rep. 634; Mercer v. Corbin, 117 Ind. 450; Purple v. Greenfield, 138 Mass. 1; Reg. v. Justin, 24 Ont. Rep. 827; Swift v. Topeka, 43 Kan. 671.

[3] McCarthy v. Chicago, 53 Ill. 38; Wood v. Mears, 12 Ind. 515.

[4] Com. v. Passmore, 1 Serg. & R. 217.

[5] Graves v. Shattuc, 85 N. H. 257; State v. Pratt, 52 Minn. 131.

[6] Matthews v. Kelsey, 58 Me. 56.

[7] Davis v. Winslow, 51 Me. 264; Franklin Wharf Co. v. Portland, 67 Me. 46; State v. Pratt, 52 Minn. 131.

giving the common council power to control and regulate the construction of buildings and to regulate the manner of using streets and pavements, it may require the owner or contractor for a building to erect a covered passage-way over the sidewalk in front of a building in process of construction as soon as the first story is completed.[1] Neither the acquiescence of a city in an obstruction or private use of a street by a citizen, nor laches in resorting to legal remedies, nor the statute of limitations, nor equitable estoppel, nor prescription, can defeat the right to maintain a suit in equity to remove the obstructions.[2]

§ 103. *Power to improve streets.*—The legislative power may control and improve the streets when deemed necessary. This power when duly exercised by ordinance will override any license previously given by which the control of the street has been surrendered to any individual or corporation. The right of a city to improve its streets by regrading or otherwise is so essential to its growth and prosperity that the common council of a city can no more deprive itself of that right than it can of its power to legislate for the health, safety and morals of the community. It is a legislative power which cannot be contracted away.[3] An ordinance authorizing a railroad company to erect new bridges of a certain construction, provided it shall

---

[1] Smith v. Milwaukee Builders' Exchange, 91 Wis. 360, 30 L. R. A. 504.

[2] Webb v. Demopolis, 95 Ala. 116, 21 L. R. A. 63; Elliott, Roads and Streets, p. 667 *et seq.* As to adverse possession of a highway, see Meyer v. Graham, 33 Neb. 566, 18 L. R. A. 146, note; Teass v. St. Albans, 38 W. Va. 1, 19 L. R. A. 802, note.

[3] In re Opening First Street, 66 Mich. 42; Bush v. Portland, 19 Oreg. 45, 20 Am. St. Rep. 789; Northern Trans. Co. v. Chicago, 99 U. S. 635; Wabash Ry. Co. v. Defiance, 167 U. S. 88. The legislature of Connecticut passed an act abolishing grade crossings as a menace to public safety. The supreme court of Connecticut held that as grade crossings are in the nature of nuisances, the legislature had a right to cause them to be abated, and to require either party to pay the whole or any portion of the expense; and that it was the settled policy of the state to abolish grade crossings as rapidly as it could reasonably be done, and that all general laws and police regulations affecting railroad corporations were binding upon them without their assent. In affirming this decision the supreme court in N. Y. & N. E. Ry. Co. v. Bristol, 151 U. S. 556, said: "That the governmental power of health protection cannot be contracted away, nor can the exercise of rights granted, nor the use of property be withdrawn from the implied liability to governmental regulation in particulars essential to the preservation of the community from injury." See, also, Wabash Ry. Co.

build sufficient approaches and grade to the bridges and keep them in repair, constitutes a mere license, and not a contract that the bridges or approaches shall remain any particular length of time or that the city will not make new requirements.[1] The power to grade is a continuing power.[2]

§ 104. *Gas and water pipes.*— A city may use the streets for the purpose of laying down gas pipes and water mains.[3] When the supplying of gas and water is let to a contractor, the city may authorize him to tear up the streets in such a manner as is necessary in order to lay pipes and mains. The right to authorize the use of the public streets for such purposes, however, must be directly conferred upon the municipality.[4]

§ 105. *Projecting doors, windows and porches.*— Strictly a person has no right to project his buildings over the line of the street. But a city may be authorized to enact an ordinance which will permit the owners of lots abutting on a street to extend bay-windows and porticos a certain distance over the line. In such a case the adjoining property owner who suffers some inconvenience thereby cannot recover damages.[5] So it

v. Defiance, 167 U. S. 88; Davis v. New York, 14 N. Y. 506; Milhau v. Sharp, 27 N. Y. 611, 84 Am. Dec. 314; Coleman v. Second Ave. Ry. Co., 38 N. Y. 201; Detroit v. Ft. Wayne & D. L R. Co., 95 Mich. 456, 20 L. R. A. 79; C., B. & Q. R. Co. v. Quincy, 139 Ill. 355; Roanoke Gas Co. v. Roanoke, 88 Va. 810. In the Wabash Railway case the court said: "While municipalities, when authorized so to do, doubtless have the power to make certain contracts with respect to the use of their streets, which are obligatory upon them (N. O. Gas L. Co. v. La. L. & H. Co., 115 U. S. 650; N. O. W. W. Co. v. Rivers, 115 U. S. 674; City R. Co. v. Citizens' St. Ry. Co., 166 U. S. 557; Indianapolis v. Ind. Gas L. Co., 66 Ind. 396; Indiana v. Consumers' Gas Trust Co., 140 Ind. 107, 27 L. R. A. 514), the general rule to be extracted from the authorities is that the legislative power vested in municipal bodies is something which cannot be bartered away in such a manner as to disable them from the performance of their public functions."

[1] Wabash Ry. Co. v. Defiance, 167 U. S. 88. As to liability for the cost of changing the grade at a railroad crossing, see Kelley v. Minneapolis, 57 Minn. 294, 26 L. R. A. 92.

[2] Goesler v. Georgetown, 6 Wheat. (U. S.) 593.

[3] Norwich Gas Co. v. Norwich City Gas Co., 25 Conn. 19; Nelson v. La Porte, 33 Ind. 258; Milhau v. Sharp, 27 N. Y. 611, 15 Barb. 193; New Orleans v. Clark, 95 U. S. 644.

[4] State v. Cincinnati Gas Co., 18 Ohio St. 262; Quincy v. Bull, 106 Ill. 337.

[5] Livingston v. Wolf, 136 Pa. St. 519, 20 Am. St. Rep. 937; Garrett v. Janes, 65 Md. 260. See Salisbury v. Andrew, 128 Mass. 336.

may authorize the construction of doors and windows in such manner as to open out upon the street, and of cellars under the sidewalk, with grating and trap-doors opening into the street.[1] Under authority to make "salutary and needful bylaws" and to regulate "the erection and maintenance of balustrades or other projections upon the roof or sides of buildings," a corporation cannot prohibit the maintenance of door-steps in the highway which were placed there under the authority of a statute.[2]

§ 106. *Railroads in streets.*— The legislature may, unless restricted by the constitution, authorize the use of the public streets by a railroad, and may delegate this power to a municipal corporation.[3] "The power of municipalities to authorize railroads to use their streets may be derived either from express grant or by necessary implication. It is a question of some doubt whether the general authority over the streets which is usually given to them empowers them to grant to street railway companies the right to use their streets; but the better rule seems to be that it does.[4] It is believed, however, that the ordinary powers of municipal corporations to regulate and improve their streets and to prevent their obstruction are not in themselves sufficient to enable municipalities to grant the right to use their streets to ordinary commercial railroads,[5] although it has been held that a city may grant such

[1] Irvine v. Wood, 51 N. Y. 224, 10 Am. Rep. 603; O'Linda v. Lathrop, 21 Pick. 292.

[2] Cushing v. Boston, 128 Mass. 330, 35 Am. St. Rep. 393. As to overhanging obstructions and poles in streets in general, see Hawkins v. Sanders, 45 Mich. 491 (awning); Beecher v. People, 38 Mich. 289, 31 Am. Rep. 316 (roof); Reimer's Appeal, 100 Pa. St. 182, 45 Am. Rep. 373 (bay-window); City of Allegheny v. Zimmerman, 95 Pa. St. 287, 40 Am. Rep. 649 (liberty pole); Wellington v. Gregson, 31 Kan. 99, 47 Am. Rep. 482 (post); Day v. Milford. 5 Allen (Mass.), 98 (awning); Salisbury v. Herchenroder, 106 Mass. 458, 8 Am. Rep. 354; French v. Brunswick, 21 Me. 29 (rope); Jones v. Boston, 104 Mass. 75, 6 Am. Rep. 194 (sign); Bohen v. Waseca, 32 Minn. 176, 50 Am. Rep. 564 (awning).

[3] Kennelly v. Jersey City (a trolley system), 57 N. J. L. 293, 26 L. R. A. 281; Koch v. N. Ave. Car Co., 75 Md. 222, 15 L. R. A. 377; Hudson R. T. Co. v. Waterveldt Tp., 135 N. Y. 393, 17 L. R. A. 674; Trustees v. Milwaukee, etc. Co., 77 Wis. 158; Hine v. Keokuk, etc. R. Co., 42 Iowa, 636.

[4] Atchison St. R. Co. v. Mo. Pac. R. R. Co., 31 Kan. 660; Detroit City R. Co. v. Detroit, 64 Fed. Rep. 628; State v. Carrigan, etc. R. Co., 85 Mo. 263.

[5] Ruttles v. Covington, 10 Ky. L. Rep. 766, 10 S. W. Rep. 644; Newell v. Minneapolis, etc. R. Co., 35 Minn.

a right when it is given sole and exclusive control of its streets.¹ It is clear that it cannot grant such a right when a railroad is for the mere private use of an individual."²

§ 107. *Conditions imposed.*— The municipality may attach to a grant such conditions as it deems advisable in order that the use of the streets for purposes of ordinary travel may not be unnecessarily interfered with. Thus, it may regulate the location of railway tracks and telegraph poles, and prescribe rules and regulations for the protection of persons and vehicles.³ Such a grant is taken subject to its burdens, which include such as may be imposed in the future by the exercise of governmental and police powers.⁴

A railway company does not lose its property in the rails by laying them in a public street, and a rival corporation has no right to use them without its consent.⁵ A city is sometimes empowered to grant the right to use the streets for railway purposes upon the condition that the consent of a certain portion of the owners of abutting property be first obtained. Such a provision is a limitation upon the power of the municipality to grant the license.⁶ An agreement to pay a property owner for his consent is invalid.⁷

112; Stanley v. Davenport, 54 Iowa, 463, 37 Am. Rep. 216; Daly v. Georgia, etc. R. Co., 80 Ga. 793, 12 Am. St. Rep. 286.

¹ Kistner v. Indianapolis, 100 Ind. 210.

² Elliott on Railroads, vol. III, § 1077; Glessner v. Anheuser-Busch Ass'n, 100 Mo. 508; Heath v. Des Moines, etc. R. Co., 61 Iowa, 11; Gustafson v. Hamm, 56 Minn. 334.

³ Fath v. Tower Grove, etc. R. R. Co., 105 Mo. 537, 13 L. R. A. 74; State v. Trenton, 53 N. J. L. 132, 11 L. R. A. 410; New Orleans v. N. O. etc. Ry. Co., 40 La. Ann. 587, 4 So. Rep. 512; Detroit v. Detroit City Ry. Co., 37 Mich. 558; Electric Ry. Co. v. Grand Rapids, 84 Mich. 257; Philadelphia v. Ridge Ave. Ry. Co., 143 Pa. St. 444. May require electric cars to be in charge of conductors. State v. Sloan, 48 S. C. 21, 25 S. E. Rep. 898.

⁴ City of Allegheney v. Millville, etc. Ry. Co., 159 Pa. St. 411, 28 Atl. Rep. 202; Pittsburg, etc. Ry. Co. v. Chicago, 159 Ill. 309, 42 N. E. Rep. 781; Textor v. B. & O. Ry. Co., 59 Md. 63, 43 Am. Rep. 340.

⁵ Jersey City, etc. Ry. Co. v. Railroad Co., 20 N. J. Eq. 61.

⁶ Roberts v. Easton, 19 Ohio St. 78; McCarthy v. Chicago, etc. R. R. Co., 112 Ill. 611; Hunt v. Chicago, etc. Ry. Co., 121 Ill. 638; Kennelly v. Jersey City, 57 N. J. L. 293, 26 L. R. A. 281. The permission must be to a legally incorporated company. If given to one not legally in existence, it does not become effective upon incorporation. Homestead St. Ry. Co. v. Pittsburgh, etc. Ry. Co., 166 Pa. St. 162, 27 L. R. A. 388.

⁷ Doane v. Chicago City R. R. Co., 160 Ill. 22, 35 L. R. A. 588.

In a recent well-considered case[1] the following propositions of law were deduced from the cases: (1) If the right of a railroad to occupy the streets of a town or city be dependent solely upon the action of such town or city, the latter may, in granting its consent, prescribe terms for the breach of which the right granted may be forfeited. The power that creates a corporate right may limit its enjoyment.[2] (2) When the law of a state grants permission to railroads to use the streets of towns and cities, but requires the assent of the authorities of such municipal corporation, if the town or city in giving such consent annexes thereto conditions which may operate upon breach thereof to forfeit the license granted, and if such terms are embodied in a separate contract signed by the railroad company, it will be enforced by the courts.[3]

When by the law of a state a railroad company is granted the privilege of constructing its road upon the streets of towns or cities with the assent of the authorities of such towns or cities, the local authorities may, in connection with the consent given, prescribe terms requiring the railroad company to perform such work and do such things as may be necessary to preserve the streets as highways for public use; the things thus prescribed being within the powers granted to such municipal corporation by its charter.[4] But a city cannot impose a condition to the effect that the privilege shall be forfeited unless the road is completed within a specified time to a designated point outside of the city, when the legislature has given the railway company the right to use the streets of the city upon obtaining the consent of the municipality.[5]

[1] Galveston & W. R. Co. v. Galveston (Tex.), 39 S. W. Rep. 96, 36 L. R. A. 33. The authorities upon municipal power to impose conditions when giving consent to a railway in its streets are collected in the notes to this case.

[2] State v. Madison St. Ry. Co., 72 Wis. 612, 1 L. R. A. 771.

[3] Pacific Ry. Co. v. Leavenworth, 1 Dill. C. C. 393; Indianola v. G. W., T. & P. R. Co., 56 Tex. 594.

[4] N. C. R. Co. v. Baltimore, 21 Md. 93; Indianapolis & C. R. Co. v. Lawrenceburg, 34 Ind. 304.

[5] In Galveston & W. R. Co. v. Galveston (Tex., 1897), 39 S. W. Rep. 96, 36 L. R. A. 33, the court said: "It is not denied that the state might have granted to railroad companies the right to occupy the streets and highways without any condition. Therefore the superior authority over this subject rests with the state legislature. The legislature did, in clear and unambiguous terms, grant to railroad companies the right to occupy the streets of towns or cities upon the condition that the consent of such city or town should be first

§ 108. *Telegraph and telephone poles.*— Telegraph and telephone poles cannot be erected in a street or highway without authority, and the municipality has no authority to grant the privilege unless it has been expressly authorized so to do by the legislature.[1]

§ 109. *Additional servitudes — Compensation to abutting owners.*— When a burden is imposed upon a street in addition to that for which it was dedicated, the abutting owners who are injured thereby are entitled to compensation. Many uses are now considered proper which in former times would have been treated as foreign to the purposes of a street or highway.[2] It has often been held that when the fee of the highway is in the public, or in the municipality in trust for the public, the legislature may authorize the use of a street for railway purposes without compensation to the owners of abutting property; but that when the fee is in the abutter and the public has only an easement, the abutter is entitled to compensation when an additional servitude is imposed upon the street.[3] But the tendency is to consider the location of the fee as immaterial, and to award damages to the owners of abutting property whenever an additional burden is imposed upon the street or highway.[4]

§ 110. *Railways as additional burdens.*— The construction of an ordinary steam railway along a street or highway is, according to the prevailing rule, such a change of use as will entitle the owner of abutting property to compensation.[5] But

obtained. When the city of Galveston gave its consent for the railroad company to construct its road over the streets of the city, the condition precedent prescribed by the legislature was fulfilled, and the statutory right attached in favor of the railroad company."

[1] Com. v. Boston, 97 Mass. 555; Irwin v. Great Southern Tel. Co., 37 La. Ann. 63; Julia Bldg. Ass'n v. Bell Tel. Co., 88 Mo. 258.

[2] See the language of Mr. Justice Mitchell in Cater v. N. W. Tel. Exch. Co., 60 Minn. 539, 63 N. W. Rep. 111. The interest of an adjoining land-owner in a highway is "property" within the meaning of a constitutional provision that property cannot be taken without compensation. Pearsall v. Eaton Co. Supervisors, 74 Mich. 558, 4 L. R. A. 193; Gargan v. Louisville, etc. R. Co., 89 Ky. 212, 6 L. R. A. 340.

[3] Dillon, Mun. Corp., § 702; Indianapolis, etc. Ry. Co. v. Hartley, 67 Ill. 439, 16 Am. Rep. 624.

[4] Theobald v. Louisville, etc. Ry. Co., 66 Miss. 279, 4 L. R. A. 735; Dillon, Mun. Corp. (6th ed.), § 704 a.

[5] Elliott, Roads and Streets, p. 160, and cases cited.

more difficult questions arise when we come to consider ordinary street railways. The decisions are not in entire accord, but when the fee of the street is in the public, it may be taken as the law that such a railway is not an additional servitude.[1] According to the great weight of authority, electric street railways are governed by the same principles as ordinary street railways.[2] In reference to the poles used by an electric railway the supreme court of Michigan said:[3] They "are a necessary part of the system. Where they do not interfere with the owner's access to and the use of his land, we see no rea-

[1] Fobes v. Rome, W. & O. R. Co., 121 N. Y. 505, 8 L. R. A. 453, annotated; People v. Kerr, 27 N. Y. 188; Storey v. N. Y. Elev. Ry. Co., 90 N. Y. 122; Lehr v. Metr. Elev. Ry. Co., 104 N. Y. 268; Eichels v. Evansville St. Ry. Co., 78 Ind. 261. See Cooley, Const. Lim. 545.

[2] Howe v. West End St. Ry. Co., 167 Mass. 46; Taggart v. Newport St. Ry. Co., 16 R. I. 668, 7 L. R. A. 205; Lockhart v. Railway Co., 139 Pa. St. 419; Halsey v. Rapid Tr. St. Ry. Co., 47 N. J. Eq. 380, 20 Atl. Rep. 859; State v. Trenton R. Co., 58 N. J. L. 666, 33 L. R. A. 129; Detroit City Ry. Co. v. Mills, 85 Mich. 634; Koch v. North Ave. Ry. Co., 75 Md. 222, 15 L. R. A. 377. In Kennelly v. Jersey City, 57 N. J. L. 293, 26 L. R. A. 281, the court said: "A fundamental question lying at the basis of matters which we must consider in passing upon the objections of the prosecutor is whether the trolley system of propelling street cars, involving as it does the erection of poles and wire on land the fee of which is private property, is within the public easement over urban highways. In our judgment it is. That easement includes the right to use the streets for purposes of passage by the public, and therefore to employ any means directly conducive to that end which do not substantially interfere with the customary use of the street by any portion of the public, or with the recognized rights of abutting owners. The cars propelled by the trolley system do not materially differ either in appearance or use from the ordinary horse cars. They are permitted to go along the streets in such manner only as is compatible with customary modes of travel by others of the public (Newark Pass. R. Co. v. Block, 55 N. J. L. 605), and the tracks, poles and wires cause no greater detriment to adjoining property than do the tracks, sewers, pipes, posts and trees which indisputably the public may authorize to be placed in the streets. These considerations, we think, lead to the conclusion reached by the learned vice-chancellors of this state in Halsey v. Rapid Street R. Co., 47 N. J. Eq. 380, 391, and Paterson Horse R. Co. v. Grundy, 51 N. J. Eq. 213, 228, and by the learned chancellor in West Jersey R. Co. v. Camden & W. R. Co., 52 N. J. 31, 29 Atl. Rep. 423, that the adoption of the trolley system for the conveyance of passengers through the streets of a city does not necessitate the invasion of any private rights." See Placke v. Union Depot Co. (Mo., 1897), 41 S. W. Rep. 915. An electric street railway upon a highway is an additional servitude. Conastota Knife Co. v. Newington Tramway Co., 69 Conn. 146, 36 Atl. Rep. 1107.

[3] Detroit City Ry. Co. v. Mills, 85 Mich. 634.

son why they should be held to constitute an additional servitude. Certainly they constitute no injury to his reversionary interest. To constitute an additional servitude, therefore, they must be an injury to the present use and enjoyment of the land. But they do not obstruct the light or his vision as do the structures of an elevated railroad. Neither they nor the cars they assist in moving cause the noise, steam, smoke and dirt which are produced by steam cars. They do not interfere with his going and coming at his pleasure when placed as they can and must be so as to give him free access." A surface street railway operated by steam motor engines, but used exclusively for carrying passengers, and stopping upon the street crossings after the manner of an ordinary street railway, is not an additional burden upon the street.[1] The same conclusion has been reached by the courts of Illinois with reference to an elevated railway.[2]

§ 111. *Telegraph and telephone poles as servitudes.*— The authorities are not in harmony on the question whether telegraph and telephone poles constitute an additional burden upon a public street or highway. In some cases the location of the fee is made the test.[3] In Missouri it was held that an injunction would not issue to restrain the erection of a proper telegraph pole in front of a man's premises, when the fee was in the abutter.[4] The Missouri decisions were followed in Louisiana, and the same rule prevails in New Jersey, Michigan and Massachusetts.[5] In Minnesota it was held by a divided court that telephone poles constructed along the side of a country highway, the fee of which was in the abutter, do not constitute an additional servitude upon the highway.[6] But the weight of

[1] Newell v. Railway Co., 35 Minn. 112, 59 Am. Rep. 303. As to waterpipes in a street, see Kincaid v. Indianapolis Nat. Gas Co., 124 Ind. 577, 8 L. R. A. 602; Sterling's Appeal, 111 Pa. St. 35; Note to Western R. Co. v. Ala. etc. R. Co., 17 L. R. A. 474, 96 Ala. 272.

[2] Doane v. Lake Street Elev. R. Co., 165 Ill. 510, 46 N. E. Rep. 510, 36 L. R. A. 97.

[3] See Keasby, Electric Wires, p. 73.

[4] Gay v. Mut. U. T. Co., 12 Mo. App. 485 (1882); Forsyth v. B. & O. Tel. Co., 12 Mo. App. 494; Julia Building Ass'n v. Bell Tel. Co., 88 Mo. 258.

[5] Erwin v. G. S. Tel. Co., 87 La. Ann. 63; Halsey v. Rapid Tr. Ry. Co., 47 N. J. Eq. 380, 20 Atl. Rep. 859; People v. Eaton, 100 Mich. 208; Pierce v. Drew, 136 Mass. 75; McCormick v. District of Columbia, 4 Mackey, 396, 54 Am. Rep. 284, and note.

[6] Cater v. N. W. Tel. Exch. Co., 60

authority sustains the view that telegraph and telephone lines constitute an additional servitude upon the streets of a city.[1] But there is no question as to the right of the abutting owner to relief for any substantial obstruction to his right of access or interference with his enjoyment of the street.

II. Taxation and Special Assessments.

§ 112. *Power of taxation.*—The power of taxation is an attribute of sovereignty. In contemplation of law it is always imposed by the state, although it may act through the agency of a public corporation.[2] Almost all municipal corporations have power to levy taxes for certain purposes. It is ordinarily conferred in express terms,[3] but like other powers it may be implied. Thus, when a municipal corporation is expressly empowered to borrow money, it has implied authority to levy a tax to raise the money to meet the obligation.[4] But the mere fact of incorporation does not carry with it the power of taxation.[5] The power can be legally exercised for public purposes

Minn. 539, 63 N. W. Rep. 111. Chief Justice Start, dissenting, said: "The adjudged cases upon this subject are conflicting, but the later cases and the weight of authority sustain the doctrine that a telegraph or telephone line along the highway, where the fee thereof is in the abutting owner, is foreign to its use and an additional servitude, for which such owner is entitled to compensation; and that the legislature cannot authorize the imposition of such servitude without also providing for such compensation."

[1] Eels v. American T. & T. Co., 143 N. Y. 133, 38 N. E. Rep. 202; W. U. Tel. Co. v. Williams, 86 Va. 696, 8 L. R. A. 429; Chesapeake P. Tel. Co. v. Mackenzie, 74 Md. 36, 21 Atl. Rep. 690. 28 Am. St. Rep. 219, and note; Stowers v. Postal Tel. & C. Co., 68 Miss. 559, 12 L. R. A. 864; B. & W. R. Co. v. Hartley, 67 Ill. 439; Willis v. Erie L. & T. Co., 37 Minn. 347; Board of Trade T. Co. v. Barnet, 107 Ill. 507; American T. & T. Co. v. Pearce, 71 Md. 535, 7 L. R. A. 200. Congress may confer the right upon a telegraph company to construct its lines over all post roads, and under this power "a telegraph company can obtain a right of way for its poles and wires through and along the streets of a city without the consent of the municipality." Southern Bell Tel. Co. v. City of Richmond, 78 Fed. Rep. 858, and cases cited therein.

[2] Whiting v. West Point, 88 Va. 905, 15 L. R. A. 860, note.

[3] See Ould v. Richmond, 23 Gratt. 464, 14 Am. Rep. 139.

[4] United States v. New Orleans, 98 U. S. 381. And see Lowell v. Boston, 111 Mass. 454.

[5] Cooley Taxation (2d ed.), 464, and cases cited. In Minot v. West Roxbury, 112 Mass. 1, the court said: "It is well settled by our own decisions that towns derive all their authority to tax their inhabitants from the statutes; if the authority to tax for a particular purpose is not found there, either in express terms or by

only.[1] Being a governmental power it cannot be granted in perpetuity, but may be revoked at any time.[2] A municipality cannot, even for a consideration,[3] exempt certain property from taxation without special legislative authority.[4]

§ 113. *Nature of special assessments.*— The special form of taxation known as local assessments has some features which distinguish it from general taxation.[5] Although much criticised and sometimes disapproved of, it is now settled that the legislature may authorize municipal corporations to levy special assessments upon property so situated as to be specially benefited by certain public improvements. In order, however, that a municipality may exercise this power it must be able to show legislative authority therefor. Ordinarily the statute provides in detail the manner in which the power is to be exercised. But when the power is conferred in general words it confers all the authority essential to the execution of the power by the ordinary and appropriate methods.[6] Such assessments are a peculiar species of taxation, "standing apart from the general burden imposed for state and municipal purposes, and governed by principles which do not apply universally. The general levy of taxes is understood to exact contribution in return for the general benefits of government; and it promises nothing to the persons taxed beyond what may be anticipated from an administration of the laws for individual protection and the general public good. Special assessments, on the other hand,

necessary implication, it does not exist." Coolidge v. Brookline, 114 Mass. 592. And see Drummer v. Cox, 165 Ill. 648, 46 N. E. Rep. 716.

[1] Lowell v. Boston, 111 Mass. 454; Lund v. Chippewa Co., 93 Wis. 640, 84 L. R. A. 131; Wisconsin Keeley Inst. Co. v. Milwaukee Co., 95 Wis. 153, 70 N. W. Rep. 68, 36 L. R. A. 55; People v. Mayor, 4 N. Y. 421; Doggert v. Colgan, 92 Cal. 53, 14 L. R. A. 474, and cases in note; Fallbrook Irrigation District v. Bradley, 164 U. S. 112.

[2] Williamson v. New Jersey, 130 U. S. 190; New Orleans v. Waterworks, 142 U. S. 79.

[3] Austin v. Austin Gas Co., 69 Tex.

180. But see Grant v. Davenport, 36 Iowa, 396.

[4] Whiting v. West Point, 88 Va. 905, 15 L. R. A. 860, and note; Altgelt v. San Antonio, 81 Tex. 436,·16 L. R. A. 383; State v. Hannibal & St. J. R. Co., 75 Mo. 209; New Orleans v. New Orleans, etc. Co., 35 La. Ann. 548.

[5] That an assessment for benefits is in the nature of a tax is no longer questioned. Sargent v. Tuttle, 67 Conn. 162, 34 Atl. Rep. 1028, 32 L. R. A. 822. But power to tax will not authorize a local assessment. Macon v. Patty, 57 Miss. 378.

[6] Raleigh v. Pease, 110 N. C. 32, 17 L. R. A. 33L

are made upon the assumption that a portion of the community is to be specially and particularly benefited, in the enhancement of the value of property peculiarly situated as regards a contemplated expenditure of public funds; and in addition to the general levy they demand that special contribution in consideration of the special benefit shall be made by the persons receiving it. The justice of demanding the special contribution is supposed to be evident in the fact that the persons who are to make it, while they are made to bear the cost of a public work, are at the same time to suffer no pecuniary loss thereby, their property being increased in value by the expenditure to an amount at least equal to the sum they are required to pay. This is the idea that underlies all these levies."[1] The levy of such an assessment must not be confounded with the exercise of the power of eminent domain.[2]

§ 114. *Their constitutionality.*—The cases in which the constitutionality of local assessments has been discussed turn largely upon the construction of the language of the particular constitution under consideration, and upon the method of apportionment.[3] The right to levy such assessments is as well established as it is possible by judicial decisions to establish any legal principle.[4] They do not constitute a taking of property without due process of law or without compensation to the owner.[5] Due process of law does not require a judicial proceeding. There must be an orderly proceeding by a tribunal provided by law, but the determination of the proceeding, and the tribunal, rests with the legislature. It is essential, however, that the

---

[1] Cooley, Taxation, p. 606; Duluth v. Dibblee, 62 Minn. 18; Brooks v. Baltimore, 48 Md. 265. Mr. Burroughs (Taxation, p. 460) says: "An assessment for improvements is not considered as a burden, but as an equivalent or compensation in the enhanced value which the property derives from the improvement."

[2] Raleigh v. Pease, 110 N. C. 32; Lewis, Eminent Domain, § 4. For a history of the principle and a discussion of the difference between general taxation and local assessments, see Macon v. Patty, 57 Miss. 378. For a discussion of the justice and equity of this system of taxation, see Municipality v. Dunn, 10 La. Ann. 57; Elliott, Roads and Streets, § 370; Hare, Am. Const. Law, vol. I, p. 301.

[3] State v. Reis, 38 Minn. 371; Stinson v. Smith, 8 Minn. 366.

[4] See many cases cited in a note to Ivanhoe v. Enterprise, 35 L. R. A. 58, 29 Oreg. 245.

[5] Hoyt v. East Saginaw, 19 Mich. 39; Pray v. North Liberties, 31 Pa. St. 69; Bridgeport v. Railway Co., 36 Conn. 255; Holton v. Milwaukee, 31 Wis. 27.

owner shall at some stage of the proceeding have an opportunity to be heard. If such provision is made, and the owner has the opportunity to be heard upon the question of what proportion of the tax shall be assessed upon his land, there is not a taking of the property without due process of law.[1] "When the opportunity to be heard respecting the assessment is afforded the taxpayer in an action, there has been given him all that the guaranty of due process of law requires and secures; and he has nothing to complain of in regard to such process."[2] The manner of giving notice of the proceedings may be prescribed by the legislature and may be by publication.[3] It is not necessary that there should be a provision for appeal from the decision of the determining body. As said by the supreme court of Pennsylvania, such assessments " have always been regarded as a species of taxation, which within well-defined limits is constitutional and proper, without provision for such appeals from the action of those intrusted with the duty of making and revising such assessments. The principle is too firmly settled by a long line of cases to be now changed."[4]

§ 115. *Purposes for which local assessments may be levied — Benefits.*— The purposes for which special assessments may be made are numerous. There must exist the ordinary elements of taxation, and in addition thereto the improvement upon which the assessment is based must be productive of special local benefit to the property upon which it is assessed.[5] The

[1] Duluth v. Dibblee, 62 Minn. 18.
[2] Reclamation Dist. v. Goloman, 65 Cal. 635, 4 Pac. Rep. 678; Paulson v. City of Portland, 149 U. S. 30; McMillan v. Anderson, 95 U. S. 37; Spencer v. Merchant, 125 U. S. 345; Overing v. Foote, 65 N. Y. 262; Stewart v. Palmer, 74 N. Y. 183; People v. Hager, 52 Cal. 171. As to right of owner to interpose objections to regularity of proceedings after judgment of confirmation, see Kochersperger v. Markley, 166 Ill. 48, 46 N. E. Rep. 742.
[3] Paulson v. City of Portland, *supra;* Lent v. Tillson, 140 U. S. 316; County of Hennepin v. Bartleson, 37 Minn. 343. As to sufficiency of notice, see Lawrence v. Webster, 167 Mass. 513, 46 N. E. Rep. 123. As to necessity for notice, Landis v. Borough of Vineland (N. J.), 37 Atl. Rep. 965.
[4] Oil City v. Oil City Boiler Works, 152 Pa. St. 348; Harrisburg v. Segelbaum, 151 Pa. St. 172; Michener v. Philadelphia, 118 Pa. St. 535; Hammett v. Philadelphia, 65 Pa. St. 146.
[5] In re Wash. Ave., 69 Pa. St. 352; Allen v. Drew, 44 Vt. 174; Title Guarantee & T. Co. v. Chicago, 162 Ill. 505. The general rule is that a local assessment is constitutional only when it confers a special bene-

local improvement must partake of a permanent nature, and the benefit must flow from an actual improvement.[1] Hence, a local assessment should not be made for sprinkling streets,[2] or for the maintenance and repair of boulevards and pleasure ways.[3] But such assessments are often made, and it is said that they may be made for any purpose that tends to make a street more suitable and convenient for the use of the public, such as grading,[4] changing a grade,[5] paving,[6] altering or widening streets,[7] or constructing sidewalks.[8] Assessments to pay the cost of repaving a street are generally sustained.[9] So the expense of constructing drains in order to carry off stagnant water which may become detrimental to health may be met by the levy of special assessments.[10] And "where any considerable tract of land owned by different persons is in a condition precluding cultivation by reason of excessive moisture, which drains would relieve, it may well be said that the public has such an interest in the improvement and the consequent advancement of the general interests of the locality as will justify the levy of assessments upon the owners for drainage purposes. Such a case

---

fit. The cases are collected in a note, 14 L. R. A. 756. The contrary doctrine is held in Re Bonds of Madeira Irrigation District, 92 Cal. 296, 14 L. R. A. 755.

[1] In re Bonds of Madeira Irr. Dist., 92 Cal. 296, 14 L. R. A. 755.

[2] Chicago v. Blair, 149 Ill. 310, 24 L. R. A. 412, and cases cited in note. *Contra*, State v. Reis, 38 Minn. 371, where the court said: "The only essential elements of a 'local improvement' are those which the term implies, viz., that it shall benefit the property on which the cost is assessed in a manner local in its nature and not enjoyed by property generally in the city. If it does this,— rendering the property more attractive and comfortable, and hence more valuable for use,— then it is an improvement."

[3] Crane v. West Chicago Park Com., 153 Ill. 348, 26 L. R. A. 311. An assessment may be made to pay the expenses of sweeping a street. Reinken v. Fuehring, 130 Ind. 382, 15 L. R. A. 624.

[4] Wray v. Pittsburgh, 46 Pa. St. 365.

[5] La Fayette v. Fowler, 34 Ind. 140.

[6] Schenley v. Com., 36 Pa. St. 29; Petition of Burmeister, 76 N. Y. 174. In Dewey v. Des Moines (Iowa), 70 N. W. Rep. 605, it is held that a street-paving improvement is a public improvement which will support a special assessment upon abutting owners regardless of benefits.

[7] Jones v. Boston, 104 Mass. 461.

[8] Flint v. Webb, 25 Minn. 93; Sloane v. Beebe, 24 Kan. 343; White v. People, 94 Ill. 604.

[9] Willard v. Presburg, 14 Wall. 676; Sheley v. Detroit, 45 Mich. 431; Gurnee v. Chicago, 40 Ill. 165; Matter of Phillips, 60 N. Y. 16; In re Smith, 99 N. Y. 424. *Contra*, see Hammett v. Philadelphia, 65 Pa. St. 146: Wistar v. Philadelphia, 80 Pa. St. 505.

[10] Reeves v. Wood Co., 8 Ohio St. 333; People v. Haines, 49 N. Y. 587.

would seem to stand upon the same solid ground with assessments for levee purposes, which have for their object to protect lands from falling into a condition of uselessness.[1] But under the rule of strict construction of powers to tax, authority to drain lands for public health, and to lay assessments therefor, will not support an assessment the main cost of which is for filling in land."[2] Under power to make and maintain highways and streets by special assessments, a city has authority to levy such assessments for the construction of sewers and culverts on the theory that they are simply street improvements.[3] So the cost of laying water pipes may be levied upon property benefited thereby. "The benefits are local, as the use of the water must necessarily be mostly restricted to the property on the lines both for domestic purposes and the extinguishment of fires. The effect of supplying the streets with water is to enhance the value of dwelling-houses thereon."[4]

§ 116. *Method of apportionment.*— The cost of a public improvement may be met in part by a general tax and in part by special assessment levied upon the property particularly benefited. In fixing the basis of apportionment between individuals, there are two methods in common use:

1. An assessment made by assessors or commissioners appointed for the purpose under legislative authority, who are to view the estates and levy the expense in proportion to the benefits which in their opinion the estates will receive from the improvements proposed.

2. An assessment by some definite standard fixed upon by the legislature itself, and which is applied to estates by measurements of length, quantity or value.[5]

The determination of the question whether an improvement is general or local is a legislative question, and the action of a city council pursuant to authority vested in it by the legisla-

[1] French v. Kirkland, 1 Paige, 117; Hager v. Supervisors, 47 Cal. 222; Hager v. Reclamation Dist., 111 U. S. 701; Fallbrook Irrigation District v. Bradley, 164 U. S. 112.
[2] Cooley, Taxation, p. 618; Petition of Van Buren 79 N. Y. 384. As to levees, see Williams v. Commack, 27 Miss. 209.
[3] Hungerford v. Hartford, 39 Conn. 279; Wright v. Boston, 9 Cush. 233; Grinnell v. Des Moines, 57 Iowa, 144.
[4] Allentown v. Henry, 73 Pa. St. 404.
[5] Cooley, Taxation, 638.

ture is not subject to review by the courts. These questions must necessarily be left to the judgment of men. Thus, where the charter provided that it should be determined by a board of public works, the court said: "Their judgment is final and conclusive, and cannot be reviewed by the district court or any other tribunal unless shown to be fraudulent in fact, or unless it is made up upon a demonstrable mistake of fact."[1] With reference to a similar case the supreme court of Michigan said: "These officers acted within the scope of their powers, and the record contains no evidence of fraud, corrupt motive or favoritism. The presumption is that in making the district and the assessment the officers of the municipality acted in good faith, and have correctly and faithfully exercised the discretion vested in them. In such case, where mistake or abuse of discretion is not manifest or demonstrable, the determination of municipal officers in whom such discretion is vested is conclusive and not reviewable by the courts."[2]

§ 117. *By benefits.*— The right to assess for benefits, as we have seen, is no longer open to question. When the assessment is apportioned according to the benefits accruing to the property, the legislature or the municipality, when duly authorized, may determine over what territory the benefits are diffused, or it may provide for the appointment of assessors or commissioners with authority to make the assessment upon such lands as in their judgment are specially benefited. As stated in the preceding section, the determination of questions of fact in these proceedings, when free from fraud or manifest mistake, is not open to review by the courts.[3] It must not be understood, however, that any assessment or apportionment which the legislature or commissioners may make will be permitted to stand by the court. The proceedings must comply strictly

---

[1] State v. Board of Public Works, 27 Minn. 442; State v. District Court, 29 Minn. 62; Spencer v. Merchant, 100 N. Y. 585; Michner v. Philadelphia, 118 Pa. St. 535. The findings of commissioners will not be disturbed by courts save for manifest error. In re Amberson Ave. (Pa.), 36 Atl. Rep. 854 (1897).

[2] Powers v. City of Grand Rapids, 98 Mich. 393, 57 N. W. Rep. 250. As to the effect of fraud in the determination to pave a street, see Dewey v. Des Moines (Iowa), 70 N. W. Rep. 605.

[3] Dewey v. Des Moines (Iowa), 70 N. W. Rep. 605, and cases cited.

with the requirements of the statute. The improvement must be of a public nature, and the benefit accruing must result especially to the property upon which the assessment is made. A work of general benefit cannot be treated as a special benefit and the costs assessed upon certain property.[1]

§ 118. *The frontage rule.*— The apportionment of benefits according to what is known as the frontage rule is very common. Under it the line of frontage is taken as the most practical test of probable benefits. When applied to city property it is probably as equitable as any other system that can be adopted. As said by a recent writer: "The system which leads to the least mischievous and unjust consequences is that which takes into account the entire line of the way improved and apportions the expense according to the frontage; for it takes into consideration the benefit to each property owner that accrues from the improvement of the entire line of the way, and does not impose upon the lot-owner an unjust portion of the burden."[2] The right to apportion assessments according to this rule is no longer open to controversy.[3] It seems, however, that it is not applicable to farm lands or suburban property.

[1] Baltimore v. Hughes, 1 Gill & J. 265. See Thomas v. Gaines, 35 Mich. 155; Seely v. Pittsburgh, 82 Pa. St. 360, 22 Am. Rep. 760; In re Wash. Ave., 69 Pa. St. 352; Title Guarantee & T. Co. v. Chicago, 162 Ill. 505. See the statement of the rule and its exception in Raleigh v. Pease, 110 N. C. 32.

[2] Elliott, Roads and Streets, § 396.

[3] Sheley v. Detroit, 45 Mich. 431; Palmyra v. Morton, 25 Mo. 594; Rutherford v. Hamilton, 97 Mo. 543; Farrar v. St. Louis, 80 Mo. 379; Galesburg v. Searles, 114 Ill. 217; White v. People, 94 Ill. 604; Craw v. Tolono, 96 Ill. 255, 35 Am. Rep. 143; Springfield v. Green, 120 Ill. 269; Springfield v. Sale, 127 Ill. 359; O'Reilley v. Kingston, 114 N. Y. 439; Bacon v. Savannah, 86 Ga. 301; Whiting v. Townsend, 57 Cal. 515; Palmer v. Stumph, 29 Ind. 329; Parker v. Challis, 9 Kan. 155. Modified by combining valuation and frontage in Newman v. Emporia, 41 Kan. 583; Ludlow v. Cincinnati S. R. Co., 78 Ky. 357; State v. Gardner, 34 N. J. L. 327; Corry v. Holtz, 29 Ohio St. 320; M'Gee v. Com., 46 Pa. St. 358; Beaumont v. Wilkesbarre, 142 Pa. St. 198; Davis v. Lynchburg, 84 Va. 861; State v. Reis, 38 Minn. 371; State v. Norton, 63 Minn. 497; Raleigh v. Peace, 110 N. C. 32, 17 L. R. A. 330, and note, where these and many other cases are cited. The contrary was held in McBean v. Chandler, 9 Heisk. (Tenn.) 349; Peay v. Little Rock, 32 Ark. 31, and Chicago v. Larned, 34 Ill. 253. The latter case was overruled by the decisions cited in the preceding note. Railroad property may be taxed on the basis of frontage for sewer and water connection improvements. Palmer v. Danville, 166 Ill. 42, 46 N. E. Rep. 629.

With reference to such an assessment the supreme court of Pennsylvania says that it is "unequal, unjust and unconstitutional."[1] But the entire cost of the improvement in front of a lot cannot be levied upon that lot. Such a proceeding violates every principle of equality and apportionment.[2]

§ 119. *Property exempt from taxation.*— Although local assessments are made by virtue of the taxing power they are not taxes within the meaning of the word as used in statutes exempting certain property from taxation.[3] Express words are necessary to exempt from general taxation or special assessment.[4] In the following cases the language used was held not to include assessments for local improvements: Taxation of every kind,[5] taxes of every kind,[6] all taxation,[7] all taxes, either by state, parish or city,[8] all public taxes,[9] rates and assessments,[10] all and every county road, city and school tax,[11] exempt from taxation of every description,[12] taxes, charges and imposi-

---

[1] Philadelphia v. Rule, 93 Pa. St. 15; Seely v. Pittsburgh, 82 Pa. St. 360, 22 Am. Rep. 760; McKeesport v. Soles, 178 Pa. St. 363, 35 Atl. Rep. 927. In Garham v. Conger, 85 Ky. 583, the system of local assessments is held not to apply to rural lands when it is sought to levy the cost of expenses of street improvements upon them. Under certain conditions, however, farm lands may be subjected to an assessment. Thus, although the laying of water supply pipes in a street on which a farm abuts may not benefit the farm in its present condition, it is subject to assessment for benefits if the value is thereby increased for any use for which the land is adapted. Clark v. Chicago, 166 Ill. 84, 46 N. E. Rep. 730, distinguishing Hutt v. Chicago, 132 Ill. 352, and Edwards v. Chicago, 140 Ill. 440.

[2] Moutz v. Detroit, 18 Mich. 495; Morrison v. St. Paul, 5 Minn. 108; State v. Jersey City, 37 N. J. L. 128; Davis v. Litchfield, 145 Ill. 313, 21 L. R. A. 563, note. *Contra,* Weeks v. Milwaukee, 10 Wis. 258; Warren v. Henley, 31 Iowa, 31.

[3] Ford v. Delta, etc. Co., 164 U. S. 662; Farwell v. Des Moines (Iowa, 1897), 35 L. R. A. 63; In re Mayor of New York, 11 John. 77; Baltimore v. Cemetery Co., 7 Md. 517; Oliver Cemetery Co. v. Philadelphia, 93 Pa. St. 129; Bridgeport v. Railway Co., 36 Conn. 255; Chicago v. Baptist Theo. Union, 115 Ill. 245; Atlanta v. First Presb. Church, 86 Ga. 730, 12 L. R. A. 852, and cases in note.

[4] Lima v. Cemetery Ass'n, 42 Ohio St. 128.

[5] Sheehan v. Good Samaritan Hospital, 50 Mo. 155, 11 Am. Rep. 112.

[6] Ill. Cent. Ry. Co. v. Decatur, 126 Ill. 92, 1 L. R. A. 613.

[7] Winona & St. P. Ry. Co. v. Watertown, 1 S. Dak. 46, 44 N. W. Rep. 1072.

[8] La Fayette v. Male Orphans' Asylum, 4 La. Ann. 1.

[9] Buffalo City Cemetery v. Buffalo, 46 N. Y. 506.

[10] Northern Liberties v. St. John's Church, 13 Pa. St. 104.

[11] Illinois & M. Canal v. Chicago, 12 Ill. 403.

[12] Patterson v. Society, 24 N. J. L. 385.

tions,[1] charges and impositions,[2] any tax or public imposition whatever,[3] a tax on franchises in lieu of all other taxes,[4] exempt from taxation,[5] exempt from all taxation by state or local laws for any purpose whatever.[6] Land owned by a railroad company and held in anticipation of being needed for railroad purposes at an indefinite future time is not exempt from assessments for street improvements under a statute providing for the payment of a percentage of the gross earnings in lieu of other taxes and assessments.[7] An assessment is not invalidated by exempting certain property belonging to the state.[8]

§ 120. *Collection of assessments.*— Special assessments must be collected in the way provided in the statute. It is generally provided that the contractor who does the work shall look to the assessment on the lot for his compensation. It is sometimes provided that the contractor shall make the collection; and in such case there is no liability on the part of the city. When, however, it is provided that the city shall make the collection it acts as a representative of the contractor, and is not liable to him unless its officers fail in their duty and thus prejudice the rights of the contractor.[9] Thus, when it is provided that the contractor shall perform the work and furnish the materials required under his contract according to the plans and specifications, and be entitled to his pay when the fund for that purpose shall be assessed, levied and collected by the regular agencies of the city, he has a right to rely upon the implied obligation of the city to use with due diligence its own agencies in procuring the means to satisfy his claims. If the city neglects to perform its duty he may recover such damages from it as he

[1] State v. Newark, 27 N. J. L. 185.
[2] Baltimore v. Proprietors, 7 Md. 517.
[3] Bridgeport v. N. Y. & N. H. Ry. Co., 36 Conn. 255, 4 Am. Rep. 63.
[4] Boston Seamen's Friend Society v. Boston, 116 Mass. 181, 19 Am. Rep. 153; Roosevelt Hospital v. New York, 84 N. Y. 108.
[5] Zable v. Louisville Baptist Orphans' Home, 92 Ky. 89, 13 L. R. A. 668.
[6] The cases with reference to church property are collected in note to Atlanta v. First Presb. Church, 86 Ga. 730, 13 L. R. A. 85℥.
[7] In re Assessment for Grading Prior Ave. (Minn.), 71 N. W. Rep. 27.
[8] Doyle v. Austin, 47 Cal. 353; Worcester Co. v. Worcester, 116 Mass. 193. The cases are reviewed in Atlanta v. First Presb. Church, *supra*.
[9] Chambers v. Satterlee, 40 Cal. 497; Lovell v. St. Paul, 10 Minn. 290. If the city agrees to collect the assessment and fails to do so it is liable to the contractor. Morgan v. Dubuque, 28 Iowa, 575.

suffers by reason of such neglect.¹ So a city is liable to a contractor for damages occasioned to him by reason of its mistake in the construction of the law, as where the ordinance under which the assessment was made was held void, and some of the claims for benefits were outlawed before a re-assessment could be made.² When the proper authorities have accepted the work as satisfactory it is conclusive, and the property owner cannot defend against the assessment by showing that the work is not properly performed. "No misconstruction nor malconstruction of the work arising from the incapacity, the honest mistake or the fraud of the contractor would invalidate the assessment or relieve the parties assessed from the obligation to pay it. In this respect the property owners assessed under the provisions of the law for the cost of a sewer must stand upon the same footing with parties assessed for taxes for the public benefit. They take the hazard incident to all public improvements of their being faulty or useless through the incapacity or fraud of public servants."³ The amount of the assessment should be made a lien upon the land benefited and a method provided for its sale.⁴

§ 121. *Personal liability for assessments.*— The English statutes make local assessments a charge upon the land and also authorize a personal action against "the present and future owner of the property."⁵ In many states such a liability has been imposed and been unquestioned,⁶ while in others it has been sustained after full consideration.⁷ But most of the latest cases support the view that no personal judgment can be entered against the owner of the land benefited. The reason for this rule is thus stated by the supreme court of California:⁸ "To say that the owner of land bordering upon an improved

¹ Reilly v. City of Albany, 112 N. Y. 30, 19 N. E. Rep. 508.
² Denny v. City of Spokane, 48 C. C. A. 282, 79 Fed. Rep. 719.
³ State v. Jersey City, 29 N. J. Law, 441; Cooley, Taxation, 671.
⁴ McInery v. Reid, 23 Iowa, 410. See Morrison v. Hershire, 32 Iowa, 271.
⁵ Bermonsey v. Ramsey, L. R. 6 C. P. 247.
⁶ Emery v. Bradford, 29 Cal. 75, and cases cited in note to Ivanhoe v. Enterprise, 29 Oreg. 245, 35 L. R. A. 60.
⁷ Dewey v. Des Moines (Iowa), 70 N. W. Rep. 805 (1897); Furwell v. Manufacturing Co. (Iowa), 66 N. W. Rep. 177 (1896).
⁸ Taylor v. Palmer, 31 Cal. 241. To the same effect are Dempster v. People, 158 Ill. 36; Ill. Cent. R. R. Co. v. People, 161 Ill. 244; Shepherd v. Sullivan, 166 Ill. 78, 46 N. E. Rep. 720; Raleigh v. Peace, 110 N. C. 32, 17 L.

street can be made personally liable for the payment for the improvement is equivalent to saying that his entire estate, real, personal or remote from it, whether within the corporate limits or without, whether benefited or not, shall be held responsible for the tax, which, in turn, is equivalent to saying that his entire estate may be taxed for the improvement, in direct contradiction to the very terms of the power." In some states a personal judgment not to exceed the value of the property is allowed,[1] while in others the liability is limited to the amount of the fund realized from the sale of the land.[2] Under the prevailing rule the only judgment allowable is for the enforcement of the lien upon the land in the exact manner specified by the law.[3]

R. A. 330; Ivanhoe v. Enterprise, 29 Oreg. 245, 35 L. R. A. 58, and note. Neeman v. Smith, 50 Mo. 525; Shaw v. Pickett, 26 Vt. 482; St. Louis v. Allen, 53 Mo. 44. In Craw v. Tolono, 96 Ill. 255, 35 Am. Rep. 143, the court said: "A man who owns real estate within a state or municipality necessarily subjects that property to the lawful rules and regulations of the state or municipality; but he does not thereby subject the rest of his fortune not within such state or municipality to the jurisdiction of such municipality, unless he is a citizen or resident of such state or municipality or transacts business therein." See Noonan v. Stillwater, 33 Minn. 198.

[1] See Broadway Church v. McAtee, 8 Bush (Ky.), 508, 8 Am. Rep. 408.
[2] Moale v. Baltimore, 61 Md. 224.
[3] Pleasant Hill v. Dasher, 120 Mo. 675; Clinton v. Henry Co., 115 Mo. 557. The right to a personal judgment under a statute giving power to collect assessments "in the same manner as other taxes are collected" is doubted in McCrowell v. Bristol, 89 Va. 652, 20 L. R. A. 653.

CHAPTER VIII.

PARTICULAR POWERS — CONTINUED.

I. THE POWER OF EMINENT DOMAIN.
§ 122. Definition.
123. May be delegated.
124. What may be taken.
125. Must be for public use.
126. Property already appropriated to public use.
127. Meaning of property.
128. What constitutes a "taking."
129. The proceedings.
130. The tribunal.
131. Notice.
132. The compensation.
133. Consequential injuries.
134. Benefits.
135. Manner of payment.
136. Right of appeal.

II. JUDICIAL POWER.
137. Power to establish court.

§ 138. Jurisdiction.
139. Qualifications of judges and jurors.
140. Procedure — Jury trial.

III. CORPORATE OR PRIVATE POWERS.
141. In general.
142. Right to hold property.
143. Parks and cemeteries.
144. Wharves and ferries.
145. Water and lights.
146. Power to own and operate gas, light and water plants.
147. Nature of the power.
148. The acquisition of the plant.
149. Contracts between the municipality and franchise companies.

I. THE POWER OF EMINENT DOMAIN.

§ 122. *Definition.*— The power of eminent domain is "that superior right of property pertaining to the sovereignty by which the private property acquired by its citizens under its protection may be taken or its use controlled for the public benefit, without regard to the wishes of its owners. More accurately, it is the rightful authority which exists in every sovereignty to control and regulate those rights of a public nature which pertain to its citizens in common and to appropriate and control individual property for the public benefit as the public safety, necessity, convenience or welfare may demand."[1]

It grows out of the necessities of government and is the offspring of political necessity.[2] It is distinct from the police power and the power of taxation.[3]

[1] Cooley, Const. Lim. (6th ed.) 643; Lewis, Eminent Domain, ch. 1.
[2] Kohl v. United States, 93 U. S. 367.
[3] Nichols v. Bridgeport, 23 Conn. 189.

§ 123. *May be delegated.*— The right to exercise the power of eminent domain may be delegated to public or private corporations.[1] Such a grant must, however, be strictly construed.[2] When the power is clearly conferred the courts will not determine the propriety of its exercise.[3]

§ 124. *What may be taken.*— A grant of the power of eminent domain in general terms authorizes the taking of private property, but it is only when there is express or clearly implied authority for this purpose that it will be held to authorize the taking of public property.[4] Every species of property may be taken under this power. Thus, the state, or a body to which the power has been delegated, may, when necessary for a public purpose, take lands,[5] houses,[6] piers,[7] bridges,[8] streams of water[9] and corporate property and franchises.[10] Riparian rights are property which cannot be taken without compensation.[11] Thus, the riparian rights of the lower owners upon the banks of a stream cannot, except in aid of navigation, be taken by the state for a public purpose without compensation.[12] The legislature may determine the quantity of estate which shall be taken,[13] or it may delegate this power to a municipality.[14] It may authorize the taking of the fee [15] or of a mere easement.[16] When necessary a city may condemn lands situated beyond the corporate limits.[17]

[1] Kansas City v. Marsh Oil Co. (Mo., 1897), 41 S. W. Rep. 943; Allen v. Jones, 47 Ind. 438; Cooley, Const. Lim. (6th ed.) 662.
[2] Alexandria, etc. Ry. Co. v. Alexandria, 75 Va. 780; Leeds v. Richmond, 102 Ind. 372.
[3] Dunham v. Hyde Park, 75 Ill. 371.
[4] Seattle & Mont. R. Co. v. State, 7 Wash. 150, 22 L. R. A. 217.
[5] Bliss v. Hosmer, 15 Ohio, 44.
[6] Wells v. Somerset, etc. R. Co., 47 Me. 345.
[7] In re Union Ferry, 98 N. Y. 139. A lease of the wharves of a port may be taken. Duffy v. New Orleans, 49 La. Ann. 114.
[8] Northampton Bridge Case, 116 Mass. 442.
[9] Reusch v. Chicago, etc. Ry. Co., 57 Iowa, 685.
[10] West River Bridge Co. v. Dix, 6 How. (U. S.) 507.
[11] Rumsey v. N. Y. & N. E. Ry. Co., 130 N. Y. 88, 15 L. R. A. 618, annotated.
[12] Kaukauna Water Power Co. v. Green Bay Canal Co., 142 U. S. 254; Patten Paper Co. v. Kaukauna Water Power Co., 90 Wis. 370, 28 L. R. A. 443.
[13] Brooklyn Park Com'rs v. Armstrong, 45 N. Y. 234; Wyoming Coal Co. v. Price, 81 Pa. St. 156.
[14] Powers' Appeal, 29 Mich. 504.
[15] Haldeman v. Pennsylvania Ry. Co., 50 Pa. St. 425.
[16] Kellogg v. Malin, 50 Mo. 496; Clark v. Worcester, 135 Mass. 226.
[17] Thompson v. Moran, 44 Mich. 602.

§ 125.]　　　PARTICULAR POWERS.　　　121

§ 125. *Must be for public use.*— It is only for public use and upon compensation made that private property may be taken under the power of eminent domain. What is a public use is always a question of law. The expediency or necessity of the exercise of the power is a political question which must be determined by the legislature,[1] or a body to which the power is delegated,[2] and its action will not be reviewed by the courts unless there is gross error or extreme wrong results therefrom.[3] Public roads and streets,[4] parks[5] and squares,[6] markets,[7] cemeteries,[8] school buildings,[9] water and gas plants,[10] sewers and drains,[11] almshouses and other public buildings,[12] are illustrations of public uses for which private property may be taken under the power of eminent domain. The use of water for the purpose of irrigation is a public use.[13] Land cannot be taken for a purely private road. But the rule is probably otherwise where the road is to some extent public, as, for instance, where a road is opened at the instance of a private person who agrees to keep it in repair, although the public is permitted to use it.[14]

---

[1] Paxton, etc. Co. v. Farmers' Co., 45 Neb. 884, 29 L. R. A. 853; Dingley v. Boston, 100 Mass. 558; Ryerson v. Brown, 35 Mich. 333, 24 Am. Rep. 564; In re St. Paul Ry. Co., 34 Minn. 227. On the general subject of public uses for which property may be taken under the power of eminent domain, see Wisconsin Water Co. v. Winans, 85 Wis. 26, 20 L. R. A. 662; Pittsburgh, etc. Co. v. Benwood Iron Works, 31 W. Va. 710, 2 L. R. A. 680; Barre Ry. Co. v. Montpelier, etc. Ry. Co., 61 Vt. 1, 4 L. R. A. 785.

[2] New York, etc. R. Co. v. Long, 69 Conn. 424.

[3] Waterloo Mfg. Co. v. Shannahan, 128 N. Y. 345.

[4] Wild v. Deig, 43 Ind. 455; Bankhead v. Brown, 25 Iowa, 540; Elliott, Road and Streets, § 146.

[5] In re Mayor of New York, 99 N.Y. 569; South Park Com'rs v. Williams, 51 Ill. 57.

[6] Owners v. Mayor, 15 Wend. (N. Y.) 374.

[7] In re Application of Cooper, 38 Hun (N. Y.), 515.

[8] Balch v. County Com'rs, 103 Mass. 106.

[9] Williams v. School District, 37 Vt. 271.

[10] Lake Pleasanton Water Co. v. Contra Costa Water Co., 67 Cal. 659; Bailey v. Woburn, 126 Mass. 416; Tyler v. Hudson, 147 Mass. 609; State v. Eau Claire, 40 Wis. 533; In re Deering, 93 N. Y. 651.

[11] Norfleet v. Cromwell, 70 N. C. 634, 16 Am. Rep. 787; Bancroft v. Cambridge, 126 Mass. 438.

[12] Lewis, Eminent Domain, § 174.

[13] Bankhead v. Brown, 25 Iowa, 545; Welton v. Dickson, 38 Neb. 767, 32 L. R. A. 496; Latah Co. v. Peterson, 2 Idaho, 1118, 16 L. R. A. 81; Varner v. Martin, 21 W. Va. 533.

[14] Paxton & Hersby Co. v. Farmers', etc. Co., 45 Neb. 884, 29 L. R. A. 853; Lindsay Irr. Co. v. Mehrtens, 97 Cal. 676. As to flowage of land, see Turner v. Nye, 154 Mass. 579, 14 L. R. A. 487, and note.

Land may be taken for a useful purpose which serves to satisfy a public want, notwithstanding the fact that the element of ornament or beauty may be a controlling consideration.[1]

§ 126. *Property already appropriated to public use.*— Property which is already appropriated to a public use cannot be taken for another public use unless the statute clearly confers authority to make a second seizure.[2] Thus, under a general power, a city cannot excavate a canal across a railway yard where there are numerous tracks. "In determining whether a power generally given is meant to have operation upon lands already devoted by legislative authority to a public purpose," said Folger, J.,[3] "it is proper to consider the nature of the prior public work, the public use to which it is applied, the extent to which that use would be impaired or diminished by the taking of such part of the land as may be demanded by the subsequent public use. If both uses may not stand together, with some tolerable interference which may be compensated for by damages paid; if the latter use when exercised must supersede the former, it is not to be implied from a general power given, without having in view a then existing and particular need therefor, that the legislature meant to subject lands devoted to a public use already in exercise to one which might thereafter arise. A legislative intent that there should be such an effect will not be inferred from a gift of power made in general terms."

Under general power one railway company cannot lay a track longitudinally along an existing track of another road.[4] But it may make necessary crossings over another road.[5] A public cemetery cannot be taken for highway purposes without express authority.[6] But a part of a school lot may be taken

[1] Higginson v. Nahant, 11 Allen, 532; Gardner v. Newburg Tp., 2 Johns. Ch. 162; Eldridge v. Smith, 34 Vt. 482.
[2] Cincinnati, etc. R. Co. v. Belle Centre, 48 Ohio St. 273, 27 N. E. Rep. 464; Old Colony Ry. Co. v. Farmington Water Co., 153 Mass. 561, 13 L. R. A. 333. The legislature will not be deemed to have authorized the taking of such property unless the intention is clearly expressed in the statute. People v. Thompson, 98 N. Y. 6.
[3] In re Buffalo, 68 N. Y. 167.
[4] Boston & M. R. R. Co. v. Lowell, etc. R. Co., 124 Mass. 368.
[5] St. Paul, etc. Co. v. Minneapolis 35 Minn. 141; Minneapolis W. R. Co. v. M. & St. L. R. Co., 61 Minn. 502. But see Sharon R. Co.'s Appeal, 122 Pa. St. 533, and cases cited.
[6] Evergreen Cemetery Ass'n v. New Haven, 43 Conn. 234.

when what remains is not rendered wholly useless.[1] The works and franchises of a water company may be condemned by a city on the ground that they are required for a use of a higher and wider scope. "All property within the state is subject to the right of the legislature to appropriate for a reasonable and necessary use upon a just compensation being provided to be made therefor, and there can be no distinction in favor of corporations whose franchises and operations impart to them a *quasi*-public character."[2]

§ 127. *Meaning of "property."* — The word "property," as now understood, includes all rights which pertain to the ownership of things.[3] In a leading case[4] it appeared that after paying the owner of land for the damages resulting from laying out a railroad across his land, the company in building its road made a deep cut through a ridge north of the land which protected it from high water in a neighboring river. In times of high water, stone and gravel were washed through the cut upon the plaintiff's land, and it was held that he could recover for this damage, notwithstanding the fact that the road had been constructed with due care. In this case, which has been pronounced "the most satisfactory and best considered case which can be found in the books on this subject,"[5] will be found a full discussion of what is meant by property and what is a taking of property within the meaning of the constitution.

§ 128. *What constitutes a taking.*— It is not necessary that there should be a physical taking of the property. It may be by restricting the use or depriving the owner of an incorporeal right,[6] such as by the flowing of lands or the diversion of a stream.[7] The owner of land abutting on a navigable stream

---

[1] Easthampton v. County Com'rs, 164 Mass. 424.
[2] In re Brooklyn, 143 N. Y. 596, 26 L. R. A. 270.
[3] Arnold v. Hudson R. Co., 55 N. Y. 661; Morrison v. Semple, 6 Binn. (Pa.) 94; Denver v. Bayer, 7 Col. 113. See an article by Mr. Sedgwick, in North Am. Rev., Sept. 1882, vol. 135, p. 253.
[4] Eaton v. Boston, etc. R. Co., 51 N. H. 504.
[5] Grand Rapids Booming Co. v. Jarvis, 30 Mich. 308, Christiancy, J.
[6] Pumpelly v. Green Bay, etc. Co., 13 Wall. (U. S.) 166; Stephens v. Proprietors of Canal, 12 Mass. 466; Grand Rapids Booming Co. v. Jarvis, 30 Mich. 308.
[7] Baltimore, etc. R. Co. v. M'Gruder, 34 Md. 79, 6 Am. Rep. 310; Pettigrew v. Evansville, 25 Wis. 223.

cannot be deprived of all access to the same without proper compensation,[1] although it was at one time held that when the title to the bed of the stream was in the state there was no taking when the water front was appropriated for a public purpose.[2] A change of the grade of a street is not a taking of the property of abutting owners for public use.[3] It was at one time held that there was no taking unless there was an actual physical appropriation of the property or divestiture of the title. The damage, in order to constitute a taking, must be of such a nature as to give a cause of action on common-law principles. Thus, there can be no recovery for damages resulting from the location of a jail, although it may result in actual injury to property.[4]

§ 129. *The proceedings.*—The manner in which private property may be taken for public use is always provided by statute. This statutory proceeding must be strictly followed. It may be instituted by the state or by some person or body to which the power has been delegated. It is generally commenced by the filing of a petition signed by a certain number of persons possessing the requisite qualifications. This petition must show all the jurisdictional facts and substantially comply with the statute, although it is not necessary that it should be technically accurate.[5]

§ 130. *The tribunal.*—It is necessary that some impartial tribunal exercising judicial power be provided for assessing the damages to be awarded.[6] It may consist of a court, a court and jury, or commissioners selected by the court.[7] It is not necessary, however, that it should be a tribunal exercising judicial functions only.[8] The constitutional right to a jury trial has no application to proceedings for the condemnation

[1] Railway Co. v. Renwick, 102 U. S. 180.
[2] Tomlin v. Dubuque, etc. Ry. Co., 32 Iowa, 106, 7 Am. Rep. 126.
[3] Talbot v. New York & Harlem R. R. Co., 151 N. Y. 155; Transportation Co. v. Chicago, 99 U. S. 635.
[4] Burwell v. Vance Co., 93 N. C. 73.
[5] State v. Morse, 50 N. H. 9; In re Grove Street, 61 Cal. 438. The petition must contain an allegation that there is a necessity for taking the property. Colville v. Judy, 73 Mo. 651; In re Road in Sterritt Township, 114 Pa. St. 637.
[6] Ames v. Lake Superior, etc. Co., 21 Minn. 241; Clifford v. Commissioners, 59 Me. 262.
[7] State v. Jones, 109 U. S. 513.
[8] Shue v. Commissioners, 41 Mich. 638.

of property under the power of eminent domain.[1] In some states, however, the constitution provides for a jury trial in such cases.[2] It has been held that this provision requires an ordinary jury of twelve men,[3] and that the legislature cannot authorize a verdict by a majority thereof.[4]

§ 131. *Notice.*—The property of an individual cannot be taken for public use without due process of law, and this requires that he shall have notice of the proceedings.[5] There must be "an orderly proceeding adapted to the nature of the case, in which the citizen has an opportunity to be heard and to defend, enforce and protect his rights. A hearing or an opportunity to be heard is absolutely essential."[6] The substance of the notice must be such as the law requires, and it must be given in the prescribed manner.[7] When not otherwise provided it may be by advertisement in a newspaper.[8] "The manner of the notification is immaterial, but the notification is indispensable."[9] It must be given to those who have a vested interest of record in the estate, but it need not be given to mere lienholders or to the holders of a contingent or inchoate interest.[10] Thus, it need not be given to a judgment creditor,[11]

[1] Kohl v. United States, 91 U. S. 375; New York, etc. R. Co. v. Long, 64 Conn. 424; Martin v. Tyler, 4 N. Dak. 278, 25 L. R. A. 838; Brugerman v. True, 25 Minn. 123; Backus v. Lebanon, 11 N. H. 19, 35 Am. Dec. 466. See Lewis, Eminent Domain, § 311. For a discussion of "due process of law," see Mo. Pac. Ry. Co. v. Humes, 115 U. S. 512.

[2] Paul v. Detroit, 32 Mich. 108; Williams v. Pittsburg, 88 Pa. St. 71.

[3] Mitchell v. Illinois, etc. Ry. Co., 58 Ill. 286.

[4] Jacksonville, etc. Ry. Co. v. Adams 33 Fla. 608, 24 L. R. A. 272.

[5] The contrary is held in Illinois, Maryland and Mississippi. Johnson v. Joliet, etc. R. Co., 23 Ill. 202; George's Creek Coal Co. v. New Central Coal Co., 40 Md. 425; Stewart v. Board of Police, 25 Miss. 479.

[6] Mr. Justice Field, in Windsor v. McVeigh, 98 U. S. 274.

[7] Stewart v. Palmer, 74 N. Y. 183; Wurts v. Hoagland, 114 U. S. 606; Neeld's Road, 1 Pa. St. 353; Lewis, Em. Dom., § 364.

[8] Birge v. Chicago, etc. Ry. Co., 65 Iowa, 440; Morgan v. Chicago, etc. Ry. Co., 36 Mich. 428; Huling v. Kaw Valley R. Co., 130 U. S. 559. As to the effect of allowing a jury trial in an appellate court, see Thorp v. Witham, 65 Iowa, 506, and cases cited, § 140, *infra.*

[9] Petition of De Puyster, 80 N. Y. 565; Wilkins v. St. Paul, 16 Minn. 271; State v. Chicago, etc. Ry. Co., 80 Iowa, 586. The reasons for the rule are well stated in Cupp v. Commissioners, 19 Ohio St. 173.

[10] Girard v. Omaha, etc. Ry. Co., 14 Neb. 270.

[11] Gambel v. Stolte, 59 Ind. 446; Watson v. N. Y. etc. Ry. Co., 47 N. Y. 157.

or to the holder of the dower interest;[1] but it must be given to a mortgagee,[2] and to both a landlord and his tenant.[3] But this is largely governed by the language of the statute. As a general rule, "all persons who have any proprietary interest in the property taken or proposed to be taken should be made parties to the proceedings, and also all other persons, if any, who are required to be made parties by statute."[4] .

§ 132. *The compensation.*— The compensation allowed should be the full reasonable value of the interest taken. In determining the value of land appropriated for public purposes "the same considerations are to be regarded as in a sale of property between private parties. The inquiry in such cases must be, what is the property worth in the market, viewed not merely with reference to the uses to which it is at the time applied, but with reference to the use to which it is at the time adapted; that is to say, what is it worth from its availability for valuable uses. Property is not to be deemed worthless because the owner allows it to go to waste, or to be regarded as valueless because he is unable to put it to any use. Others may be able to use it and make it subserve the necessities or conveniences of life. Its capability of being made thus available gives it a market value which can be readily estimated. So many and varied are the circumstances to be taken into account in determining the value of property taken for public purposes, that it is perhaps impossible to formulate a rule to govern the appraisement in all cases. Exceptional circumstances will modify the most carefully guarded rules; but as a general thing we should say that the compensation to the owner is to be estimated by reference to the uses for which the property is suitable, having regard to the existing business or wants of the community, or such as may be reasonably expected in the immediate future."[5] The improvements upon the property should be taken into consideration.[6] Some cases hold that the owner

[1] City v. Kingsboro, 101 Ind. 290.
[2] Voegtly v. Pittsburgh, etc. Ry. Co., 2 Grant's Cas. (Pa.) 243.
[3] For a full treatment of this subject, see Lewis, Em. Dom., ch. XII.
[4] Sherwood v. City, 109 Ind. 410; Severin v. Cole, 38 Iowa, 463.
[5] Boom Co. v. Patterson, 98 U. S. 403, Field, J.; Laurence v. Boston, 119 Mass. 126; Commissioners v. Railway Co., 63 Iowa, 297; Chapman v. Oshkosh, etc. Ry. Co., 33 Wis. 629; King v. Minneapolis, 32 Minn. 224.
[6] Jacksonville, etc. Ry. Co. v.

is entitled to the market value for the use to which the land may be most advantageously applied and for which it would sell for the highest price in the market.[1] Sentimental valuations based upon associations cannot be taken into consideration, as it is impossible to measure such matters in money.[2] The jury in condemnation proceedings cannot rely upon their own judgment in the matter of damages and reject the evidence of competent witnesses.[3]

Neither the diminished value of a stock of merchandise, nor the loss of profits caused by removal made necessary by the taking of real estate, is a proper element of damage.[4] The cost of adjusting a bridge erected by a railway company for the purpose of carrying its track over a street-crossing, after the street has been widened by the city under the power of eminent domain, is a proper element of damages to be allowed the company in proceedings to condemn a portion of its property for the purpose of such widening, notwithstanding the fact that an ordinance provides that the company shall erect and maintain the bridge at its own expense.[5]

§ 133. *Consequential injuries.*— The damages resulting to the property of a person by the lawful exercise by another of his legal rights is not a taking of the property of the former. This question arises when the state engages in the improvement of rivers and highways. The prevailing doctrine is that there can be no recovery for injuries resulting from the change of the grade of a street. So the owner of a fishery which is reduced in value by improvements made in a navigable stream has no remedy.[6] Mr. Justice Miller says:[7] "The

---

Walsh, 106 Ill. 253. The cost of repairs upon a toll bridge which has been taken by the county cannot be considered. Mifflin Bridge Co. v. Juniata Co., 144 Pa. St. 235, 13 L. R. A. 431.

[1] King v. Minneapolis Ry. Co., 32 Minn. 224. Where a bridge is taken by a county the measure of damages is the value of the property to the owners and not to the county taking it. The owners are entitled to recover not only the cost of the structure, but also the value of the franchise. Montgomery Co. v. Schuylkill Bridge Co., 110 Pa. St. 54.

[2] Cooley, Const. Lim. (6th ed.) 697.

[3] Peoria Gas L. Co. v. Peoria R. Co., 146 Ill. 372, 21 L. R. A. 373.

[4] Becker v. Phil. etc. R. Co., 177 Pa. St. 252, 25 L. R. A. 593.

[5] Kansas City v. Kansas City Belt R. Co., 102 Mo. 633, 10 L. R. A. 851.

[6] Parker v. Mill Dam Co., 20 Me. 353, 37 Am. Dec. 56; Commonwealth v. Look, 108 Mass. 452.

[7] Pumpelly v. Green Bay, 13 Wall.

doctrine that for a consequential injury to the property of an individual for the prosecution of improvements of roads, streets, rivers and other highways, there is no redress . . . is a sound one in its proper application to many injuries to property; . . . but we are of opinion that the decisions referred to have gone to the uttermost limit of sound judicial construction in favor of this principle, and in some cases beyond it, and that it remains true that where real estate is actually invaded by superinduced additions of water, earth, sand, or other material, or by having any artificial structure placed on it so as to effectually destroy or impair its usefulness, it is a taking within the meaning of the constitution, and that this proposition is not in conflict with the weight of judicial authority in this country, and certainly not with sound principles."

§ 134. *Benefits.*— The cases are conflicting upon the question of the right to set off benefits which are special to particular land, against the damages awarded. Certain cases hold that such benefits cannot in any case be offset against the injury sustained by the land-owner;[1] and this principle has been incorporated in some constitutions.[2] Others allow a set-off only against incidental injuries sustained,[3] while still others allow such a set-off against the value of the land as well as against incidental injuries.[4] But benefits to be allowed in any case must be of a kind not common to the public at large.[5]

§ 135. *Manner of payment.*— In the absence of a constitutional requirement to the contrary, it is sufficient if an adequate and certain remedy is provided whereby the land-owner may compel payment of damages.[6] In a recent case[7] the court said: "Under constitutional provisions declaring that private property shall not be taken for public use without just compensa-

166; Talbot v. N. Y. & Harlem R. R. Co., 151 N. Y. 155.
[1] Israel v. Jewett, 29 Iowa, 475.
[2] See Newmann v. Metropolitan, etc. Ry. Co., 118 N. Y. 618.
[3] Robbins v. Milwaukee, etc. Co., 6 Wis. 637; Shawneetown v. Mason, 82 Ill. 337; Shipley v. Baltimore, etc. R. Co., 34 Md. 336.
[4] Putnam v. Douglas Co., 6 Oreg.

328, 25 Am. Rep. 627; Root's Case, 77 Pa. St. 276.
[5] Commissioners v. Johnson, 71 N. C. 398; Lipes v. Hand, 104 Ind. 503. On the general question, see Elliott, Roads and Streets, § 189, and cases cited.
[6] Sage v. Brooklyn, 89 N. Y. 189.
[7] Martin v. Tyler, 4 N. Dak. 278, 25 L. R. A. 838.

tion, and silent as to the time of payment, it has generally, if not universally, been held that when property was thus taken by a private corporation, payment must precede the taking; but where the property was taken directly by the state or a municipality of the state, it has generally been held a sufficient compliance with the provision if the compensation was definitely ascertained and made a charge upon the municipal fund for which the credit of the municipality was pledged." But the party must not be required to resort to a lawsuit in order to collect his money.[1] Judge Cooley says:[2] "Whenever the necessary steps have been taken on the part of the public to select the property to be taken, locate the public work and declare the appropriation, the owner becomes absolutely entitled to the compensation, whether the public proceed at once to occupy the property or not. If a street is legally established over the land of an individual, he is entitled to demand payment of the damages without waiting for the street to be opened."[3] When the law expressly requires that the money shall be paid before the property is taken, there can be no valid taking until after the payment is made.[4]

§ 136. *Right of appeal.*— It is for the legislature to say whether the land-owner shall have a right to appeal from the determination of the tribunal which is established to determine his damages.[5] It may provide for an appeal or it may make the decision final. The trial in the appellate court is *de novo.*[6] The appeal vacates the decision appealed from.[7] The usual remedy for reviewing erroneous proceedings is by *certiorari*, and under it only questions of law are considered.[8]

[1] Shepardson v. Milwaukee, etc. R. Co., 6 Wis. 605.
[2] Cooley, Const. Lim. (6th ed.) 696.
[3] Rogers v. Bradshaw, 20 Johns. 744; Bloodgood v. Mohawk, etc. R. Co., 18 Wend. 9, 31 Am. Dec. 313; Brock v. Hishen, 40 Wis. 674; Long v. Fuller, 68 Pa. St. 170. The same rule has been adopted in Minnesota and Michigan, where the constitution requires that compensation shall be first paid or secured. State v. Messenger, 27 Minn. 119; State v. Bruggerman, 81 Minn. 493; People v.
Southern Mich. Ry. Co., 3 Mich. 496.
[4] Martin v. Tyler, 4 N. Dak. 278, 25 L. R. A. 838.
[5] Simms v. Hymmes, 121 Ind. 534; Matter of State Reservation, 132 N. Y. 734; Fass v. Seehawer, 60 Wis. 525; Harwood v. Shaw, 126 Ill. 53.
[6] Hardy v. McKinney, 107 Ind. 367.
[7] Minneapolis v. Northwestern Ry. Co., 32 Minn. 452.
[8] Farmington River Water-Power Co. v. County Com'rs, 112 Mass. 206; Tiedt v. Carstensen, 61 Iowa, 334.

II. JUDICIAL POWER.

§ 137. Power to establish courts.— By the common law municipal corporations have power to establish courts for the purpose of determining controversies of limited and local importance. The early charters "contained grants of courts of various degrees and importance; the mayor and aldermen were in some instances made magistrates *ex officio* and authorized to hold courts of quarter sessions, and these grants were accompanied or not, as the case might be, by a clause called the '*non-intromittant*' clause, which ousted the jurisdiction of the county magistrates. In some cases towns were made counties by themselves; in some cases there was no limitation at all upon the extent of the town jurisdiction; they might try all crimes and inflict any punishment up to death; in other cases they were confined within narrower limits."[1]

The grant of power to hold a court imposes a duty upon the municipality.[2] In the United States these courts are known by various names, such as municipal, mayor's, recorder's and police courts. Their creation and jurisdiction rest with the legislature, which may modify and change their jurisdiction at will.[3] The legislature must, of course, act in accordance with constitutional provisions. When the constitution confers upon the legislature authority to create "other courts" than those named in the constitution, it may erect municipal courts for the trial of offenses against municipal ordinances and confer upon them the general powers of justices of the peace within the limits of the municipality.[4]

§ 138. Jurisdiction.— The jurisdiction of municipal courts ordinarily extends to the enforcement of municipal ordinances and the recovery of penalties for a breach thereof and to controversies between individuals when the amount involved does not exceed a specified amount.[5] They are often empowered to de-

---

[1] Stephens, Hist. Crim. Law of Eng., I, p. 116.
[2] Rex v. Mayor of Hastings, 5 Barn. & Ald. 692.
[3] Boyd v. Chambers, 78 Ky. 140.
[4] State v. Young, 30 Kan. 445; Shafer v. Muma, 17 Md. 331. See Fawcett v. Pritchard, 14 Wash. 604.
A municipal court cannot sit outside of the corporation limits. Herschoff v. Beverly, 43 N. J. L. 139.
[5] Fox v. Ellison, 43 Minn. 41; Henderson v. Davis, 106 N. C. 88; People v. Lawrence, 82 Cal. 182; State v. Wright, 80 Wis. 648; Brown v. Jerome, 102 Ill. 371.

termine civil suits where the amount involved does not exceed five hundred dollars, and when title to land is not involved. As a rule they have no equity jurisdiction. In some instances, however, the jurisdiction of city courts is by statute made as extensive as that of the district and circuit courts.[1] When the jurisdiction is not co-extensive with the limits of a municipality, the court is not properly a municipal court. But the fact that it is called by that name is not material when the constitution authorizes the creation of inferior courts, and the court created comes within this designation.[2]

§ 139. *Qualifications of judges and jurors.*— The common-law rule that the municipality cannot be a suitor in its own court and that a member of the corporation cannot sit as judge or juror in a suit in which the corporation is interested[3] is not enforced in the United States. It is considered that the interest which each citizen has in the result of such litigation is too inconsiderable to give rise to any prejudice.[4]

§ 140. *Procedure—Jury trial.*— The procedure in municipal courts is ordinarily of a summary nature, as the number and comparative unimportance of the offenses tried renders the system of jury trial impracticable. The constitutional right to a jury trial has never been understood to apply to violations of city ordinances. The violations of such ordinances are not criminal offenses or crimes as those words are understood in constitutional law. The constitutional guaranty that "the right of trial by jury shall remain inviolate" does not prevent the enforcement of municipal ordinances by a summary pro-

[1] Bledsoe v. Gary, 95 Ala. 70, 10 So. Rep. 502. As to jurisdiction in cases of violation of game laws, see State v. Synott, 89 Me. 41; bastardy, Williams v. State, 112 Ala. 688; forcible entry and unlawful detainer, Suchaneck v. State, 45 Minn. 26.
[2] Shaffel v. State (Wis.), 72 N. W. Rep. 888 (1897).
[3] City of London v. Wood, 12 Mod. 674; Reg. v. Rogers, 2 Lord Raym. 777.
[4] City Council v. Pepper, 1 Rich. (S. C.) 364; State v. Wells, 46 Iowa, 662; Montezuma v. Minor, 73 Ga. 484. But see Omaha v. Olmstead, 5 Neb. 446; Kemper v. Louisville, 14 Bush, 87. It is held that in an action in a state court to which a municipal corporation is a party, a taxpayer of the corporation cannot serve as a juror unless his common-law liability has been expressly or impliedly removed by statute. Dively v. Elmira, 51 N. Y. 506; Boston v. Baldwin, 139 Mass. 315; Kindinger v. Saginaw, 59 Mich. 355. See Beach, Pub. Corp., sec. 1289.

cedure;[1] but the legislature cannot confer upon municipal corporations the power to proceed summarily and try persons for the commission of criminal offenses against the laws of the state.[2] It is generally held in the state courts that the constitutional right of a jury trial is not denied if the defendant, who is convicted summarily in an inferior court, has a right to appeal to a higher court where he can obtain a jury trial;[3] but the supreme court of the United States, in a recent case,[4] said: "We cannot assent to that interpretation of the constitution, except in that class or grade of offenses called petty offenses, which, according to the common law, may be proceeded against summarily in any tribunal legally constituted for that purpose. The guaranty of an impartial jury to the accused in a criminal prosecution, conducted either in the name or by or under the authority of the United States, secures to him the right to enjoy that mode of trial from the first moment, and in whatever court he is put on trial for the offense charged."

Actions for violations of city ordinances are sometimes brought in the name of the state[5] and sometimes in the name of the corporation.[6]

III. CORPORATE OR PRIVATE POWERS.

§ 141. *In general.*—The private or corporate powers conferred upon municipal corporations must have some relation to their public duties. They cannot properly be authorized to engage in a speculative or purely private mercantile business, for the sole purpose of earning money in competition with individ-

[1] Callan v. Wilson, 127 U. S. 540; State v. Lee, 29 Minn. 445; State v. Robitshek, 60 Minn. 123; State v. Harris, 50 Minn. 128; Hollenbeck v. Marshalltown, 62 Iowa, 21; State v. Glenn, 54 Md. 571.
[2] Tierney v. Dodge, 9 Minn. 166. For the history of courts of summary jurisdiction, see Stephens' Hist. Crim. Law, I, p. 122.
[3] Jones v. Robins, 8 Gray, 329; Maxwell v. Board, 119 Ind. 20; Emporia v. Volmer, 12 Kan. 622.
[4] Callan v. Wilson, 127 U. S. 540, 556.

[5] State v. Powell, 97 N. C. 417. Although the prosecution is in the name of the state the offenses are against the city, and a notice of appeal must be served on the city attorney and not on the attorney-general. State v. Sexton, 42 Minn. 154. The state as such has no interest in a prosecution for a violation of a city ordinance. State v. Robitshek, 60 Minn. 123.
[6] Williams v. Com., 4 B. Mon. (Ky.) 146; Davenport v. Bird, 34 Iowa, 524; Ex parte Holwedell, 74 Mo. 395.

uals. An examination of the cases will show that the corporate powers ordinarily and properly conferred upon these bodies, and under and by virtue of which they acquire property, are intended to aid the corporations to perform their duties to the public. Originally the income from this property was expected to pay the expenses of administering the government of the city. The greater the wealth of the corporation in income-producing property the less the necessity for resorting to taxation of the people. The importance of the distinction between the public and private property of a municipality is of greatest importance in considering the question of legislative control, and of liability to individuals for negligence in the care of such property. These subjects are elsewhere considered in detail.

§ 142. *Right to hold property.*— A public corporation may purchase and hold such property as is reasonably necessary to enable it to execute its powers.[1] The power is ordinarily conferred in express words. A provision authorizing the council to purchase real estate necessary "for the use, convenience and improvement of the city" does not authorize it to buy land as a place for holding fairs. The mere fact that from the use of such land for annual fairs collateral advantages would accrue to the city will not bring the purchase within the contemplation of the act.[2] Power to maintain public schools and to purchase, hold and dispose of real, personal and mixed property for the benefit of the town will authorize the purchase of real estate upon which to construct a school-house.[3] Authority to purchase the property owned and operated by an electric light company as a part of its plant will not authorize the purchase of property used by the company for an entirely different purpose.[4] The power of a corporation to convey,[5] mort-

[1] Richmond, etc. Co. v. West Point (Va., 1897), 27 S. E. Rep. 460; McDonald's Ex'r v. Murdock, 15 How. (U. S.) 363; Ketchum v. Buffalo, 14 N. Y. 356; West Chicago Park Com'rs v. McMullen, 134 Ill. 170, 25 N. E. Rep. 676; Proprietors of Jeffrey's Neck v. Inhabitants, 153 Mass. 42, 26 N. E. Rep. 239.

[2] Eufalie v. McNab, 67 Ala. 588, 42 Am. Rep. 118.

[3] Tacoma v. Tacoma L. & W. Co., 15 Wash. 499, 46 Pac. Rep. 1119.

[4] Allen v. La Fayette, 89 Ala. 641, 9 L. R. A. 497.

[5] Knox Co. v. Goggin, 105 Mo. 182, 16 S. W. Rep. 684; Ft. Wayne v. Lake Shore, etc. R. Co. (Ind.), 18 L. R. A. 367, 32 N. E. Rep. 215.

gage¹ or lease² its private property differs in no essential particular from that of a natural person under like circumstances; but property dedicated to a public use cannot be alienated without express legislative authority.³

It is now settled that a public corporation may be empowered to take and hold private property for municipal uses, and that it will be protected in its ownership to the same extent as would a private owner under the same circumstances. It was early held that a public corporation could not be deprived of property which it held for purposes of revenue without compensation. The cases generally arose on the question of the power of the legislature to dispose of this property without the consent of the municipality.⁴ Under the provision of the constitution of Ohio which prohibits a city from raising money for or loaning its credit to or in aid of any company, corporation or association, a city is not permitted to invest the public funds in property of which another is part owner. The court said:⁵ "The mischief which this section interdicts is a business partnership between a municipality or subdivision of the state and individuals or private corporations or associations. It forbids the union of public and private capital or credit in any enterprise whatever."

§ 143. *Parks and cemeteries.*— A cemetery has been held to belong to a city in its private or corporate capacity. Thus, in a recent case⁶ where the subject is fully discussed, the court said: "The city of Boston is possessed of much other property

¹ Belcher's S. R. Co. v. Grain Elev. Co., 101 Mo. 192, 13 S. W. Rep. 822; Hand v. Newton, 92 N. Y. 88.
² State v. Laclede Gas Co., 102 Mo. 472, 22 Am. St. Rep. 789.
³ Mowry v. Providence, 16 R. I. 422, 16 Atl. Rep. 511; Lord v. Oconto, 47 Wis. 386; Merriweather v. Garrett, 102 U. S. 472; Ft. Wayne v. Lake Shore, etc. R. Co., *supra.*
⁴ Terrill v. Taylor, 9 Cranch (U. S.), 43; Pawlet v. Clark, 9 Cranch (U. S.), 292; Dartmouth College v. Woodward, 4 Wheat. (U. S.) 518; Montpelier v. East Montpelier, 29 Vt. 12; People v. Ingersoll, 58 N. Y. 1; Philadelphia v. Fox, 54 Pa. St. 169; Town of Milwaukee v. City of Milwaukee, 12 Wis. 93; Grogan v. San Francisco, 18 Cal. 519. The development of the doctrine as illustrated in the above and other cases is detailed in Goodnow, Municipal Home Rule, ch. 9.
⁵ Ampt v. Cincinnati (Ohio St.), 35 L. R. A. 737; Walker v. Cincinnati, 21 Ohio St. 13, 8 Am. Rep. 24. See, also, Bates v. Bassett, 60 Vt. 530, 1 L. R. A. 66. As to the right to lease a part of a public building, see State v. Hart (Ind.), 33 L. R. A. 118, note.
⁶ Mt. Hope Cemetery v. Boston, 158 Mass. 509.

which in a certain sense, and to a certain extent, is held for the benefit of the public, but in other respects is held more like the property of a private corporation. Notably among these may be mentioned its system of water-works, its system of parks, its markets, its hospital and its library. In establishing all these the city has not acted strictly as an agent of the state government for the accomplishment of general public or political purposes, but with special reference to the benefit of its own inhabitants. If its cemetery is under legislative control, so that a transfer of it without compensation can be required, it is not easy to see why the other properties mentioned are not also; and all the other cities and towns which own cemeteries or other properties of the kinds mentioned might be under a similar liability."[1]

§ 144. *Wharves and ferries.*—A city cannot carry on a public wharf or ferry and charge tolls and fees for its use without special authorization by the legislature.[2] "It is a power of a special and extra-municipal nature."[3] The right to erect and regulate wharves and appoint wharfingers includes the right to impose and collect toll;[4] but the right to erect, repair and regulate wharves, with fixed rates of wharfage, does not authorize a city to lease a wharf or to farm out its revenues and authorize the lessee to fix the rates of wharfage. Where a street extending to navigable water is dedicated to public use, the corporation may extend it into the water by the construction of a wharf, without reference to the title of the land under water.[5] The rights which a municipality acquire under the grant of a right to build wharves and charge wharfage are

---

[1] That parks are in the nature of private property, see People v. Detroit, 28 Mich. 228; State v. Schweick, 19 So. Rep. 97. *Contra,* Davos v. Portland Water Com., 14 Oreg. 98. See § 33, *supra.*

[2] Webb v. Demopolis, 95 Ala. 116, 21 L. R. A. 62; The Geneva, Am. Law Reg., Sept., 1883, annotated; Railroad Co. v. Ellerman, 105 U. S. 166; Turner v. People's Ferry, 21 Fed. Rep. 90; Williams v. New York Ferry Co., 105

N. Y. 419; Snyder v. Rockport, 6 Ind. 237.

[3] Dillon, Mun. Corp., § 67; The Wharf Case, 3 Bland Ch. 361; The Empire State, 1 Newb. Adm. 541.

[4] Municipality v. Pease, 2 La. Ann. 538; Muscatine v. Hershey, 18 Iowa, 39. As to the proper uses of a public wharf, see Illinois v. Canal Co., 2 Dill. (C. C.) 70.

[5] Keokuk v. Keokuk P. Co., 45 Iowa, 196.

held to be private rights in so far that it cannot be required to permit the use of its wharf without compensation,[1] and the same principle has been applied to a ferry franchise.[2]

§ 145. *Water and lights.*— The power to light the streets and public places of a municipality is commonly conferred upon the corporation by the charter.[3] The city generally enters into a contract with an individual or corporation for a supply of water, gas or electric light for a certain period. When not restricted by some provision of the charter the time may be determined by the city council, subject to the limitation of reasonableness.

The power to grant franchises has been already considered.[4] When such grants are made, the grantor may reserve a large power of regulation and control. Under such a reservation the municipality may regulate the rates and charges which may legally be made by public service corporations. Thus, the state may determine the rates which may be charged by a railway corporation. But the rates fixed by a state railway commission must be reasonable, and this is a judicial and not a legislative question.[5] The same principle governs the action of a municipality, when acting under proper authority, in determining the rates which may be charged by franchised companies for water, gas, electric light and telephone service. But the courts will not permit the property to be confiscated under the pretense of regulating rates.[6] The municipality

[1] New Orleans M. & T. Co. v. Ellerman, 105 U. S. 166. The court said: "Whatever powers the municipal body rightfully enjoys over the subject are derived from the legislature. They are merely administrative and may be revoked at any time, not touching, of course, any property of the city actually acquired in the course of administrations. The sole ground of the right of the city to collect wharfage at all is that it is a reasonable compensation which it is allowed by law to charge for the actual use of the structures provided at its expense for the convenience of vessels engaged in the navigation of the river." Cannon v. New Orleans, 20 Wall. (U. S.) 577.

[2] Benson v. Mayor, 10 Barb. (N. Y.) 223. *Contra,* Rober v. McWhorter, 17 Va. 214.

[3] Newport v. Newport Gas Co., 84 Ky. 466; Minneapolis Gas Light Co. v. Minneapolis, 36 Minn. 159.

[4] § 85, *supra.* See, also, Andrews v. Nat. F. & P. Works (C. C. A.), 61 Fed. Rep. 782, and Westerly Waterworks Co. v. Westerly, 80 Fed. Rep. 611.

[5] Chicago, M. & St. P. Ry. Co. v. Minnesota, 134 U. S. 418.

[6] State v. Cincinnati Gas Co., 18 Ohio St. 262; Norwich Gas Co. v. Gas Co., 25 Conn. 19; State v. Gas

must be able to show legislative autnority to regulate rates, when the power is not expressly reserved at the time the franchise is granted. Authority to light the streets and furnish the inhabitants with gas and other light and "to regulate and control the use thereof" will not authorize an ordinance fixing the price at which gas shall be furnished the city and its inhabitants.[1] To permit a city which is itself a large user of gas, and which has not reserved the power, to determine the price which the company shall receive for it, seems contrary to accepted principles.[2]

§ 146. *Power to own and operate gas, light and water plants.* It has been held[3] that municipal corporations have inherent power to provide for lighting the streets, alleys and public places. If so, "unless their discretion is controlled by some express statutory restriction, they may in their discretion provide that form of light which is best suited to the wants and financial condition of the corporation. . . . We see no good reason why they may not also, without statutory authority, provide and maintain the necessary plant to generate and supply the electricity required. Possessing power to do the lighting carries with it incidentally the further power to procure or furnish whatever is necessary for the production and dissemination of the light. . . . We can see no good reason why it may not also at the same time furnish it to the inhabitants to light their residences and places of business. To do so is, in our opinion, a legitimate exercise of the police power for the preservation of property and health." But express authority is generally required.[4] There is no question of the power of

---

Co., 29 Wis. 452; Sherwood v. C. W. Co., 90 Cal. 635; State v. Gas Light Co., 102 Mo. 472; Manhattan Trust Co. v. Dayton Nat. Gas Co., 55 Fed. Rep. 181.

[1] Tacoma G. & E. L. Co. v. Tacoma, 14 Wash. 288, 44 Pac. Rep. 655; St. Louis v. Bell Tel. Co., 96 Mo. 623, 2 L. R. A. 278; In re Prior, 55 Kan. 724, 29 L. R. A. 398.

[2] Foot & Everett, Incorporated Companies, I, p. 211. See note on legislative power to fix tolls, rates and prices, Winchester & L. T. Co. v. Croxton, 98 Ky. 739, 33 L. R. A. 177. As to manner of assessing and collecting water rates, see Kelsey v. Marquette Fire & Water Com'rs (Mich., 1897), 71 N. W. Rep. 589.

[3] Crawfordsville v. Brader, 130 Ind. 149, 14 L. R. A. 268 (1891). The contrary rule is announced in Spaulding v. Peabody, 153 Mass. 129, 10 L. R. A. 357.

[4] Dillon, Mun. Corp., §§ 146, 561.

the legislature to authorize cities to purchase or construct such plants.¹ It is simply a question of public policy. In Massachusetts it is held that the general law confers no power upon towns to maintain electric light plants.²

Power to provide for "lighting the streets,"³ or "to provide the city with water,"⁴ will authorize a city to construct its own plant for that purpose. The erection of an electric light plant to supply a city with light for use in the streets and public places and in the homes and places of business of the inhabitants is a municipal purpose for which bonds may be issued.⁵ There is authority to the effect that under power to light the city a municipality can purchase and operate its own plant, but cannot furnish its inhabitants with light, because this would be engaging in a private enterprise.⁶ But, as has been said,⁷ for a city to meet the demand for wholesome water "is to perform a public act and confer a public blessing. . . . It is not strictly a governmental or municipal function which every municipality is under obligation to assume and perform, but it is very closely akin to it, and should always be recognized as within the scope of its authority unless excluded by some positive law. . . . It cannot be said that the city in doing so is engaging in a private enterprise or performing a municipal

¹ Mitchell v. Negaunee (Mich., 1897), 71 N. W. Rep. 646; Opinion of Justices, 150 Mass. 392, 8 L. R. A. 487; Linn v. Chambersburg, 160 Mass. 511, 25 L. R. A. 217; Peabody v. Westerly Water Works Co. (R. I., 1897), 37 Atl. Rep. 807. Supplying the inhabitants with light and water is a municipal function which may properly be delegated to a municipality. Brenham v. Brenham Water Co., 67 Tex. 542; Opinion of Justices, 150 Mass. 392, 8 L. R. A. 487; Tacoma v. Tacoma L. & W. Co., 15 Wash. 499; Long v. Duluth, 48 Minn. 280, 51 N. W. Rep. 913; State v. Hamilton, 47 Ohio St. 52, 23 N. E. Rep. 935. As to lighting public buildings, see St. Paul G. L. Co. v. McCardy, 62 Minn. 509.

² Spaulding v. Peabody, 153 Mass. 129, 26 N. E. Rep. 421.

³ Parkersburg Gas Co. v. Parkersburg, 30 W. Va. 435; Saginaw G. L. Co. v. Saginaw, 28 Fed. Rep. 252; Crawfordsville v. Braden, 130 Ind. 149, 28 N. E. Rep. 849, 14 L. R. A. 268.

⁴ Atlantic City W. W. v. Atlantic City, 39 N. J. Eq. 367; Hall v. Houghton, 8 Mich. 451; Smith v. Mayor, 88 Tenn. 464; Putnam v. Grand Rapids, 58 Mich. 417.

⁵ Jacksonville v. Electric Light Co., 36 Fla. 229, 30 L. R. A. 540.

⁶ Mauldin v. Greenville, 33 S. C. 1, 8 L. R. A. 291.

⁷ Smith v. Nashville, 88 Tenn. 464, 7 L. R. A. 469; Fire Ins. Co. v. Keeseville, 148 N. Y. 46; Jacksonville Elec. L. Co. v. Jacksonville (Fla.), 30 L. R. A. 540; Thompson-Houston Elec. L. Co. v. Newton, 42 Fed. Rep. 723.

function for a private end." A city with authority to furnish water for its inhabitants has no authority to carry water outside of its limits for the purpose of supplying the inhabitants of another municipality.[1] But when a town succeeds to the business of a water company under a statute which authorizes it to furnish water to any person or corporation within its limits, it may deliver water to the corporation within its limits, although a part of the water is used beyond the city limits and in another municipal corporation.[2]

§ 147. *Nature of the power.*— It has been generally held that when a municipal corporation engages in the business of manufacturing gas and supplying and selling gas and water to its inhabitants it is engaged in a business of a private nature.[3] But the New York court of appeals has recently held[4] that such power is granted to municipalities for public use, and that as a result the corporation is not liable for damages resulting from nonuser or misuser of the power. The action was brought by an insurance company against the village for damages alleged to have been caused by the failure of the village to keep the city water-works system in proper condition. The court, after stating the distinction between the public and private powers which are ordinarily conferred upon municipal corporations, said: "When we find that the power conferred has relation to public purposes and is for the public good, it is to be classified as governmental in its nature, and it appertains to the corporation in its political character. When it relates to the accomplishment of private corporate purposes in which the public is indirectly concerned, it is private in its nature, and the municipal corporation in respect to its exercise is regarded as a legal individual. In the former case the corporation is exempt from all liability whether for nonuser or misuser; while in the latter case it may be held to that degree of

---

[1] Haupt's Appeal, 125 Pa. St. 211, 3 L. R. A. 536.

[2] Lawrence v. Meecham, 166 Mass. 206, 44 N. E. Rep. 247.

[3] Illinois Trust & Sav. Bank v. Arkansas City, 76 Fed. Rep. 271; Bailey v. New York, 3 Hill (N. Y.), 531, 38 Am. Dec. 669; Cincinnati v. Cameron, 33 Ohio St. 336; Helena Consol. Water Co. v. Steele (Mont., 1897), 49 Pac. Rep. 382, 37 L. R. A. 412; Western Sav. Fund Soc. v. Philadelphia, 31 Pa. St. 183, 72 Am. Dec. 730. See §§ 22, 43.

[4] Fire Ins. Co. v. Village of Keeseville, 148 N. Y. 46.

responsibility which would attach to an ordinary private corporation." The fact that water rents were paid by the inhabitants was held not to show that the corporation was engaged in private business. "The imposition of water rents is but a mode of taxation and a part of the general scheme for raising revenue with which to carry on the work of government. If profits accrue over the expense of maintaining the system, they go to benefit the public by lessening the general burden of taxation. . . . There is nothing connected with the work which is not of a governmental and public nature. It is in no sense a private business; and the authority to construct the work was given it by the legislature, not at its own particular instance or application, but because it was one of the political divisions of the state and as such was entitled to exercise it. . . . No interest was designed to be subserved other than that of adding to the powers of a community carrying on a local government."

§ 148. *The acquisition of the plant.*— Without express legislative authority a municipal corporation cannot grant an exclusive franchise to a company which will prevent the corporation from establishing a plant for the purpose of supplying itself with gas or water.[1] Under certain circumstances the franchise of a water company may be exclusive as to other companies, and yet not prevent the city from supplying water by works constructed by itself, although it may thus impair the value of the water company's franchise.[2] The reservation in the grant of a franchise to a water company of a *right* to purchase the plant at any time after the lapse of a stated period imposes no duty upon the town to purchase, and does not justify the inference that the city can only provide itself with water-works by purchasing from the company.[3] It has recently been held that a statute allowing a city to acquire a water plant only by purchase from private parties to whom it has granted a franchise or with whom it has entered into a contract is in violation of

---

[1] Long v. City of Duluth, 49 Minn. 280.
[2] Lehigh Water Co.'s Appeal, 102 Pa. St. 515. An exclusive statutory franchise to provide a city with water is assignable. San Luis Water
Co. v. Estrada (Cal., 1897), 48 Pac. Rep. 1075.
[3] Long v. Duluth, 49 Minn. 280; Syracuse Water Co. v. Syracuse, 116 N. Y. 167, 22 N. E. Rep. 381.

a constitutional provision prohibiting the legislature from levying a tax upon the people of a municipality for a municipal purpose without their consent.[1] A city may condemn the plant of a private gas or water company under the power of eminent domain.[2]

§ 149. *Contracts between municipality and franchise companies.*— Until within recent times it was customary for public corporations to enter into contracts with persons or corporations for a supply of water or lights for a term of years. Exclusive franchises were often granted to corporations. In some instances they entered into contracts with the companies, whereby the municipality deprived itself of the power to construct plants for the purpose of supplying itself and its inhabitants. In other cases the contract reserved to the city the right to purchase the plant of the company at a fixed valuation at the end of a definite period, or provided that the plant should become the property of the city at the termination of the franchise by lapse of time. The present tendency is toward the construction or acquisition of such plants by municipalities. Cities now commonly own and operate their own water-works, and in many cases manufacture and sell gas and electric light to the inhabitants. In acquiring the plants the municipality must not violate the contracts it has made with the persons to whom it has granted franchises. In Pennsylvania it is held that when a borough has contracted with a water company for a supply of water and reserved the right to purchase the plant after twenty years, and the company has laid its pipes and mains in the streets, it cannot during that period erect and maintain a system of water-works of its own and thus depreciate the value of the company's plant.[3]

If a valid contract is created it will be protected and enforced. If a city is engaged in a business of a private nature when it manufactures and sells water, gas or light to its in-

---

[1] Helena Consolidated Water Co. v. Steele (Mont., 1897), 49 Pac. Rep. 382, 37 L. R. A. 412.

[2] In re Brooklyn, 143 N. Y. 596, 26 L. R. A. 271.

[3] Metzger v. Beaver Falls, 178 Pa. St. 1; White v. Meadville, 177 Pa. St. 643, 34 L. R. A. 567; Wilson v. Borough of Rochester, 180 Pa. St. 509. As to power to make a contract excluding itself from competition with a water company for a term of years, see Westerly Water Works Co. v. Westerly, 80 Fed. Rep. 611.

habitants, its transactions are governed by the principles of private law. But the tendency illustrated by recent decisions to hold that power to supply water and lights is a governmental power may lead to a different conclusion. A public corporation cannot by contract deprive itself of its legislative power. All attempts to do so are ineffectual and may be disregarded.

But the legislative grant to a corporation or individual of special privileges may be a contract when the language is so explicit as to require such a construction. If, however, one of the conditions of the grant be that the grantor may revoke or alter it, there is no violation of the contract when the grant is revoked or altered.[1] Such grants will be strictly construed.

[1] Hamilton Gas Light Co. v. Hamilton City, 146 U. S. 258. This case was decided under the Ohio statute. One section provided that any city might erect gas works when it deemed it expedient. Another section provided that on the failure of a city gas company to extend its lines, make connections and perform certain duties, the charter of the company might be declared forfeited and the city be at liberty to establish and maintain gas works of its own. In State v. City of Hamilton, 47 Ohio St. 52, it was held that the city might erect gas works without reference to the failure of an existing gas company to perform its duties. The decision was affirmed in Hamilton Gas Light Co. v. Hamilton City, supra. The court said: "The contention is that such legislation [the first section above referred to] is within the constitutional inhibition of state laws impairing the obligation of contracts. This view is inadmissible. The statutes in force when the plaintiff became a corporation did not compel the city to use the gas light furnished by the plaintiff. The city was empowered to contract with the plaintiff for lighting streets, lanes, squares and public places within its limits, but it was under no legal obligation to make a contract of that character, although it could regulate by ordinance the price to be charged for gas light to be supplied by the plaintiff and used by the city or its inhabitants. It may be that the stockholders of the plaintiff supposed, at the time it became incorporated and when they made their original investment, that the city would never do what evidently is contemplated by the ordinance of 1889. And it may be that the erection and maintenance of gas works by the city at the public expense, and in competition with the plaintiff, will ultimately impair, if not destroy, the value of the plaintiff's works for the purposes for which they were established. But such consideration cannot control the legal rights of the parties. As said by this court in Curtis v. Whitney, 13 Wall. 68, 70: 'Nor does every statute which affects the value of a contract impair its obligation. It is one of the contingencies to which parties look now in making a large class of contracts, that they may be affected in many ways by state and national legislation.'"

"We are forbidden," said Mr. Justice Harlan,[1] "to hold that a grant, under legislative authority, of an exclusive privilege for a term of years, of supplying a municipal corporation and its people with water drawn by means of a system of waterworks from a particular stream of water, prevents the state from granting to other persons the privilege of supplying, during the same period, the same corporation and people with water drawn in like manner from a different stream or river."

[1] Stein v. Bienville Water Supply Co., 141 U. S. 67.

CHAPTER IX.

MUNICIPAL SECURITIES.

I. WARRANTS AND ORDERS.
§ 150. Power to issue.
151. Form.
152. Negotiability.
153. Effect of acceptance.
154. Presentment and demand.
155. Payable out of particular fund.
156. Rights of indorser.
157. Defenses.

II. MUNICIPAL BONDS.
158. Power of public *quasi*-corporations.
159. Power of municipal corporations.
160. Ratification of illegal bonds.
161. Liability for money received.
162. Right to restrain issue of illegal bonds.

a. PURPOSES FOR WHICH BONDS MAY BE ISSUED.
163. Must be a public purpose.
164. What are public purposes.
165. Railways.
166. Private purposes.
167. How determined.

b. CONDITIONS PRECEDENT TO LEGAL ISSUE.
§ 168. In general.
169. Consent of the people.
170. Manner of obtaining consent.
171. Majority of voters.
172. Location and completion of road.

c. ESTOPPEL.
173. When estoppel arises.
174. Authority of officers.
175. Estoppel by conduct; illustrations.
176. By judgment.

d. RIGHTS OF BONA FIDE HOLDERS.
177. Who are such.
178. Defenses available against a *bona fide* holder.
179. Recitals in bonds.
180. Effect of recitals—continued.
181. Authority of officials to make recitals.
182. Recital that bonds have been issued "in conformity to law."
183. Excessive issues.

I. WARRANTS AND ORDERS.

§ 150. *Power to issue.*—Counties, towns and municipal corporations have implied authority to issue instruments in the form of vouchers for money due, certificates of indebtedness for services rendered or property furnished, or orders by one officer of the municipality upon another. Such instruments are necessary and proper in carrying on the administration and anticipating the payment of taxes.[1] But in order to be

[1] Mayor v. Ray, 19 Wall. 477; Shawnee Co. Com'rs v. Carter, 2 Kan. 115.

valid, such warrants must be issued for a legal purpose and for the amount actually due. They cannot be discounted.[1]

§ 151. *Form.*—Warrants are commonly in the form of an order drawn by one officer upon another, by which the drawer authorizes the payment of a certain sum of money to the payee. Statutes prescribing the form are commonly held to be directory.[2]

§ 152. *Negotiability.*—In a few cases it has been held that warrants, when negotiable in form, have all the attributes of negotiable paper,[3] but the overwhelming weight of authority is to the effect that such instruments are not commercial paper within the meaning of the law merchant, and that the purchaser takes subject to any defenses which were available between the original parties.[4] "Although negotiable instruments," says Mr. Justice Gray,[5] "they belong to a peculiar class of such instruments, being made by a municipal corporation, and having no validity unless issued for a purpose authorized by law. . . . To invest such documents with the character and incidents of commercial paper, so as to render them in the hands of *bona fide* holders absolute obligations to pay, is an abuse of their true character and purpose." With reference to the power to issue such obligations Mr. Justice Miller says:[6] "It seems to us to be a question quite distinct from that of incurring indebtedness for improvements actually authorized and undertaken, the justice and validity of which

[1] Erskine v. Steele Co., 4 N. D. 339, 28 L. R. A. 645; Foster v. Coleman, 10 Cal. 278; Bauer v. Franklin Co., 51 Mo. 205; Arnott v. Spokane, 6 Wash. 442.
[2] Burton v. Harvey Co. Bank, 28 Kan. 390.
[3] Kelley v. Mayor, 4 Hill (N. Y.), 263; Crawford Co. v. Wilson, 7 Ark. 214; Hancock v. Chicot Co., 32 Ark. 575. See Fairchild v. Ogdensburgh, etc. Ry. Co., 15 N. Y. 337; Garvin v. Wiswell, 83 Ill. 215.
[4] Beardsley v. Steinberg (Mont.), 49 Pac. Rep. 499 (1897); Police Jury v. Britton, 15 Wall. (U. S.) 566; Mayor of Nashville v. Ray, 19 Wall. (U. S.) 478; Claiborne Co. v. Brooks, 111 U. S. 400; Emery v. Mariaville, 50 Me. 315; Sturtevant v. Liberty, 46 Me. 457; Shirk v. Pulaski Co., 4 Dill. (U. S.) 209; Clark v. Des Moines, 19 Iowa, 199; People v. Johnson, 100 Ill. 537, 39 Am. Rep. 63; Goodnow v. Ramsey Co., 11 Minn. 31 (Gil. 12); School District v. Stough, 4 Neb. 357; Hubbard v. Town of Linden, 48 Wis. 674; Eaton v. Berlin, 49 N. H. 219; Hyde v. Franklin Co., 27 Vt. 185; Erskine v. Steele Co., 4 N. D. 339, 28 L. R. A. 645.
[5] District of Columbia v. Cornell, 130 U. S. 655.
[6] Police Jury v. Britton, 15 Wall. (U. S.) 566.

may always be inquired into. It is a power which ought not to be implied from the mere authority to make such improvements. It is one thing for county or parish trustees to have the power to incur obligations for work actually done in behalf of the county or parish and to give proper vouchers therefor, and a totally different thing to have the power of issuing unimpeachable paper obligations which may be multiplied to an indefinite extent. It would be an anomaly justly to be deprecated for our limited territorial boards, charged with certain objects of local administration, to become the fountains of commercial issue capable of floating about in the commercial whirlpool of our great cities."

§ 153. *Effect of acceptance.*— A creditor is not obliged to accept a warrant in payment of his claim against a corporation, but if he does accept it and parts with it he loses his right of action on the original debt.[1] But the original holder of an unpaid or dishonored warrant may abandon it and sue on the original claim.[2]

§ 154. *Presentment and demand.*— In the absence of any provision to the contrary, municipal obligations are payable at the municipal treasury.[3] Until demand there is no default.[4] It is hence the duty of the holder of such instruments to present them to the proper officer for payment before bringing suit;[5] and the fact of presentment, demand and non-payment, or facts which will excuse the same, must be alleged and proven. A warrant is due immediately upon presentation and demand although there is no money in the treasury with which to pay it.[6] In a leading case it was said: "There is nothing in the charter which favors the notion that the liability of the city

[1] Dalrymple v. Whitingham, 26 Vt. 347. *Contra*, Lyell v. Lapeer Co., 6 McLean (C. C.), 446.

[2] Paddock v. Symonds, 11 Barb. (N. Y.) 117; Dyer v. Covington Tp., 19 Pa. St. 200; Varner v. Nobleborough, 2 Me. 121, 11 Am. Dec. 48. In Allison v. Juniata Co., 50 Pa. St. 351, it was held that the action must be upon the original claim.

[3] Friend v. Pittsburgh, 131 Pa. St. 305, 6 L. R. A. 636.

[4] Pekin v. Reynolds, 31 Ill. 529, 28 Am. Dec. 244; Dalrymple v. Whitingham, 26 Vt. 345; Central v. Wilcoxen, 3 Colo. 566; East Union Tp. v. Ryan, 86 Pa. St. 459.

[5] Varner v. Nobleborough, 2 Me. 126, 11 Am. Dec. 48.

[6] International Bank v. Franklin Co., 65 Mo. 105, 27 Am. Rep. 241; Terry v. Milwaukee, 15 Wis. 543; Mills Co. Nat. Bank v. Mills Co., 67 Iowa, 697.

for road debts is conditioned upon the existence of road funds
in the treasury. For road debts the city is absolutely and un-
conditionally liable as for other debts. This liability cannot
be controlled or varied by the form in which the warrant may
be drawn or worded by the municipal officers."[1]

§ 155. *Payable out of a particular fund.*— When the law
requires that a warrant shall be drawn on a specified fund it
cannot be made a general charge upon the treasury. The
holder of such warrant must look to the particular fund for
payment.[2] A warrant containing the words "Charge the same
to the account of Union Avenue" is payable out of a particular fund.[3] A warrant containing a clause, "payable out of
any money not otherwise appropriated,"[4] or "it being for the
appropriate part of the surplus revenue,"[5] is payable uncon-
ditionally. So a warrant payable "for jail purposes."[6] A
distinction must be observed between orders drawn payable
out of a particular fund and those which are simply chargeable to a particular account.[7]

§ 156. *Rights of indorser.*— The title to a warrant passes by
indorsement, and the assignee may sue in his own name,[8] although he stands in no better position than did the original
holder.[9] He must, however, show that the consideration for the
warrant was such an obligation as the corporation had authority to incur.[10]

§ 157. *Defenses.*— When payment of a warrant is made in
good faith the corporation is released from further liability.[11]
If re-issued after being paid it is void in the hands of an innocent purchaser.[12] But there must be some act evidencing an

[1] Clark v. Des Moines, 19 Iowa, 199.
[2] Campbell v. Polk Co., 76 Mo. 57; Boro v. Phillips Co., 4 Dill. (U. S. C. C.) 216; M'Cullough v. Mayor, 23 Wend. (N. Y.) 458; People v. Wood, 71 N. Y. 371.
[3] Lake v. Williamsburgh, 4 Denio (N. Y.), 520.
[4] Campbell v. Polk Co., 3 Iowa, 467.
[5] Pease v. Cornish, 19 Me. 191.
[6] Montague v. Horton, 12 Wis. 668.
[7] Clark v. Des Moines, 19 Iowa, 199; Pease v. Cornish, 19 Me. 191.

[8] Kelley v. Mayor, 4 Hill (N. Y.), 263; Great Falls Bank v. Farming-ton, 41 N. H. 32; Clark v. Des Moines, 19 Iowa, 199.
[9] Matthis v. Town of Cameron, 62 Mo. 504.
[10] School District v. Thompson, 5 Minn. 280; Goodnow v. Ramsey Co., 11 Minn. 31 (Gil. 12). See Polk v. Tunica, 52 Miss. 422.
[11] Sweet v. Carver Co., 16 Minn. 106.
[12] Board of Commissioners v. Standley (Colo.), 49 Pac. Rep. 23 (1897);

intent to cancel the warrant. Thus, the mere receiving of a warrant in payment of taxes is not of itself payment.[1] Want of authority is always a defense to an action on a warrant.[2] Although "a warrant signed by the proper officer *prima facie* imports validity and a subsisting cause of action, it is always competent for a municipal corporation, even after the issuance of a warrant on the treasury, to set up the defense of *ultra vires*."[3] So the authority of the officer issuing the warrant is always open to inquiry.[4] The statute of limitations runs from the time of demand and refusal.[5] Where there is want of power to borrow money there can be no recovery on warrants issued therefor, although the money received was used for a purpose for which the corporation had power to contract a debt.[6]

II. MUNICIPAL BONDS.

§ 158. *Power of public quasi-corporations.*— Legislative authority is necessary to authorize counties, townships and school districts to borrow money and issue negotiable bonds, or to issue negotiable bonds in aid of any public enterprise. It must be clearly conferred but may be implied. Thus, a county may issue bonds under express power to make a donation of "money or other securities" for the benefit of a state insane asylum.[7] Such bodies exist for purposes of local and police regulation, and having the power to levy taxes to defray all public charges created, they have no implied power to make commercial paper of any kind unless it is clearly implied from some express power which cannot be fairly exercised without it.[8] It is a

Chemung Bank v. Chemung Co., 5 Denio (N. Y.), 517.
[1] Wiley v. Greenfield, 30 Me. 452.
[2] Sault Ste. Marie v. Van Dusen, 40 Mich. 429; Jefferson Co. v. Arrighi, 54 Miss. 668; Nash v. St. Paul, 11 Minn. 174 (Gil. 110).
[3] Cheeney v. Town of Brookfield, 60 Mo. 53; Thomas v. Richmond, 12 Wall. (U. S.) 349; Salamanca Tp. v. Jasper Co. Bank, 22 Kan. 696.
[4] Taft v. Pittsford, 28 Vt. 286; First Nat. Bank v. Saratoga Co., 106 N. Y. 488.
[5] Clark v. Iowa City, 20 Wall. (U. S.) 583; Brewer v. Otoe Co., 1 Neb. 373; Leech v. Wilson Co., 68 Tex. 353.
[6] Allen v. Intendant of La Fayette, 89 Ala. 641, 9 L. R. A. 497.
[7] Lund v. Chippewa Co., 93 Wis. 640, 67 N. W. Rep. 927, 34 L. R. A. 131. See, also, as to implied power, Carter Co. v. Linton, 120 U. S. 517. Power to issue bonds payable in gold coin is not conferred on a county by a statute not prescribing the kind of money in which the bonds shall be paid. Burnett v. Maloney, 97 Tenn. 697, 34 L. R. A. 541.
[8] Goodnow v. Ramsey Co., 11 Minn. 31; Board of Education v. Blodgett.

power distinct from that of incurring indebtedness for improvements actually authorized; as it is one thing to have the power to incur a debt and to give proper vouchers therefor, and a totally different thing to have the power of issuing obligations unimpeachable in the hands of third persons.[1] Thus, the power to build a court-house does not include the power to issue municipal bonds in payment therefor.[2] But upon this last proposition the cases are not uniform, as it has been held that the power to contract debts carries with it the power to agree with creditors as to the time and manner of payment and the issue of negotiable bonds.[3]

§ 159. *Power of municipal corporations.*— The powers of cities and incorporated towns are somewhat more liberally construed, but notwithstanding this fact the rule is that the power to borrow money and to issue negotiable paper does not belong to such a corporation as an incident of its creation.[4] It is held, however, that express power to borrow money carries with it implied power to issue negotiable bonds.[5] Power to

---

155 Ill. 441, 31 L. R. A. 70; Police Jury v. Britton, 15 Wall. (U. S.) 566. The mere failure to provide means for paying the bonds does not render the enabling statute invalid. Stockton v. Powell, 29 Fla. 1, 15 L. R. A. 42.

[1] Claiborne Co. v. Brooks, 111 U. S. 400.

[2] Hill v. Memphis, 134 U. S. 198; Young v. Clarendon Tp., 132 U. S. 340; Kelley v. Town of Milan, 127 U. S. 139; Dent v. Cook, 45 Ga. 323; Knapp v. Hoboken, 39 N. J. L. 394; Hamlin v. Meadville, 6 Neb. 227; Goodnow v. Ramsey Co., 11 Minn. 31 (Gil. 12). In Rushville Gas L. Co. v. City of Rushville, 121 Ind. 206, 6 L. R. A. 315, the court said with reference to public corporations other than school districts, "issuing bonds to pay for property purchased is a very different thing from issuing bonds to obtain money."

[3] Williamsport v. Commonwealth, 84 Pa. St. 487, 24 Am. Rep. 208; First Municipality v. McDonough, 2 Rob. (La.) 244; Bank of Chillicothe v. Mayor, 7 Ohio (pt. 2), 31; Douglass v. Virginia City, 5 Nev. 122; Richmond v. McGirr, 78 Ind. 192; Holmes v. Shreeveport, 31 Fed. Rep. 113.

[4] Mayor v. Ray, 19 Wall. (U. S.) 468; Merrill v. Monticello, 138 U. S. 673; Hill v. Memphis, 134 U. S. 198; Hewitt v. School District, 94 Ill. 528.

[5] Comanche Co. v. Lewis, 133 U. S. 198; Seybert v. Pittsburgh, 1 Wall. (U. S.) 272; Commonwealth v. Pittsburgh, 34 Pa. St. 496; Evansville v. Evansville, etc. Ry. Co., 15 Ind. 395; Galena v. Corwith, 48 Ill. 423, 95 Am. Dec. 557; De Vose v. Richmond, 18 Gratt. 338, 98 Am. Dec. 646. See Merrill v. Monticello, 138 U. S. 673; Brenham v. German American Bank, 144 U. S. 191, and cases cited; Farr v. City of Grand Rapids (Mich., 1897), 70 N. W. Rep. 411. Power to issue bonds to take up floating indebtedness, see Morris v. Taylor (Oreg., 1897), 49 Pac. Rep. 23.

issue bonds will authorize their issue in the usual form of negotiable bonds payable to bearer.[1] It is not, however, implied from express authority to subscribe for stock in a railway corporation,[2] or from a grant of power to appropriate money to aid in the construction of a railroad, with authority to levy a tax to provide the money to meet the appropriation.[3] It is well settled that a public corporation cannot, without express authority, issue its negotiable bonds in aid of a railway corporation.[4]

§ 160. *Ratification of illegal bonds.*— An *ultra vires* act cannot be ratified by any act of the corporation.[5] Thus, where a corporation, in pursuance of a compromise agreement, consented to the entry of a decree in favor of the validity of certain bonds, the court said: "The act of the mayor in signing that agreement could give no validity to the bonds if they had none at the time the agreement was made. The want of authority to issue them extended to a want of authority to declare valid. The mayor had no such authority. The decree of the court was based solely on the declaration of the mayor, in the agreement, that the bonds were valid; and that declaration was of no more effect than the declaration of the mayor in the bill in chancery that the bonds were invalid. The adjudication in the decree cannot, under the circumstances, be set up as a judicial determination of the validity of the bonds.[6] This was not

[1] West Plains Tp. v. Sage, 32 U. S. App. 725, 69 Fed. Rep. 943; Austin v. Nalle, 85 Tex. 520.
[2] Hill v. Memphis, 134 U. S. 198; Kelly v. Milan, 127 U. S. 139; Norton v. Dyersburg, 127 U. S. 160; Claiborne Co. v. Brooks, 111 U. S. 400; Milan v. Tennessee Cent. Ry. Co., 11 Lea (Tenn.), 330.
[3] Concord v. Robinson, 121 U. S. 165, and cases cited in preceding note.
[4] Young v. Clarendon Tp., 132 U. S. 340; Brenham v. German American Bank, 144 U. S. 173; Claiborne Co. v. Brooks, 111 U. S. 400; Town of Coloma v. Eaves, 92 U. S. 484; Pitzman v. Freeburg, 92 Ill. 111; Delaware Co. v. McClintock, 51 Ind. 325; Missis- sippi, etc. R. R. Co. v. Camden, 23 Ark. 300; Clay v. Nicholas Co., 4 Bush (Ky.), 154; Williamson v. Keokuk, 44 Iowa, 88; Hawkins v. Carroll Co., 50 Miss. 735; Reineman v. Covington, etc. Ry. Co., 7 Neb. 310; Pennsylvania Ry. Co. v. Philadelphia, 47 Pa. St. 189; Fisk v. Kenosha, 26 Wis. 23; New Orleans, etc. Ry. Co. v. Dunn, 51 Ala. 128.
[5] Ottawa v. Carey, 108 U. S. 110; Lewis v. Shreveport, 108 U. S. 282; Daviess Co. v. Dickinson, 117 U. S. 657; Mills v. Gleason, 11 Wis. 470, 78 Am. Dec. 721; Blen v. Bear River, etc. Co., 20 Cal. 602, 81 Am. Dec. 132.
[6] Russell v. Place, 94 U. S. 606; Manhattan L. Ins. Co. v. Broughton, 109 U. S. 121.

the case of the submission to a court of a question for its decision on the merits; but it was a consent in advance to a particular decision by a person who had no right to bind the town by such a consent, because it gave life to invalid bonds; and the authorities of the town had no more power to do so than they had to issue the bonds originally." [1]

But when power to issue exists, and the bonds are rendered invalid by reason of some irregularity, they may be ratified by the act of the corporation.[2] The legislature may validate an illegal issue of bonds if at the time of the passage of the curative act it has constitutional authority to authorize an original issue of such bonds.[3]

§ 161. *Liability for money received.*—Although the cases are not uniform, the rule may be considered as established that when a corporation has issued illegal bonds, and received and applied the proceeds thereof to an authorized purpose, an action will lie against the corporation for money had and received, although there can be no recovery upon the bond.[4] As stated in a recent case,[5] municipal corporations are liable to actions of implied *assumpsit* with respect to money or property received by them and applied beneficially to their authorized objects, through contracts which are simply unauthorized as distinguished from contracts which are prohibited by their charters or some other law bearing upon them, or are *malum in se*, or violative of public policy.

[1] Kelley v. Town of Milan, 127 U. S. 139, per Blatchford, J.

[2] Bolles v. Brimfield, 120 U. S. 759; Anderson v. Santa Anna Co., 116 U. S. 356; Otoe Co. v. Baldwin, 111 U. S. 1; Black v. Cohen, 52 Ga. 621; Bridgeport v. Housatonic Ry. Co., 15 Conn. 475; Mills v. Gleason, 11 Wis. 493, 78 Am. Dec. 721; Comer v. Folsom, 13 Minn. 219 (Gil. 205); Kunkle v. Town of Franklin, 13 Minn. 127 (Gil. 119), 97 Am. Dec. 226. By payment of interest. Brown v. Bon Homme Co. (S. D.), 46 N. W. Rep. 173.

[3] Sykes v. Columbus, 55 Miss. 115; Katzenberger v. Aberdeen, 121 U. S. 172. A municipal subscription to the stock of a railway company or in aid of the construction of a railroad, made without authority previously conferred, may be confirmed and legalized by subsequent enactment, when legislation of that character is not prohibited by the constitution, and when that which is done would have been legal had it been done under legislative sanction previously given. Grenada Co. v. Brogden, 112 U. S. 261, 7 Am. & Eng. Corp. Cas. 329.

[4] Bangor Sav. Bank v. Stillwater, 49 Fed. Rep. 721; Argenti v. San Francisco, 16 Cal. 255; Morton v. Nevada, 41 Fed. Rep. 582; Chapman v. Douglas Co., 107 U. S. 348; Salt Lake City v. Hollister, 118 U. S. 256.

[5] Allen v. The Intendant of La Fayette, 89 Ala. 641, 9 L. R. A. 497.

§ 162. *Right to restrain issue of illegal bonds.*— Where no adequate remedy at law exists, a taxpayer may restrain the illegal issue of bonds which would be valid in the hands of an innocent holder for value.[1] But if they are of such a character as to be void even in the hands of an innocent holder, the taxpayer cannot suffer any loss by reason of their issue, and hence cannot maintain an action for injunction.[2]

a. PURPOSES FOR WHICH BONDS MAY BE ISSUED.

§ 163. *Must be a public purpose.*— The money with which to pay maturing bonds must be raised by taxation; and it follows from the general rule governing taxation that negotiable bonds can be issued for public purposes only.[3] "The legislature," said Chief Justice Black,[4] " has no constitutional right to create a debt, or to levy a tax, or to authorize any municipal corporation to do it, in order to raise money for a private purpose. No such authority passed to the general assembly by the general grant of legislative power. This would not be legislation. Taxation is a mode of raising money for public purposes. When it is prostituted to objects in no way connected with public interest or welfare, it ceases to be taxation and becomes plunder."

§ 164. *What are public purposes.*— A public corporation may properly incur a debt and issue bonds for the purpose of paving streets,[5] constructing water-works,[6] supporting public schools,[7]

[1] Harrington v. Town of Plainview, 27 Minn. 224; Flack v. Hughes, 67 Ill. 384; Hodgman v. Chicago, etc. Ry. Co., 20 Minn. 48; English v. Smock, 54 Ind. 115, 7 Am. Rep. 215.

[2] McCoy v. Briant, 53 Cal. 247; East Oakland Tp. v. Skinner, 94 U. S. 256.

[3] Parkersburg v. Brown, 106 U. S. 487; Loan Ass'n v. Topeka, 20 Wall. 655; City of Eufaula v. McNab, 67 Ala. 588; Baltimore, etc. Ry. Co. v. Spring, 80 Md. 510, 27 L. R. A. 72.

[4] Sharpless v. Mayor of Philadelphia, 21 Pa. St. 147, 59 Am. Dec. 759.

[5] Gladstone v. Throop, 71 Fed. Rep. 341, 37 U. S. App. 481; Rogers v. Burlington, 3 Wall. 654; In re Washington Ave., 69 Pa. St. 352; People v. Flagg, 46 N. Y. 401.

[6] Land, L. & L. Co. v. Brown, 73 Wis. 294, 3 L. R. A. 473; Yesler v. Seattle, 1 Wash. 308. As to irrigation bonds, see § 112; Hughson v. Crane, 115 Cal. 404; Falmouth Irrigation District v. Bradley, 164 U. S. 112.

[7] Read v. Plattsmouth, 107 U. S. 568; Hensley v. People, 82 Ill. 544; Richards v. Raymond, 92 Ill. 612, 34 Am. Rep. 151; Board of Education v. State, 26 Kan. 44.

§ 165.]   MUNICIPAL SECURITIES.   153

constructing public buildings,[1] acquiring electric light plant,[2] and, under express legislative authority, to aid in celebrating some great national event, such as the Columbian Exposition,[3] or the anniversary of its incorporation,[4] or for the entertainment of distinguished visitors upon such occasions.[5] But no implied authority exists to appropriate money for such purposes.[6] The treatment of habitual drunkards in a private institution, which is subject to visitation and inspection, is not a public purpose for which a county can be required to pay.[7]

§ 165. *Railways.*—Railways are of such a public character that a public corporation may be authorized to aid in their construction, either by subscription to their capital stock or by donation, and the issue of negotiable bonds in payment of such subscription or donation.[8] The public has an interest in such roads when they belong to a corporation as clearly as it would if they were free or if tolls were payable to the state. Travel and transportation are cheapened by it to a degree far exceeding all the charges. This advantage the public has in addition to those of rapidity, comfort and increase of trade.[9]

[1] Leavenworth v. Miller, 7 Kan. 479. Public park. People v. Detroit, 28 Mich. 228, 15 Am. Rep. 202; People v. Chicago, 51 Ill. 17, 2 Am. Rep. 278.

[2] Electric Light Co. v. Jacksonville, 36 Fla. 229, 30 L. R. A. 540.

[3] Daggett v. Colgan, 92 Cal. 53, 14 L. R. A. 474, and note.

[4] Hill v. Easthampton, 140 Mass. 381.

[5] Tatham v. Philadelphia, 11 Phil. 276.

[6] Hodges v. Buffalo, 2 Denio (N. Y.), 110; Hood v. Lynn, 1 Allen (Mass.), 103; The Liberty Bell, 23 Fed. Rep. 843. See Hayes v. Douglas County, 92 Wis. 429, 31 L. R. A. 213.

[7] Wisconsin Keeley Institute Co. v. Milwaukee Co. (Wis.), 70 N. W. Rep. 68, 36 L. R. A. 54. See § 97, *supra*.

[8] Norton v. Dyersburg, 127 U. S. 139; Concord v. Robinson, 121 U. S. 165; Gelpcke v. Dubuque, 1 Wall. (U. S.) 175; Quincy, etc. Ry. Co. v. Morris, 84 Ill. 410; Pine Grove Tp. v. Talcott, 19 Wall. (U. S.) 666, reversing People v. Salem, 20 Mich. 452, 4 Am. Rep. 400; Thompson v. Lee County, 3 Wall. (U. S.) 327; Dickinson v. Neely, 30 S. C. 587, 3 L. R. A. 672; Whiting v. Sheboygan, etc. Ry. Co., 25 Wis. 167, 3 Am. Rep. 30; Davidson v. Ramsey County, 18 Minn. 482; Ex parte Selma, etc. Ry. Co., 45 Ala. 696, 6 Am. Rep. 722; Society of Savings v. New London, 29 Conn. 174; Renick v. Davenport, 47 Iowa, 511; Hallenbeck v. Hahn, 2 Neb. 377; Wullenwaber v. Dunigan, 30 Neb. 877, 13 L. R. A. 811; Nelson v. Haywood Co., 87 Tenn. 781, 4 L. R. A. 648. The Michigan court adheres to the decision in People v. Salem. *supra*, although it was reversed by the supreme court of the United States. People v. State Treasurer, 23 Mich. 499; Thomas v. Port Huron, 27 Mich. 320.

[9] Sharpless v. Mayor of Philadelphia, 21 Pa. St. 147, 59 Am. Dec. 759.

But bonds issued by a county for the benefit of an insolvent railroad company, with a provision that legal claims against the company held by residents of the county shall first be paid out of the proceeds, are void.[1] "The effect and scope of the act is simply to levy a tax upon the property of the citizens of the county to pay to certain residents of the county the claims due to them by an insolvent railway company. This is a private purpose and not one of the objects of taxation."

In most of the cases no distinction is made between a subscription to the stock of and a donation to the railway company;[2] but it has been held that while a subscription to stock is valid, a gift for the same purpose is invalid.[3] The road to be aided need not be in the municipality and may be in another state.[4]

§ 166. *Private purposes.*— The public has no such interest in manufacturing and mining enterprises as will justify the exercise of the power of taxation in their aid. And it follows that bonds issued for such purposes are invalid.[5] Thus, a city

[1] Baltimore, etc. Ry. Co. v. Spring, 80 Md. 510, 27 L. R. A. 72.

[2] In Davidson v. Ramsey Co., 18 Minn. 482 (Gil. 432), the court said: "So far as the question of power is concerned we think it quite unimportant whether the money to be raised is to be given to the company or loaned to it, or applied to pay for subscriptions to stock. Stewart v. Polk Co., 30 Iowa, 9. As remarked by Chief Justice Black in Sharpless v. Mayor of Philadelphia, 21 Pa. St. 147 and 169, the right to tax depends upon the ultimate use, purpose and object for which the fund is raised. . . . The purpose of constructing a railroad is a public purpose; . . . and if it is thought to be better that an outright gift of money should be made than that the city should become a stockholder in the road, there is nothing to prevent the former course from being adopted."

[3] Whiting v. Sheboygan, etc. Ry. Co., 35 Wis. 167, 8 Am. Rep. 30; Sweet v. Hulbert, 51 Barb. (N. Y.) 312.

[4] Bell v. Mobile, etc. Ry. Co., 4 Wall. (U. S.) 598; Chicago, etc. Ry. Co. v. Otoe Co., 16 Wall. (U. S.) 667; Walker v. Cincinnati, 21 Ohio St. 14, 8 Am. Rep. 24; St. Jo. etc. Ry. Co. v. Buchanan Co., 39 Mo. 485. See 72 Mo. 329.

[5] Loan Ass'n v. Topeka, 3 Dill. 376, 20 Wall. (U. S.) 655; Osborne v. Adams Co., 106 U. S. 181, 109 U. S. 1; Parkersburg v. Brown, 106 U. S. 487, 2 Am. & Eng. Corp. Cas. 263; Blair v. Cuming Co., 111 U. S. 363; Brodhead v. Milwaukee, 19 Wis. 624, 88 Am. Dec. 711; Weismer v. Douglas, 64 N. Y. 91, 21 Am. Rep. 586; Bissell v. Kankakee, 64 Ill. 249, 21 Am. Rep. 554; Tyler v. Beacher, 44 Vt. 648, 8 Am. Rep. 398; Allen v. Jay, 60 Me. 124, 11 Am. Rep. 185. In State v. Osawkee Tp., 14 Kan. 418, 19 Am. Rep. 99, it was held that money might lawfully be appropriated to provide destitute farmers with seed grain; but the contrary was held in State v. Nelson Co. (N. Dak.), 45 N. W. Rep. 33, 8 L. R. A. 283, and In re House Roll No. 284,

cannot legally incur a debt and issue bonds for the purpose of aiding in the construction of a dam over a river within the limits of the municipality, in order to aid in developing the manufacturing interests of the city.[1]

§ 167. *How determined.*— It is well settled that the courts must determine whether the particular purpose under consideration is public or private,[2] and in so doing they must be guided largely by considerations of public policy.[3]

b. CONDITIONS PRECEDENT TO LEGAL ISSUE.

§ 168. *In general.*— The issue of bonds by public corporations is ordinarily authorized upon certain specified conditions. Such conditions may be imposed by the constitution, an act of the legislature, or by the corporate authorities. Those imposed by the constitution or act of the legislature must be strictly complied with or the bonds will be invalid.[4] But where the law provided that bonds should not "be valid and binding until such conditions precedent had been complied with," it was held that they might be complied with after the bonds were issued.[5] After there has been substantial performance of the conditions, the validity of the bonds is not affected by subsequent acts.[6] Such conditions may be imposed by the corporation although not required to do so by the law.[7] But an innocent purchaser of

81 Neb. 505. In Lowell v. Boston, 111 Mass. 454, 15 Am. Rep. 39, it was held a city has no power to issue bonds in aid of persons suffering from a flood or fire.

[1] Mather v. Ottawa, 114 Ill. 659, 11 Am. & Eng. Corp. Cas. 248; Ottawa v. Carey, 108 U. S. 110.

[2] In re Townsend, 39 N. Y. 171.

[3] Perry v. Keene, 56 N. H. 514. In Weismer v. Douglas Co., 64 N. Y. 91, 21 Am. Rep. 586, Mr. Justice Folger said: "When we come to ask, in any case, what is a public purpose, the answer is not always ready nor easy to be found. It is to be conceded that no pinched or meager sense may be put on the words, and that if the purpose designated by the legislature lie so near the border line as that it may be doubtful on which side it may be domiciled, the court may not set their judgment against that of the law-makers."

[4] Leavenworth, etc. Ry. Co. v. Platte Co., 42 Mo. 171; Essex Co. Ry. Co. v. Lunenburg, 49 Vt. 143; Town of Eagle v. Kohn, 84 Ill. 292; Belo v. Forsythe Co., 76 N. C. 489.

[5] Town of Eagle v. Kohn, 84 Ill. 292.

[6] Hodgman v. Chicago, etc. Ry. Co., 23 Minn. 153.

[7] Mason v. Shawneetown, 77 Ill. 533; California, etc. Ry. Co. v. Butte Co., 18 Cal. 671; Hodgman v. Chicago, etc. Ry. Co., 20 Minn. 48, 23 Minn. 153; Coe v. Railway Co., 27 Minn. 197.

bonds issued under such conditions is not required to see that they have been complied with.[1] When conditions have been submitted to and approved by the voters of a municipality they cannot be waived by the municipal officials,[2] but must be resubmitted to the people.[3] But it seems that if it is generally known that the conditions have not been complied with, and the bonds are allowed to issue without objection, it will be held to amount to a waiver.[4] The power to determine when conditions have been performed is an official trust which cannot be delegated by the corporate authorities.[5]

§ 169. *Consent of the people.*— A common condition precedent to the issue of bonds is that the consent of a certain proportion of the voters or taxpayers shall first be obtained at a general or special election. This is now required in most of the states. But a popular vote does not confer power to issue aid bonds in the absence of a valid enabling act.[6] This condition must be strictly complied with;[7] but irregularities which do not affect the result of the election will not invalidate the bonds in the hands of an innocent purchaser for value.[8] Reasonable certainty only in the manner of voting is necessary.[9]

§ 170. *Manner of obtaining consent.*— When a majority of the voters of a municipality are authorized by law to incumber the property of all in aid of some public purpose, the record of the proceedings must affirmatively show that the statutory authority has been followed according to its terms.[10] Thus,

[1] Nelson v. Haywood Co., 87 Tenn. 781, 4 L. R. A. 648, 659.
[2] Hodgman v. Chicago, etc. Ry. Co., 20 Minn. 48, 23 Minn. 153.
[3] Town of Platteville v. Galena, 43 Wis. 493; State v. Montgomery, 74 Ala. 226; Douglas Co. v. Walbridge, 38 Wis. 179; State v. Daviess Co., 64 Mo. 30.
[4] Leavenworth, etc. Ry. Co. v. Douglas Co., 18 Kan. 169.
[5] Jackson Co. v. Brush, 77 Ill. 59; Knox Co. v. Nichols, 14 Ohio St. 260.
[6] Allen v. Louisiana, 103 U. S. 80; Hayes v. Holly Springs, 114 U. S. 120.

[7] Louis v. Bourbon Co., 12 Kan. 186. See State v. Saline Co., 48 Mo. 390, 8 Am. Rep. 108.
[8] Johnson Co. v. Thayer, 94 U. S. 631; Commissioners v. Shorter, 50 Ga. 489; State v. Hordey, 39 Kan. 657, 18 Pac. Rep. 942. Mere informality in conducting the election will not overcome the presumption that the holder is a *bona fide* holder. Pana v. Bowler, 107 U. S. 539.
[9] Ranney v. Baeder, 50 Mo. 600.
[10] Rich v. Mentz Tp., 134 U. S. 623; Cowdry v. Caneadea, 16 Fed. Rep. 532.

where the proceeding is by petition, the petition required by the law must be absolute,[1] must contain all the facts required by the law,[2] and be signed by the requisite number [3] of duly qualified citizens.[4] A petition showing the consent of a "majority of taxpayers" is not sufficient when the law requires the consent of a majority of taxpayers exclusive of those taxed for dogs and highway purposes only.[5] A required election must be called by the persons designated in the law [6] and notice must be given in the manner directed.[7] When the notice is required to be given by the supervisors, it may be by order of the board signed by the clerk.[8] The notice must state the subject-matter to be voted on with reasonable certainty. Thus, an article in a warrant for a town meeting "to see if the town will loan its credit to aid in the construction" of a railroad is sufficient.[9] But a notice which does not state the amount of bonds proposed to be issued, the interest or the time or place of payment thereof, but merely the time of election and the object of the bonds, is insufficient.[10] A general notice of election need not state the places at which the election will be held when the general election law requires that notices to be posted in each precinct shall contain such statement.[11] The conditions in the bonds must follow the notice.[12]

§ 171. "*Majority of voters.*"— A majority of the legal voters satisfies a statute which requires a majority of the taxpayers.[13] The consent of the "inhabitants" means the consent of the legal voters.[14] A majority of the legal voters means a majority of those voting at an election duly called and held.[15] A major-

[1] Craig v. Township of Andes, 93 N. Y. 405. *Contra*, Bittinger v. Bell, 65 Ind. 445.
[2] People v. Spencer, 55 N. Y. 1; Wellsborough v. New York, etc. Ry. Co., 76 N. Y. 182.
[3] People v. Oldtown, 88 Ill. 202.
[4] People v. Cline, 63 Ill. 394.
[5] Rich v. Mentz Tp., 134 U. S. 623.
[6] Jacksonville R. R. Co. v. Virden, 104 Ill. 339.
[7] George v. Oxford Tp., 16 Kan. 72.
[8] Lawson v. Milwaukee, etc. Ry. Co., 30 Wis. 597.
[9] Belfast v. Brooks, 60 Me. 569;

Bowen v. Mayor of Greensboro, 79 Ga. 709.
[10] Packwood v. Kittitas Co., 15 Wash. 88, 33 L. R. A. 673, 45 Pac. Rep. 640.
[11] Packwood v. Kittitas Co., *supra*.
[12] Skinner v. Santa Rosa (Cal.), 29 L. R. A. 512.
[13] Hannibal v. Fauntleroy, 105 U. S. 408.
[14] Walnut Tp. v. Wade, 103 U. S. 683.
[15] St. Joseph Tp. v. Rogers, 16 Wall. 644; Cass Co. v. Johnston, 95 U. S. 360, overruling Harshman v. Bates, 92 U. S. 569. The supreme court of

ity of the qualified electors means a majority of the registered voters.[1] Two-thirds of the qualified voters means two-thirds of those who vote.[2] A purchaser of county bonds need look no further than the record made by the county board of their determination that the requisite number of votes has been cast.[3]

§ 172. *Location and completion of roads.*— Where bonds are to be used to aid in the construction of a railroad it is commonly made a condition precedent to their lawful issue and delivery that the road to be aided shall be located on a certain line or completed to a designated point. Such conditions must be complied with before the bonds are earned.[4] A condition that the company shall, before a certain date, "have completed, ironed and equipped its road from said village of W. to the city of M., and have the same in operation for the transportation of passengers and freight," is substantially complied with by so constructing the road to within a quarter of a mile of the village of W. and from that point entering the town over the line of another company and using its depot.[5] The completion of a road to within three-quarters of a mile of the opposite bank of the Mississippi river is not performance of a condition requiring the completion of the road to a town on the opposite side of the river, but the railway company cannot in such case be required to construct a bridge across the river. It is sufficient if it provides such facilities for crossing as at the time of the contract were usual and customary under the circumstances in railroad transportation and as were reasonably adequate

Missouri has held the statute under consideration in the above case unconstitutional. State v. Harris, 96 Mo. 29, 22 Am. & Eng. Corp. Cas. 43: Carroll Co. v. Smith, 111 U. S. 556; People v. Warfield, 20 Ill. 160; People v. Wiant, 48 Ill. 263; Griffin v. Inman, 57 Ga. 370. "The majority of such electors," as used in section 1, article 2, constitution of Minnesota, means the majority of the electors voting at the election. Taylor v. Taylor, 10 Minn. 107 (Gil. 81); Everett v. Smith, 22 Minn. 53; Belknap v. Louisville (Ky.), 34 L. R. A. 256.

[1] Sutherland v. Town of Goldsboro, 96 N. C. 49; McDowell v. Mass. etc. Co., 96 N. C. 514.
[2] State v. St. Joseph, 37 Mo. 270.
[3] Portland, etc. Ry. Co. v. Hartford, 58 Me. 23; Woonsocket, etc. Ry. Co. v. Sherman, 8 R. I. 504; Stockton, etc. Ry. Co. v. Stockton, 51 Cal. 328; Virginia, etc. Ry. Co. v. Lyon Co., 6 Nev. 68; Dickinson v. Neely, 30 S. C. 587, 3 L. R. A. 672.
[4] Valley Co. v. McLean, 49 U. S. App. 131, 79 Fed. Rep. 728.
[5] State v. Clark, 23 Minn. 422. And see Mo. Pac. Ry. Co. v. Tygard, 84 Mo. 263, 54 Am. Rep. 97.

and convenient.[1] Whether the time of completion is material will depend upon the language of the statute. When not made of the essence of the contract the municipality will be liable on the bonds if it actually receives the benefits sought by the contract.[2] Thus, a railway company does not forfeit its right to a donation by its failure to complete its road within the designated time when the prescribed expenditure has been made within the township limit.[3] The actual location of the road may be made a condition precedent to the submission of the question of aid to the voters.[4] In such a case, if the conditions are not complied with and the bonds are nevertheless issued, they are invalid unless held by *bona fide* purchasers without notice.[5]

C. ESTOPPEL.

§ 173. *When estoppel arises.*— It has been stated that want of power is always a defense to an action on municipal securities, even as against a *bona fide* holder. The validity of such instruments is ordinarily attacked on the grounds: First, because issued or used for other than public purposes; second, because the enabling statute is unconstitutional; or third, because of non-compliance with conditions imposed by the enabling act or the issuing corporation. But the corporation may by its acts place itself in a position where it cannot avail itself of what would

---

[1] Hodgman v. Chicago, etc. Ry. Co., 20 Minn. 48. See Winona v. Thompson, 24 Minn. 199, and Winona v. Cowdry, 93 U. S. 612.
[2] Nevada Bank v. Steinmetz, 61 Cal. 301; Kansas City Ry. Co. v. Alderman, 47 Mo. 349; Portage Co. v. Wis. etc. Ry. Co., 121 Mass. 460; People v. Holden, 82 Ill. 93; McManus v. Duluth, C. & W. R. Co., 51 Minn. 30; German Savings Bank v. Franklin Co., 128 U. S. 526.
[3] Nixson v. Campbell, 106 Ind. 47.
[4] Cass v. Jordan, 95 U. S. 373; Treadwell v. Hancock Co., 11 Ohio St. 183.
[5] Purdy v. Lansing, 128 U. S. 557; Millen v. Lansing, 11 Fed. Rep. 829. In Wilson Co. v. First Nat. Bank, 103 U. S. 770, it was held that it was not necessary that there should have been a definite and final survey and location of the entire line of road before the election. All that was necessary was a substantial location designating the termini and general direction of the road and an estimate of the cost of construction. In some of the state courts, however, a much stricter rule is applied. Thus, where a condition required the construction of a road within twelve hundred feet of a mill, it was held that its construction within two thousand feet was not a compliance with the conditions. Virginia, etc. R. R. Co. v. Lyon Co., 6 Nev. 68. Federal courts disregard fractions of miles in such cases. Johnson Co. v. Thayer, 94 U. S. 631.

but for the doctrine of estoppel be a good defense. No estoppel can arise, however, against the defense of want of power.[1] Even a *bona fide* holder for value is bound to take notice of the law under which the bonds are issued.[2]

§ 174. *Authority of officers.*— A public corporation is not estopped to deny the authority of persons who assume to act for it; and it follows that purchasers of bonds must assume the risk of the genuineness of signatures and official character.[3] Mr. Justice Bradley said:[4] "The plea that the city is estopped by the acts of its officers, by the resolutions of the city council, or by the negotiable form or matter in the bonds themselves, from denying the authority of such officers to pledge the faith of the city in aid of said plank-road and to issue the bonds in question, cannot be maintained. Public officers cannot acquire authority by declaring that they have it. They cannot thus shut the mouths of the public whom they represent. The officers and agents of private corporations intrusted by them with the management of their own business and property may estop their principals and subject them to the consequences of their unauthorized acts. But the body politic cannot be thus silenced by the acts or declarations of its agents. I hold it to be a sound proposition that no municipal or political body can be estopped by the acts or declarations of its officers from denying their authority to bind it."

§ 175. *Estoppel by conduct — Illustrations.*— A municipality may by its course of dealing be estopped to interpose a defense growing out of an irregular exercise of power. Under such

[1] Aspinwall v. Daviess Co., 22 How. (U. S.) 364; Marsh v. Fulton Co., 10 Wall. (U. S.) 676; Loan Ass'n v. Topeka, 20 Wall. (U. S.) 655; Force v. Town of Batavia, 61 Ill. 100; Bissell v. Kankakee, 64 Ill. 249, 21 Am. Rep. 554; Town of Douglass v. Niantic Sav. Bank, 97 Ill. 228; Williamson v. Keokuk, 44 Iowa, 88: Lamoille, etc. Ry. Co. v. Fairfield, 51 Vt. 257. Mr. Simonton (Mun. Bonds, § 192) says: "The true meaning of the term 'want of power' is the total lack of authority in the corporation to act, and every act done by the municipal corporation without power is void and cannot be made valid by any act of the corporation or its officers."

[2] Barnett v. Dennison, 145 U. S. 136; Ottawa v. Carey, 108 U. S. 110; Force v. Town of Batavia, 61 Ill. 100.

[3] Merchants' Bank v. Bergen Co., 115 U. S. 348; Brown v. Bon Homme Co., 1 S. Dak. 216, 46 N. W. Rep. 173; Coler v. Cleburne, 131 U. S. 162; Flagg v. School District, 4 N. Dak. 30, 25 L. R. A. 363, 58 N. W. Rep. 499.

[4] Chisholm v. Montgomery, 2 Wood (C. C.), 584.

circumstances the holder of the bonds is entitled to the same protection as a *bona fide* holder.[1] Thus, an estoppel may arise by the corporation retaining the consideration, such as stock, received for the bonds, and paying interest on the bonds.[2] But it must be remembered that such acts do not create an estoppel when no power to issue the bonds existed. If the legislature was without power to authorize the issue of bonds and the enabling statute is therefore invalid, the mere payment of interest or other such acts cannot create or supplement the power which is lacking.[3] Failure to enjoin the issue of bonds, followed by long acquiescence, has been held to work an estoppel.[4] But when suit was brought twelve years after the issue of the bonds to secure a correction of their form, and it appeared that the town' officers had been culpably negligent, the relief was granted as against the defendants, who knew all the facts and were trying to obtain an unfair advantage.[5] The mere execution and delivery of bonds will not estop the corporation from asserting the non-performance of conditions precedent.[6]

[1] Rogers v. Burlington, 3 Wall. (U. S.) 654; Bissell v. Jeffersonville, 24 How. (U. S.) 287; Bennington v. Park, 50 Vt. 178; N. H. etc. Ry. Co. v. Chatham, 42 Conn. 465; Steines v. Franklin Co., 48 Mo. 167, 8 Am. Rep. 87.

[2] Alvord v. Syracuse Savings Bank, 98 N. Y. 599, 8 Am. & Eng. Corp. Cas. 598; People v. Cline, 63 Ill. 394; Ray Co. v. Vansycle, 96 U. S. 675; State v. Clinton Co., 6 Ohio St. 280. In Pendleton Co. v. Amy, 13 Wall. (U. S.) 297, it appeared that the county issued bonds without a popular vote as required by law. After holding the stock which it received for the bonds for seventeen years the county was held estopped to defend, although the bonds contained no recitals. In Moulton v. Evansville, 25 Fed. Rep. 382, the court said: "While it is unquestionably true that the payment of interest will not validate a bond issued without authority of law, yet in cases where the objection is, not a want of power to issue, but of compliance with a condition in respect to which there may be an estoppel by recitals or other act by the city officials, such payment of interest ought to have and has been held to have great weight." See, also, the remarks of Judge Drummond in Portsmouth Savings Bank v. Springfield, 4 Fed. Rep. 276. The payment of interest on all the bonds issued is not a ratification of those issued in excess of the constitutional limit. Daviess Co. v. Dickinson, 117 U. S. 657.

[3] Loan Ass'n v. Topeka, 20 Wall. (U. S.) 655.

[4] Supervisors of Marshall Co. v. Schenck, 5 Wall. (U. S.) 781; Meyer v. Muscatine, 1 Wall. (U. S.) 384, *Contra*, as to mere failure to enjoin. McPherson v. Foster, 43 Iowa, 48, 22 Am. Rep. 215.

[5] Town of Essex v. Day, 52 Conn. 483, 11 Am. & Eng. Corp. Cas. 265.

[6] Buchanan v. Litchfield, 102 U. S. 278. But see Mutual Ben. Life Ins. Co. v. Elizabeth, 42 N. J. L. 235.

11

§ 176. *By judgment.*— A judgment against a corporation on a contract, although by default, closes the question of the power of the corporation to make the contract. Hence, "in an action to enforce the collection of a judgment, or the collection of bonds or coupons issued in payment of a judgment against a municipal or *quasi*-municipal corporation, the judgment conclusively estops the corporation from making the defense that the original indebtedness evidenced by it was in excess of the amount which the corporation had the power to create, under the limitation of the constitution of the state in which it was incorporated."[1]

d. RIGHTS OF BONA FIDE HOLDERS.

§ 177. *Who are such.*— A *bona fide* holder of municipal securities is one who purchases for value without notice of any defect or is the successor of one who was such a purchaser.[2] A purchaser for value from a *bona fide* holder is entitled to all the rights of such holder, although such purchaser has notice of existing equities.[3] A purchaser is not charged with constructive notice of defenses by the pendency of an action to determine the validity of the bonds;[4] nor by the fact that the bonds were issued in violation of an injunction issued in a proceeding to which he was not a party.[5] The presence of overdue coupons on a bond will not charge the purchaser with notice of defenses;[6] but when the bond states that default in the payment of interest will render the bond due and payable, the presence of unpaid coupons is notice that the whole amount

---

[1] Board of Commissioners v. Platt (C. C. A.), 70 Fed. Rep. 572; Last Chance Min. Co. v. Tyler Min. Co., 157 U. S. 683; Cutler v. Houston, 158 U. S. 423; Sioux City, etc. St. R. Co. v. Osceola Co., 45 Iowa, 168, 52 Iowa, 26; Edmondson v. School District (Iowa), 67 N. W. Rep. 671; Howard v. Huron (S. D.), 59 N. W. Rep. 833, 60 N. W. Rep. 803. In Board of Commissioners v. Pratt, *supra*, the court said: "The cases of Commissioners v. Loague, 129 U. S. 493, and Kelly v. Town of Milan, 21 Fed. Rep. 842, 127. U. S. 138, are not in conflict with this decision. The opinion and the effect of the decision in the former case are explained and limited in Franklin Co. v. German Sav. Bank, 142 U. S. 98."

[2] McClure v. Oxford Tp., 94 U. S. 429.

[3] Rollins v. Gunnison Co., 49 U. S. App. 399, 80 Fed. Rep. 682; Cromwell v. Sac Co., 96 U. S. 51; Suffolk Sav. Bank v. Boston, 149 Mass. 364, 4 L. R. A. 516; Lynchburg v. Slaughter, 75 Va. 57.

[4] Scotland Co. v. Hill, 132 U. S. 107.

[5] Carroll Co. v. Smith, 111 U. S. 556.

[6] Cromwell v. Sac Co., 96 U. S. 58.

of the bond is due.[1] But a purchaser is bound to take notice of the provision of the constitution, the laws of the state,[2] the requirements of the statute under which the bonds are issued,[3] the public records in relation to the issue,[4] and of what appears upon the face of the instrument.[5]

§ 178. *Defenses available against a bona fide holder.*— When bonds are issued in pursuance of powers conferred by the legislature they are valid commercial instruments; but if issued without authority they are invalid even in the hands of *bona fide* holders for value. Want of power to issue the securities is the only defense which can be successfully interposed to a suit by a *bona fide* holder for value who acquired the bond before maturity in reliance upon recitals contained therein and without notice, actual or constructive, of defenses.[6]

§ 179. *Recitals in bonds.*— As between the original parties the question of compliance with conditions precedent to the lawful issue of bonds is always open to investigation. Every holder of bonds is required to know the law under which they were issued and the terms and conditions imposed by the law upon the corporation as limitations upon its power. Hence, when the enabling statute provides that the bonds shall be void unless the conditions are complied with, every holder takes with notice of this provision and must satisfy himself of the fact of compliance,[7] as bonds issued in violation of the express terms of the statute are invalid even in the hands of an inno-

---

[1] Mayor v. City Bank, 58 Ga. 587. As to what is sufficient to put a purchaser on inquiry, see Parsons v. Jackson, 99 U. S. 434; Crow v. Oxford Tp., 119 U. S. 215.

[2] Knox Co. v. Aspinwall, 21 How. (U. S.) 539.

[3] Manhattan Co. v. Ironwood, 43 U. S. App. 369, 74 Fed. Rep. 585; Bank v. School District No. 53; 3 N. Dak. 496, 28 L. R. A. 642; Barnett v. Dennison, 145 U. S. 136. In McClure v. Oxford Tp., 94 U. S. 429, the court said: "Every dealer in municipal bonds which upon their face refer to the statute under which they were issued is bound to take notice of the statute and of all its requirements."

[4] Brown v. Ingalls Tp., 81 Fed. Rep. 485. See § 183, *infra*.

[5] Brown v. Bon Homme Co., 1 S. Dak. 216, 46 N. W. Rep. 173; Aurora v. West, 22 Ind. 88; Gilson v. Dayton, 123 U. S. 59.

[6] St. Joseph Tp. v. Rogers, 16 Wall. 644; Brenham v. German American Bank, 144 U. S. 173; Bissell v. Kankakee, 64 Ill. 249.

[7] German Sav. Bank v. Franklin Co., 128 U. S. 526; Anthony v. Jasper Co., 4 Dill. (C. C.) 136; Bailey v. Tabor, 5 Mass. 286, 4 Am. Dec. 57. See § 183 as to overissue.

cent purchaser for value.* But when the law contemplates that certain officials shall determine when the prescribed conditions are complied with, and such officials certify to the facts, the innocent purchaser of the bonds is entitled to rely upon such certificate.² The rule, as established by many decisions, is thus stated by Judge Dillon:³ "If upon a true construction of the legislative enactment conferring the authority (to issue the bonds upon certain condition), the corporations or certain officers or a given body or tribunal are invested with power to decide whether the conditions precedent have been complied with, then it may well be that their determination of a matter *in pais* which they are authorized to decide will, in favor of the bondholder for value, bind the corporation." This rule applies to non-negotiable as well as to negotiable bonds.⁴

§ 180. *Effect of recitals — continued.*—The rule stated in the preceding section has been frequently approved by the supreme court of the United States. Thus, in a leading case,⁵ Mr. Justice Strong said, with reference to the language of Judge Dillon: "This is a very cautious statement of the doctrine. It may be stated in a slightly different form,— when the legislative authority has been given to a municipality or to its officers to subscribe to the stock of a railroad company and to issue bonds in payment, but only on some precedent condition, such as a popular vote in favor of the subscription; and where it may be gathered from the legislative enactment that the officers of the municipality were invested with power to decide whether the condition precedent has been complied with, their recital that it has been, made in bonds issued by them and held by a *bona fide* purchaser, is conclusive of the fact,

¹ Aspinwall v. Daviess Co., 22 How. (U. S.) 364; Moore v. Mayor, 73 N. Y. 238, 29 Am. Rep. 134.
² Second Ward Sav. Bank v. City of Huron, 80 Fed. Rep. 661; Evansville v. Dennett, 161 U. S. 434.
³ Mun. Corp., I, § 523.
⁴ Flagg v. School District, 4 N. Dak. 30, 25 L. R. A. 363, 58 N. W. Rep. 499.
⁵ Town of Coloma v. Eaves, 92 U. S. 484. A corporation cannot be heard to deny that the bonds were issued for the purpose stated on their face. National Life Ins. Co. v. Board of Education, 62 Fed. Rep. 783. The first and leading case upon the subject of the effect of recitals is Commissioners of Knox Co. v. Aspinwall, 21 How. (U. S.) 539, decided in 1858. It has never been overruled although attacked in dissenting opinions in later cases. See Town of Coloma v. Eaves, *supra*.

and binding upon the municipality; for the recital is itself a decision of the fact by the appointed tribunal." Hence the municipality may, by proper recitals made by duly authorized officials, be estopped from availing itself of the defense of irregularities in the election held to authorize the issue of bonds,[1] that the consent of the requisite number of taxpayers has not been duly obtained,[2] or that the authority to make the stock subscription has expired before the subscription was made.[3]

§ 181. *Authority of officials to make recitals.*— It is only when the officers have authority to determine whether or not conditions have been complied with that their recital of the fact of performance estops the corporation from showing nonperformance. If no authority exists, the purchaser has no more right to rely upon their recital than upon the certificate of a stranger. Hence, where the validity of the bonds depends upon an estoppel claimed to arise upon the recitals in the instrument, the question being as to the existence of the power to issue them, it is necessary to establish that the officers executing the bonds had lawful authority to make the recitals and to make them conclusive. The ground of the estoppel is the recitals and official statements of those to whom the law refers the public for authentic and final information on the subject.[4] It is not necessary that the authority to determine the facts should be conferred on the officers in express terms, as it is enough that the whole control of the matter be given to the officers named.[5]

§ 182. *Recital that bonds have been issued " in conformity to law."*— " It is not necessary," says the supreme court of the United States,[6] " that the recital should enumerate each partic-

---

[1] Moran v. Miami Co., 67 U. S. 722; Bissell v. Jeffersonville, 24 How. (U. S.) 287; Pana v. Bowler, 107 U. S. 529, 12 Am. & Eng. Ry. Cas. 563.

[2] Town of Venice v. Murdock, 92 U. S. 494.

[3] Moultrie Co. v. Rockingham Sav. Bank, 92 U. S. 631.

[4] Dixon Co. v. Field, 111 U. S. 83; German Sav. Bank v. Franklin Co., 128 U. S. 526; Coffin v. Kearney Co. Com'rs, 57 Fed. Rep. 137; Brown v. Bon Homme Co., 1 S. Dak. 216, 46 N. W. Rep. 173; Flagg v. School District, 4 N. Dak. 30, 25 L. R. A. 363, 58 N. W. Rep. 499.

[5] Bernards Tp. v. Morrison, 133 U. S. 523; Coler v. Dwight School Tp., 3 N. Dak. 249, 55 N. W. Rep. 587; Fulton v. Riverton, 42 Minn. 895; Brownell v. Greenwich, 114 N. Y. 518, 4 L. R. A. 685.

[6] Dixon Co. v. Field, 111 U. S. 83.

ular fact essential to the existence of the obligation. A general statement that the bonds have been issued in conformity with the law will suffice, so as to embrace every fact which the officers making the statement are authorized to determine and certify. This is the rule which has been constantly applied by this court in the numerous cases in which it has been involved. The differences in the results of the judgments depended upon the question whether in the particular case under consideration a fair construction of the law authorized the officers issuing the bonds to ascertain, determine and certify the existence of the facts upon which their power, by the terms of the law, was made to depend, not including, of course, that class of cases in which the controversy related not to the conditions precedent on which the right to act depended, but upon conditions affecting only the mode of exercising a power admitted to have come into being."[1]

In a case where the bonds under consideration recited that they were issued "in pursuance" of the statute, Mr. Justice Harlan said:[2] "Legislative authority for an issue of bonds being established by reference to the statute, and the bonds reciting that they were issued in pursuance of the statute, the utmost which plaintiff was bound to show, to entitle him *prima facie* to judgment, was the due appointment of the commissioners and execution by them in fact of the bonds. It was not necessary that he should in the first instance prove either that he paid value or that the conditions preliminary to the exercise by the commissioners of the authority conferred by statute were in fact performed before the bonds were issued. The one was presumed from the possession of the bonds, and the other was established by the statute authorizing an issue of bonds and by proof of the due appointment of commissioners and their execution of the bonds with the recital of their

[1] The facts which the corporation is not permitted, as against a *bona fide* holder, to question in the face of a recital in the bond of their existence are those connected with or growing out of the discharge of the ordinary duties of such of its officers as were invested with authority to execute them and which the statute conferring the power made it their duty to ascertain and determine before the bonds were issued. Northern Trust Co. v. Porter Tp., 110 U. S. 608; Brown v. Bon Homme Co., 1 S. Dak. 216, 46 N. W. Rep. 173.

[2] Montclair v. Ramsdell, 107 U. S. 147.

compliance with the statute."[1] A recital that the bonds were executed pursuant to an order of the county court is equivalent to an express statement that the ordinance is in conformity with the statute.[2]

§ 183. *Excessive issues.*—When the constitution provides that public corporations shall not issue bonds in an amount greater than a specified percentage of the valuation of the taxable property within the corporation limits, to be ascertained by the official valuation for the purposes of taxation, it fixes a limit beyond which the power to issue bonds cannot be conferred. Bonds issued in excess of such limit are void in the hands of *bona fide* holders,[3] notwithstanding the fact that they contain a recital that they are issued under and pursuant to the constitution of the state. But when the legislature is the source of the law creating the limitation a different rule seems to apply. After declaring the limitation, it creates or designates a board or an officer as the authority which is to determine whether the condition precedent to the issue has been complied with. In such case the power which limits or restricts may suspend the restriction or limitation. The facts to be determined by the official, such as the amount of taxable property and the amount of existing indebtedness, are extrinsic facts, which bear not so much upon the power to issue the bonds as upon the question whether or not they should be issued at the time in question.[4] Hence, when the designated officials have determined these questions and issued the bonds, with full recitals of compliance with the law, they are valid in the hands of innocent holders for value although for an amount in excess of the statutory limit.[5] But when the limitation is based upon a public record, such as an assessment roll, the pur-

---

[1] Bernards Tp. v. Morrison, 133 U. S. 523; Chaffee Co. Com'rs v. Potter, 142 U. S. 355; Cotton v. New Providence, 47 N. J. L. 401.

[2] Wesson v. Saline Co., 34 U. S. App. 080, 73 Fed. Rep. 917.

[3] Dixon Co. v. Field, 111 U. S. 83; Dillon, Mun. Corp., sec. 529; Lake Co. v. Graham, 130 U. S. 674; Buchanan v. Litchfield, 102 U. S. 278; Daviess Co. v. Dickinson, 117 U. S.

657; Stockdale v. Wayland School District, 47 Mich. 226.

[4] Prince v. Crocker, 166 Mass. 347, 44 N. E. Rep. 446, 32 L. R. A. 610; Sherman v. Simons, 109 U. S. 735; Lake Co. v. Graham, 130 U. S. 674; Oregon v. Jennings, 119 U. S. 74.

[5] Marcy v. Oswego Tp., 92 U. S. 637; New Providence v. Halsey, 117 U. S. 336.

chaser of bonds is bound to take notice of such facts as the official records disclose concerning the valuation of taxable property.

In a case of overissue of bonds under a constitutional provision it was said: [1] "When the authority to create the debt at all, or beyond a given amount, is made to depend upon official records, the same rule in regard to recitals in bonds given for the debt should not be applied. Every holder of such bonds is charged with a knowledge of the provisions of the law relating to their issuance, and the law points to the records as evidence of the existence of the facts required to authorize their issuance, or to limit the amount of the debt the city may create. Such records and not the recitals in the bonds must be looked to by every one who proposes to deal in the bonds."

[1] Citizens' Bank v. City of Terrell, 78 Tex. 456, 14 S. W. Rep. 1003; Quaker City Nat. Bank v. Nolan Co., 59 Fed. Rep. 660. In Frances v. Howard Co., 54 Fed. Rep. 487, the court said: "All the decisions of the supreme court of the United States from Dixon Co. v. Field, 111 U. S. 83, to Sutcliffe v. Board, 147 U. S. 230, agree that the purchasers of bonds issued by municipalities under authority of laws which limit the amount of bonds to be issued to a certain percentage of the assessment rolls are charged with notice of the amount of bonds which can be validly issued based on such assessment rolls." Valley Co. v. McLean, 49 U. S. App. 131, 79 Fed. Rep. 728. In Shaw v. Independent School District, 40 U. S. App. 475, 77 Fed. Rep. 277, it was held that the purchaser could not rely on the recitals when the public records showed that the constitutional limit of indebtedness had been reached.

CHAPTER X.

MUNICIPAL INDEBTEDNESS.

§ 184. Power to incur debts.
185. The meaning of indebtedness.
186. Contingent obligations.

§ 187. Contracts requiring annual payments.
188. Anticipation of revenues.

§ 184. *Power to incur debts.*—A public corporation may incur a debt whenever it is incident to the exercise of a power to do some specified thing which it is authorized to do. In the absence of limitation the amount of the debt which may be created rests in the discretion of the corporation, but municipal carelessness and extravagance have led to the general adoption of constitutional or charter provisions which limit the amount of legal indebtedness which may be incurred. This limit is determined in various ways, but ordinarily the corporation is prohibited from becoming indebted in an amount greater than a specified percentage on the assessed valuation of the real property within its limits. When such provisions are directed to the legislature they have no effect upon the powers already possessed by corporations. But when directed to the municipalities they repeal all charter provisions inconsistent therewith.[1] A person dealing with such bodies must take notice of limitations upon their power to contract debts,[2] and must determine for himself whether the legal limit has been reached.[3]

§ 185. *The meaning of indebtedness.*—Such prohibitions are generally held to apply to indebtedness of all kinds, express and implied, current and bonded.[4] But the authorities are far

---

[1] List v. Wheeling, 7 W. Va. 501; East St. Louis v. People, 124 Ill. 655, 23 Am. & Eng. Corp. Cas. 408.

[2] People v. May, 9 Colo. 80, 13 Am. & Eng. Corp. Cas. 307; French v. Burlington, 42 Iowa, 614.

[3] La Porte v. Gamewell Fire Alarm Tel. Co., 146 Ind. 466; 45 N. E. Rep. 588; Law v. People, 87 Ill. 385; Atlantic City W. W. Co. v. Read, 50 N. J. L. 665.

[4] Litchfield v. Ballou, 114 U. S. 190; Lake Co. v. Rollins, 130 id. 662, 26 Am. & Eng. Corp. Cas. 465. Obligations payable out of a particular fund and for which the fund only is liable do not create a debt against the corporation. Quill v. Indianap-

from uniform. In some states it includes compulsory obligations incurred for books and records which the county is required by law to purchase,[1] while in others it is confined to such as are voluntarily incurred.[2] Again, there is a conflict on the question whether it includes obligations incurred for the current expenses of the municipality. In some states a corporation is not permitted to incur a liability for ordinary current expenses after the constitutional limit of indebtedness has been reached.[3] Necessity is no excuse for contracting a debt in excess of the limit.[4] Thus, a city which has reached the limit cannot enter into a valid contract for a supply of water for a fixed annual amount unless provision is made for the raising of the money to meet the obligation as it accrues, by taxation.[5] A city cannot issue bonds for the purpose of erecting water-

olis, 124 Ind. 202, 7 L. R. A. 681; Board v. Harrell (Ind., 1897), 46 N. E. Rep. 124; Baker v. Seattle, 2 Wash. 576. Liabilities arising *ex delicto* are not to be included. Bartle v. Des Moines, 38 Iowa, 414.

[1] Barnard v. Knox Co., 105 Mo. 382, 13 L. R. A. 244, reversing Potter v. Douglas Co., 87 Mo. 240; Lake Co. v. Rollins, 130 U. S. 662, reversing Rollins v. Lake Co., 34 Fed. Rep. 845; Prince v. Quincy, 105 Ill. 138; Council Bluffs v. Stewart, 51 Iowa, 385; McAleer v. Angell (R. I., 1897), 36 Atl. Rep. 588. In People v. May, 9 Colo. 80, the court says: "The limitation being applicable to all debts, irrespective of their form, it follows that, in determining the amount of the county indebtedness, county warrants are to be taken into account, and any warrant which increases the indebtedness over and beyond the limit fixed is in violation of the constitution and void."

[2] Barnard v. Knox Co., 37 Fed. Rep. 503, 2 L. R. A. 426, note; Grant Co. v. Lake Co., 17 Oreg. 453; McCracken v. San Francisco, 16 Cal. 591; Thomas v. Burlington, 69 Iowa, 140; Rauch v. Chapman (Wash.), 36 L. R. A. 407.

[3] Beard v. Hopkinsville (Ky.), 23

L. R. A. 402, and elaborate note; Prince v. Quincy, 105 Ill. 138, 44 Am. Rep. 785; Sackett v. New Albany, 88 Ind. 473, 45 Am. Rep. 467; Saleno v. Neosho (Mo.), 27 L. R. A. 769; Baltimore v. Gill, 31 Md. 375; French v. Burlington, 42 Iowa, 614; Council Bluffs v. Stewart, 51 id. 385; Appeal of Erie, 91 Pa. St. 398. *Contra*, Grant v. Davenport, 36 Iowa, 396; Corpus Christi v. Woessner, 58 Tex. 462; Laycock v. Baton Rouge, 85 La. Ann. 475. In Carter v. Thorson (S. Dak.), 24 L. R. A. 734, it was held that a constitutional provision prohibiting "the incurring of indebtedness, except in pursuance of appropriations," did not prevent the legislature from incurring or directing the incurring of indebtedness for the usual and current administration of state affairs, without having first made an appropriation for that specific purpose. Hence a contract for doing the public printing is not "incurring an indebtedness."

[4] Sackett v. New Albany, 88 Ind. 473, 45 Am. Rep. 467.

[5] State v. Atlantic City, 49 N. J. L. 558; Prince v. Quincy, 105 Ill. 138, 44 Am. Rep. 785; Salem Water Co. v. Salem, 5 Oreg. 30.

works under such conditions although it will acquire property in exchange for said bonds equal in value to the amount of the bonds and productive of revenue.[1] Nor can a city make a valid contract to rent a market house for a stated rental which is in excess of the annual revenues received from the market.[2] But when a debt already exists a city may issue new bonds for its payment and for the interest to accrue thereon.[3] But if the proceeds of the new bonds are not used to pay the old bonds a new debt is created.[4] When a judgment has been obtained

---

[1] In Scott v. Davenport, 34 Iowa, 208, the court said: "But the fact that the property for which the debt was contracted is valuable, and a source of profit and revenue, does not remove or change the character of the indebtedness. The purchaser, having become bound to pay, has incurred an indebtedness which he may be compelled to pay. Being thus bound, he is in debt, no matter what amount of property he may have received in consideration for his obligation."

[2] Appeal of Erie, 91 Pa. St. 398.

[3] Powell v. Madison, 107 Ind. 106 (funding bonds); Palmer v. Helena (Mont.), 47 Pac. Rep. 209.

[4] Doon Tp. v. Cummins, 142 U. S. 366; Anderson v. Insurance Co., 88 Iowa, 579. In Burkholtz v. Dinnie (N. D., 1897), 72 N. W. Rep. 931, it was held that the indebtedness cannot be increased beyond the limit, although the debt is incurred for the purpose of refunding the indebtedness of the municipality. The debt was temporarily increased, and this might be permanent, owing to the loss or diversion of the fund created by the sale of the refunding bonds. Chief Justice Corliss said: "We are unable to discover any sound basis for the view which, in the teeth of a declaration that the indebtedness shall never — i. e., shall not for a day or an hour — exceed a certain percentage of assessed valuation, considers a temporary excess as not within the prohibition. The fact that other debts equal in amount are subsequently paid with the money does not destroy the fact that the debt has been for a season increased beyond the constitutional limit. We do not wish to be understood as holding that refunding bonds cannot be issued to take the place of the old bonds which have matured. An exchange of bond for bond would not even temporarily increase the indebtedness of the city one dollar. It would be merely the substitution of one obligation for another. It would be analogous to the giving of a renewal note at a bank. If the action which the city officials proposed to take was a mere exchange of new city bonds for old city bonds, we would hold such action to be legal upon the facts in this record. Nor do we consider it necessary that an exchange of bond for bond should be made. We think that the mere execution of refunding bonds may be authorized even beyond the debt limit, and that they may then be put on the market and sold, on the condition that they are not to be delivered until an equal amount of the old bonds are surrendered. The resolution might provide that, simultaneously with the delivery of the refunding bonds and the payment of the cash therefor, there should be at hand an equal amount of the old bonds, to be then and there extinguished by the use of the cash so re-

upon an obligation not within the prohibition, bonds may be issued for its satisfaction without increasing the indebtedness of the municipality.[1] When suitable provision has been made for the discharge of an obligation, or the money is in the treasury to meet it, the drawing of a warrant upon the treasury for the payment of such obligation or claim does not create a debt.[2] The amount of a sinking fund must be deducted from the apparent debt of a city in order to ascertain its total indebtedness.[3] So park-board certificates secured by mortgage on real estate and payable out of a fund arising from assessments for benefits are not a part of the indebtedness of the city.[4]

§ 186. *Contingent obligations.*— An obligation payable in the future is as much a debt as though due immediately.[5] The time when it comes into existence, and not when due, must be

ceived and delivered up to the city as part of the same transaction. But the purpose of the city officials is something radically different from an exchange or a sale guarded in the manner specified. Their plan is to sell the bonds of the city, thus increasing the indebtedness thereof against the prohibitions of the constitution, and leaving uncertain the question whether the old debt will be fully extinguished, or whether a dollar of it will be paid. The scheme is to pay the old debt with the proceeds of the new; but there is no absolute certainty, although there may be a probability, that this will be done. Nothing short of a certainty that the debt will not be increased permanently will suffice, and even that will not suffice if it is temporarily augmented beyond the constitutional limit. We admit that there appear to be some decisions opposed to our ruling. It can probably be said that the weight of authority is against our view. See City of Poughkeepsie v. Quintard, 136 N. Y. 275, 32 N. E. Rep. 764; Powell v. City of Madison, 107 Ind. 106, 8 N. E. Rep. 31; Board of Com'rs of Marion Co. v. Board of Com'rs of Harvey Co., 26 Kan. 181, 201; Opinion of the Justices, 81 Me. 602, 18 Atl. Rep. 291; Hotchkiss v. Marion, 12 Mont. 218, 29 Pac. Rep. 821; Los Angeles v. Teed, 112 Cal. 319, 44 Pac. Rep. 580; Miller v. School Dist. (Wyo.), 39 Pac. Rep. 879; Palmer v. City of Helena (Mont.), 47 Pac. Rep. 209. But in one of these cases no question of constitutional prohibition was involved. City of Poughkeepsie v. Quintard, 136 N. Y. 275, 32 N. E. Rep. 764. In none of the cases was the inhibition of the fundamental law so sweeping in terms as ours."

[1] Board of Com'rs v. Platt (C. C. A.), 79 Fed. Rep. 567; Sioux City v. Weare, 59 Iowa, 95.
[2] Springfield v. Edwards, 84 Ill. 626.
[3] Kelly v. Minneapolis, 63 Minn. 125, 65 N. W. Rep. 115, 30 L. R. A. 281. As to what should be included, see Wade v. Oakmont, 165 Pa. St. 479; New York Bank v. Grace, 102 N. Y. 313; Thomas v. Burlington, 69 Iowa, 140; Austin v. Seattle, 2 Wash. 667.
[4] Kelly v. Minneapolis, *supra*.
[5] Law v. People, 87 Ill. 385.

considered in applying the rule of limitation upon indebtedness.[1] The character of the obligation as a liability is not affected by the fact that it is not to be paid until some condition has been performed by the payee. Thus, where a city obligated itself to pay a sum of money upon the completion of a certain work, the court said: "It cannot be said that the indebtedness did not come into being until the work was completed and accepted by the city. The city bound itself to pay for the work when it should be completed, and it could be compelled to do so if the work should be done according to contract."[2] In another case it was said:[3] "It is believed not only to apply to a present indebtedness, but also to such as is payable on a contingency at some future day, or which depends on some contingency before a liability is created. But it must appear that such contingency is sure to take place irrespective of any action taken or option exercised by the city in the future. That is, if a present indebtedness is incurred, or obligation assumed, which without further action on the part of the city has the effect to create such an indebtedness at some future day, such are within the inhibition of the constitution. But if the fact of the indebtedness depends upon some act of the city, or upon its volition, to be exercised or determined at some future date, then no present indebtedness is incurred, and none will be until the period arrives and the required act or option is exercised, and from that time only can it be said there exists an indebtedness."

§ 187. *Contracts requiring annual payments.*— Some very difficult questions have arisen under these limitations upon indebtedness in connection with contracts which require the corporation to pay a fixed annual or monthly sum during a period of years for water, lighting, the disposal of sewage and such other purposes. Many of the authorities are in conflict with the principles stated in the preceding section. But careful attention must be given the particular charter under con-

---

[1] La Porte v. Gamewell F. A. Tel. Co., 146 Ind. 466, 45 N. E. Rep. 588.
[2] Culbertson v. Fulton, 127 Ill. 30; Springfield v. Edwards, 84 Ill. 626; Beard v. Hopkinsville, 95 Ky. 239, 23 L. R. A. 402, with elaborate note on what constitutes indebtedness.
[3] Burlington Water Co. v. Woodward, 49 Iowa, 62. But see Keihl v. City of South Bend, 76 Fed. Rep. 921.

sideration, as the right may be determined by provisions relating to taxation and appropriations. The supreme court of Michigan said:[1] "There can be no doubt, in our opinion, that this whole contract obligation is a liability to the full extent of the thirty years' rental. And it is equally clear that all unpaid sums will be aggregated until paid." The contract was therefore held void. The same conclusion has been reached in Ohio,[2] New Jersey,[3] Oregon,[4] Montana[5] and Minnesota.[6] On the other hand, Illinois,[7] Pennsylvania,[8] Massachusetts,[9] Iowa,[10] New York,[11] Indiana,[12] Oklahoma,[13] California[14] and Missouri[15] hold such contracts not in violation of the prohibition. "We base our views," says the supreme court of California, "upon the conviction that at the time of entering into the contract no debt or liability is created for the aggregate amount of the

[1] Niles W. W. v. Niles, 59 Mich. 312.
[2] State v. Medbery, 7 Ohio St. 523.
[3] Atlantic City W. W. v. Read, 49 N. J. L. 558, 50 N. J. L. 665.
[4] Salem W. W. v. Salem, 5 Oreg. 29.
[5] Davenport v. Kleinschmidt, 6 Mont. 502.
[6] Kichli v. Minn. Brush Electric Co., 58 Minn. 418.
[7] East St. Louis v. East St. Louis Gas L. Co., 98 Ill. 415, 38 Am. Rep. 97.
[8] In re Erie's Appeal, 91 Pa. St. 398; Wade v. Oakmont Borough, 165 Pa. St. 479; Brown v. City of Cory, 175 Pa. 528, 34 Atl. Rep. 854.
[9] Weston v. Syracuse, 17 N. Y. 110.
[10] Smith v. Dedham, 144 Mass. 177.
[11] Grant v. Davenport, 36 Iowa, 396.
[12] La Porte v. Gamewell F. A. Tel. Co., 146 Ind. 466, 45 N. E. Rep. 588; Crowder v. Town of Sullivan, 128 Ind. 486, 28 N. E. Rep. 94; Valparaiso v. Gardner, 97 Ind. 1. See Indianapolis v. Wann, 144 Ind. 175, 4 N. E. Rep. 901, 31 L. R. A. 743.
[13] Territory v. Oklahoma, 2 Okla. 158.
[14] McBean v. Fresno (Cal., 1897), 31 L. R. A. 794.
[15] Lamar Water & E. L. Co. v. City of Lamar, 128 Mo. 188, 32 L. R. A. 157. In Saleno v. City of Neosho, 127 Mo. 627, 27 L. R. A. 709, the court said: "In construing the words used in that instrument, in the absence of some restriction placed upon their meaning, they must be given such meaning as is generally accorded to them. A debt is understood to be an unconditional promise to pay a fixed sum at some specified time, and is quite different from a contract to be performed in the future, depending upon a condition precedent which may never be performed, and which cannot ripen into a debt until performed. Here the hydrant rental depended upon the water supply to be furnished to defendant, and if not furnished, no payment could be required. . . . A number of cases have been cited by defendant. The weight of decisions, and which we regard to be the proper view of the question, is that such a contract is not prohibited, even if the total amount which the corporation will have to pay will, with the other debts of the municipality, exceed the statutory or constitutional limit. Only the annual payment of the year when the calculation is made should be considered as a debt." Simonton, Municipal Bonds, § 60.

instalments to be paid under the contract, but that the sole debt or liability created is that which arises from year to year in separate amounts as the work is performed." Where a city contracted for a fire-alarm system at a time when it was indebted beyond the constitutional limit and had no money in the treasury at the time when the contract was made or the work accepted, the contract was held to create a liability within the prohibition, notwithstanding the fact that there was money in the treasury at the time fixed for payment.[1]

§ 188. *Anticipation of revenues.*— In some states a municipality which has reached its constitutional limit of indebtedness is permitted to anticipate the collection of the revenues appropriated to its use by drawing warrants against taxes levied but not collected. The result is a substantial appropriation and assignment of the amount drawn to the holder of the warrant. In order that such warrants may not increase the indebtedness of the municipality it is necessary that the tax should not only be levied but that the warrant be drawn on the particular fund and be in legal effect sufficient to discharge the city.[2]

[1] In La Porte v. Gamewell F. A. Tel. Co., *supra,* the court said: "When a municipal corporation contracts for a usual and necessary thing, such as water or light, and agrees to pay for it annually or monthly as furnished, the contract does not create an indebtedness for the aggregate sum of the instalments, since the debt for each year or month does not come into existence until it is earned. The earning of each year's or month's compensation is essential to the existence of the debt. If the city can pay this indebtedness when it comes into existence, without exceeding the constitutional limit, there is no indebtedness, and therefore no violation of the constitution. But if the indebtedness of the city already equals or exceeds the constitutional limit, and the current revenues are not sufficient to pay said indebtedness when it comes into existence, including other expenses for which the city is liable, an indebtedness is thereby created, and there is a violation of the constitution." Walla Walla Water Co. v. City of Walla Walla, 60 Fed. Rep. 957; Keihl v. City of South Bend, 76 Fed. Rep. 921.

[2] State v. Parkinson, 5 Nev. 17; Springfield v. Edwards, 84 Ill. 626; Law v. People, 87 Ill. 885; French v. Burlington, 42 Iowa, 614.

BOOK III.

OF THE MODE AND AGENCIES OF CORPORATE ACTION.

CHAPTER XI.

OF THE MANNER OF EXERCISING CORPORATE POWER.

§ 189. Charter provisions.
190. Meaning of terms.
191. Statutory directions.

§ 192. Procedure in the enactment of ordinances.
193. Where no mode is prescribed.
194. Illustrations.

§ 189. *Charter provisions.*— The charter ordinarily provides for the various methods by which the corporation shall exercise the powers conferred upon it. Certain powers may be exercised through designated boards or officials without reference to the city council. But as a general rule, all powers, whether police or contractual, are exercised through the body in which is vested the legislative function.[1] The formal expression of the will of this body is evidenced by an ordinance or resolution.[2]

§ 190. *Meaning of terms.*— The words "ordinance" and "by-law" are practically synonymous,[3] although in the United States the word "by-law" is ordinarily limited in its application to the law of private corporations.[4] An ordinance is "a local law prescribing a general and permanent rule,"[5] while a

[1] Terre Haute v. Lake, 43 Ind. 480; Saxton v. St. Joseph, 60 Mo. 153.
[2] Day v. Jersey City, 19 N. J. Eq. 412; Creighton v. Marson, 27 Cal. 613; Alton v. Mulledy, 21 Ill. 76. It must be by a vote embodied in some distinct and definite form. Schumm v. Seymour, 24 N. J. Eq. 143.
[3] Bills v. Goshen, 117 Ind. 221, 3 L. R. A. 261; National Bank of Commerce v. Grenada, 44 Fed. Rep. 262.
[4] Kepner v. Commonwealth, 40 Pa. St. 124; Taylor v. Lambertville, 43 N. J. Eq. 112. An ordinance is "the law of the inhabitants of the corporate place or district made by themselves, or the authorized body, in distinction from the general law of the country or the statute law of the particular state." 1 Dillon, Mun. Corp., § 307; Willcox, Corp. 73; 2 Kyd, Corp. 93, 98; Commonwealth v. Turner, 1 Cush. (Mass.) 493.
[5] Citizens' Gas & Mining Co. v. Ellwood, 114 Ind. 336.

resolution is of a special or temporary character and is ordinarily enacted with less formality.[1] Comparing the different terms Chief Justice Shaw said:[2] "'Regulation' is the most general of them all, meaning any rule for the ordering of affairs public or private; and it thus becomes the generic term from which all the others are defined, specified and differentiated. 'Ordinance' is the next most general term, including all forms of regulation by civil authority, even acts of parliament. With us its meaning is usually confined to corporation regulations. Ordinances are all sorts of rules and by-laws of municipal corporations. 'Resolution' is only a less solemn or less usual form of an ordinance. It is an ordinance still if there is anything intended to regulate the affairs of a corporation."

§ 191. *Statutory directions.*—Where a power is conferred by statute and the manner of its exercise is prescribed, all other modes are impliedly prohibited.[3] Such directions must be strictly and literally complied with, as they are in effect limitations upon the grant.[4]

§ 192. *Procedure in the enactment of ordinances.*—Statutory directions as to the procedure to be observed in the enactment of ordinances are mandatory, and if not complied with the ordinance is void.[5] But if the mode of procedure is left to the

[1] Blanchard v. Bissell, 11 Ohio St. 96; State v. Bayonne, 35 N. J. L. 335; Kepner v. Commonwealth, 40 Pa. St. 124.
[2] Commonwealth v. Turner, 1 Cush. 493; Kepner v. Commonwealth, 40 Pa. St. 130.
[3] Des Moines v. Gilchrist, 67 Iowa, 211; Zottman v. San Francisco, 20 Cal. 96, 81 Am. Dec. 96.
[4] State v. Newark, 25 N. J. L. 399; Iowa Land Co. v. County of Sac, 39 Iowa, 149; Mayor v. Porter, 18 Md. 284, 79 Am. Dec. 686; Ferguson v. Halsell, 47 Tex. 42; Sadler v. Eureka Co., 15 Nev. 44; Glass Co. v. Ashbury, 49 Cal. 571; McCoy v. Briant, 53 Cal. 248. In Zottman v. San Francisco, 20 Cal. 96, 81 Am. Dec. 96, Field, C. J., said: "When the mode in which their power on any given subject can be exercised is prescribed by their charter the mode must be followed. The mode in such cases constitutes the measure of the power." An ordinance is not invalidated by the failure of the clerk to comply with a statute requiring him to place his certificate on the journal of the proceedings and on the ordinance, when all other requirements are complied with. Brohme v. Monroe, 106 Mich. 401, 64 N. Y. 204.
[5] Jacksonville v. Ledwith, 26 Fla. 163, 9 L. R. A. 69; Altoona v. Bowman, 171 Pa. St. 307; Bloom v. Xenia, 32 Ohio St. 461; Welker v. Potter, 18 Ohio St. 85; Blanchard v. Bissell, 11 Ohio St. 101; Cantril v. Sainer, 59 Iowa, 26; Herzo v. San Francisco, 33

municipal body it may be determined by an ordinance, and the mode so provided must be observed in the enactment of all ordinances.[1] There seems to be a tendency toward allowing municipalities to provide their own rules of procedure.[2]

§ 193. *Where no mode is prescribed.*— When a power exists and the manner of exercising it is not declared, the council may proceed either by way of ordinance or resolution.[3] As a general rule, however, it may be said that all general and permanent acts should be in the form of ordinances,[4] while ministerial acts may be by resolution.[5] The difference is not so much in the nature of the act as in the manner of enactment. Both are legislative acts; and when it appears that a resolution was passed with all the formalities required for an ordinance, it is generally held valid as an ordinance.[6] Where a contract which

Cal. 134; Smith v. Emporia, 27 Kan. 528; State v. Newark, 25 N. J. L. 399; Danville v. Shelton, 76 Va. 325. As to requirement of a majority vote, see Ill. T. & Sav. Bank v. Arkansas City, 76 Fed. Rep. 271, 34 L. R. A. 518. If in the charter it is required that there shall be a publication of an ordinance between the second and third reading, such publication may be shown *aliunde* the records of the council. State v. New Brunswick, 58 N. J. L. 255. See ch. XII.

[1] Swindell v. State, 143 Ind. 153.

[2] See Smith v. People, 162 Ill. 534, 38 L. R. A. 470.

[3] Crawfordsville v. Braden, 130 Ind. 149, 30 Am. St. Rep. 214, 14 L. R. A. 268; Butler v. Passaic, 44 N. J. L. 171; State v. Jersey City, 27 N. J. L. 493; Green v. Cape May, 41 N. J. L. 46; Burlington v. Dennison, 42 N. J. L. 165; Quincy v. Chicago, etc. R. Co., 92 Ill. 23; Indianapolis v. Imbery, 17 Ind. 175; First Municipality v. Cutting, 4 La. Ann. 336; Halsey v. Rapid Tr. Co., 47 N. J. Eq. 380, 20 Atl. Rep. 859; Robinson v. Franklin, 1 Humph. 156, 34 Am. Dec. 625 and note; McGavock v. Omaha, 40 Neb. 64, 58 N. W. Rep. 543.

[4] A common council should act by ordinance in organizing a fire department, in promoting a plan of government for it, or in prescribing the manner of the election of its officers and their duties. But it may act by resolution in purchasing the fire-engine. Green v. Cape May, 41 N. J. L. 46. See the following cases, which, however, are controlled by statute: City of Paterson v. Barnett, 46 N. J. L. 62; Grimmell v. Des Moines, 57 Iowa, 144.

[5] Somer v. Philadelphia, 35 Pa. St. 231; San Francisco Gas Co. v. San Francisco, 6 Cal. 190.

[6] Sheuck v. Borough, 181 Pa. St. 191; Tipton v. Norman, 72 Mo. 380; Rumsey Mfg. Co. v. Schell City, 21 Mo. App. 175; Gas Co. v. San Francisco, 6 Cal. 190; Somer v. Philadelphia, 35 Pa. St. 231; Drake v. Hudson River R. Co., 7 Barb. (N. Y.) 539; Municipality v. Cutting, 4 La. Ann. 335. In City of Delphi v. Evans, 36 Ind. 90, the court said: "We do not regard the name or form of the order as of the substance of the thing. It may be done by an ordinance, by a motion or resolution; but whatever mode may be adopted, it must comply with the requirements of the charter." A resolution to have the

the municipality is authorized to enter into is not required to be made in the form of an ordinance, it may be by resolution.[1] But an act which the charter specifically requires to be done by ordinance cannot legally be done by resolution,[2] although one that is authorized to be done by resolution may be done by ordinance.[3]

§ 194. *Illustrations.*— An ordinance has been held necessary to authorize the grading of a street,[4] to change the width of a sidewalk,[5] to appoint a commission to assess damages resulting from the widening of a street,[6] to fix the compensation of officers,[7] to provide for the payment of license fees,[8] to authorize the specific improvement of city property under a general power to pass all proper and necessary laws providing for improvements,[9] or to direct the construction of a public work generally.[10]

On the other hand, the council may by resolution authorize the construction of a sewer,[11] remove the clerk of the corporation,[12] authorize the opening of a new street,[13] the purchase of fire apparatus,[14] the acceptance of a dedication,[15] the improvement of a street,[16] the laying of a tax for a specific pur-

---

effect of a law must be passed with all the formalities required in the enactment of a law. Thus, money cannot be appropriated by a joint resolution when the constitution requires that no money can be drawn except in pursuance of appropriations made by law. May v. Rice, 91 Ind. 546; Burritt v. Commissioners of State Contracts, 120 Ill. 322.

[1] Illinois Trust & Sav. Bank v. Arkansas City, 76 Fed. Rep. 271.

[2] Cape Girardeau v. Forgen, 30 Mo. App. 551. A resolution is not the legal equivalent of an ordinance. City of Paterson v. Barnett, 46 N. J. L. 62.

[3] Los Angeles v. Waldren, 65 Cal. 283.

[4] State v. Bayonne, 35 N. J. L. 335.

[5] Cross v. Mayor of Morristown, 18 N. J. Eq. 305, decided under a statute granting to the common council the power to pass ordinances to regulate the sidewalks and streets.

[6] State v. Bergen, 33 N. J. L. 39, 72.

[7] Central v. Sears, 2 Colo. 589; Smith v. Com., 41 Pa. St. 335.

[8] See People v. Cratty, 93 Ill. 181.

[9] Zottman v. San Francisco, 20 Cal. 96.

[10] Indianapolis v. Miller, 27 Ind. 394.

[11] State v. Jersey City, 27 N. J. L. 493.

[12] Landow West v. Burtram, 26 Ont. Rep. 161.

[13] Somer v. Philadelphia, 35 Pa. St. 231.

[14] Green v. Cape May, 41 N. J. L. 45.

[15] State v. Elizabeth, 37 N. J. L. 432.

[16] Indianapolis v. Imbery, 17 Ind. 175, where the court said: "The manner in which the order or determination of the council that a given street or alley, or part thereof, shall be improved, is to be expressed, is

pose,[1] or confirm the past acts of agents of the municipality.[2] So, when an ordinance requires a license and authorizes the council to fix the license fee as it shall from time to time think proper, the fee may be fixed by resolution.[3] No rules of any particular value can be laid down on this subject, as each case must be determined after a careful examination of the charter under which the council is acting.

not pointed out in the paramount law."
[1] It is an act of "a temporary character and prescribes no permanent rule of government." Blanchard v. Bissell, 11 Ohio St. 103.

[2] Egan v. Chicago, 5 Ill. App. 70.
[3] City of Burlington v. Putnam Ins. Co., 31 Iowa, 102; Arkadelphia Lumber Co. v. City of Arkadelphia, 56 Ark. 370, 19 S. W. Rep. 1053. See People v. Cratty, 93 Ill. 181.

CHAPTER XII.

OF THE FORM AND ENACTMENT OF ORDINANCES.

§ 195. The form.
196. The title.
197. The enacting clause.
198. The penalty.
199. Need not recite authority.
200. Council meeting.
201. Introduction — Notice.
202. Readings.
203. Suspension of the rules.
204. Presumption as to regularity.
205. Signing.
206. Approval.
207. Approval — Illustrations.

§ 208. The executive veto.
209. Necessity for publication.
210. Publication, when directory.
211. *Ultra vires* acts of officials.
212. Manner of publication.
213. Designation of paper.
214. Location of paper — "Printed and published in the city."
215. Manner and sufficiency.
216. Distinction between publication and notice.
217. Time and period.
218. Proof of publication.

§ 195. *The form.*— An ordinance should properly take the form of a statute, although this is not essential to its validity, as it is sufficient if it contains the substance of an ordinance and is properly enacted.[1] There should be a title, an enacting clause, a repealing clause, and a provision fixing the time when the ordinance will take effect. Certain requirements as to form are commonly found in charters and statutes.

§ 196. *The title.*— It is generally provided that the ordinance shall relate to but one subject, which shall be expressed in the title. Such provisions, like those found in constitutions relating to statutes, are intended to guard against fraud and surprise and are governed by the same rules of construction.[2] Constitutional provisions with reference to the title of a statute do not apply to municipal ordinances unless expressly made applicable thereto.[3]

[1] Rumsey Mfg. Co. v. Schell City, 21 Mo. App. 175.

[2] Esling's Appeal, 89 Pa. St. 205; State v. Cantiney, 34 Minn. 1; Bergman v. St. Louis, etc. R. Co., 88 Mo. 678; Stebbins v. Mayor, 38 Kan. 573, 16 Pac. Rep. 745. Such provisions are mandatory. Missouri Pac. R. Co. v. City of Wyandotte, 38 Kan. 573, 23 Pac. Rep. 950. The construction of the ordinance cannot be controlled by the title. State v. Benerly, 45 N. J. L. 289.

[3] In re Haskell, 112 Cal. 412, 32 L. R. A. 527; Tarkio v. Cook Co., 120 Mo. 1, 41 Am. St. Rep. 678; People v.

§ 197. *The enacting clause.*— An ordinance should show on its face that it was passed by a body having authority to pass it.[1] Properly there should be an enacting clause, as "Be it enacted by the Common Council of ———." But the absence of such clause is not fatal, even when required by the charter, as the record of the passage of the ordinance is a sufficient declaration that it is the act of the council.[2]

§ 198. *Penalty.*— An ordinance must contain provisions for a definite penalty, as this cannot be left to the discretion of the court.[3] This penalty must be reasonable in amount in view of the nature of the offense.[4] It is sufficiently definite if it fixes the maximum amount of the penalty, as "it is in harmony with our system of jurisprudence to allow the court or jury trying the cause to fix the penalty within the bound prescribed, with the right to vary in amount according to the gravity of the offense."[5] It has been held that the precise penalty for the infraction of a police ordinance must be provided for in the ordinance, and that an ordinance which provides

---

Wagner, 86 Mich. 594, 24 Am. St. Rep. 141; People v. Hanrahan, 75 Mich. 611, 4 L. R. A. 751. See Re Thomas, 53 Kan. 659, 37 Pac. Rep. 171.

[1] Hawkins v. Huron, 2 U. P. C. C. P. 72.

[2] People v. Murray, 57 Mich. 396; Cape Girardeau v. Riley, 52 Mo. 424; People v. Lee, 112 Ill. 112. A charter clause requiring that an ordinance shall contain an enacting clause is directory only, and its omission will not invalidate an ordinance. Tarkio v. Cook, 120 Mo. 1, 25 S. W. Rep. 202, 41 Am. St. Rep. 678; St. Louis v. Foster, 52 Mo. 313. *Contra*, Galveston, etc. R. Co. v. Harris (Tex. Civ. App.), 36 S. W. Rep. 776. The omission of the name of the town from the enacting clause will not invalidate the ordinance if it appears from the title that it was an ordinance of the particular town and is shown that it was regularly passed and in other respects conforms to the statutory requirements. State v. Fountain, 14 Wash. 236. The authorities on the question of the effect of the omission of an enacting clause from a statute are conflicting. In State v. Patterson, 98 N. C. 660; State v. Rogers, 10 Nev. 250; Burritt v. Commissioners, 120 Ill. 322, and May v. Rice, 91 Ind. 46, it is held that the constitutional requirement of an enacting clause is mandatory. McPherson v. Leonard, 29 Md. 377, and Cape Girardeau v. Riley, 52 Mo. 424, hold such a provision directory only. See, also, Watson v. Carey, 6 Utah, 150, and Hill v. Boyland, 40 Miss. 618.

[3] State v. Worth, 95 N. C. 615; Bowman v. St. John, 43 Ill. 337; Melick v. Washington, 47 N. J. L. 254; State v. Zigler, 32 N. J. L. 204; In re Frazee, 63 Mich. 396.

[4] In re Frazee, 63 Mich. 396; Mobile v. Yuille, 3 Ala. 137; Re Ah Yon, 88 Cal. 99, 11 L. R. A. 408.

[5] Bills v. Goshen, 117 Ind. 221, 3 L. R. A. 261. And see Atkins v. Phillips, 26 Fla. 281, 10 L. R. A. 158.

§ 199.] FORM AND ENACTMENT OF ORDINANCES. 183

that a justice of the peace may impose a penalty between two specified limits is invalid.[1] It is sometimes provided that conviction for the violation of an ordinance shall work a forfeiture of a license. It has been recently held that a city cannot enact such an ordinance, because it would operate as an extinguishment of a right which can only be legally extinguished by the city council. Thus, an ordinance which provided that a conviction of a violation of its provisions should operate as a revocation of a liquor license was held to be an unauthorized delegation of authority to revoke a license, which by the charter was conferred exclusively upon the city council.[2] But such an ordinance was sustained in Minnesota without reference to this objection. It was there held that the provision for the revocation of the license was not a part of the penalty, and did not change the grade of the offense. It was held that the granting of the license was a mere privilege, and that the provision in the charter that conviction of the licensee for a violation of the liquor ordinance should work a revocation was valid. The court said:[3] "While the revocation by the court follows conviction as a consequence of the violation of the ordinance, it has no more the purpose or effect of punishment than if the license were revoked by the mayor or city council, neither of whom has power to impose punishment for the offense. There is a plain distinction between the withdrawal of a special privilege, which has been abused, the termination of a mere license, and the penalty which the law imposes as a punishment for crime. The constitutional provision limiting the jurisdiction of justices of the peace by the measure of the 'punishment' which may be imposed has no reference to any such incidental consequences."[4]

§ 199. *Need not recite authority.*— An ordinance need not recite the authority under which it is enacted.[5] Nor need it recite the fact of compliance with conditions precedent to the right to enact the ordinance.[6] Where the authority is to pass

[1] State v. Ocean Grove Camp Meeting Ass'n, 57 N. J. L. 110, 35 Atl. Rep. 794.
[2] State v. Rahway, 58 N. J. L. 578.
[3] State v. Harris, 50 Minn. 128.
[4] State v. Larson, 40 Minn. 62.
[5] Methodist E. Church v. Baltimore, 6 Gill, 391, per Dorsey, C. J.; Com. v. Fahey, 5 Cush. 408.
[6] Cronin v. People, 82 N. Y. 318; Coates v. New York, 7 Cow. 585; Rex v. Harrison, 3 Burr. 1328.

an ordinance if found necessary the ordinance need not recite the necessity,[1] unless the charter requires it to be so stated.[2]

§ 200. *Council meeting.*— A valid ordinance can only be enacted at a legally convened meeting of a properly constituted council or legislative body vested with authority to pass the same and acting in accordance with statutory formalities.[3]

§ 201. *Introduction — Notice.*— Where the charter provides that an ordinance must be introduced at a previous meeting it cannot be materially amended and passed at the subsequent meeting; the amendment must have been previously introduced.[4] Nor under such provision can an ordinance be passed at an adjourned meeting.[5]

§ 202. *Readings.*— A provision requiring every ordinance to be read at three different meetings before its final passage is mandatory.[6] A reading by the title for at least one of the three readings is a sufficient compliance with such a require-

---

[1] Stuyvesant v. Mayor, 7 Cow. (N. Y.) 588; Young v. St. Louis, 47 Mo. 492; Kiley v. Forsee, 57 Mo. 390; Platter v. Elkhart Co., 103 Ind. 360.

[2] Hoyt v. East Saginaw, 19 Mich. 39.

[3] County of San Luis Obispo v. Hendricks, 71 Cal. 242; Jacksonville v. Ledwith, 26 Fla. 163, 9 L. R. A. 69. The rules of parliamentary law need not be observed unless required by the charter. McDonald v. State, 80 Wis. 411; McGraw v. Whitson, 69 Iowa, 348; St. Louis, etc. Co. v. Gill, 54 Ark. 105, 11 L. R. A. 452.

[4] State v. Bergen, 33 N. J. L. 39. In State v. Jersey City, 34 N. J. L. 429, the court said: "The object of the provision requiring such previous introduction would be wholly frustrated if an ordinance could be so materially amended and passed at the same meeting, and its sanction might in all cases be evaded under the guise of an amendment. See State v. City of Hudson, 29 N. J. L. 475. For effect of an indefinite postponement, see Zeiler v. Central R. Co., 84 Md. 304, 34 L. R. A. 469.

[5] "An adjourned meeting is a continuation of the same meeting, and at such adjourned meeting the council may do any act which might have been done if no adjournment had taken place. The meeting of May 2d, at which the ordinance was introduced, was not a meeting previous to that of May 9th, at which it was passed, but a continuation of the same meeting; and as the ordinance could not have been passed on May 2d, neither could it be passed on May 9th." Staates v. Washington, 44 N. J. L. 605.

[6] Weil v. Kerfield, 54 Cal. 111. But see Barton v. Pittsburgh, 4 Brew. (Pa.) 373. The two-thirds of the members required to dispense with a regular reading means two-thirds of the members voting if they are not less than a majority which constitutes a quorum. Zeiler v. Central R. Co., 84 Md. 304, 34 L. R. A. 469.

ment.[1] A newly-constituted council may take up an ordinance which was read twice in the preceding council, give it a third reading and pass it.[2] A reading may be at a special or adjourned meeting.[3] Where a charter requires an ordinance to be published for a certain time and in a certain manner between its second and third readings, it cannot lawfully be amended in any material respect and read again without the vote required by the charter.[4] An ordinance which requires that all ordinances shall be read three times before being passed and that no ordinance shall be read the third time and passed on the same day on which it was introduced cannot be repealed by a mere majority vote.[5]

§ 203. *Suspension of the rules.*— All provisions regulating the passage of an ordinance under a suspension of the rules must be strictly observed. When the rules are so suspended but one ordinance can be passed under such suspension.[6]

§ 204. *Presumption as to regularity.*— All meetings of the council are presumed to be regularly conducted. Thus, where it is the duty of the mayor to preside at a council meeting, it will be presumed that he was present and presided.[7]

§ 205. *Signing.*— The signing of an ordinance by a clerk of the council is a ministerial act, and if he refuses to comply with the requirement the presiding officer may appoint a deputy to sign the same.[8] Nor is the signature of the mayor generally necessary to the validity of an ordinance which has been regularly passed and recorded.[9] But a statute may, by its express terms, make the mayor's signature essential to the validity of the ordinance. But a requirement that the mayor shall au-

---

[1] State v. Camden, 58 N. J. L. 515, 33 Atl. Rep. 846.
[2] McGow v. Whitson, 69 Iowa, 348.
[3] Cutcamp v. Utt, 60 Iowa, 156.
[4] State v. Newark, 30 N. J. L. 303.
[5] Swindell v. Moxey, 143 Ind. 153, 42 N. E. Rep. 528.
[6] Bloom v. Xenia, 32 Ohio St. 460.
[7] Martin v. State, 23 Neb. 371, 36 N. W. Rep. 554, Maxwell, C. J., dissenting.
[8] Preston v. Manvers, 21 U. C. Q. B. 626.
[9] Martindale v. Palmer, 52 Ind. 411; State v. Henderson, 38 Ohio St. 644. It is sometimes expressly provided that if the mayor neglects or refuses to sign the ordinance it shall become a law without his signature. Saleno v. Neosho, 127 Mo. 627, 27 L. R. A. 679, 48 Am. St. Rep. 653.

thenticate all ordinances by his signature is merely directory.[1] A direction in a city charter that a bill shall be signed in open session is mandatory.[2] Under a statute providing that "no bill shall become a law until the same is signed by the president of the board of aldermen or the mayor," and that "the mayor shall preside at all meetings of the board of aldermen," signing by the mayor as such only, is sufficient.[3] When an ordinance is required to be signed by the presiding officer and attested by the clerk, the defect cannot be remedied by motion.[4]

§ 206. *Approval.*—The requirement of the executive approval must be distinguished from that of signing. Such approval is generally made essential to the validity of an ordinance, and when such is the case all proceedings under an ordinance which has neither been approved nor passed over a veto are void.[5] "Whenever, either by constitutional or legislative requirement, the president of the United States, the governor of a state or the mayor of a city is required to approve an act of congress, or of a legislature, or of a common council, the word 'approve' means more than the unexpressed mental acquiescence of the individual in the propriety of what has been done; it means that the officer, in his official capacity as the guardian of the interests of the community, having in view its welfare, and not his personal wish or advantage, shall consider the proposed legislation and determine that it is proper, and make that fact known to all men with absolute certainty by some visible, unmistakable and enduring mark, to wit, by written declaration attested by his signature."[6] Where the charter provides that the approval of the mayor shall be by his signature, his approval cannot be shown in any other way.[7] It has been held

---

[1] Blanchard v. Bissell, 11 Ohio St. 96; Stevenson v. Bay City, 26 Mich. 44; Martindale v. Palmer, 52 Ind. 411; McKenzie v. Wooley, 39 La. Ann. 944; Opelousas v. Andrus, 87 La. Ann. 699.

[2] Barber Asphalt Pav. Co. v. Hunt, 100 Mo. 22, 18 Am. St. Rep. 530.

[3] Becker v. Washington, 94 Mo. 375. See Worth v. Springfield, 78 Mo. 108.

[4] Bills v. City of Goshen, 117 Ind. 221, 20 N. E. Rep. 115.

[5] People v. Schroeder, 76 N. Y. 160; Dey v. Jersey City, 19 N. J. Eq. 414. Necessity of approval of order or resolution. Shaub v. Lancaster, 156 Pa. St. 362, 21 L. R. A. 691.

[6] New York, etc. R. Co. v. City of Waterbury, 55 Conn. 19, per Pardee, J.

[7] "It is enough to say . . . that

there must be a formal and literal presentation for approval or veto, and that a requirement, therefore, cannot be waived by the mayor.[1] The express charter requirement that the ordinance shall be submitted to the mayor before it becomes law is mandatory.[2] And if the statute prescribes the manner in which the measure shall be approved, the approval in that manner cannot be dispensed with. Though the mayor puts the resolution, declares it adopted, and in fact signs and approves it, this is not in such a case sufficient.[3]

§ 207. *Approval — Illustrations.* — Where the council has power to pass "by-laws, ordinances, resolutions and regulations," and the charter requires that "by-laws and ordinances" shall be approved by the mayor, the requirement extends to resolutions.[4] But a provision requiring all ordinances and resolutions to be presented to the mayor for his approval does not apply to the appointment of the officers of the council.[5] It is sufficient if the ordinance be approved by the "acting president of the board of aldermen," in the mayor's absence, where it is provided by statute that such officer shall for the time being perform the duties of mayor, with all his rights, powers and jurisdiction.[6]

§ 208. *The executive veto.* — When an ordinance is vetoed there can be but one reconsideration;[7] and where the charter provides that "at the next meeting of the council after a disapproval by the mayor it shall proceed to reconsider the resolution,". it cannot be postponed to a subsequent meeting."[8]

the charter provides but one mode for the mayor to attest his approval of resolutions, to wit, by his signature. It is impossible to substitute for that any other evidence that as an alderman or as a private person he approved or consented to the resolutions." Gilfillan, C. J., in State v. District Court, 41 Minn. 518. *Contra,* Woodruff v. Stewart, 63 Ala. 209. The signature affixed to the journal of the council is not a sufficient approval. Graham v. Carondelet, 33 Mo. 262.
[1] State v. Newark, 25 N. J. L. 399.

[2] Bubridge v. Astoria, 25 Oreg. 417, 42 Am. St. Rep. 796.
[3] Whitney v. Port Huron, 88 Mich. 268, 26 Am. St. Rep. 291.
[4] Kepner v. Com., 40 Pa. St. 124. But see Blanchard v. Bissell, 11 Ohio St. 103.
[5] McDermott v. Miller, 45 N. J. L. 251.
[6] Saleno v. Neosho, 127 Mo. 627, 27 L. R. A. 769.
[7] Sauk v. Philadelphia, 8 Phila. (Pa.) 118.
[8] Peck v. Rochester, 3 N. Y. Supp. 873.

Where an ordinance is passed over the veto it takes effect without further act of the executive.

§ 209. *Necessity for publication.*— It is commonly required that all ordinances shall be published before taking effect. This just and reasonable provision must be complied with in order to give validity to the law.[1] Under such a provision actual notice is not the equivalent of publication.[2] Provisions relating to publication are strictly construed when applied to police ordinances which affect the personal rights and liberties of the citizen. Under a constitutional provision that no person shall be punished save under a law established and promulgated prior to the commission of the offense, an ordinance must be published for such a time as will give the public a reasonable opportunity to become acquainted with its provisions.[3] The legislature may provide that the failure to publish an ordinance within a stated time shall not affect its validity, but it can have no retroactive effect.[4]

A provision in a city charter that the ayes and noes shall be called and published whenever the vote of the council is taken on any proposed improvement involving a tax or assessment upon the people is directory — "the essential requirement being the determination of the improvement and not the form or manner of expressing that determination."[5]

§ 210. *Publication directory.*— In Massachusetts, statutes providing for the publication of ordinances are held to be directory. Thus, when ordinances were required to be "published two weeks successively in three newspapers published in

[1] Meyer v. Fromm, 108 Ind. 208; Napa v. Esterly, 61 Cal. 509; Wahn v. Philadelphia, 99 Pa. St. 330; Higby v. Bunce, 10 Conn. 567; Barnett v. Newark, 28 Iowa, 62; Schwartz v. Oshkosh, 55 Wis. 490; Elizabethtown v. Lefler, 23 Ill. 90; Stillwater v. Moor (Oklahoma, 1893), 33 Pac. Rep. 1024. But see Elmendorf v. Mayor, 25 Wend. (N. Y.) 693.

[2] O'Hare v. Parker River (N. Dak.), 47 N. W. Rep. 380; National Bank of Commerce v. Grenada, 44 Fed. Rep. 262.

[3] A publication for seven days is sufficient. Pitts v. Opelika, 79 Ala. 527. For an illustration of the effect of a requirement of publication of an administrative ordinance, see Stuhr v. Hoboken, 47 N. J. L. 147. It is not necessary to publish books and maps referred to in an ordinance. Napa v. Esterly (Cal.), 16 Pac. Rep. 256.

[4] Schweizer v. Liberty, 82 Mo. 309.

[5] Striker v. Kelley, 7 Hill (N. Y.), 9, 2 Denio, 323; Indianola v. Jones, 29 Iowa, 282; St. Louis v. Foster, 52 Mo. 513; Elmendorf v. Mayor, etc., 25 Wend. 693.

the city," Morton, C. J., said[1] that, as there is no provision that the ordinance shall not take effect until published, "the provision requiring publication is directory; it contemplates a publication after the ordinance is enacted, and a compliance with it is not a condition precedent to the validity of the ordinance."

§ 211. *Ultra vires acts of officials.*— When an ordinance is passed and published in the mode prescribed by the charter, it is valid although the city officials exceeded their authority in incurring a debt for the publication.[2]

§ 212. *Manner of publication.*— When no method of publication is prescribed it seems that posting copies in public places is sufficient.[3] But publication is generally directed to be made in a newspaper published or having a general circulation in the municipality. A statute requiring "legal notices and advertisements" to be published in certain kinds of newspapers has no application to city ordinances.[4]

§ 213. *Designation of paper.*— The designation of the paper must be by the proper authority. Thus, where a town is given discretion to publish the ordinances in either of three specified classes of papers, a publication made in a paper belonging to one of the classes by order of the town clerk is ineffectual.[5] But where the council neglects to designate a paper and the law requires the clerk of the board of aldermen to publish resolutions and ordinances of the kind in question, the clerk may make a legal publication in any paper published in the city.[6]

§ 214. *Location of paper —"Printed and published in the city."*— A paper is printed and published in the city although some of the press-work is done elsewhere.[7] A statute which requires publication in a newspaper of the town for a specified

---

[1] Com. v. Davis, 140 Mass. 485; Com. v. McCafferty, 145 Mass. 384, 14 N. E. Rep. 451. See, also, Sacramento v. Dillman, 102 Cal. 107, 36 Pac. Rep. 385.

[2] Kimble v. Peoria, 140 Ill. 156, 29 N. E. Rep. 723.

[3] Queen v. Justices, 4 Q. B. 522, 29 Moak's Eng. Rep. 61.

[4] Pittsburg v. Reynolds, 48 Kan. 360, 29 Pac. Rep. 757.

[5] Higby v. Bunce, 10 Conn. 436, 567. See Chicago v. McCoy, 136 Ill. 344, 11 L. R. A. 413.

[6] In re Darkin, 10 Hun (N. Y.), 269.

[7] Bayer v. Hoboken, 44 N. J. L. 131.

period is complied with by publication in a paper prepared and edited expressly for publication in the town and having its principal circulation there, although it is printed elsewhere and sent to the town in bundles for distribution.[1] But there can be no valid "publication" in a paper which has no circulation in a town although it is entirely printed there.[2]

§ 215. *Manner and sufficiency.*— It is not necessary to publish along with the ordinance the law which is the authority for its enactment.[3] The publication may be in connection with the other proceedings of the council.[4] The distribution of printed copies of an ordinance along with a newspaper is a compliance with a statute requiring publication in the paper.[5] Inaccuracies in printing are immaterial if the meaning is clear from the context.[6]

§ 216. *Distinction between publication and notice.*— There is a manifest distinction to be observed between the publication of a notice and the publication of an instrument, a statute or ordinance. A notice requires no particular collocation of words so long as it conveys a clear idea of its subject, but a statute or ordinance has no legal existence except in the language in which it is passed.[7] Hence, where a notice is by statute required to be published in a paper printed in the German language, the notice must be printed in the German language; but when a statute or ordinance is required to be published in the same paper it must, in default of legislative direction to the contrary, be printed in the English language.[8]

§ 217. *Time and period.*— When no time is designated publication may be made at any time.[9] A provision for publica-

---

[1] Tisdale v. Town of Minonk, 46 Ill. 9.
[2] Haskell v. Bartlett, 34 Cal. 281. Where publication is directed to be made in an *adjoining* municipality in the absence of any local newspaper, a leading paper in a large city not far distant which circulates in the municipality may be resorted to in preference to the local paper of a village lying nearer in point of fact than the city." Gallerno v. Rochester, 46 U. C. Q. B. 279.
[3] People v. Board of Supervisors, 27 Cal. 655.
[4] Law v. People, 87 Ill. 389.
[5] Ex parte Bedell, 20 Mo. App. 125.
[6] Moss v. Oakland, 88 Ill. 100. See How v. People, 88 Ill. 389.
[7] State v. Mayor, 54 N. J. L. 111, 22 Atl. Rep. 1004, 14 L. R. A. 62.
[8] State v. Mayor, *supra.*
[9] St. Paul v. Colter, 12 Minn. 41, 90 Am. Dec. 278. The charter provided that "the council shall cause all publications made by authority of

tion for a certain time before taking effect requires but one insertion.[1] A requirement of publication "for five successive days" in a daily newspaper is complied with by publication for five successive week days, although a Sunday intervenes on which there was no issue.[2] The day of issue and delivery of the paper is the first day of the period regardless of the date of the paper.

A requirement of publication "for at least one week" in a newspaper published in the city is complied with by one publication if the paper is a weekly paper, but if made in a daily paper it must appear in each issue for one week.[3]

§ 218. *Proof of publication.*— It is commonly provided that proof of publication may be made by the certificate of the clerk under the seal of the corporation. A mere memorandum entered on the ordinance is insufficient as a certificate.[4] Where the publication must be in a paper "published in the city," there must be proof of publication and of the place of publication.[5]

the city to be inserted in the first column of the third page of the newspaper doing the city printing." The ordinance was passed May 4th, and not published until September 9th following, between which dates several meetings of the council had taken place.

[1] Hoboken v. Gear, 27 N. J. L. 267; State v. Hardy, 7 Neb. 377; Commonwealth v. Mathews, 122 Mass. 60.

[2] Ex parte Fisk, 72 Cal. 125; Taylor v. Palmer, 31 Cal. 240. When the publication is required to be in the official paper of the city it is sufficient if it is published as often as the paper is issued. Richter v. Harper, 95 Mich. 221, 54 N. W. Rep. 768.

[3] Union P. R. Co. v. Montgomery, 49 Neb. 429, 68 N. W. Rep. 619.

[4] Thus, in Hutchins v. Mt. Vernon, 40 Ill. App. 19, it was held that the words " published July 17, 1890. Attest, B. B. Slade," was "nothing more than a memorandum of the fact and date, so that thereafter a certificate thereof might be readily made when required."

[5] Hutchins v. Mt. Vernon, 40 Ill. App. 19.

CHAPTER XIII.

THE VALIDITY OF ORDINANCES.

§ 219. General statement.
220. Under express power.
221. Motives of legislative body.
222. Ordinances valid in part.
223. Nature of an ordinance.
224. Injunctions — Invalid ordinances.

I. GENERAL PRINCIPLES GOVERNING VALIDITY.

225. Must conform to charter.
226. Must be constitutional.
227. Must conform to law.
228. Must not contravene common right.
229. Must be general and impartial.
230. Must not be oppressive.
231. Must be reasonable.
232. Reasonableness a question for the court.
233. Presumption of reasonableness.

II. ILLUSTRATIONS OF VALID AND INVALID ORDINANCES.

234. Laying pipes in streets.

§ 235. Location and speed of vehicles.
236. Handling of trains.
237. Regulation of street railways.
238. Parades, music, and speaking in public places.
239. Licenses.
240. Discrimination against non-residents.
241. Regulation of markets.
242. Regulation of liquor traffic.
243. Fire regulations.
244. Quarantine regulations — Second-hand clothing.
245. Hotel runners and hackmen.
246. Miscellaneous decisions.

III. ORDINANCES WHICH PROHIBIT ACTS WITHOUT THE CONSENT OF CERTAIN OFFICIALS.

247. General statement.
248. Cases sustaining such ordinances.
249. Delegation of authority.
250. Nature of act prohibited.
251. Uniform conditions — Unjust discrimination.

§ 219. *General statement.*— An ordinance may be void because of want of power in the corporation to enact it, the failure to observe prescribed formalities in its enactment, or because contrary to certain general principles of law. As a rule the questions arise upon the validity of ordinances enacted under general authority to legislate with reference to a certain subject-matter. Thus, when a city is granted the power to regulate and control its streets, it is authorized to exercise the general power by means of ordinances enacted in accordance with the provisions of the charter and the general rules of law.

§ 220. *Under express power.*— When the legislature specifically authorizes the passage of a particular ordinance, the courts will not inquire into the question of its reasonableness. The only questions which can then arise are those which go to the power of the legislature.[1] Hence, the power of a court to declare ordinances void for reasons which would not apply equally well to a statute is practically restricted to cases in which the legislature has not legislated on the subject-matter of the ordinance, and consequently to cases in which the ordinance was passed under a supposed incidental power of the corporation.[2]

§ 221. *Motives of council.*— The courts have no power to inquire into the motives of members of the legislature which enacted a law.[3] This principle applies as well to a city council as a state legislature.[4] But notwithstanding this the courts will not sustain an ordinance the enactment of which was procured by fraud and bribery.[5] As said by Judge Dillon:[6] "It would be disastrous to apply the analogy to its full extent. Municipal bodies, like the directories of private corporations, have too often shown themselves capable of using their powers fraudulently for their own advantage or to the injury of others. We suppose it to be a sound proposition that their acts, whether in the form of resolutions or ordinances, *may be impeached for fraud* at the instance of persons injured thereby."

---

[1] Phillips v. Denver, 19 Colo. 179, 41 Am. St. Rep. 230; Champer v. Greencastle, 138 Ind. 339, 46 Am. St. Rep. 390. In Beiling v. Evansville, 144 Ind. 644, 35 L. R. A. 272, the court said: "It is well settled that when the adoption of a municipal ordinance or by-law is expressly authorized by the legislature, and when the express grant of power is not in conflict with a constitutional prohibition or fundamental principles, it cannot be successfully assailed as unreasonable in a judicial tribunal."

[2] Skaggs v. Martinsville, 140 Ind. 476, 49 Am. St. Rep. 209, 33 L. R. A. 781; Coal Float v. Jeffersonville, 112 Ind. 19; Ex parte Chan Yen, 60 Cal. 79; Brooklyn v. Breslau, 57 N. Y. 591; State v. Clark, 54 Mo. 17; Hayne v. Cape May, 50 N. J. L. 55. "Where an ordinance is based upon a general power, and its provisions are more specific and detailed than the expression of the power conferred, the court will look into the reasonableness of such provisions." State v. Trenton, 53 N. J. L. 132, 20 Atl. Rep. 1076. And see Howes v. Chicago, 158 Ill. 653, 30 L. R. A. 225, and Darlington v. Ward, 48 S. C. 570.

[3] Cooley, Const. Lim., § 186; Wright v. Defrees, 8 Ind. 298.

[4] Buell v. Ball, 20 Iowa, 282; Freeport v. Marks, 59 Pa. St. 253.

[5] State v. Cin. Gas Co., 18 Ohio St. 262.

[6] Dillon, Mun. Corp. (4th ed.), I, § 311.

§ 222. *Ordinances valid in part.*— Certain sections or parts of sections of an ordinance may be held invalid without affecting the validity of what remains, if the parts are not so interblended and dependent that the vice of one necessarily vitiates the others. It is only necessary "that the good and bad parts be so distinct and independent that the invalid parts may be eliminated and that what remains contain all the essentials of a complete ordinance."[1] The fact that the penal provision for the enforcement of an ordinance is void does not invalidate its other provisions, the valid part being complete and independent of the void portion.[2] As said by the supreme court of the United States, with reference to statutes: "These are cases where the parts are so distinctly separable that each can stand alone, and where the court is able to see and to declare that the intention of the legislature was that the part pronounced valid should be enforceable, even though the other part should fail. To hold otherwise would be to substitute for the law intended by the legislature one they may never have been willing themselves to enact."[3]

An ordinance may be valid as to certain persons or sales and invalid as to others.[4] Thus, an ordinance which forbids the sale of malt liquors, which the corporation has power to do, and also of spirituous liquors, which it has not power to do, is valid as to the former and invalid as to the latter.[5] So, where the general law permits the sale of liquor in quantities of five gallons or more without a license, an ordinance which prohibits all sale of liquors without a license is valid as to sales in quantities of less than five gallons.[6] But when the remaining part of the ordinance does not express the legislative intent,[7]

[1] In re Bizzell, 112 Ala. 210, 21 So. Rep. 371; City of Detroit v. Fort Wayne, etc. R. Co., 95 Mich. 456, 35 Am. St. Rep. 580, 20 L. R. A. 79; Ex parte Stephen, 114 Cal. 278.
[2] Magenan v. Fremont, 30 Neb. 843, 9 L. R. A. 786.
[3] Pointdexter v. Greenhow, 114 U. S. 305; State v. Webber, 107 N. C. 962, 22 Am. St. Rep. 020; In re Wong Hane, 108 Cal. 080, 49 Am. St. Rep. 138; City of Tarkio v. Cook, 120 Mo. 1, 41 Am. St. Rep. 678; In re Haskell, 112 Cal. 412, 32 L. R. A. 527; State v. Hardy,

[7] Neb. 377; St. Louis v. St. Louis Ry. Co., 89 Mo. 44; Belleville v. Citizens' Horse Car Co., 153 Ill. 171, 26 L. R. A. 681; Danversberger v. Pendergast, 128 Ill. 229; Koch v. North Ave. R. Co., 75 Md. 222, 15 L. R. A. 377.
[4] Ex parte Cowert, 92 Ala. 94, 9 So. Rep. 225.
[5] Eldora v. Burlingame, 62 Iowa, 32; Cantril v. Sainer, 59 Iowa, 26.
[6] State v. Priester, 43 Minn. 373.
[7] In re Wong Hane, 108 Cal. 080, 49 Am. St. Rep. 138.

§ 223.]   VALIDITY OF ORDINANCES.   195

or the objectionable part is the compensation for or inducement to the unobjectionable part, so that it is apparent that the latter part would not have been enacted alone, the whole is invalid.[1]

§ 223. *The nature of an ordinance.*— A municipal ordinance is a local law prescribing a general rule of action, and is as binding upon the people within the municipality as are the acts of the legislature upon the citizens of the state.[2] When applicable to every part of the city it is a general law, and not in conflict with a constitutional provision prohibiting local legislation.[3] It is binding upon all who are within the limits of the municipality;[4] and any person who contracts with reference to a matter governed by an ordinance is charged with notice

---

[1] Gilbert-Arnold Land Co. v. Superior, 91 Wis. 353, 64 N. W. Rep. 999; Jacksonville v. Leadwith, 26 Fla. 163, 23 Am. St. Rep. 558, and note to City of Tarkio v. Cook, 120 Mo. 1, 41 Am. St. Rep. 678, 683.

[2] New Orleans Water Works v. New Orleans, 164 U. S. 481; Buffalo v. New York, etc. Ry. Co., 152 N. Y. 276, 46 N. E. Rep. 496; Citizens' Gas & Min. Co. v. Elmwood, 114 Ind. 332; Bills v. Goshen, 117 Ind. 221, 3 L. R. A. 261. "Ordinances are not merely rules or regulations in the ordinary sense of those terms; but, as the derivation of the word would indicate, they are in the nature of laws, being decreed by a body vested with definite legislative authority coupled with the power to enforce obedience to its enactment." Horr & Bemis, Mun. Pol. Ord., sec. 12; Hopkins v. Mayor, 4 M. & W. 461, 640, per Lord Abinger; Village of St. Johnsbury v. Thomson, 59 Vt. 301; State v. Tryon, 39 Conn. 183; Beardon v. Madison, 73 Ga. 184; Des Moines Gas Co. v. Des Moines, 44 Iowa, 508; Starr v. Burlington, 45 Iowa, 87; St. Louis v. Buffinger, 19 Mo. 13; Jones v. Insurance Co., 2 Daly (N. Y.), 307; McDermott v. Board, 5 Abb. Pr. (N. Y.) 422; Gabel v. Houston, 29 Tex. 336; Burmeister v. Howard, 1 Wash. 207. A city council "is a miniature general assembly, and their authorized ordinances have the force of laws passed by the legislature of the state." Scott, J., in Taylor v. Carondelet, 22 Mo. 105; St. Louis v. Foster, 52 Mo. 513. Contracts between the inhabitants of a city in violation of the provisions of a valid ordinance are illegal and cannot be enforced. Milne v. Davidson, 5 Mart. N. S. (La.) 586. But see Baker v. Portland, 58 Me. 199, 10 Am. L. Reg. (N. S.) 559, note.

[3] Foster v. Police Com'rs, 102 Cal. 183, 41 Am. St. Rep. 194.

[4] City Ry. Co. v. Mayor, 77 Ga. 731, 4 Am. St. Rep. 106. In Bott v. Pratt, 33 Minn. 323, the court, by Vanderberg, J., said: "An ordinance which a municipal corporation is authorized to make is as binding upon all persons within the corporate limits as any statute or other laws of the commonwealth, and all persons interested are bound to take notice of their existence. Heland v. Lowell, 3 Allen (Mass.), 407; Vandines' Case, 6 Pick. 187; Gilmore v. Holt, 4 Pick. 257; Johnson v. Simonton, 33 Cal. 242, 249." Compare Henry v. Sprague, 11 R. I. 457, 23 Am. Rep. 502.

of its provisions.¹ But police ordinances, although their violation may be punished by fine and imprisonment, are only *quasi-criminal* laws.² They are not criminal laws within the general meaning of the term, although the procedure for their enforcement is generally criminal in form and may be in the name of the state. Hence, a conviction under an ordinance for keeping a house of ill-fame is not a bar to a conviction for the same offense under the general law of the state.³ The violation of one ordinance is not properly a crime against public law.⁴ Hence a defendant when prosecuted under an ordinance is not entitled to a jury trial.⁵ But the courts are not always consistent, at least in the use of language. Thus, it was said⁶ of ordinances: "They come strictly within the definition of 'crimes or criminal offenses.' The terms 'crime,' 'offense' and 'criminal offense' are all synonymous, and ordinarily used interchangeably, and include any breach of law established for the protection of the public, as distinguished from an infringement of mere private rights, for which a penalty is imposed or punishment inflicted in any judicial proceeding." But the same court held⁷ that a city council might lawfully enact an ordi-

¹ North Birmingham v. Colderwood, 89 Ala. 247, 18 Am. St. Rep. 105; Sylvester Coal Co. v. St. Louis, 130 Mo. 323, 32 S. W. Rep. 649. In Ewing v. Webster City (Iowa), 72 N. W. Rep. 511 (1897), the court said: "It is the established rule of this state that, for most purposes at least, the violation of a municipal ordinance enacted by authority of the state is a crime, and that proceedings for its punishment are criminal."

² State v. Webber, 107 N. C. 962, 22 Am. St. Rep. 920; State v. Boneil, 42 La. Ann. 1110, 21 Am. St. Rep. 413.

³ State v. Lee, 29 Minn. 407, 13 N. W. Rep. 913; State v. Harris, 50 Minn. 128; Wragg v. Penn Tp., 94 Ill. 23; Shafer v. Mumma, 17 Md. 331; Brownville v. Cook, 4 Neb. 105. See an extensive note to State v. Robitshek, in 33 L. R. A. 33.

⁴ Ex parte Holdenell, 74 Mo. 401; Platteville v. McKennan, 54 Wis. 487;

City of Goshen v. Craxton, 34 Ind. 239.

⁵ Byers v. Com., 42 Pa. St. 89; Howe v. Plainfield, 8 Vroom (N. J.), 151; Mankato v. Arnold, 36 Minn. 62, 30 N. W. Rep. 505; State v. West, 42 Minn. 147, 43 N. W. Rep. 845; State v. Harris, 50 Minn. 128, 52 N. W. Rep. 387.

⁶ State v. West, 42 Minn. 147.

⁷ State v. Robitshek, 60 Minn. 123, 61 N. W. Rep. 1023, 33 L. R. A. 33, annotated. The court said: "Prosecutions thereunder are in the name of the state by express provision of the charter, as a matter of convenience; and they are, at most, merely *quasi-criminal* in form. They are simply local police regulations or by-laws for the government of the municipality, and have no reference to or connection with the administration of the criminal laws of the state. Originally the only method of enforcing them was by civil action, brought by the

nance which in effect prohibited any one not a policeman from instituting a prosecution for failing to keep a saloon closed on Sunday, on the ground that "municipal ordinances are not criminal statutes; that violations thereof are not crimes, nor are such violations governed by the rules of the criminal law, save in certain specified exceptional particulars."

§ 224. *Injunctions — Invalid ordinances.*— The passage of an ordinance is a legislative act, and it is well settled that the legislative acts of a municipal corporation will not be restrained by injunction.[1] But when an ordinance is invalid and the case falls within any of the common heads of equity, a court will enjoin the enforcement of the ordinance in order to protect private rights.[2] Ordinances are penal in their nature, and the validity of criminal laws will not be tested by injunction; but this rule is "subordinate to the general principle that equity will grant relief where there is not a plain, adequate and complete remedy at law, and when it is necessary to prevent an irreparable injury."[3] Thus, an injunction was granted to restrain the enforcement of an invalid ordinance which imposed certain restrictions upon articles of merchandise and subjected the seller to an action for a violation of the ordinance.[4] But where the plaintiff had been twice convicted and fined for violating an ordinance requiring grain to be weighed on city scales and had appealed, and pending the appeal brought a suit to restrain the city from further prosecuting him or any of his customers on the ground that the ordinance was void, the injunction was denied on the ground that the plaintiff could avoid a multiplicity of suits by obeying the ordinance pending the appeal, and that the loss and convenience which he would thereby suffer would not be so great as to warrant the interference of a court of equity.[5]

The general principle has been announced that a municipal

municipality in its own name to recover such penalty as was prescribed for a violation."

[1] New Orleans Water Works v. New Orleans, 164 U. S. 471; Des Moines Gas Co. v. Des Moines, 44 Iowa, 505; High, Inj., § 1246.

[2] New Orleans Water Works v. New Orleans, 164 U. S. 471; Baltimore v. Radicke, 49 Md. 217.

[3] Austin v. Austin Cemetery Ass'n, 87 Tex. 330. See Vegelahn v. Guntner, 167 Mass. 92.

[4] Sylvester Coal Co. v. St. Louis, 130 Mo. 323, 51 Am. St. Rep. 556.

[5] Ewing v. Webster City (Iowa), 72 N. W. Rep. 511 (1897).

corporation will be enjoined from performing a threatened act which constitutes a manifest abuse of its discretion, to the oppression of the citizens.[1]

I. GENERAL PRINCIPLES GOVERNING VALIDITY.

§ 225. *Must conform to charter.*— As all ordinances are enacted for the purpose of carrying into effect powers granted by the charter, it necessarily follows that they must in all things conform to the charter.[2]

§ 226. *Must not contravene the constitution.*— Municipal ordinances are subject to the restrictions imposed by the constitution of the state and of the United States, and when repugnant to either are void.[3] Thus, an ordinance impairing the obligation of a contract,[4] or taking property without due process of law,[5] or making unjust discriminations between citizens, in violation of the fourteenth amendment to the constitution,[6] or attempting to regulate interstate commerce, is void.[7] It seems that a person has a constitutional right to associate with criminals, and an ordinance forbidding any one knowingly to associate with persons having the reputation of criminals is an invasion of the constitutional right of personal liberty.[8] An ordinance which authorizes a fire warden to arrest and detain any person who, at a fire, without sufficient excuse refuses to obey his orders is unconstitutional as depriving the person of his liberty without due process of law.[9] An ordinance discriminating against the

[1] Atlanta v. Halleday, 96 Ga. 546, 26 S. E. Rep. 509.
[2] People v. Armstrong, 73 Mich. 288, 16 Am. St. Rep. 578; Thompson v. Carroll, 22 How. (U. S.) 422; Thomas v. Richmond, 12 Wall. (U. S.) 349; Com. v. Roy, 140 Mass. 432; Garden City v. Abbott, 34 Kan. 283; State v. Nashville, 15 Lea (Tenn.), 697; State v. Municipal Court, 32 Minn. 329; Rothschild v. Darien, 69 Ga. 503; Breinger v. Beloibere, 44 N. J. L. 350.
[3] Ex parte Felchlin, 96 Cal. 360, 31 Am. St. Rep. 223; Phillips v. Denver, 19 Colo. 179, 41 Am. St. Rep. 230; Mt. Pleasant v. Vancise, 43 Mich. 361;

Baldwin v. Smith, 82 Ill. 162; Illinois Central R. R. Co. v. Bloomington, 76 Ill. 447; Vance v. Little Rock, 30 Ark. 435; Judson v. Reardon, 16 Minn. 435.
[4] Savings Society v. Philadelphia, 31 Pa. St. 175; Kansas City v. Corrigan, 86 Mo. 67.
[5] Baldwin v. Smith, 82 Ill. 162.
[6] State v. Dering, 84 Wis. 585, 36 Am. St. Rep. 948.
[7] Moran v. New Orleans, 112 U. S. 69.
[8] Ex parte Smith, 135 Mo. 223, 33 L. R. A. 606.
[9] Judson v. Reardon, 16 Minn. 431 (Gil. 387).

§ 227.] VALIDITY OF ORDINANCES. 199

Chinese in granting laundry licenses is void as contravening the fourteenth amendment.[1]

§ 227. *Must conform to law.*— Ordinances must not only conform to the charter and the constitution, but when enacted in pursuance of implied power they must be consistent with the general laws and policy of the state.[2] If contrary to the general laws or declared policy of the state they are void.[3]

A grant of power to a municipal corporation to make by-laws for its own government and the regulation of its own police "cannot be construed as imparting to it power to repeal the laws in force or to supersede their operation by any of its ordinances. Such a power, if not expressly conferred, cannot arise by mere implication unless the exercise of the power given be inconsistent with the previous law and does necessarily operate as its repeal *pro tanto*. Nor can the assumption be indulged that the legislature intended that an ordinance passed

---

[1] Yick Wo v. Hopkins, 118 U. S. 356; In re Tie Lay, 26 Fed. Rep. 611. See, also, Soon Hing v. Crowley, 113 U. S. 703; Barbey v. Connolly, 113 U. S. 27. An ordinance declaring steamboats emitting dense smoke a nuisance is valid as affecting boats on the Chicago river. Harmon v. Chicago, 110 Ill. 400. A penalty for violating an ordinance is not a debt within the meaning of the constitutional provision prohibiting imprisonment for debt. Hardenbrock v. Town of Legonier, 95 Ind. 70.

[2] Burg v. Chicago, etc. Ry. Co., 90 Iowa, 106, 48 Am. St. Rep. 419; Kratzenberger v. Law, 90 Tenn. 235, 25 Am. St. Rep. 681. See note to this case in 13 L. R. A. 185. Volk v. Newark, 47 N. J. L. 117; Lozier v. Newark, 48 N. J. L. 452; Robinson v. Mayor of Franklyn, 1 Humph. (Tenn.) 156; May v. Cincinnati, 1 Ohio St. 268; Canton v. Nist, 9 Ohio St. 439; 34 Am. Dec. 625; Carr v. St. Louis, 9 Mo. 191; Du Bois v. Augusta, Dudley (Ga.), 30; Adams v. Mayor, etc., 29 Ga. 56; Southport v. Ogden, 23 Conn. 128; Wirth v. Wilmington, 68 N. C. 24; State v. Austin, 114 N. C. 855, 41 Am. St. Rep. 817; Wood v. Brooklyn, 14 Barb. (N. Y.) 425. In Flood v. State, 19 Tex. App. 584, it is said: "An ordinance, to be valid, unless such legislative authority be given for its enactment, must not conflict with the statute, but must conform to the laws of the state." An ordinance which prohibits traffic in intoxicating liquors is not an illegal interference with business. Fanner v. Alliance, 29 Fed. Rep. 169; Markle v. Akron, 14 Ohio, 586. An ordinance enacted under the police power, prescribing a penalty for the non-observance of Sunday in the conduct of certain business, is not repugnant to the state law because it exempts from its operation certain occupations not exempted by the state law. Theisen v. McDaniel, 34 Fla. 440, 26 L. R. A. 234. The king cannot authorize the making of a by-law contrary to the law of the realm. Chief Justice Hobart, in Norris v. Staps (1617), Hob. 210.

[3] See Walker v. City of Aurora, 140 Ill. 402, 29 N. E. Rep. 741.

by the city should be superior to or take the place of the general law of the state upon the same subject."[1]

A general law does not repeal an existing special law unless such clearly appears to have been the legislative intention. Thus, a grant of power to provide for the punishment of a designated offense, contained in a city charter, is not repealed by a subsequently enacted general statute providing for the prosecution of the same offense throughout the state.[2] But the powers granted must be exercised in conformity to the general criminal laws. Thus, under authority to prohibit variety shows, a city cannot group together a certain number of acts in themselves lawful, and by calling the result a variety show prohibit the performance.[3]

When an ordinance is specifically authorized by the charter it has the effect of a special law of the legislature within the limits of the municipality, and supersedes the general law. It operates to repeal the general law on the principle that provisions of different statutes which are in conflict with one another cannot stand together; and in the absence of anything showing a different intent on the part of the legislature, general legislation upon a particular subject is repealed by subsequent special legislation upon the same subject.[4]

§ 228. *Must not contravene common right.*—It is said that there can be no implied power to enact an ordinance which contravenes common right. It is somewhat difficult to determine what is meant by a common right, and no clear defini-

[1] March v. Com., 12 B. Mon. (Ky.) 25, Simpson, C. J. See Sutton's Hospital Case, 10 Reports, 31a; Rex v. Maidston, 3 Burr. 1837.
[2] State v. Labatate, 39 La. Ann. 513, 2 So. Rep. 550; Covington v. St. Louis, 78 Ill. 548. *Contra*, Southport v. Ogden, 23 Conn. 128. In People v. Hariahan, 75 Mich. 611, it was held that a subsequent general law did not, by implication, work the repeal of a special law on the same subject although inconsistent with it. An act of the legislature making the offense of keeping a house of ill-fame a felony and punishable as such was held not to repeal by implication a provision of the charter of Detroit authorizing the common council to prohibit, prevent and suppress the keeping of such houses and ordinances enacted thereunder.
[3] Ex parte Bell, 32 Tex. Cr. Rep. 308, 42 Am. St. Rep. 778.
[4] St. Johnsbury v. Thompson, 59 Vt. 300; In re Snell, 58 Vt. 207; State v. Clark, 54 Mo. 17; Mark v. State, 97 N. Y. 572; State v. Morristown, 33 N. J. L. 57. See § 69.

tion is found in the cases. There certainly can be no common right to do an act which the legislature has forbidden.[1]

§ 229. *Must be general and impartial.*— Ordinances should be general in their nature and impartial in their operation. Unwarranted discrimination or oppressive interference in particular instances will render an ordinance invalid.[2] An ordinance prohibiting a specified railroad corporation from running locomotives by steam on a certain street does not contravene this principle, when no other person or corporation has the right to run locomotives on that street. Hence, said the court, "no other person or corporation is or can be in a like situation, except with the consent of the city. On this account the ordinance, while apparently limited in its operation, is in effect general, as it applies to all who can do what is prohibited."[3] An ordinance containing a grant may reserve the right to impose restrictions not imposed upon other persons or corporations. Such ordinances are necessarily several and independent of each other, and the conditions imposed and requirements exacted are necessarily different, as the conditions and circumstances vary.[4]

§ 230. *Must not be oppressive.*— An ordinance which is unjust and oppressive in its character and operation is invalid.[5]

---

[1] The principle of the above section is recognized in Anderson v. City of Wellington, 40 Kan. 173, 2 L. R. A. 110, 10 Am. St. Rep. 175; In re Flaherty, 105 Cal. 558, 27 L. R. A. 529; Hayden v. Noyes, 5 Conn. 391. But there is no common right to do that which is prohibited by a valid ordinance. City Council v. Ahrens, 4 Strob. (S. C.) L. 241; Dillon, § 325.

[2] Detroit v. Ft. Wayne, etc. Ry. Co., 95 Mich. 456, 20 L. R. A. 79; Phillips v. Denver, 19 Colo. 179, 41 Am. St. Rep. 230; Lindall v. Covington, 90 Ky. 444, 29 Am. St. Rep. 393; In re Flaherty, 105 Cal. 559, 27 L. R. A. 529; Ex parte Chin Tan, 60 Cal. 78; Zaume v. Mound City, 103 Ill. 552; Ingaman v. Chicago, 78 Ill. 405; Champer v. Greencastle, 138 Ind. 339, 46 Am. St. Rep. 390. That an ordinance manifestly intended as a sanitary regulation is made to apply only to a part of the city does not render it invalid, if that part is so situated as to require particular and exceptional provisions. Com. v. Patch, 97 Mass. 221.

[3] Railway Co. v. Richmond, 96 U. S. 521.

[4] Detroit v. Ft. W. etc. Ry. Co., 95 Mich. 456, 20 L. R. A. 79. An ordinance which prohibits certain occupations on Sunday is valid, although it excludes certain other occupations from its operation. See Theisen v. McDaniel, 34 Fla. 440, 26 L. R. A. 234.

[5] Mayor v. Beasly, 1 Humph. (Tenn.) 232; Mayor v. Winfield, 8 Humph. (Tenn.) 707; St. Louis v. Weber, 44

Thus, an ordinance which compelled the substitution of a cement sidewalk in the place of a plank walk in front of a twenty-acre vacant lot, the plank walk having been laid only six months before in conformity with an ordinance, and being still safe, sufficient and in good condition, was held void, because unreasonable, unjust and oppressive.[1]

§ 231. *Must be reasonable.*— Probably the most important general rule affecting ordinances enacted under implied authority is that which makes their validity dependent upon their reasonableness.[2] When the ordinance is passed under specific authority, the question of its reasonableness cannot be raised. In all other cases an unreasonable ordinance is invalid, and the question of reasonableness must be determined in the light of the particular circumstances. An ordinance may be reasonable and valid as to one state of facts and circumstances, and unreasonable and invalid when applied to facts and circumstances of a different character.[3]

§ 232. *Reasonableness a question for the court.*— The question of the reasonableness of an ordinance must be decided by the court with due regard to all existing circumstances and conditions, the object sought to be attained, and the necessity for the adoption of the ordinance.[4] It may be determined by an inspection of the ordinance or after hearing evidence. But such evidence must be directed to the court and not to the jury.[5]

Mo. 547; Baltimore v. Radicke, 49 Md. 217; St. Louis v. Fitz, 53 Mo. 582; Commissioners v. Gas Co., 12 Pa. St. 318.

[1] Hawes v. Chicago, 158 Ill. 653, 30 L. R. A. 225. For applications of the same principle, see Davis v. Litchfield, 145 Ill. 313, 21 L. R. A. 563; Palmer v. Danville, 158 Ill. 156; Bloomington v. Latham, 142 Ill. 462, 18 L. R. A. 487.

[2] Johnson v. Mayor of Croyden (1886), 16 Q. B. D. 708, 7 Eng. Rul. Cas. 278, and many early cases cited in the English and American notes. Many cases are also collected in a note to 35 Am. Rep. 702.

[3] State v. Sheppard, 64 Minn. 287, 36 L. R. A. 305.

[4] Hawes v. Chicago, 158 Ill. 653, 30 L. R. A. 225; Lake View v. Tate, 130 Ill. 247, 6 L. R. A. 58; Kipp v. Paterson, 26 N. J. L. 298; Railway Co. v. East Orange, 41 N. J. L. 127; State v. Orange, 50 N. J. L. 389, 13 Atl. Rep. 240; Ex parte Frank, 52 Cal. 606; Kneedler v. Norristown, 100 Pa. St. 368; Com. v. Worcester, 3 Pick. 462; Neier v. Missouri Pac. Ry. Co., 12 Mo. App. 25; St. Louis v. Webber, 44 Mo. 547.

[5] State v. Trenton, 53 N. J. L. 132, 20 Atl. Rep. 1076. In Evison v. C., M. & St. P. Ry. Co., 45 Minn. 370.

§ 233. *Presumption of reasonableness.*— The presumption is in favor of the reasonableness of the ordinance.[1] The party asserting its illegality must set forth the facts in his pleading and sustain the burden of proof.[2] It requires a clear and strong case to justify the court in holding an ordinance invalid when the corporation is acting within the apparent scope of its authority. As said in a recent case, "The judicial power to declare it void can only be exercised when from the inherent character of the ordinance, or from evidence taken showing its operation, it is demonstrated to be unreasonable."[3]

In assuming the right to judge of the reasonableness of an exercise of corporate power, courts will not look closely into mere matters of judgment where there may be a reasonable difference of opinion. It is not to be expected that every power will be exercised with the highest discretion, and, when it is plainly granted, a clear case should be made to authorize an interference on the ground of unreasonableness.[4] "This,

Mr. Justice Mitchell said: "An ordinance is in the nature of a local statute, and it would seem anomalous to leave it to the jury to determine whether a law is valid. Certainly, if the invalidity is apparent on the face of the statute or ordinance, it has always been held a question of law for the court, and we cannot perceive why a rule should be different where the invalidity is made to appear from extrinsic facts. Any other rule would lead to the embarrassing result that, upon the same state of facts, one jury might hold an ordinance valid and another jury hold it invalid." In Clason v. Milwaukee, 30 Wis. 316, and Austin v. Austin Cemetery Ass'n, 87 Tex. 330, 47 Am. St. Rep. 114, it was held that where the question of reasonableness depended upon the existence of certain facts of which the court had not judicial knowledge, such facts might be submitted to the jury. But in Mercer County v. Fleming, 111 Cal. 46, it was said that the question must be determined from an inspection of the ordinance, and that evidence could not be received to show the manner in which it was or might be enforced. See, also, State v. Fourcade, 45 La. Ann. 717, 40 Am. St. Rep. 249.

[1] Mayor v. Dry Dock R. Co., 133 N. Y. 104; People v. Creiger, 138 Ill. 401, 28 N. E. Rep. 812.

[2] State v. Fourcade, 45 La. Ann. 717, 40 Am. St. Rep. 249.

[3] State v. City of Trenton, 53 N. J. L. 132, 20 Atl. Rep. 1076; Paxton v. Sweet, 30 N. J. L. 196; Lewis v. Newton, 75 Fed. Rep. 884; Littlefield v. State, 42 Neb. 223, 47 Am. St. Rep. 697; Mayor v. Dry Dock, etc. Ry. Co., 133 N. Y. 104, 28 Am. St. Rep. 609; White v. Kent, 11 Ohio St. 550; Com. v. Patch, 97 Mass. 221; Van Hook v. Selma, 70 Ala. 361. Contemporaneous construction cannot be considered when the meaning is clear from the language of the act. Wesson v. Collins, 72 Miss. 844, 18 So. Rep. 360, 917.

[4] St. Louis v. Webber, 44 Mo. 547; Kansas City v. Cook, 30 Mo. App. 660; Duluth v. Mallett, 43 Minn. 204.

we think, is the true rule," said Crockett, J., " and it proceeds upon the theory that, under a general grant of power to a municipal corporation to pass ordinances on a given subject, it will be presumed that it was not intended to clothe it with power to pass an ordinance which is clearly unreasonable, unjust, oppressive, partial and unfair; or which contravenes public policy or is in restraint of trade. But an ordinance will not be presumed invalid on either of these grounds unless in a plain case."[1]

II. ILLUSTRATIONS OF VALID AND INVALID ORDINANCES.

§ 234. *Laying pipes in streets.*— An ordinance prohibiting the opening of streets for the purpose of laying gas mains between the first of December and the first of the following March is reasonable,[2] although an ordinance entirely prohibiting the opening of a paved street for the purpose of laying pipes from the main to the opposite side of the street is unreasonable, as it would tend to increase the price of gas by requiring mains to be laid on each side of the street.[3]

§ 235. *Location and speed of vehicles.*— A city may reasonably require stages or other such vehicles to keep off certain narrow and crowded streets,[4] or prohibit vehicles containing perishable produce to stand in a public street longer than twenty minutes between certain hours of the day.[5] So it may properly provide that a hackney coach shall not stand within thirty feet of any public place of amusement,[6] and that vehicles used for hire shall occupy only certain designated stands.[7] The speed

[1] Ex parte Frank, 52 Cal. 606, 28 Am. Rep. 642; Grand Rapids v. Braudy, 105 Mich. 670, 32 L. R. A. 116; Swift v. Topeka, 43 Kan. 671, 8 L. R. A. 772.

[2] Commissioners v. Gas Co., 12 Pa. St. 318; Commissioners v. North Liberties Gas Co., 2 Jones, 318.

[3] Commissioners v. North Liberties Gas Co., 2 Jones, 318. An ordinance regulating the stringing of wires in a city, which provides that "whenever it shall be necessary to cross the line of any existing telephone line or lines . . . the person or company making such crossing shall supply all necessary safeguards for the same," is reasonable. State v. Janesville, etc. Ry. Co., 87 Wis. 72, 41 Am. St. Rep. 23.

[4] Com. v. Stodder, 2 Cush. 563; Com. v. Mulhall, 162 Mass. 496, 44 Am. St. Rep. 387.

[5] Com. v. Brooks, 109 Mass. 355. An ordinance prohibiting vehicles from standing in the street more than twenty minutes applies to licensed peddlers. Com. v. Fenton, 139 Mass. 195, 29 N. E. Rep. 653.

[6] Com. v. Robertson, 5 Cush. 430.

[7] Com. v. Matthews, 122 Mass. 60.

of vehicles on streets may be regulated,[1] even without express authority.[2] But an ordinance prohibiting driving on a street at a speed of more than six miles an hour is unreasonable when applied to the members of a salvage corps when responding to an alarm of fire.[3]

§ 236. *Handling of trains.*— A city may regulate the running of railway trains across and over its streets, but the ordinances must be reasonable and take into consideration the various conditions existing in different parts of the city.[4] An ordinance limiting the speed to six miles per hour is reasonable;[5] but a limitation to four or six miles an hour is unreasonable when applied to that part of the road in the suburbs of the city, where the road is securely fenced on each side and there is but one grade crossing.[6] Ordinances forbidding trains from standing across a public street longer than two minutes,[7] or from stopping on a street crossing for any other purpose than to prevent accident in the face of immediate danger,[8] or requiring railway companies to keep flagmen at dangerous crossings,[9] or

Fixing the fare which may be charged by coaches. Com. v. Gage, 118 Mass. 328. Imposing a moderate tax upon all vehicles used on the streets. St. Louis v. Green, 70 Mo. 562. The place may be determined by a marshal or policeman. Veneman v. Jones, 118 Ind. 41, 20 N. E. Rep. 644; St. Paul v. Smith, 27 Minn. 364.

[1] State v. Sheppard, 64 Minn. 287, 36 L. R. A. 305, and note; Scudder v. Hinshaw, 134 Ind. 56; Com. v. Adams, 114 Mass. 323, 19 Am. Rep. 362; People v. Little, 86 Mich. 125.

[2] Reynolds v. Mandain, 4 Harr. (Del.) 317; Mittelstadt v. Morrison, 76 Wis. 265.

[3] State v. Sheppard, 64 Minn. 287.

[4] Lake View v. Tate, 130 Ill. 247, 6 L. R. A. 268; Evison v. Chicago, etc. R. Co., 45 Minn. 370, 11 L. R. A. 434; Buffalo v. New York, etc. R. Co., 152 N. Y. 276, 46 N. E. Rep. 496; Prewitt v. Missouri, etc. Ry. Co., 134 Mo. 615, 36 S. W. Rep. 667; Larkin v. Burlington, etc. Ry. Co., 85 Iowa, 492; Gratiot v. Mo. Pac. Ry. Co., 116 Mo. 450, 16 L. R. A. 189; Pennsylvania Co. v. Horton, 132 Ind. 187; Burg v. Chicago, etc. R. Co., 90 Iowa, 106.

[5] Knoblauch v. Railway Co., 31 Minn. 402; Buffalo v. New York, etc. Ry. Co., 152 N. Y. 276, 46 N. E. Rep. 496; Com. v. Worcester, 3 Pick. 461; Gahagan v. Railway Co., 1 Allen, 187.

[6] Evison v. Chicago, etc. Ry. Co., 45 Minn. 370; Burg v. Chicago, etc. Ry. Co., 90 Iowa, 106, 48 Am. St. Rep. 419. See Larkin v. Burlington, etc. Ry. Co., 85 Iowa, 492, 52 N. W. Rep. 480. Local trains may be excepted from the operation of an ordinance. Buffalo v. New York, etc. Ry. Co., 152 N. Y. 276, 46 N. E. Rep. 496.

[7] State v. Mayor, etc., 37 N. J. L. 348; Borough v. Alabama, etc. Ry. Co. (Ala.), 13 So. Rep. 141.

[8] Duluth v. Mallett, 43 Minn. 204.

[9] Railway Co. v. East Orange, 41 N. J. L. 127. In Village of Ravenna v. Pennsylvania Co., 45 Ohio St. 118,

prohibiting boys and others not connected with the train service from getting on or off moving trains within the city limits,[1] are reasonable and valid. But ordinances requiring railway companies to keep flagmen by day and red lanterns by night at ordinary crossings where there is no unusual danger,[2] or prohibiting a railway company between 6 A. M. and 11 P. M. from moving its cars across the street for the purpose of being distributed in their yards, without regard to whether they are stopped on the street, are unreasonable.[3] So an ordinance which requires a railroad company, whose only scheduled train at night passes at eight o'clock, to light each street which it crosses with an electric light from dark to dawn, is unreasonable and void.[4]

§ 237. *Regulation of street railways.*— Street railways are subject to a variety of regulations that are rendered reasonable and necessary by reason of the conditions surrounding their business. Thus, they may by ordinance be required to make quarterly reports of the number of passengers,[5] to pave the sides of the streets through which they run,[6] and to provide a driver and conductor on each car.[7]

§ 238. *Parades, music, and speaking in public places.*— It is very doubtful whether a city can, under the general power over its streets, prohibit their use for the purpose of parades and processions. But it may regulate such uses by prescribing the time and manner of the use, and may make the right conditional upon the consent of certain officials. But the actions of the official must be governed by a prescribed general rule. It cannot be left to the arbitrary discretion of the official.[8] An

12 N. E. Rep. 445, it was held that municipal corporations in Ohio have no power to compel a railway company to keep a watchman at their crossings. See Pittsburg, etc. R. Co. v. Crown Point (Ind.), 35 L. R. A. 684.

[1] Reardon v. Madison, 73 Ga. 184.
[2] Toledo, etc. R. Co. v. Jacksonville, 67 Ill. 37, 10 Am. Rep. 611.
[3] Birmingham v. Alabama, etc. Ry. Co., 98 Ala. 134, 13 So. Rep. 141.
[4] Cleveland, etc. R. Co. v. Connersville (Ind., 1897), 38 L. R. A. 175.

[5] St. Louis v. St. Louis Ry. Co., 89 Mo. 44.
[6] City v. Erie Pass. Ry. Co., 7 Phil. 321.
[7] South Cov. etc. Ry. Co. v. Berry, 93 Ky. 43, 18 S. W. Rep. 1026; State v. Trenton, 53 N. J. L. 132, 20 Atl. Rep. 1076.
[8] See § 247, *post*; State v. Dering, 84 Wis. 585, 36 Am. St. Rep. 948, 19 L. R. A. 859, annotated; In re Frazee, 63 Mich. 396, 6 Am. St. Rep. 310. Street parades cannot be prohibited

ordinance prohibiting street parades with shouting and music without the permission of a city officer, but excepting certain organizations from its operation, is unreasonable.[1] The same objection exists to an ordinance which forbids any person not acting under the orders of a military officer to play any musical instrument in the street on Sunday.[2] But an ordinance forbidding the beating of drums and shouting on the streets without a permit from the mayor was recently held valid.[3] So a city may prohibit speaking in a public park without such a permit.[4] The supreme court of Massachusetts said: "For the legislature absolutely or conditionally to forbid public speaking in a highway or public park is no more an infringement of the rights of a member of the public than for the owner of a private house to forbid it in his house. When no proprietary rights interfere the legislature may end the right of the public to enter upon the public place by putting an end to the dedication to public uses. So it may take the less step of limiting the public use to certain purposes.[5] If the legislature had power under the constitution to pass a law in the form of the present ordinance, there is no doubt that it could authorize the city of Boston to pass the ordinance, and it is settled by the former decision."

§ 239. *Licenses.*—The principles which govern the granting of licenses have already been considered. There must be something connected with the business to be licensed which gives rise to the necessity for some degree of supervision. Hence a license may reasonably be required from those who sell milk,[6]

(Rich v. Naperville, 42 Ill. App. 222; Bloomington v. Richardson, 38 Ill. App. 60; People v. Rochester, 44 Hun (N. Y.), 166; Anderson v. Wellington, 40 Kan. 173, 2 L. R. A. 110; State v. Hughes, 72 N. C. 25), but may be regulated in order to prevent their becoming a public annoyance. Charliton v. Fitzsimmons, 87 Iowa, 226; Com. v. Plaisted, 148 Mass. 375; State v. White, 64 N. Y. 48; Roderick v. Whitson, 51 Hun (N. Y.), 620; White v. State (Ga., 1897), 37 L. R. A. 642.

[1] State v. Dering, 84 Wis. 585.

[2] Johnson v. Mayor of Croyden, 16 Q. B. D. 708, 7 Eng. Rul. Cas. 278.

[3] In re Flaherty, 105 Cal. 558, 27 L. R. A. 529.

[4] Davis v. Com., 167 U. S. 43, 162 Mass. 510, 44 Am. St. Rep. 389, 26 L. R. A. 712.

[5] See Dill. Mun. Corp., §§ 398, 407, 651, 656, 666; Brooklyn Park Com'rs v. Armstrong, 45 N. Y. 234, 243, 244, 6 Am. Rep. 70.

[6] People v. Mulholland, 82 N. Y. 324; State v. Nelson (Minn.) 68 N. W. Rep. 1066. See § 78.

peddle goods from house to house,[1] sell papers on the street,[2] sell articles in certain streets,[3] or engage in certain kinds of business, such as butchers[4] and cattle dealers.[5] The amount of license fee which can be exacted as a police measure varies according to the nature of the occupation licensed. It must not exceed a sum which is sufficient to reimburse the municipality for the probable trouble and expense of issuing the license and inspecting and regulating the business.[6] Thus, a license fee of $300 for an auctioneer,[7] $20 for a peddler[8] and $200 for a butcher[9] has been held unreasonable. But when the amount of the license fee is determined by the state through legislative enactment, its reasonableness cannot be determined by the courts.[10]

§ 240. *Discrimination against non-residents.*— An ordinance which discriminates against a non-resident by requiring a larger license fee from a non-resident than from a resident is unreasonable and void.[11] There must be no discrimination between those engaged in the same business or between residents and non-residents.[12]

[1] State Center v. Barnstein, 66 Iowa, 249.
[2] Com. v. Elliott, 121 Mass. 367.
[3] Nightingale, Petitioner, 11 Pick. 168.
[4] St. Paul v. Coulter, 12 Minn. 41 (Gil. 16).
[5] St. Louis v. Know, 6 Mo. App. 247. In this case the dealer was required to have a certificate of good moral character.
[6] North Hudson Co. R. Co. v. Hoboken, 41 N. J. L. 81. If the amount exacted is unreasonably large in view of the purpose for which it is to be paid, the ordinance is void. Littlefield v. State, 42 Neb. 223, 47 Am. St. Rep. 697.
[7] Mankato v. Fowler, 32 Minn. 364.
[8] State Center v. Barrenstein, 66 Iowa, 249.
[9] St. Paul v. Coulter, 12 Minn. 41. See State v. Wheelock (Iowa), 64 N. W. Rep. 621, 30 L. R. A. 429. For many authorities on the limit of the amount of license fees, see note to State v. French (Mont.), in 30 L. R. A. 415.
[10] State v. Harrington, 68 Vt. 622, 34 L. R. A. 100.
[11] Muhlenbrinck v. Com., 44 N. J. L. 365; State v. City of Orange (N. J.), 13 Atl. Rep. 240; Borough of Sayre v. Phillips, 148 Pa. St. 482, 24 Atl. Rep. 76; State v. Ocean Grove, etc. Ass'n, 55 N. J. L. 507, 26 Atl. Rep. 798. The real objection to these ordinances is not an unreasonable exercise of power, but that they are unconstitutional.
A city may, by ordinance, fix the number of hours which its workmen shall work on the public works; but it cannot make a violation of the ordinance an indictable offense. State v. McNally, 48 La. Ann. 1450, 21 So. Rep. 27, 36 L. R. A. 533.
[12] City of Indianapolis v. Bieler, 138 Ind. 30, 36 N. E. Rep. 857; Clement v. Town of Casper (Wy.), 85 Pac. Rep. 472.

§ 241. *Regulation of markets.*— A city may reasonably provide by ordinance that wagons loaded with produce shall not remain in the market place for more than twenty minutes during certain hours;[1] that persons not licensed occupants of stalls shall not offer meats for sale in less than certain quantities;[2] or that fresh beef shall not be sold in less than quarters except between dawn and 9 A. M.[3] An ordinance fixing a penalty for each hour that a wagon is kept in a public market is unreasonable.[4]

§ 242. *Regulation of liquor traffic.*— A municipality may make reasonable regulations with reference to the sale of intoxicating liquors without violating the constitutional right of equal protection and privilege.[5] Thus, it may limit the districts or precincts of a city in which liquor may be sold.[6] Druggists may be prohibited from selling liquor except for medicinal purposes.[7] It may provide by ordinance that no license shall be issued to any person until he obtains the consent of two-thirds of the freeholders residing within three miles of his proposed place of business,[8] or that the granting of a license shall be dependent upon the consent of the county officials.[9] The reasonableness of an ordinance requiring saloons to close at a certain hour must be determined by the size of the municipality and the character of its population. Ordinances requiring them to close at nine,[10] ten[11] and eleven,[12] from 10:30 P. M. to 5 A. M.;[13] and from midnight to 5 A. M.,[14] have been held reasonable. But an ordinance forbidding licensed retailers to sell between 6 P. M. and 6 A. M. is unreasonable, as it "deprives a party of several hours of daylight in which

[1] Com. v. Brooks, 100 Mass. 55.
[2] St. Louis v. Weber, 44 Mo. 547.
[3] Bowling Green v. Carson, 10 Bush (Ky.), 164.
[4] Com. v. Wilkins, 121 Mass. 356.
[5] Giozza v. Tiernan, 148 U. S. 657; Ex parte Hayes, 98 Cal. 555, 20 L. R. A. 701; Decie v. Brown, 167 Mass. 290, 45 N. E. Rep. 765.
[6] In re Wilson, 32 Minn. 145; State v. Clark, 28 N. H. 176. It may limit the license to one for each thousand of the population. Decie v. Brown, 167 Mass. 290.
[7] Provost City v. Shurtleff, 4 Utah, 15, 5 Pac. Rep. 302.
[8] Metcalf v. State, 76 Ga. 208.
[9] Wagner v. Town of Garrett, 118 Ind. 114; State v. Hellmon, 56 Conn. 190.
[10] Smith v. Knoxville, 3 Head (Tenn.), 245.
[11] State v. Washington, 44 N. J. L. 605; Ex parte Wolf, 14 Neb. 24; Morris v. Rome, 10 Ga. 532.
[12] Decker v. Sergeant, 125 Ind. 404.
[13] State v. Welch, 36 Conn. 215.
[14] Brighton v. Toronto, 12 U. C. 433.

he is forbidden to exercise a right conferred by the state."[1] So an ordinance requiring such persons to close their doors and cease selling whenever "any denomination of Christian people are holding divine service" is void.[2] An ordinance which prohibits the employment of women in saloons is a reasonable exercise of the power to regulate such places;[3] but when the constitution provides that no person shall be disqualified by reason of sex from pursuing any lawful occupation, an ordinance forbidding the proprietors of drinking saloons to permit any females to be employed in their places after a certain hour is invalid.[4]

§ 243. *Fire regulations.*— Power to establish fire limits and prohibit the erection of certain kinds of buildings within such limits must be reasonably exercised. Hence an ordinance which absolutely prohibits the altering, repairing or rebuilding of any frame building within certain limits whenever the amount to be expended exceeds $300 is arbitrary and unreasonable, and practically amounts to the taking of the property without due process of law.[5]

§ 244. *Quarantine regulations — Second-hand clothing.*— The business of dealing in second-hand clothing is a proper one for police regulation.[6] In the absence of an epidemic showing an apparent necessity therefor, an ordinance prohibiting any one from bringing second-hand clothing into a town, or exposing it for sale therein, without furnishing proof that it did not come from an infected district, is an unreasonable restraint of trade.[7]

---

[1] Ward v. Greenville, 8 Bax. (Tenn.) 228.
[2] Gilham v. Well, 64 Ga. 192. See State v. Strauss, 49 Md. 288.
[3] Bergman v. Cleveland, 39 Ohio St. 651; State v. Considine, 16 Wash. 358, 47 Pac. Rep. 755.
[4] In re M'Guire, 57 Cal. 604. See Black, Intox. Liq., § 236.
[5] First Nat. Bank v. Sarles, 129 Ind. 201, 28 Am. St. Rep. 185. As to the power to establish fire limits under the general welfare clause, see Kaufmann v. Stein, 138 Ind. 49, 46 Am. St. Rep. 368.
[6] State v. Taft, 118 N. C. 1190, 32 L.

R. A. 122; Greensborough v. Ehrenruch, 80 Ala. 579, 60 Am. Rep. 130; Weil v. Record, 24 N. J. Eq. 169; State v. Long Branch, 42 N. J. L. 364, 36 Am. Rep. 518; State v. Segel, 60 Minn. 507; Marmet v. State, 45 Ohio St. 63. A very clear abuse of the police power must be shown in order to justify a court in declaring ordinances regulating the business of pawnbrokers, junk-dealers and dealers in second-hand goods unreasonable and void. Grand Rapids v. Braudy, 105 Mich. 670, 32 L. R. A. 116.
[7] Town of Kosciusko v. Stomberg, 68 Miss. 469, 9 So. Rep. 297.

§ 245. *Hotel runners and hackmen.*—A city may regulate the conduct of hackmen, hotel runners and porters. An ordinance limiting the number of hackmen who may stand in front of a hotel is reasonable when there are other hack-stands in the city.[1] Such persons may be forbidden to solicit business at the depots and railway platforms within the city limits. But a city cannot interfere with the reasonable regulations of the railway companies for the handling of passengers. Thus, an ordinance which forbids hotel runners from going within twenty feet of the train, although permitted to do so by the rules of the company, is invalid.[2]

§ 246. *Miscellaneous decisions.*—An ordinance forbidding smoking in street cars is a reasonable exercise of the power to protect the public health and to suppress nuisances.[3] The decisions are in conflict upon the question of the right of the city to require the owners of lots to clean the snow from the sidewalk in front of their premises at their own expense.[4] An ordinance requiring all restaurants to close at ten o'clock at night is reasonable under certain conditions.[5] An ordinance which requires the keepers of boarding-houses, restaurants and hotels to furnish the city with the names of all persons boarding or lodging at their houses is reasonable.[6] A city may require pawnbrokers to furnish the police with a record of all property received and a description of the persons from whom received.[7] So it may prohibit pawnbrokers from purchasing the articles upon which they make loans of money.[8] An ordinance which requires the proprietors of theaters to pay a police officer two dollars per night for attendance at theaters for the purpose of preserving

[1] Montgomery v. Parks (Ala.), 21 So. Rep. 452.
[2] Nappeau v. People, 19 Mich. 352.
[3] State v. Huydenham, 42 La. Ann. 483, 7 So. Rep. 621.
[4] In support of the power, see Goddard's Case 16 Pick. 504, 28 Am. Dec. 259. *Contra*, Bridley v. Bloomington, 88 Ill. 554, 30 Am. Rep. 566; Chicago v. O'Brien, 111 Ill. 532, 53 Am. Rep. 640. As to the liability of owners for damages for injuries occasioned by failure to remove ice and snow from sidewalk as required by statute, see Flynn v. Canton Co., 40 Md. 312, 17 Am. Rep. 603.
[5] State v. Freeman, 38 N. H. 426.
[6] Topeka v. Boutwell, 53 Kan. 20, 27 L. R. A. 593.
[7] Kansas City v. Garnier, 57 Kan. 412, 46 Pac. Rep. 707. The decisions on the power to regulate the business of pawnbrokers, junk dealers, etc., are collected in a note to Grand Rapids v. Braudy, 105 Mich. 670, 32 L. R. A. 116.
[8] Kuhn v. Chicago, 30 Ill. App. 203.

order is unreasonable and void.[1] When a city furnishes gas and water to its inhabitants for a compensation it may provide by ordinance that the gas or water may be stopped after ten days' default in the payment of the bill and until the same is paid.[2] An ordinance requiring that garbage shall be removed in water-tight closed carts or wagons, which shall be marked with the word "garbage," is reasonable.[3] The owner of a lot may be required to remove filth from a private way adjoining his land although he did not place it there.[4] An ordinance which prohibits any person from permitting drunkards or disorderly persons from assembling at or remaining in his "house, tavern, inn, saloon, cellar, shop, office or other residence or place of business" is unreasonable and void because not limited to places which require police supervision, nor to assemblages of immoral persons.[5]

III. ORDINANCES WHICH PROHIBIT ACTS WITHOUT THE CONSENT OF CERTAIN OFFICIALS.

§ 247. *General statement.*—Municipalities often enact ordinances which assume to make the legality of an act depend upon the previously obtained consent of a designated official. In the earlier decisions such ordinances were sustained without special reference to this feature. The present tendency, however, is towards treating the provision as an improper delegation of authority, as contravening common right, or as failing to provide uniform and impartial conditions, thus placing it in the power of the official to discriminate between citizens entitled to equal rights before the law. Such ordinances may be roughly thrown into five classes:

1. Those which divide persons into classes without reference to their character or qualifications, placing on one side of the dividing line those who are permitted to pursue their business by the consent of the official, and on the other side those from whom that consent is withheld. Such ordinances are almost universally held invalid.

[1] Waters v. Leach, 3 Ark. 110.
[2] Com. v. Philadelphia, 132 Pa. St. 238.
[3] People v. Gordon (Mich.), 45 N. W. Rep. 658.
[4] Com. v. Cutler, 156 Mass. 52, 29 N. E. Rep. 1140.
[5] Grand Rapids v. Newton (Mich., 1890), 85 L. R. A. 226; Ex parte Smith (Mo., 1896), 33 L. R. A. 606.

2. Those in which discretion is granted to public officials to determine the qualifications of applicants for licenses, where the fitness of the applicant is left to the judgment of the officer. Such ordinances are held valid, as they call for the exercise of discretion of a judicial nature.

3. Those which prescribe uniform conditions, and authorize some official to determine whether such conditions have been complied with. There can be no objection to ordinances of this kind, as the duties delegated to the officer are of a ministerial character.

4. Those which assume to regulate the doing of lawful acts, and give some officer discretion and power to grant or refuse permission.

5. Those which authorize and empower some officer to arbitrarily authorize or forbid an act illegal under the general terms of the ordinance or the laws of the state.

The two latter classes will be considered in the following sections.

§ 248. *Cases sustaining such ordinances.*— As above stated, ordinances containing this provision have often been sustained, but generally without the question under consideration being raised.[1] In a recent California case[2] an ordinance which made it unlawful to beat a drum upon a traveled street without special permission from the president of the board of trustees was held valid. In answer to the contention that the ordinance was oppressive and gave too much power to an officer, the court said: "Laws are not made upon the theory of the total depravity of those who are elected to administer them; and the presumption is that municipal officers will not use these small powers villainously and for the purpose of mischief and oppression." The same court sustained an ordinance which prohibited the repair or alteration of any wooden building within designated fire limits without written permission of

---

[1] This is true of Hume v. New Haven, 40 Conn. 478; Nightingale's Petition, 11 Pick. 168; Vanderbilt v. Adams, 7 Cow. 349; Pedrick v. Bailey, 12 Gray, 161. These cases are cited in the recent case of In re Flaherty, 105 Cal. 558, 27 L. R. A. 529, but are of little value in support of the proposition contended for.

[2] In re Flaherty, 105 Cal. 528, 27 L. R. A. 529. See Barbier v. Connelly, 113 U. S. 27.

certain officers, on the ground that the provision was necessary in order to avoid the hardships incident to the literal enforcement of the prohibition; and that as no general rule could be established, it was proper to leave the power to the official, who would not "be presumed to exercise it wantonly or for the purpose of profit or oppression."[1]

Ordinances which require an applicant for a saloon license to obtain the consent of a certain number of voters or residents in the vicinity of his proposed place of business are generally sustained.[2] But a city council cannot delegate the power to grant licenses to the mayor.[3] Nor can it grant to the mayor the power to determine the district within which licenses may be granted.[4] But it may authorize him to grant a license when certain prescribed conditions have been complied with.[5]

§ 249. *Delegation of authority.*— Such ordinances are very frequently held invalid as attempts to delegate legislative power. Thus, an ordinance which delegated to the owners of one-half the ground in any block the power to determine whether a livery-stable should be erected therein was held invalid.[6]

---

[1] Ex parte Feske, 72 Cal. 125, citing Barbier v. Connelly, 113 U. S. 27; Soon Hung v. Crowley, 113 U. S. 703, and distinguishing Yick Wo v. Hopkins, 118 U. S. 356. See, also, Easton Com. v. Covey, 74 Md. 262; Com. v. Brooks, 109 Mass. 355. Where a park board had authority to "govern and regulate the parks" and to "make rules for the government thereof," a rule which forbade "harangues, orations or loud outcries" in a park "except with the prior consent of the board" was held valid in Com. v. Abraham, 156 Mass. 57. See § 238, *supra.*

[2] Whitten v. Covington, 43 Ga. 421; In re Bickenstaff, 70 Cal. 35; House v. State, 41 Miss. 737; Grousch v. State, 42 Ind. 547; State v. Brown, 19 Fla. 563; Jones v. Hilliard, 68 Ala. 300. But in Re Christianson, 43 Fed. Rep. 243, an ordinance which required the applicant to obtain the consent of a majority of the board of police commissioners or of not less than twelve citizens owning real estate in the block, was held invalid on the ground that it left to the persons named the power to control the liquor traffic, and as vesting in them arbitrary discretion. See, also, Quong Woo, 13 Fed. Rep. 229.

[3] Kinmundy v. Mayor, 72 Ill. 463; State v. Bayonne, 44 N. J. L. 114; Trento v. Clayton, 50 Mo. 541.

[4] State v. Cantler, 33 Minn. 69; In re Wilson, 23 Minn. 28.

[5] Swarth v. People, 129 Ill. 621; Bradley v. Rochester, 54 Hun (N. Y.), 140; State v. Redmon, 43 Minn. 250.

[6] St. Louis v. Russell, 116 Mo. 248, 20 L. R. A. 721, note. This principle will be found discussed in many of the cases cited under this general subject. *Vide* Anderson v. Wellington and In re Frazee, *supra.* Contra, Chicago v. Stratton, 162 Ill. 494,

§ 250. *Nature of prohibited act.*— The validity of such an ordinance is sometimes made to turn upon the nature of the act prohibited thereby. If it is an act which no citizen has the inherent right to do, and which the municipality may absolutely prohibit, it may grant the privilege under such conditions as it sees proper. In considering a town order which prohibited the keeping of swine "without a permit in writing first obtained from the board of health," Mr. Justice Holmes said: "We are at a loss to see how it affects the validity of the order that the board expressly reserved to themselves a power to do what they could have done even if the prohibition had been absolute; or how the defendants are put in a worse position by the order contemplating the possibility that the board of health may grant them a written permit than if it had excluded that possibility."[1] But when the act can only be regulated the conditions imposed must be general and uniform, and this principle is violated by an ordinance which makes the exercise of the right subject to the arbitrary discretion of any person.[2]

---

35 L. R. A. 84. This case contains a discussion of the question of the validity of laws which are made dependent upon a contingency, and cites Locke's Appeal, 72 Pa. St. 491; People v. Hoffman, 116 Ill. 587, 56 Am. Rep. 793.

[1] Inhabitants of Quincy v. Kennard, 151 Mass. 563; In re Flaherty, 105 Cal. 558; Ex parte Tuttle, 91 Cal. 589; In re Guerrero, 69 Cal. 88. It is upon this theory that ordinances providing that the issuing of liquor licenses shall depend upon obtaining the consent of certain officials are sustained. Ex parte Christianson, 85 Cal. 208.

[2] In re Frazee, 63 Mich. 369; State v. Dering, 84 Wis. 585, 19 L. R. A. 858; Anderson v. Wellington, 40 Kan. 173, 2 L. R. A. 110. In State v. Dering, *supra,* the court said: "It is susceptible of being applied to offensive and improper uses, made subversive of the rights of the private citizen, and it interferes with and abridges their privileges and immunities, and denies them the equal protection of the law and the enjoyment of their undoubted rights. In the exercise of the police power the common council may in its discretion regulate the exercise of such rights in a reasonable manner, but cannot suppress them directly or indirectly, by attempting to submit the power of doing so to the mayor or any other officer. The discretion with which the council is vested is a legal discretion, to be exercised within the limits of the law, and not a discretion to transcend it, or to confer upon any city officer an arbitrary authority, making him in its exercise a petty tyrant. Such ordinances or regulations to be valid must have an equal and uniform application to all persons, societies or organizations similarly circumstanced, and not be susceptible of unjust discriminations, which may be arbitrarily practiced to the hurt, prejudice or

§ 251. *Uniform conditions — Unjust discrimination.* — Although ordinances of this kind are generally said to be unreasonable, the real objection is that they are unconstitutional because in violation of the fourteenth amendment to the constitution of the United States, which prohibits the enactment of any law which abridges the privileges or immunities of citizens or denies to any person the equal protection of the laws.[1] If the conditions upon which the consent of the official is to be given are determined and are uniform and applicable to all citizens, the ordinance is valid; but if its enforcement rests in the uncontrolled discretion of any officer or city council, it is invalid.[2] Thus, an ordinance that provides that no one shall maintain a market within certain limits without the permission of the city council is invalid because the discretion is in no way regulated or controlled, and no conditions are prescribed upon which permission shall be granted.[3] So an ordinance which provides that it shall be unlawful for any person or persons, club or association of any kind to parade the streets of the city with any flag or flags, banners, transparencies, drums, horns or other musical instruments without first having procured permission of the city council so to do is an encroachment upon the constitutional rights of citizens.[4] So an ordinance which makes it unlawful for any person to parade the streets of the city shouting, singing and beating drums or other musical instruments, or doing any other act designed or calculated to attract an unusual crowd, without the written consent of the mayor, is invalid because not fixing uniform and impartial conditions and improperly delegating power.[5] Where the ordinance prohibited dairies within certain designated limits with-

annoyance of any." City of St. Paul v. Lawton, 61 Minn. 537; State v. McMahon (Minn., 1897), 72 N. W. Rep. 79. (Requirement that a "permit" shall be obtained before removing contents of privy vault.) This provision does not give "any arbitrary discretion by which to withhold a permit from a suitable person properly equipped to do the work."

[1] State v. Dering, 84 Wis. 585; 19 L. R. A. 858. This equal protection of the laws is a pledge of the "protection of equal laws." Yick Wo v. Hopkins, 113 U. S. 369.

[2] In re Frazee, 63 Mich. 396; Chicago v. Trotter, 136 Ill. 430.

[3] State v. Du Barry, 44 La. Ann. —, 11 So. Rep. 718; followed in State v. Deffes, 44 La. Ann. 45, 12 So. Rep. 841.

[4] Rich v. City of Naperville, 42 Ill. App. 222.

[5] Anderson v. City of Wellington, 40 Kan. 173, 2 L. R. A. 110.

out the consent of the city council, the court said:[1] "The discretion vested in the city council by the ordinance is in no way regulated or controlled. There are no conditions prescribed upon which permission may be granted. It is within the power of the city council to grant the privilege to some and deny it to others. The discretion vested in the council is purely arbitrary and may be exercised in the interest of the favored few. It may be controlled by partisan considerations, race prejudices or personal animosities. It lays down no rules by which its impartial execution can be secured."

[1] State v. Mahner, 43 La. Ann. 496, 9 So. Rep. 840.

CHAPTER XIV.

GOVERNING BODIES, OFFICERS AND AGENTS.

§ 252. Distribution of powers.
253. The corporate meeting.
254. Notice of corporate meetings.
255. The common council.
256. Place of meeting.
257. Majority and quorum.
258. Who are officers.
259. Election and appointment.
260. Qualifications.
261. Conditions precedent to entering upon an office.
262. Relation of officer to corporation.
263. Incompatible offices.
264. Illustrations.
265. Officers *de facto*.
266. Officers *de facto* — Continued.
267. Compensation.
268. Compensation — *De facto* officers.
269. Increase of salary — Misdemeanor.

§ 270. Compensation of employees — Attorneys.
271. The mayor.
272. Control by the courts.
273. Holding over after expiration of term.
274. Resignation.
275. Amotion.
276. Removal — Express authority — Proceedings.
277. Personal liability on contracts.
278. Liability in tort.
279. Liability of officers acting judicially.
280. Liability of recorder of deeds.
281. Liability of sheriff.
282. Liability of highway officers.
283. Liability of various officers.
284. Liability for loss of public funds.
285. Manner of trying title to an office.

§ 252. *Distribution of powers.*— The nature of a corporation is such that it must necessarily exercise its powers through some representative or agent. Under the town-meeting system there must be administrative and executive officers to carry into effect the expressed will of the general body. Under the representative system the city council and various officers act as the agents of the corporation. In a wide sense the council represents the corporation, and early charters incorporated the mayor and the members of the council instead of the people of a particular locality. The distribution of powers and duties among the various boards and officers is made by the charter of a corporation. It also determines the constitution of the council and the manner of its organization. In some cities large powers are vested in boards which act under the general supervision of the council. These boards, however, are often distinct public corporations charged with a portion of local administration, and possessed of the power to pass by-laws which have the effect of municipal ordinances. Thus, the public schools, the park system and the general subject of the public health are commonly placed under the control of subordinate corporations known as school boards, park boards and boards of health.

§ 253. *The corporate meeting.*— The affairs of a corporation must be transacted at a meeting of the corporate body.[1] Under the town-meeting system this means a meeting of all the qualified inhabitants of the corporation. But the business of the ordinary municipal corporation is transacted by a select or representative body called the common council. Its members are elected by the qualified electors of the corporation at an election duly called for that purpose. Under this system the electors have no power to bind the corporation at a public or general meeting. They can act only through their legally constituted representatives. The composition of these representative or corporate meetings is generally provided for by statute. At common law a valid meeting required the presence of the mayor or other head officer, a majority of the members of each select or definite class, and some members of the indefinite body usually called the commonalty, or of each of the indefinite classes if there were more than one. If there was no indefinite class and the governing body consisted of a select class or of more than one select class, a majority of each select class must be present. The presence of the mayor in a select assembly of this kind was not necessary unless expressly required; but where a common council existed the presence of the mayor or head officer was necessary.

§ 254. *Notice of corporate meetings.*— Where the charter provides for the time of regular meetings, it is not necessary that

[1] Dey v. Jersey City, 19 N. J. Eq. 412. In vol. 7, Eng. Rul. Cas. 337, the rule is thus stated: "At common law, and in the absence of special contract, the acts of a corporation are those of a duly-constituted meeting, to which (unless there is a fixed time of meeting) all the corporators must be summoned, and if the corporation consists of a definite number the major part must attend."

special notice thereof be given members. If, however, it is intended to transact business at any other time, it is necessary that special notice be served upon each member, designating the time and place, if other than the regular place of meeting, and the general character of the business to be transacted. The notice must be given by some one having authority to call the meeting. Generally, however, notice is waived by the presence and consent of every one entitled to receive the notice.[1] Charter provisions with reference to notice of meeting must of course govern in all cases. Such provisions with reference to the calling of town meetings are strictly construed. Thus, it is held that notice is essential to a valid meeting, and that a *de facto* meeting not duly warned or notified is invalid, although all who are entitled to notice attend.[2] Such notice must be sufficient to fairly indicate the object of the meeting and the nature of the business to be transacted.

§ 255. *The common council.*—The common council is the most important of the agencies through which municipal corporations act. It exercises legislative power and controls the general policy of the municipality.[3] Under one form of organization the council has extensive administrative power, makes contracts, appoints officials, and is the general administrative as well as governing body. Under another form its duties are purely legislative, and the work of administration is largely left to officers elected by the people for that purpose. The common form is a single body with a membership determined by the charter and elected by the people from defined districts within the municipality. The mayor is sometimes the presiding officer of the council; but more commonly the council elects its own officers.[4] The constitution of the council, its powers, meetings and procedure are ordinarily determined by the city

[1] Lord v. Anoka, 36 Minn. 176. But the mere attendance of a quorum is not sufficient. Every member has a right to be present. Beaver Creek v. Hastings, 52 Mich. 528.

[2] Bloomfield v. Charter Oak Bank, 121 U. S. 121, 130; Sherwin v. Bugbee, 17 Vt. 337; Hayward v. School District, 2 Cush. (Mass.) 419; Stow v. Wyse, 7 Conn. 214, 18 Am. Dec. 99.

[3] Central Bridge Corp. v. Lowell, 15 Gray (Mass.), 106, 116, note.

[4] State v. Kiichli, 53 Minn. 147, 19 L. R. A. 779. Power of legislative assembly to remove speaker, see In re Speakership, 15 Colo. 500, 11 L. R. A. 240.

charter. It must act as a unit at a regularly called meeting. The right of the mayor to preside over the council is a franchise, which may be tested by *quo warranto* but not by a bill in chancery to enjoin.[2] When the power is vested in the "mayor and aldermen" the council cannot legislate alone. Under the English system the mayor was an integral part of the council and no business could be transacted in his absence. Hence all business could be stopped by the wrongful withdrawal of one of the constituent parts of the body.[3] But this rule has no application to public corporations in this country.[4] The mayor cannot adjourn a council beyond a time at which the law requires a certain city official to be elected.[5]

§ 256. *Place of meetings.*— The validity of corporate acts or the action of municipal officials may depend upon whether the action was taken at the place designated by the statute. Thus, a law requiring boards of supervisors to meet "at the court-house" was not complied with by a meeting held in a building near the court-house, which opened into the court-house inclosure and was used as an office by the clerk and sheriff.[6] A statute requiring a town meeting to be held in the "school-house" means within the walls of the school-house.[7]

§ 257. *Majority and quorum.*— As above stated the common-law doctrine is that a majority of those present at a legally called meeting of the indefinite body will bind the whole body.[8] This rule applies to New England town meetings and to corporate bodies consisting of definite members. A majority of those elected constitutes a legal quorum unless otherwise pro-

[1] Dey v. Jersey City, 19 N. J. Eq. 412. As to manner in which a board of police must act, see Baltimore v. Poultney, 25 Md. 18.

[2] Cochran v. McCleary, 22 Iowa, 75 (Dillon, J.); In re Sawyer, 124 U. S. 200 (Gray, J., citing many cases).

[3] King v. Williams, 2 Maule & Sel. 141.

[4] Martindale v. Palmer, 52 Ind. 411; Kimball v. Marshall, 44 N. H. 465.

[5] Tillman v. Otter, 93 Ky. 600, 29 L. R. A. 110.

[6] Harris v. State, 72 Miss. 960, 33 L. R. A. 85.

[7] Chamberlain v. Dover, 13 Me. 466, 29 Am. Dec. 517. For further illustrations, see Hall v. Ray, 40 Vt. 576, 94 Am. Dec. 440; Moody v. Moeller, 72 Tex. 635; Marion Co. Com'rs v. Barker, 25 Kan. 258, and cases cited in note to Harris v. State, 33 L. R. A. 85.

[8] Damon v. Granby, 2 Pick. 345; State v. Binder, 38 Mo. 450; Cushing, Leg. Assem., § 247. See note to Lawrence v. Ingersoll, 6 L. R. A. 309.

vided by the charter.[1] A quorum is that number which, when assembled in the proper place, will enable a body to transact business.[2] If a quorum is present and a majority of the quorum votes in favor of a measure it will prevail, although an equal number is present and refrains from voting. It is not the majority of the whole number of members present that is required. All that is requisite is a majority of the number of members necessary to constitute a quorum.[3] Mr. Justice Lamar said:[4] "The rule on the subject has been well stated by Dillon:[5] 'As a general rule, it may be stated that not only where the corporate power resides in a select body, as a city council, but where it has been delegated to a committee or agents, then, in the absence of special provisions otherwise, a minority of the select body or of the committee or agents are powerless to bind the majority or do any valid act. If all the members of the select body or committee or if all of the agents are assembled, or if all have been duly notified and the minority refuse or neglect to meet with the others, a majority of those present may act, provided those present constitute a majority of the whole number. In other words, in such a case a major part of the whole is necessary to constitute a quorum, and a majority of the quorum may act. If the major part withdraw so as to leave no quorum, the power of the minority to act is, in general, considered to cease.'" Where a council consists of eight members, five being a quorum, and the mayor has the casting vote in case of a tie, and four members vote one way and four refuse to vote, the mayor is entitled to the deciding vote.[6] In

[1] Heiskell v. Baltimore, 65 Md. 125, 57 Am. Rep. 308; Barnert v. Patterson, 48 N. J. L. 395.
[2] Heiskell v. Baltimore, 65 Md. 125, 57 Am. Rep. 308.
[3] Rushville Gas Co. v. Rushville, 121 Ind. 206, 23 N. E. Rep. 72, 6 L. R. A. 315; State v. Ballin, 144 U. S. 1; State v. Green, 37 Ohio St. 227; Launtz v. People, 113 Ill. 137, 55 Am. Rep. 405; Everett v. Smith, 22 Minn. 53. "The exercise of law-making power is not stopped by the mere silence and inaction of some of the law-makers who are present." Attorney-General v. Sheppard, 62 N. H. 383; State v. Dillon, 125 Ind. 65, 25 N. E. Rep. 136. See note to Hooper v. Creager, 84 Md. 197. In Lawrence v. Ingersoll, 88 Tenn. 52, 6 L. R. A. 309, it was held that a majority *of those present at a meeting* of a select body consisting of a definite number of voters must concur in order to do any valid act.
[4] Brown v. District of Columbia, 127 U. S. 579.
[5] Mun. Corp., § 283.
[6] Launtz v. People, 113 Ill. 137, 55 Am. Rep. 405.

a council of twelve, seven is the smallest number that can hold a legal meeting, but when seven are present four may bind the council.[1] Authority to remove an officer by a two-thirds vote of the council means a two-thirds vote of the legal quorum.[2] Authority to settle rules of procedure does not confer authority to determine what number shall be a quorum, and the rule of the common law will govern.[3] Acts done when less than a quorum is present are void.

§ 258. *Who are officers.*— A public officer is one who is selected to discharge a public duty, and who receives compensation therefor from some source.[4] File clerks, janitors, officers of justice courts and the like are mere employees and the courts will not determine their rights in *quo warranto* proceedings.[5] Commissioners appointed to refund the bonded indebtedness of a township are mere financial agents and not public officers.[6] The president of a city council is not necessarily an officer of the city, but may be only an officer or servant of the council that selected him.[7] The members of the detective department of the district police force are public officers and not mere employees.[8] But the question whether a certain person is a public officer or merely an employee must in many cases be determined from an examination of the statute providing for the office and prescribing its duties. The distinction between state and municipal officers has been elsewhere considered.[9] The question often arises under the provisions of law which forbid one person holding more than one office, a state and municipal office,

---

[1] Ex parte Wilcocks, 7 Cowan (N. Y.) 403; Buell v. Buckingham, 16 Iowa, 284.

[2] Warnock v. La Fayette, 4 La. Ann. 419; State v. Porter, 113 Ind. 79; Cooley, Const. Lim., p. 169; Journals of United States Senate, 1st Sess., 43d Cong., 418.

[3] Heiskell v. Baltimore, 65 Md. 125, 57 Am. Rep. 308. Also Zeiler v. Central R. Co., 84 Md. 304, 34 L. R. A. 469.

[4] Henley v. Lyme, 5 Bing. 91; Ogden v. Raymond, 22 Conn. 379, 59 Am. Dec. 429. Many definitions and authorities are cited in State v. Spaulding (Iowa, 1897), 72 N. W. Rep. 288. See, also, many cases cited in note to McCornick v. Pratt, 8 Utah, 294, in 17 L. R. A. 243. See, also, State v. Kiichli, 53 Minn. 147; State v. Dillon, 32 Fla. 545, 22 L. R. A. 124; State v. Anderson, 45 Ohio St. 196, 12 N. E. Rep. 656.

[5] Trainor v. Board of Auditors, 89 Mich. 162, 15 L. R. A. 95.

[6] Travelers' Ins. Co. v. Oswego, 59 Fed. Rep. 58, 7 C. C. A. 69.

[7] State v. Kiichli, 53 Minn. 147, 54 N. W. Rep. 1069.

[8] Brown v. Russell, 166 Mass. 14, 33 L. R. A. 253.

[9] § 30 *et seq.*

a state and federal office, or under the common law which forbids one person from holding inconsistent offices.

§ 259. *Election and appointment.*— The manner in which the officers of public corporations are to be elected or appointed is always provided in the charter or general law. The members of a city council are always elected by the people, and this is generally true of the mayor. The treasurer, comptroller, attorney and members of boards are sometimes elected by the people and sometimes by the council. Subordinate officers are generally appointed by the mayor and confirmed by the council or elected by the council. The power to appoint to office is not an inherent executive function.[1] The transfer from a council to the mayor " of all executive power now vested by law in the city council or in either branch thereof " authorizes the mayor to appoint a superintendent of buildings.[2] When the power of appointment is vested in the mayor there is no implied requirement of confirmation by the council.[3] After having confirmed an appointment the council cannot reconsider its action and refuse to confirm.[4] A council the term of whose life is one year may create and appoint to an office the term of which exceeds one year.[5]

§ 260. *Qualifications.*— The qualifications necessary to the holding of an office are determined by the constitution or by the statutes of the state, and the possession of such qualifications is as essential to the right to hold an office as is appointment or election.[6] An alien cannot hold an office; but a nonresident is eligible to office unless the contrary is provided by statute.[7] As a general rule it is held that women are ineligible to office unless the right is expressly conferred upon them.[8]

[1] Fox v. McDonald, 101 Ala. 51, 46 Am. St. Rep. 98, 21 L. R. A. 529; State v. Boucher, 3 N. Dak. 389, 21 L. R. A. 539; People v. Freeman, 80 Cal. 233, 13 Am. St. Rep. 122, and note on p. 127.
[2] Attorney-General v. Varnum, 167 Mass. 477, 46 N. E. Rep. 1.
[3] State v. Doherty, 16 Wash. 382, 47 Pac. Rep. 958.
[4] State v. Wadham, 64 Minn. 318, 67 N. W. Rep. 64. Power to appoint court-house and city hall commissioners, see State v. Ermentrout, 63 Minn. 105, 65 N. W. Rep. 251.
[5] State v. Anderson, 58 N. J. L. 515, 33 Atl. Rep. 840.
[6] Nanson v. Grizzard, 96 N. C. 203.
[7] Com. v. Jones, 12 Pa. St. 365; State v. George, 23 Fla. 585.
[8] Bradwell v. Illinois, 16 Wall. 130; Robinson's Case, 131 Mass. 376; Hough v. Cook, 44 Iowa, 039; State v. Gorton, 33 Minn. 345.

The tendency, however, is to confer the right in certain cases; and under certain constitutions, which are silent upon the subject, the general right has been admitted.[1] Reasonable property qualifications may be required in the absence of constitutional restriction.[2] When the qualifications are fixed by the constitution, the legislature cannot impose others as a condition to the holding of office.[3] Thus, a statute requiring members of a police commission to be members of a party having the highest or next highest representation in the common council is unconstitutional.[4] So a statute assuming to grant special privileges to freeholders in addition to those granted by the constitution is class legislation and void.[5] A number of statutes have been enacted which provide that veterans shall be given the preference over other citizens in the matter of appointment to office. Such statutes are probably valid when applied to mere employees, and invalid when applied to public officers.[6]

[1] Jeffries v. Harrington, 11 Colo. 191.

[2] Darrow v. People, 8 Colo. 417.

[3] McCrary, Elections, § 312; Barker v. People, 3 Cowan (N. Y.), 685, 15 Am. Dec. 322.

[4] Rathbone v. Wirth, 150 N. Y. 459, 34 L. R. A. 403.

[5] State v. Goodville, 30 W. Va. 179, 6 L. R. A. 621. In support of the proposition that the legislature cannot impose upon voters other qualifications than those fixed by the constitution, see Kansas City v. Whipple, 136 Mo. 475, 35 L. R. A. 746; Stockton v. Powell, 29 Fla. 1, 15 L. R. A. 42; State v. Dillon, 32 Fla. 454, 22 L. R. A. 124; Buckner v. Gordon, 81 Ky. 665; Short v. Maryland, 80 Md. 392.

[6] Sullivan v. Gilroy, 55 Hun (N. Y.), 285; People v. French, 52 Hun (N. Y.), 464; Opinion of Justices, 145 Mass. 587; State v. Delaney (N. J., 1893), 25 Atl. Rep. 946. In Brown v. Russell, 166 Mass. 14, 43 N. E. Rep. 1005, 33 L. R. A. 253, the court said: "Can the legislature constitutionally provide that certain public offices and employments which it has created shall be filled by veterans in preferment to all other persons, whether the veterans are or are not found or thought to be actually qualified to perform the duties of the offices and employments by some impartial and competent officer or board charged with some public duty in making the appointments? If such legislation is not constitutional as regards public offices, the question incidentally may arise whether a distinction can be made between public offices and employments by the public which are not offices. Public offices are created for the purpose of effecting the ends for which government has been instituted, which are the common good and not the profit, honor or private interest of any man, family or class of men. In our form of government it is fundamental that public offices are a public trust, and that the persons to be appointed should be selected solely with a view to the public welfare." It was held that the members of the police force were

§ 261. *Conditions precedent to entering upon an office.*— An office must be accepted, but no particular form of acceptance is necessary. The mere entering upon the office is sufficient.[1] At common law it was an indictable offense to refuse to accept an office, but for obvious reasons this rule has become of little importance.[2] When the taking of an oath is made a condition precedent to admission to an office the officer possesses no rights until this requirement is complied with.[3] But a failure to take the oath within the time fixed by law does not *ipso facto* create a vacancy. He may take the oath at any time before any steps are taken to have a vacancy declared.[4] The form of oath is ordinarily prescribed, and must be substantially followed.[5] The filing of a bond with sufficient sureties is almost universally made a condition precedent to the right to enter upon an office which requires the care and custody of money or property. Unless the statute makes the filing of a bond within a designated time a condition precedent to the right to the office, the failure to file within such time will not work a forfeiture of the right or create a vacancy. In such case the officer may file his bond after he has entered upon the duties of the office.[6]

In some states it is held that one who can qualify at the time when called upon to assume the duties of an office is eligible to the office although he was under some disability on the day of election. This, on the theory that "it is an eligible officer the law requires, and any person who can qualify himself to take and hold the office is eligible at the time of the election."[7]

public officers and that the act was unconstitutional. See State v. Miller (Minn.), 68 N. W. Rep. 732 (preference to veterans on public works). In State v. Barrows (Minn., 1898), 73 N. W. Rep. 704, such a statute was construed, but its constitutionality was not questioned. See note to Louisville, etc. Co. v. N. R. Co., 14 L. R. A. 579, for cases on equality of privileges, etc.

[1] Smith v. Moore, 90 Ind. 294.
[2] See Hinze v. People, 92 Ill. 406.
[3] People v. McKinney, 52 N. Y. 374.
[4] State v. Ruff, 4 Wash. 234, 16 L. R. A. 140.

[5] Davis v. Berger, 54 Mich. 692; Olney v. Pierce, 1 R. I. 292; State v. Trenton, 35 N. J. L. 485.
[6] Knox Co. v. Johnson, 124 Ind. 145, 7 L. R. A. 684, and cases cited in decision; Launtz v. People, 113 Ill. 137. Many authorities are reviewed and cited in Holt Co. v. Scott (Neb., 1898), 73 N. W. Rep. 681. See, also, note to Com. v. Johnson, 19 Am. St. Rep. 96. As to the right of a comptroller to refuse to approve the bond of an officer, see State v. Shannon, 133 Mo. 139.
[7] State v. Van Beek, 87 Iowa, 569, 19 L. R. A. 622; State v. Smith, 14 Wis.

This rule is adopted by congress with reference to the qualifications of its members.[1] But the stronger reasons appear to be with the courts which hold that the person must be eligible at the time of his election as well as at the time of entering upon the office.[2] When the constitution imposes a disability upon a member of the legislature "during the time for which he is elected" to hold any office, the disability continues until the expiration of the full period for which he was elected, notwithstanding his resignation as a member of the legislature.[3]

§ 262. *Relation of officer to corporation.*— The members of a city council, like all other corporate officers, are trustees for the public interest. They must act solely with reference to

497; State v. Trumpf, 50 Wis. 103; Privet v. Bickford, 26 Kan. 53, 40 Am. Rep. 301; State v. Murray, 29 Wis. 96, 9 Am. Rep. 489; Vogel v. State, 107 Ind. 374.

[1] Cushing, Law and Prac. Leg. Ass., p. 79; McCrary, Elections, § 311.

[2] State v. Williams, 99 Mo. 291, 12 S. W. Rep. 905; Taylor v. Sullivan, 45 Minn. 309, 11 L. R. A. 272. In State v. Moores (Neb., 1898), 73 N. W. Rep. 299, it was held that the word "eligible" relates to the capacity to be elected or chosen to an office as well as to hold the office. The court said: "To hold that the disqualification has reference alone to the time of assuming the duties of public office is to disregard the etymology of the word 'eligible.' The definition given it in the Standard Dictionary is: 'Capable of being chosen; qualified for selection or election; fit for or worthy of choice or adoption.' The word is similarly defined in the Century and other dictionaries. The term 'eligible,' as employed in the constitution, should be given its plain and ordinary signification; and, when so construed, there is no escaping the conclusion that it means capable of being elected or chosen. Neither the framers of the constitution, nor the people in adopting it, intended to permit a person to be elected to a public office who at the time was disqualified from entering upon the duties thereof, and run the risk of the removal of the disability between the day of election and the commencement of the official term. One who is in default as collector and custodian of public money or property is disqualified from being legally elected to any office of profit or trust under the constitution or laws of the state. This is the plain and natural construction of the language of the constitution. These views find abundant support in the authorities. See Territory v. Smith, 3 Minn. 240 (Gil. 164); Taylor v. Sullivan, 45 Minn. 309, 47 N. W. Rep. 802; State v. Clarke, 3 Nev. 566; Searcy v. Grow, 15 Cal. 117; People v. Leonard, 73 Cal. 230, 14 Pac. Rep. 853; Drew v. Rogers (Cal.), 34 Pac. Rep. 1081; In re Corliss, 11 R. I. 638; Carson v. McPhetridge, 15 Ind. 327; Jeffries v. Rowe, 63 Ind. 592; Hill v. Territory (Wash. T.), 7 Pac. Rep. 63. There is a division in the authorities upon the subject, but the ones cited above and those in line therewith are believed to be sustained by the better logic." See People v. Rogers (Cal.), 46 Pac. Rep. 740, 50 Pac. Rep. 668.

[3] State v. Sutton, 63 Minn. 147, 65 N. W. Rep. 262, 30 L. R. A. 630.

the best interests of the community. Thus, in making improvements, erecting public buildings, and similar acts, it must consult only the interests of the people. Hence, although a lot has been sold to the city at a price much below its value on the understanding that the city hall would be built upon it, a court of equity will not enforce specific performance of the contract when there is available a more ample and favorable site which can be procured for the purpose. A city council cannot bind subsequent city officials to erect a public building upon a particular lot if such officials believe that the lot is not a suitable site for the building.[1]

An official may not take advantage of his position and of the knowledge acquired by reason thereof to make a profit for himself to the detriment of the corporation. Thus, if a member of a board appointed to select a suitable site for a public building purchases for himself a tract of land which he knows the board considers suitable for municipal purposes, and sells it to the board at an advanced price, he is liable to the city for damages occasioned thereby. So, if he procures the purchase of a lot by an agent for this purpose, with the knowledge and co-operation of the agent, both principal and agent are liable.[2] But it is quite well established that the officers controlling the affairs of a public corporation may contract with ministerial officers of the corporation unless such contracts are prohibited by statute.[3] But an officer cannot contract with himself personally.[4]

§ 263. *Incompatible offices.* — By the common law, if one while occupying a public office accepts another which is incompatible with it, the first *ipso facto* terminates, without judicial proceedings or any other act of the incumbent. The acceptance of the second office operates as a resignation of the first.[5]

[1] Kendall v. Frey, 74 Wis. 26, 17 Am. St. Rep. 118.
[2] Short v. Symes, 150 Mass. 298, 15 Am. St. Rep. 204.
[3] United States v. Brindle, 110 U. S. 688; McBride v. Grand Rapids, 47 Mich. 236; Board of Com'rs v. Mitchell, 131 Ind. 370, 15 L. R. A. 520. Contracts which do not involve a conflict of interests are not invalid

unless made so by statute. Niles v. Muzzy, 33 Mich. 61, 20 Am. Rep. 670.
[4] Fort Wayne v. Rosenthal, 75 Ind. 156, 39 Am. Rep. 127.
[5] Milward v. Thatcher, 2 T. R. 81, 7 Eng. Rul. Cas. 320 (the leading case); Rex v. Pateman, 2 T. R. 777; Rex v. Patteson, 4 B. & Ad. 9; People v. Carrique, 2 Hill (N. Y.), 93; Mechem, Pub. Off., § 420; Throop, Pub. Off.,

Under this rule the question of compatibility must be determined by the courts. When the law forbids the holding of two offices at the same time, or the holding of two lucrative offices, or a state and federal office, the effect is the same. "In each case the holding of the two offices is illegal; it is made so in one case by the policy of the law and in the other by absolute law. In either case the law presumes that the officer did not intend to commit the unlawful act of holding both offices, and a surrender of the first is implied."[1] The common-law rule assumes that the offices are derived from a common source. But state authorities cannot declare a federal office vacant because the incumbent has accepted a state office when the constitution prohibits the holding of both at the same time.[2] The incompatibility does not consist in the physical inability of one person to discharge the duties of the two offices. There must be some inconsistency in the functions of the offices; some conflict in the duties required of the officer; as where one has supervision of the other, or is required to deal with, control or assist the other. As said by Judge Folger,[3] "Where one office is not subordinate to the other nor the relations of the one to the other such as are inconsistent and repugnant, there is not that incompatibility from which the law declares that the acceptance of the one is the vacation of the other. The force of the word in its application to this matter is that from the nature and relations to each other of the two places they ought not to be held by the same person, from the contrariety and antagonism which would result in the attempt by one person to faithfully and impartially discharge the duties of one toward the incumbent of the other. Thus, a man may not be landlord and

---

§ 80. "The acceptance of the incompatible office . . . absolutely terminates the original office, leaving no shadow of title in the possessor, whose successor may be at once elected or appointed, neither *quo warranto* nor motion being necessary." Dillon, Mun. Corp., § 225. "An exception is made to the general rule in those cases in which an officer cannot vacate the first office by his own act, upon the principle that he will not be permitted to do indirectly what he could not do directly." Mechem, Pub. Off., § 421.

[1] State v. Bus, 135 Mo. 325, 33 L. R. A. 616; State v. Draper, 45 Mo. 355.

[2] De Turk v. Com., 129 Pa. St. 151, 15 Am. St. Rep. 703, 5 L. R. A. 853, note.

[3] People v. Green, 58 N. Y. 295; State v. Goff, 15 R. I. 507, 2 Am. St. Rep. 921; State v. Bus, 135 Mo. 325, 33 L. R. A. 616; Folz v. Kerlin, 105 Ind. 221.

tenant of the same premises. He may be landlord of one farm and tenant of another, though he may not at the same hour be able to do the duty of each relation. The offices must subordinate one the other, and they must *per se* have the right to interfere one with the other, before they are incompatible at common law." But an officer who has given bond for the faithful performance of his duties cannot relieve himself from its responsibilities by resignation. Thus, where a tax collector accepted the incompatible office of selectman, the court said:[1] "The acceptance of an office by one disqualified to hold it by reason of holding an incompatible office is not necessarily a resignation of the prior office, unless it is made so by special statutory or constitutional provision." A person may hold any number of offices if they are not incompatible or not forbidden by statute.[2]

§ 264. *Illustrations.*— There are many cases illustrating the rule that a person cannot hold two offices which are incompatible. The following have been held incompatible: Governor and member of the legislature;[3] sheriff and justice of the peace;[4] member of prudential committee and auditor of a school district;[5] governor and mayor of a city;[6] state treasurer and justice of the peace;[7] secretary and recorder of a city;[8] constable and justice of the peace;[9] councilman and city marshal;[10] justice of the peace and deputy-sheriff;[11] township trustee and postmaster;[12] postmaster and county judge;[13] alderman and member of congress;[14] jurat and town clerk;[15] city clerk and township supervisor.[16]

[1] Attorney-General v. Marston, 66 N. H. 485, 13 L. R. A. 670.
[2] Badeau v. United States, 130 U. S. 439; Converse v. United States, 21 How. (U. S.) 470.
[3] Barnum v. Gilman, 27 Minn. 466, 38 Am. Dec. 304.
[4] Stubbs v. Lee, 64 Me. 195, 18 Am. Rep. 251.
[5] Cotton v. Phillips, 56 N. H. 220.
[6] Attorney - General v. Common Council of Detroit (Mich.), 71 N. W. Rep. 632, 37 L. R. A. 211.
[7] State v. Hutt, 2 Ark. 282.
[8] State v. Brinkerhoff, 66 Tex. 45.
[9] Magie v. Stoddard, 25 Conn. 565, 68 Am. Dec. 375.
[10] State v. Hoyt, 2 Oreg. 246.
[11] State v. Goff, 15 R. I. 505, 2 Am. St. Rep. 921, note.
[12] Foltz v. Kerlin, 105 Ind. 221, 55 Am. Rep. 197.
[13] Hoglan v. Carpenter, 4 Bush (Ky.), 89.
[14] People v. Common Council, 77 N. Y. 503, 33 Am. Rep. 659.
[15] Milward v. Thatcher, 2 T. R. 81, 7 Eng. Rul. Cas. 320, annotated.
[16] Northway v. Sheridan (Mich.), 69 N. W. Rep. 82.

The following offices have been held compatible: A deputy-sheriff in a city and a director of the public schools of the city;[1] clerk of the circuit court and clerk of the county court;[2] school director and judge of elections;[3] clerk of the district court and court commissioner;[4] crier and messenger of a court;[5] member of the assembly and clerk of the court of special sessions.[6]

A lucrative office is one where pay is affixed to the performance of the duties.[7] The offices of township trustee,[8] recorder and county commissioner,[9] supreme court reporter,[10] school trustee of an incorporated town,[11] are "lucrative offices."

Park commissioners are officers under the city government, within the meaning of a provision that city officers shall not be eligible to the legislature, where the power to appoint or suspend them is vested in the city council, and they are required to take the constitutional oath of office and are prohibited from holding any other office.[12] If an office is purely municipal, the officer is not within a constitutional provision declaring that no person shall hold more than one lucrative office at the same time.[13] A county commissioner is not an officer of the commonwealth and cannot be impeached.[14]

§ 265. *Officers de facto.*—A *de facto* officer is one who discharges the duties of an office under color of title.[15] There can be no *de facto* officer where the *de jure* officer is in possession of the office.[16] The doctrine that the acts of *de facto* officers

---

[1] State v. Bus, 135 Mo. 325, 33 L. R. A. 616.
[2] State v. Lusk, 48 Mo. 242.
[3] In re District Attorney, 11 Phila. 645.
[4] Kenney v. Goergen, 36 Minn. 90.
[5] Preston v. United States, 37 Fed. Rep. 417.
[6] People v. Green, 58 N. Y. 295.
[7] State v. Kirk, 44 Ind. 401.
[8] Fultz v. Kerlin, 105 Ind. 221.
[9] Dailey v. State, 8 Blackf. (Ind.) 329.
[10] Kerr v. Jones, 19 Ind. 351.
[11] Chambers v. Barnard, 127 Ind. 365, 11 L. R. A. 613, note.
[12] People v. State Board of Commissioners, 129 N. Y. 360, 14 L. R. A. 646, annotated.
[13] Chambers v. Barnard, 127 Ind. 365, 11 L. R. A. 613.
[14] Opinion of Justices, 167 Mass. 599, 46 N. E. Rep. 118.
[15] The acts of a *de facto* officer before the title to the office is determined are valid and cannot be collaterally assailed. Hamlin v. Kassafer, 15 Oreg. 456, 3 Am. St. Rep. 176; Jewel v. Gilbert, 64 N. H. 13, 10 Am. St. Rep. 357.
[16] As to liability of sureties on the bond of an officer *de facto*, see Holt Co. v. Scott (Neb., 1898), 73 N. W. Rep. 681. In Jones v. Scanland, 6

are valid[1] applies to the acts of members of the governing body of a municipal corporation.[2] The doctrine, however, has no application to a case where the acts of the officer are challenged at the outset and before any person has been or can be misled or any right of either a public or private character accrued.[3] Before there can be a *de facto* officer there must be a *de jure* office. In a case where it was sought to sustain the acts of certain commissioners who were appointed under an unconstitutional act Mr. Justice Field said:[4] "The doctrine which gives validity to acts of officers *de facto*, whatever defect there may be in the legality of their appointment or election, is founded upon considerations of policy and necessity, for the protection of the public and individuals whose interests may be affected thereby. Offices are created for the benefit of the public, and

Humph. (Tenn.) 195,— an action upon an official bond,— it was said: "Although the election of a person as sheriff was void, and his induction into office illegal by reason of his having then been a defaulter to the treasury, and he did not thereby become sheriff *de jure*, yet he became sheriff *de facto*, and those who voluntarily bound themselves for the faithful performance of his duties, as sureties, cannot absolve themselves from their obligation by insisting that he was no sheriff." In the case of State v. Rhoades, 6 Nev. 352, it was announced: "Where a state treasurer, re-elected in 1866, accepted a new commission and took a new oath, and continued to discharge the duties of the office, but failed to file a new official bond within the time prescribed by law, *held*, that he was an officer *de facto*, and holding as of the new term; and that the sureties on the new bond afterwards filed were estopped from denying that he was holding as of the new term *de jure*. . . . A person discharging the duties of a public office under color of right is an officer *de facto*, and not a mere intruder. . . . Where a person discharges the duties of an office as an officer *de facto*, and not as a mere intruder, he and his sureties are estopped by the recitals in his official bond from denying that he is entitled to the office."

[1] School District v. Smith, 67 Vt. 566, 32 Atl. Rep. 484.
[2] Williams v. Boynton, 147 N. Y. 426, 42 N. E. Rep. 184.
[3] Decorah v. Bullis, 25 Iowa, 12; Lover v. Glochlin, 28 Wis. 364; People v. Nostrand, 46 N. Y. 378. In the leading case of State v. Carroll, 38 Conn. 449, 9 Am. Rep. 409, the court said: "An officer *de facto* is one whose acts, though not those of a lawful officer, the law, upon principles of policy or justice, will hold valid, so far as they involve the interests of the public or third persons, where the duties of the office were exercised . . . under color of a known election or appointment, void because the officer was not eligible, . . . such ineligibility being unknown to the public." Holt Co. v. Scott (Neb.), 73 N. W. Rep. 681, and many cases cited by the court.
[4] Norton v. Shelby Co., 118 U. S. 425; People v. Hecht, 105 Cal. 621, 27 L. R. A. 203.

private parties are not permitted to inquire into the title of persons clothed with the evidence of such offices and in apparent possession of their powers and functions. For the good order and peace of society, their authority is to be respected and obeyed until in some regular mode prescribed by law their title is investigated and determined. It is manifest that endless confusion would result if in every proceeding before such officers their title could be called in question. But the idea of an officer implies the existence of an office which he holds. It would be a misapplication of terms to call one an officer who holds no office, and a public office can exist only by force of law. This seems to us so obvious that we should hardly feel called upon to consider any adverse opinion on the subject but for the earnest contention of plaintiff's counsel that such existence is not essential, and that it is sufficient if the office be provided for by any legislative enactment however invalid. Their position is that a legislative act, though unconstitutional, may in terms create an office, and nothing further than its apparent existence is necessary to give validity to the acts of its assumed incumbent. . . . An unconstitutional act is not a law; it confers no rights; it imposes no duties; it affords no protection; it creates no office; it is in legal contemplation as inoperative as though it had never been passed. . . . For the existence of a *de facto* officer there must be an office *de jure*. . . . Where no office legally exists the pretended officer is merely an usurper, to whose acts no validity can be attached." A mere intruder cannot be regarded as an officer *de facto*.[1]

§ 266. *De facto officers — Continued.*— Two persons cannot be officers *de facto* for the same office at the same time. If an office is filled and the duties pertaining thereto are performed by an officer or a body *de jure*, another person or body, although claiming the officer under color of title, cannot be an officer or body *de facto*, and the relations of the parties cannot be changed by the physical ousting of the body or officer *de jure* from the room where the business is transacted.[2] One is not a *de facto*

[1] Dabney v. Hudson, 68 Miss. 292, 24 Am. St. Rep. 276; Hamlin v. Kassafer, 15 Oreg. 456, 3 Am. St. Rep. 176. See note in 4 Am. St. Rep. 147. One who assumes to perform the duties of a public office without an attempt to qualify is without color of title. Creighton v. Com., 83 Ky. 147.

[2] In re Gunn, 19 L. R. A. 519; Mc-

officer who has not the reputation of being such an officer, and whose acts and authority as such officer are not generally recognized or acquiesced in, and who does not exercise the duties of the office under such circumstances of continuance, reputation, acquiescence or otherwise as to afford a reasonable presumption that he was such officer.[1] One who is appointed to an office from which the incumbent was never legally removed, and who retained possession of the property of the office and continued to discharge its duties, is not an officer *de facto*.[2] A person who has been elected to an office in a manner consistent with an honest misapprehension of the law, and not in palpable disregard of its provisions, is an officer *de facto* although the election may be held invalid.[3] The members of a commission duly appointed to prepare a city charter are *de facto* officers, although not possessing the necessary qualification of five years' residence.[4] When the right of confirmation is vested in the council, a person appointed by the mayor and wrongfully placed in possession of an office without the consent of the council is a mere intruder.[5]

§ 267. *Compensation.*— The compensation of public officers is governed entirely by the charter or statute. It is under the control of the legislature, and in the absence of constitutional restrictions it may be increased, diminished or entirely taken away at any time.[6] It follows that an officer can recover no compensation for services rendered unless it was provided for by law at the time the office was accepted.[7] When a statute

Chaon v. Leavenworth County, 8 Kan. 438; State v. Blossom, 19 Nev. 312.

[1] State v. Pinkerman, 63 Conn. 176, 22 L. R. A. 563; Hamlin v. Kassafer, 15 Oreg. 456, 3 Am. St. Rep. 176.

[2] Halgren v. Campbell, 82 Mich. 255, 9 L. R. A. 408.

[3] State v. Mayor of Atlantic City, 52 N. J. L. 332, 8 L. R. A. 697.

[4] People v. Hecht, 105 Cal. 621, 27 L. R. A. 203.

[5] Kempster v. City of Milwaukee (Wis., 1897), 72 N. W. Rep. 743.

[6] Cooley, Const. Lim., § 276; Swan v. Buck, 40 Miss. 268; People v. Morrell, 21 Wend. (N. Y.) 563.

[7] McCumber v. Waukesha Co., 91 Wis. 442, 65 N. W. Rep. 51; Locke v. City of Central, 4 Colo. 65, 34 Am. Rep. 66; Langdon v. Casselton, 30 Vt. 285; Romero v. United States, 24 Ct. of Cl. 331, 5 L. R. A. 69; Kinney v. United States, 60 Fed. Rep. 883. When no salary is attached to the office of mayor, an incumbent of the office cannot collect fees for services rendered in the capacity of a justice of the peace. Howland v. Wright Co., 82 Iowa, 164, 47 N. W. Rep. 1086. See Prince v. City of Fresno, 88 Cal. 407, 26 Pac. Rep. 606.

allowing an officer compensation admits of two interpretations it should be construed strictly against the officer.[1] It is generally provided, however, that the salary shall not be increased or diminished during the term of office.[2] An officer cannot recover extra compensation for extra services imposed upon him after he has entered upon the performance of his duties. In a recent case the supreme court of Iowa said:[3] "By the act of the legislature authorizing the creation of boards of health the mayor was made a member of said board and its chairman. While additional duties were thus imposed upon the mayor no additional compensation was allowed therefor. This he knew when he accepted the office, and he is bound to perform the duties of the office for a salary fixed, and cannot legally claim additional compensation for additional services, even though they be subsequently imposed upon him; and it matters not that the salary was inadequate."[4]

§ 268. *Compensation — De facto officers.*— The general rule is that the salary follows the legal title to the office. Hence, only an officer who is legally elected or appointed to an office can maintain an action to collect the salary.[5] Thus, a police officer cannot recover for salary during a period when he was wrongfully prevented from performing the duties of his posi-

---

[1] United States v. Clough, 55 Fed. Rep. 373, 5 C. C. A. 140.

[2] Such a constitutional provision does not apply to police officers. Mangam v. Brooklyn, 98 N. Y. 585, 5 Am. Rep. 705.

[3] State v. Olinger (Iowa, 1897), 72 N. W. Rep. 441.

[4] People v. Vilas, 36 N. Y. 459; Mayor v. Kelley, 98 N. Y. 467; Marshall Co. v. Johnson, 127 Ind. 238, 26 N. E. Rep. 821; Pierie v. Philadelphia, 139 Pa. St. 573, 21 Atl. Rep. 90. An assignment by a public officer of his unearned salary as security for a debt is contrary to public policy and void. The reasons for this rule apply with greater force to fees payable to an officer, as for example a sheriff, upon the due performance of public duty which cannot be discharged by any other officer. "If he could assign to one he could to many, and every purchaser would be entitled to the rights of assignees of claims against individuals, and in the case of conflicting interests or of disputes between the officer and his alleged transferee the government would have to decide at its peril between them, or be subjected to litigation. . . . An officer having assigned his interest in a compensation to become due him for future public services would have less interest in the punctual and efficient performance of his duties, and in the case of improvident assignments might be without the ability to discharge them." Bowery Nat. Bank v. Wilson, 122 N. Y. 478, 9 L. R. A. 706.

[5] Phelan v. Granville, 140 Mass. 386.

tion, unless he can prove that he was legally appointed.[1] As a general rule, an officer who has been prevented through no fault of his own from performing the duties of his office can recover his salary during the interim, and cannot be compelled to account for wages earned in other and different employments.[2] But under a charter providing that police officers shall be paid "for the time engaged in active service," an officer improperly removed and afterwards reinstated is not entitled to pay pending reinstatement.[3] After an officer has performed services under a legal election or appointment, he may recover from the corporation the salary which is by law affixed to the office. But the relation between a public corporation and its officer is not based upon contract, and there is nothing to prevent the corporation from abolishing the office and thus depriving the officer of his salary for the unexpired term.[4]

A *de facto* officer cannot maintain an action for salary.[5] But the general rule probably is that the payment of salary to a *de facto* officer before the claim to the office has been determined against him by a competent tribunal will defeat the right of the *de jure* officer to recover the salary from the corporation.[6] Where this rule prevails the remedy of the *de jure*

[1] Yorks v. City of St. Paul, 62 Minn. 250, 64 N. W. Rep. 565.

[2] Fitzsimmons v. Brooklyn, 102 N. Y. 536, 7 N. E. Rep. 878.

[3] Wilkinson v. Saginaw (Mich., 1897), 70 N. W. Rep. 142.

[4] In City Council of Augusta v. Sweeny, 44 Ga. 463, 9 Am. Rep. 172, the court said: "The right of an incumbent to an office does not depend on any contract in the sense of a bargain between him and the public. His right depends on the law under which he holds. If that law be one capable of being repealed by the power which acts, the right of the officer is gone. That clause of the bill of rights in our constitution which prohibits the passage of a law affecting private rights, or rather the varying of a general law by special legislation so as to affect private rights, cannot affect this question, since this law or ordinance of council which was repealed was not itself a general law, but a law creating a particular office, which the power creating it had the same power to abolish as it had to create." State v. Pinkerman, 63 Conn. 176, 22 L. R. A. 653. But see State v. Friedley, 135 Ind. 119, 21 L. R. A. 634, cited in § 276, *infra*. A salaried officer cannot set off his salary against a claim by the city against him for moneys collected by him in his official capacity. New Orleans v. Finnerty, 27 La. Ann. 681, 21 Am. Rep. 569.

[5] Andrews v. Portland, 79 Me. 484, 10 Am. St. Rep. 280; Romero v. United States, 24 Ct. of Cl. 331, 5 L. R. A. 69. See note, 54 Am. Rep. 730.

[6] Creely Co. v. Milne, 36 Neb. 801, 19 L. R. A. 689, ann.; Nichols v. McLean, 101 N. Y. 526, 54 Am. Rep. 730; State v. Clark, 52 Mo. 508; Parker v. Dakota Co., 4 Minn. 59 (Gil. 39); Steu-

officer is against the *de facto* officer.[1] But the more logical rule is that the *de jure* officer is entitled to recover for the salary notwithstanding it has been paid to a *de facto* officer.[2]

§ 269. *Increase of salary — Misdemeanor.—* In some states it is made a misdemeanor for a member of a city council to vote upon any question in which he is interested. Under a charter which provided that no alderman "shall vote on any question in which he is directly or indirectly interested," and a statute which provided that "when the performance of an act is prohibited by any statute and no penalty for the violation of such statute is imposed, the doing of such act is a misdemeanor," it was held that an alderman who voted for an increase of his salary was guilty of a misdemeanor. The court

benville v. Culp, 38 Ohio St. 18, 43 Am. Rep. 417; Michel v. New Orleans, 32 La. Ann. 1094; Saline Co. Com'rs v. Anderson, 20 Kan. 298, 27 Am. Rep. 171; Wayne Co. Auditor v. Benoit, 20 Mich. 176; Demarest v. New York, 147 N. Y. 203, 41 N. E. Rep. 405.

[1] Bier v. Gorell, 30 W. Va. 95, 8 Am. St. Rep. 17. In Kreitz v. Behrensmeyer, 149 Ill. 496, 24 L. R. A. 59, the court said: "An examination of the decisions of the courts of that country shows a uniform declaration of the principle that a *de jure* officer has the right of action to recover against an officer *de facto* by reason of the intrusion of the latter into his office and his receipt of the emoluments thereof. Among others, the following opinions of English courts may be referred to as sustaining this right of recovery: Vaux v. Jeffren, 2 Dyer, 114; Arris v. Stukely, 2 Mod. 260; Lee v. Drake, 2 Salk. 468; Webb's Case, 8 Coke, 45. By the adoption of the common law of England the principle announced in these cases was adopted as the law of this state, for the principle is of a general nature and applicable to our constitution. On the basis of a sound public policy, the principle commends itself for the reason that one would be less liable to usurp or wrongfully retain a public office and defeat the will of the people or the appointing power, as loss would result from wrongful detention or usurpation of an office. The question has frequently been before the courts of the different states and of the United States, and the great weight of authority sustains the doctrine of the common law." Citing United States v. Addison, 6 Wall. 291; Dolan v. New York, 68 N. Y. 74, 23 Am. Rep. 163; Glasscock v. Lyons, 20 Ind. 1, 83 Am. Dec. 299; Kessel v. Zeiser, 102 N. Y. 114, 55 Am. Rep. 769; Nichols v. McLean, 115 N. Y. 526, 54 Am. Rep. 730; People v. Miller, 24 Mich. 458, 9 Am. Rep. 131; Hunter v. Chandler, 45 Mo. 452; People v. Smythe, 28 Cal. 21; Pettit v. Rossau, 15 La. Ann. 239. *Contra*, Stuher v. Kern, 44 N. J. L. 181, 43 Am. Rep. 353.

[2] State v. Carr, 129 Ind. 44, 13 L. R. A. 177; Andrews v. Portland, 79 Me. 485, 10 Am. St. Rep. 280; Ward v. Marshall, 96 Cal. 153, 30 Pac. Rep. 113; Memphis v. Woodward, 12 Heisk. (Tenn.) 499, 27 Am. Rep. 750; Kempster v. City of Milwaukee (Wis., 1897), 72 N. W. Rep. 743.

said: "It is not necessary that any injurious consequences should have resulted from the misconduct of the officers. The crime consists in a perversion of their powers and duties to the purposes of fraud and wrong; and they are punishable although no injury resulted to any individual, and no money was drawn from the treasury by reason of the vote to increase the salaries."[1] A provision that the salary of an officer shall not be reduced during his term of office does not prevent its reduction between the time of his appointment and of entering upon the duties of the office.[2]

§ 270. *Compensation of employees — Attorneys.*— The principles governing the compensation of public officers have no application to ordinary employees.[3] Where the salary of a city attorney is fixed by law, he can receive no other compensation for services rendered.[4] But unless restrained by its charter, a public corporation may employ an attorney to transact its legal business, and may be compelled to pay a reasonable compensation for such services.[5] When a city has authority to allow its attorney "fees," it may allow him a commission on all moneys collected in civil and criminal cases.[6] A provision that the salary of a city attorney shall not be increased during his term of office prevents an increase in his salary although the city passes from the second to the first class during his term of office.[7] A county attorney may receive extra compensation for services rendered out of the county under the direction of the county commissioners.[8]

---

[1] State v. Shea (Iowa, 1897), 72 N. W. Rep. 300. As bearing upon the question see State v. Van Aucken (Iowa), 68 N. W. Rep. 454; Duty v. State (Ind. App.), 36 N. E. Rep. 655; People v. Bogart, 3 Park. Crim. Rep. 143. In Macy v. City of Duluth (Minn., 1897), 71 N. W. Rep. 687, it is held that under the city charter a poundmaster cannot recover on an implied contract for use and occupation of premises furnished by him to the city for use as a public pound.

[2] Wesch v. Common Council (Mich., 1895), 64 N. W. Rep. 1051.

[3] City of Ellsworth v. Rossiter, 46 Kan. 237, 26 Pac. Rep. 674.

[4] Liddy v. Long Island City, 104 N. Y. 218; Hayes v. Oil City, 11 Atl. Rep. 63. The duty of a city attorney to attend to "all suits, matters and things" in which the city is interested is not limited to suits in any particular courts. Buck v. Eureka, 109 Cal. 504, 30 L. R. A. 409.

[5] State v. Patterson, 40 N. J. L. 186; Langdon v. Casselton, 30 Vt. 385.

[6] Austin v. Johns, 62 Tex. 179.

[7] Barnes v. Williams, 53 Ark. 205, 13 S. W. Rep. 845. As to the fees of a city attorney, see, also, Smith v. Waterbury, 54 Conn. 174, 7 Atl. Rep. 17.

[8] Leavenworth County v. Brewer,

§ 271.] GOVERNING BODIES, OFFICERS AND AGENTS.

§ 271. *The mayor.*— The mayor is the general executive officer of the corporation, although he sometimes performs the judicial duties of a justice of the peace. His court is not a court of record, and the corporate seal need not be attached to a warrant issued by him.[1] Conferring the jurisdiction of a justice of the peace upon a mayor does not contravene the provision of the constitution that no person charged with the exercise of powers properly belonging to either the executive, legislative or judicial department shall exercise any functions pertaining to either of the others, as this applies only to the different departments of the state government.[2] The executive duties of the mayor pertain to him only as an officer of the corporation. Where the mayor presides over the city council he is ordinarily given the right to vote under certain circumstances. Where two official newspapers are to be chosen by the council and three papers receive the votes of four aldermen each, the mayor in casting the deciding vote may vote for two papers.[3] If there is no limitation upon the right of the mayor to cast the deciding vote, it may be upon the question of the choice of a candidate for office as well as upon a question of general legislation.[4] If the mayor is a lawyer by profession and there is no collusion or fraud, he may recover for services rendered in his professional capacity in defending a suit against the city under the authority of a resolution of the council.[5] The compensation of a mayor cannot be entirely taken away under the authority of an ordinance authorizing the council to change the same.[6] It is no part of the duties of the mayor to aid private individuals in obtaining their right to examine the books of other city officials, although the mayor is entitled to investigate such books himself and to give the information so acquired to the public. The obstruction of an executive officer in the exercise of his lawful right to examine the books of a public office for a lawful purpose is an indictable

---

9 Kan. 307; White v. Polk, 17 Iowa, 413; Hoffman v. Greenwood County, 23 Kan. 307.

[1] Santo v. State, 2 Iowa, 155, 63 Am. Dec. 487; Scott v. Fishbate, 117 N. C. 265, 30 L. R. A. 696.

[2] People v. Provines, 34 Cal. 518.

[3] Wooster v. Mullins, 64 Conn. 340, 25 L. R. A. 694.

[4] State v. Pinkerman, 63 Conn. 176, 22 L. R. A. 653.

[5] Mayor v. Muzzy, 33 Mich. 61.

[6] State v. Nashville, 15 Lea (Tenn.), 697, 54 Am. Rep. 427.

offense.[1] In the absence of the mayor the officer who is by law designated for the purpose exercises all the powers of the mayor.[2]

§ 272. *Control by the courts.*— Like other natural and artificial bodies, a municipal council exercises its authority subject to the control of the courts. This control, however, will not be extended to cases in which the council has exercised proper discretionary power, as the court will not substitute its judgment for that of the persons in whom the discretion is vested. But the rule is limited by the restriction "that the discretion must be exercised within its proper limits for the purposes for which it is given, and from the motives by which alone those who gave the discretion intended that its exercise should be governed."[3] Thus, where power is given to a board of supervisors to fix water rates, it is intended that the rate of compensation fixed shall be reasonable and just, and if the rates are fixed so low as to amount to practical confiscation of the property of the water company the court will provide a remedy.[4] A court of equity will not interfere or revise the discretion and judgment of a common council as to the place and manner of the erection of a public building.[5] Such questions necessarily require the exercise of discretion and judgment by the council. Although a board of aldermen is made the sole judge of the qualification, election and return of its own members, its action is subject to the supervision of the courts.[6] Such power is judicial in its nature; and the council will be required to observe the limits of its jurisdiction, and to exer-

[1] Tryon v. Pingree (Mich., 1897), 70 N. W. Rep. 905, 37 L. R. A. 222.

[2] Datz v. Cleveland, 52 N. J. L. 188, 7 L. R. A. 431. An order of the mayor, not required to be in writing, may be by letter or orally, in any manner which is understood by all parties as a direction. Eichenloub v. St. Joseph, 113 Mo. 385, 18 L. R. A. 590.

[3] Davis v. Mayor of New York, 1 Duer, 451; People v. Sturtevant, 9 N. Y. 263, 59 Am. Dec. 536.

[4] Spring Valley W. W. v. San Francisco, 82 Cal. 286, 16 Am. St. Rep. 116. See § 145, *supra.*

[5] Kendall v. Frey, 74 Wis. 26, 17 Am. St. Rep. 118.

[6] State v. Gates, 35 Minn. 385; Com. v. Allen, 70 Pa. St. 465: State v. Kemp, 69 Wis. 470, 2 Am. St. Rep. 753. Some authorities sustain the rule that where the body is given power to judge of the election and qualification of its members the court has no reviewing power. Linegar v. Rittenhouse, 94 Ill. 208; State v. Marlowe, 15 Ohio St. 114; Mayor v. Morgan, 7 Mart. (N. S.) 1, 18 Am. Dec. 232.

cise its power regularly. If a council refuses to obey a *mandamus* ordering the payment of a claim, those members who voted against such payment may be punished for contempt of court.[1]

§ 273. *Holding over after expiration of term.*— Unless the contrary is expressly provided, an officer elected or appointed for a fixed term is entitled to continue in office until his successor is elected and qualified.[2] Hence, one whose term of office is for a specified period "and until his successor is elected and qualified" will remain in office if the person who is elected to succeed him has not the necessary legal qualifications.[3] A constitutional provision that "the general assembly shall not create any office the tenure of which shall be more than four years" does not prevent the incumbent of an office from holding until his successor is elected and qualified.[4] The incumbent will hold over when there is a failure to elect his successor.[5] But when the failure is due to the neglect of the incumbent to perform some duty imposed upon him by law, such as to give notice of an election, he cannot hold over.[6]

§ 274. *Resignation.*— At common law an officer cannot resign his office at his pleasure. "As civil officers are appointed for the purpose of exercising the functions and carrying on the operations of government and maintaining public order, a political organization would seem to be imperfect which should allow the depositaries of its power to throw off their responsibilities at their own pleasure. This certainly was not the doctrine of the common law. In England a person elected to a municipal office was obliged to accept it and perform its duties, and he

---

[1] State v. Judge, 39 La. Ann. 43, 58 Am. St. Rep. 153; Board of Com. v. Sellew, 99 U. S. 624.

[2] State v. Smith, 87 Mo. 158; People v. Rodgers (Cal.), 46 Pac. Rep. 740, reversed 50 Pac. Rep. 668; State v. Bulkeley, 61 Conn. 287, 14 L. R. A. 657; State v. Harrison, 113 Ind. 440; Kimberlain v. Tow, 130 Ind. 120, 14 L. R. A. 858; McMillin v. Richards, 45 Neb. 786, 64 N. W. Rep. 242; State v. Fagin, 42 Conn. 32.

[3] Taylor v. Sullivan, 45 Minn. 309, 22 Am. St. Rep. 709, 11 L. R. A. 272. See People v. Rodgers, *supra*.

[4] State v. Harrison, 113 Ind. 234, 3 Am. St. Rep. 663.

[5] Lafferty v. Huffman (Ky.), 35 S. W. Rep. 123, 32 L. R. A. 203.

[6] People v. Bartlett, 6 Wend. (N. Y.) 422. A contrary rule would enable the officer to profit by his own carelessness or wrong.

subjected himself to a penalty by refusal. An office was regarded as a burden which the appointee was bound, in the interest of the community and the government, to bear. And from this it follows of course that after an office was conferred and assumed it could not be laid down without the consent of the appointing power. This was required in order that the public interests might suffer no inconvenience for the want of public servants to execute the laws."[1] The acceptance of a resignation may be manifested by a formal declaration or by the appointment of a successor. "To complete a resignation," says Mr. Willcock, "it is necessary that a corporation manifest their acceptance of the offer to resign, which may be done by an entry in the public books, or electing another person to fill the place, treating it as vacant."[2] In some jurisdictions it is held that the holding of office is not compulsory, and that a resignation takes effect without acceptance, and that a successor may be appointed without the formality of an acceptance of the resignation.[3] When it is provided that an incumbent shall hold office until his successor is qualified, he is not relieved from the duties of the office even by the acceptance of his resignation.[4]

§ 275. *Amotion.*— Amotion relates to officers, and disfranchisement to corporators or members of a corporation. The former is the removal of an officer from his office without depriving him of his membership in the corporation. The latter is the depriving a member of his membership in the corporation.[5] The English doctrine of disfranchisement is not applicable to municipal corporations in this country. At common

---

[1] Willcock, Corp., p. 129; Grant, Corp., pp. 221, 223, 268; Dillon, Mun. Corp., I, § 163; Rex v. Bower, 1 Barn. & Cress. 585; Rex v. Burder, 4 T. R. 778; Rex v. Lone, 2 Stra. 920; Rex v. Jones, 2 Stra. 1146; Hope v. Henderson, 4 Dev. (N. C.) L. 1; Van Orsdale v. Hazard, 3 Hill (N. Y.) 243; State v. Ferguson, 31 N. J. L. 170. The common-law rule is in force in some states. State v. Clayton, 27 Kan. 442, 41 Am. Rep. 413; Hope v. Henderson, 15 N. C. 29, 25 Am. Dec. 677; Coleman v. Sands, 87 Va. 689.

[2] Willcock, Corp., p. 230; Edwards v. United States, 103 U. S. 471.

[3] Reiter v. State, 51 Ohio St. 74, 23 L. R. A. 681; People v. Porter, 6 Cal. 26; State v. Lincoln, 4 Neb. 260; State v. Clark, 3 Neb. 560; Bunting v. Willis, 27 Gratt. 144, 21 Am. Rep. 338.

[4] People v. Barnett Tp., 100 Ill. 332; Jones v. Jefferson, 66 Tex. 573; United States v. Green, 53 Fed. Rep. 769; Badger v. United States, 93 U. S. 599.

[5] Willcock, Mun. Corp., § 703; Dillon, Mun. Corp., I, § 238; Kyd, Corp. 50-94; Angell & Ames, Corp., ch. XII.

law a corporation has implied power to remove a corporate officer for just cause. In the leading case[1] Lord Mansfield said that there are three sorts of offenses for which an officer or corporator may be discharged: 1. Such as have no immediate relation to his office, but are in themselves of so infamous a nature as to render the offender unfit to execute any public franchise. 2. Such as are only against his oath and the duty of his office as a corporator, and amount to breaches of the tacit condition annexed to his franchise or office. 3. The third sort of offense for which an officer or corporator may be displaced is of a mixed nature, as being an offense not only against the duty of his office, but also a matter indictable at common law. For the first sort of offenses there must be a previous conviction upon an indictment. When the offense is merely against his duty as a corporator he can only be tried for it by the corporation. Whether under the English cases there can be a removal for offenses of the third class before a conviction in a court of justice is uncertain.[2] Only acts of a serious nature will justify removal under the incidental power of a corporation.[3]

§ 276. *Removal — Express authority, proceedings.*— Unless limited by positive provisions of law, the power of removal is an incident of the power of appointment.[4] The incumbent holds during the pleasure of the appointive power, and subject

[1] Rex v. Richardson, 1 Burr. 517, 538. The English cases are reviewed in Richard v. Clarkburg, 30 W. Va. 491. In Ellison v. Raleigh, 89 N. C. 125, the court said: "We have been unable to find any precedent for depriving a member of his place by the action of a municipal body of which he is a member for any pre-existing impediment affecting his capacity to hold the office."

[2] "The cases decided are considered to favor this view, viz.: If the act is criminal and single in its nature, so that a conviction or acquittal in the courts of law will necessarily determine the guilt or innocence of the party, there must be a conviction, but otherwise there may be a removal without, or independent of, a conviction." Dillon, Mun. Corp., I, § 251, n.; Willcock, Mun. Corp. 249; Kyd, Corp. 88–94.

[3] Evans v. Philadelphia Club, 50 Pa. St. 107. A summary of English cases will be found in Ang. & Ames, Corp., sec. 427.

[4] Newsome v. Cooke, 44 Miss. 352, 7 Am. Rep. 686; Williams v. Brewster, 148 Mass. 256; People v. Robb, 126 N. Y. 180; People v. Cain, 84 Mich. 223; Trainor v. Wayne County Auditors, 87 Mich. 162, 15 L. R. A. 95, annotated; State v. Kiichli, 53 Minn. 147, 54 N. W. Rep. 1069, 19 L. R. A. 779.

to removal at any time without notice or hearing.[1] In such cases the appointing power only can remove except for malfeasance by judicial decree.[2] "The authorities are all to the effect that a grant of power to remove either for cause or at discretion carries with it the exclusive power to hear and decide; and whereas the courts are entirely powerless where the power is discretionary, they are equally so where it is for cause, if the grantee of the power acts within its limits and upon notice, if notice is required; if the removal is for a cause designated by or following within the grant, the grantee or depositary of the removing power is the sole judge of the sufficiency of the evidence to justify the removal."[3] But where the incumbent holds office for a definite term, he can be removed only for cause, after a hearing upon specific charges.[4] The legislature may authorize the removal of non-elective officers at the will of the appointing power,[5] but the holder of an elective office cannot be deprived of his right to the office without due process of law, which requires notice and a hearing.[6] But

[1] People v. Mayor, 82 N. Y. 491; State v. McGarry, 21 Wis. 496; State v. McQuay, 12 Wash. 554, 14 Pac. Rep. 897. Where the statute fixes a term longer than is permitted by the constitution, the incumbent holds during the pleasure of the appointing power. Lewis v. Lewelling, 53 Kan. 510, 23 L. R. A. 510.

[2] Carr v. State, 111 Ind. 1.

[3] State v. Johnson, 30 Fla. 433, 18 L. R. A. 414.

[4] Kennard v. Louisiana, 92 U. S. 480; Foster v. Kansas, 112 U. S. 201; People v. Hayden, 113 N. Y. 198; Wilson v. Dullan, 53 Mich. 392. Where by the charter of a city it is provided that elective officers shall not be removed except for cause, the courts will not presume that the legislature intended that appointed officers might be removed without cause. In the absence of express words conferring upon the common council the power to remove an officer without cause, it will be presumed that the legislature intended that every officer appointed for a fixed period should be entitled to hold his office until the expiration of such period unless removed therefrom for cause after a fair trial. Hallgren v. Campbell, 82 Mich. 255, 9 L. R. A. 408.

[5] Trainor v. Board of Auditors, 98 Mich. 162, 15 L. R. A. 95; People v. Witlock, 92 N. Y. 191.

[6] Denver v. Barrow, 13 Colo. 460, 16 Am. Rep. 215; Rex v. Richardson, 1 Burr. 540; People v. Brooklyn, 100 N. Y. 64. "When an officer is appointed during pleasure, or where the power of removal is discretionary, the power to remove may be exercised without notice or hearing. But where the appointment is during good behavior, or where the removal can only be for certain specified causes, the power of removal cannot . . . be exercised unless there be a formulated charge against the officer, notice to him of the accusation, and a hearing of the evidence in support of the charge and an opportunity given the party of making defense." Dillon, Mun.

notice is dispensed with by an appearance and answer to the charge or by a total desertion of the place.[1] Some courts hold that the power to remove from office is judicial in its nature,[2] while others hold that it is administrative,[3] on the theory that the office is conferred upon the incumbent as a public agent, and that he has no property rights in the same. If it is of a judicial nature the officer is entitled to a hearing upon specific charges.[4] The charge need not, however, be as specific as an indictment;[5] and while the rules governing judicial proceedings should be observed, they may be liberally applied.[6] The power of the governor to remove municipal officers is derived from the statute.[7] The power to remove includes the power of temporary suspension pending trial.[8] In such case it is the duty of the governor to notify the officer of the cause of suspension and to give him an opportunity to be heard, and to reinstate him if the evidence does not sustain the charge.[9] When the statute enumerates the causes for which an officer may be removed, it impliedly excludes all others except such as are of a similar nature.[10] The misconduct must be of such a character

Corp., I, § 250; Field v. Com., 32 Pa. St. 478; Willard's Appeal, 4 R. L 595.

[1] Willcock, Mun. Corp. 265; Dillon, Mun. Corp, I, § 254. Where a statute provides that a person may be removed from office when in the opinion of the appointing power "he is incompetent to execute properly the duties of his office, or when on charges and evidence they shall be satisfied that he has been guilty of official misconduct or habitual or wilful neglect of duty," it is not necessary to prefer charges or to notify a person before removing him for incompetency. Trainor v. Board of Auditors, 87 Mich. 162, 15 L. R. A. 95.

[2] State v. Pritchard, 36 N. J. L. 101; Dullan v. Wilson, 53 Mich. 392; State v. Peterson, 50 Minn. 241.

[3] State v. Hawkins, 44 Ohio St. 98; Donahue v. County of Wills, 100 Ill. 94.

[4] People v. Steward, 74 Mich. 411, 16 Am. St. Rep. 644; Wood v. Varnum, 83 Cal. 46.

[5] State v. Superior, 90 Wis. 612, 64 N. W. Rep. 304; People v. French, 102 N. Y. 583; People v. Therrein, 80 Mich. 187.

[6] People v. McClave, 123 N. Y. 512, 35 N. E. Rep. 1047.

[7] People v. Mirton, 19 Colo. 565, 24 L. R. A. 201; Speed v. Detroit, 98 Mich. 360, 22 L. R. A. 842; Mechem, Pub. Off., § 447.

[8] State v. Peterson, 50 Minn. 239; Westberg v. Kansas City, 64 Mo. 493; Shannon v. Portsmouth, 54 N. H. 183. But see State v. Jersey City, 25 N. J. L. 537. The suspension cannot be indefinitely without pay. Gregory v. New York, 113 N. Y. 416.

[9] State v. Johnson, 30 Fla. 433, 18 L. R. A. 410. The notice is not a judicial writ, nor need it be authenticated by the great seal. Attorney-General v. Jochim, 99 Mich. 358, 23 L. R. A. 699.

[10] Dullam v. Wilson, 53 Mich. 392, 51 Am. Rep. 128; Wellman v. Board, 84 Mich. 558, 47 N. W. Rep. 559; State v. Jersey City, 25 N. J. L. 537; State

as to affect the performance of the duties of the office.¹ The causes usually designated are wilful neglect of duty, incompetence, habitual drunkenness and corruption in office.² The misconduct which will justify removal must consist of acts and conduct relating to the office from which the removal is sought.³ The office is vacated by a legal and authorized amotion. A judge whose term of office is fixed by the constitution cannot be deprived of his office by a statute which attempts to abolish the judicial district to which he belongs.⁴

§ 277. *Personal liability on contracts.*— The courts are frequently called upon to determine the individual liability of municipal officers upon instruments signed by such officers with their official designation added. If such instruments are made with authority and intent to bind the municipality, the corporation is liable. But both the corporation and officer may be liable on the same instrument. If, for example, the selectmen of a town offer a reward for the arrest and conviction of a criminal, and such public officers sign their names individually, with the designation "Selectmen of Milton," they do not, by adding their official designation, take away from their names their ordinary significance as proper names, and make of their collective signatures a composite unit. The promise being otherwise in the usual and proper form for a personal undertaking, they are personally liable.⁵ If it appears from the instrument that the officer did not intend to assume personal liability, he will not be rendered liable by the fact that the instrument

v. Gary, 21 Wis. 496. This will depend upon the intent of the legislature as gathered from the statute. People v. Higgins, 15 Ill. 110.

¹ Clapp v. Board of Police, 72 N. Y. 415; Rogers v. Morrill, 55 Kan. 737, 42 Pac. Rep. 555.

² State v. Savage, 89 Ala. 1, 7 L. R. A. 426.

³ Speed v. Detroit, 98 Mich. 360, 22 L. R. A. 842. A register of deeds may be removed for making a false certificate as to the condition of the title, although the making of such certificate is not part of the duties of his office. State v. Leach, 60 Me.

58, 11 Am. Rep. 172. Receiving a bribe is "disorderly conduct" within the meaning of a provision conferring upon the council authority to expel a member for disorderly conduct. State v. Jersey City, 25 N. J. L. 536. An expelled member of a city council may be re-elected, and cannot thereafter be again expelled for the same offense. State v. Jersey City, *supra.*

⁴ State v. Friedley, 135 Ind. 119, 21 L. R. A. 634.

⁵ Brown v. Bradlee, 156 Mass. 28, 15 L. R. A. 509.

§ 278.]   GOVERNING BODIES, OFFICERS AND AGENTS.   247

is invalid in so far as it purports to bind the corporation.[1] But where the signers of the note made the promise "as trustees of school district" they are not individually liable, the intention to bind the school district being plain.[2] If the promise of a public agent is connected with a subject fairly within the scope of his authority, it will be presumed to have been made officially and in his public character, unless it clearly appears that he intended to bind himself personally.[3] For example, if gravel is sold on the credit of the town upon the order of a surveyor of highways who has authority to make the purchase, the town and not the surveyor is responsible.[4] But if an overseer of the poor, in contracting for the support of a pauper, engages that he will be responsible for the payment of the charges, and credit is given on his personal promise, he is liable.[5]

§ 278. *Liability in tort.*— An officer charged with discretionary power is not responsible in damages unless it be shown that he has acted arbitrarily and in clear violation of law.[6] It is a general rule that an action for neglect of an official duty can be maintained against ministerial officers only. "There are, however, many cases of powers not discretionary, for the manner of whose performance there can be no responsibility to individuals. The sheriff, for example, is under no responsibility to individuals for any neglect of duty in respect to the execution of a convict, though in such a matter he is allowed no discretion. Plainly, it is not only because duties are discretionary that officers are exempt from civil suits in respect to their performance. No man can have any ground for private action until some duty owing to him has been neglected. The rule of official responsibility, then, may be stated thus: If the duty imposed upon an officer is a duty to the public, a failure to perform it or an inadequate or erroneous performance is a public injury and must be redressed, if at all, in some form of public

[1] Willitt v. Young, 82 Iowa, 292, 11 L. R. A. 115.
[2] Sanborn v. Neal, 4 Minn. 126, 77 Am. Dec. 502; Lyon v. Adamson, 7 Iowa, 509.
[3] Parks v. Ross, 11 How. (U. S.) 362.
[4] Brown v. Rundlett, 15 N. H. 360.
And see Hall v. Lauderdale, 46 N. Y. 70.
[5] Ives v. Hulet, 12 Vt. 314; King v. Butler, 15 Johns. (N. Y.) 281.
[6] Boutte v. Emer, 43 La. Ann. 980, 15 L. R. A. 63. As to liability for arrest without warrant, see note in 8 L. R. A. 529.

prosecution. But if, on the contrary, the duty is a duty to an individual, then the neglect to perform it properly is an individual wrong and may support an individual action for damages."[1] One who has actually exercised the functions of a public officer is estopped to deny, for the purpose of escaping liability, that he properly held the office. And so the rule respecting the disability of officers applies not only to those who hold the office of right, but also to those who are officers *de facto* only.[2] Immunity from private suits depends not upon the grade of the office but upon the nature of the duty. A policeman, for example, is one of the lowest in grade of public officers, but if by reason of his neglect of duty a breach of the peace results and loss accrues to an individual the latter cannot hold him liable for his neglect. If a highway commissioner declines to lay out a road which an individual desires, or discontinues one which it is for his interest to have retained, there is a damage to the individual, but no wrong to him. Damage alone does not constitute a wrong.[3] If the officer fails to regard sufficiently the interests of individuals in his official action, it is a breach of public duty of which the state alone can complain.[4]

§ 279. *Liability of officers acting judicially.*—The rule that judicial officers cannot be held personally liable for the improper or erroneous performance of their duties when acting within their jurisdiction[5] shields the members of an equalizing board, or board of review of assessments, from liability for damages for corruptly and oppressively increasing the valuation of certain property.[6] The same rule protects inspectors of fruits and meats acting in the interest of the public health;[7] assessors on whom is imposed the duty of valuing property for the purpose of a levy of taxes;[8] officers empowered to lay out, alter and discontinue highways;[9] members of a town board in decid-

[1] Cooley, Elements of Torts, 146; Moss v. Cummings, 44 Mich. 359.
[2] Billingsley v. State, 14 Md. 869; Trescott v. Moan, 50 Me. 347.
[3] Waterer v. Freeman, Hob. 266.
[4] Sage v. Laurain, 19 Mich. 137.
[5] Lange v. Benedict, 73 N. Y. 12; Yates v. Lansing, 5 Johns. 282, 9 Johns. 395, 6 Am. Dec. 290, annotated; Mostyn v. Fabrigas, Cowp. 161; Smith's L. C. 1027; Jordan v. Hansom, 49 N. H. 199, 6 Am. Rep. 508.
[6] Steele v. Dunham, 26 Wis. 393.
[7] Fath v. Koeppel, 72 Wis. 289, 7 Am. St. Rep. 867.
[8] Weaver v. Devendorf, 3 Den. (N. Y.) 117; Cooley on Taxation, 551 et seq.
[9] Sage v. Laurain, 19 Mich. 137.

ing upon the allowance of claims,[1] and all officers exercising judicial powers, whatever they may be called. The members of a board of street commissioners, in determining upon work and adopting plans and specifications therefor, act as judicial officers and are amenable to the public alone for errors, negligence or misfeasance in the matters within their jurisdiction. But if, after adopting the plans and specifications, they undertake to carry them out practically and to do the work themselves, employing agents and servants, they are liable to third persons for negligence or misfeasance, as they act in a ministerial capacity.[2] The tendency is toward abolishing the distinction between the liability of judges of superior and inferior courts. Thus, it is held that a justice of the peace is protected from personal liability for judicial acts in excess of his jurisdiction if he acts in good faith.[3] So a constable is not liable for executing a writ on a justice's judgment if the justice is not liable.[4] A mayor is not liable for an erroneous order maliciously made if the making of such an order was within his jurisdiction.[5]

§ 280. *Liability of recorder of deeds.*— With regard to certain offices the public is incidentally benefited by the performance of duties to individuals, instead of individuals being benefited by the performance of public duties. For example, the recorder of deeds is a public officer; but in recording conveyances and furnishing abstracts or notice from the record to those who request them and tender the legal fees, he performs duties to individuals only, the performance of which the state is not expected to enforce. The breach of the duty is a wrong to the individual, and the right to private action follows as of course.[6] By refusing to record a conveyance tendered to him for that purpose with the proper fees, or if, having undertaken to record the instrument, he records it inaccurately, the recorder

[1] Wall v. Trumbull, 16 Mich. 228.
[2] Robinson v. Rohr, 73 Wis. 436, 2 L. R. A. 366.
[3] Austin v. Vrooman, 128 N. Y. 229, 14 L. R. A. 138, annotated; Williamson v. Lacy, 86 Me. 80, 25 L. R. A. 506; Thompson v. Jackson, 93 Iowa, 376, 27 L. R. A. 92, annotated; Bishop, Non-Contract Law, § 783; Cooley, Torts, § 419; Brooks v. Morgan, 86 Mich. 576. But see Bradley v. Fisher, 13 Wall. (U. S.) 335; Houlden v. Smith, 3 Moore, P. C. C. 75; Grumon v. Raymond, 1 Conn. 40, 6 Am. Dec. 200.
[4] Scott v. Fishbate, 117 N. C. 265, 30 L. R. A. 696.
[5] Thompson v. Jackson, 93 Iowa, 376, 27 L. R. A. 92.
[6] Clark v. Miller, 54 N. Y. 528; Kirth v. Howard, 24 Pick. 202.

commits an actionable wrong. There is a conflict of authority on the question as to who is entitled to maintain an action for damages resulting from recording an instrument incorrectly. As between the grantee in a deed incorrectly recorded and another person claiming under a subsequent conveyance by the same grantor which has been recorded while the first record remained uncorrected, it has been held that the grantee in the first deed is not to be prejudiced by the recorder's error.[1] So under a statute which made the deed operative as a record from the time it was delivered by the grantee for the purpose, a similar ruling was made.[2] Probably, however, the cost of the new record would be the measure of recovery, unless the erroneous record stands in the way of a sale by the grantee, or in some such way works actual damage. If, however, the deed were lost or destroyed, the grantee's title would incur a double danger, and the question of remote and proximate cause would be involved. But in many of the states by statute a purchaser is bound to look no further than the record, and he must suffer whose deed has been incorrectly recorded.[3] A recorder may be responsible for recording papers not entitled to record if he is aware that the record is unauthorized and if it may cause a legal injury.[4] He is liable also if he gives an erroneous certificate which it is his duty to give and to a person having a right to it, that being an official act. But if the giving of the certificate is not an official act he is not liable.[5] And whatever liability is incurred in such a case is to the person for whom the certificate is made and not to his grantee.[6]

[1] Merrick v. Wallace, 19 Ill. 486. But see Ritchie v. Griffiths, 1 Wash. 429, 12 L. R. A. 384.

[2] Mims v. Mims, 35 Ala. 23; Chandler v. Scott, 127 Ind. 226, 10 L. R. A. 875.

[3] Ramsey v. Riley, 13 Ohio, 157.

[4] Van Schaick v. Sigel, 60 How. Pr. 122; Mallory v. Ferguson, 50 Kan. 685, 22 L. R. A. 99 and note.

[5] Mallory v. Ferguson, *supra;* Frost v. Beekman, 1 Johns. Ch. 288.

[6] See Satterfield v. Malone, 35 Fed. Rep. 445, 1 L. R. A. 35. For rulings on this point under the statutes of the respective states see the following cases: Mims v. Mims, 35 Ala. 23; Fouche v. Swain, 80 Ala. 153; Oats v. Walls, 28 Ark. 244; Myers v. Spooner, 55 Cal. 262; Weese v. Barker, 7 Colo. 181; Hine v. Robbins, 8 Conn. 347; Shepherd v. Burkhalter, 13 Ga. 447; Benson v. Green, 80 Ga. 230; Cook v. Hall, 6 Ill. 579; Worcester Nat. Bank v. Cheeney, 87 Ill. 602; Gilchrist v. Gough, 63 Ind. 588; Miller v. Bradford, 12 Iowa, 19; Miller v. Ware, 31 Iowa, 524; Poplin v. Mundell, 27 Kan. 159; Payne v. Pavey, 29 La. Ann. 116; Lewis v. Koltz, 30 La. Ann. 259; Handley v. Howe, 22 Me. 562; Hill v. McNichol, 76 Me. 315; Bryden v. Campbell, 40 Md. 338; Gil-

§ 281. *Liability of sheriff.*— A sheriff in serving a civil process is charged with duties only to the parties to the proceeding. He is liable to the plaintiff[1] for refusal or neglect to serve process, or want of diligence in such service, or for neglect or refusal to return process,[2] or for making a false return,[3] or for neglect to pay over moneys collected.[4] If the officer has levied upon property he must keep the property with reasonable care, and his breach of this duty affords ground for an action on behalf of each party to the writ.[5] If the sheriff is directed to levy upon goods of a person named, he must at his peril ascertain who the real defendant is and make service upon him.[6] In deciding as to the identity of the real owner he is not exercising a judicial function, and is liable if on execution against one person he by mistake seizes the goods of another. A sheriff is generally responsible for the misfeasance or non-feasance of his deputies. The deputy, however, is not such a private agent as to make the sheriff responsible when the deputy is employed to do something because of his office which the law does not require the sheriff officially to perform, as in serving a distress warrant[7] or selling the property on foreclosure of a chattel mortgage.[8] The law imposes no duty on a deputy as such. For omissions to act, therefore, he is not responsible, not being bound to act. For tortious acts of a deputy under color of the officer's authority, not only the deputy, but the officer himself, is liable. "Whenever the plaintiff must state the official character of the party sued, as one of the allegations on which the defendant's liability depends, the principal only is responsible. But where the *corpus delicti* is a thing of active wrong and a trespass *per se* unless justified, then the hand that does or pro-

lespie v. Rogers, 146 Mass. 612; Sinclair v. Slawson, 44 Mich. 127; Parrott v. Shaubhut, 5 Minn. 331; Terrell v. Andrew Co., 44 Mo. 309; Converse v. Porter, 45 N. H. 399; Musser v. Hyde, 2 W. & S. 314; Shelle v. Bryden, 114 Pa. St. 147; Throckmorton v. Price, 28 Tex. 609; Sawyer v. Adams, 8 Vt. 172; Bigelow v. Topliff, 25 Vt. 282; Shove v. Larsen, 22 Wis. 142; Lombard v. Culbertson, 59 Wis. 433. See Ritchie v. Griffith, 1 Wash. 429, 12 L. R. A. 384, and note.

[1] Howe v. White, 49 Cal. 658.
[2] State v. Schar, 50 Mo. 393.
[3] State v. Finn, 87 Mo. 310.
[4] Norton v. Nye, 56 Me. 211; Nash v. Muldoon, 16 Nev. 404.
[5] Abbott v. Kimball, 19 Vt. 551, 47 Am. Dec. 708.
[6] Screws v. Watson, 48 Ala. 628. See, also, Thomas v. Markman, 43 Neb. 843, 62 N. W. Rep. 206.
[7] Moulton v. Moulton. 5 Barb. 286.
[8] Door v. Mickley, 16 Minn. 20 (Gil. 8).

cures the act is liable."[1] But in cases where deputy-sheriffs are appointed by the sheriff subject to the approval of the judge of the circuit court, his power of appointment comes from the state and his authority is derived from the law.[2]

§ 282. *Highway officers.*— If a ministerial officer has the funds at his command with which to discharge the duty incumbent upon him, he is responsible to parties injured by his neglect. But he cannot be in fault unless the funds are provided for the purpose, or unless by virtue of his office he may raise the necessary means by levying a tax or in some other mode. Thus, commissioners having charge of the cutting and keeping open of public drains will be liable, after the drains are once cut, if they suffer them to become obstructed to the injury of neighboring lands when they have the means at their command to keep them open.[3] The decisions are conflicting as to the liability to individuals of an officer who has charge of the duty of making and repairing highways and public bridges. In an early New York case, where an individual, injured in consequence of a bridge being out of repair, had brought suit against the overseer of highways, it was held that the overseer's duty was owing to the public and not to individuals.[4] This decision has been followed in several states,[5] but by later decisions in New York highway commissioners are held responsible to individuals for failure to keep the public ways in repair so far as they have the means of doing so. "Defective bridges are dangerous," said the court in an important case, "and travelers generally have no means of knowing whether they are safe or not. They have to rely upon the fidelity and vigilance of the highway officers, who are the only persons whose duty it is to see that the bridges are in repair."[6] A similar liability exists in other states by statute.[7]

[1] Coltraine v. McCaine, 3 Dev. Law (N. C.), 308, 24 Am. Dec. 256.
[2] State v. Bus, 125 Mo. 335, 33 L. R. A. 616.
[3] Child v. Boston, 4 Allen, 41, 81 Am. Dec. 680.
[4] Bartlett v. Crozier, 17 Johns. 449, 8 Am. Dec. 428.
[5] See Dunlap v. Knapp, 14 Ohio St. 64; McConnell v. Dewey, 5 Neb. 385; Lynn v. Adams, 2 Ind. 143.
[6] Hover v. Barkhoof, 44 N. Y. 113, 125.
[7] See Hathaway v. Hinton, 1 Jones (N. C.), 243; County Com'rs v. Gibson, 36 Md. 229.

§ 283. *Liability of various officers.*— The members of a board of health are personally liable for damages occasioned by the negligent manner of removing one afflicted with a contagious disease, without proof of malice or gross negligence.[1] A supervisor is personally liable for damages resulting from his neglect to report a claim to a county board after allowance.[2] A clerk of court is liable for damages occasioned by his neglect to put a case on the docket,[3] and for approving an appeal bond with a penalty less than that required by law,[4] or for failing to enter a judgment properly.[5] The purchasers of meat who rely upon the inspection of a public inspector may maintain an action against the inspector for damages caused by the neglect of his duty.[6]

§ 284. *Liability for loss of public funds.*— In some states an officer is regarded as the debtor of the corporation and not as a bailee or trustee of funds intrusted to his care, and is liable for such funds, without reference to the cause of their loss. This is the rule of liability in those states where the officer has the right to use the money as his own and to retain any interest or profit that the funds may earn. It has no application where the officer is considered as a trustee charged with certain duties and responsibilities and where he is held to have no right to the income of the funds. In some states it is made a felony for the officer to use the public funds directly or indirectly, or to receive or to agree to receive interest for their use or deposit.[7] In other cases the officer is held liable on broad grounds of public policy, and the obligations resting upon him are made absolute and unconditional because a different construction would open up the door for fraudulent practices and evasions by public officials. Many of the cases holding officials liable for public funds, lost without their fault or negligence, are decided under local statutes, but a number

[1] In Aaron v. Broils, 64 Tex. 316, 53 Am. St. Rep. 764, it was held that while the board of health, mayor and marshal of a city might remove from the city persons afflicted with small-pox, they were liable for negligence in doing so, and for removing them in stormy weather and putting them in an unsafe and unprotected tent, whereby they were so exposed that death ensued.
[2] Clark v. Miller, 54 N. Y. 528.
[3] Brown v. Lester, 21 Miss. 392.
[4] Billings v. Lafferty, 31 Ill. 318.
[5] Douglass v. Yallup, Burr. 722.
[6] Hayes v. Porter, 22 Me. 371.
[7] State v. Copeland, 96 Tenn. 296, 31 L. R. A. 844.

of them rest squarely on principles of public policy. "It shocks the sense of justice," said the court in a recent case,[1] "that the public officials should be held to any greater liability than the old rule of the common law which exacted proof of misconduct or neglect. It is at this point, however, that the question of public policy presents itself, and it may well be asked whether it is not wiser to subject a custodian of the public moneys to the strictest liability rather than open the door for the perpetration of frauds in numberless ways impossible of detection, thereby placing in jeopardy the enormous amount of the public funds constantly passing through the hands of disbursing agents." Hence the court in this case held that a supervisor who acted in good faith and without negligence was liable for public moneys lost by the failure of a firm of private bankers with whom the money had been deposited. In other cases the liability of the officer is made to turn upon the terms of his bond, and is construed as having been enlarged by the bond and made an absolute engagement to pay over the money in any event and under every contingency. This rule has been adopted in many cases on the authority of an important decision of the supreme court of the United States, where it was held that an officer under bond to "keep safely" must make good the public funds stolen from him without his fault.[2] This stringent rule was modified, however, in a later decision of that tribunal, where it was held that an officer was excused by the act of God or the public enemy.[3]

[1] Tillinghast v. Merrill, 151 N. Y. 135, 34 L. R. A. 678.
[2] United States v. Prescott, 44 U. S. 589. To the same effect are United States v. Dashiel, 71 U. S. 182; United States v. Morgan, 52 U. S. 154; Boyden v. United States, 80 U. S. 17; State v. Nevin, 19 Nev. 162; State v. Lanier, 31 La. Ann. 423; Jefferson Co. Com'rs v. Lineberger, 3 Mont. 231, 35 Am. Rep. 562; Redwood Co. Com'rs v. Tower, 28 Minn. 45; State v. Blair, 76 N. C. 78; Hancock v. Hazzard, 12 Cush. 112, 59 Am. Dec. 171; State v. Harper, 6 Ohio St. 607, 67 Am. Dec. 363. These are principally cases where the money had been stolen from the office or house of the official, in some cases where it had been placed in a private safe, and in others where it had been taken from a safe furnished by the county. The same rule has been adopted in other instances where the money had been lost through the failure of a bank in which it had been deposited. State v. Moore, 74 Mo. 413, 41 Am. Rep. 322; State v. Powle, 67 Mo. 395, 29 Am. Rep. 512; Ward v. Colfax Co., 10 Neb. 293, 35 Am. Rep. 477; Lowry v. Polk Co., 51 Iowa, 50, 33 Am. Rep. 113; State v. Croft, 24 Ark. 560; Havens v. Lathene, 75 N. C. 505.
[3] United States v. Thomas, 82 U. S.

The tendency of the authorities is to revert to the common-law rule of liability and to hold the officer intrusted with public funds, not an insurer against loss, but "liable only if he acts without proper diligence, caution, prudence and good faith." "We believe," said the court in one case,[1] "the true rule is that a public officer who receives money by virtue of his office is a bailee and that the extent of his obligation is that imposed by law; that when unaffected by constitutional or legislative provisions his duty and liability is measured by the law of bailment. If a more stringent obligation is desired, it must be prescribed by statute; that his official bond does not extend to such obligation, but its office is to secure the faithful and prompt performance of his legal duties."

§ 285. *Manner of trying title to office.*— The title to an office cannot be determined in a collateral proceeding, although sufficient inquiry may be made to determine whether the occupant is a mere intruder.[2] If one in possession of an office seeks to have a court review the proceeding of a board of aldermen which interferes with his enjoyment of the office, the proper

---

337. Mr. Justice Bradley, delivering the opinion in this case and treating of the contention that the bond forms the basis of a new rule of responsibility, called attention to the distinction between an absolute agreement to do a thing and a condition to do the same thing inserted in the bond, and said: "The condition of an official bond is collateral to the obligation or penalty; it is not based on a prior debt nor is it evidence of a debt, and the duty secured thereby does not become a debt until default is made on the part of the principal. Until then, as we have seen, he is a bailee, though a bailee resting under special obligations. The condition of his bond is not to pay a debt but to perform a duty about and respecting certain and specific property which is not his and which he cannot use for his own purposes."

[1] See Wilson v. People, Pueblo & A. V. R. Co., 19 Colo. 199, 22 L. R. A.

449. See cases cited where, by the constitution and the statutes, the common-law liability of certain officers was increased. State v. Walsen, 17 Colo. 170; McClure v. La Platte Com'rs, 19 Colo. 122. In York County v. Watson, 15 S. C. 1, 40 Am. Rep. 675, a county treasurer was held not responsible for public moneys deposited in a bank which had borne a good reputation. The court said that the public officer was no more responsible than a private trustee would be under like circumstances. In Cumberland County v. Pennell, 69 Me. 357, 31 Am. Rep. 284, a county treasurer was held not liable for money taken from his safe in his office by robbers who had first beaten him. See, also, Strout v. Pennell, 74 Me. 262; State v. Houston, 78 Ala. 576, 56 Am. Rep. 59; State v. Copeland, 96 Tenn. 296, 31 L. R. A. 844.

[2] United States v. Alexander, 46 Fed. Rep. 728.

remedy is *certiorari*. When the title of one in possession is to be tried, the proper remedy is *quo warranto* and not *mandamus*.[1] The title to an office cannot be tried in an action of replevin for property belonging to the office. As a general rule the appropriate remedy for the particular case is provided by statute.[2]

[1] Denver v. Darrow, 13 Colo. 460, 16 Am. St. Rep. 215, and note. The writ of *mandamus* being a prerogative writ and not a writ of right may be granted or not, in the discretion of the court. Reg. v. Churchwardens, 1 App. Cas. 611, 35 L. T. 381. That *quo warranto* is the appropriate remedy to settle title to office conclusively, see Rex v. Mayor of Colchester, 2 T. R. 259, 7 Eng. Rul. Cas. 328; Leeds v. Atlantic City, 52 N. J. L. 333; Matter of Gardner, 68 N. Y. 467; Duane v. McDonald, 41 Conn. 517; St. Louis Co. Court v. Sparks, 10 Mo. 117, 45 Am. Dec. 355; Bonner v. State, 7 Ga. 473; People v. Kilduff, 15 Ill. 492; Frey v. Michie, 68 Mich. 323; State v. Choate, 11 Ohio, 511; State v. De Gress, 53 Tex. 387; Com. v. Meeser, 44 Pa. St. 341; State v. Dunn, Minor, 46, 12 Am. Dec. 25; State v. Oates, 86 Wis. 634, 39 Am. St. Rep. 912; Brown v. Turner, 70 N. C. 93. In some states *mandamus* is used for this purpose. See Luce v. Board of Examiners, 153 Mass. 108; Dew v. Judges, 3 Hen. & Munf. 1, 8 Am. Dec. 639; Harwood v. Marshall, 9 Md. 83; Lawrence v. Ingersoll, 88 Tenn. 52, 17 Am. St. Rep. 870; Boston v. Wilson, 4 Tex. 400. "*Quo warranto* lies to oust an illegal incumbent from an office, not to induct the legal officer into it." State v. Sone, 16 R. I. 620. The validity of the acts of an officer *de facto* can be questioned only by a direct proceeding in *quo warranto* to determine title to his office. Walcott v. Wells, 21 Nev. 47, 37 Am. St. Rep. 478.

[2] Hallgren v. Campbell, 82 Mich. 255, 9 L. R. A. 408.

BOOK IV.

THE LIABILITIES OF PUBLIC CORPORATIONS.

CHAPTER XV.

LIABILITY ON CONTRACTS.

§ 286. General liability.
287. Presentation and demand.
288. The doctrine of *ultra vires*.
289. Estoppel — Contract executed by one party.
290. Contract within scope of general powers.

§ 291. Contract in part *ultra vires*.
292. Liability on implied contract.
293. Illustrations.
294. Right to recover back illegal taxes.
295. Payment must be compulsory.
296. Voluntary payment.

§ 286. *General liability.*— A public corporation is liable upon a contract which is within the scope of its chartered powers when duly made by the proper officers in the same manner and to the same extent as a private corporation or a natural person. It may be sued like any individual, and may resort to the courts to enforce its rights and redress its wrongs.[1]

§ 287. *Presentation and demand.*— Municipal charters ordinarily contain a provision that no action shall be commenced on any "claim" or "claim or demand" until the same shall have been presented for allowance to the city council.[2] Similar provisions often limit the time within which an action may be brought against the corporation.[3] While the words "claim" and "demand" have a very wide significance, they are not construed as including claims arising out of torts.[4] At common law it is not necessary to present a claim arising on tort before bringing suit.[5] If the council neglects to act upon a demand

---

[1] Buffalo v. Bettinger, 76 N. Y. 393.
[2] Kelley v. Madison, 43 Wis. 638.
[3] McGaffin v. Cohoes, 74 N. Y. 387.

[4] Nance v. Falls City, 16 Neb. 85; Flieth v. Wausau, 93 Wis. 448.
[5] Green v. Spencer, 67 Iowa, 410.

within the sixty days fixed by the charter, it is equivalent to a refusal to allow it.[1]

§ 288. *The doctrine of ultra vires.*—A public corporation derives all its powers from its charter, and the general rule is that it cannot bind itself by any contract in excess of the powers thus conferred upon it.[2] Hence it necessarily follows that *ultra vires* contracts are not enforceable.[3] This doctrine has with good reason been applied with greater strictness to municipal bodies than to private corporations, and in general a municipality is not estopped from denying the validity of a contract made by its officers when there was no authority for the making of such contract.[4] The harshness of the rule has in practice led to the adoption of certain modifications which seem

[1] Fleming v. Appleton, 55 Wis. 90.

[2] City of Eufaula v. McNab, 67 Ala. 588; Swift v. Falmouth, 167 Mass. 115, 45 N. E. Rep. 184; Alleghaney Co. v. Parrish, 93 Va. 615, 25 S. E. Rep. 882. Much of the apparent confusion in the law of *ultra vires* is due to the use of the words in different senses. It is used to characterize (1) an act of the directors or officers in excess of their authority as agents of the corporation; (2) an act of the majority of the stockholders in violation of the rights of the minority; (3) an act done in disregard of the requirements of the charter; (4) an act which the corporation has not the power to do, as being in excess of the corporate powers. In a recent work it is said: "For a time, whenever an element of uncertainty in the views expressed by the courts as to whether or not the doctrine should be applied only to the acts of a corporation as such, or whether it should not also be applied to acts of the directors or officers which were in excess of the authority given them in the management of the internal affairs of the corporation. In the former sense only is the doctrine legitimately applicable." Reece, Ultra Vires, § 17. In Camden, etc. R. Co. v. May's Land-ing, etc. Co., 48 N. J. L. 530, the court said: "In its legitimate use, the expression *ultra vires* should be applied only to such acts as are beyond the powers of the corporation itself." See dissenting opinion. In Chicago, etc. R. Co. v. Union Pac. R. Co., 47 Fed. Rep. 15, Mr. Justice Brewer said: "Two propositions are settled. One is that a contract by which a corporation disables itself from performing the functions and duties undertaken and imposed by its charter is, unless the state which creates it consents, *ultra vires*. . . . The other is that the powers of a corporation are such, and such only, as its charter confers; and an act beyond the measure of those powers as either expressly stated or fairly implied is *ultra vires*. . . . These two propositions embrace the whole doctrine of *ultra vires*. They are its alpha and omega."

[3] Cooley, Const. Lim., p. 261; Dillon, Mun. Corp., I, § 457.

[4] Newberry v. Fox, 37 Minn. 141, 51 Am. St. Rep. 830; Sutro v. Pettit, 74 Cal. 332, 5 Am. St. Rep. 442; Thompson, Corp., V, § 5069. For a strict application of the rule see Mayor of Nashville v. Sutherland, 92 Tenn. 335, 19 L. R. A. 619.

necessary in order to do justice between the parties. It has thus been materially modified by the application of the doctrines of estoppel and implied contract.

§ 289. *Estoppel— Contract executed by one party.*— The general rule is that there can be no estoppel when the contract is illegal in the sense of being forbidden by law, or where there is a total want of power on the part of the corporation.[1] But where an act is in its external aspects within the general powers of a corporation, but is unauthorized because it is done with a secret unauthorized intent, the defense of *ultra vires* will not avail against a stranger who in good faith dealt with the corporation without notice of such intent.[2] Although there is some conflict of authorities, the logical rule would seem to be that, when the corporation is estopped to assert the defense of *ultra vires*, the liability thus enforced is on the contract.[3] Thus, it was said that "although there might be a defect of power in a corporation to make contracts, yet if a contract made by it is not in violation of its charter or of any statute prohibiting it, and the corporation has by its promise induced the party relying on the promise and in execution of the promise to expend money and perform his part thereof, the corporation *is liable on the contract.*"[4] A party who is sued on a contract with the city may defend on the ground that the city had no power to make the contract.[5] There can be no recovery upon a contract

---

[1] In King v. Mahaska Co., 75 Iowa, 329, it was held that a contractor for the building of a court-house could not recover for extra work where it created a cost in excess of the amount which the people had voted for the law. In Goose River Bank v. Willow Lake School Township, 1 N. Dak. 26, it was held that a school teacher who lacked the necessary legal qualifications could not recover for services rendered.

[2] Dillon, Mun. Corp., I, § 936.

[3] It is uncertain whether there is an action *on the contract.* See Dillon, Mun. Corp., I, § 414, note, and the cases cited in the next note; Thompson, Corp., V, § 5968; Central Tp. Co. v. Pullman Palace Car Co., 139 U. S. 22.

[4] State Board of Agriculture v. Citizens' St. Ry. Co., 47 Ind. 407, 17 Am. Rep. 702. This language is quoted with approval by Mr. Justice Strong in Hitchcock v. Galveston, 96 U. S. 351, in Columbus Water Works v. Mayor of Columbus, 48 Kan. 99, 15 L. R. A. 354, and in Illinois Tr. & Sav. Bank v. Arkansas City, 76 Fed. Rep. 271, 40 U. S. App. 257, 34 L. R. A. 518. In Boss Machine Works v. Park Co. Com'rs, 115 Ind. 234, the court said: "The doctrine of *ultra vires* does not absolve municipal corporations from the principle of common honesty."

[5] Montgomery City Council v. Montgomery, etc. Ry. Co., 81 Ala. 76.

which is illegal in the sense of being absolutely prohibited by law.[1]

§ 290. *Contracts within scope of general powers.* — Cities often enter into contracts which are within the scope of their general powers, but which are made in an irregular manner, or contain *ultra vires* conditions or provisions. A mere irregularity in the exercise of power cannot be asserted as a defense against one who has in good faith parted with value for the benefit of the corporation.[2] In a well known case[3] it appeared that the city had entered into a contract with certain contractors, by the terms of which they were to pave its streets and receive the negotiable bonds of the city in payment therefor. The city had power to pave the streets but not to issue the bonds. In an action for damages for a breach of the contract the court said: "The present is not a case in which the issue of the bonds was prohibited by any statute. At most, the issue was unauthorized. At most, there was a defect of power. The promise to give bonds to the plaintiffs in payment of what they undertook to do was therefore, at furthest, only *ultra vires;* and in such a case, though specific performance of an engagement to do a thing transgressive of its corporate power may not be enforced, the corporation can be held liable on its contract. Having received benefit at the expense of the other contracting party, it cannot object that it was not empowered to perform what it promised in return in the mode in which it promised to perform." Elsewhere the court said: "They are not suing upon the bonds, and it is not necessary to their success that they should assert the validity of those instruments. It is enough for them that the city council have power to enter into a contract for the improvement of the sidewalk; that such a contract was made with them; that under it they have proceeded to furnish materials and do work as well as to assume

[1] McDonald v. New York, 68 N. Y. 23, 23 Am. Rep. 144; Argenti v. San Francisco, 16 Cal. 256.

[2] Moore v. New York, 73 N. Y. 238. The distinction between cases where the contract is entirely outside of the granted powers and cases where the particular contract is within the general scope of the corporate pow-

ers, but *ultra vires* because of some particular circumstance, is fully explained by Chief Justice Sawyer in Miner's Ditch Co. v. Zellerbach, 37 Cal. 543, 99 Am. Dec. 300. See, also, Northwestern Union Packet Co. v. Shaw, 37 Wis. 655, 19 Am. Rep. 781.

[3] Hitchcock v. Galveston, 96 U. S. 341.

liability; that the city has received and now enjoys the benefit of what they have done and furnished; that for these things the city promised to pay; and that after having received the benefit of the contract the city has broken it. It matters not that the promise was to pay in a manner not authorized by law. If payments cannot be made in bonds because their issue is *ultra vires*, it would be sanctioning rank injustice to hold that payment need not be made at all. Such is not the law. The contract between the parties is in force so far as it is lawful."

§ 291. *Contract in part ultra vires.*— An entire contract is not necessarily invalid because a part thereof is *ultra vires*. It is said that a court should not destroy a contract made by parties further than some good reason requires.[1] Thus, where a city had power to provide for gas, and entered into a contract with a corporation to furnish it for the city, and as a part of the contract granted to the corporation the exclusive right to use the streets, it was held that the granting of the exclusive franchise was beyond the power of the city. But the court said:[2] " No reason occurs to us why, under this state of facts, the gas company or its successors may not waive the exclusive right and recover the remainder of the consideration which the city promised to pay. The grant of this exclusive right was neither immoral nor illegal. It was merely *ultra vires*. We know of no rule of law nor of morals which relieves the recipient of the substantial benefits of a partially-executed contract from the obligation to perform or pay that part of the consideration which he can perform or pay because the performance of an insignificant portion of it is beyond his power. On the other hand, the true rule is and ought to be the converse of that proposition. It is that when a part of a divisible contract is *ultra vires*, but neither *malum in se* nor *malum prohibitum*, the remainder may be enforced, unless it appears from a consideration of the whole contract that it would not have been made independently of the part which was void."[3]

[1] In East St. Louis v. East St. Louis Gas Co., 98 Ill. 415, it appeared that the city had entered into a contract to furnish lights for a number of years. This contract was held beyond its powers, but the court held that there could be a recovery for the lights actually furnished. See the statement of the rule in Brown v. Atchison, 39 Kan. 54.

[2] Illinois Trust & Sav. Bank v. Arkansas City, 76 Fed. Rep. 271, 40 U. S. App. 257, 34 L. R. A. 518 (Sanborn, J.).

[3] Oregon St. Nav. Co. v. Winsor,

§ 292. *Liability on implied contract.*— The strict doctrine of *ultra vires* is further modified by the rule that when a contract has been performed by one party and money or property has thus come into the possession of the corporation and been applied to its use, the law presumes a contract to restore such property to the rightful owner.[1] This implication is based on the theory that "the obligation to do justice rests upon all persons, natural and artificial; and if the county obtains the money or property of others without authority, the law, independent of any statute, will compel restitution or compensation." In one of the leading cases[2] Chief Justice Field said: "The doctrine of implied municipal obligation applies to cases where money or other property of the party is received under such circumstances that the general law, independent of express contract, imposes the obligation upon the city to do justice with respect to the same. If the city obtains money of another by mistake or without authority of law it is its duty to refund it, not from any contract entered into by it on the subject, but from the general obligation to do justice which binds all persons, natural or artificial. If the city obtains other property which does not belong to her, it is her duty to restore it; or if used by her, to render an equivalent to the true owner from the like general obligation; the law, which always intends justice, implies a promise. In reference to money or other property it is not difficult to determine, in any particular case, whether liability in respect to the same has attached to the the city. The money must have gone into the treasury or have been appropriated by her; and when it is property other than money, it must have been used by her or under her control. But with reference to services rendered the case is different. There, acceptance must be evidenced by ordinance[3] to that effect. If not originally authorized, no liability can attach upon any ground of implied contract. The acceptance upon

20 Wall. (U. S.) 64; Regan v. Farmers' Loan & Trust Co., 154 U. S. 362; Western Union T. Co. v. Burlington, etc. R. Co., 11 Fed. Rep. 1, and note; Saginaw G. L. Co. v. Saginaw, 28 Fed. Rep. 529.

[1] Marsh v. Fulton Co., 10 Wall. (U. S.) 376; Louisiana v. Wood, 102 U. S. 294; Chapman v. Douglass Co., 107 U. S. 355; Schipper v. Aurora, 121 Ind. 154, 6 L. R. A. 318; Pittsburgh, etc. Ry. Co. v. Keokuk, etc. Co., 131 U. S. 371.

[2] Argenti v. San Francisco, 16 Cal. 255.

[3] Or other appropriate act.

§ 293.]   LIABILITY ON CONTRACTS.   263

which alone the obligation to pay could arise would be wanting." An *ultra vires* contract does not become lawful by being executed; but while the courts will not disturb such a contract so far as executed, it may be disaffirmed by either party upon making restitution of what has been received under it. If the party so disaffirming fails to make restitution, the other party may recover the property or its value in an action upon an implied contract.[1]

§ 293. *Illustrations.*— When a municipal corporation sells property and gives a deed which passes no title and receives the person's money and appropriates it to its own use, the purchaser may recover back the purchase-money.[2] When a city has authority to borrow money and places in the hands of a broker bonds apparently valid, but which are in fact invalid, and the bonds are sold and proceeds received by the city, the transaction is the borrowing of money, and the purchaser of the bonds may disregard them and sue the city for money had and received.[3] As the bonds are wholly void they need not be tendered back.[4] So, where a city without authority exchanges its bonds for the bonds of a railroad company, it is not liable on the bonds; but if value has been received by the city it can be recovered in an action for money had and received.[5] Where a county was authorized to purchase lands, but not to give notes secured by mortgage for the purchase price, it was held that the county held the title to the land as trustee for the vendor, and that unless the sum due was paid within a reasonable time, having reference to the necessity for raising the money by taxation, the county would be compelled to reconvey the land.[6] The person who furnishes necessaries to a pauper whom the municipality is under legal obligation to support can recover for the same from the municipality.[7] So a city is liable for the value

[1] Marble Co. v. Harvey, 92 Tenn. 115; Central Trans. Co. v. Pullman P. C. Co., 139 U. S. 60.

[2] Pimental v. San Francisco, 21 Cal. 352. In Massachusetts one who loans money to a town in a way not authorized by statute cannot recover it back, although the town used the money to pay its debts. Agawam Nat. Bank v. South Hadley, 128 Mass. 503.

[3] Louisiana v. Wood, 102 U. S. 294, 5 Dillon, C. C. 122.

[4] Paul v. Kenosha, 22 Wis. 266.

[5] Thomas v. Port Hudson, 27 Mich. 320.

[6] Chapman v. Douglass Co., 107 U. S. 349.

[7] Seagraves v. Alton, 13 Ill. 366.

of the property of an individual which it uses in the care of the indigent.[1]

§ 294. *Right to recover back illegal taxes.*—A number of states have statutes which authorize the recovery of money paid for illegal taxes.[2] In the absence of such statutory provisions, cities, villages, counties and towns for which a tax has been collected may, under certain circumstances, be liable in an action by the party from whom the tax has been collected. Such actions are usually brought in *assumpsit* for money had and received.[3] In the absence of statutory authority such an action can only be maintained when the following conditions are found to concur:

1. The tax must have been illegal and void, and not merely irregular.
2. It must have been paid under compulsion or the legal equivalent.
3. It must have been paid over by the collecting officer and have been received to the use of the municipality.[4]

And to these, says Judge Cooley,[5] should perhaps be added:

4. The party must not have elected to proceed in any remedy he may have had against the assessor or collector.[6]

§ 295. *Payment must be compulsory.*— The assessment must not only be void, and the corporation actually receive the money, but the payment must also be compulsory. That is, it

[1] Nashville v. Toney, 10 Lea (Tenn.), 643. In Gas Co. v. San Francisco, 9 Cal. 453, the city was held liable for gas furnished with the knowledge of the council, although no ordinance or resolution had been passed authorizing it to be furnished. A city is liable on *quantum meruit*, in the absence of a statute to the contrary, in the same manner as an individual. Peterson v. Mayor, 17 N. Y. 449.

[2] See Cooley, Taxation, 804.

[3] Grand Rapids v. Blakely, 40 Mich. 367.

[4] First Nat. Bank v. Americus, 68 Ga. 119.

[5] Cooley, Taxation, p. 805; Dillon, Mun. Corp., I, § 940. See opinion of

Chief Justice Shaw in Lincoln v. Worcester, 8 Cush. (Mass.) 55.

[6] Ware v. Percival, 61 Me. 391. A demand is not necessary before bringing suit to recover back illegal taxes unless made so by statute. Look v. Industry, 51 Me. 375. Interest is recoverable from the date of demand, but not before. Boston & Co. v. Boston, 4 Met. (Mass.) 181. If only a part of the tax was illegal the recovery will be limited to that part, if capable of being distinguished. Torrey v. Millbury, 21 Pick. (Mass.) 64. The burden of showing illegalities is on the party who counts upon them. Douglasville v. Johns, 62 Ga. 423.

must be made upon direct and immediate compulsion and under such circumstances that the party can save himself and his property only by paying the illegal demand.[1] As stated by Judge Dillon,[2] the coercion must consist of some "actual or threatened exercise of power possessed or believed to be possessed by the party exacting or receiving the payment over the person or property of another, from which the latter has no other means or reasonable means of immediate relief except by making payment."

§ 296. *Voluntary payment.*— A voluntary payment made with a full knowledge of all the facts and circumstances of the case, although made under a mistaken view of the law, cannot be recovered back. As stated by the supreme court of the United States:[3] "Where a party pays an illegal demand with a full knowledge of all the facts which render such demand illegal without an immediate and urgent necessity therefor, or unless to release his person or property from detention, or to prevent an immediate seizure of his person or property, such payment must be deemed to be voluntary and cannot be recovered back. And the fact that the party at the time of making the payment filed a written protest does not make the payment involuntary."[4] A payment to avoid a sale under an unconstitutional statute is voluntary.[5] But some overt act is necessary, and the mere issuing of tax warrants or a threat to collect the tax is not compulsion.[6] It is not necessary, however, for the tax-

---

[1] Union Pac. Ry. Co. v. Dodge Co., 98 U. S. 541; Preston v. Boston, 12 Pick. (Mass.) 7; Briggs v. Lewiston, 29 Me. 472; Grim v. School District, 57 Pa. St. 433.

[2] Dillon, Mun. Corp., II, § 944.

[3] Union Pac. Ry. Co. v. Dodge Co., 98 U. S. 541; Lamborn v. Dickinson Co., 97 U. S. 181; Dunnell Mfg. Co. v. Newell, 15 R. I. 233. There is a strong tendency toward giving relief against a mistake of law. See Story, Eq. Jur., § 212a; Cooper v. Phipps, L. R. 2 H. L. 149; Doniell v. Sinclair, L. R. 6 App. Cas. 181, 190.

[4] Sowles v. Soule, 59 Vt. 131; Shane v. St. Paul, 26 Minn. 543; Powell v. St. Croix Co., 46 Wis. 210; Babcock v. Fond du Lac, 58 Wis. 231; Goddard v. Seymour, 30 Conn. 349. Protest alone cannot change a voluntary into an involuntary payment. Sonoma Co. Tax Case, 13 Fed. Rep. 789; Merrill v. Austin, 53 Cal. 379.

[5] Detroit v. Martin, 34 Mich. 170; Phelps v. Mayor of New York, 112 N. Y. 216, 2 L. R. A. 625. Such an assessment does not create a cloud upon the title. Wells v. Buffalo, 80 N. Y. 253.

[6] Union Pac. Ry. Co. v. Dodge Co., 98 U. S. 541; Dunnell Mfg. Co. v. Newell, 15 R. I. 233.

payer to wait until his goods are sold or even seized.[1] In Iowa money paid under pr*test for illegal taxes is considered as paid under compulsion.[2] So it has been held that taxes paid under a void law to a person who appeared authorized to collect the tax can be recovered although it was paid without protest.[3] So one who by force of a statute is unable to place a deed of record because of the existence of illegal taxes charged against it may pay the taxes in order to secure the recording of the deed without such payment being deemed voluntary.[4]

[1] Atwell v. Zeluff, 26 Mich. 118.
[2] Thomas v. Burlington, 69 Iowa, 140. See Robinson v. Ruggles, 50 Iowa, 240.
[3] Tuttle v. Everett, 51 Miss. 27.
[4] State v. Nelson, 41 Minn. 25, 4 L. R. A. 300, annotated. In this case the court said: "It has always been considered that the payment under protest of an illegal tax or demand to an officer armed with a warrant authorizing him to enforce the payment by imprisonment or by seizure and sale of property, and who is about to so exercise his authority, is not voluntary and may be recovered back. Dakota County v. Parker, 7 Minn. 207; Seeley v. Westport, 47 Conn. 294; Allen v. Burlington, 45 Vt. 202; Nickodemus v. East Saginaw, 25 Mich. 456; Ruggles v. Fond du Lac, 53 Wis. 436; Smith v. Farrelly, 52 Cal. 77; Guy v. Washburn. 23 Cal. 111; Grim v. Weissenberg School District, 57 Pa. St. 433. Nor is this proposition applicable merely with respect to personal property. The same is true, as it obviously ought to be, when real property is involved. See cases above cited, especially Seeley v. Westport, Guy v. Washburn; also Stephlan v. Daniel, 27 Ohio St. 527; Valentine v. St. Paul, 34 Minn. 446. Nor is it necessary, in order to constitute compulsory as distinguished from a voluntary payment, that the unlawful demand be made by an officer who is prepared to enforce it by process. There may be that kind and degree of necessity or coercion which justifies and virtually requires payment to be made of the illegal demands of a private person who has it in his power to seriously prejudice the property rights of another, and to impose upon the latter the risk of suffering great loss if the demand be not complied with. This is illustrated in the case of Fargusson v. Winslow, 34 Minn. 384, and cases cited." The payment of an illegal water charge under threat that the water would be shut off, which would result in closing the plaintiff's foundry, is such "moral duress" as to make the payment compulsory. Westlake v. St. Louis, 77 Mo. 47. The fact that an ordinance subjects a person to a fine of §25 a day for selling liquor without a license made the payment of an illegal license fee compulsory. Marshall v. Snediker, 25 Tex. 460.

CHAPTER XVI.

LIABILITY FOR TORT—GOVERNMENTAL AND CORPORATE DUTIES.

§ 297. Nature of corporation.
298. Nature of duty.
299. Discretionary powers.
300. Imposed and assumed duties.
301. Liability for acts of agents — Respondeat superior.
302. *Ultra vires* torts.
303. Ratification of *ultra vires* acts.
304. Increase of liability by contract.
305. General rules.

I. SOLELY GOVERNMENTAL DUTIES.
306. Definition.
307. Neglect to enact or enforce laws.
308. Suspension of ordinances.
309. Liability for acts of a mob.

§ 310. Acts of police officers.
311. Prevention of fires.
312. Destruction of property to prevent spread of fire.
313. Acts of firemen.
314. Acts of board of health — Care of hospital.
315. Care of criminals.
316. Care of the indigent.
317. Care of school buildings.

II. SOLELY CORPORATE DUTIES.
318. Rule of liability for negligence.
319. As owner of property.
320. Illustration — Wharves.
321. Private business enterprises, gas and water.

§ 297. *Nature of corporation.*— In considering the liability of public corporations for torts the distinction between municipal corporations proper, such as chartered cities, and public *quasi*-corporations, such as counties and towns, is of great importance. The question of liability in many cases depends upon the nature of the corporation, although the real basis for the distinction between the liability of municipal corporations and counties and towns is found in the nature of the duties imposed upon them.

§ 298. *Nature of duty.*— The distinction between governmental and corporate powers has been often referred to in the course of this work.[1] A municipal corporation exercises both corporate and governmental powers, while public *quasi*-corporations exercise governmental powers only. As a general rule there is no liability for negligence in the exercise of governmental powers. Hence the liability of a municipal corporation

[1] See § 22; also Lloyd v. New York, v. New York, 3 Hill (N. Y.), 531, 38
5 N. Y. 369, 55 Am. Dec. 347; Bailey Am. Dec. 669.

in a particular case will depend upon the nature of the power being exercised. It will be held liable for a negligent exercise of its strictly corporate powers, but not liable for a negligent exercise of purely governmental powers. More difficult questions arise when a municipal corporation is exercising powers of a governmental nature for the special benefit of the particular municipality. The liability in a particular case may be effected by the manner in which the duty is imposed and the means of performance. Careful attention must in all cases be given the statutes of the state, as the common-law rules of liability to which reference is made in this chapter have in many states been very materially modified.

§ 299. *Discretionary powers.*— A municipal corporation is not liable for injuries caused by the negligence of its officers or agents in the discharge or the omission to discharge duties which are purely discretionary.[1] Its action in such a case is final, although it may appear that it seriously misjudged the public interest. Illustrations of cases in which such corporations are entitled to exercise discretion are found in the change of grade of a street,[2] opening and closing a street,[3] making a crossing at a particular place,[4] or where reasonable and proper regulations are temporarily suspended to the detriment of individual citizens.[5]

§ 300. *Imposed and assumed duties.*— The fact that the duty has been imperatively imposed by the legislature or has been voluntarily assumed by the municipality under authority of law is not material as affecting the question of liability resulting from negligence in the performance of the duty. Thus, where a city provides and maintains a workhouse solely for the public service and for the general good in providing for the care and support of offenders for whose maintenance it was responsible, the fact that the city was not compelled by law to provide such an establishment and that it acted voluntarily does not affect its liability for its acts in connection therewith.[6]

[1] Howsman v. Trenton Water Works, 119 Mo. 304, 23 L. R. A. 146.
[2] Transportation Co. v. Chicago, 99 U. S. 635.
[3] Bauman v. Campau, 58 Mich. 444.
[4] Smith v. Gould, 61 Wis. 31.
[5] See Burford v. Grand Rapids, 53 Mich. 98, 51 Am. Rep. 105. In this case the city designated a particular street for coasting.
[6] Curran v. Boston, 151 Mass. 505, 8 L. R. A. 243. See Tindley v. Salem, 137 Mass. 171.

§ 301. Liability for acts of agents — Respondeat superior. — A city is not liable for damages resulting from the negligent exercise of a governmental power.[1] Neither is it responsible for the torts of a public officer when engaged in the performance of a public governmental duty, nor of a specific duty imposed upon the officer by statute. In the latter case the officer derives his authority from the law and not from the corporation, and is not the representative of the corporation.[2] The doctrine of *respondeat superior* applies to the acts of the agents of a public corporation when acting for the corporation and within the scope of their authority.[3] But the corporation is not liable for the acts of officers who are not under its control or engaged in the performance of its duties. The officers may, in such cases, be personally liable for the negligent performance of ministerial duties. When, however, a public officer is engaged in the performance of duties which rest upon the corporation, his acts may bind the corporation in a particular case, although it would not be generally liable for his negligence. Thus, a city is not liable for damages caused by the tortious acts of a policeman, but it may be liable for damages caused by a defect in a street when a police officer has negligently failed to report the defect.[4] A corporation is liable neither for the acts of independent boards who do not act for it and are not subordinate to it, nor of subordinate boards which exercise governmental power.[5]

---

[1] Wood, Master and Servant, § 463.

[2] In Sievers v. San Francisco, 115 Cal. 648, the court said: "In a learned and very instructive note to Goddard v. Hartwell, 80 Am. St. Rep. 373, Mr. Freeman, after careful and critical review and analysis of many authorities, deduces and expresses the rule of liability for the acts of an officer of a municipality in the following language: 'When an officer of a municipality has no other authority than that intrusted to him by law, and he acts beyond that authority and permits a tort whereby a citizen is injured either in person or property, the tort is the act of the officer only and ordinarily no recovery of damages could be had except against him.'" It was therefore held that the city was not liable for damages occasioned by an erroneous fixing of a street grade eight feet above the official grade. The court further said: "When the injury results from the wrongful act or omission of an officer charged with the duty prescribed and limited by law, the officer is not treated as the servant or agent of the corporation in the performance of those duties so enjoined, but is held to be the servant and agent of and controlled by the law, and for his acts the municipality would not be liable."

[3] Field v. Des Moines, 39 Iowa, 575.

[4] Kunz v. Troy, 104 N. Y. 344, 10 N. E. Rep. 442.

[5] Bulger v. Eden, 82 Me. 352; Kuhn

Such independent boards are not, in general, held liable for the negligent acts of their servants.[1] "To determine whether there is municipal responsibility, the inquiry must be whether the department whose misfeasance or nonfeasance is complained of is a part of the machinery for carrying on municipal government, and whether it was at the time engaged in the discharge of a duty or charged with a duty primarily resting upon the municipality."[2] The manner in which the members of a board are appointed is important, but not decisive upon this question.[3] It is not easy to determine when a municipality is liable for the negligence of a contractor. It certainly cannot relieve itself from the duty which rests upon it by transferring that duty to a contractor. The corporation must see that the public is properly protected, and if the contractor fails to perform this duty the city is responsible for the resulting damages.[4] But when the negligence relates to a matter with reference to which the corporation is under no special obligation, the liability rests upon the contractor alone.[5] In jurisdictions where there is no

v. Milwaukee, 93 Wis. 263; Bryant v. St. Paul, 33 Minn. 289.

[1] O'Leary v. Board of Commissioners, 79 Mich. 281, 19 Am. St. Rep. 169; Elmore v. Drainage Commissioners, 135 Ill. 269, 25 N. E. Rep. 1010; Anne Arundel County v. Diwell, 54 Md. 350, 39 Am. Rep. 393 (county commissioners).

[2] Pettengill v. Yonkers, 116 N. Y. 558. In O'Brien v. New York, 15 N. Y. Supp. 520, it is held that under the statute the city is not liable for the negligence of aqueduct commissioners. In District of Columbia v. Woodbury, 136 U. S. 450, the District of Columbia was held liable for the negligence of street commissioners who were ultimately responsible to congress. In Kobs v. Minneapolis, 22 Minn. 159, the city was held liable for the negligence of a street commissioner appointed by the common council.

[3] District of Columbia v. Woodbury, 136 U. S. 450. It has been held that the corporation is liable when it appoints the officer and the duty to be performed is for the benefit of the corporation. New York v. Bailey, 2 Denio, 433 (engineer and water commissioners); Tarney v. New York, 12 Hun, 542 (board of health); Walsh v. New York, 41 Hun, 299 (trustees of Brooklyn bridge). So where the duty is imposed upon the corporation and the officers or department acts as the agent. Niven v. Rochester, 76 N. Y. 619 (commissioners of public works); Barnes v. District of Columbia, 91 U. S. 540 (board of public works); Ehrgott v. New York, 96 N. Y. 264 (park commissioners).

[4] Turner v. Newburgh, 109 N. Y. 301; Jefferson v. Chapman, 127 Ill. 438; Circleville v. Neuding, 41 Ohio St. 465; Hinck v. Milwaukee, 46 Wis. 565, 32 Am. Rep. 735; Grant v. Stillwater, 35 Minn. 242.

[5] Harvey v. Hillsdale, 86 Mich. 330, 49 N. W. Rep. 141; Van Winter v. Henry County, 61 Iowa, 684. See, further, Herrington v. Lansingburg, 110 N. Y. 145; Depot v. Simmons, 112 Pa. St. 384.

duty resting upon the corporation to keep the streets in proper condition, there is no liability for acts of negligence of a public officer engaged in the construction of a street.[1]

§ 302. *Ultra vires torts.*— The rule that a principal is civilly liable for the acts of his agents when acting in the line of their employment is applicable to municipal corporations. The acts must, however, be within the general powers of the corporation,[2] and not of a purely governmental nature. "A municipal corporation is liable for the acts of its agents injurious to others when the act is in its nature lawful and authorized, but is done in an unlawful manner or in an unauthorized place, but it is not liable for injuries or tortious acts which are in their nature unlawful and prohibited."[3] The principle of non-liability of public corporations for torts *ultra vires* is firmly established,[4]

---

[1] Jensen v. Waltham, 166 Mass. 344 (assistant superintendent of streets); McCann v. Waltham, 163 Mass. 344 (laborer employed by superintendent of streets). A city is not liable for acts of its servants in operating a passenger elevator in a city hall. Snider v. St. Paul, 51 Minn. 466. Where a contractor in paving a street unnecessarily deposits earth upon an abutting lot, the corporation is not liable to the owner of the lot. Fuller v. Grand Rapids, 105 Mich. 529, 63 N. W. Rep. 530. A city is bound to give its workmen a reasonably safe place in which to work and is liable to them for damages resulting from a failure to do so. Norton v. New Bedford, 166 Mass. 48.

[2] Smith v. Rochester, 76 N. Y. 506; Stoddard v. Saratoga Springs, 127 N. Y. 261; Love v. Raleigh, 116 N. C. 296, 28 L. R. A. 192 (fireworks managed by officers of municipality); Moffett v. Asheville, 103 N. C. 237; Haag v. Vanderburg County, 60 Ind. 511; Elliott, Roads and Streets, p. 355; McCarthy v. Boston, 135 Mass. 197; Seele v. Deering, 79 Me. 343. The rule of *respondeat superior* has no application when the officer or agent of a corporation acts in the discharge of governmental duties. Anderson v. East, 117 Ind. 126, 2 L. R. A. 712 (annotated).

[3] Worley v. Columbia, 88 Mo. 106.

[4] A municipal corporation is not liable for the malfeasance or negligence of its officers or employees when acting under the authority of its ordinances and within the scope of its charter powers. Hines v. Charlotte, 72 Mich. 278, 1 L. R. A. 844; Robinson v. Rohr, 73 Wis. 436, 2 L. R. A. 366, note; Culver v. Streator, 130 Ill. 238, 6 L. R. A. 270, and note on "Municipal corporation not liable except for its own negligence;" Lincoln v. Boston, 148 Mass. 578, 3 L. R. A. 257, note. The liability, if it exists, is the creature of statute. Anderson v. East, 117 Ind. 126, 2 L. R. A. 712. The well-known case of Salt Lake City v. Hollister, 118 U. S. 256, restricts the doctrine of *ultra vires* when applied to municipal corporations. It was there held that the city could not recover back money paid as a tax for distilling spirits, although the act of engaging in the business was wholly *ultra vires* the corporation. See comment on this case in Dillon, Mun. Corp., II, § 793, note. The doctrine is not consistently ap-

although it is often explained away in practice. It has been held that a town is not liable for damages resulting from building a dam without corporate power[1] or under an unconstitutional statute.[2] So a city is not liable for the torts of officers committed under the apparent authority of an ordinance which the corporation had no power to enact.[3] But the corporation is sometimes held liable for acts done by it under a claim of authority which is afterwards shown to be unfounded.[4] A

plied and municipal corporations are often held liable for *ultra vires* acts. Thus, in Stanley v. Davenport, 54 Iowa, 463, 37 Am. Rep. 216, the city was held liable for damages resulting from its unauthorized act in allowing a steam motor to go upon a street. As to liability when it has granted licenses without authority, see § 381, *infra*. As to liability on *ultra vires* contracts, see § 288, *supra*.

[1] In Anthony v. Adams, 1 Met. (Mass.) 284, the county commissioners ordered a dam built and it was constructed by the selectmen without a vote or other action of the town. It was held that the town was not liable for negligence in this case.

[2] Albany v. Cunliff, 2 N. Y. 165. But see Schussler v. Hennepin Co. (Minn., 1897), 70 N. W. Rep. 6. In Board of Commissioners v. Duprez, 87 Ind. 509, Mr. Justice Elliott said: "There is a fatal defect in the complaint. It is not shown that the bridge was one which the county had authority to build. It is settled that a public corporation cannot be held liable for injuries resulting from an act done by its officers beyond its power and jurisdiction. There is in this respect a well-defined distinction between public and private corporations. Browning v. Board, 44 Ind. 11; Haag v. Board, 60 Ind. 511, 28 Am. Rep. 654; Driftwood & Co. v. Board, 72 Ind. 226; Cummins v. City of Seymour, 79 Ind. 491, 41 Am. Rep. 226. A public corporation is not liable for injuries caused by the unsafe condition of a bridge which its officers had no authority to build. 2 Dill. Mun. Corp. (3d. ed.), § 970 (4th ed., § 1017). There is nothing showing that the bridge formed any part of a highway or that the place where it was built was one where the county had authority to build a bridge. Where negligence is the ground of an action against a public corporation, it is necessary to show a duty and its breach. Neither a county nor a city can be made responsible for negligence in maintaining a bridge or highway unless there rests upon it some duty."

[3] Field v. Des Moines, 39 Iowa, 575, 579.

[4] In Thayer v. Boston, 19 Pick. (Mass.) 511, the court said: "There is a large class of cases in which the rights of both the public and of individuals may be deeply involved in which it cannot be known at the time the act is done whether it is lawful or not. The event of a legal inquiry in a court of justice may show that it was unlawful. Still if it was not known and understood to be unlawful at the time; if it was an act done by the officers having competent authority, either by express vote of the city government or by the nature of the duties and functions with which they are charged by their offices, to act upon the general subject-matter; and especially if the act was done with an honest view to obtain for the public

city is liable for the trespasses or malicious injuries committed by its agents when engaged in the execution of its powers.[1] The city has no power to call a political meeting, and one who is injured by the careless discharge of a cannon at a meeting called and managed by the city council has no right of action against the city.[2] In the absence of express power a public corporation has no right to expend money for public celebrations, and there is no liability for injuries resulting from the explosion of fireworks on such occasions. It has been held that this is true where the fireworks were exhibited under a permit granted by the municipal authorities under an ordinance prohibiting anything of the kind without such a permit.[3] Where such exhibitions, however, amount to a nuisance the city is liable for injuries resulting therefrom.[4]

The fact that work is being done by the day when the charter requires that it shall be done by contract is no defense to an action for negligence.[5] The city has been held not liable for placing an obstruction in the street without authority,[6] although it has been held liable for injuries resulting from unlawfully licensing persons to allow a wagon to stand in the street.[7] The former decision is inconsistent with the duty of caring for the street. A city is liable for trespass in attempting to acquire a lot as a site for a public building in an unlawful manner when it has power to acquire it lawfully.[8] A city is not liable for injuries received by a prisoner while engaged in working with other prisoners under the direction of the chief

some lawful benefit or advantage,— reason and justice obviously require that the city, in its corporate capacity, should be liable to make good the damage sustained by an individual in consequence of the acts thus done." To the same effect is Schussler v. Hennepin Co. (Minn., 1897), 70 N. W. Rep. 6.

[1] Allen v. Decatur, 23 Ill. 372; Manners v. Haverhill, 135 Mass. 165; Leeds v. Richmond, 102 Ind. 372.

[2] Morrison v. Lawrence, 98 Mass. 219; Findley v. Salem, 137 Mass. 171, 50 Am. Rep. 289 (celebration of a holiday under direction of the city); Ball v. Woodbine, 61 Iowa, 83, 47 Am. Rep. 803 (where the fireworks were discharged by citizens with the participation of the town officers, who made no attempt to stop it).

[3] Fifield v. Phœnix (Ariz.), 24 L. R. A. 430. See § 308.

[4] The persons were acting under express authority. Spiers v. Brooklyn, 89 N. Y. 6, 21 L. R. A. 640.

[5] Donahoe v. Kansas City, 136 Mo. 657; Collinsworth v. New Whatcom, 16 Wash. 224, 47 Pac. Rep. 439.

[6] Redford v. Coggeshall (R. I.), 36 Atl. Rep. 89.

[7] Cohen v. New York, 118 N. Y. 532.

[8] Oklahoma v. Hill (Okl.), 50 Pac. Rep. 243.

of police, who acted without authority in requiring the prisoner to work.[1]

§ 303. *Ratification of ultra vires acts.*— If a corporation is not liable for an *ultra vires* tort because in excess of its power it cannot make itself liable by ratification of the act after it has been done by its agents;[2] but it may become liable by the adoption or ratification of acts which were beyond the powers of the agents but within the scope of the powers of the corporation. Such ratification may be express or it may be inferred from circumstances such as receiving the benefit of the wrongful act. Thus, a county may become liable for the *ultra vires* acts of its officers by adopting them in its answer.[3] And it was held that a county which constructed a dam under the authority of an unconstitutional act of the legislature is liable for damages occasioned thereby when it assumes the entire responsibility for the same and asserts the validity of its acts in its answer.[4]

§ 304. *Increase of liability by contract.*— The officers of a city cannot lawfully contract to extend its liability for negli-

[1] Royce v. St. Louis (Utah), 49 Pac. Rep. 290.
[2] Hodges v. Buffalo, 2 Denio (N. Y.), 110; Mitchell v. Rockland, 52 Me. 118; Moore v. New York, 73 N. Y. 238; Trescott v. Waterloo, 26 Fed. Rep. 592.
[3] Wilde v. New Orleans, 12 La. Ann. 15.
[4] Schussler v. County Commissioners of Hennepin County (Minn., 1897), 70 N. W. Rep. 6. The county not only failed to plead that the acts complained of were *ultra vires*, but adopted and ratified them and insisted that they were right, proper and legal and insisted that the acts were performed under a public necessity. The court said: "It is therefore not a mere act of negligence of the board of county commissioners in the performance of an official duty, but an active and affirmative tort, done under claim of statutory authority and duty, and justified upon such grounds by defendant, and that it was performed within the scope of the board's official duty. . . . It insists upon retaining the benefits of the illegal acts of its officers. It is not willing that the wrong shall cease, but aggressively insists that it will make no reparation for its past tort, and that it has a legal right to enjoy in the future all the benefits secured through an unconstitutional law. . . . We may concede the general rule to be that the defendant would not be responsible for the unauthorized and unlawful acts of its officers done *colore officii;* but where the defendant expressly authorizes such act, or, when done, adopts and ratifies it, and retains and enjoys its benefits and persists in so doing, it is liable in damages." Citing Thayer v. Boston, 19 Pick. (Mass.) 511. The rule of these cases must be regarded as an exception to the general rule that a corporation is not responsible for torts *ultra vires* its legal powers.

gence in a particular instance beyond that imposed by the law. Hence, a contract entered into between a city and a party from whom it purchased a right of way, to the effect that the city would have the sewer so constructed as to prevent water from flowing back on the grantor's premises, was held void in so far as it assumed to guaranty the grantor against damages, without reference to the manner in which the work of the city was done.[1] A city is not liable for the failure to extinguish fires,[2] although it owns the water-works and receives an income therefrom; and in the absence of an express charter authority a contract imposing such liability upon the city is void.[3] Where an action was brought against the city based upon the neglect of the water-works company to supply sufficient water to extinguish a fire, and it appeared that the city had taken from the water-works company a bond to indemnify it against damages that might result from the water company's negligence in the construction and management of its works, the court said:[4] "Indemnification against liability must always be regarded as having reference to existing grounds of liability and not as serving to create new ones. Besides, the city could not assume liability for negligence in cases where the law did not impose a liability. The contract then must be construed as covering cases only where an action might be maintained against the city independent of the contract."

§ 305. *General rules.*—Subject to statutory modifications, it may safely be stated as a general rule that:

1. A public corporation is not liable for failing to exercise or for improperly exercising its purely governmental powers.

2. A municipal corporation, when dealing with property held by it as a private owner, is liable as an individual owner.

[1] Nashville v. Sutherland, 92 Tenn. 335, 19 L. R. A. 619, note on *ultra vires*.

[2] Springfield F. & M. Co. v. Keeseville, 148 N. Y. 46, 30 L. R. A. 660; Mendel v. Healey, 28 W. Va. 233, 57 Am. Rep. 664, where the city was empowered to maintain a sufficient number of reservoirs "to supply water in case of fire;" Grant v. Erie, 69 Pa. St. 420, 8 Am. Rep. 272. See §§ 147, 311.

[3] Black v. Columbia, 19 S. C. 412, 45 Am. Rep. 785.

[4] Van Horne v. Des Moines, 63 Iowa, 447; Becker v. Keokuk Water Works, 79 Iowa, 419. The taking of a bond from a railroad company which is about to lay its tracks in the streets of the city to save the city harmless from the results of the negligence of the company does not increase the liability of the city. Terry v. Richmond (Va., 1897), 38 L. R. A. 834.

3. A municipal corporation is liable for negligence in the discharge of ministerial or specified duties, not discretionary or governmental, assumed in consideration of the privileges conferred by its charter, although there are no special awards or advantages.

4. In many states by the common law, and in some states by statute, a municipal corporation is liable for failure to keep streets, alleys, roads, sidewalks and bridges in repair. No such liability rests upon counties and townships at common law.

I. SOLELY GOVERNMENTAL DUTIES.

§ 306. *Definition.*—Solely governmental duties are such as involve the exercise of governmental power and are assumed for the exclusive benefit of the public. The sovereign acts of a government cannot be submitted to the judgment of the courts. The government is not a subject of private law. "The rule that a tort creates a liability for damages is a rule of private law; it therefore applies to the relations of the private law only. The position of the state, when it acts in the exercise of sovereign and governmental functions, is, however, entirely beyond the sphere of private law, and must be judged by different standards. . . . Governmental functions do not create civil causes of action."[1] The state, directly or through its corporate agencies, "gives such protection from law-breakers, from fire, from disease and from other common evils as the power, energy and faithfulness of the government shall compass." A person can have no civil action from damages resulting from his being badly governed.[2]

[1] Freund, "Private Claims against the State," Political Science Quarterly, VIII, p. 648.

[2] Many cases in support of the rule that a municipal corporation is exempt from liability when acting as the agent of the state and exercising governmental power are collected and reviewed in Donaher v. City of Brooklyn, 51 Hun (N. Y.), 563, and in Moflitt v. City of Asheville, 103 N. C. 237, 14 Am. St. Rep. 810 and note. In Terry v. Richmond (Va., 1897), 38 L. R. A. 834, the rule is thus stated:

"The duty of a municipal corporation to see that the streets and sidewalks are in a safe condition, and its sewers and drains are kept in good order, and that its other like municipal obligations are cared for, is a purely ministerial and absolute corporate duty, assumed in consideration of the privilege conferred by its charter; and the law holds the municipality responsible for an injury resulting from a negligent discharge of that duty or the negligent omission to discharge it, but ex-

§ 307. *Neglect to enact or enforce laws.*— A corporation is not liable for a failure to enact or neglect to enforce or observe its own laws and ordinances.[1] Hence there is no liability for damages resulting from a failure to enforce an ordinance against the use of fireworks,[2] against allowing sunken vessels to remain in a river,[3] against allowing swine to run at large,[4] against nuisances,[5] against coasting on the streets,[6] or against the erection of certain kinds of buildings within the fire limits,[7] or against creating a nuisance.[8]

§ 308. *Suspension of ordinances.*— It rests with the corporation to determine whether it will exercise its governmental

---

empts it from liability for the exercise of governmental or discretionary powers." Richmond v. Long, 17 Gratt. 375, 94 Am. Dec. 461; Petersburg v. Applegarth, 28 Gratt. 343, 26 Am. Rep. 357; Elliott, Roads and Streets, pp. 504, 532; Dillon, Mun. Corp., II, §§ 1046, 1049; Tiedeman, Mun. Corp., § 349; Cooley, Torts, p. 733; Stevens v. Muskegon (Mich.), 69 N. W. Rep. 227; Eddy v. Granger, 19 R. I. 105; Commissioners v. Allman, 142 Ind. 58.

[1] Harmon v. St. Louis (Mo.), 38 S. W. Rep. 1102; Fowle v. Alexandria, 3 Pet. (U. S.) 398; Wheeling v. Plymouth, 116 Ind. 158; Forsyth v. Atlanta, 45 Ga. 152; Burford v. Grand Rapids, 53 Mich. 98, 51 Am. Rep. 105. In Anderson v. East, 117 Ind. 126, the rule is thus stated: "A municipal corporation is an instrumentality of government and is not liable for a failure to exercise legislative or judicial powers, nor for an improper or negligent exercise of such powers. . . . In one thing all unite, and that is in affirming that no recovery can in any event be had where the negligence of the municipal corporation consists in failing to perform a legislative, judicial or discretionary duty or in simply performing such a duty in an improper method."

[2] McDade v. Chester, 117 Pa. St. 414, 2 Am. St. Rep. 681; Hubbell v. City of Viroqua, 67 Wis. 343, 58 Am. Rep. 866 (shooting-gallery under a license); Robinson v. Greenville, 42 Ohio St. 625, 51 Am. Rep. 857; Ball v. Woodbine, 61 Iowa, 83, 47 Am. Rep. 805.

[3] Coonley v. Albany, 57 Hun, 327.

[4] Levy v. New York, 1 Sandf. (N. Y.) 465. But a city may be liable for allowing cattle to run at large in the streets under circumstances which amount to a nuisance. Cochrane v. Frostburg, 81 Md. 54, 31 Atl. Rep. 703, 27 L. R. A. 728. In Mayor v. Marriott, 9 Md. 174, 66 Am. Dec. 326, it was held that where a statute conferred a power upon a public corporation to be exercised for the public good the exercise of that power is not discretionary but imperative. Hence, in Cochrane v. Frostburg, 81 Md. 54, 43 Am. St. Rep. 479, a city was held liable for damages caused by a cow running at large in the street where the city had power to restrain by ordinance.

[5] Davis v. Montgomery, 51 Ala. 139; Butz v. Cavanaugh, 137 Mo. 503, 38 S. W. Rep. 1102.

[6] Wilmington v. Von Degrift (Del.), 29 Atl. Rep. 1047, 25 L. R. A. 538.

[7] Harman v. St. Louis, 137 Mo. 494, 38 S. W. Rep. 1104.

[8] Moran v. Palace Car Co., 134 Mo. 641, 56 Am. St. Rep. 543.

powers. It may entirely fail to act or it may temporarily suspend an ordinance without becoming liable for injuries resulting thereby to individuals. Thus, there is no liability when an ordinance is suspended and a fire is started by boys exploding fireworks,[1] or for damages caused by a runaway horse which was frightened by fireworks;[2] or to a person who is injured by cattle allowed to run at large in the streets under a suspended ordinance.[3] A distinction, however, is sometimes made between the mere suspension of an ordinance and the granting of a license to an individual to do an otherwise forbidden thing.[4]

§ 309. *Liability for acts of a mob.*— In the absence of a statute there is no liability on the part of a public corporation for negligence in failing to protect the lives and property of the citizens from mob violence.[5] In many states, however, statutes have been enacted giving a right of action against a municipality for damages caused by the destruction of property by a mob.[6] The right, however, is purely statutory, and may be taken away at any time before or after the damage has been sustained.[7] A statute providing that the corporation shall be

[1] Hill v. Charlotte, 72 N. C. 55, 21 Am. Rep. 451.
[2] Lincoln v. Washburn, 148 Mass. 578, 3 L. R. A. 257. As to liability for injuries caused by the firing of a cannon in a public street by the permission but without the express license of the corporation, see Robinson v. Greenville, 42 Ohio St. 625, 51 Am. Rep. 857, note. As to liability for failure to prevent a nuisance, see Faulkner v. Aurora, 85 Ind. 130, 44 Am. Rep. 1; Pierce v. New Bedford, 129 Mass. 534, 37 Am. Rep. 387; Schultz v. Milwaukee, 49 Wis. 254, 35 Am. Rep. 779. A city is liable for injuries to property by an explosion of fireworks under a permit constituting a dangerous public nuisance. Speir v. Brooklyn, 139 N. Y. 6, 21 L. R. A. 641. This case is not in accordance with the weight of authority. See note to Scanlon v. Wedger, in 16 L. R. A. 395; also next section.
[3] Rivers v. Augusta, 67 Ga. 376, 88 Am. Rep. 787. *Contra*, Cochrane v. Frostburg, 81 Md. 54, 48 Am. St. Rep. 479.
[4] McCaull v. Manchester, 85 Va. 579, 2 L. R. A. 691.
[5] Western Reserve College v. Cleveland, 12 Ohio St. 375; Robinson v. Greenville, 42 Ohio St. 625; Gianfortone v. New Orleans, 61 Fed. Rep. 64, 24 L. R. A. 592 (the authorities are collected in a note to this case); Hart v. Bridgeport, 13 Blatchf. 289; Prather v. Lexington, 13 B. Mon. 559, 56 Am. Dec. 585.
[6] Darlington v. New York, 31 N. Y. 164, 88 Am. Dec. 248; Palmer v. Concord, 48 N. H. 211, 97 Am. Dec. 605. In Allegheny County v. Gibson, 90 Pa. St. 397, 35 Am. Rep. 670, it was held that under the statute the county was liable to a non-resident for the value of property destroyed by a mob while passing through the county.
[7] State v. New Orleans, 109 U. S.

liable for the destruction of property by a mob will not sustain an action for the taking of human life.[1] A party cannot recover if he had previous knowledge of the intended attempt to destroy his property, unless he or his agent gave notice of such intention to the officials whose duty it was to guard the property.[2] The party must use due diligence on his own part to prevent the injury,[3] but he will not be presumed to have acted illegally or improperly.[4] The constitutionality of such statutes has been frequently called in question and uniformly sustained.[5] It is not the duty of a person to employ an armed force to protect his property, and he cannot be charged with negligence because he declined to take human life. It is no defense under such a statute that the mob was composed of the employees of the plaintiff.[6]

§ 310. *Acts of police officers.*— Police officers act solely in relation to the governmental duty of the state to preserve order, and no liability rests upon the corporation for their negligence in the performance of such duties.[7] Thus, a city is not liable

285; New Orleans v. Abagznatto, 62 Fed. Rep. 240, 26 L. R. A. 329. For construction of such a statute, see Adams v. Salina (Kan.), 48 Pac. Rep. 918. For definition of a "riot," see Aron v. City of Wausau (Wis., 1898), 74 N. W. Rep. 354; 2 Whart. Cr. Law (10th ed.), § 1537.

[1] Jolly v. Hawesville, 89 Ky. 279; Gianfortone v. New Orleans, *supra*, and note.

[2] Allegheny County v. Gibson, 90 Pa. St. 397; Moody v. Niagara County, 46 Barb. (N. Y.) 659.

[3] Chadbourne v. Newcastle, 48 N. H. 196; Eastman v. New York, 5 Robt. (N. Y.) 389; Underhill v. Manchester, 45 N. H. 214; Hill v. Rensselaer County, 119 N. Y. 344.

[4] Palmer v. Concord, 48 N. H. 211, 97 Am. Dec. 605.

[5] Pennsylvania Co. v. Chicago, 81 Fed. Rep. 317; Darlington v. New York, 31 N. Y. 164, 88 Am. Dec. 248; Hagerstown v. Sehner, 37 Md. 180.

[6] Spring Valley Co. v. Spring Valley, 65 Ill. App. 571.

[7] Woodhull v. New York, 150 N. Y. 450; Taylor v. Owensboro, 98 Ky. 271; Gullikson v. McDonald, 62 Minn. 278; Kies v. Erie, 135 Pa. St. 144; Kimball v. Boston, 1 Allen, 417; Calwell v. Boone, 51 Iowa, 687; Perkins v. New Haven, 53 Conn. 214; Dargan v. Mobile, 31 Ala. 469, 70 Am. Dec. 505. In Culver v. Streator, 130 Ill. 238, 6 L. R. A. 270, the court said: "Police officers appointed by the city are not its agents or servants so as to render it responsible for their unlawful or negligent acts in the discharge of their duties. Accordingly it has been held that the city is not liable for an assault and battery committed by its police officers, though done in an attempt to enforce an ordinance (Buttrick v. Lowell, 1 Allen, 172); nor for illegal or oppressive acts of officers committed in the administration of an ordinance (Odell v. Schroeder, 58 Ill. 353); nor for an arrest made by them which is illegal for want of a warrant (Pollock v. Louisville, 13 Bush, 221; Cook v.

for damages resulting from an unlawful arrest;⁶ the act of a drunken policeman in assaulting a citizen;² allowing a horse to escape and be killed while attempting to make an arrest for fast driving;³ nor the wanton and malicious killing of a dog under the pretense of enforcing an ordinance.⁴ So where an officer whose duty it is to kill unmuzzled dogs, by his recklessness in attempting to discharge such duty injures an individual, the corporation is not liable for damages.⁵

§ 311. *Prevention of fires.*— The obligation to prevent the destruction of property by fire is solely governmental.⁶ "As a part of the governmental machinery of the state, municipal corporations legislate and provide for the customary local conveniences of the people, and in exercising these discretionary functions the corporations are not called upon to respond in damages to individuals either for omissions to act or for the mode of exercising powers conferred on them for public purposes and to be exercised at discretion for the public good."⁷ The protection of all the buildings in a city or town from destruction or injury by fire is for the benefit of all the inhabitants and for their protection from a common danger.⁸ A city is not an insurer of the property of its inhabitants. The

Macon, 54 Ga. 468; Harris v. Atlanta, 62 Ga. 290); nor for their unlawful acts of violence, whereby, in the exercise of their duty in suppressing an unlawful assembly, an injury is done to the property of an individual (Stewart v. New Orleans, 9 La. Ann. 461, 61 Am. Dec. 219; Durgan v. Mobile, 31 Ala. 469)." Cobb v. Portland, 55 Me. 381, 92 Am. Dec. 598. There is no liability for acts of police when attempting to enforce an illegal ordinance. Easterly v. Town of Erwin (Iowa), 68 N. W. Rep. 919. No liability of city to one who is injured while aiding the police to make an arrest. Cobb v. Portland, 55 Me. 381.

¹ Attaway v. Cartersville, 68 Ga. 740; Peters v. Lindsborg, 40 Kan. 654; Gullikson v. McDonald, 62 Minn. 278; City of Caldwell v. Prunelle, 57 Kan. 511. The policeman is personally liable for making a malicious arrest. Bolton v. Velines (Va.), 26 S. E. Rep. 847.

² McElroy v. Albany, 65 Ga. 387, 38 Am. Rep. 791. Nor for unnecessary violence in making an arrest. Calwell v. Boone, 51 Iowa, 687.

³ Elliott v. Philadelphia, 75 Pa. St. 342, 15 Am. Rep. 591.

⁴ Moss v. Augusta, 93 Ga. 797.

⁵ Culver v. Streator, 130 Ill. 238, 6 L. R. A. 270; Whitefield v. Paris, 84 Tex. 431, 15 L. R. A. 783 (annotated).

⁶ Edgerly v. Concord, 59 N. H. 78; Welsh v. Rutland, 56 Vt. 228; Hayes v. Oshkosh, 33 Wis. 314, 14 Am. Rep. 760.

⁷ Edgerly v. Concord, 62 N. H. 8.

⁸ Wheeler v. Cincinnati, 19 Ohio St. 19, 2 Am. Rep. 368.

extent and manner of the exercise of the power to prescribe regulations governing a fire department must necessarily be determined by the judgment and discretion of the proper municipal authorities, and for any defect in the execution of such powers the corporation cannot be held liable to individuals.[1] It is not, therefore, liable for neglect of duty on the part of fire companies or their officers charged with the duty of extinguishing fires. When a municipal corporation undertakes to furnish water to be used as a protection against fire, it acts in its governmental capacity, and is not liable in damages for injury caused by lack of water or a defect in the hydrants or other machinery of the fire or water department. By accepting a statute authorizing the maintenance of a system of waterworks and constructing its water-works under it, a city does not "enter into any contract with or assume any liability to the owners of property to furnish means or water for the extinguishment of fires upon which an action can be maintained."[2]

§ 312. *Destruction of property to prevent spread of fire.*— By the common law, under the principle expressed in the maxim *salus populi suprema lex*, an individual or a corporation might destroy houses or other private property to prevent the spread of a conflagration without being responsible to the owner for the value of the property so destroyed.[3] Thus, Lord Coke says: "For the Commonwealth, a man shall suffer damage; as for the saving of a city or town, a house shall be plucked down if the next be on fire.[4] This every man may do without being liable for an action." It must appear, however, that there was a reasonable necessity for such destruction.[5] It is not un-

[1] Mendel v. Wheeling, 28 W. Va. 253, 57 Am. Rep. 665; Heller v. Sedalia, 53 Mo. 159, 14 Am. Rep. 444; Van Horne v. Des Moines, 63 Iowa, 447, 50 Am. Rep. 750; Grant v. Erie, 69 Pa. St. 420, 8 Am. Rep. 272; Patch v. Covington, 17 B. Mon. (Ky.) 722, 66 Am. Dec. 186; Black v. Columbia, 19 S. C. 412, 45 Am. Rep. 785; Howsman v. Trenton Water Co., 119 Mo. 304, 23 L. R. A. 146 (annotated).

[2] Tainter v. Worcester, 123 Mass. 311, 25 Am. Rep. 90; Springfield Fire Ins. Co. v. Keeseville, 148 N. Y. 46, 30 L. R. A. 660, and cases cited in preceding note.

[3] Bowditch v. Boston, 101 U. S. 16; McDonald v. Red Wing, 13 Minn. 38; Field v. Des Moines, 39 Iowa, 575.

[4] Mouse's Case, 12 Coke, 13, 63.

[5] In Bishop v. Macon, 7 Ga. 200, 50 Am. Dec. 400, it was held that the property owner could maintain an action against the city in *assumpsit* for the value of property that might have been saved; but this decision has been questioned. See cases cited in next note.

common for the law to designate certain officers who are to determine when an emergency exists and to order the destruction of private property under such circumstances. Corporations are also frequently made liable by statute for the value of property thus destroyed.[1] It must appear clearly that there is an intention to charge the corporation, and the party seeking his remedy must proceed under the statute.[2] The destruction of property under a necessity of this nature is not the taking of private property for a public use for which compensation must be made under the constitution.

§ 313. *Acts of firemen.*— The officers and men of a city fire department are public officers or agents for whose negligence the corporation is not liable.[3] This is true whether the injury for which it is sought to recover damages results from the negligent acts or omissions of firemen while engaged in their proper duty of extinguishing fires, in keeping the department apparatus in order,[4] or in the management and care of the appliances of the department when not in actual service. Thus, there can be no recovery for the value of property destroyed by fire started by sparks escaping from a steam fire-engine while used in extinguishing a fire;[5] nor for an injury to a person resulting from the bursting of hose;[6] nor for damages caused by a runaway horse frightened by the escape of steam from a fire-engine;[7] nor for an injury resulting from the negligent

[1] For a full discussion of general questions of liability, see Field v. Des Moines, 39 Iowa, 575, 18 Am. Rep. 46; McDonald v. Red Wing, 13 Minn. 38 (Gil. 25).

[2] Keller v. Corpus Christi, 50 Tex. 614, 32 Am. Rep. 613. In People v. Brisbane, 76 N. Y. 558, 32 Am. Rep. 337, it was held that where the statute provides that compensation shall be made for a building blown up or destroyed by order of a designated officer, the owner of another building across the street which was wrecked by the explosion, but which was not intended to be destroyed, cannot recover, although the destruction of his building was the natural and probable result of the explosion.

[3] Grube v. St. Paul, 34 Minn. 402; Wilcox v. Chicago, 107 Ill. 337, 47 Am. Rep. 434, and cases cited in following notes. The rule of *respondeat superior* has no application in such a case. Jewett v. New Haven, 38 Conn. 368, 9 Am. Rep. 382; Fisher v. Boston, 104 Mass. 87, 6 Am. Rep. 196.

[4] Welsh v. Rutland, 56 Vt. 228, 48 Am. Rep. 762.

[5] Hayes v. Oshkosh, 33 Wis. 314, 14 Am. Rep. 760.

[6] Fisher v. Boston, 104 Mass. 87, 6 Am. Rep. 196.

[7] Burrill v. Augusta, 78 Me. 118, 57 Am. Rep. 788.

driving of a fireman on the way to a fire;[1] nor for injuries inflicted while the firemen are practicing in the streets[2] or engaged in a parade,[3] or thawing a hydrant,[4] or by allowing a ladder to project from an engine house over the sidewalk.[5] The fact that firemen engaged in the extinguishing of fires are members of a voluntary association and not paid firemen does not change the rule as to the liability of the city for their negligence.[6] The city is not liable for the negligence of the members of a fire patrol[7] nor of a board of fire commissioners.[8] There may, however, be instances where, on other grounds, a corporation is liable in damages for injuries resulting from the negligent acts of its firemen or police officers. Thus, a city may be liable for damages resulting from an obstruction wrongfully placed and allowed to remain in a highway by a fire department.[9] It is the duty of the corporation to keep the highway safe for the use of travelers, and a city is liable for damages resulting from allowing a nuisance to exist in a highway after due notice thereof. Hence, if a police officer leaves a trap-door open in a sidewalk in front of a police station, and as a result an individual is injured, the city is liable.[10] This liability, however, is based not upon the act of the officer, but upon the negligence on the part of the city in failing to care for its property.

§ 314. *Boards of health — Care of hospitals.* — The duties of a board of health are public and not corporate, and the city is therefore not liable for negligence of officers in the discharge of

---

[1] Wilcox v. Chicago, 104 Ill. 334, 47 Am. Rep. 434; Greenwood v. Louisville, 13 Bush, 226, 26 Am. Rep. 263

[2] Thomas v. Findley, 6 Ohio C. C. 241; Gillespie v. Lincoln, 35 Neb. 34, 16 L. R. A. 349.

[3] Rope drawn across the street. Simon v. Atlanta, 67 Ga. 618, 44 Am. Rep. 739.

[4] Welsh v. Rutland, 56 Vt. 228, 48 Am. Rep. 762.

[5] Dodge v. Granger, 17 R. I. 664. For further illustrations of the principle see cases cited in note to this case, in 15 L. R. A. 781.

[6] Torbush v. Norwich, 38 Conn. 225, 9 Am. Rep. 395.

[7] Boyd v. Insurance Patrol of Philadelphia, 113 Pa. St. 269. In Newcomb v. Boston Protection Dept., 151 Mass. 215, 24 N. E. Rep. 39, it was held that such an organization was a private corporation and liable for the negligence of its agents.

[8] O'Leary v. Board, 79 Mich. 281, 7 L. R. A. 170.

[9] See opinion of Tillinghast, J., in Dodge v. Granger, 17 R. I. 664, 15 L. R. A. 781.

[10] Carrington v. St. Louis, 89 Mo. 208.

such duties.[1] Hence, a city is not liable for negligence of those in charge of its public hospitals,[2] or engaged in handling garbage;[3] nor is it liable for the negligence of the county physician.[4] Where the board of health is a separate body, its members and officers are not the agents of the corporation, and their negligence is not its negligence. Hence, the neglect or carelessness of a quarantine officer upon whom the public imposes the duty of preventing the spread of disease creates no liability against the corporation.[5]

§ 315. *Care of criminals.*— A city is not liable to a person who is confined in a city prison for damages occasioned by negligence of the officers or the bad sanitary condition of the prison.[6] Nor is it liable for injuries occasioned by the destruction of a jail by fire occasioned by the negligence of its officers.[7] Nor is a county liable for injuries caused by defective machinery used in a state prison;[8] nor for the death of a convict due to the negligence of a foreman.[9] The city is not liable for

[1] Bryant v. St. Paul, 33 Minn. 289, 53 Am. Rep. 31; Love v. Atlanta, 95 Ga. 129, 51 Am. St. Rep. 64; Orlando v. Pragg, 31 Fla. 111, 34 Am. St. Rep. 17, 25; Whitfield v. Paris, 84 Tex. 431, 31 Am. St. Rep. 69, note; Hughes v. Monroe County, 147 Ill. 49.

[2] Benton v. Trustees of Boston City Hospital, 140 Mass. 13; Brown v. Vinalhaven, 65 Me. 402; White v. Marshfield, 48 Vt. 20; McDonald v. Mass. Gen. Hospital, 120 Mass. 432 (a charitable corporation). But see 12 R. I. 411.

[3] Kuehn v. Milwaukee, 92 Wis. 263.

[4] Summers v. Davis County, 103 Ind. 263; Sherbourne v. Yuba County, 21 Cal. 113; Bates v. Houston (Tex.), 37 S. W. Rep. 383.

[5] Forbes v. Escambria Board of Health, 28 Fla. 26, 13 L. R. A. 549. In Ogg v. Lansing, 35 Iowa, 495, 14 Am. Rep. 499, the plaintiff was asked by the health officer to assist in moving a coffin which contained the body of a person who had died of the smallpox, which was known to the officer. The plaintiff caught the disease, and from him it was contracted by his children. It was held that he had no cause of action against the city for their death.

[6] Hughes v. Lawrenceburg (Ky.), 37 S. W. Rep. 257; La Clef v. City of Concordia, 41 Kan. 323, 13 Am. St. Rep. 385; Lindley v. Pope County (Iowa), 50 N. W. Rep. 975; Gulliken v. McDonald, 62 Minn. 278. But see Shields v. Durham, 118 N. C. 450. In Virginia incorporated cities and towns, but not counties, are required to exercise the same care over prisons as over their streets and sewers, and are liable for negligence. Edwards v. Pocahontas, 47 Fed. Rep. 268.

[7] Brown v. Guyandotte (W. Va.), 12 S. E. Rep. 1207, 11 L. R. A. 121; Hughes v. Lawrenceburg (Ky.), 37 S. W. Rep. 257.

[8] Alamango v. Albany County, 25 Hun (N. Y.), 551.

[9] Nisbit v. Atlanta, 97 Ga. 650. See Royce v. Salt Lake City (Utah), 49 Pac. Rep. 290.

personal injuries suffered by an inmate of the city work-house while engaged in unloading coal, although the city derives a certain amount of revenue from the employment of the inmates of the prison.[1]

§ 316. *Care of the indigent.*—When a public corporation undertakes to care for the poor, it acts in its governmental capacity and is not liable for negligence in connection therewith.[2]

§ 317. *Care of school buildings.*—A public *quasi*-corporation, acting on behalf of the state and having no separate fund, is not liable for negligence in the care of the school buildings.[3] Thus, such a corporation is not liable for an injury caused by a broken lightning rod[4] or an uncovered cellar.[5] School trustees are state officers and not the agents of the corporation. In some cases a liability exists on the part of the officers, but trustees are not liable unless they have some means of providing funds for keeping the property in repair.[6] The question of the liability of a municipal corporation which owns its school buildings and has a fund from which to provide for their care will be considered hereafter.

II. Solely Corporate Duties.

§ 318. *Rule of liability for negligence.*—The rule is settled that when municipal corporations are not in the exercise of their purely governmental functions, for the sole and immediate benefit of the public, but are exercising as corporations private

---

[1] Cerran v. Boston, 151 Mass. 505, 8 L. R. A. 243. In this case the court, after stating the rule that municipal corporations are not liable in private actions for omissions or neglects in the performance of a public duty imposed by law, nor for that of their servant engaged therein, said: "Nor do we see any reason why the city should be held responsible because some revenue is derived from the labor of the inmates. It is required by the statute that these inmates should be kept at work, but the institution is not conducted with a view to a pecuniary profit."

[2] Maximilian v. Mayor, 62 N. Y. 160 (commissioners of charities); Brennan v. Guardians of Limerick Union, L. R. 2 C. L. 42. As to negligence in care of poor farm, see Neff v. Wellesly, 148 Mass. 487, 2 L. R. A. 500; Symonds v. Clay County, 71 Ill. 355 (injuries caused by fire in the poor-house).

[3] Lane v. Woodbury, 58 Iowa, 462.

[4] Donovan v. Board of Education, 85 N. Y. 117.

[5] Diehm v. Cincinnati, 25 Ohio St. 305; Hamm v. New York, 70 N. Y. 460.

[6] Finch v. Board of Education, 30 Ohio St. 37.

franchise powers and privileges which belong to them for their immediate corporate benefit, or dealing with property held by them for their corporate advantage, for a profit, although it inures ultimately to the benefit of the general public, they become liable for the negligent exercise of such powers precisely as are individuals.[1]

§ 319. *As owner of property.*— When a corporation is the owner of private property it is chargeable with the same duties and obligations in respect thereto as if it were a private corporation or individual.[2] Thus, if it so manages a market as to render it a nuisance it is liable in damages to those who are injured thereby.[3] So, if it maintains a farm, in order to more economically support its poor, it is liable for injuries caused by its negligence in connection therewith.[4] A municipal corporation is not ordinarily liable to individuals for the manner in which it cares for a public building, but if instead of using the building for public purposes exclusively it rents a portion of it for private purposes and receives an income therefrom, it is liable for its negligence in and about the building in the same manner as though it owned the property in its private corporate capacity.[5] A city is responsible in damages for the death of a child caused by the dangerous condition of a lot owned by the city and but partially inclosed from the street.[6] When a city owns a ceme-

---

[1] Shearman & Redfield, Neg., § 286; Jones, Neg. of Mun. Corp., ch. 5; Dillon, Mun. Corp., § 954; Welsh v. Rutland, 56 Vt. 228, 48 Am. Rep. 762.

[2] Oliver v. Worcester, 102 Mass. 489. And see note to Riddell v. Proprietors (7 Mass. 169) in 5 Am. Dec. 43; Neff v. Wellesley, 148 Mass. 487, 2 L. R. A. 500.

[3] Suffolk v. Parker, 79 Va. 660, 52 Am. Rep. 640, and cases cited in note; Weymouth v. New Orleans, 43 La. Ann. 344. In Barron v. Detroit, 94 Mich. 601, 19 L. R. A. 452, it was held that where no duty rested upon the corporation to construct a market, it was liable for the same degree of care, in respect to plans and construction, as private individuals.

[4] Moulton v. Scarborough, 71 Me. 267, 36 Am. Rep. 308. The injury was caused by a ram kept by the town for breeding purposes, but negligently allowed to run at large. Compare Hollenbeck v. Winnebago Co., 95 Ill. 148, 35 Am. Rep. 151, and note; French v. Boston, 129 Mass. 592.

[5] Warden v. New Bedford, 131 Mass. 23, 41 Am. Rep. 185. Also where a building in a public common was rented. Oliver v. Worcester, 102 Mass. 489. Degree of care required in construction of a building, see Flori v. St. Louis, 69 Mo. 341, 33 Am. Rep. 504.

[6] The lot was allowed to become flooded with water in which the child was drowned. Pekin v. McMaben, 154 Ill. 141, 27 L. R. A. 206. See Seben v. Chicago, 165 Ill. 371; Omaha v. Richards, 49 Neb. 244.

tery and derives an income therefrom, it is liable for damages caused by a lack of due care in its management.[1]

§ 320. *Illustrations — Wharves.* — When a city owns and receives an income from wharves it must keep them in a condition suitable for use, and is hence liable for damages resulting from a want of care in this respect.[2] This applies to the approaches to a dock or pier of which the corporation has charge,[3] and the duty is toward all persons approaching the same from the land or from the water.[4]

§ 321. *Private business enterprises — Gas and water.* — When a municipal corporation engages in a business enterprise or undertakes to carry on any business or perform any work for its citizens for compensation, it is held to the same responsibility for negligence that the law imposes upon private corporations doing the same or similar work.[5] This principle applies where the corporation maintains a public wash-house and renders it liable for injuries caused by defective machinery used therein.[6] So, if the corporation manufactures and sells gas for a compensation, it is liable in the same manner as a private corporation.[7] The weight of authority supports the doctrine that powers conferred upon municipal corporations to establish water and fire departments are in their nature legislative and governmental.[8] It has been said,[9] on the authority of an early New York case,[10]

---

[1] Toledo v. Cone, 41 Ohio St. 149.

[2] Seaman v. New York, 80 N. Y. 239; Nickerson v. Tirrell, 127 Mass. 236; Willey v. Alleghany City, 118 Pa. St. 490.

[3] Barber v. Abendroth, 102 N. Y. 406.

[4] Kennedy v. New York, 73 N. Y. 365.

[5] Jones, Neg. of Mun. Corp., sec. 41; Thompson, Neg., p. 738; City Council v. Lombard (Ga.), 25 S. E. Rep. 772.

[6] Cowley v. Sunderland, 6 H. & N. 565.

[7] Western Savings Society v. Philadelphia, 31 Pa. St. 175.

[8] Springfield F. & M. Co. v. Keeseville, 148 N. Y. 46; Edgerly v. Concord, 62 N. H. 8; Taintor v. Worcester, 123 Mass. 311.

[9] See Jones, Neg. of Mun. Corp., sec. 40.

[10] Bailey v. New York, 3 Hill (N. Y.), 531. These cases proceed upon the principle that "a city or town which is charged with a public duty in consideration of valuable franchises is liable to indemnify an individual who suffers any special injury from a neglect of the city; and that a city or town which derives any emolument from the exercise of powers conferred upon it is liable in like manner for the negligent or unskilful exercise of the powers by its agents or for the neglect of a duty which is consequent upon having ex-

that when a municipal corporation maintains water-works and supplies water for a compensation, it is engaged in a private enterprise and liable in the same manner as a private corporation; but the authority of this case is virtually destroyed by a recent case [1] in which it is held that when an incorporated village avails itself of the permissible legislative authority to construct and maintain a system of water-works, the power is to be regarded as exclusively for public purposes and as belonging to the corporation in its public political character; that the corporation was therefore not liable for neglect to exercise reasonable care and diligence in respect to the maintenance of the work, and that it was not made a private business by the fact that water rents were paid to the corporation by the inhabitants.

But it has been held that a municipal corporation is liable for damages caused by water escaping from the mains or reservoirs through the negligence of the city; and where the injury was caused by a defective water-box in a street the court said: [2] "The cause of the accident was the improper condition of the water-box or the negligence of the defendant in maintaining it in a proper condition. This places the neglect upon the defendant, as the owner and the manager of the aqueduct, and not as having the supervision and charged with the duty of repairing the highway at that point. For an injury caused by the failure to repair the highways within the limits the defendant is not liable. But for an injury caused by a failure to properly maintain its aqueduct it is liable." But this liability cannot in any case be so extended as to make the corporation liable for the non-performance or the negligent performance of purely

ercised them; and in such cases the officers engaged in the execution of the powers are to be regarded as the agents of the city or town." Aldrich v. Tripp, 11 R. I. 141, 23 Am. Rep. 434.

[1] Springfield F. & M. Co. v. Keeseville, *supra*. In Smith v. Philadelphia, 81 Pa. St. 38, 22 Am. Rep. 731, it was held that the amount of water rent paid was the measure of damages which could be recovered for the failure of the city to supply the plaintiff with water. No damages can be recovered for being deprived of the water.

[2] Stock v. Boston, 149 Mass. 410. In Hand v. Brookline, 126 Mass. 324, Gray, C. J., said: "If the water escaping from the aqueduct by reason of its negligent and imperfect construction had injured buildings or property, there could be no doubt of the right of the owner to recover damages against the town. The fact that the injury occasioned was within the limits of a highway where the person injured has a lawful right to be, affords no grounds for exempting the town from liability."

governmental duties.¹ Thus, a city is not bound to protect the property of its citizens from fire, and it cannot be held in damages for a failure to supply the necessary water to extinguish a fire, or for defects of any kind or character in the hydrants or other machinery which it provides for the purpose of extinguishing fires.² The electrical bureau of a city from which it receives fees from grants of privileges to private persons is of such a private nature as to render the city liable for the negligence of its servants.³

¹ Wilkins v. Rutland, 61 Vt. 336. See Grimes v. Keene, 52 N. H. 335.
² Mendel v. Wheeling, 28 W. Va. 233.
³ Bodge v. Philadelphia, 167 Pa. St. 492.

CHAPTER XVII.

MUNICIPAL DUTIES RELATING TO GOVERNMENTAL AFFAIRS.

§ 322. General statement.
323. Common-law duty to repair highways.
324. Conflicting rules — Chartered municipalities.
325. Liability of counties and towns.
326. Extent of duty to care for highways.
327. Lighting the streets.
§ 328. Necessary obstructions.
329. Illustrations.
330. Lack of funds as a defense.
331. Liability for acts of licensees.
332. Care of sidewalks.
333. Obstructions on sidewalk.
334. Ice and snow on highways.
335. Care of bridges.
336. Notice.

§ 322. *General statement.*— While public corporations are not liable for negligence in connection with the performance of solely governmental duties, and are liable for negligence in connection with solely municipal duties, more difficult questions are presented when we come to consider their liability for duties which are ministerial in their nature but which relate to governmental affairs. Illustrations of duties of this character are found in connection with highways, sewers, bridges and other public works. The decisions are very conflicting, and the defects or uncertainties of the common law have in many cases been cured by statutes.

§ 323. *Common-law duty to repair highways.*— The control of highways rests primarily with the state, but it is almost universally imposed upon public corporations through which the highways run. The decisions upon the question of the implied liability of such corporations for injuries resulting from neglect to perform the duty of keeping the highways in reasonably safe condition are so conflicting that little more can be done than to classify them. It will be found that the liability or non-liability is made to depend upon the nature of the corporation or the nature of the duty to be performed, and the means within the control of the corporation for performing the duty. The student must in all cases, however, consult the statutes of the state.

§ 324. *Conflicting rules — Chartered municipalities.*—In the New England states it is almost universally held that no implied liability attaches to a county, town or even a chartered municipality for failing to keep the highways in proper condition. In the leading Massachusetts case,[1] the authorities are elaborately discussed by Chief Justice Gray and the statement made that such liability is not recognized by the English cases. This conclusion, however, has been criticised,[2] and there are strong reasons for believing that the common law, as declared by the English courts, was otherwise. What may be called the rule of the case of Russell v. Men of Devon, as construed by Chief Justice Gray, has been followed in a number of states.[3] But the implied liability of chartered municipalities, although not generally of public *quasi*-corporations, for negligence in the care of highways, is recognized by a strong current of authority

---

[1] Hill v. Boston, 122 Mass. 344, 23 Am. Rep. 332. See the early cases of Riddell v. Proprietors of Locks, 7 Mass. 169; Mower v. Leicester, 9 Mass. 237.

[2] This doctrine rests upon the authority of Russell v. Men of Devon, 2 T. R. 667. The early English authorities are reviewed in Jones on Neg. of Mun. Corp., §§ 15–19. In Thomas v. Sorrell, Vaughan, 330, decided in the latter half of the seventeenth century, we find the following statement by Chief Justice Vaughan: "And note, if a man have particular damage by a foundrous way, he is generally without remedy, though the nuisance is to be punished by the king. The reason is, because a foundrous way, a decayed bridge or the like, are commonly to be repaired by some township, vill, hamlet or a county, who are not corporate, and therefore no action lies against them for a particular damage, but their neglects are to be presented, and they punished by fine to the king. But if a particular person or body corporate be to repair a certain highway or portion of it, or a bridge, and a man is endamaged particularly by the foundrousness of the way or decay of the bridge, he may have his action against the person or body corporate who ought to repair, for his damage, because he can bring his action against them; but where there is no person against whom to bring his action, it is as if a man be damaged by one that cannot be known."

[3] Fort Smith v. York, 52 Ark. 84; Winbigler v. Los Angeles, 45 Cal. 36; Chope v. Eureka, 78 Cal. 588, 4 L. R. A. 327, two judges dissenting. A number of authorities are cited in note to this case. Beardsley v. Hartford, 50 Conn. 529, 47 Am. Dec. 677; Aldrich v. Gorham, 77 Me. 287; Moore v. Abbot, 32 Me. 46; Detroit v. Blackeby, 21 Mich. 84; Eastman v. Meredith, 36 N. H. 284; Elliott v. Lisbon, 57 N. H. 27; Pray v. Jersey City, 32 N. J. Law, 394; Wild v. Paterson, 47 N. J. Law, 406; Wixon v. Newport, 13 R. I. 454, 43 Am. Rep. 35 (injury caused by defect in school-house); Young v. Charleston, 20 S. C. 116, 47 Am. Rep. 827; Wilkins v. Rutland, 61 Vt. 336; Welsh v. Rutland, 56 Vt. 228; Cairncross v. Pewaukee, 78 Wis. 66, 10 L. R. A. 473; Robinson v. Rohr, 73 Wis. 436, 2 L. R. A. 366.

in the states outside of New England.[1] This doctrine has been adopted by the supreme court of the United States,[2] which will, however, follow the decisions of the highest court of the state from which an appeal is taken.[3]

§ 325. *Liability of counties and towns.*—By a very decided weight of authority, there is no liability on the part of counties and townships for the care of highways unless such liability is created by statute.[4] In some states there is no liability even when the duty to repair rests upon such corporation, as this

[1] Dillon, Mun. Corp., sec. 1017; Jones, Neg. of Mun. Corp., sec. 57; Smoot v. Wetumpka, 24 Ala. 112; Montgomery v. Wright, 72 Ala. 411; Denver v. Dunsmore, 7 Colo. 328; Denver v. Williams, 12 Colo. 475; Larson v. Grand Forks, 3 Dak. 307; Anderson v. Wilmington (Del.), 19 Atl. Rep. 509; Tallahassee v. Fortune, 3 Fla. 19, 52 Am. Dec. 358; Brunswick v. Braxton, 70 Ga. 193; Anderson v. East, 117 Ind. 126, 2 L. R. A. 325; Knightstown v. Musgrove, 116 Ind. 121, 9 Am. St. Rep. 827; Goshen v. England, 119 Ind. 368, 5 L. R. A. 253; Protestant Episcopal Church v. Anamosa, 76 Iowa, 538, 2 L. R. A. 606; Chicago v. Keefe, 114 Ill. 222; Kansas City v. Bermingham, 45 Kan. 212, 25 Pac. Rep. 569; Topeka v. Tuttle, 5 Kan. 186; Greenwood v. Louisville, 13 Ky. 226; Cline v. Crescent City R. Co., 41 La. Ann. 1031, 6 So. Rep. 851; Baltimore v. Marriott, 9 Md. 160; Kennedy v. Cumberland, 65 Md. 514; Welter v. St. Paul, 40 Minn. 460, 12 Am. St. Rep. 752, and note; Shartle v. Minneapolis, 17 Minn. 308 (Gil. 284); Whitfield v. Meridian, 66 Miss. 570, 4 L. R. A. 834, 14 Am. St. Rep. 596; Haniford v. Kansas City, 103 Mo. 172; Maus v. Springfield, 101 Mo. 613, 20 Am. St. Rep. 634; Sullivan v. Helena, 10 Mont. 134, 25 Pac. Rep. 94; Ponca v. Crawford, 18 Neb. 551, 28 Neb. 762, 8 Am. St. Rep. 144; Lincoln v. Smith, 29 Neb. 228. This case is elaborately annotated in 10 L. R. A. 735; McNally v. Cohoes, 127 N. Y. 350; Ehrgott v. New York, 96 N. Y. 264; McDonough v. Virginia City, 6 Nev. 431; Bunch v. Edenton, 90 N. C. 431; Shelby v. Clagett, 46 Ohio St. 549; Cleveland v. King, 132 U. S. 295; Sheridan v. Salem, 14 Oreg. 328; Farquar v. Roseburg, 18 Oreg. 271, 17 Am. St. Rep. 732, note; Brookville v. Arthurs, 130 Pa. St. 501; Knoxville v. Bell, 12 Lea (Tenn.), 157; Galveston v. Posnainsky, 62 Tex. 118; Levy v. Salt Lake City, 3 Utah, 63; McCoull v. Manchester, 85 Va. 579, 2 L. R. A. 691; Morgan v. Morley, 1 Wash. 464; Phillips v. Ritchie County, 31 W. Va. 477.

[2] District of Columbia v. Woodbury, 136 U. S. 450; Barnes v. District of Columbia, 91 U. S. 540.

[3] Detroit v. Osborne, 135 U. S. 492.

[4] Hill v. Boston, 122 Mass. 344; Templeton v. Linn County, 22 Oreg. 313, 15 L. R. A. 730; Bates v. Rutland, 62 Vt. 178, 9 L. R. A. 363; Perry v. John, 79 Pa. St. 412; Peters v. Fergus Falls, 35 Minn. 549; Dosdall v. Olmsted Co., 30 Minn. 96; Young v. Charleston, 20 S. C. 116, 47 Am. Rep. 827; Elliott, Roads and Streets, p. 42. In Dillon, Mun. Corp., II, § 997, it is said: "In the United States there is no common-law obligation resting upon *quasi*-corporations such as counties, townships and New England towns to repair highways, streets or bridges within their limits, and they are not obliged to do so unless by force of statute."

duty is purely governmental.[1] The rule of non-liability of counties and towns is adopted in many states where the decisions impose the liability upon municipal corporations proper.[2] The distinction between the liability of municipal corporations and public *quasi*-corporations in this respect is well established, although it rests upon very unsatisfactory reasons.[3] It is not universal, however, as some states impose a liability upon counties[4] and even townships,[5] especially in connection with the care of bridges.[6] Of course there is no corporate liability when the duty to care for highways is imposed upon certain officials and not upon the corporation. Under such circumstances the corporation is not liable for the negligence of the officers unless made so by statute.[7]

§ 326. *Extent of duty to care for highways.*— Where the law imposes the duty to care for streets upon municipal corporations, it is bound to exercise reasonable care to see that they are in safe condition,[8] but it is not an insurer of their safety.[9] The street must be public[10] and under the control of the corporation.[11]

---

[1] Altnow v. Town of Libley, 30 Minn. 186, 44 Am. Rep. 191; Stilling v. Thorp, 54 Wis. 528.

[2] Thompson, Neg., I, p. 615; Dillon, Mun. Corp., I, § 1023; Jones, Neg. Mun. Corp., ch. 8. Conflicting authorities are cited in a note to Eastman v. Clackamas County. 32 Fed. Rep. 24.

[3] Elliott, Roads and Streets, p. 319 and cases cited.

[4] Shadler v. Blair County, 136 Pa. St. 488; Anne Arundell County v. Duckett, 20 Md. 468.

[5] Dean v. New Milford Tp., 5 W. & S. (Pa.) 545.

[6] Howard County Commissioners v. Legg, 93 Ind. 523, 47 Am. Rep. 390; Wilson v. Jefferson County, 13 Iowa, 181. But see Green v. Harrison County, 61 Iowa, 311.

[7] Monk v. New Utrecht, 104 N. Y. 552; Reardon v. St. Louis County, 36 Mo. 555; Scales v. Chattahoochee County, 41 Ga. 225.

[8] Raymond v. Lowell, 6 Cush. (Mass.) 524, 53 Am. Dec. 57, note. When the city authorizes a railway company to occupy a street which is thereby rendered in an unsafe condition, a person who is injured may proceed against the city or the railway company. The primary liability is on the city. Zanesville v. Fannan, 53 Ohio St. 605, 53 Am. St. Rep. 664; Eyler v. Commissioners, 49 Md. 257, 33 Am. Rep. 249. A railway which has torn up a street must restore it to its former condition, and if it fails to do so it is liable for damages for injuries. Louisville, etc. R. Co. v. Pritchard, 131 Ind. 564, 11 Am. St. Rep. 395, and cases cited in note; State v. St. Paul, etc. R. Co., 35 Minn. 131, 59 Am. Rep. 313.

[9] Hunt v. New York, 109 N. Y. 134; Burns v. Bradford, 137 Pa. St. 361, 11 L. R. A. 726.

[10] Carpenter v. Cohoes, 81 N. Y. 21, 37 Am. Rep. 468; Veale v. Boston, 135 Mass. 187.

[11] Taylor v. Woburn, 130 Mass. 494; Hart v. Red Cedar, 63 Wis. 634; Will

It must have been accepted by the corporation after being dedicated by the owner of the land.[1] If the city has assumed the care of a street, it is responsible thereafter for its condition, although the street may not be technically under the care of the city. The entire width of the street must be kept in a safe condition.[2] This rule, however, does not apply to a country highway, where the duty extends only to the traveled part of the road.[3] There may be instances, however, where the corporation would be liable for injuries resulting to one traveling outside of the limits of the highway; as, "where there is no visible boundary to the line of the street and a portion of the roadway traveled on is so near the actual line (although really outside thereof) as to induce the belief in any one exercising reasonable care that he is within such line."[4] That part of the road which is kept open to travel must be kept in a reasonable safe condition,[5] although in order to do so it may be necessary to protect the public from danger by obstructions or excavations on adjoining land.[6] It is for the jury to determine whether, under the circumstances of the particular case, the obstruction was of such a nature that the highway was not in a suitable state of repair, and whether the corporation was negligent in not removing the obstruction.[7]

§ 327. *Lighting the streets.*— Where a city is required by a statute or by its charter to light its streets, it is, of course, liable

v. Village of Mendon (Mich.), 66 N. W. Rep. 58; City of Chadron v. Glover, 43 Neb. 732, 62 N. W. Rep. 62.

[1] Ivory v. Deerpark, 116 N. Y. 476; Estelle v. Lake Crystal, 27 Minn. 243.

[2] Monongahela City v. Fischer, 111 Pa. St. 9. The corporation must keep the streets in the outskirts of the city clear for such a width as the public necessity and convenience requires. Village of Rankin v. Smith, 63 Ill. App. 522.

[3] Perkins v. Fayette, 68 Me. 152; Fitzgerald v. Berlin, 64 Wis. 203; Campbell v. Race, 7 Cush. 408.

[4] Jewhurst v. Syracuse, 108 N. Y. 303. A city must use reasonable care to prevent pedestrians from falling into excavations on private property adjacent to the sidewalk. Wiggin v. St. Louis, 135 Mo. 558. But there is no liability for injuries suffered by one who goes outside of an unfenced highway when the whole of the highway is in safe condition. McHugh v. St. Paul (Minn.), 70 N. W. Rep. 5.

[5] Aston v. Newton, 134 Mass. 507; Stafford v. Oskaloosa, 57 Iowa, 748.

[6] Rooney v. Randolph, 128 Mass. 580.

[7] Hubbard v. Concord, 35 N. H. 52, 69 Am. Dec. 520; Seeley v. Litchfield, 49 Conn. 134, 44 Am. Rep. 213; Michigan City v. Boeckling, 122 Ind. 39; Goodfellow v. New York, 100 N. Y. 15; Foxworthy v. Hastings, 25 Neb. 133; Hill v. Fond du Lac, 56 Wis. 242.

for injuries caused by its neglect to do so; but wnere no such duty is imposed on it by the legislature, it is not liable for omitting to light the streets,[1] although the fact that a street is not lighted may be material upon the question of negligence where it was partially obstructed or out of repair.[2] It is the duty, however, of the corporation to place lights near obstructions or excavations temporarily placed in the streets.[3]

§ 328. *Necessary obstructions.*— There are many obstructions which may be placed or allowed to be placed in a public street which do not constitute defects or nuisances. If they do not unnecessarily interfere with the primary purpose for which streets are dedicated, they do not render the way unsafe in the eye of the law. Thus hydrants,[4] hitching-posts,[5] door-steps[6] and stepping-stones[7] are not in themselves objects which render a street unsafe. The public must adapt itself to the fact of their existence, and if they are properly located and cared for the city is not liable for injuries occasioned by them. The same rule applies to car tracks and merchandise and building material temporarily placed in a street.[8] They constitute obstructions, but they are necessary, and when properly guarded[9] may be allowed to remain in a street for a reasonable time[10] without rendering the municipality liable for injuries occasioned thereby.[11] But unnecessary obstructions must not be allowed

---

[1] Dillon, Mun. Corp., II, § 1010; Freeport v. Isbell, 83 Ill. 440; Gould v. Topeka, 32 Kan. 485; Cleveland v. King, 132 U. S. 295; McHugh v. St. Paul (Minn.), 70 N. W. Rep. 5.

[2] Elliott, Roads and Streets, p. 457; Lyon v. Cambridge, 136 Mass. 419.

[3] McCoull v. Manchester, 85 Va. 579; Wilson v. White, 71 Ga. 506, 51 Am. Rep. 269. In Sinclair v. Baltimore, 59 Md. 592, it was held that the city need not place lights upon building material which had been left in the street.

[4] Ring v. Cohoes, 77 N. Y. 83.

[5] Macomber v. Taunton, 100 Mass. 255.

[6] Cushing v. Boston, 128 Mass. 330.

[7] Kingston v. Dubois, 102 N. Y. 219.

[8] Callanan v. Gilman, 107 N. Y. 360.

[9] Bauer v. Rochester, 35 N. Y. St. Rep. 959; Olson v. Chippewa Falls, 71 Wis. 558; Wilson v. White, 71 Ga. 506, 51 Am. Rep. 269.

[10] Pettengill v. Yonkers, 116 N. Y. 558.

[11] Cleveland v. King, 132 U. S. 295; Nolan v. King, 97 N. Y. 565; Klatt v. Milwaukee, 53 Wis. 196. A corporation is not relieved from liability by the fact that the person who was allowed to place the obstruction in the street agreed to protect the public. Cleveland v. King, *supra;* Farquar v. Roseberg, 18 Oreg. 271, 17 Am. St. Rep. 272; Boucher v. New Haven, 40 Conn. 456.

to remain in the street, as the city must "keep all streets, sidewalks and crossings in a reasonably safe condition and free from all unnecessary and dangerous obstruction, so as not to endanger the persons of those lawfully using the same."[1] The size or location of the object is immaterial if it renders the street unsafe.[2]

§ 329. *Illustrations.*— Municipal corporations have been held liable for injuries occasioned by negligently leaving a road scraper in a street,[3] wires across a highway,[4] mud piled in a street and allowed to freeze,[5] projecting nails in a plank street,[6] a projecting water plug,[7] a wagon standing in the street under a license,[8] unguarded holes or excavations,[9] no matter by whom made,[10] a hole caused by the breaking of a water pipe,[11] an open culvert,[12] slippery objects under certain circumstances,[13] excavations and embankments adjoining the street which render it unsafe,[14] a collision caused by the narrowing of a street by an

[1] Glantz v. Bend, 106 Ind. 305; Village of Ponca v. Crawford, 23 Neb. 662, 8 Am. St. Rep. 144, note.
[2] McCool v. Grand Rapids, 58 Mich. 41.
[3] Whitney v. Town of Ticonderoga, 127 N. Y. 40, 27 N. E. Rep. 403.
[4] Hayes v. Hyde Park, 153 Mass. 514, 12 L. R. A. 249.
[5] Champaign v. Jones, 132 Ill. 304.
[6] Michigan City v. Boeckling, 122 Ind. 39.
[7] Scranton v. Catterson, 94 Pa. St. 202.
[8] Cohen v. New York, 113 N. Y. 532. In this case the court said: "We do not say that this principle of responsibility would render the city liable in every case of a mistaken exercise of power authorizing the use or occupancy of a public street by an individual. We confine ourselves to the decision of this case, and we simply say that when the city, without the pretense of authority, and in direct violation of a statute, assumes to grant to a private individual the right to obstruct the public highway while in the transaction of his private business, and for such privilege takes compensation, it must be regarded as itself maintaining a nuisance so long as the obstruction is continued by reason of and under such license."
[9] Barr v. Kansas City, 105 Mo. 550.
[10] Savannah v. Donnelly, 71 Ga. 258.
[11] Hopkins v. Ogden City, 5 Utah, 390, 16 Pac. Rep. 596.
[12] O'Gorman v. Morris, 26 Minn. 267.
[13] Cromarty v. Boston, 127 Mass. 329, 34 Am. Rep. 381.
[14] Barnes v. Chicopee, 138 Mass. 67, 52 Am. Rep. 259. In Puffer v. Orange, 122 Mass. 389, 23 Am. Rep. 368, the court said: "A town is bound to erect barriers or railings where a dangerous place is in such close proximity to the highway as to make traveling on the highway unsafe. But it is not bound to do so to prevent travelers from straying from the highway, although there is a dangerous place at some distance from the highway which they may reach by so straying." Hudson v. Marlborough, 154 Mass. 218, 28 N. E. Rep. 147.

embankment.[1] Obstructions which have a natural tendency to frighten horses being driven along the highway are generally viewed as defects, and the corporation held liable for injuries resulting therefrom.[2] As a general rule no distinction is made between cases where the obstruction or defect was due to the act of the corporation or the act of private individuals. The right of action against the city rests upon the duty of the city to keep the streets in a reasonably safe condition,[3] and this duty cannot be shifted upon the property owners.

[1] Fopper v. Wheatland, 59 Wis. 623; Flagg v. Hudson, 142 Mass. 280.

[2] Morse v. Richmond, 41 Vt. 435, 98 Am. Dec. 600 (statutory duty — see an elaborate note to this case); Dimock v. Suffield, 30 Conn. 129; Rushville v. Adams, 107 Ind. 475, 57 Am. Rep. 124; Cairncross v. Pewaukee, 78 Wis. 66, 10 L. R. A. 473; Campbell v. Stillwater, 32 Minn. 308; Thompson, Neg., § 1011; Shearman & Red. Neg., § 169. The city is liable if the object has a natural tendency to frighten horses of ordinary gentleness and training. Piollet v. Simmers, 106 Pa. St. 95, 51 Am. Rep. 496. For contrary decisions, see Bowes v. Boston, 155 Mass. 344, 15 L. R. A. 365, and Agnew v. Corunna, 55 Mich. 428, 54 Am. Rep. 388 (boulders in street). A steam-engine, as a means of locomotion in a highway, is not necessarily a nuisance. Where the use of one frightens horses the right of action for injuries will depend upon the question of negligence. Macomber v. Nichols, 34 Mich. 212, 22 Am. Rep. 522. But see Stanley v. Davenport, 54 Iowa, 463, 37 Am. Rep. 216. In Omaha v. Richards, 49 Neb. 244, the court said: "A case quite analogous in principle to the one at bar is City of Chicago v. Hesing, 83 Ill. 204. That was an action to recover damages for the death of a child about four years old." The third paragraph of the syllabus reads thus:

"It is gross negligence on the part of the city to leave a ditch filled with water about five feet deep in a public and frequented street bordering on a sidewalk without any guards to prevent children from falling into the same, and if a child is drowned by falling into the same the city will be liable." The same principle was held and tried in the Village of Carterville v. Cook, 129 Ill. 152; Brennan v. City of St. Louis, 92 Mo. 482; City of Indianapolis v. Emmelman, 108 Ind. 530; Nichols v. City of St. Paul, 44 Minn. 494; Hawley v. City of Atlantic, 92 Iowa, 172, 60 N. W. Rep. 519; Reed v. City of Madison, 83 Wis. 171; Gibson v. Huntington, 38 W. Va. 177. See, also, for a similar case, Seben v. City of Chicago, 165 Ill. 371. In Kies v. Erie, 169 Pa. St. 598, it appears that the plaintiff was injured by the large doors of a firehouse suddenly opening out, and the court said: "If the operation of these doors with reasonable care would have provided against danger and accident to the passers-by, the city is liable. If the necessary and natural and probable operation of these doors was dangerous, even though accompanied by the use of ordinary care on the part of the employees, the city is liable for such results."

[3] But see Baltimore v. O'Donnell, 54 Md. 110.

§ 330. *Lack of funds as a defense.*— A public corporation is not liable for damages caused by its failure to repair a street where it has neither the means nor the corporate power to procure the means necessary for making such repairs;[1] but "want of funds to repair a street will not excuse a city for its neglect in regard to them unless it has exhausted all the means at its command to raise funds or to make the repairs and unless the accident could not have been prevented by guards or signs."[2] If it has not the means of keeping the street in proper condition, it should either close the street or protect the public by means of guards or other proper and necessary signs.[3]

§ 331. *Liability for acts of licensees.*— The rule is that a municipal corporation is not liable for injuries resulting from the acts of its licensees unless the license is granted without authority[4] or the acts so licensed are admittedly dangerous.[5] The liability in such cases must be distinguished from the mere failure to prevent the doing of an act which is an exercise of

---

[1] Hines v. Lockport, 50 N. Y. 236; Weed v. Ballston Spa, 76 N. Y. 329; Ivory v. Deerpark, 116 N. Y. 476; Whitfield v. Meridian, 66 Miss. 570, 14 Am. St. Rep. 596. The defense of want of means to make repairs must be pleaded. Netzer v. Crookston, 59 Minn. 244.

[2] Jones, Neg. of Mun. Corp., sec. 75; Dillon, Mun. Corp., II, § 1017; Elliott, Roads and Streets, p. 445; Delger v. St. Paul, 14 Fed. Rep. 567; Birmingham v. Lewis, 92 Ala. 352, 9 So. Rep. 243; Lord v. Mobile (Ala.), 21 So. Rep. 366.

[3] Monk v. New Utrecht, 104 N. Y. 552. Knowledge that there is no money in the treasury by one who is hurt by a defective sidewalk is not notice of the defects. Village of Ponca v. Crawford, 23 Neb. 662, 8 Am. St. Rep. 144.

[4] Cohen v. New York, 113 N. Y. 532.

[5] As by authorizing a lunatic to sell gunpowder. Cole v. Nashville, 4 Sneed (Tenn.), 162. In Wheeler v. Plymouth, 116 Ind. 158, 9 Am. St. Rep. 837, 18 N. E. Rep. 532, the court said: "It is quite well settled that a municipal corporation is not liable for the acts of its licensees, unless it is shown that they were authorized to perform an act dangerous in itself." The cases cannot be reconciled, but the test seems to be, Did the city merely fail to prohibit the act by appropriate legislation or for the time being suspend its legislation, and thus, by failing to prohibit, consent (Lincoln v. Boston, 148 Mass. 578, 3 L. R. A. 257), or did it affirmatively authorize the act? If the authority given is in general terms, it will be presumed that the licensee will exercise due care and the city will not be responsible for his negligence (Little v. Madison, 49 Wis. 605); but if the city licenses a dangerous act, or acts beyond its general authority in licensing an act which it has no power to license, it is liable for damages resulting therefrom.

legislative discretion.[1] The corporation may exercise its discretion on the question of forbidding certain conduct without being liable for damages which would have been avoided had the conduct been forbidden.[2] Thus, the corporation is not liable because it fails to prevent persons from coasting on streets, although such a use of the streets is manifestly dangerous to the public.[3] But a city may be liable if, without authority, it allows a wagon to stand in the street[4] or a steam motor to use the street.[5]

§ 332. *Care of sidewalks.*— A municipal corporation is liable for injuries resulting from the improper condition of a sidewalk which is under its care,[6] although it was constructed by a private corporation or individual.[7] It is its duty to keep the sidewalks in a reasonably safe condition both day and night for the uses for which they are designed.[8] This duty exists in the case of all sidewalks under the control of the city, although what would amount to negligence in one locality might be proper care in another.[9] The liability is the same in respect to walks built by private persons or situated on private property, if they are under the care and control of the corporation.[10] This duty cannot be imposed upon the lot owner in such a manner as to relieve the corporation from its responsibility.[11]

[1] Carthage v. Frederick, 122 N. Y. 268, 19 Am. St. Rep. 490.
[2] Little v. Madison, 49 Wis. 605.
[3] Burford v. Grand Rapids, 53 Mich. 98, 51 Am. Rep. 105 (under permission of an ordinance); Lafayette v. Timberlake, 88 Ind. 330; Schultz v. Milwaukee, 49 Wis. 254, 35 Am. Rep. 782; Calwell v. Boone, 51 Iowa, 687, 83 Am. Rep. 154; Steele v. Boston, 123 Mass. 583; Wilmington v. Van Degrift (Del.), 29 Atl. Rep. 1047, 25 L. R. A. 538.
[4] Cohen v. New York, 113 N. Y. 532.
[5] Stanley v. Davenport, 54 Iowa, 463, 37 Am. Rep. 216.
[6] Roe v. Kansas City, 100 Mo. 190. As to liability for defective construction or the adoption of a dangerous plan, see *infra*, § 340.
[7] Hutchings v. Sullivan (Me.), 37 Atl. Rep. 883; Salisbury v. Ithaca, 94 N. Y. 27.
[8] City v. Nash (Neb.), 69 N. W. Rep. 964.
[9] South Omaha v. Powell (Neb.), 70 N. W. Rep. 391; Waggener v. Point Pleasant, 42 W. Va. 798; City of Flora v. Naney, 136 Ill. 45, 26 N. E. Rep. 645; Fulliam v. Muscatine, 70 Iowa, 436, 30 N. W. Rep. 861.
[10] Graham v. Albert Lea, 48 Minn. 201, 50 N. W. Rep. 1108; Foxworthy v. Hastings, 31 Neb. 825, 48 N. W. Rep. 901; Mansfield v. Moore, 124 Ill. 133; Jewhurst v. Syracuse, 108 N. Y. 303.
[11] Betz v. Limingi, 46 La. Ann. 1113, 46 Am. St. Rep. 344; Rochester v. Campbell, 123 N. Y. 405; Brookville v. Arthurs, 130 Pa. St. 501; Keokuk v. Independent District, 53 Iowa, 352,

By the weight of authority the imposition of the duty to care for the sidewalk upon the owner of adjoining property does not render the lot owner liable to individuals or relieve the municipality.¹ The owner is, of course, liable for his own acts of negligence, as where he places an obstruction in the street;² but the mere fact that he is so liable, or that he is liable over to the corporation,³ does not relieve the corporation from its liability to persons injured by reason of the street being in an unsafe condition.⁴ Some courts hold that a statute which imposes the duty of keeping the sidewalk in repair upon the owners of adjoining property is unconstitutional.⁵ Where a charter made it the duty of the lot owner to construct the sidewalk in front of his property and to keep the same in repair, and provided that if he failed to do so the city might do the work and charge the expense against the property, and that when an injury resulted from any defect in a sidewalk which was due to the wrong, default or negligence of any person other than the city such person should be primarily liable for the damages, it was held that the owner was not liable for a mere failure to keep the sidewalk in repair.⁶ Reasonable care requires that the corporation shall make such inspection of the sidewalks

---

30 Am. Rep. 220; Noonan v. Stillwater, 33 Minn. 198; Davenport v. Ruckman, 37 N. Y. 568. The mere fact that the charter made it the duty of the city to repair the sidewalks at the expense of the lot owner does not make the owner primarily liable for injuries caused by negligence. Fife v. Oshkosh, 89 Wis. 540; Sommers v. Marshfield, 90 Wis. 59. No obligation to repair streets or sidewalks rests upon the owners of abutting property at common law. Rochester v. Campbell, 123 N. Y. 405, 20 Am. St. Rep. 760, and note.

¹ Lord v. Mobile (Ala.), 21 So. Rep. 366; Flynn v. Canton Co., 40 Md. 321, 17 Am. Rep. 603; Zanesville v. Fannan, 53 Ohio St. 605, 53 Am. St. Rep. 664 (liability of city and railway company); Sioux City v. Weare, 59 Iowa, 95; Westfield v. Mayo, 122 Mass. 100, 23 Am. Rep. 292; Dillon,

Mun. Corp., I, §§ 1035, 1037. The crosswalks are a part of the sidewalk. Goodfellow v. New York, 100 N. Y. 15. See under statute, Hoyt v. Danbury, 69 Conn. 341.

² Rochester v. Campbell, 123 N. Y. 405, 10 L. R. A. 393; Calder v. Smalley, 66 Iowa, 219.

³ City of Pawtucket v. Bray (R. I.), 37 Atl. Rep. 1.

⁴ Noonan v. Stillwater, 33 Minn. 198; Kellogg v. Janesville, 34 Minn. 132. Joint action may be maintained against city or lot owner, where there is a neglect to perform a common duty. Peoria v. Simpson, 110 Ill. 294, 51 Am. Rep. 683; Stebbins v. Keene Township, 55 Mich. 552; McConnell v. Osage City, 80 Iowa, 293.

⁵ Noonan v. Stillwater, *supra*.

⁶ Selleck v. Tallman, 93 Wis. 246; Toutloff v. Green Bay, 91 Wis. 490.

from time to time as is reasonably necessary to guard against the results of the natural decay of the material of which they are constructed.[1] The duty to keep the sidewalks in a reasonably safe condition is at common law owing to every person who uses the streets for the ordinary purposes for which they are designed.[2]

§ 333. *Obstructions on sidewalks.*— A corporation must exercise reasonable care to protect the public from being injured by obstructions which are necessarily and properly placed on sidewalks and in the streets. The owner of land abutting upon a public street is permitted to encroach on the primary right of the public to a limited extent and for a temporary purpose, owing to the necessities of the case. Two facts must, however, exist to render the encroachment lawful: the obstruction must be reasonably necessary for the transaction of business and it must not unnecessarily interfere with the rights of the public.[3] The corporation must keep the streets as safe as practicable under such circumstances.[4] The corporation is not an insurer against all defects in its sidewalks.[5] Thus, stepping-stones for persons alighting from carriages,[6] or slight unevenness or depression in the sidewalks,[7] are not defects; but loose planks[8] and large holes[9] are such defects as will render the city liable for damages occasioned thereby. The city must provide rea-

---

[1] Kellogg v. Janesville, 34 Minn. 132; Peoria v. Simpson, 110 Ill. 294, 51 Am. Rep. 683; McConnell v. Osage City, 80 Iowa, 293; Stebbins v. Keene Township, 55 Mich. 552.

[2] Duffy v. Dubuque, 63 Iowa, 171; Maguire v. Spence, 91 N. Y. 302. When the liability is the creature of statute it extends only to travelers; but the word is given a liberal construction and it is held to include every one who has occasion to pass over the highway for any purpose of business, convenience or pleasure. It must be kept "safe and convenient for all persons having occasion to pass over it while engaged in any of the pursuits or duties of life." Blodgett v. Boston, 8 Allen, 237; Reed v. Madison, 83 Wis. 171, 17 L. R. A. 733.

The question is discussed in Duffy v. Dubuque, 63 Iowa, 171, and in Langlois v. Cohoes, 58 Hun (N. Y.), 226.

[3] Flynn v. Taylor, 127 N. Y. 596; Callanan v. Gilman, 107 N. Y. 360. See District of Columbia v. Woodbury, 136 U. S. 450.

[4] Nolan v. King, 97 N. Y. 565.

[5] Burns v. Bradford City, 137 Pa. St. 361, 11 L. R. A. 726.

[6] Dubois v. Kingston, 102 N. Y. 219.

[7] Witham v. Portland, 72 Me. 539; Childrey v. Huntington, 34 W. Va. 459, 11 L. R. A. 313.

[8] Moon v. Ionia, 81 Mich. 535, 46 N. W. Rep. 25; Armstrong v. Ackley, 71 Iowa, 76.

[9] Tice v. Bay City, 84 Mich. 461, 47 N. W. Rep. 1062.

sonable guards and railings to prevent people from being injured by cellar-ways and area-ways entered from the street.[1] It must also protect them from dangers arising from structures overhead, such as awnings,[2] poles,[3] sign-boards,[4] and the like.

§ 334. *Ice and snow on highways.*— The liability for damages resulting from the presence of ice and snow in a public street is governed very much by locality. It is well settled, however, that in the absence of any structural defect mere slipperiness is not such a defect in a street as will render the municipality liable.[5] In some parts of the country it is held that the corporation must keep its sidewalks free from ice and snow, while in other localities, where the climate is such that this would be imposing an undue burden upon the municipality, it is held that no liability exists unless the ice or snow is allowed to accumulate in ridges or inequalities so as to form an obstruction in the street.[6] The duty is not affected by the fact that the ice is in part the result of artificial causes, as water escaping from a hose used by firemen.[7] The liability

[1] Maguire v. Spence, 91 N. Y. 303; Day v. Mt. Pleasant, 70 Iowa, 193. But see Beardsley v. Hartford, 50 Conn. 529, 47 Am. Rep. 677; Elliott, Roads and Streets, p. 453.

[2] Bohen v. Waseca, 32 Minn. 176, 50 Am. Rep. 564; Bieling v. Brooklyn, 120 N. Y. 98.

[3] Norristown v. Moyer, 67 Pa. St. 355.

[4] Langan v. Atchison, 35 Kan. 318, 57 Am. Rep. 165; Kutz v. Troy, 104 N. Y. 344. As to the distinction between the liability in case of objects attached to and forming a part of the sidewalk and other overhanging objects, see West v. Lynn, 110 Mass. 514.

[5] Chicago v. McGiven, 78 Ill. 347; Harrington v. Buffalo, 121 N. Y. 147; Bell v. York, 31 Neb. 842, 48 N. W. Rep. 878; Broburg v. Des Moines, 63 Iowa, 523, 19 N. W. Rep. 340, 50 Am. Rep. 756; Grossenbach v. Milwaukee, 65 Wis. 31, 56 Am. Rep. 614; Rolf v. Greenville, 102 Mich. 544.

[6] Henkes v. Minneapolis, 42 Minn. 530; Stanke v. St. Paul (Minn.), 73 N. W. Rep. 629; Cook v. Milwaukee, 27 Wis. 191; Kinney v. Troy, 108 N. Y. 567; Hausmann v. Madison, 85 Wis. 187, 21 L. R. A. 263, annotated; Huston v. Council Bluffs (Iowa), 60 N. W. Rep. 1130, 36 L. R. A. 211; Paulson v. Pelican, 79 Wis. 445, 48 N. W. Rep. 715, and cases cited in preceding note. An accumulation of snow or ice on a sidewalk, allowed to remain after actual notice of the danger, will render the city liable for damages caused thereby. Virginia v. Plummer, 65 Ill. App. 419. Piling snow on both sides of a railway track is negligence. Ellis v. Lewiston, 89 Me. 60. But see Hutchinson v. Ypsilanti, 103 Mich. 12, 61 N. W. Rep. 279. Liable for injuries caused by snow on sidewalk. Fife v. Oshkosh, 89 Wis. 540.

[7] Henkes v. Minneapolis, 42 Minn. 530.

has been held to exist where ice is formed on a sloping sidewalk[1] or where it is caused by an accumulation of water due to a structural defect in the walk.[2] The owner of the adjoining property may be required to remove snow and ice from the sidewalk under a penalty,[3] but cannot be made liable to individuals for, injuries received by reason of this neglect to comply with the requirements of such an ordinance.[4] The fact that a country road was impassable for a period of three months because of snow will not render the town liable for injuries received by a person trying to pass over the road.[5] There is no liability for a defect in a road made by travelers around a snowdrift.[6] A person who attempts to pass over a sidewalk which is dangerous by reason of ice, when he might avoid the same by passing around it, is guilty of contributory negligence.[7]

§ 335. *Care of bridges.*— Bridges are ordinarily a part of the highway,[8] and it is for the corporation to decide whether or not they shall be built.[9] Where, however, a public corporation

[1] Pinkham v. Topsfield, 104 Mass. 78. See Nichols v. St. Paul, 44 Minn. 494 (sloping street).
[2] Gillrie v. Lockport, 122 N. Y. 403.
[3] Carthage v. Frederick, 122 N. Y. 269, 19 Am. St. Rep. 490, 10 L. R. A. 178; Paxson v. Sweet, 13 N. J. L. 196. But see Chicago v. O'Brien, 111 Ill. 532, 53 Am. Rep. 640, and § 246, *supra.* In City of Port Huron v. Jenkinson, 77 Mich. 414, 18 Am. St. Rep. 409, an ordinance which made it a crime for the owner of a lot to neglect to build a sidewalk in front of the lot, without reference to his ability to do so, was held invalid.
[4] Rochester v. Campbell, 123 N. Y. 405; Heeney v. Sprague, 11 R. L. 456, 23 Am. Rep. 502, and the elaborate decision in Flynn v. Canton Co., 40 Md. 312, 17 Am. Rep. 603. As to civil liability created by violation of one ordinance, see Hartford v. Talcott, 48 Conn. 525.
[5] Burr v. Plymouth, 48 Conn. 460.
[6] Bogie v. Waupun, 75 Wis. 1.

[7] Erie v. Magill, 101 Pa. St. 616, 47 Am. Rep. 739, annotated; Quincy v. Barker, 81 Ill. 300; Belton v. Boston, 54 N. Y. 245; Shaefler v. Sandusky, 33 Ohio St. 246.
[8] Goshen v. Myers, 119 Ind. 196. "In this country the power of municipal corporations to build them and their authority over them are wholly statutory, and their duties in respect to them are either prescribed by statute or spring from their powers. There is no common-law responsibility on municipal corporations in respect to the repair of bridges within their limits; but where bridges are part of the streets and built by the municipal authorities under powers given to them by the legislature, they are liable for defects therein on the same principles and to the same extent as for defective streets." Dillon, Mun. Corp., II, § 728.
[9] Quinton v. Burton, 61 Iowa, 471; Orth v. Milwaukee, 59 Wis. 336.

is required by a mandatory statute to construct a bridge, the duty may be compelled by *mandamus*.¹ The corporation must exercise reasonable care during the construction of the bridge by placing proper guards and railings in the streets and around the approaches.² The location of a bridge is a governmental act, but a corporation has been held liable for locating a bridge so as to injure adjoining property, on the theory that the government has no right to undertake the work in a negligent manner.³ During the process of construction the corporation is under the same obligation to exercise reasonable care as an individual under the same circumstances.⁴ All public works must be so constructed as to withstand the ordinary storms of the locality,⁵ and as to afford a reasonably safe passage-way for the public, using it in the ordinary manner.⁶ But provision need not be made for supporting extraordinary weights.⁷ It must be so protected by proper guards and railings as to avoid injury to persons using the bridge in the exercise of ordinary care;⁸ that is, the corporation is under obligation to construct and maintain a reasonably safe structure.⁹

§ 336. *Notice.*— Before a municipal corporation can be held liable for an injury resulting from a defective street which was not caused by its act or with its permission,¹⁰ it must appear that it had actual or constructive¹¹ notice of such defect in time

¹ State v. Northumberland, 46 N. H. 156.
² Mullen v. Rutland, 55 Vt. 77; The Modock, 26 Fed. Rep. 718.
³ Hartford County v. Wise, 75 Md. 38.
⁴ Perry v. Worcester, 6 Gray, 544, 66 Am. Dec. 431; Doherty v. Braintree, 148 Mass. 495.
⁵ Allen v. Chippewa Falls, 52 Wis. 430, 38 Am. Rep. 748; Chicago, etc. Co. v. Sawyer, 69 Ill. 285, 18 Am. Rep. 618, note.
⁶ Wabash v. Pearson, 120 Ind. 426; Wilson v. Granby, 47 Conn. 59.
⁷ Monongahela Bridge Co. v. Pittsburgh, 114 Pa. St. 478; Moore v. Kenockee Tp., 75 Mich. 332.
⁸ Corbalis v. Newberry Tp., 132 Pa. St. 9. Where the liability is to travelers imposed by statute, the side-rails need not be sufficient to sustain the weight of one who leans upon them; they are supposed to be for the purpose of warning only. See Stickney v. Salem, 3 Allen, 374. *Contra*, Langlois v. Cohoes, 58 Hun, 226.
⁹ Jordan v. Hannibal, 87 Mo. 673; Ferguson v. Davis County, 57 Iowa, 601.
¹⁰ If the defective condition of the street is due to the negligence of the corporation, notice is not essential. A city must take notice of the tendency of wood to decay. Furnell v. St. Paul, 20 Minn. 117 (Gil. 101); Springfield v. Le Claire, 49 Ill. 476; Barton v. Syracuse, 36 N. Y. 54.
¹¹ The fact that a defect in a sidewalk on a prominent thoroughfare

to have repaired it or protected passers-by from injury.[1] But the corporation is chargeable with knowledge of a condition of its streets which it is its duty to possess,[2] and it is sufficient to establish the existence of facts from which notice will be inferred or circumstances from which the defect might have been known.[3]

---

has existed for several months is constructive notice of its condition. Moore v. Minneapolis, 19 Minn. 300 (Gil. 259). Evidence that the sidewalk in or near the place of the accident was in generally bad condition is competent on the issue of notice. Gude v. Mankato, 30 Minn. 256; Sterling v. Merrill, 124 Ill. 522; Cook v. Anamosa, 66 Iowa, 427.

[1] Moore v. Minneapolis, 19 Minn. 300 (Gil. 258); Burleson v. Reading, 117 Mich. 115, 68 N. W. Rep. 294; L'Herault v. Minneapolis (Minn.), 73 N. W. Rep. 73; Jones v. Clinton (Iowa), 69 N. W. Rep. 418; Snyder v. Albion (Mich.), 71 N. W. Rep. 475.

[2] Carstesen v. Town of Stratford, 67 Conn. 428.

[3] Lincoln v. Smith, 28 Neb. 762; Gillvie v. Lockport, 122 N. Y. 403; Lorence v. Ellensburg, 13 Wash. 341, 52 Am. St. Rep. 42.

CHAPTER XVIII.

THE CONSTRUCTION AND CARE OF PUBLIC WORKS.

§ 337. Care of public property.
338. Surface waters.
339. Drainage and sewers.
340. The plan of a public work.

§ 341. Direct injury to property.
342. The construction and care of sewers.
343. Consequential damages.

§ 337. *Care of public property.*— The rule of non-liability of a municipal corporation for negligence in the care of public buildings is thus stated by Mr. Justice Morton:[1] "A city is not liable to a private citizen for an injury caused by any defect or want of repair in a city or town hall or other public building erected and used solely for municipal purposes or for negligence of its agents in the management of such buildings. This is because it is not liable to private actions for omission or neglect to perform a corporate duty imposed by general laws upon all cities and towns alike from the performance of which it derives no compensation. But when a city or town does not devote such building exclusively to municipal uses, but lets it or a part of it for its own advantage and emolument, by receiving rents or otherwise, it is liable while it is so let in the same manner as a private owner would be." This rule prevails in the New England states generally, and exempts counties from liability for injuries caused by neglect to keep the public buildings in repair.[2] The liability has, however, been imposed by statute in many states, and even in the absence of statute the authorities are not uniform. Thus, a city has been held liable for injuries caused by the negligent condition of the court-house,[3] defective plumbing in a school building,[4] an open cellar

[1] Worden v. New Bedford, 131 Mass. 23. See, also, Eastman v. Meredith, 36 N. H. 284; Wixon v. Newport, 13 R. I. 454; Hill v. Boston, 122 Mass. 344.
[2] Dosdale v. Olmstead County, 33 Minn. 96, 44 Am. Rep. 185; Kincaid v. Hardin County, 53 Iowa, 430, 36 Am. Rep. 236; Downing v. Mason County, 87 Ky. 208; Shepard v. Pulaski County (Ky.), 18 S. W. Rep. 15.
[3] Galvin v. New York, 112 N. Y. 223.
[4] Briegel v. Philadelphia, 135 Pa. St. 451, 30 Am. & Eng. C. C. 501, note; Wixon v. Newport, 13 R. I. 454.

of a police station,[1] a well maintained for public use,[2] a fire engine,[3] a public dumping yard,[4] and of trees belonging to the city.[5] But there is no liability for damages caused by the bursting of fire-hose caused by the negligence of the firemen,[6] the unsafe condition of a hydrant which resulted in injury to property of a citizen,[7] or the unsafe handling of a dumping truck while engaged in collecting the refuse of the city.[8]

§ 338. *Surface waters.*— By the common law any person may erect barriers to prevent surface water from coming upon his land, although it is thereby made to flow upon the land of another to his damage. This doctrine has been adopted in a number of states,[9] while others adhere to what is known as the civil-law rule, which holds the lower estate chargeable with a servitude for the benefit of the upper estate, to permit the surface waters to flow over it *as it has been accustomed to do.*[10] Where the common-law rule prevails, cities and towns, as the owners of lands for highways and other public purposes, have the same right to obstruct and repel the flow of surface water

---

[1] Carrington v. St. Louis, 89 Mo. 208.
[2] Danaher v. Brooklyn, 119 N. Y. 241. But the city is not the insurer of the quality of the water, and in order to authorize a recovery on such grounds it is necessary to show wilful misconduct or culpable neglect.
[3] Lafayette v. Allen, 81 Ind. 166. In this case the city was held liable to an engineer who was put at work on a defective engine. *Contra,* see Wild v. Paterson, 47 N. J. L. 406.
[4] Fort Worth v. Crawford, 74 Tex. 404.
[5] Jones v. New Haven, 34 Conn. 1.
[6] Fisher v. Boston, 104 Mass. 87, 6 Am. Rep. 196.
[7] Welsh v. Rutland, 56 Vt. 228, 48 Am. Rep. 762. *Contra,* Jenny v. Brooklyn, 120 N. Y. 164.
[8] Condict v. Jersey City, 46 N. J. L. 157.
[9] Gannon v. Hargadon, 10 Allen, 106, Bigelow, C. J. See, also, Chadeayne v. Robinson, 55 Conn. 345; Murphy v. Kelley, 68 Me. 521; Edwards v. Charlotte R. R. Co., 39 S. C. 472, 22 L. R. A. 246; Hanlin v. Chicago, etc. Co., 61 Wis. 515; Jones v. Hannoran, 55 Mo. 462; Mo. Pac. R. Co. v. Keys, 55 Kan. 205, 49 Am. St. Rep. 249, and note. The common law regards surface water as the common enemy which each proprietor may turn from his own land. The description was first used in Rex v. Com'rs of Sewers, 8 Barn. & Cress. 355. See an article in 23 Am. Law Rev. 372. See for common-law rule, Mayor v. Sikes, 94 Ga. 30, 47 Am. St. Rep. 132. The cases governing surface water are collected in an exhaustive note to Gray v. McWilliams, 98 Cal. 157, in 21 L. R. A. 593.
[10] Domat, Civil Law (Cush. ed.), § 1583; Lambert v. Alcorn, 144 Ill. 313, 21 L. R. A. 611; Gray v. McWilliams, 98 Cal. 157, 21 L. R. A. 593; Farris v. Dudley, 78 Ala. 124.

as other proprietors.¹ A corporation has less power over natural water-courses than over ordinary surface waters. To be a water-course "there must be a stream usually flowing in a particular direction, though it need not flow continually. It may sometimes be dry. It must flow in a definite channel, having a bed, sides and banks, and usually discharge itself in some other stream or body of water."² A natural watercourse cannot be obstructed and the waters turned back upon the land of another proprietor.³ Every proprietor of land on a water-course is entitled to the employment and use of the stream substantially in its natural flow, subject only to such interruptions as are necessary and unavoidable in its reasonable and proper use by other proprietors.⁴ A corporation must so construct its public works as not to interfere with or obstruct the waters of a natural stream, and in the absence of a statute expressly authorizing such obstruction it is liable for real and substantial damages occasioned to individuals by its torts.⁵ It is also established by the weight of authority that a municipal corporation is liable for damages if it collects surface water and causes it to be discharged with increased volume and force upon the property of an individual where it would not have gone by natural causes.⁶

§ 339. *Drainage and sewers.*— A municipal corporation is not liable for damages resulting from a failure to exercise its discretionary or governmental power to improve its streets by constructing sewers or drains for the purpose of carrying off

¹ Hoyt v. Hudson, 27 Wis. 656, 9 Am. Rep. 473; Inman v. Tripp, 11 R. I. 520; Wakefield v. Newell, 12 R. I. 75; Murray v. Allen (R. I.), 38 Atl. Rep. 497.

² Dixon, C. J., in Hoyt v. Hudson, 27 Wis. 656, 661, 9 Am. Rep. 473.

³ Emery v. Lowell, 104 Mass. 13.

⁴ See Warren v. Westbrook Mfg. Co., 86 Me. 32, 26 L. R. A. 284.

⁵ Perry v. Worcester, 6 Gray, 544, 66 Am. Dec. 431, and note; Gilman v. Laconia, 55 N. H. 130, 20 Am. Rep. 175.

⁶ Kauffman v. Griesemer, 26 Pa. St. 407, 67 Am. Dec. 437; Beach v. Gaylord, 43 Minn. 466; Conner v. Woodfill, 126 Ind. 85; Rathke v. Gardner, 134 Mass. 14; Rychlicki v. St. Louis, 98 Mo. 497; Kobs v. Minneapolis, 22 Minn. 159; Pyre v. Mankato, 36 Minn. 373, 1 Am. St. Rep. 671, note. In Davis v. Crawfordsville, 119 Ind. 1, 12 Am. St. Rep. 361, it was held that a city is liable in damages for collecting water in artificial channels and casting it in a body upon the property of others, but not liable for consequential damages caused by grading and improving its streets, unless the work is done negligently.

surface water and sewage.[1] In determining the time when such public improvements shall be made, and the claims of various localities, it acts in a governmental capacity, and is not liable to any one for its action or non-action.[2] The authorities are not entirely in accord, but the prevailing rule seems to be that a city is not liable for damages occasioned by changing the flow of surface water when it results from a proper exercise of a legal power to grade the streets, or in constructing other public improvements.[3]

§ 340. *The plan of a public work.*— It has often been said that a city is not liable for any defect or want of efficiency in the plan adopted for a sewer or other public improvement,[4] but this general statement must be modified in the light of recent decisions. In deciding whether a system shall be adopted and in what part or parts of a city it shall be constructed, the corporation acts free from liability to individuals for consequential damages. But it must exercise reasonable care and skill in adopting the plan as well as in the work of mechanical construction.[5] This requires that it shall use care in selecting ad-

---

[1] Cochrane v. Malden, 152 Mass. 365; Noble v. St. Albans, 56 Vt. 522; Springfield v. Spence, 39 Ohio St. 665; Weis v. Madison, 75 Ind. 241.

[2] Mills v. Brooklyn, 32 N. Y. 489; Cummins v. Seymour, 79 Ind. 491, 41 Am. Rep. 618; Henderson v. Minneapolis, 32 Minn. 319. It is not the duty of a city to construct sewers in order to relieve the property of individuals from surface water. Jordan v. Benwood (W. Va.), 26 S. E. Rep. 266; Montgomery v. Gilmer, 33 Ala. 116, 70 Am. Dec. 562.

[3] See § 338, *supra;* also Burns v. Cohoes, 67 N. Y. 204; Templeton v. Voshloe, 72 Ind. 134, 37 Am. Rep. 150; Davis v. Crawfordville, 119 Ind. 1; O'Brien v. St. Paul, 25 Minn. 331. See Dillon, Mun. Corp., II, § 1042, and cases cited. See § 343 as to consequential damages.

[4] The leading case is Mills v. Brooklyn, 32 N. Y. 489. The authorities are collected in an extensive note to Perry v. Worcester, 6 Gray, 544, 66 Am. Dec. 431, 435. The author of the note says that the weight of authority (1886) is in favor of the view that the city acts judicially in adopting the plan of drainage. It will be observed that in Mills v. Brooklyn, 32 N. Y. 495, the court said that the plaintiff's condition was no worse than it would have been had no sewer been built.

[5] North Vernon v. Voegler, 103 Ind. 314; Evansville v. Decker, 84 Ind. 325, 43 Am. Rep. 86; Seifert v. Brooklyn, 101 N. Y. 136; Indianapolis v. Huffer, 30 Ind. 235; Seymour v. Cummins, 119 Ind. 148, 5 L. R. A. 126; Rochester White Lead Co. v. Rochester, 3 N. Y. 463; Van Pelt v. Davenport, 42 Iowa, 308; Chicago v. Seben, 165 Ill. 371. There is no responsibility when reasonable care is exercised to employ a competent engineer to devise the plan. Diamond Match Co. v. New Haven, 55 Conn. 510. The

visers and engineers[1] and in adopting a system reasonably adequate for the work which, in the light of the history of the locality, will be required of it.[2] That is, there may be such a lack of care and skill in devising the plan as to amount to actionable negligence. But if such care is used in adopting the plan there is no liability for damages resulting to individuals from the mere fact that the plan proves defective or insufficient. If, however, after the system is constructed it proves inadequate to do the work, and with knowledge of that fact the corporation continues to maintain it, and individuals are thereby damaged, it is liable therefor,[3] as a city has no immunity from legal responsibility for maintaining a nuisance.

§ 341. *Direct injury to property.*— It has already been stated that a municipality has no right, in the exercise of its power over its streets, to collect water and sewage and deposit it in

rule that a city is not liable for injuries occasioned by the plan adopted should not be so extended as to relieve "the city from liability when the plan devised and put in operation leaves the city's streets in a dangerous condition for public use." Tiedeman, Pub. Corp., § 350, quoted in approval in Chicago v. Seben, 165 Ill. 371. In Omaha v. Richards, 49 Neb. 244, the court said: "It was the duty of the city to have constructed the sewer and street in question in such a manner as to provide a proper and adequate outlet for the water that might have been reasonably expected to come down this ravine. In failing to do so, the city authorities were guilty of negligence."

[1] Rochester White Lead Co. v. Rochester, 3 N. Y. 463; Diamond Match Co. v. New Haven, 55 Conn. 510.

[2] Beatrice v. Leary, 45 Neb. 149, 50 Am. St. Rep. 547; Allen v. Chippewa Falls, 52 Wis. 430, 38 Am. Rep. 748. In Spangler v. San Francisco, 84 Cal. 12, the court said: "It was the duty of the city, when it does provide waterways, to provide such as are suffi-cient to carry off the water that might reasonably be expected to accumulate." Citing Damour v. Lyon City, 44 Iowa, 276; Powers v. Council Bluffs, 50 Iowa, 197; Schroeder v. Baraboo, 93 Wis. 95, 67 N. W. Rep. 27.

[3] Netzer v. Crookston, 59 Minn. 244; Tate v. St. Paul, 56 Minn. 527; Seifert v. Brooklyn, 101 N. Y. 136. In Netzer v. Crookston, *supra*, the court said, with reference to Tate v. St. Paul: "The principle on which that case was really decided is that, even though the defect in the sewer is of legislative origin, yet where it is clearly demonstrated by experience, after sufficient trial, that the sewer is, under ordinary conditions, insufficient for its purpose, the city is liable for maintaining it; that while it is not liable for the original error, which was legislative, it is liable for persisting in that error after sufficient trial and experience, which is ministerial. A city cannot justify itself for maintaining a nuisance unless it can show legislation to do the act. Miles v. Worcester, 154 Mass. 511; Harper v. Milwaukee, 30 Wis. 365; Noonan v. Albany, 79 N. Y. 470.

increased quantities upon the private property of an individual.[1] Such an act is a *direct invasion of a property right,* and the corporation is liable for the resulting damages, regardless of the fact that the sewer was constructed in accordance with the plan adopted.[2] "To determine when and upon what plan a public improvement shall be made is," says Chief Justice Gilfillan, "unless the charter otherwise provides, left to the judgment of the proper municipal authorities, and is in its nature legislative; and although the power is vested in the municipality for the benefit and relief of property, error of judgment as to when or upon what plan the improvement shall be made, resulting only in incidental injury to the property, will not be ground of action; as if, in grading streets to the authorized grades, the plan of the grading is inadequate to drain a lot of its surface water, or even if it makes it more difficult and expensive for the owner to drain it, or makes access to the lot more difficult, that is a result incidental to the improvement. But for a direct invasion of one's right of property, even though

[1] Seifert v. Brooklyn, 101 N. Y. 136; Lynch v. New York, 76 N. Y. 60; Hitchins v. Frostburg, 68 Md. 100. A city may be enjoined from discharging water on private lands. Field v. West Orange, 36 N. J. Eq. 118. *Contra,* see Heth v. Fond du Lac, 63 Wis. 228; Gilluly v. Madison, 63 Wis. 518. There is no liability for damages caused by water percolating from gullys into adjacent cellars. Kennison v. Beverly, 146 Mass. 467, § 338, *supra*.

[2] Tate v. St. Paul, 56 Minn. 527; Seifert v. Brooklyn, 101 N. Y. 136; Ashley v. Port Huron, 35 Mich. 296; Weis v. Madison, 75 Ind. 241; Gillison v. Charleston, 16 W. Va. 282, 37 Am. Rep. 763; Boston Belting Co. v. Boston, 149 Mass. 44; Burford v. Grand Rapids, 53 Mich. 98; Evansville v. Decker, 84 Ind. 325, 43 Am. Rep. 86; Rychlicki v. St. Louis, 98 Mo. 497, 4 L. R. A. 594, note; Chapman v. Rochester, 110 N. Y. 273, 1 L. R. A. 296, with note on liability for the pollution of waters. In Tate v. St. Paul, 56 Minn. 527, the court said: "Judge Dillon, in his work on Municipal Corporations (4th ed.), §§ 1047 to 1051, approves the rule laid down in more recent decisions by some of our ablest courts, that if a sewer, *whatever its plan,* is so constructed as to cause a positive and direct invasion of private property, as by collecting and throwing upon it to its damage water or sewage which would not otherwise have flowed or found its way there, the corporation is liable. . . . It is impossible to answer the reasoning of these cases, especially where the injury complained of constitutes a taking, that making one's premises a place of deposit for the surplus waters in the sewers in times of high water, or creating a nuisance upon them so as to deprive the owner of the beneficial use of his property, is an appropriation requiring compensation to be made." See Weaver v. Mississippi & R. R. Boom Co., 28 Minn. 534.

contemplated by or necessarily resulting from the plan adopted, an action will lie; otherwise it would be taking private property for public use without compensation. Thus, if in cutting a street down to a grade the soil of an abutting lot is precipitated into the cut, or if in filling up the grade the slope of the embankment is made to rest on private property, that is a direct invasion of property rights which cannot be justified, even though the plan adopted contemplates or will necessarily produce the result."

§ 342. *The construction and care of sewers.*— When the corporation ceases to act judicially or legislatively and begins to act ministerially it is liable for damages caused by its negligence. The liability for damages caused by its neglect to exercise reasonable care in the construction[1] or maintenance of drains and sewers over which it has control[2] is recognized even in the states which impose no liability upon the corporation for want of care in the management of its highways.[3] The distinction has been placed on the grounds that the city acts

[1] A city acts ministerially in the construction of a sewer. Montgomery v. Gilmer, 33 Ala. 116, 70 Am. Dec. 502. See note to Perry v. Worcester, 66 Am. Dec. 434, 442.

[2] Monticello v. Fox (Ind. App.), 28 N. E. Rep. 1025; Kosmak v. New York, 117 N. Y. 361, 22 N. E. Rep. 945. See note, 66 Am. Dec. 436, where many cases are cited. As to liability when a sewer is in part on private property, see Stoddard v. Saratoga Springs, 127 N. Y. 261. In Schroeder v. City of Baraboo, 93 Wis. 95, 101, the court said: "It may be stated generally as the law that where private property is flooded by water and sewage, whether such property be on the grade of the street or below such grade, either by such water and sewage, after having been collected in such sewer or drain, escaping therefrom to such property by reason of the negligent construction of such drain or sewer or want of proper repair of the same, or by negligent dis-

continuance thereof by closing up the outlet, the city is liable. Such is the doctrine of Gilluly v. Madison, 63 Wis. 518, and to the same effect are Hitchins v. Frostburg, 68 Md. 100; Defer v. Detroit, 67 Mich. 346. And this is so though the sewer or drain be originally constructed wholly or in part only by private parties, if the municipality assumes the control and maintenance of it. Taylor v. Austin, 52 Minn. 247."

[3] Bates v. Westborough, 151 Mass. 174, 23 N. E. Rep. 1070, 7 L. R. A. 156; Gilman v. Laconia, 55 N. H. 130, 20 Am. Rep. 175; Weller v. St. Paul (Minn.), 12 Am. St. Rep. 754, note; Davis v. Crawfordville, 119 Ind. 1, 12 Am. St. Rep. 361, note; Hazzard v. Council Bluffs, 79 Iowa, 106; Seifert v. Brooklyn, 101 N. Y. 136; Judge v. Meriden, 38 Conn. 90; Gilluly v. Madison, 63 Wis. 518; Owens v. City of Lancaster, 182 Pa. St. 257, 38 Atl. Rep. 858; Blizzard v. Danville, 175 Pa. St. 479.

voluntarily in constructing sewers and involuntarily in constructing highways,[1] and that the interest of the corporation in the sewers is so distinct from that of the public at large that it practically owns them and is therefore liable for their care.[2] The corporation is not required to exercise extraordinary care to keep its sewers in proper condition.[3] As in the case of highways, it is not liable unless it has actual or constructive notice of the defect,[4] but it is required to exercise reasonable care in inspecting the works in order to discover defects.[5]

§ 343. *Consequential damages.*— That which the legislature legally authorizes cannot be wrongful. Hence, when a corporation acts within the limits of its power and jurisdiction and pursuant to a valid act of the legislature, and with reasonable care and skill, it is not responsible for consequential damages to private property or persons.[6] Thus, there is no liability for damages caused by establishing or changing the grade of streets.[7] The state has absolute control over the streets and highways, and all adjoining property is held subject to the condition that the grade may be changed. The reason for this rule is thus stated in a leading case:[8] "Those who purchase house-lots bordering upon streets are supposed to calculate the chances of such elevations and reductions as the increasing population of a city may require in order to render the passage to and from the several parts of the city safe and convenient;

---

[1] Rowe v. Portsmouth, 56 N. H. 291; Winn v. Rutland, 52 Vt. 481.

[2] Bates v. Westborough, 151 Mass. 174; Child v. Boston, 4 Allen, 41.

[3] Netzer v. Crookston, 59 Minn. 244.

[4] Haus v. Bethlehem, 134 Pa. St. 12, 19 Atl. Rep. 437.

[5] Vanderslice v. Philadelphia, 103 Pa. St. 102. A city must use reasonable care when it is constructing sewers to avoid injury to individuals. When the work is in the hands of a contractor the weight of authority is to the effect that both the city and the contractor are liable for injuries caused by negligence regarding excavations in the streets. See Pearson v. Zable, 78 Ky. 170; Welsh v. St. Louis, 73 Mo. 71.

[6] Dillon, Mun. Corp., II, § 987; Callendar v. Marsh, 1 Pick. (Mass.) 417; Alexander v. Milwaukee, 16 Wis. 264; Terry v. Richmond (Va.), 27 S. E. Rep. 429, 38 L. R. A. 834; Powell v. Wytheville (Va.), 27 S. E. Rep. 805.

[7] Callendar v. Marsh, 1 Pick. 417; Green v. Reading, 9 Watts (Pa.), 382; Lee v. Minneapolis, 22 Minn. 13; Abel v. Minneapolis (Minn.), 70 N. W. Rep. 851. This rule is recognized in every state except Ohio. See McCombs v. Akron Council, 15 Ohio, 474; Cohen v. Cleveland, 43 Ohio St. 190.

[8] Callendar v. Marsh, 1 Pick. 417; Northern Transportation Co. v. Chicago, 99 U. S. 635.

and as their purchase is always voluntary they may indemnify themselves in the price of the lot which they buy or take the chance of future improvements, as they see fit. They are presumed to foresee the changes which public necessity or convenience may require." The rule is the same although the property owner has constructed buildings with reference to such grade,[1] and his access is entirely cut off. Changing the grade under such circumstances is not taking the property for public use.[2] It has been said that a municipal corporation is liable for damages caused to private property by grading streets, "when a private owner of the soil over which the streets are laid, if improving it for his own use," would be liable.[3] On this principle an abutting owner can recover damages from a municipality for removing the natural support of his land.[4] But the prevailing rule is that there is no common-law liability for damages, although the street is so graded as to cause the earth to fall in.[5] A remedy is now generally provided for by statute. In such cases it is exclusive of all other remedies.[6]

---

[1] Henderson v. Minneapolis, 32 Minn. 319. The power to make a grade and improve streets is a continuing power. Karst v. St. Paul, etc. R. Co., 22 Minn. 118.

[2] Northern Transportation Co. v. Chicago, 99 U. S. 635. See Dillon, Mun. Corp., II, § 995b.'
But when the constitution provides for compensation when property is taken or "damaged," there can be a recovery. See Searles v. Lead (S. Dak., 1897), 39 L. R. A. 345, note, and cases cited.

[3] O'Brien v. St. Paul, 25 Minn. 331; Armstrong v. St. Paul, 30 Minn. 299.

[4] O'Brien v. St. Paul, 25 Minn. 331; Nichols v. Duluth, 40 Minn. 389.

[5] See Dillon, Mun. Corp., II, § 990, note.

[6] Heiser v. New York, 104 N. Y. 68; Cole v. Muscatine, 14 Iowa, 296.

CHAPTER XIX.

ACTIONS AND PROCEEDINGS.

§ 344. The right to sue and be sued.
345. Notice of claim.
346. *Mandamus.*
347. *Mandamus* to enforce duties toward creditors.
348. Further illustrations of the use of *mandamus.*

§ 349. *Quo warranto.*
350. Remedy in equity.
351. *Certiorari.*
352. Levy of execution on corporate property.
353. Liability to garnishment.

§ 344. *The right to sue and be sued.*— The right to sue and be sued is a power incidental to all public corporations. A question has sometimes arisen in connection with *quasi*-corporations, but if such bodies are corporations they may sue and be sued in the same manner as municipal corporations. The name in which actions shall be brought is governed by the charter. They are sometimes brought in the corporate name or in the name of the inhabitants, the mayor, the county commissioners or trustees. This must be determined by examination of the charter or laws of the state.[1]

§ 345. *Notice of claim.*— Municipal charters generally provide that no action shall be maintained against the corporation unless a statement in writing signed by the person injured or claiming to be injured by the wrong and the circumstances thereof and the amount of damages claimed shall be presented to the proper officer within a designated time. As already stated, the words "claim or demand," when used in such a statute, do not apply to a tort.[2] An action to recover back illegal taxes paid under protest sounds in tort, although in form an action on an implied contract.[3]

[1] With reference to the right to sue a county, see Ward v. Hartford County, 12 Conn. 404; Whittaker v. Tuolumne County, 96 Cal. 100, 30 Pac. Rep. 1010. As to the right of county commissioners to sue, see County of Tipton v. Kimberlin, 108 Ind. 449, 9 N. E. Rep. 407. As to the right of a village to sue, see Buffalo v. Harling, 50 Minn. 551, 52 N. W. Rep. 931.

[2] § 287, *supra.*

[3] Flieth v. City of Wausau, 93 Wis. 446; Ruggles v. Fond du Lac, 53 Wis. 436.

§ 346. *Mandamus.*— The writ of *mandamus* will issue to a public corporation or its officers to compel the performance of a duty clearly enjoined upon them by law when there is no other specific legal remedy adequate to enforce the rights of the relator or of the public.[1] It is not as formerly a prerogative writ,[2] but in modern practice "is nothing more than an action at law between the parties. . . . The right to the writ and the power to issue it has ceased to depend on any prerogative power, and it is now regarded as an ordinary process in cases to which it is applicable. It is a writ to which every one is entitled when it is the appropriate process for asserting the right he claims."[3] It will issue only where there is a clear legal right in the relator,[4] a corresponding duty in the defendant,[5] and the want of any other adequate and sufficient legal remedy.[6] It

[1] State v. Whitesides, 30 S. C. 579, 3 L. R. A. 777, annotated; People v. Crotty, 93 Ill. 180; Baker v. Marshall, 15 Minn. 177 (Gil. 136); State v. Southern Minn. Ry. Co., 18 Minn. 40 (Gil. 21). In Bassett v. Atwater, 65 Conn. 355, 32 L. R. A. 575, Andrews, C. J., said: "*Mandamus*, although it is an extraordinary legal remedy, is in the nature of an equitable interference, supplementing the deficiencies of the common law. It will ordinarily be issued where a legal duty is established and no other sufficient means exists for enforcing it. When the object sought can be equally well obtained by other means, as by an action, or by some other form of proceeding, then *mandamus* will not lie. Thus, the enforcement of merely private obligations, such as those arising from contracts, are not within its scope." *Mandamus* cannot usurp the functions of an appeal or writ of error. State v. Buhler, 90 Mo. 560. It must be remembered that the writ of *mandamus* is regulated by statute in many states and that the tendency is toward extending its use. The writ may under some statutes be used whenever it will afford a proper and sufficient remedy, although there may be another specific remedy. See People v. Commissioners of Highways, 130 Ill. 482, 6 L. R. A. 161; People v. Crotty, *supra*.

[2] See § 285, *supra*, note; High, Extr. Legal Rem., §§ 350, 606. But it is not a writ of right granted *ex debito justitiœ*, but of sound judicial discretion, to be granted or withheld according to circumstances.

[3] Taney, C. J., in Kentucky v. Dennison, 24 How. (U. S.) 66, 97; Illinois Central Ry. Co. v. People, 143 Ill. 434, 19 L. R. A. 119.

[4] State v. McCabe, 74 Wis. 481, 43 N. W. Rep. 322; People v. State Board of Canvassers, 129 N. Y. 360, 14 L. R. A. 646; People v. Stevens, 5 Hill (N. Y.), 616; Phœnix Iron Co. v. Com., 113 Pa. St. 563.

[5] Com. v. Pittsburgh, 34 Pa. St. 496.

[6] State v. Whitesides, 30 S. C. 579, 3 L. R. A. 777; Ray v. Wilson, 29 Fla. 342, 14 L. R. A. 773; State v. Manitowoc, 52 Wis. 423; People v. Chenango County, 11 N. Y. 563; State v. Langlie, 5 N. Dak. 594, 32 L. R. A. 723. As to the existence of another specific remedy under the statute, see People v. Commissioners of Highways, 130 Ill. 482, 6 L. R. A. 161. An ordinary action at law against

will therefore not issue to compel the performance of a duty which is doubtful or discretionary. Thus, it will not issue to a mayor to compel him to issue a license, when the issuance of such license is within his sound legal discretion.[1] Judge Dillon says:[2] "If the inferior tribunal, corporate body or public agent or officer has a discretion and acts and exercises it, the discretion cannot be controlled by *mandamus;* but if the inferior tribunal, body, officer or agents refuse to act in cases where the law requires them to act, and the party has no other legal remedy, and where in justice there ought to be one, a *mandamus* will lie to set them in motion, to compel action; and in proper cases the court will settle the legal principles which should govern, but without controlling the discretion of the subordinate jurisdiction, body or officer." Thus, the ministerial act of approving a bond will not be enforced by *mandamus.*[3] The writ never lies to enforce private contracts.[4]

§ 347. *Mandamus to enforce duties toward creditors.—Mandamus* is the proper remedy to compel a public corporation to perform its legal duties toward its creditors.[5] As a general

a county was held not a specific and adequate remedy to defeat a *mandamus* to compel a county treasurer to pay a warrant out of funds in his possession. Ray v. Wilson, 29 Fla. 342, 14 L. R. A. 773, with note on "*Mandamus* to compel payment of municipal debt by custodian of municipal funds." In State v. Ames, 31 Minn. 440, it was said that such a suit would be neither speedy nor adequate. It has usually been held, however, that *mandamus* will not be allowed when suit will lie against the municipality. See Lexington v. Mulliken, 7 Gray (Mass.), 280; State v. Bridgman, 8 Kan. 307; Sessions v. Boykin, 78 Ala. 328. But see People v. Mead, 24 N. Y. 114.

[1] Sherlock v. Stuart, 96 Mich. 193, 21 L. R. A. 580; State v. Tippecanoe Co., 45 Ind. 501; Deehan v. Johnson, 141 Mass. 23.

[2] Dillon, Mun. Corp., II, § 832. As to the right to issue a *mandamus* to the governor and other state officers, see People v. Governor, 29 Mich. 320, note, 18 Am. Rep. 89; Rice v. Austin, 19 Minn. 103, 18 Am. Rep. 330; State v. Kirkwood, 14 Iowa, 162; State v. Stone, 120 Mo. 428, 23 L. R. A. 194; Mauran v. Smith, 8 R. I. 192, 5 Am. Rep. 564. The discretionary power of building bridges and making local improvements will not be controlled by *mandamus.* State v. Essex County, 23 N. J. L. 214.

[3] Knox County v. Johnson, 124 Ind. 145, 7 L. R. A. 684. It is uncertain whether the act of approving an official bond is judicial or ministerial. The authorities are cited in this case.

[4] Florida, etc. R. Co. v. State, 31 Fla. 482, 20 L. R. A. 419; Parrott v. Bridgeport, 44 Conn. 180. See note, 3 L. R. A. 265.

[5] Meriwether v. Garrett, 102 U. S. 472; Baltimore v. Keeley Institute, 81 Md. 106, 27 L. R. A. 647; Thomas v. Mason, 39 W. Va. 526, 26 L. R. A. 727.

rule, the writ will not issue when the creditor has a right to an execution and levy on the property of the corporation or of its citizens, unless the creditor, by virtue of his contract, is entitled to the levy of a special tax for the payment of his debt.[1] In some states the writ will issue before the creditor has obtained judgment;[2] but in the federal courts, when the creditor is not entitled to a specific tax, there must be a judgment and the return of an execution *nulla bona* before a writ of *mandamus* will issue.[3] The writ is then in the nature of an execution[4] and may be directed to the corporation or its officers, and its execution cannot be interfered with by the state authorities.[5] After judgment, *mandamus* and not a bill in equity is the proper remedy to compel the levy of a tax for the payment of the judgment.[6] The illegality of the debt is not a defense to *mandamus* proceedings to enforce payment of the judgment.[7] But where the town authorities consented to a judgment in favor of certain bondholders, and it appeared that there was no authority to issue the bonds, *mandamus* to compel the levy of a tax to pay the judgment was refused.[8] The writ does not confer new authority,[9] and therefore a corporation can only be compelled to exert its legal powers. If it has no power to raise money by taxation, it cannot be compelled to levy a tax.[10]

[1] Knox County v. Aspinwall, 24 How. (U. S.) 376.
[2] Com. v. Pittsburgh, 34 Pa. St. 496; Rahway Savings Institution v. Rahway, 49 N. J. L. 384.
[3] Heine v. Levee Commissioners, 19 Wall. (U. S.) 655; Riggs v. Johnson County, 6 Wall. (U. S.) 166; State v. Manitowoc, 52 Wis. 423.
[4] Howard v. City of Huron, 5 S. Dak. 539, 26 L. R. A. 493.
[5] Supervisors v. Rogers, 7 Wall. (U. S.) 175. Under extraordinary circumstances, as where all the municipal officers resign, the United States court will appoint a commissioner to levy and collect the tax. This question and the effect of resignations are considered in Badger v. United States, 93 U. S. 599; Amy v. Watertown, 130 U. S. 301; Leavenworth County Commissioners v. Sellew, 99 U. S. 624; Dillon, Mun. Corp., II, § 861.
[6] Louisiana v. Police Jury, 111 U. S. 716; Rock Island County v. United States, 4 Wall. (U. S.) 435.
[7] Howard v. Huron, 5 S. D. 539, 26 L. R. A. 493.
[8] Union Bank v. Com'rs of Oxford, 119 N. C. 214.
[9] Rosenthal v. Board of Canvassers, 50 Kan. 129, 10 L. R. A. 157; State v. Secrest, 33 Minn. 381. *Mandamus* will not be allowed to compel the performance of an act for the purpose of accomplishing an illegal end. State v. Hill, 32 Minn. 275.
[10] Brownville v. Loague, 129 U. S. 493; United States v. Macon County Court, 99 U. S. 582.

§ 348. *Further illustrations of the use of mandamus.*— Subject to the general rules stated in the preceding section, *mandamus* is the proper remedy to compel the payment of the salary of an official,[1] the levy of an assessment as directed by the charter,[2] the issue of bonds to pay for a public improvement,[3] the prosecution of a public improvement,[4] the admission to an office,[5] the restoration of an officer wrongfully removed or suspended,[6] the holding of an election as required by law[7] or according to the method prescribed by a particular statute,[8] the holding by a municipal council of a meeting and the election of an officer as required by the charter,[9] a board to meet and canvass votes,[10] a canvassing board to omit certain illegal ballots,[11] officers to turn over funds actually in their possession,[12]

[1] Baker v. Johnson, 41 Me. 15.
[2] Reock v. Newark, 33 N. J. L. 129.
[3] People v. Flagg, 46 N. Y. 401. See People v. Batchellor, 35 N. Y. 128, 13 Am. Rep. 480.
[4] People v. Brooklyn Council, 22 Barb. (N. Y.) 404.
[5] State v. Rahway, 33 N. J. L. 111; Ellison v. Raleigh, 89 N. C. 125. But *mandamus* is not the proper remedy to try title to an office. See People v. Detroit, 18 Mich. 338; Biggs v. McBride, 17 Oreg. 640, 5 L. R. A. 115; State v. Atlantic City, 52 N. J. L. 332, 8 L. R. A. 697; Fleming v. Guthrie, 32 W. Va. 1, 3 L. R. A. 57, annotated. In Harwood v. Marshall, 9 Md. 83, it was held that *mandamus* was the proper remedy to try the title to an office when, by reason of the delay incident to the remedy by *quo warranto*, relief would be ineffectual. See Dillon, Mun. Corp., II, § 846, and § 285, *supra*.
[6] State v. Jersey City, 25 N. J. L. 536. *Mandamus* is not the proper remedy to restore to office a person who has been wrongfully removed and whose successor has been elected and enters upon the duties of the office. People v. New York Infants' Asylum, 122 N. Y. 190, 10 L. R. A. 381.
[7] People v. Fairbury, 51 Ill. 149.

[8] State v. Wrightson, 56 N. J. L. 126, 22 L. R. A. 548.
[9] Lamb v. Lynd, 44 Pa. St. 336.
[10] Rosenthal v. State Board of Canvassers, 50 Kan. 129, 19 L. R. A. 157. To compel the board to disregard certain returns which, although regular on their face, is admittedly the result of an illegal canvass. People v. Rice, 129 N. Y. 449, 14 L. R. A. 643, note. To correct the return by omitting certain irregular ballots. State v. Board of County Canvassers, 129 N. Y. 395. But not to count ballots which have passed beyond their control. State v. Waggoner, 34 Neb. 116, 15 L. R. A. 740.
[11] People v. Board of County Canvassers, 129 N. Y. 395, 14 L. R. A. 624. But it will not issue to compel a board to count ballots according to the provision of an unconstitutional statute. Maynard v. Board of District Canvassers, 84 Mich. 298, 11 L. R. A. 332.
[12] Duval County Commissioners v. Jacksonville (Fla.), 29 L. R. A. 416. But *mandamus* will not issue to compel what cannot be done. Hence, if an officer has wrongfully put it out of his power to turn over funds, there is no remedy by *mandamus*.

to call a new election where the prior election was inoperative,[1] to compel the acceptance of an office,[2] the payment of a warrant by the county treasurer,[3] to proceed in a legal manner and divide a county,[4] to compel a board of supervisors to include certain items in estimates of expenses of the county for the current year,[5] to compel highway commissioners to remove a certain fence from across a public highway when the facts which render the existence of the fence illegal are conceded,[6] the issue of warrants in payment of referee's fees,[7] the delivery of the office room, books and records of an office to a public officer,[8] to compel a member of a board to meet with the other members and elect an officer,[9] to compel county officers to hold their office at the legal county seat,[10] or to compel a mayor to recognize a person as a member of the city council.[11] But *mandamus* will not issue to compel a county treasurer to certify that all taxes are paid when certain illegal taxes remain unpaid,[12] or to compel township trustees to sign bonds issued and

[1] State v. South Kingston, 18 R. I. 258, 22 L. R. A. 65.
[2] People v. Williams, 145 Ill. 573, 24 L. R. A. 492, annotated.
[3] Ray v. Wilson, 29 Fla. 342, 14 L. R. A. 773.
[4] People v. Broom, 138 N. Y. 95, 20 L. R. A. 81.
[5] State v. Robinson, 35 Neb. 401, 17 L. R. A. 383.
[6] Brokaw v. Bloomington Township Commissioners, 130 Ill. 482, 6 L. R. A. 161, annotated.
[7] Guthrie v. Territory, 1 Okla. 188, 21 L. R. A. 841.
[8] To defeat a *mandamus* in such a case it must appear that the incumbent has a colorable title and is in possession under a claim of right. Stevens v. Carter, 27 Oreg. 553, 35 L. R. A. 343; State v. Johnson, 35 Fla. 2, 35 L. R. A. 357. See elaborate note in 35 L. R. A. 343, on "*Mandamus* to compel surrender of office." State v. Sherwood, 15 Minn. 221, 2 Am. Rep. 116; State v. Churchill, 15 Minn. 455 (Gil. 369); Merrill, Mandamus, § 142. But the writ will be denied when it will become necessary to determine the title of the *de facto* incumbent. State v. Williams, 25 Minn. 340.
[9] Statutes which specify a time within which a public officer is to perform an official act regarding the rights and duties of others are generally directory. Thus, where the law requires that township trustees shall meet on a certain day and elect a county superintendent, and they are unable to act for want of a quorum, an absent member will be required by *mandamus* to attend at a later date. Wampler v. State (Ind., 1897), 38 L. R. A. 829; State v. Smith, 22 Minn. 218.
[10] State v. Langlie, 5 N. Dak. 594, 32 L. R. A. 723. The proceedings were to determine whether the county seat had been legally changed.
[11] Swindell v. State, 143 Ind. 153, 35 L. R. A. 50. See Lawrence v. Ingersoll, 88 Tenn. 52, 6 L. R. A. 308.
[12] State v. Nelson, 41 Minn. 25, 4 L. R. A. 300.

§ 349.] ACTIONS AND PROCEEDINGS. 321

placed in the hands of a third person and afterwards held to have been issued under an unconstitutional statute.[1]

§ 349. *Quo warranto.*— *Quo warranto* is the proper proceeding by which to determine whether a public trust or franchise is being exercised without authority.[2] When a person is in possession of an office under color of right, the validity of his title can in general be tested only on an information in the nature of a *quo warranto.*[3] In this proceeding the court will go behind the certificate of election or commission and inquire into the validity of the election or appointment.[4] It is the proper writ by which to test the right of a person to preside over a meeting of a municipal body[5] or the right to a seat in the city council.[6] It is generally held in this country that the question whether a public corporation has been legally created can be tested in a proceeding of this nature brought against one exercising an office in the corporation.[7] If it appears in such a proceeding that no corporation either *de jure* or *de facto* exists, the relator is entitled to judgment.[8] Under the English practice the information for usurping a franchise by a corporation must be brought against the corporation, but for usurping a franchise to be a corporation it must be against the persons usurping it,[9] although an exception to the rule seems to

---

[1] State v. Whitesides, 30 S. C. 579, 3 L. R. A. 777.

[2] It was originally a prerogative writ, but the tendency is to reduce it to the position of an ordinary action. It does not, however, issue as a matter of course, as it is an intraordinary remedy.

[3] § 285, *supra;* State v. Sullivan, 45 Minn. 309, 11 L. R. A. 272; State v. Bulkeley, 61 Conn. 287, 14 L. R. A. 657; People v. Londoner, 13 Colo. 303, 6 L. R. A. 444.

[4] Cochran v. McCleary, 22 Iowa, 75.

[5] Com. v. Meeser, 44 Pa. St. 341.

[6] People v. Thatcher, 55 N. Y. 525.

[7] People v. Carpenter, 24 N. Y. 86; State v. Parker, 25 Minn. 215. In England the information is refused when it appears that no corporation exists. The leading case is Rex v. Saunders, 3 East, 119.

[8] State v. Weatherby, 45 Mo. 17; State v. McReynolds, 61 Mo. 203.

[9] People v. Richardson, 4 Cow. (N. Y.) 91, 109, note. Proceedings in the nature of *quo warranto*, for the purpose of restraining a corporation from an unlawful exercise of franchises, must be against the corporation, and not merely against the officers and agents. State v. Somerby, 42 Minn. 55. It has been held that the relator, by making the corporation a defendant under its corporation name, is estopped to deny its corporate existence. People v. Spring Valley, 129 Ill. 169. *Contra,* State v. Tracy, 48 Minn. 497.

be made in the case of municipal corporations.¹ The proceedings to arrest the usurpation of a franchise rest in the sound discretion of the attorney-general² of the state, and the granting of the writ rests in the sound discretion of the court or judge.³ The following rules have been stated as those which should guide in the issuance of this writ:⁴ First, the relator must not be a mere stranger coming in to disturb a corporation with which he has no concern. Second, he must not have concurred in the act of which he now complains as illegal. Third, unless there is fraud or intentional violation of law, it must appear that public or private interests will not be seriously affected by the ouster of the incumbent.

§ 350. *Remedy in equity.*— Before a court of equity will use its powers by injunction to prevent a public corporation from exceeding or abusing its powers, it must be made to appear that the case falls within one of the recognized heads of equity jurisprudence, such as fraud, irreparable injury, want of an adequate remedy at law or the prevention of a multiplicity of suits.⁵ There appears to be a tendency, however, to extend this jurisdiction,⁶ and it is well recognized that the court will see that a corporation performs all its duties in reference to property

---

¹ State v. Cincinnati, etc. Gas Co., 18 Ohio St. 262. An association, although not incorporated, may be ousted by *quo warranto* from acting "as a corporation." State v. Ackerman, 51 Ohio St. 163, 24 L. R. A. 298.

² Robinson v. Jones, 14 Fla. 256. It must be prosecuted by, and not merely with the consent of, the attorney-general when the object is to test the right of a corporation to exercise a franchise. State v. Tracy, 48 Minn. 497, 51 N. W. Rep. 613. It will issue, however, without the consent of the attorney-general when the private person has an interest in himself distinct from that of the public, as a right to an office. In re Barnum, 27 Minn. 466.

³ People v. Waite, 70 Ill. 25.

⁴ Depue, J., in State v. Tolon, 33 N. J. L. 195, quoted in Dillon, Mun. Corp., II, § 901.

⁵ Brooklyn v. Meserole, 26 Wend. (N. Y.) 132; Haywood v. Buffalo, 14 N. Y. 534; Minnesota Linseed Oil Co. v. Palmer, 20 Minn. 424. The writ of prohibition is sometimes used to restrain the imposition of illegal fines and penalties. An injunction is directed to an individual and a writ of prohibition to an inferior court. Smith v. Whitney, 116 U. S. 167; Bluffton v. Silver, 63 Ind. 262. It will not issue when there is a remedy by appeal or *certiorari*. State v. Withrow, 108 Mo. 1; Turner v. Forsyth, 78 Ga. 683.

⁶ Dillon, Mun. Corp., II, § 908. A public corporation may also be indicted for nonfeasance or misfeasance in the performance of public duties imposed by law. McClain, Crim. Law, I, § 183 and cases cited.

which it holds in trust.[1] Suits to prevent public corporations from exceeding their authority, or to have their illegal acts set aside or corrected, are properly brought in the name of the attorney-general of the state, or in the name of the state on the relation of some interested person.[2] On the theory that a public corporation is a trustee for the inhabitants, a taxpayer may file a bill in equity on behalf of himself and other taxpayers to prevent the corporation from acting *ultra vires* or from fraudulently disposing of the property of the corporation or creating a debt which the taxpayers will be called upon to pay.[3] In New York, however, a citizen or taxpayer cannot maintain a suit to restrain or avoid a corporate act alleged to be illegal, unless he is able to show that he will suffer some damage special and peculiar to himself, distinct from that of other inhabitants.[4] But every taxable inhabitant, and perhaps every citizen, says Judge Dillon,[5] has such an interest to prevent or avoid illegal or unauthorized corporate acts that he may be a relator on whose application the proper public officer may, on behalf of the public, file the requisite bill in cases which fall within the jurisdiction of equity, to enjoin the menaced wrong; or, if it has been consummated, to relieve against it. A court of equity will, at the suit of one or more taxpayers, enjoin a municipality from collecting an illegal tax on real property.[6] The mere fact that the sale would create a cloud on the title is sufficient to confer jurisdiction upon the court.[7] The court will not generally in-

[1] Attorney-General v. Boston, 123 Mass. 460.

[2] State v. Saline County, 51 Mo. 350, 11 Am. Rep. 454; Attorney-General v. Detroit, 26 Mich. 262. In People v. Field, 58 N. Y. 491 (Tweed cases), it was held that an action to recover money illegally taken from the city of New York could not be maintained in the name of the attorney-general of the state; § 37 note, *supra*.

[3] Crampton v. Zabriskie, 101 U. S. 601; New London v. Brainard, 22 Conn. 552; The Liberty Bell, 23 Fed. Rep. 843; Baltimore v. Gill, 31 Md. 375. As to the right to enjoin a threatened misapplication of funds, see Place v. Providence, 12 R. I. 1;

Newmeyer v. Missouri, etc. Ry. Co., 52 Mo. 81, 14 Am. Rep. 394, note.

[4] Doolittle v. Broome County, 18 N. Y. 155; Roosevelt v. Draper, 23 N. Y. 318.

[5] Dillon, Mun. Corp., II, § 921; Chicago v. Union Building Ass'n, 102 Ill. 379.

[6] Dows v. Chicago, 11 Wall. (U. S.) 108; State Railway Tax Cases, 92 U. S. 575.

[7] Holland v. Baltimore, 11 Md. 186. It is considered that there is an adequate remedy at law in the case of personal property. Dodd v. Hartford, 25 Conn. 231; Youngblood v. Sexton, 32 Mich. 406, 2 Am. Rep. 65; Milwaukee v. Koeffler, 116 U. S. 219.

terfere to prevent the collection of an illegal tax on personal property,[1] and will never interfere where the tax is merely irregular.[2]

§ 351. *Certiorari.*—The writ of *certiorari* lies to inferior courts and officers exercising power of a judicial nature to review judicial proceedings when no right of appeal or other specific mode of review is provided.[3] It is a common-law remedy and exists in such cases, although not provided for by statute.[4] Its application, however, has in some cases been extended beyond its proper function at common law by statute and judicial decision. The other remedy referred to in such a statute has been held to be one which will enable the relator to have the proceedings complained of annulled as void and as not including a mere right to sue an officer acting under the void order.[5] The proceedings of a public corporation, so far as they are of a judicial nature, may be reviewed and errors of law corrected by *certiorari*,[6] but it is not a substitute for an appeal and cannot be used unless aided by statute for the purpose of correcting errors of fact.[7] Thus, the legality of convictions in municipal courts,[8] of local assessments[9] or the opening of a street[10] may be thus determined when no other mode of review is provided by law. The common-law rule that only judicial acts can be reviewed under the writ has been somewhat relaxed by some of our courts, and it has been used to test the acts of municipal corporations, whether judicial or legislative.[11]

But there are exceptions to this rule. See Allen v. Baltimore & Ohio Ry. Co., 114 U. S. 311.

[1] Milwaukee v. Koeffler, 116 U. S. 219.

[2] Stone v. Mobile, 57 Ala. 61.

[3] In re Wilson, 32 Minn. 145; State v. St. Paul, 34 Minn. 250; Attorney-General v. Northampton, 143 Mass. 589; State v. The Judge, etc., 43 La. Ann. 1089, 10 L. R. A. 248; Tomlinson v. Board of Equalization, 88 Tenn. 1, 6 L. R. A. 207; State v. Hughes County, 1 S. D. 292, 10 L. R. A. 588. It must be remembered that the use of this writ is regulated by statute in many states. The writ of *certiorari* will not be granted for the purpose of reviewing nugatory proceedings. State v. Village of Lambertson, 37 Minn. 362. For a history of the writ of *certiorari*, see an article by Prof. Goodnow, "The Writ of Certiorari," Pol. Sci. Quar., VI, 492.

[4] People v. New York, 2 Hill (N. Y.), 9.

[5] State ex rel. v. Rose, 4 N. D. 319, 26 L. R. A. 593.

[6] Collins v. Davis, 57 Iowa, 256; Oshkosh v. State, 59 Wis. 425; Jackson v. Michigan, 9 Mich. 111.

[7] State v. Bill, 13 Ired. (N. C.) L. 373.

[8] Taylor v. Americus, 39 Ga. 59.

[9] State v. Newark, 25 N. J. L. 399.

[10] Dwight v. Springfield, 4 Gray, 107.

[11] Camden v. Mulford, 26 N. J. L. 49.

§ 352. *Levy of execution on corporate property.*— The nature of the powers conferred upon public corporations requires that they shall not be subject to the ordinary remedies provided for the collection of debts against individuals. In order that they may properly provide for the local government of the community, it is essential that the property held for public uses shall be exempt from execution. Hence, on grounds of public policy, it is held that neither the property, the revenues raised by taxation or by fines and penalties, nor tax judgments can be seized under execution upon a judgment against the corporation.[1] The property and income of a municipal corporation are so closely related to that of the state that they partake of the state's exemption from federal taxation;[2] but private property not held in trust or dedicated to a public use may be sold on execution to satisfy a judgment against the city.[3] Thus, the water-works[4] or the city hall,[5] owned by a city, are not subject to sale on execution. Nor can a mechanic's lien be imposed upon the public property of a corporation.[6] In the New England states, by common law or immemorial usage, a judgment against a town may be satisfied out of the individual property of the citizens.[7]

On *certiorari* the evidence returned may be considered only for the purpose of determining whether it will justify the finding—not whether the superior court would have reached the same conclusion. Jackson v. People, 9 Mich. 111. The proceedings of a board of health condemning a nuisance are not reviewable when the board is not required to take evidence, but may act upon its own inspection. People v. Yonkers Board of Health, 140 N. Y. 1, 23 L. R. A. 481.

[1] Brown v. Gates, 15 W. Va. 131; Overton Bridge Co. v. Means, 33 Neb. 857, 51 N. W. Rep. 240, 29 Am. St. Rep. 514; Sherman v. Williams, 84 Tex. 421, 19 S. W. Rep. 606; Morrison v. Hinkson, 87 Ill. 587, 29 Am. Rep. 77; Emery Co. v. Burresen, 14 Utah, 328, 37 L. R. A. 732 (county); Klein v. New Orleans, 99 U. S. 149. A statute naming corporations among those subject to garnishment does not apply to a county. State v. Tyler, 14 Wash. 495, 45 Pac. Rep. 31.

[2] United States v. Baltimore & Ohio R. Co., 17 Wall. (U. S.) 322.

[3] Brown v. Gates, 15 W. Va. 131; New Orleans v. Home Ins. Co., 23 La. Ann. 61; Davenport v. Peoria Ins. Co., 17 Iowa, 276; Hart v. New Orleans, 12 Fed. Rep. 292.

[4] New Orleans v. Morris, 105 U. S. 600.

[5] Ellis v. Pratt City, 113 Ala. 541, 33 L. R. A. 264. The exemption from levy or attachment applies to the proceeds of insurance on the city hall.

[6] Foster v. Fowler, 60 Pa. St. 27; Charnock v. Colfax, 51 Iowa, 70; Klein v. New Orleans, 99 U. S. 149; Leonard v. Brooklyn, 71 N. Y. 493.

[7] Bloomfield v. Charter Oak Bank, 121 U. S. 121; Beardsley v. Smith, 16

§ 353. *Liability to garnishment.*— On grounds of policy, public corporations are generally held not liable to garnishment with respect to their revenues and the salaries of their officials. In some states this rule has been established on principle,[1] in others the exemption is based upon statutory provisions,[2] and in some states garnishment is allowed.[3] An officer cannot subject the funds of a municipality to garnishment in a suit to collect his salary from the corporation.[4] Nor can a city be garnished by a creditor of one of its officers or employees.[5] An officer's salary, when not exempt on other grounds, may be reached by proceedings supplemental to execution.[6] So a judgment debtor may be ordered to assign to his creditor a debt due him from a municipality.[7] Where the controversy is between a creditor of the corporation and a creditor of its creditor, there is every reason for holding that the cor-

Conn. 367, 41 Am. Dec. 147. Elsewhere, in the absence of statute, there is individual liability on the part of citizens for the debts of the corporation. Rees v. Watertown, 19 Wall. (U. S.) 107; Meriwether v. Garrett, 102 U. S. 472; Kincaid v. Hardin Co., 53 Iowa, 430.

[1] Burnham v. Fond du Lac, 15 Wis. 211; Merrell v. Campbell, 49 Wis. 535; Erie v. Knapp, 29 Pa. St. 173; Roeller v. Ames, 33 Minn. 132; Merwin v. Chicago, 45 Ill. 133; Bireus v. Harper, 59 Ill. 21; McDougall v. Hennepin Co., 4 Minn. 184 (Gil. —); Underhill v. Calhoun, 63 Ala. 216. See note to 24 Am. St. Rep. 73. The conflicting authorities are reviewed in Drake on Attachment (7th ed.), § 516. Garnishment of taxes due from an individual. Egerton v. Third Municipality, 1 La. Ann. 435. A city may waive its exemption by appearing. Clapp v. Davis, 25 Iowa, 315.

[2] As in Iowa. See Jenks v. Township, 45 Iowa, 554.

[3] See Davis v. Grover, 38 N. J. L. 104; Whidden v. Drake, 5 N. H. 13; Newark v. Funk, 15 Ohio St. 462; Bray v. Wallingford, 20 Conn. 416 (town); Seymour v. School District, 53 Conn. 502 (county); Adams v. Tyler, 121 Mass. 380 (county); Wales v. Muscatine, 4 Iowa, 302 (incorporated city); Laredo v. Nalle, 65 Tex. 359.

[4] Baltimore v. Root, 8 Md. 95. In Waterbury v. Commissioners, 10 Mont. 515, 24 Am. St. Rep. 67, it is held that a county is liable to garnishment for a debt due by it to its officers, under a statute declaring that all "persons." To the same effect, Newark v. Funk, 15 Ohio St. 462.

[5] School District v. Gage, 39 Mich. 484; Wallace v. Lawyer, 54 Ind. 501, 23 Am. Rep. 661; Clark v. Mobile, 36 Ala. 621 (salary of teacher); Roeller v. Ames, 33 Minn. 132 (mayor); McLellan v. Young, 54 Ga. 399, 21 Am. Rep. 276; Bank v. Dibrell, 3 Sneed (Tenn.), 379. *Contra,* Rodman v. Musselman, 12 Bush (Ky.), 354, 23 Am. Rep. 724. By statute salary of policeman is subject to garnishment. City Council v. Van Dorn, 41 Ala. 505.

[6] Roeller v. Ames, 33 Minn. 132.

[7] Knight v. Nash, 22 Minn. 456.

poration should not be required to become involved in the controversy. But when the corporation is the debtor, there seems to be no sufficient reason why its creditors should be deprived of the remedy which the law gives to the creditors of natural persons and private corporations.[1]

[1] A city is subject to garnishment for an ordinary debt due by it to a third person. City of Laredo v. Nalle, 65 Tex. 359; Droz v. Baton Rouge, 36 La. Ann. 340; Walker v. Cook, 129 Mass. 577; State v. Eberly, 12 Neb. 616; Dillon, Mun. Corp., I, § 101.

INDEX.

References are to pages.

ABUTTERS —
    rights of, in street, 97.
    duty to repair sidewalk, 299, 300.

ACTION (see ch. XIX) —
    right to sue, 315.
    filing claim as a condition precedent to, 315.

AGRICULTURAL LANDS —
    annexation of, 42, 43.

AMENDMENT —
    of charter, whether special legislation, 64, 65.

AMOTION (see OFFICER) —
    relates to officers, 242.
    implied grounds of, 243.
    under express statute, 243.
    power of removal, whether judicial, 245.
    suspension, 245.
    removal by appointing power, 245.
    causes of removal, 245, 246.
    proceedings, notice, 244.

AMUSEMENTS —
    regulation of, 89.

ANNEXATION (see BOUNDARIES).

APPEAL —
    in condemnation proceedings, 129.

APPOINTMENT TO OFFICE (see OFFICES AND OFFICERS).

APPORTIONMENT (see SPECIAL ASSESSMENTS) —
    of benefits under special assessments, 112.

ARBITRATION, 82.

ASSESSMENTS —
    see SPECIAL ASSESSMENTS, 107.

ATTORNEY —
    compensation of, 238.

ATTORNEY-GENERAL —
    control over *quo warranto* proceedings, 324.

B.

BAY WINDOWS—
projecting over sidewalk, 100.

BENEFITS—
as set-off against damages in condemnation proceedings, 128.

BIBLE—
use of, in public schools, 83.

BICYCLES—
right to use streets, 98.

BIDDERS—
rights and remedies of, 78.

BOARDS—
powers vested in, 218, 219.

BONA FIDE HOLDERS (see BONDS)—
of municipal bonds, 162.
defenses available against, 163.
right to rely on recitals, 163.

BONDS—
power of public *quasi*-corporations to issue, 148.
power of municipal corporations, 149.
authority to issue negotiable bonds, 148.
may be invalid, 148.
bonds payable in gold coin, 148, n.
distinguished from power to incur debt, 149.
implied power to issue bonds, 149, 150.
railway aid bonds, 150.
ratification of illegal bonds, 150, 151.
cannot ratify an act *ultra vires* the corporation, 150.
liability for value received for illegal bonds, 150, 262.
action for money had and received, 150.
right to restrain issue of illegal negotiable bonds, 152.
bonds illegal in hands of innocent purchaser, 152.
can be issued for public purposes only, 152.
what are such purposes, 152.
paving streets, 152.
constructing water-works, 152.
support of public schools, 152.
constructing public buildings, 153.
acquiring electric light plants, 153.
celebrating Columbian Exposition, 153.
entertainment of visitors, 153.
no implied authority to use money for such purposes, 153.
treatment of habitual drunkards, 94, 153.
construction of railways, 153, 154.
distinction between subscriptions and donations to, 154.

References are to pages.

BONDS (continued) —
 manufacturing enterprises, private, 154.
 construction of a dam to aid manufacturing enterprise, 154, 155.
 whether purpose public to be determined by court, 145.
 conditions precedent to legal issue, 155 *et seq.*
 how imposed, 155.
 when imposed by corporation, right of innocent holder, 156.
 waiver of condition by officials, 156.
 delegation of power to determine performance of condition, 156.
 consent of people as a condition, 156.
 such consent does not confer power, 156.
 statutory authority must be followed, 156, 157.
 effect of irregularities in voting, 156.
 contents of petition, 157.
 manner of calling election, 157.
 notice, 157.
 majority of voters, meaning of, 157.
 "inhabitants" means legal voters, 157.
 majority of qualified electors, 157, 158.
 two-thirds of qualified voters, 158.
 location or completion of road as a condition, 158.
 illustrations, 158.
 time of completion, when material, 159.
 estoppel, 159.
 no estoppel against defense of want of power, 159.
 no estoppel to deny authority of officers, 160.
 by conduct, 160.
 by retaining consideration, 161.
 acquiescence, 161.
 payment of interest, 161.
 estoppel by judgment, 162.
 who are *bona fide* holders, 162.
 constructive notice of defenses, 162.
 issue in violation of an injunction, 162.
 presence of overdue coupons, 162.
 must take notice of laws of state, 163.
  of public records, 163.
  of what appears on face of the bonds, 163.
 defenses against a *bona fide* holder, 163.
 want of power, 163.
 estoppel by recitals, 163, 164.
 statement of rule by Dillon, 164.
 bonds issued in violation of an express statute, 163.
 statement of rule by Mr. Justice Strong, 164.
 authority of officers to make recitals, 165.
 grounds of the estoppel, 165.
 recital that bonds have been issued "in conformity to law," 165.
  "in pursuance of statute," 166.
  in pursuance of an order of county court, 167.

References are to pages.

BONDS (continued)—
over-issues, 167.
beyond constitutional limitation, 167.
beyond legislative limitation, 167.
when authority is made to depend upon facts of record, 168.
facts which appear upon assessment rolls, 168.

BOUNDARIES—
determination of, by legislature, 21, 41.
legislative power to change, 41.
effect of change on corporate existence, 44.
disposition of public property when no legislative apportionment is made, 44 and note.
change of, not an amendment of charter, 26.
annexation of territory, 41.
what territory can be annexed, 42.
contiguous territory, 41.
agricultural lands, 42.
cannot annex territory of another corporation, 43.
division of territory, 44.
apportionment of property and debts upon division, 44.

BREACH OF OFFICIAL DUTY—
when cause for removal from office, 245.

BRIDGES (see NEGLIGENCE)—
part of highway, 303.
construction of, compelled by *mandamus*, 304.
reasonable care required in construction, 304.
must be a reasonably safe structure, 304.
guards and railings, 304.
location of, a governmental act, 304.
constructed to withstand ordinary storms, 304.
not to support extraordinary weights, 304.
negligence in case of, 272.

BUILDING—
moving through street, 98.

BUILDING MATERIAL—
in streets, 98.

BY-LAW—
synonymous with ordinance, 176.

C.

CELEBRATIONS—
right to appropriate money for, 153.

CEMETERIES—
as corporate property, 134.

References are to pages.

CERTIORARI —
    nature of writ, 324.
    its history, 324, n.
    reviews proceedings of a judicial nature, 324.
    a common-law remedy, 324.
    extended by statute, 324.
    meaning of "other remedy," 324.
    not a substitute for an appeal, 324.

CHARTER —
    not a contract, 24.
    subject to change by legislature, 24.
    may be submitted to vote of inhabitants, 24.
    as determining powers, 176.

CHARTER POWERS (see POWERS).

CITY LIMITS —
    see BOUNDARIES, 50.

CLASSIFICATION —
    as a basis for legislation, 55.
    based upon number, 57.
    based upon population, 58, 59.

COASTING (see NEGLIGENCE) —
    liability for injuries caused by, 269, 299.

COMPENSATION (see OFFICERS) —
    upon taking property by eminent domain, 126.
    rule for determining, 126, 127.
    improvement, 126.
    valuations founded on sentiment, 127.
    loss of profits, 127.
    diminished value of merchandise caused by removal, 127.
    of officers, 234, 235.
    of mayor, 239.

COMPULSORY INCORPORATION —
    consent of inhabitants, 14.
    by direct legislative action, 14.

CONDITIONS PRECEDENT (see BONDS) —
    to entry on office, 226.
    to issue of bonds, 155.
    by what authority imposed, 155.
    rule of construction, 155.
    consent of people, 156.
    manner of obtaining consent, 156.
    "majority of voters," "inhabitants," meaning of, 157.
    location of railroad, 158.
    oath of office, 226.
    official bond, 226.

CONFLAGRATION —
    destruction of building to prevent, 281.

References are to pages.

CONSEQUENTIAL DAMAGES (see NEGLIGENCE; SEWERS) —
liability for, 813.
resulting from exercise of legal right, 127.
as by change of street grade, 127.

CONSTITUTIONAL LIMITATIONS (see ch. IV) —
upon legislative power over corporations, 46.
corporations created for municipal purposes, 46.
general laws, definition, 47.
requirement of a uniform system of government, 48.
object of such a provision, 48.
does not prohibit classification, 48.
same powers possessed by all corporations; law is general, 49.
not intended to secure uniformity in exercise of police power, 50.
special law to legalize defective incorporation, 50.
illustrations under provision requiring uniformity, 50.
laws of a general nature shall have uniform operation, 51.
effect of this provision, 51.
its construction, 51.
does not prevent proper classification, 52.
illustrations, 52.
local-option laws, 54.
classification, 55.
must have a basis in reason, 55.
illustrations of proper basis, 56, 57.
class may contain but one member, 57.
geographical conditions as a basis, 58.
population, 58.
illustrations, 59.
possible accession to a class, 60.
regulation of the "business" and "affairs" of a corporation, 61, 62.
prohibition of special legislation when a general law can be made applicable, 63.
whether a judicial or legislative question, 63.
amendment or repeal of charters, 64.
an evasion of the constitutional provision, 65.

CONSTRUCTION —
grant of power of eminent domain, construed strictly, 120.
of grants of power, 69.

CONTIGUOUS TERRITORY (see BOUNDARIES) —
right to annex, 51.

CONTINGENT OBLIGATIONS —
as increasing indebtedness, 172.

CONTRACTOR (see TORTS) —
liability for negligence of, 270.

CONTRACTS (see LEGISLATIVE CONTROL) —
legislative control over, 34.
charter not a contract, 34.

INDEX.

References are to pages.

CONTRACTS (continued)—
grants of power, revocable, 84.
no vested rights in license fees, 84.
contract between corporation and third persons, 35.
power of taxation, part of contract, 35.
effect of changing manner of levying tax, 35.
exemption of certain property from taxation, 36.
rights of creditors in sinking fund, 36.
limitation of indebtedness as a part of contract, 36.
compulsory contracts, 37.
power to make, 75.
to limit legislative power, 76.
to interfere with duty to preserve public health, 76.
revocation of, by corporation, 76.
letting to lowest bidder, 76.
necessary under charter provision only, 77.
lowest responsible bidder, 77.
remedy of bidder, 78, 79.
remedy of taxpayer, 78.
for term of years, 79.
extending beyond life of council, 79.
creating monopoly, 80.
grant of exclusive privileges, 80.
liability of corporation on, 257.
personal liability of officers on, 246.
ultra vires contracts, 247.
estoppel, when executed by one party, 259.
irregularly executed contracts, 260.
within scope of general power, 260.
contracts in part *ultra vires*, 261.
implied contracts, liability on, 262.
when value received, 262, 263.
illustrations, 263.
recovery back of illegal taxes, 264.
must be compulsory, 264.
must be involuntary, 265.

CONTROL OF STREETS—
by legislature, 96.

CORPORATE DUTIES (see NEGLIGENCE)—
negligence in connection with, 285.

CORPORATE POWERS—
distinguished from public powers, 28, 132.
powers properly conferred, 132.
right to own private property, 133, 134.
electric light plant, 133.
right to convey its property, 134.
cannot be taken from it without compensation, 134.

References are to pages.

CORPORATE POWERS (continued)—
cemeteries, 134.
parks, 134, 135, n.
wharves, 135.
ferries, 135.
ownership of water and lighting plants, 136, 137.
may be authorized to purchase, 138.
nature of the power, 139, 140.
manner of acquiring plant, 140.

COUNCIL—
motives of, in enacting ordinance, 193.
exercises legislative power, 220.
its administrative powers, 220.
its organization, 220.
must act as a unit, 221.
place of meeting, 221.
majority of, 221.
quorum of, 221, 222.
power of appointment, 224.

COUNTIES (see NEGLIGENCE)—
liability for care of streets and roads, 292.

COURT (see MUNICIPAL COURT)—
mayor's court, 239.

CREATION OF CORPORATIONS—
by legislative authority only, 17.
manner of action, 20.
determination of boundaries, 21, 41.
compulsory incorporation, 18.
by United States, 18.
by general law, 20.
by special act, 20.

CREDITORS (see BONDS)—
rights of, 35, 36.
aided by *mandamus*, 317.

CRIMINALS—
liability for negligence in care of, 284.

D.

DAIRIES—
prohibition of, within certain limits, 216.

DAMAGES (see NEGLIGENCE).

DEBTS (see BOUNDARIES)—
apportionment of, 55.

DE FACTO OFFICERS (see OFFICER)—
who are, 232, 233, 234.

INDEX. 337

References are to pages.

DELEGATION OF POWER—
of legislative authority, 70, 214.
DEMAND, 146, 315.
DEPUTIES—
liability of, 251.
DISCRETION (see LEGISLATIVE CONTROL)—
in granting permits, must be uncontrolled, 216, 217.
DISCRIMINATION—
unjust, by city officials in granting privileges, 216.
DISSOLUTION—
of corporation by legislature, 44.
property and debts upon, 41.
may be dissolved by legislature, 41, 44.
disposition of property upon, 29.
DONATION—
to railroads, 154.
DRAINAGE (see SEWERS)—
of lands, assessments for, 111.
DRUNKARDS AND DISORDERLY PERSONS—
regulating assembling of, 212.
DUAL CHARACTER OF MUNICIPAL CORPORATIONS, 22.

E.

ELECTRIC RAILWAY, 105.
ELECTRICAL BUREAU—
private business, 289.
ELECTIONS—
mandamus to compel, 320.
ELEVATED RAILWAYS—
as servitude, 106.
EMINENT DOMAIN—
subject treated in ch. VIII, p. 119 *et seq.*
definition, 119.
distinct from police power, 119.
distinct from power of taxation, 119.
distinct from special assessment, 109.
may be delegated, 120.
grant of power of, strictly construed, 120.
generally private property only taken, 120.
may take public property, 120.
may take every species of property, 120, 123.
illustrations—lands, houses, stream of water, etc., 120.
riparian rights. 120.
legislature to determine quantity of estate, 120.

22

References are to pages.

EMINENT DOMAIN (continued) —
   may take fee or a mere easement, 120.
   lands situated beyond corporate limit, 120.
   taken for public use only, 121.
   public use a question of law, 121.
   necessity for taking, a legislative question, 121.
   reviewed by courts only when gross error, 121.
   illustrations of public uses, 121.
   land for private road, 121.
   land for ornamental purposes, 122.
   property already appropriated to public use, 122.
   construction of grant, 122.
   railroad crossings, 122.
   cemetery, for highway, 122.
   right to condemn franchise of a water company, 123, 141.
   meaning of "property," 123.
   what is a taking, 123, 314.
   physical taking not essential, 123, 124.
   right to take water front, 124.
   change of street grade, 124.
   the proceedings to condemn, 124.
   statutory, strictly followed, 124.
   hearing necessary, 125.
   the petition, 124.
   the tribunal, 124.
   no right to trial by jury, 124, 125.
   notice necessary to due process of law, 125.
   by whom given, 125, 126.
   by advertisement, 125.
   compensation, 126, 127.
   must be full reasonable value, 126.
   improvements, 126.
   sentimental considerations, 126.
   consequential damages, 127.
   benefits, right to set off, 128.
   time of payment of damages, 128, 129.
   right of appeal, 129.
   review by *certiorari*, 129.

EMPLOYEE —
   distinguished from officer, 225.

ENACTING CLAUSE —
   to ordinance, 182, n.

EQUITY (see INJUNCTION) —
   injunction to prevent abuse of corporate power, 322.
   proceedings in name of attorney-general, 323.
   in name of some interested person, 323.
   proceeding by taxpayer, 323.

References are to pages.

EQUITY (continued) —
　case must fall under recognized head of equity, 322.
　duties in connection with property held in trust, 322.
　sale of real property under illegal tax, 323.
　of personal property, 323, 324.

ESTOPPEL (see BONDS) —
　when it arises, 159.
　want of power to issue bonds, no estoppel, 159.
　no estoppel to deny authority of officers, 160.
　by conduct, 160.
　illustrations, 161.
　retaining consideration, 161.
　by payment of interest, 161.
　by acquiescence, 161.
　by judgment, 162.
　by recitals, 163, 164. See RECITALS.
　to defend against *ultra vires* contract, 259.

EXCLUSIVE FRANCHISE (see FRANCHISE).

EXCLUSIVE PRIVILEGES (see CONTRACTS)
　cannot be granted without express legislative authority, 80.
　not favored, 81.
　doubts resolved against, 81.
　to operate street railways, 81.
　to provide water supply, 81.

EXECUTION —
　public property of corporation not subject to, 325.
　private property of corporation, 325.
　rule in New England states, 325.

EXEMPTION —
　from taxation, 115.
　from local assessments, 116.

F.

FAILURE TO ENFORCE ORDINANCES (see ORDINANCE).

FAST DRIVING —
　by members of salvage corps, 205.

FEE (see LICENSE).

FERRY FRANCHISES —
　subject to legislative control, 28.
　power to maintain ferry may be revoked, 29.

FINAL JUDGMENT —
　in *mandamus*, 318.

FIRE —
　destruction of building to prevent spread of, 281.

340   INDEX.

References are to pages.

FIRE LIMITS —
power to establish, 210.
must be reasonably exercised, 210.
repair of building within, 212.

FIREMEN (see NEGLIGENCE) —
negligence of, 282.

FIRE PATROL —
negligence of, city not liable for, 283.

FIREWORKS —
damages by, liability of corporation, 271, n., 278, n.

FLAGMAN —
at railway crossings, 205, 206.

FRANCHISE —
of being a corporation, 2.
of water and light company, 140.
exclusive franchise, 140, 141, 143.

FREEHOLDERS —
special privileges to, 225.

FRONTAGE —
as basis for apportioning local assessment, 114.

FUNDS AND REVENUE (see TAXATION) —
legislative control over, 33.
revenue of a county, not its property, 33.
fund for disabled officer, control over, 33.

G.

GARBAGE —
regulating manner of removal, 212.

GARNISHMENT —
public corporations, when liable to, 326, 327.

GAS AND WATER WORKS (see CORPORATE POWERS) —
ownership of, by corporation, 136, 137.
liability of corporation for negligence in connection with, 28?

GENERAL LAWS (see CONSTITUTIONAL LIMITATIONS) —
definition of, 47, 58.

GENERAL WELFARE CLAUSE —
construction of, 75.

GOVERNMENTAL DUTIES (see NEGLIGENCE) —
what are, 276.

GRADE OF STREET (see STREET) —
damages occasioned by change of, 313, 314.
whether a taking of property, 124, 127, 314.

References are to pages.

H.

HABITUAL DRUNKARDS—
 power to provide for treatment of, 94.

HACKMEN—
 regulation of, 211.

HEALTH (see POLICE POWER)—
 corporate powers in relation to, 86.
 quarantine regulations, 210.
 must not be prohibitory of lawful business, 210.
 smoking in street-cars, 211.

HEALTH OFFICERS—
 liability for negligence of, 283.

HIGHWAYS (see NEGLIGENCE)—
 duty to keep in repair, 290 *et seq.*

HIGHWAY OFFICERS (see OFFICER)—
 personal liability of, 252.
 when no funds, 252.
 for defective ways and bridges, 252.

HOLDING OVER—
 by officers, 241.

HORSE—
 objects in street liable to frighten, 297.

HOSPITALS—
 care of, 283.

HOTEL RUNNERS—
 regulation of, 211.

I.

ICE AND SNOW (see NEGLIGENCE)—
 in street and highway, 302.
 right to require lot-owner to remove from sidewalk, 303.
 liability for injuries occasioned by, 303.

ILLEGAL TAXES—
 may be recovered back, 264.
 when paid involuntarily and under compulsion, 264, 265.
 not when merely irregular, 264.
 what constitutes coercion, 265.
 effect of protest, 265.
 necessity of overt act, 265.
 paid in order to get a deed recorded, 266.

IMPLICATION—
 creation of corporation by, 19.

References are to pages.

IMPLIED CONTRACT —
for money had and received, 151.
consideration for illegal bonds, 151.
liability on, 262.
modifies strict doctrine of *ultra vires*, 262, 263.
to pay back illegal taxes, 264.
payment must have been compulsory, 264.

IMPLIED POWERS, 67.
see POWERS.

INCOMPATIBLE OFFICES, 228.
see OFFICES AND OFFICERS.

INCORPORATION (see CREATION OF CORPORATIONS).

INDEBTEDNESS (see ch. X) —
power to incur, 169.
limitations upon, 169.
measured by percentage of assessed valuation, 169.
notice of such limitations, 169.
meaning of indebtedness, 169.
compulsory obligations, 170.
current expenses, 170.
necessity no excuse, 170.
county warrants, 170, n, 172.
obligations in exchange for property, 170, 171.
agreement to pay rent for market-house, 171.
bonds to pay old debt, 171.
if not used for that purpose are void, 171.
to pay a judgment, 172.
amount of sinking fund to be deducted, 172.
park board certificates, 172.
contingent obligations, 172, 173.
time when created governs, 172.
when contingency depends upon act of corporation, 172.
contracts requiring annual payments, 172.
conflicting decisions, 173.
warrants drawn against future taxes, 175.

INDICTMENT —
of corporation, 322, n.

INDORSEMENT —
of warrant, 147.

INFORMATION —
in nature of *quo warranto*, 321.

INJUNCTION (see EQUITY) —
against enforcement of void ordinance, 197.

INSPECTION —
of sidewalks, 300, 301.

INTOXICATING LIQUORS —
control over sales of, 91.

References are to pages.

J.

JUDGE —
    of municipal courts, 131.

JUDGMENT —
    public property cannot be sold under, 325.
    estoppel by, 162.

JUDICIAL OFFICERS (see OFFICER) —
    liability of, 248.

JURISDICTION —
    over streets, 96.
    of municipal courts, 130.

JURY TRIAL —
    no right to, in condemnation proceedings, 124, 125.
    provided for by certain constitutions, 125.
    this means an ordinary jury of twelve, 125.
    right to, in summary proceedings, 131.
    no right to, in suits for violation of city ordinances, 131, 196.
    when right exists in appellate court, 132.

L.

LAND (see EMINENT DOMAIN; SPECIAL ASSESSMENTS).

LEGISLATIVE CONTROL —
    the general rule, 22.
    as applied to counties and townships, 22.
    limited application to municipal corporations, 23.
    dual character of municipal corporations, 23.
    in matters of governmental nature, 23.
    private or corporate powers, 23.
    local self-government, 24.
    control over municipal charters, 26.
    charters are not contracts, 26.
    when corporation is a trustee, 26.
    may submit proposed amendments to the people, 26.
    public property, control over, 26.
    property acquired by eminent domain, 26.
    highways, use of may be regulated by legislature, 27.
    municipality has no property interest in street, 27.
    control may be transferred to park commissioners, 28.
    may withdraw ferry franchise, 28.
    over private property of corporation, 28.
    over property when corporation is dissolved, 29.
    over public officers, 29.
    police officials, 30.
    may control their appointment and payment, 30.

References are to pages.

LEGISLATIVE CONTROL (continued) —
    municipal board of police, 31.
    over park commissioners, 31.
    over board of public works, 31.
    over board of water commissioners, 31.
    officers to lay out streets, 32.
    the mayor, 32.
    over the funds and revenues, 33.
    over contracts, 34, 35, 45, 46.
    rights of persons contracting with corporation, 35.
    right of a creditor entitled to a tax, 35.
    changes in manner of levying the tax, 35.
    effect of exempting property, 35.
    over a sinking fund, 36.
    amount of municipal indebtedness, 36.
    may impose certain obligations on the corporation, 37.
    when for a public purpose, 37.
    compulsory taxation, 38.
    may not be imposed for a local corporate purpose, 39.
    cannot be compelled to subscribe for work in a private corporation, 39.
    payment of a just debt, 39.
    control over boundaries, 41.
    may annex contiguous territory, 41.
    may not annex non-contiguous lands, 41.
    may delegate the power to municipality, 42.
    illustrations of annexation, 43.
    may provide for apportionment of property and debts upon division of territory, 44.
    control over municipal courts, 130.
LEVY OF SPECIAL TAX —
    compelled by *mandamus*, 318.
LIABILITIES (see CONTRACTS; TORTS).
LICENSEES (see NEGLIGENCE) —
    liability of corporation for acts of, 298.
LICENSES (see ORDINANCE; LIQUOR TRAFFIC; NEGLIGENCE) —
    power to license, 89, 214.
    when implied, 90.
    as tax on police power, 89.
    object of, under police power, 90.
    amount of fee, reasonableness, 90, 207, 208.
    occupations which may be licensed, 91.
    must be no discrimination in granting, 91, 208.
    for market privilege, 92.
    acts of licensee, liability for, 298.
LIQUOR TRAFFIC (see ORDINANCE) —
    regulation of, by ordinance, 209.
    sales limited to certain districts, 209.

References are to pages.

LIQUOR TRAFFIC (continued) —
 district cannot be determined by mayor, 214.
 druggists forbidden to sell, except for medical purposes, 209.
 consent of freeholders within three miles of place of business, 209, 214.
 closing saloons at certain hours, 209.
 closing during church hours, 209.
 license, power to grant cannot be delegated to mayor, 214.

LOCAL ASSESSMENTS (see SPECIAL ASSESSMENTS).

LOCAL-OPTION LAWS, 54.

LOCAL SELF-GOVERNMENT —
 under legislative control, 24.
 protected by constitutional provisions, 24.
 protected by decisions under certain constitutions, 24.
 tendency toward encroachment on, 24, n.

M.

MAJORITY, 221.

MANDAMUS —
 nature of the writ, 316.
 an extraordinary legal remedy, 316.
 when will issue, 316.
 not to govern official discretion, 317.
 to enforce duties toward creditors, 317.
 when creditor has right to levy on property, 318.
 judgment as a condition precedent to issue, 318.
 rule in federal courts, 318.
 when in nature of an execution, 318.
 to compel levy of a tax, 318.
 defense against, 318.
 confers no new authority, 318.
 to compel payment of officer's salary, 319.
 the levy of an assessment, 319.
 admission to an office, 319.
 the holding of an election, 319.
 further illustrations of its use, 319, 320.
 not, as a rule, the remedy to try title to office, 256, 319.
 to compel use of certain text-book, 83.
 to compel letting of contract to lowest bidder, 78.

MANNER OF EXERCISING POWER (see ORDINANCE) —
 when determined by charter, 176.
 statutory directions must be observed, 177.
 when no mode prescribed, 178.
 by ordinance or by-law, 178, 179.

MARKETS —
 definition of, 92.
 power to establish and regulate, 92, 209, 216.

References are to pages.

MARKETS (continued) —
under supervision of police, 92.
requirement of license for keeping, 92.
prohibition of sales of articles during certain hours, 92, 209.
cannot require producers to sell their produce from market stalls, 93.

MAYOR (see OFFICES AND OFFICERS) —
right to preside over council, 220.
right to vote, 239.
to appoint to office, 224.
general executive head, 239.
mayor's court, 239.
right to compensation for services as lawyer, 239.
right to examine books of city officials, 239.

MEETING —
of corporation, 219.
essentials of valid, 219.
notice of, 219.
of common council, place of, 221.

MISDEMEANOR —
to vote for increase of salary, 237.

MOB (see NEGLIGENCE).

MOTIVE OF COUNCIL —
power of courts to consider, 193.

MULTIPLICITY OF SUITS —
as basis of equity jurisdiction, 322.

MUNICIPALITY —
the English municipality, 13, 14.
its origin and history, 13.
organization, 13.
the American municipality, 15.
its history, 15.

MUNICIPAL CORPORATIONS —
definition, 5.
counties, when municipal corporations, 5.
school district, when, 6, 7.
creation of, 17.
    by the United States, 18.
    by prescription, 20.
    by implication, 19.
    by territorial legislature, 19.
manner of legislative action, 20.
boundaries, 21.
name, 21.
dual nature of, 23.

References are to pages.

MUNICIPAL COURTS (see JURY TRIAL; COURTS; JUDICIAL OFFICERS)—
    power of municipal corporation to establish, 130.
    duty on corporation, 130.
    control of legislature over, 130.
    jurisdiction, 130.
    court cannot sit outside of city limits, 130, n.
    qualification of judge and jurors, 131.
    procedure of a summary nature, 131.
    right to jury trial, 131.

N.

NAME—
    of corporation, 21.

NEGLIGENCE (see TORTS)—
    distinction between governmental and corporate powers, 267, 268.
    increase of liability by contract, 274.
    general rules, 275.
    in performance of solely governmental duties, 276.
    when acting as agent of the state, 276.
    failure to exercise a power, 277.
    neglect to enforce an ordinance, 277.
    acts done under suspended ordinance, 277.
    explosion of fireworks, 278.
    cattle running at large, 278.
    acts of a mob, 278.
    action given by statute, 278.
    acts of police officers, 279.
    failure to prevent fires, 280, 289.
    destruction of property to prevent spread of fire, 281.
    acts of firemen, 282.
    negligent handling of fire apparatus, 282.
    negligent driving, 283.
    negligence of fire patrol, 283.
    further illustrations, 283.
    negligence of members of board of health, 283.
    negligence of health officers, 284.
    care of hospital, 284.
    care of prisoners, 284.
    for injuries to prisoners, 284.
    care of the poor, 285.
    care of public school buildings, 285.
    solely corporate duties, 285.
    liable for negligence in some manner as individuals, 286.
    as owner of property, 286.
    in management of a market, 286.
    in management of public building leased for profit, 286.
    in connection with management of poor farm, 286.
    condition of lot owned by city, 286.

References are to pages.

NEGLIGENCE (continued) —
in management of a cemetery, 286.
condition of a wharf, 287.
defective machinery in a public work-house, 287.
when manufacturing and selling gas as an individual, 287.
in supplying water, acts in governmental capacity, 287, 288.
condition of water-box and mains, 288.
in case of highways, 290.
authorities conflicting as to liability of municipalities, 290, 291.
rule in New England states, 291.
the English rule, 291.
liability of public *quasi*-corporations, 292.
duty governmental, 293.
distinction between liability of municipal corporation and counties and towns, 293.
exceptions to the general rule, 293.
when duty is imposed on certain officials, 293.
extent of duty to care for highways, 293, 294, 301.
reasonable care required, 293.
street must be public, 293.
entire width of street must be safe, 294.
rule as to country roads, 294.
lighting of the streets, 294.
failure to light as evidence of negligence, 295.
necessary obstructions allowed, 295.
illustrations of such obstructions, 295, 296.
things having a tendency to frighten horses, 297.
when obstruction placed by an individual, 297.
basis of right of action against city, 297.
lack of funds to repair, 298.
duty of corporation when no funds, 298.
acts of licensees, liability for, 298.
distinguished from mere failure to act, 298, 299.
when granted without authority, 298.
where acts are admittedly dangerous, 298.
sidewalks, care of, 299.
when constructed by individual, 299.
duty cannot be shifted to lot-owner, 299, 300, 303.
owner liable for his own acts of negligence, 300.
inspection of sidewalks, 300.
natural decay of material, 301.
corporation not an insurer of safety of sidewalks, 301.
what are defects in sidewalk, 301.
guards for cellar-ways, 301.
awnings, signboards, etc., 302.
ice and snow, 302.
rule affected by climate of locality, 302.
mere slipperiness not a defect, 302.

References are to pages.

NEGLIGENCE (continued) —
    when accumulated in ridges, 302.
    snow in country road, 302.
    care of bridges, 303.
    reasonable care required in construction and care of, 304.
    need provide for ordinary weights only, 304.
    notice of defect necessary to liability, 204.
    actual or constructive notice, 304.
    construction and care of public buildings, 306.
    in construction of public works, see ch. XVIII.
    collection and discharge of surface water, 308.

NEGOTIABILITY —
    of bonds, 149.
    of warrants, 145.

NON-RESIDENCE —
    discrimination against, 91, 208.

NOTICE —
    of corporate meeting, 219, 220.
    in condemnation proceedings, 125.
    of claim against corporation, 315.
    in proceedings to levy special assessments, 109, 110.
    manner of giving, 125.
    by advertisement, 125.
    by whom given, 125, 126.
    statement of general rule, 126.
    of defective condition of highway, 304.
    actual or constructive, 304, 305.

NUISANCES (see POLICE POWER) —
    what are, 297.
    power to abate, 88.
    must be an actual nuisance, 88.
    merely saying a thing is a nuisance not sufficient, 88.
    judicial determination ordinarily required, 89.
    must depend upon circumstances, 89.
    remedy by indictment or injunction, 89.

O.

OATH —
    condition precedent to entry on office, 226.
    effect of failure to take, 226.
    form of, 226.

OBSTRUCTIONS IN STREETS, 98.

OCCUPATIONS —
    licensing of, 91.

References are to pages.

OFFICIAL BOND —
time of filing, 226.
condition precedent to entry in office, 226.
effect of failure to file, 226.

OFFICES AND OFFICERS —
various kinds of officers, 29.
distinction between state and municipal officers, 29.
public officials, state officers, 30.
control of legislature over appointment, 30.
the mayor a municipal officer, 32.
a state officer within certain constitutional provisions, 32.
members of board of public works, 31.
park commissioner, control over, 31.
who are, 223.
mere financial agents, 223.
president of city council, 223.
members of detective department, 223.
distinction between municipal and state, 29, 223.
relation to corporation, 227.
must not make a personal profit out of his position, 228.
election and appointment of, 224.
power to appoint, 224.
qualifications of, 224.
alien, 224.
non-resident, 224.
women, 224.
property qualifications, 225.
membership in political party, 225.
preference to veterans, 225.
conditions precedent to entering on office, 226.
acceptance, 226.
taking an oath, 226.
effect of failure to take oath, 226.
form of oath, 226.
filing a bond, 226.
effect of failure to file bond, 226.
time of qualification, election or entry on office, 226.
incompatible offices, 228.
what are, questions for the courts, 229.
cannot hold, common-law rule, 228, 229.
lucrative offices, 229.
illustrations of compatible and incompatible offices, 230, 231.
de facto officers, 231, 234.
reputation of, essential, 234.
when acts of, are valid, 232.
must be a *de jure* office, 232.
officer appointed under unconstitutional act, 232.
one elected at illegal election, 234.

OFFICES AND OFFICERS (continued)—
  lack of necessary qualification, 234.
  when no confirmation, 234.
  compensation, 234.
  governed by statute, 234.
  under legislative control, 234.
  recoverable in action, 236.
  no implied right to, 234.
  no compensation for extra services, 235.
  of *de facto* officers, 235.
  salary follows legal title, 235.
  not recoverable by *de facto* officer, 236.
  office may be abolished, 236.
  remedy of *de jure* officer after salary paid to *de facto* officer, 236.
  increase of salary, 237.
  compensation of employees, 237.
  of attorneys, 237.
  the mayor, see MAYOR.
  judicial control over officer, 240.
  over discretionary acts, 240.
  over common council, 240.
  holding over by officer, 241.
  when successor is without legal qualification, 241.
  when failure to elect successor, 241.
  resignation, 241.
  common-law rule, 241, 242.
  acceptance of resignation, 242.
  amotion, 242.
  disfranchisement, 242.
  common ground for removal, 243.
  removal incident to power of appointment, 243.
  where incumbent holds for fixed term, 244.
  power of removal, whether judicial, 245.
  right to hearing on charges, 244, 245.
  elective officers, 244.
  when term of office is fixed by constitution, 246.
  non-elective officers, control of legislature over, 244.
  power of governor to remove, 245.
  temporary suspension, 245.
  misconduct, what is, 246.
  effect of a legal amotion, 246.
  personal liability of officers on contracts, 246.
  both officer and corporation may be liable, 246.
  liability in tort, 247.
  when charged with discretionary power, 247.
  liability of ministerial officer, 247.
  no liability for breach of public duty, 248.
  officers acting judicially, 248.

References are to pages.

OFFICES AND OFFICERS (continued) —
illustrations of such, 248, 249.
distinction between liability of judges of superior and inferior court, 249.
liability of recorder of deeds, 249.
        sheriff, 251.
        highway officer, 252.
        member of board of health, 253.
        supervisors, 253.
        clerk of court, 253.
        inspector of meats, 253.
liability for loss of public funds, 253.
conflicting rules, 253, 254.
officer liable absolutely, 253.
liable for results of negligence, 253, 254.
tendency of authorities, 255.
manner of trying title to office, 255, 256.

ORDINANCE —
definition, 176.
nature of an ordinance, 195.
when a general law, 195.
contracts made with reference thereto, 195.
binding on all within limits, 195.
procedure in enactment of, 177, 196.
police ordinances *quasi*-criminal law, 196.
when may be determined by council, 178.
no right to jury trial, 196.
general acts should be by ordinance, 178.
are legislative acts, 178.
must act by, when, 179.
form of, 181.
the title, 181.
constitutional provision as to title of statutes, 181.
the enacting clause, 182.
when necessary, 182, n.
penalty, 182.
must be reasonable, 182.
discretion of court as to, 182.
provision for forfeiture of a license on conviction, 183.
not a part of the penalty, 183.
necessity for recitals in ordinance, 183.
must be enacted at legal meeting of council, 184.
introduction of, 184.
provisions for reading before final passage, 184.
suspension of rules, 185.
presumption that meeting of council was regular, 184.
signing by clerk, 184.
signature of mayor, 184.

References are to pages.

ORDINANCE (continued) —
   requirement that bill shall be signed in open session, 186.
   executive approval, 186.
   must be in manner provided for, 186, 187.
   the executive veto, 187.
   publication, 188.
   notice not the equivalent of publication, 188, 190.
   when publication directory, 188.
   illegal debts incurred for publication, 189.
   manner of publication, 189.
   designation of paper, 189.
   paper "printed or published in the city," 189.
   place of printing, 189, 190.
   manner and sufficiency of publication, 190.
   time and period of publication, 190.
   proof of publication, 191.
   validity of ordinances, 192 (treated in ch. XIII).
   ordinances enacted under express power, 193.
   motives of council, 193.
   acts impeachable for fraud, when, 193.
   may be valid in part, 194.
   good and bad parts must be distinct, 194.
   valid as to certain persons only, 194, 205.
      as to certain sales, 194.
   prosecution under, in name of state, 196, n.
   injunction against enforcement of invalid ordinance, 197.
   validity, general principles, 198.
   must conform to charter, 198.
   must be constitutional, 198.
   must conform to law, 199.
   must not contravene common right, 200.
   must be general and impartial, 201.
   must not be oppressive, 201.
   must be reasonable, 202.
   reasonableness, a question for the court, 202.
   presumption of reasonableness, 203.
   pipes, laying of in street between certain dates, 204.
   locating vehicles on certain streets, 204.
   speed of vehicles, 204, 205.
   driving by members of salvage corps, 205.
   handling of trains over streets and crossings, 205, 206.
   limiting speed of trains within limits, 205.
   boys getting on moving trains, 206.
   regulation of street railways, 206.
   reports of passengers, 206.
   parades and speaking in streets, 206, 207.
   music, 206.
   regulated, not prohibited, 206.

References are to pages.

ORDINANCE (continued) —
arbitrary discretion of officials, 206, 207.
fixing license fees, 207, 208.
discrimination against non-residents, 208.
regulation of liquor traffic, 208.
fire regulations, 210.
quarantine regulations, 210.
regulation of second-hand clothing business, 210.
hotel runners and hackmen, 211.
smoking in street-cars, 211.
removing snow from sidewalk, 211.
closing restaurants at certain hour, 211.
reporting names of boarders, 211.
reports by pawnbrokers, 211.
shutting off gas or water for non-payment of rent, 212.
garbage, manner of removal of, 212.
prohibiting certain persons from frequenting saloons, etc., 212.
validity dependent upon consent of officials, 212.
when an improper delegation of authority, 214.
classification of such ordinances, 212.
decisions sustaining such ordinance, 212.
when dependent upon nature of act, 215.
beating drums in street, 213.
consent of residents to issue of saloon license, 214.
prohibiting repair of wooden building, 213.
conditions imposed must be general and uniform, 212.
unjust discrimination, 212.
act of officer must be governed by general rules, 216.
suspension of, 277.

ORNAMENTAL USE (see EMINENT DOMAIN) —
taking land for, 122.

P.

PARADES —
right to use street for, 206, 216.
ordinance requiring consent of official, 216.

PARK COMMISSIONERS —
may be given control of streets, 26.

PARKS —
as corporate property, 134, 135, n.
use of, for public meetings, 207.

PAUPERS —
care of, 94.

PAVEMENT —
a local improvement, 111.

INDEX. 355

References are to pages.

PAWNBROKERS —
  may be required to pay a license, 91.
  may be required to report business done, 211.

PAYMENT —
  manner of, in condemnation proceedings, 128.

PENALTY (see ORDINANCES) —
  provided in ordinances, 182.
  revocation of license as part of, 183.

PERSONAL LIABILITY —
  of public officers, 249 *et seq.*
  for local assessment, 117, 118.

PLAN OF PUBLIC WORK (see SEWERS; NEGLIGENCE) —
  negligence in adoption of, 309.

POLICE OFFICERS (see NEGLIGENCE; OFFICERS; LEGISLATIVE CONTROL).

POLICE POWER (see LICENSES; MARKETS; HABITUAL DRUNKARDS; NUISANCES) —
  nature and scope of, 83.
  to what extends, 84.
  limitations upon, 84.
  discretion of body exercising, 84.
  regulation of occupations and amusements, 85.
  harmless business cannot be prohibited, 85.
  certain occupation, illegal *per se*, 85.
  regulation of liquor business, 85.
  the protection of health, 86.
  slaughter-houses, regulation of, 86.
  burial of the dead, 86.
  care of sinks and cesspools, 86.
  quarantine regulations, 86.
  artesian water, 87.
  prescribed standard for articles of food, 87.
  destruction of dead trees, 87.
  requirement that samples of milk be furnished for inspection, 87.
  dealing in second-hand clothing, 87, 88.
  nuisances, 88.
  abatement of, 88.
  must be a nuisance in fact, 88.
  depends upon circumstances, 89.
  regulation of wharves, 89.
  licenses, 89.
  may be as tax or under police power, 89.
  amount of, under police power, 89.
  regulation of markets, 92.
  prevention of fires, 93.
  fire limits, 93.
  destruction of buildings, 93.
  care of indigent and infirm, 94, 95.
  treatment of habitual drunkards, 94, 95.

References are to pages.

POPULATION —
as a basis of classification, 58, 59.

POWERS (see CONTRACT; CORPORATE POWERS; EXCLUSIVE FRANCHISES; EMINENT DOMAIN; POLICE POWER; TAXATION; SPECIAL ASSESSMENTS) —
distribution of, 218.
classification of powers, 67.
derived from charter, 67.
cannot be increased or diminished by the corporation, 68.
judicial comment on theory of corporate powers, 68.
construction, 69.
usage not a source of power, 70.
powers requiring exercise of discretion cannot be delegated, 70.
ministerial powers may be delegated, 70.
illustrations, 70, 71.
manner of granting power to corporations, 72.
practice of enumerating powers granted, 72.
powers commonly granted, 73.
statutory requirement as to manner of exercising power, 73.
exercise of, beyond corporate limits, 74.
authority over drainage system, 74.
inspection of dairy herd, 74.
to enact ordinances, 74.
under general welfare clause, 75.
to contract, 75.
cannot by contract limit legislative power, 76.
powers of a private nature, 76.
to revoke a contract, 76.
to enter into contract which would create a nuisance, 76.
to revoke a contract, 76.
to ratify contract, 76.
letting of, to lowest bidder, 76.
remedy of bidder, 78.
contract for term of years, 79.
exclusive privileges, 80.
to borrow money, 81.
to compromise a claim, 82.
to arbitrate a claim, 82.
of school board as to text-books, 82.
to acquire site for market, 93.

PRESCRIPTION —
creation of corporation by, 20.

PRESENTMENT —
of warrant, 146.

PRIVATE CORPORATION —
how created, 2.
for benefit of members, 2.

References are to pages.

PRIVATE POWERS (see CORPORATE POWERS).

PRIVATE PROPERTY —
   municipal corporations may own property, 28.
   governed by private laws, 28.
   not subject to legislative control, 28.
   cannot be taken for a park without compensation, 28.

PRIVATE ROADS, 121.

PROCEEDINGS —
   in taking property for public use, 124.
   to enforce municipal ordinance, 131, 132.
   to levy special assessment, 109.
   to remove an officer, 224, 225.

PROPERTY —
   definition of, 123.
   what is, in law of eminent domain, 123.
   appropriated to public use, 122.
   right of corporation to hold, 133.

PUBLICATION (see ORDINANCES) —
   of ordinances, 188.

PUBLIC CORPORATIONS —
   created for public purposes, 2.
   classification of, 4.
   includes public *quasi*-corporations, 4.
   municipal corporations, 4.
   includes territory and inhabitants, 4.

PUBLIC FUNDS (see OFFICE) —
   liability of officer for loss of, 284.

PUBLIC PROPERTY (see NEGLIGENCE) —
   subject to control of legislature, 26.
   includes what, 26.
   on division of corporation, 44. See BOUNDARIES.
   negligence in case of, 306.
   condition of public building, 307.
   dangerous condition of school building, 306.

PUBLIC QUASI-CORPORATIONS, 6.

Q.

QUALIFICATIONS (see OFFICERS) —
   of officers, 224.
   of jurors in municipal court, 131.

QUARANTINE REGULATIONS (see POLICE POWER; HEALTH) —
   proper police regulations, 210.

QUASI-PUBLIC CORPORATIONS, 6.

References are to pages.

QUORUM —
of council or other body, 221.

QUO WARRANTO —
nature of writ, 321.
discretion of judge, 322.
rules governing its issuance, 322.
proper remedy to try title to office, 321, 356.
on right to preside over a municipal body, 321.
whether corporation legally created, 321.
proceedings against one assuming to be an officer, 321.
the English practice, 321.
usurpation of franchise, proceeding in discretion of attorney-general, 322.

R.

RAILWAY CROSSINGS (see ORDINANCE) —
speed of train at, 205.
use of, during certain hours of day, 206.

RAILWAYS (see SERVITUDES; ROADS AND STREETS) —
in streets, 100.
as additional servitude, 104, 105.
ordinary street railway, 105.
electric street railways, 105.
poles of electric railways, 105.
elevated railway, as servitude, 106.
speed of trains, 205.

READING ORDINANCE, 184.

REASONABLENESS —
of ordinance, 202. See ORDINANCE.

RECITALS IN BONDS (see BONDS) —
effect of recitals, 163, 164.
authority of officers to make, 165.
that bonds have been issued "in conformity to law," 165, 166.
effect of on overissue of bonds, 167.
when facts are to be determined by records, 168.

RECORDER OF DEEDS (see OFFICER) —
liability of, 249.
performs duties to individuals, 249.
liability for failure to record deed correctly, 250.
liability for recording paper not entitled to record, 250.
liability for giving an erroneous certificate, 250.

REMOVAL (see AMOTION; OFFICER) —
of officers, 243.

RESIGNATION (see OFFICER) —
common rule as to, 241.
necessity for acceptance of, 242.
effect of, 242.

References are to pages.

RESOLUTION—
  distinguished from ordinance, 178.
  council may act by, when, 178, 179.
  illustrations, 179.
RESTAURANT—
  time of closing, 211.
RIOT (see NEGLIGENCE).
ROADS AND STREETS (see RAILWAYS; SERVITUDES)—
  control of legislature over, 27, 96.
  may be delegated to corporation, 96.
  given to cities, counties and towns, 97.
  may be delegated to park commissioners, 26.
  title to, in corporation in trust for public, 26.
  right of people to use street, 96.
  abutting owner, rights of, 97.
  proper uses of, 97.
  necessary obstructions, 98.
  temporary uses of a street, 98.
  moving buildings in, 98.
  unloading cars, 98.
  building material, 98.
  improvement of, 99.
  right to override rights of individual in, 99.
  grading, 100.
  laying of gas and water pipes, 100.
  projecting door, windows and porches, 100, 101.
  railroads in streets, 101.
  right to authorize, 101.
  ordinary commercial railroads, 101.
  condition attached to grant of right to use street, 102, 103.
  such as tend to preserve the street, 103.
  consent of abutting owners, 102.
  agreement to pay for same, 102.
  location of tracks and telegraph poles, 102.
  grants in, subject to police power, 102.
  right of one railway to use rails of another in street, 102.
  express authority to authorize placing of telegraph poles in, 104.
  additional servitude, 104.
  railways as such, 104, 105.
  telegraph and telephone poles as servitude, 106.
  telephone poles along a country highway, 106.
  right of abutting owners to compensation, 104.

S.

SALARY (see COMPENSATION; OFFICER).
SCHOOLS (see SCHOOL BOARDS)—
  compulsory support of, 38.
  support of, a public purpose, 152.

References are to pages.

SCHOOL BOARDS (see TEXT-BOOKS) —
    powers of, purely statutory, 82.
    may prescribe text-books, 82, 83.
    use of Bible in schools, 83.
    may prescribe health regulations, 83.
    vaccination, 83.

SCHOOL BUILDINGS (see PUBLIC BUILDINGS; NEGLIGENCE) —
    dangerous condition of, liability for, 306.

SCHOOL DISTRICT (see PUBLIC SCHOOLS) —
    description of, 7.
    powers of, 7, 8.
    existence shown by prescription, 20.

SCREENS AND WINDOW BLINDS —
    requirement of in saloons, 91.

SECOND-HAND CLOTHING —
    regulating sale of, 210.

SECURITIES (see BONDS; WARRANTS).

SERVITUDES (see ROADS AND STREETS) —
    right of abutting owners, 104.
    railways as additional servitudes, 104.
    ordinary street railways, 105.
    electric railways, 105.
    poles of electric railways, 105.
    surface railway operated by steam motors, 106.
    elevated railways, 106.
    telegraph and telephone poles, 106.
    location of the fee as test, 106.
    telephone poles along country highway, 106.

SEWERS (see NEGLIGENCE) —
    failure to construct, no liability, 308.
    determination to construct, a governmental act, 309.
    adoption of plan of, 309.
    must exercise care in, 309.
    selection of engineers, 310.
    adoption of reasonably adequate system, 310.
    maintaining inadequate sewer, 310.
    when results in direct injury to property, 310.
    negligence in construction, 312.
        in maintenance, 312.
    consequential damages resulting from public works, 313.
    change of grade of street, 313, 314.
    removing natural support of land, 314.

SIDEWALKS, 300 —
    see NEGLIGENCE; ROADS AND STREETS.

SINKING FUND —
    contract rights in, 36.
    as affecting indebtedness of corporation, 172.

INDEX. 361

References are to pages.

SNOW —
  removal of, from sidewalks, 211, 302.
  in country highway, 303.

SPECIAL ASSESSMENTS, 107.
  see TAXATION.
  a form of taxation, 108.
  power to authorize, 108, 109.
  constitutionality of, 109.
  corporation has no implied power to levy, 108.
  theory of, 108, 109.
  distinguished from eminent domain, 109.
  purpose for which levied, 110.
  due process of law, 109.
  what required for, 109.
  the proceeding, notice, etc., 110.
  right of appeal, 110.
  ordinary element for valid tax, 110.
  must be a special local benefit, 110.
  not a work of general benefit, 114.
  improvement must partake of permanent nature, 111.
  sprinkling streets, 111.
  maintaining boulevards and pleasure-ways, 111.
  grading a street, 111.
  paving, 111.
  constructing sidewalk, 111.
  sprinkling, 111.
  constructing drains, 111.
  sewers and culverts, 112.
  laying water pipes, 112.
  apportionment, methods of, 112.
  by benefits, 113.
  determination of benefits by commissioners, 113.
  impeachable for fraud and manifest mistake only, 113.
  the frontage rule, 114.
  not applicable to farm or suburban property, 114.
  levied upon property exempt from taxation, 115.
  illustrations, 115, 116.
  manner of collecting assessments, 116, 117.
  when made by city, liability, 116, 117.
  acceptance of work by city, conclusive as against property owner, 117.
  personal liability of property owner, 117, 118.
  the prevailing rule, 117.

STATUTE OF LIMITATIONS —
  municipal warrants, 148.

STREETS (see ROADS AND STREETS).

STREET RAILWAYS (see ORDINANCES) —
  regulation of, 206.
  conditions imposed on, 102.

References are to pages.

STREET RAILWAYS (continued)—
provide driver and conductor on each car, 206.
reports of number of passengers, 206.

SURFACE WATER—
common-law rule in respect to, 307.
the civil-law rule, 309.
control over natural water-ways, 308.
discharge of, on land of individual, 308, 310.
as affected by change of grade, 309.

T.

TAKING—
what constitutes a, 123, 314.

TAXATION (see SPECIAL ASSESSMENTS; ILLEGAL TAXES)—
power of, 107.
may be delegated to public corporation, 110.
implied authority, 110.
exemption from, 35, 108.
property exempt from, liable to special assessments, 115.
for public purposes only, 110.
revocable, 110.
special assessment; form of taxation, 108.

TELEGRAPH AND TELEPHONE POLES—
when servitude on street, 106.

TERRITORIAL LEGISLATURE—
power to create corporation, 19.

TERRITORY (see BOUNDARIES).

TEXT-BOOKS—
may be prescribed by school boards, 82.
by the legislature, 82.
by school board commission, 82.
use of Bible as a text-book, 83.

THEATERS—
license for, 91.
policeman at, 211.

TITLE TO OFFICE—
manner of trying, 255.
by *certiorari*, 255.
by *quo warranto*, 256.

TORTS, LIABILITY FOR (see NEGLIGENCE)—
governed by nature of power or duty, 267.
distinction between governmental and corporate powers, 267.
when exercising discretionary power, 268.
when duty imposed or assumed, 268.
liability for acts of agents, 269, 271.

References are to pages.

TORTS, LIABILITY FOR (continued)—
    rule of *respondeat superior*, 269.
    officers performing duties of corporation, 269.
    acts of independent boards, 269, 270.
    acts of officers under control of boards, 269.
    acts of a contractor, 270.
    ultra vires torts, no liability for, 271.
    construction of a dam without authority, 272.
    acts of officers under void ordinance, 272.
    under unconstitutional statute, 272.
    acts done under claim of authority, 272.
    ratification of *ultra vires* torts, 274.

TOWN MEETING—
    character, 11.
    organization, 11.
    officers, 11.
    franchise, 11.
    history, 11, n.

TOWNS (see NEGLIGENCE).

TOWNSHIPS—
    history, 10.
    an administrative unit, 10.
    growth, 12.

TRIBUNAL (see COURTS; MUNICIPAL COURTS).

TROLLEY CAR SYSTEM, 105.

TRUSTEE—
    when corporation is a trustee, control of legislature, 26.
    power to hold property as trustee, 26, n.

U.

ULTRA VIRES (see CONTRACTS; TORTS)—
    the general doctrine, 258.
    its proper scope, 258, n.
    modification, 258, 259.
    by doctrine of estoppel, 259.
    when contract is within scope of general power, 260.
    contract in part *ultra vires*, 261.
    modified by doctrine of implied contract, 262.
    ultra vires torts, 271, 274.

UNCONSTITUTIONAL STATUTE—
    construction of dam under authority of, 274.

UNIFORMITY—
    of legislation, 50.
    uniform operation of laws, 51.

References are to pages.

V.

VACCINATION—
  power of school board to compel, 83.
VETERANS—
  preference, appointment to office, 225.
VETO (see ORDINANCE)—
  of ordinance, 187.

W.

WARRANTS (see ch. IX)—
  definition, 144.
  power to issue warrants, 144, 145, 148.
  form of, 145.
  not negotiable instruments, 145.
  presentment and demand, 146.
  duty of holder, 146.
  payable out of particular fund, 147.
  rights of indorser, 147.
  same as those of original holder, 147.
  payment extinguishes the debt, 147.
  cancellation, 148.
  re-issued warrant void, 147.
  defense of *ultra vires*, 148.
  authority of officer issuing, 148.
  statute of limitations, 148.
  cannot be discounted, 145.
WATER—
  may be stopped for non-payment of dues, 212.
WATER-WAYS (see SURFACE WATERS).

WATER AND LIGHTING—
  power to light the streets, 136, 138, 139.
  manner of providing water and lights, 136, 141.
  power to regulate franchise companies, 136.
  regulation of rates, 136, 137.
  power to own plants, 137, 138, 140.
  right to supply water beyond limits, 139
  acquisition of plant, 140.
  as against a company having an exclusive franchise, 140.
  reservation of right to purchase plant, 140.
  right to condemn plant, 141.
  contracts with franchise companies, 141, 142.
  grant of special privileges may be contract, 142.
  construction of such a grant, 142, 143.
WHARVES—
  legislative authority to maintain, 135.
  right to collect toll, 135.
  nature of municipal rights in, 135.

www.ingramcontent.com/pod-product-compliance
Lightning Source LLC
Chambersburg PA
CBHW022142300426
44115CB00006B/300